WHEEL OF THE YEAR
THE PAGAN YEAR ✢ THE 8 SABBAT~

Oct 31 *Samhain (sow-win) / Halloween* Cele~

December 20-22 *Yule / Winter Solstice* Sun Re~ ~e Year

Feb 2 *Brigit / Imbolc* End of Winter / Spring b~ ~tiation

March 20-22 *Eostar / Spring Equinox* Plant the garden~ ~ildren's egg hunt

May 1 *Beltane / May Day* Maypole, fertility, love, healing

June 20-22 *Summer Solstice* Longest Day / Shortest Night, burn Wicker Man

August 1-2 *Lammas / Lughnasad* Early harvest, Prepare for Winter

September 20-22 *Fall / Autumn Equinox / Mabon* Harvest-time, Day = Night

Full Moons (Esbats) and New Moons

may also be celebrated.

Publishers/Editors: V. Vale and Marian Wallace
Interviews: V. Vale and John Sulak
Supervising Editor: V. Vale
Copy Editors: Marian Wilde, Stearns Broadhead, S.M. Gray, James DeLorenzi, Donovan Bauer,
    Rick Stinson, Shauna Rogan, Holly Hinson, Mindaugis Bagdon, Kathryn Johnson, Katherin Marie
Information Technology Director: Seth Robson
Photoshop: Virgil Porter
Computer/Internet: Phil Glatz, Micah Moore
Lawyer: David S. Kahn

Design Consultants: Andrea Reider, Judy Sitz, Dave Nalesnik

Special Thanks: Valentine Wallace, Dennis & Carol Hamby, Chris Trela, Charles Gatewood,
    Elizabeth and Herbert Gunther, Deborah Nunez, Carlo Pastella, Genneire, Pesco,
    Carl Abrahamsson, Tammy Smith & Dennis Cooper, Robert Delford Brown

John Sulak (*modpagan@hotmail.com*) thanks Bruce Anderson, Dunkelwülf, Bert Huckelberry,
    Gen Ken, A. Milk, Natalie Paven, Candi Strecker, Marc Weingarten

LETTERS, ORDERS & CATALOG REQUESTS TO:
RE/SEARCH PUBLICATIONS
20 ROMOLO #B
SAN FRANCISCO, CA 94133
PH (415) 362-1465 FAX (415) 362-0742
email: *info@researchpubs.com*
www.researchpubs.com

Subscribe to our free monthly eNewsletter: *info@researchpubs.com (write "subscribe")*

Statements and allegations as set forth in this book by those interviewed are theirs alone and do not necessarily reflect the views of the editor or publisher.

©2001 RE/Search Publications
Library of Congress Catalog Number: 2001 130936
ISBN 1-889307-10-6
Printed in the U.S.A.

10   9   8   7   6   5   4   3   2   1

Interviewers V. Vale
and John Sulak

Front Cover Photo of Wynter Ravenheart by Charles Gatewood
Back Cover Photo by V. Vale Back Page Photo by Charles Gatewood
Front Page Photo supplied by Emma Reston Orr: "Johnny receives his blessing at Stonehenge ..."
Cover Design: Marian Wallace/Dave Nalesnik. Special thanks to Phil Wolstenholme

Table of Contents

WHAT PAGANISM OFFERS

Paganism is the perfect religion for anarchists. It also suits feminists, environmentalists, futurists, artists, surrealists—all who dream of social change, live for creativity not the profit motive, and hate dogma and authoritarianism. In Paganism, humor is sacred; diversity welcomed; hierarchy deprecated; activism encouraged, the body honored, and Mother Earth and every living entity revered. "Power shared" rather than "Power over" is the ruling paradigm; "Treat others as *they* want to be treated" and "Be excellent to one another!" are some of the only laws deemed necessary. Time is *cyclical* not linear, and death is as natural a part of life as birth. Here there are no rigid beliefs, Holy Bibles or Original Sin, only continuous social experimentation toward the goals of ecstatic illumination, *meaningful* ritual, long-term community, and harmony with the universe. The next stage of Modern Paganism will involve decentralized "institution"-building: more Pagan extended families, land-owning, festivals, archives and libraries, charter schools, foundations, non-profits and legal churches. In this book, fifty individuals tell why Paganism is the anti-hierarchical philosophy and religion of the future, offering wonder, joy, and celebration of all that makes us both human and divine. — *V. Vale*

A PAGAN GLOSSARY

Thanks to Oberon & Morning Glory Ravenheart, Isaac Bonewits, and books
such as J.E. Cirlot's *Dictionary of Symbols*; Lewis Spence's *Encyclopedia of Occultism*

Agnostic (Greek, "without knowledge.") "There are limits to the sphere of human intelligence . . . Man knows nothing of the Infinite and Absolute; and, knowing nothing, he had better not be dogmatic about his ignorance."—Sir Leslie Stephens

Animism The belief that all things have souls or spirit, especially phenomena of nature, e.g., "the spirit of that spring" or "the spirit that resides in that redwood tree."

Asatru Refers to the revival of "Nordic"/Northern European Paganism; see Diana Paxson's interview.

Astrology Divination system interpreting the supposed influences of the stars and planets on human affairs and destinies, depending on their positions and aspects. Chinese astrology introduces correspondences to elements, animals, etc.

Athame A ceremonial knife used in ritual.

Beltane May 1, celebration of the beginning of summer, with Maypole, games, fertility rites, May baskets, sacred marriage, the selecting of a May Queen and King. The night before is called *Walpurgisnacht*, when the door between the worlds is opened.

Bon The native Tibetan *Pagan* religion, later merged with Buddhism and Tantrism.

Botanica Occult shop serving the magickal needs of Afro-Catholic communities of Santeria, Macumba, etc. Herbs, spells, charms, votive candles, images of saints sold.

Brigit Celtic Triple Goddess of the forge/blacksmithing, poetry/inspiration, and healing. Her festival is Candlemas, Feb 1

Cernunos The Celtic horned god, shown with stag antlers. Equated with The Red Man, Faunus.

Chakra One of seven major centers of biomagnetic energy (prana) in the body.

Chalice A ceremonial cup representing the Element Water

Church of All Worlds Neo-Pagan religion founded in 1962 and incorporated March 4, 1968. Inspired by science fiction; published the highly influential *Green Egg* magazine.

Church of the Eternal Source founded by Don Harrison in 1970 and reconstructs the Mysteries of ancient Egypt and the worship of Egyptian gods and goddesses.

Cone of Power The combined psychic energy of a group mind, focused through a magickal circle, directed by a unified will and sent forth to work outside the circle. Pagan rituals often end with the raising of a cone of power.

Correspondences Various systems of correspondences link colors to musical notes, mystical relationships between music and animals, astrological signs to animals, etc.

Cosmogony Theorizing as to the *origin* of the world and the universe.

Cosmology Theorizing as to the *nature* of the universe.

Coven Usually a group of 13 or fewer Witches sharing a common tradition.

Covenant of the Goddess An international, legally incorporated, ecumenical umbrella organization of Witchcraft/Pagan groups, providing legal corporate status for otherwise unincorporated groups

Crowley, Aleister (1875-1947) Member of Golden Dawn, founded of the O.T.O., influential writer of *The Book of the Law* whose "Law of Thelema" states "Do what thou wilt shall be the whole of the law." His *Magick in Theory and Practice* is widely used in ceremonial magick.

Cult A group of people slavishly following the dictates of a single leader. *Warning signs:* Often they are isolated from non-cult members, give their incomes to the group, practice celibacy (except with the leader[s]).

Diana (Artemis/Hecate) Roman Goddess of the Moon, woods, wild animals, and the hunt.

Dianic movement Eclectic Women's traditions developed by Z. Budapest, Morgan McFarland, and others.

Drawing Down the Moon A Wiccan rite of invoking the Moon Goddess.

Druid A member of an ancient Celtic/Anglo-Saxon Pagan priesthood destroyed by the Romans. Druids worshipped in oak groves and held mistletoe to be sacred. Various reconstructionist orders now abound.

Dualism (Either/Or) Any system emphasizing two *opposed* principles, as contrasted with, for example a "both/and" system or a "thesis-antithesis-synthesis" model. Dualism is a dangerous mechanism pervasively embedded in most contemporary language usage, by which phenomena, objects, and situations are presented as "either" *this* or *that*, when in reality there could be multiform possibilities. Pagan Dualism is particularly invidious, as illustrated by the popular usage of the dualistic pair "immanence" or "transcendence"—for example, in our opinion divinity is *both* immanent *and* transcendent in our Nature-Gaia-planetary ecosystem.

Dungeons & Dragons "D & D" has become a generic term for popular role-playing games, in which players assume personas of adventurers in fantasy scenarios, encountering various monsters and pitfalls. Often draws heavily from authentic Pagan tradition/lore.

Ecstatic Latin, "out of the body."

Elements (Four) Earth, Water, Air, Fire

Eostar (Eostra). Saxon Fertility Goddess; symbols are fertile eggs and rabbits.

Equinox. One of two times each year when days and nights are equal: about March 21, September 23.

Esbat A full moon meeting or ritual.

Feng Shui Chinese system of correspondences for introducing harmony into one's environment and dwelling.

Freya (Frigga) Norse Goddess of fertility and love.

Gaia Goddess of the Earth; Mother Earth; the organic unified living entity that is our planetary biosphere; the prime deity of most Neo-Pagans.

Gerald Gardner (1884-1964) Founder of modern Witchcraft, author of *Witchcraft Today* (1954) which helped spark the modern Wiccan movement.

Golden Dawn Ceremonial magickal lodge founded in 1887 by English Freemasons including S.L. MacGregor Mathers, W.B. Yeats, Israel Regardie, Dion Fortune, A.E. Waite, and Aleister Crowley.

Great Rite Ritual sex within the magickal circle.

Green Man God of all plant life; sower of seeds.

Grimoire A compendium of spells, herb lore, charms, recipes, etc.

Hand-Fasting A Pagan Wedding ceremony. Not "til death do us part" but "for as long as love shall last."

Heathen One who lives on the heath where the heather grows. Specifically applied to rural Pagans in the U.K.

Hegemony (Greek *hegemonia,* leader—to lead) Preponderant influence or authority over. The group Reclaiming in particular seeks to combat hegemony in the workings of its group dynamics.

Hekate Greek Goddess of the Dark Moon.

Hermes (Mercury, Thoth). Greek messenger between the gods and mortals. Patron of wizards and thieves.

Hierarchy Reclaiming in particular aggressively combats hierarchy, utilizing consensus rather than voting in their decision-making, having a rotating pool of speakers in public gatherings, etc. Still working it out!

Hiving Splitting off from a magickal, Druid, Wiccan, or Pagan group to form another group.

Horned God God of animal life, love, unselfishness

Horse (or *steed*) A symbol of the animal in man; i.e., the powerful force of the instincts.

Horus Egyptian falcon god, an emanation of Ra the Sun God.

I Ching Ancient Chinese book of divination, utilizing yarrow sticks or three coins to give guidance about one's situation, or the future.

Imbolc Feb 2, the ancient Celtic festival of waxing light, dedicated to Brigit and associated with birth, menstruation, and women's mysteries. Christianized as Candlemas.

Inanna Ancient Sumerian Goddess of love, sex and war—"the Queen of Heaven and Earth."

Initiation A rite of passage into a group or religion.

Ishtar Babylonian Goddess of love, fertility, derived from the Sumerian Inanna. Called Eostre or Eostar in Europe, she gave her name to "Easter."

Isis Egyptian Goddess, Queen of Heaven, mother of Horus, wife of Osiris.

Kabala (Qabala, Caballa) Hebrew mystical lore translated, Christianized and expanded upon to become a major source of Western mainstream Occultism.

Kali Hindu Goddess of Destruction, Death and Rebirth. The Great Initiator, Portal Between Worlds.

Labyrinth A maze symbolizing the path of initiation.

Ley Lines Straight tracks on the earth connecting sacred points or power spots such as stone circles, best seen from an airplane.

Lilith Ancient Sumerian Owl Goddess.

Love "That condition in which the happiness of another person is essential to your own."—Robert A. Heinlein. Devotion with commitment.

Lughnasad (Lammas) Aug 2, the festival of first fruits, midway between Summer Solstice & Autumn Equinox.

Macumba A religion similar to Voudoun, started by African slaves in an attempt to continue their ancestral tribal religion in captivity. Now heavily overladen with Catholic symbolism.

Magick Circle Used as a focus of power for rituals, it is visualized as a doorway between dimensions.

Mandala A visual image, often in a circular design, used as a focus for associational meditation.

Maya The world of illusion; reality viewed as but a dream of the gods.

Monotheism The belief that there is only one deity who created and rules the universe. Usually omnipotent, omniscient, omnipresent, pre-existent, eternal, jealous, vengeful, wrathful, and gendered as a male patriarch.

Mudra hand gesture laden with symbolic significance

Numerology Divination or character-reading by the interpretation of numbers, which are associated with various characteristics or destinies.

Odin Norse Father-God, husband of Freya, patron of wizards. He is one-eyed, having given his other eye as a sacrifice to gain wisdom.

Orisha Yoruban term for African nature spirits or deities called "Loa" in Voudoun.

Osiris The Egyptian "Green Man" or God of Vegetation who dies and rules in the underworld as Lord of the Dead. Husband to Isis and father of Horus, his reincarnation.

Ostara (Ishtar, Astarte, Eostar) Spring Equinox, named for Saxon Fertility Goddess Eostra. Symbols are fertile eggs and rabbits.

Pagan Latin "Paganus" a peasant or country dweller. Indigenous pantheistic folk religions and peoples. Someone who worships Nature and considers life to be sacred. While primarily referential to people of European descent, it may loosely be applied to indigenous, non-monotheist peoples across the world.

Palmistry Divination by reading the lines in the palms of human hands.

Pan Pre-Christian Greek God of lust and wild Nature—goat-horned and goat-hoofed. Appropriated into the Christian Devil.

Pantheism Greek for "all divine." The belief that divinity is a quality inherent in all of Nature.

Pentacle A disk inscribed with a Pentagram or five-pointed star. It represents the element Earth.

Pentagram A five-pointed star representing the human figure with head, arms and legs. Generic symbol of Wicca or Witchcraft.

Personification The attribution of human qualities to an object.

Polytheism Belief that there are many deities.

Possession An ecstatic occurrence in which a human is apparently "possessed" by an unknown entity or personality.

Pre-Socratics Greek Pagan philosophers who left behind various insightful, aphoristic fragments of writing reflective of the cycles and transience of life.

Priest/ess. A person dedicated to the service of deities, presiding over rituals. May have additional duties such as counseling, maintenance of a temple, etc.

Ra Egyptian Sun God

Reclaiming A cutting-edge, feminist, diversity-embracing Pagan tradition founded by Starhawk and others, which incorporates public and private ritual, political activism, workshops, weekend and week-long training seminars, and "cells" in a conscious effort to enact and manifest magickal transformation within and without.

Religion (Latin "re-linking.") A body of myths, metaphors, theories and practices designed to connect individuals with Divinity.

Rhiannon Celtic Goddess of the full moon.

Rite of Passage Ritual commemoration of transitions in life, such as birth, puberty, marriage, giving birth, menopause, death.

Runes Various magickal alphabets, each letter of which contains an esoteric as well as an exoteric meaning.

Runestones (sometimes called runes) Stones marked with letters of a runic alphabet used for divination in "Casting the Runes"—also, a great story by M.R. James.

Sabbat One of eight annual festivals. The solstices and equinoxes are known as *quarters*, the others are *cross-quarters* or *Grand* Sabbats. They are outlined on page 1 of this book.

Sacrament An act, substance or food/drink regarded as inherently "holy."

Samhain (sow-en) The Great Sabbat, Oct 31-Nov 1, midway between Autumn Equinox and Winter Solstice. Celtic festival of the dead, the beginning of winter, summer's end. Sometimes celebrated with a meal of "underworld" foods: mushrooms, nuts, black olives, pork, beans, shared in total silence, where the spirits of the beloved dead are invited to join the feast and be remembered in honor.

Satan A *Christian* deity having nothing to do with Paganism. The Christian god of evil, and ruler of the Christian invention known as "hell."

Satanism An anti-religion developed in reaction to Christianity; the dark mirror side of Christianity.

Set Egyptian adversary god, murderer of Osiris and usurper of his throne.

Shakti The female principle in Hinduism.

Shaman A healer-diviner-magician member of a Pagan tribe who used altered states of consciousness to travel to the spirit realm, or Dreamtime, and do battle or gain insights to bring back.

Shinto Japanese "Pagan" animist/nature worship religion

Shrine A place of worship, usually with a small display of symbolic relics and objects.

Sigil Magickal sign or cryptic device used to identify an entity.

Skyclad Ritual nudity. "And as a sign that you be truly free, you shall be naked in your rites."—*Aradia*

Spell A complex interwoven set of mudras, mantras and mandalas, designed to achieve a magickal purpose.

Spiral Ancient Goddess symbol of emergence.

Spiral Dance A Wiccan greeting dance celebrating spiral symbolism, also a book by Starhawk.

Strega Italian or Sicilian traditional witchcraft (or witch).

Swiving The ancient rite of copulating in the plowed fields to increase their fertility by sympathetic magick.

Sword In magick, a consecrated ritual tool used for concentration and direction of energy, emblematic of Air or Fire depending on the tradition.

Synergy The combined effect of several agencies such that the whole is greater than the sum of its parts. Sometimes new properties emerge that are not present in the original components.

Talisman A manufactured object or mandala carried on one's person for the purpose of attracting good luck.

Tantra A Tibetan system of theurgical methods and training that particularly utilizes techniques for the control and direction of sexual energy.

Taoism A form of Chinese Paganism or magic system; Taoist magicians allegedly could change the weather and work various miracles. (See *The Travels of an Alchemist,* tr. Arthur Waley—a marvelous book.)

Tarot A set of 78 divination cards with illustrations into which are incorporated a vast amount of arcane symbolism. Considered by some to contain the sum total of all occult knowledge.

Thaumaturgy. The use of magick to effect changes in the reality *outside* of the magician. The scientific and technological aspects of such workings. Sometimes called sorcery. An example: weather-working.

Theagenesis (Greek, birth of the Goddess) Description of the process of the evolution of planetary consciousness as an aspect of the Gaia thesis. This term was coined by Oberon Ravenheart in 1970.

Thealogy Intellectual speculations concerning the nature of Goddess and Her relations to the world in general and humans in particular.

Theology Intellectual speculations concerning the nature of "God" and His relations to the world in general and humans in particular.

Theurgy The use of magick to effect changes in the magician's own *internal* reality. Magick used for self-actualization or personal apotheosis. Focus is on prayers, invocations, meditations.

Time, Cyclical Pagans view time as cyclic—inseparable from the changing of seasons and the cosmic rhythms of birth, growth, reproduction, aging and death. This is in direct contrast to the predominant Western concept of linear time, which embodies dubious notions and goals such as "progress," "efficiency," and "deadlines."

Totem A species of plant or animal regarded as having an ancestral or affinitive relationship to a specific tribe, family, or individual.

Tree of Life Symbolic representation of the emergent evolution of life forms.

Triskelion A three-part symbol used by Celtic Druids to signify all sacred triads, such as the Triple Goddess. National symbol of Sicily.

Undine A water elemental; also an intriguing novel by F. de La Motte Fouqué.

Voudoun (Santería, Voodoo) A transplanted tribal religious tradition brought to the West Indies and the Americas by enslaved Africans. Its rites involve ecstatic possession by ancestor archetypes (loas) and raising power to do magickal workings. Includes bird and animal sacrifices.

Walpurgisnacht Eve of Beltane. Short story by Zschökke.

Warlock Term popularized by Hollywood to indicate male Witch; the term "Witch" applies to all sexes

Weather-Working Application of psychokinesis to effect meteorological change.

Weaving The act of weaving symbolizes creation, life and growth, and was put to magical/religious use in Egypt and the Pagan cultures of Peru.

Wheel of the Year The Seasonal Round of annual festivals or Sabbats, equated with the macrocosmic Magick Circle.

Wicca The Craft; the modern practice of Witchcraft. Traditions include Gardnerians (after Gerald Gardner), Alexandrians (after Alex Sanders), Dianics (mostly women, worshipping Diana), Faeries (mostly men/queer/transgender), Shamanics, and Eclectics, who assimilate whatever they find useful from other traditions.

Witch (From Anglo-Saxon *wicce*: sorceress). A magickal shaper of reality. A practitioner of Witchcraft. In medieval and renaissance times, Witches specialized in herbalism and midwifery. The single most common ethical statement by Witches is The Wiccan Rede: "An it harm none, do as you will."

Witches Anti-Discrimination Lobby Organization founded 1970 by Dr. Leo Louis Mortello, to legally combat slander and libel against Witchcraft.

Working A thaumaturgical act.

Yin & Yang In Taoism, *yin* is the female-negative-dark-passive principle in the universe, and *yang* is the male-positive-light-active principle.

Yoga Complex body of philosophies and practices originating in India. In the West, *Hatha Yoga* is most commonly practiced; it's a set of meditative exercises aimed at keeping the spine limber and the body supple and lithe.

Zodiac The band of twelve constellations along the plane of the ecliptic through which pass the sun, moon and planets across the sky. Each constellation or astrological "sign" is given symbolic significances and associations. ◆◆◆

Starhawk

Deborah Jones Photography

Starhawk is a longtime political activist, writer, and teacher. She makes her home in the San Francisco Bay Area, frequently traveling around America and Europe to lecture, give workshops and assist in rituals. She is a founding member of Reclaiming, which has affiliates all over the world. Her latest books include *Twelve Wild Swans* and *Circle Round* (co-written with Anne Hill and Diane Baker).

Starhawk's *The Spiral Dance* was first published in 1979. It has been reprinted numerous times, updated twice, and is now considered a classic source of inspiration for the current Neo-Pagan revival. Critics described it as "one of the key volumes on contemporary American Goddess worship" and "a book of tools." Important topics such as the Goddess and the God, ritual, initiation, trance, creating sacred space, the Wheel of the Year, and "Creating Religion: Toward the Future," are discussed in lucid detail.

Reclaiming hosts an annual "Spiral Dance" at Fort Mason in San Francisco as a fund-raiser. See *www.reclaiming.org*. Interview with Starhawk by John Sulak; follow-up interview by V. Vale.

♦ *RE/SEARCH: What do you think drives people to investigate alternative spiritualities?*

♦ STARHAWK: Many of the religions in which we were raised did not actually provide what we needed spiritually. They had become focused on form, money, and their own internal bureaucracies. There is a great hunger for a spirituality that values the earth. Certainly, valuing women was important—that's probably the core reason I became a Pagan.

A lot of established religions have, over the past thirty years, made some changes and "opened up" in a lot of ways. But when I became a Pagan, in 1968, those changes had yet to occur. Probably many of them wouldn't have happened if there hadn't been a lot of challenges posed by alternative religions.

A lot of people in their teens and twenties are well aware that, unless we make some radical changes in our society and in our way of living, we're heading down an unsustainable road. The necessary social changes need to be accompanied by changes in consciousness, as well as in political and economic structures. **Changes in consciousness come about through changes in myth, ritual, and what we celebrate.** Besides, Paganism is fun!

♦ *R/S: Describe your spirituality—*

♦ S: The core of my spirituality is the understanding that the earth is alive—we're part of a living, interconnected system, a web of life that is sacred. By "sacred," I mean in the sense of what's most important to us, what we stand for, what we want to protect. Deity/spirit/sacred is not something outside of the world, it's immanent and embodied in the living world.

We focus on the earth being alive, but really, if you extend it out, so is the whole cosmos. The whole *galaxy* is a life form and a being. But we also have many different aspects of those energies and powers that sustain the universe. For the sake of convenience, we call them "Goddesses" and "Gods." They have their own personalities and their own constellations of particular energies. They work with particular issues, in particular realms, awakening resonating forces within us.

When we say "the Goddess," often what we're talking about is that whole interwoven fabric of life. So we use "the Goddess" both as an overall term, *and* to refer to specific aspects.

In Reclaiming, we often talk about "the Goddess" as being the Triple Goddess: the Maiden, the Mother and the Crone. If you look at Goddesses and Gods closely, they usually represent aspects of the cycle of birth, growth, death and regeneration that repeat over and over again throughout nature and human life. So the Maiden/Mother/Crone is one way of looking at that cycle. The God, the Green Man, who grows up and is cut down and dies and is reborn again, is another aspect of that cycle. The moon is another aspect. Plant-life is another.

♦ *R/S: How do you apply the metaphor of the Triple Goddess in your own life?*

♦ S: I'm somewhere between the Mother and the crotchety old Crone, depending on which day you see me. In human life, we go through cycles in terms of age and experience, but we also continually go back to different cycles and aspects. When I was blockading on the streets of Washington, D.C., I was the

Maiden crusading for justice. But at the same time, I was also training and teaching people—trying to pass on my experience in activism, which was more like being the Crone.

When I found myself confronting an entire squad of mounted policemen and trying to get a whole crowd to sit down so they wouldn't be trampled, I looked up at this guy on the horse and channeled the voice of *Mom:* "You people have created an incredibly dangerous situation here! What were you thinking?" So, an aspect of the Goddess can come through at any moment.

I had been training people for twenty years to sit or lie down if attacked by horses; the horses won't—or at least don't *want* to—trample you. They can slip and make a mistake, but by and large they don't. It wasn't until I was sitting under a horse that I reflected on the fact that I'd never actually *tried out* this theory before, but rather hoped that it was actually true! [laughs]

♦ *R/S: In your life, do the sacred and the mundane overlap?*

♦ S: They overlap a lot. I'm very lucky, in that most of the time I live out in the country and can spend a fair amount of time being in the garden or in the woods, just being present and communicating with the things that are around me. I also spend a fair amount of time teaching, leading rituals and speaking to groups, so I am able to be in more "sacred" states. But there *are* those other times when I'm stuck in traffic on the freeway, or trying to finish eighteen million things so I can do the next thing—when I have more jobs to do than time to do them. States of ecstasy are much harder to reach in these situations!

♦ *R/S: Your most influential book is The Spiral Dance. How many copies have sold in the past 20-odd years?*

♦ S: 310,000 copies, or maybe it was 350,000.

♦ *R/S: That's amazing. Tell us how you came to write* **The Spiral Dance**—

♦ S: By that point, I had been a feminist for many years and felt it was important for women to have other models of spirituality besides the patriarchal ones. Also, it seemed important to have models of spirituality that were earth-based and earth-centered. There's nothing in the book that's revealing secrets that shouldn't be revealed—I've never been a great one to shout, "Oh, this is so secret! This is so secret!" That really tends to support a kind of self-inflation. The real secrets of the Craft are the secrets that can't be *told* . . . because you have to *experience* them!

♦ *R/S: Some of our intelligent, open-minded yet skeptical friends ask, "What can I possibly get out of attending a Pagan gathering?"*

♦ S: Well, first of all, I think that when you do ritual together with a group of people, or even when you do it alone, it's a way of feeling a deep connection to your deepest values, and to those forces in the universe that most truly sustain and support our lives. In our tradition we work with things that are really pretty concrete, like the air and the earth and water and fire. It helps you to really, truly *value* those things that sustain our lives. And especially when you work with a community, it gives you support for your own personal growth and development, and for doing things that are sometimes quite difficult to do.

For me, I've also been a political activist for thirty years. And a lot of the reason I've been able to sustain that is we have a community of people who do that kind of thing together and who can support each other through the hard times, and who can encourage each other through the good times. And that helps you keep going, because a lot of what we do when we're really trying to change the world can get hard, and can get discouraging. Plus, it's fun! And fun—that's important! When you go to something like the big Spiral Dance where you've got people hanging off the rafters doing their invocation and dancing ecstatically—it's a helluva lot of fun!

♦ *R/S: Right. What was despicable about the New Age movement was its excessive amount of marketing hype, and excessive profits—a weekend expo could cost $500, and a $5 crystal would be priced at $50 at a New Age booth. How does Reclaiming meet its operating expenses? Unlike most churches, you don't have paid clergy, right?*

♦ S: Well, we try to balance things. We believe that people should, ideally, get paid for their work and get paid fairly and well. But we also believe that events and spiritual things should be accessible to everybody who wants to come, whether they have money or not. And so it's always a juggling act, because we live in a world in which if we do something, it often costs us money to put it on.

We have some rituals like the Spiral Dance which are a benefit for our collective for the year, that we charge money for and encourage people to pay well for. It costs no more—in fact, *less* than going to a rock concert. And if somebody shows up and says, "Hey, I just don't have fifteen bucks," we say, "Okay!"

♦ *R/S: Or you say, "Volunteer and do some work; help us clean up afterward!"*

♦ S: And when our rituals are out in a park and we're not renting a hall, then most of them are free in public. If we teach classes, we charge for the classes but we have sliding scales. When we do a week-long Witch Camp or an intensive, you just can't go somewhere for a week and get fed, housed and taught and everything else without it costing money. But we try to also offer scholarships and work exchange, and to keep the price within a reasonable range, and encourage people who don't have a lot of money to come.

We've thought a lot about this. We haven't always answered all the questions, and the answers we have come up with don't always please everybody. We still get a lot of criticism sometimes for charging money at all. But we've definitely thought about it.

♦ *R/S: You began pioneering large-scale public rituals—*

♦ S: I felt this wasn't just for a small, secret, private group to be doing—it should be offered to people. I was a political activist in the Sixties, and my natural inclination was, "If something is good, it should be shared. It belongs to the world." I feel honored that I've been able to serve people in that way.

Now there are many public rituals going on all over the Bay Area, the country, and the world. People are taking charge of their own spiritual lives, and that's very positive and important.

♦ *R/S: Can you describe the Spiral Dance?*

♦ S: It's a very simple dance in which everyone holds hands, dances into the center and then twists back out, so that in doing it you have to pass *everybody* and greet them with your eyes!

There are many different ways of doing it. Some groups start with everybody facing out, and end with everyone facing in. What we did was add an extra loop so that you spiral back in and end up in a circle, or clump close together, all facing in. As you dance you're singing and building energy that eventually rises into what we call a *cone of power.* The Spiral Dance represents the cycle of birth and renewal and regeneration—the life cycle.

♦ *R/S: That book contains "The Charge of the Goddess"—*

♦ S: "The Charge" was written by Doreen Valiente [died Sept 1, 1999]. People often think I wrote it, but I didn't. At the time I wrote *The Spiral Dance* nobody knew who had written "The Charge." I thought it was a traditional piece of liturgy that I had license to reproduce. Probably because it was in the book, people identify it with me.

"The Charge" was what actually got me into the Craft. When I was 17, a group of us had been studying witchcraft as part of a class at the Experimental College at U.C.L.A. Through it, we met some witches who read us "The Charge of the Goddess." I heard it say things like "sing, feast, dance, make music and love all in my presence, for I am the ecstasy of the spirit and I am also joy on earth." And also, **"All acts of love and pleasure are my rituals."** And "I am the beauty of the Green Earth and the White Moon, and of the stars, and of the mystery of the waters."

I thought, "Hmmm—this is what I've always believed! This is something that actually makes sense to me, spiritually. This actually speaks to the real times when I have felt I was in the presence of the sacred. This must be for me!" "The Charge" has been a very meaningful piece of writing for me.

♦ *R/S: Then you met Doreen Valiente—*

♦ S: About fifteen years ago I went to visit her in Brighton, England. She was living in Council Housing in a big bed-sitting room, surrounded by books. Her partner came in, they served us cheese and baloney sandwiches, and we talked. She was a wonderful, charming, delightful woman. She showed us the original draft of the "The Charge of the Goddess."

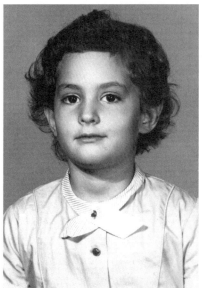

5½ years old

In many ways she was a very unpretentious person. She always said she didn't particularly like "The Charge of the Goddess" in its prose version—she preferred the poetry version. She had written that for her coven, and they said, "Nah, we don't like it. Go back and write something else." She came back with a prose version and they liked that better, as did we.

But she never really understood how important her piece of writing had become to the Craft. For years afterward, I was directing people to her to get permission to republish it, or rewrite it, or quote it. And she usually got very annoyed.

♦ *R/S: What happened after your U.C.L.A. class?*

♦ S: My friends and I met some people who began teaching us. They recommended a few books—at that time there weren't a lot. After a couple of years I drifted away from them. But when I moved to the Bay Area in 1975, I discovered a thriving Pagan community. I found other people to study and train with, and I started writing.

♦ *R/S: Did you ever have any doubts about what you were getting into?*

♦ S: There were moments. But really, I always had an underlying feeling that this was the right path for me..

♦ *R/S: You really seem to be trying to figure out how to make the "society of the future" work in a long-term way. In many so-called alternative social experiments—a horrific example being Jonestown, there's usually a guru presiding over a flock of obedient followers. Even in "socialist" groups, there's a lot of subtle jockeying for power going on. Reclaiming seems to be deliberately addressing questions like, "How do you anticipate and avoid problems involving hierarchy and hegemony, before they occur?" It seems you're "consciously" dealing with that—*

♦ S: It's not that we have always necessarily succeeded, or always have the answer, but those are definitely the questions that we're wrestling with all the time: **How do you build a group based on a different model of power?** And then, as we've grown, we're continuing to have to answer that on a larger and larger scale: How do you get people to work together and actually listen to each other and respect each other's differences…and *still* manage to come together and do something together?

♦ *R/S: The Pagan movement is growing, even though many people seem to have a negative opinion of the word "Witch." How do you address that?*

♦ S: The negative connotations of the word "Witch" stem from hundreds of years of propaganda from the churches, and then later from Hollywood, regarding what a witch supposedly is, or isn't, or is supposed to be. Either Witches are agents of the Devil/Satan, or funny creatures in pointed hats with broomsticks.

I think that for us, it's worth taking on the effort of educating people, because if you counter people's assumptions about the word "Witch," you're actually countering a lot of their assumptions about what it means to have a source of power that doesn't come from the authorities, that isn't "blessed" by the powers that be, that connect us back to our intuition and a world that is *alive* and where all the plants and animals and elements are speaking in conversation.

Paganism sort of re-enchants the world. And to me that's both a radical act and something that makes us confront a lot of our internal assumptions about power, and about who should have it. You say "Witch" and people think "woman." If you think that a woman who has power is necessarily dangerous and evil, then we're sort of back in that "old" world where only men have power, and nobody else should.

♦ *R/S: It seems that formerly only women were called Witches, while men were called Warlocks—*

♦ S: The term "Warlock" was never something that real Witches used about themselves. It's an old word that means "traitor"! It was always kind of a hokey, Hollywood usage—something used by people who were ignorant and not really connected with real Witches. We've always used "Witch" for both women and men.

♦ *R/S: Another common question is, "Are Witches Pagans? Are Pagans Witches? What's the difference?"*

♦ S: All Witches are Pagans, but not all Pagans are Witches. It's like, "All Baptists are Christians, but not all Christians are

Baptists." "Pagan" is a broad term that means "earth-based spirituality." It comes from the same root word that means land or countryside, and it refers to people who held on to their old ways after Christianity came in.

"Witch" is a more specific term for particular traditions that are goddess-centered and generally come from Western Europe or the Middle East, and that have a tie to healing, working with the land, working with magic . . . reflecting a specific sort of, or an overall sort of, style of doing ritual. Maybe you shouldn't say that, because style varies a lot from group to group.

♦ *R/S: You just hit upon another loaded word: "magic." What does that mean? A lot of people think, "Witches try to cast spells to make you do things you don't want to do, like fall in love with them."*

♦ S: The definition I like for magic comes from a woman named Dion Fortune: **"Magic is the art of changing consciousness at will."** And when we change *our* consciousness, we're able to communicate at a different level with all the other consciousness around us, in plants and animals and the natural world, and we're able to shift . . . our inner reality sometimes can make a difference in our outer reality.

But real Witches understand that . . . we have a rule that we call the Rule of Three: whatever you send out returns to you three times over. So it's basically an ethical rule that you don't cast a spell, you don't do anything to anyone that you wouldn't want done to yourselves. And making someone fall in love with you through magic isn't any more possible than making them fall in love with you in any other way. It doesn't necessarily make for a good relationship! But you could do a spell to open yourself to love in the universe, and to draw in the love that is "right" for you to come.

♦ *R/S: We've met people who say, "I only go to the Spiral Dance, but I wouldn't join any group. I'm a solitary practitioner." Do you have any comment on that?*

♦ S: Yes, a solitary is someone who works alone and does their rituals, etc, by themselves rather than joining a group or a circle or a coven. And certainly many Witches throughout history have been solitary. It's kind of like anything else in life: some people really go through life best if they're in a relationship, and other people go through life best if they're single. And for some of us, there might be times in our life when we really need a strong relationship, and other times when we really grow the most by being single for awhile. So it can vary from time to time.

I personally think you miss out a lot if you never are in a circle or coven, just like you would if you never had a relationship in life. But for some people, their spirituality is more of a private thing. Or they may just not have the time or the energy to be involved in a group.

♦ *R/S: What's the difference between a circle and a coven?*

♦ S: A circle is a group of people who get together to do ritual together. A coven is just a little more formalized, where everyone would be initiated and go through a ritual commitment to the goddess and to the group and have a very strong bond and commitment to each other. It's kind of like the difference between living together with someone *versus* getting married.

♦ *R/S: So being in a coven is like getting married—*

♦ S: Yeah! [laughs]

♦ *R/S: Regarding initiation, I have a very strong fear of, and aversion toward, authoritarianism and control over*

me by other people. I've had a "bad attitude" since early childhood—

♦ S: Good for you!

♦ *R/S: I'm actually afraid of initiation. But should I not be? Tell me why I might be interested in it—*

♦ S: Well, you probably *wouldn't* be interested, unless you felt, at a certain point in your life or your spiritual development, that it was necessary for you to grow to a new level. And there are people in the Reclaiming tradition who aren't initiated, don't believe in it, don't want to be, because of the same reason: they don't want any sense of authority over them. And there are other people for whom it's a really profound and life-changing process.

In Reclaiming, what you do is you would find just a few people that you really trust and know very well, and who know you very well. And you would ask them to initiate you, and they would give you some challenges to work on. It could be anything from reading 15 books on Witchcraft to learning to drive a car, or spending three nights in the wilderness alone. They would tailor it as something they felt you needed in order to grow. And you can accept the challenges, or reject them, or negotiate around them, but once you accept them and you do them, then they can schedule the ritual for you. In the ritual, it's really the one time in our tradition that you really have to "let go" and let somebody else take over. But again, it's very strictly limited to the people you have chosen, that you *trust* to do that.

♦ *R/S: Our friend Fakir Musafar criticized us recently: "Your* **Modern Pagans** *book is going to be a superficial piece of crap! Anyone who's really into ritual isn't going to tell you a thing that's truly deep, and important!"*

♦ S: Well, that's the "old school": that this is *all so secret,* and hush-hush, and "we have all these secret rituals and all this secret knowledge that you don't have." Again, Reclaiming tends to discredit that attitude, because we think it perpetuates a kind of hierarchy.

But again, there are a lot of things about ritual that can't be conveyed in a book, because they're *experiential.* And no matter what you do or say, words on a page just aren't going to express it. But certainly I've written enough books myself—I believe there *is* a lot you can tell. And putting what you can out in a book might encourage people to then go and have the *experience.*

♦ *R/S: You seem to be saying that to go deeper, or to access more hidden realms in yourself to unlock . . . this is facilitated and expedited by joining a few people in a coven or circle—*

♦ S: At this point, a lot of us have been doing this and experimenting and exploring for 20-30 years, so we *do* know something! You could start out without any teaching or any training and learn a lot on your own. We had some training when we started, but a lot of it is what we created on our own.

Today, you do have the option of finding people who have been doing it for a while, and learning what *they* know. And then you can take that and take it into whatever you need, you want, you might do with it . . . but you don't have to start by reinventing the wheel. Like, why do that unless you absolutely need to?! If you were studying the drum or the piano, you can learn it on your own, but it really helps to have someone show you the tricks.

♦ R/S: Don't you also have to work on changing your every-day language? Do you ever catch yourself exclaiming, under stress, "Oh, god," or "Oh, Jesus"—

♦ S: Sometimes I say, "Oh, god," but I never say "Oh, Jesus" because I wasn't raised in a Christian church. My best friend, whenever we're driving, is always grabbing the door handles and saying, "Please, Jesus!"

♦ R/S: To me, it's still kind of bowing to patriarchy to say, "Oh, god"—

♦ S: Our kids don't. They weren't raised that way. I remember my son, when he was 11 or 12, coming back from a program of Christmas carols, saying, "So now, who is this Jesus dude they all kept singing about?!" [laughs]

♦ R/S: Yes, that's the future we want—a future free of god and Jesus talk. But that patriarchal language sinks its hooks deep into our unconscious—

♦ S: Well, you can try saying, "Oh, goddess—"

♦ R/S: That's a thought. And besides, there are gods involved in goddess religion, too—

♦ S: Yes, we have lots of different images of deity: goddesses, gods, all kinds of things. For me, saying "goddess" is really about affirming the principle of life in *this* world—it's not like there's some giant lady in the sky with a skirt on! It's about valuing the process of bringing life into the world, instead of saying that Spirit is outside the world. And it's a good counter-balance to thousands of years of patriarchy and male gods. **I think that if something's out of balance, you need an extreme counterbalance for awhile. If you're on a kid's teeter-totter and you're on one end, you can't bring it into balance by sitting in the middle**—you've got to get something over on the other end—*then* you can have a balance!

♦ R/S: Some males, when they hear the term "goddess religion," immediately say something like, "Oh, so they hate men!"

♦ S: You can always whistle the old Beach Boys hit [sings]: "Two girls for every boy!"

♦ R/S: Right. If people check out a Reclaiming ritual, they'll find there are more women in attendance than men—

♦ S: Actually, it's not just in a goddess religion—in *every* religion, there are a lot more women than men. But goddess religion does attract women. I think that men who are kind of secure in who they are as men don't have any problem with that. My partner always says he feels that he as a man in the goddess religion is born out of the body of the mother, and knows her intimately; he knows her secrets, and he feels a great sense of power from that. But it's a different kind of power from being the thunderbolt-wielding, father, Zeus-type god.

♦ R/S: You call him your partner rather than your "husband"; is there a reason for that?

♦ S: He *is* my husband. We're married. But "husband" carries a whole set of connotations—many of which are negative. I like "partner" because it implies an equality.

♦ R/S: "Husband" can convey proprietary ownership implications—

♦ S: Right. And "partner" is kind of a way . . . it's sort of a state-ment of solidarity with lesbians and gay men and queer people who can't get married under our laws—even though, in a moment of latent romanticism, we did! [laughs]

♦ R/S: I suppose the same thinking applies to the term "wife," in your eyes—

♦ S: We tend to use "partner" more than "husband" and "wife." Although I do have a friend who's a gay man who always refers to his partner as his husband!

♦ R/S: Describe a typical day in the country—

♦ S: Ideally, I wake up and sit out on the deck and spend some time observing what's going on with the trees, the birds, and the garden. Then I go for a long walk. Maybe I'll come back and write, or do some other work. If I'm pressured by a writing deadline, or have a lot of work to do, I'll just wake up, grab the computer and start writing and go out for a walk later, after I've hit the exhaustion point. If my partner is there, at some point we'll have dinner or go out for a walk together. If I'm there by myself and he's in the city, I might garden, or write in the evening, or answer e-mail.

Often, there's a lot of things going on. This week, on Monday, I got up and talked to my neighbor who's my partner in beekeeping. We decided to check our hives. It turned out it was the day the bees decided to swarm, so we spent the whole day trying to capture the swarm of bees, which we finally did. Yesterday, some friends and neighbors were getting together to put on a wedding shower for someone in the neighborhood. So we cooked food and I spent the day with these wonderful women—we're all in a quilting group together.

♦ R/S: In San Francisco, you live in a shared living situa-tion in a building called "The Black Cat House." A lot of Pagans have similar shared living arrangements. How did yours begin?

♦ S: It started because a lot of us were doing political activism together in the early Eighties. We were doing a lot of blockades, and often ended up in jail. While doing that, we had such an intense sense of community and support that we wondered, "Why don't we have this in our daily lives? Why am I having a better time in jail than at home? Something is not right here!"

So we decided to live collectively. My friend Rose and I had originally lived with two other women in a smaller house for three years, but we decided we wanted a larger place. We were able to buy the house we live in now. And we formed a collective.

We've been there 15 years, and it's gone through a lot of changes and evolutions. But it's still a very supportive envi-ronment. There's a big room upstairs that we use for teaching classes, holding meetings and doing rituals. **Living collective-ly allows us to have resources we wouldn't have if we were living individually.**

I think every collective works things out differently. Right now, our group consists of me and my partner; Rose and her partner and their three-year-old; another woman, Jeanie, plus her daughter; and my friend Donna's son, who is attending San Francisco State University. Soon we'll have another old and dear friend of ours and her partner move in. I don't know—we just get along! If we have problems, we have to talk about them and work them out. We have a set of systems for keeping the house going, and keeping it clean.

♦ R/S: You have set rules for who does the cleaning?

♦ S: **We actually hire someone to come in and do the major cleaning. We all chip in for this. And I'm convinced that *this* is the secret of our collective house lasting as long as it has!** [laughs] This may or may not be politically correct, but it works for us.

We have three bathrooms, and if you need a bathroom there's usually one available. If there isn't, it's no worse than it would be in a regular family. We each have our own room, so we all have opportunities for privacy.

♦ *R/S: Speaking of privacy, do you have anything to say about sex?*

♦ S: **Sex? I'm in favor of it!** [laughs] **One of the great appeals of Paganism is it's a religion where sex is holy—it's not something dirty and nasty, it's something beautiful. Sex is something to be** *celebrated.*

The thing about being in a long-term, committed relationship is that sex gets to have this nice place in my life where I can count on it, and I don't have to go pursuing it all the time. This gives me some leeway to focus on other things.

There's also the aspect of getting to be middle-aged. I don't think age necessarily lowers your sex drive, but it does perhaps broaden your perspective. Sex is not the one overriding, driving force in your life as it can be when you're younger.

Starhawk (far right) at **Avebury** with **Pagans Against Nukes**

My focus is on having a real connection with actual nature, as opposed to *ideas* of what nature is supposed to be. And that is also a very erotic connection, a very sensual connection. I focus on activism, on taking it out into the world and making it real on every level.

♦ *R/S: What is your perspective on women's reproductive rights?*

♦ S: From a Pagan point of view, the fact that a woman can encounter this great potential to bring life into the world is one of the ways in which we directly experience the Goddess. It's one of the ways in which each of us is challenged to form our own personal ethics and choices. It's an absolutely vital spiritual necessity that women be free to make those choices without being hampered by somebody else's determination of what she should do with her body.

♦ *R/S: You were raised Jewish—what's your relation to Judaism now?*

♦ S: In many ways I identify with being Jewish. I probably practice as much Judaism as my Reformed parents did. I go to seders, I light Hanukkah candles and try to attend High Holiday services. For me, it's a way of connecting with my roots, my ancestors, and the richness of that tradition.

I'm not a really good Orthodox Jew—I don't do the whole "hide all the bread" stuff during Passover. I tend to eat bread and matzos. [laughs] The truth is, so did my mother. I'm not very strict on all those details—my grandparents would have been horrified. They were very Orthodox.

♦ *R/S: How does it feel at an indoor Jewish service in a Temple after having been priestess at big outdoor Pagan rituals?*

♦ S: It's very nice and soothing. I can go sit in the back and let *somebody else* do the whole service! [laughs] And I can experience fond memories of my childhood. It still has meaning for me, although it's different now.

♦ *R/S: Do you have any internal conflict between the two?*

♦ S: **The nice thing about being a Pagan is that you can hold a lot of contradictory beliefs all at the same time!** [laughs]

♦ *R/S: Is spell-casting an important part of Paganism?*

♦ S: Spell-casting is just one particular form of ritual. It's a very *directed* form of ritual, directed toward some specific end that you have in mind. There are times when it's very useful, but it's just one tool. It doesn't reflect the whole philosophy and understanding of what we're doing. But for many people, it's an entry point.

♦ *R/S: Do you have any advice for someone interested in Paganism?*

♦ S: Find yourself some place you can go—it might be your back yard, some corner of a park that hasn't been mowed recently, or some place where the vegetation is still a bit wild. Then make a personal commitment to spend some time there—ideally, every day if you can. But if you can't go every day, then go as often as you can, even if it's only for five or ten minutes. And don't spend that time with your eyes closed in meditation "communing with the spirit of the trees." Actually open your eyes and look at what's going on around you. Look at what's growing there. Look at what changes. Listen to the bird songs and the patterns in them. Get some tree identification books and find out what kinds of trees are growing there, and what kinds of plants and wild flowers, too.

Keep doing that over a long period of time. If you do that long enough, with enough focused attention, and actually *let* yourself be present in that spot, you'll start to see amazing things. You'll start to really understand that nature is communicating with us. All of nature is always communicating. And the Goddess will begin to reveal herself to you.

Then you can read all the books and check out all the Web sites and do all of that. But **if you're just on the Internet, and you're just reading the books, and you're not making some direct connection with nature, then you're missing the heart of what Paganism is all about.**

♦ *R/S: Are you a vegetarian?*

♦ S: No. **I've been opening my ears to the Goddess for the past 35 years and she's never once told me to be a vegetarian!** [laughs] But do I try to get meat that is "free range" or organic, and frequently buy meat from my neighbors in the country. For me this is part of understanding the whole cycle of birth and growth, and death and re-birth.

This earth is set up so we *do* eat each other—the animals and plants that we eat would not actually exist in their current forms if we were not eating them. If we stopped eating cows, it's not like they would have long happy lives in the country, eating their grass and then dying of old age. They would probably become extinct very rapidly. Their "kind" in some way made a bargain with humankind many generations ago: "Okay, you keep us, you protect us, you make our lives easier than they would be in the wild, and in return our lives will be shorter." But I do think we have to keep that bargain, in the sense of making sure the animals live good, decent lives while they're alive, and that they aren't factory-farmed and treated the way so many meat-producing animals are treated in this society.

My personal "food morality" goal is to grow at least some of my own food . . . as much as I can. I want to have that direct connection, and to eat things I actually have a relationship with. That's often a challenge for somebody who travels a lot. But I do actually grow a lot of the vegetables, salad greens, and fruits that my family and I eat.

♦ *R/S: I went to "Earth Day" recently and was chatting with a high school biology teacher who told me, "Kids today are afraid of soil. They're worried they might get their new sneakers dirty." What do you think of that?*

♦ S: I think that's a sad comment on where we've come to as a society. So many kids don't get a chance to go out and play anymore. If their families are affluent, they're in structured activities from morning until night. And if their families aren't, then they're often plunked in front of the TV set or kept in the house because the parents are afraid to let them out in the neighborhoods they live in. So they miss out on all that wonderful childhood experience, which involves actually connecting with the earth.

Even in the Pagan community, I'm amazed at how many people I meet who are afraid to get their hands dirty. Certainly, Pagans include a vast number of gardeners and people with a direct connection to the earth. But if you live in the city, you have no overriding reason to actually connect with the earth in a real and meaningful way.

♦ *R/S: How can this be remedied?*

♦ S: In *Circle Round,* a book I co-wrote with Anne Hill and Diane Baker, we present a lot of hands-on, simple ways to introduce kids to earth-based spirituality. With children, you don't want to do long, wordy rituals, or rituals where they must sit through quiet meditation. You want to get them digging in the earth, baking bread, or making something—doing things that are fun and sensual . . . activities that tie into the meaning of the seasons and the cycles, without giving them heavy-handed sermons. These things help them develop a spiritual life of their own. But they're also *fun,* and are really geared at what children like and can understand.

We've got stories for each of the holidays, we've got crafts you can do, and things you can bake, and food you can eat, and rituals that are not about standing around doing long invocations or reciting poetry. They're just very active, and often very simple. But they can give children something . . . you know, those kind of really warm, wonderful memories that you would like your kids to have when they grow up.

♦ *R/S: Are there Pagan events mainly for children?*

♦ S: The Reclaiming group in Texas is having a Witch camp this year that's a family camp for adults and children. And there

have been some people doing groups for kids at various times, or workshops or classes for kids or for families. I think that's something we could use a lot more of; it's wonderful. So—get busy!

♦ *R/S: It makes sense. Probably all parents want to raise their children better than the way they were raised—*

♦ S: Yes. I think the general Pagan style of child-rearing is pretty loving and caring and nurturing and not terribly authoritarian. Which means that our children are not always the most polite, well-behaved little children around! [laughs] But they've got a lot of spirit. There are those moments when you discover you've been raising an anti-authoritarian child, and you're an anti-authoritarian but you're also supposed to be the authority! Like, "Dammit, why aren't they listening to me?!" [laughs]

♦ *R/S: Another point about Reclaiming, or Pagan groups in general—there don't seem to be any rabid proselytizers. Pagans, in fact, appear fairly modest of demeanor—*

♦ S: We actually try to work and teach from a particular state we identify as a "neutral" state, rather than from a puffed-up, inflated state. That's part of our conscious practice; it's part of what we teach people about being a priestess or being a teacher: how to put yourself in that state where you're just a regular person, and how to keep/stay there, no matter what people perceive you as . . . because it's part of staying sane, and it also makes for better magic, better work, and *definitely* makes for better group process! [laughs]

♦ *R/S: Isn't the Reclaiming policy to teach in pairs, to try to combat authoritarian structure that can sometimes arise—*

♦ S: Right, we teach in pairs so we can always be modeling a sharing of power and a partnership. Also, so that the teachers have somebody to bounce off. Sometimes two teachers will work very differently, and people get to see that there's more than one way of doing something—

♦ *R/S: —or more than one way of thinking about something—*

♦ S: Yes. Sometimes people will really think very differently about a subject.

♦ *R/S: Again, you've made a conscious effort to encourage the embracing of diversity. At a recent Reclaiming event, a transsexual or trans-gender person was leading the event, at least for a while, and seemed to be totally accepted by everyone—*

♦ S: Yes, we try to make a conscious effort to be welcoming of a whole diversity of people who have different sexual orientations or genders or races, and—

♦ *R/S: —age, too. I've rarely seen such a wide age spectrum at a social gathering—*

Standard of the Compost Coven Photo: Sally K. Amsbury

♦ S: It's nice.

♦ *R/S: Also, there always seems to be a lot of humor at Reclaiming events. Humor is very important—*

♦ S: Yeah, that's part of our tradition, definitely. You have to be able to laugh at yourself.

♦ *R/S: Right. Without humor and self-deprecation, that's how you get the Hitlers, the Maharaji's and the whole horrible guru syndrome—*

♦ S: Reclaiming is a group of people who don't like that sort of thing!

♦ *R/S: Again, it seems like you've consciously thought about all the negative consequences that can occur with group formation, and have deliberately built in all these structures or checks-and-balances to stymie any rise of incipient authoritarianism, right?*

♦ S: Well, we've at least consciously *attempted* to do that!

♦ *R/S: But that makes a huge difference—most people don't.*

♦ S: Right. [laughs] And you know, there are times when authoritarianism still rears its head, because we've all internalized so much of it. But generally, after a while people will say, "Excuse me, but I thought we weren't about that sort of thing." "Oh—yeah, you're right!"

♦ *R/S: Can you talk about the ecstatic state—*

♦ S: It's hard to talk about. It's a feeling of energy just *pouring* through me, and of *rightness*—being in the right place. And of connectedness with all the people I'm doing the ritual with, and all those forces in Nature around me.

♦ *R/S: What do you think of the "value" of ecstatic states as personal revelation? Is it our right? Allegedly, that's a way to access some other level or dimension of consciousness. Hopefully, you can bring back from that experience insights you wouldn't have gotten otherwise—*

♦ S: I think it *is* our human right to enter into ecstatic states of consciousness. It's something that's an innate ability we all have. I actually think it's kind of a human *need* that we all have. Just like, if we're healthy and we're not injured in some way, we all have the ability to walk and run and exercise and we actually *need* to do that.

I think that any healthy society provides opportunities for people to move into ecstatic states of consciousness: states where we really understand our connectedness to all the living beings and life systems of the earth. And if we don't get that through ritual, through some kind of spiritual practice, then I think people are driven to seek it in other ways, through alcohol or drugs or some kind of weird adrenalin rush—

♦ *R/S: Raves, or extreme sports. I drove by the new baseball stadium in San Francisco and suddenly heard a huge roar go up; it made me sick. [laughs] I suppose that's as close as those fans get to an ecstatic state—*

♦ S: Well, David, my partner, my husband—*whatever the hell he is*—has this whole theory that sports actually *are* our true cultural religion, and that they *are* the way that people get ecstatic together in our major culture. Also, they sort of organize the seasons for us, but in kind of a slightly warped way.

♦ *R/S: And in a heavily consumeristic and marketing/ branded kind of way—*

♦ S: Yeah. And heavily, heavily competitive . . . in sort of a warlike way.

♦ *R/S: That's a great insight into sports. At least you credited David—*

♦ S: Yeah; it'll help preserve our marital harmony! He's writing a book about this subject.

♦ *R/S: On the issue of ways to reach ecstasy, one thing I really like about Reclaiming gatherings is that they are expressly no-alcohol, no-drug—*

♦ S: For us, this policy came out of a time in our community when a lot of people were in Alcoholics Anonymous or other 12-step programs around addictions of one sort or another. But we also found that it just created an atmosphere for our public rituals that we liked. It kind of separated out the people who were coming for some kind of serious ritual work, from the people who might just be coming to party. It kind of made a statement like, "This is fun, and it is ecstatic, but it's not just about getting high—it's about something deeper."

And it creates a safer atmosphere—especially because we *do* get into pretty deep altered states of consciousness. And you can do that, but it's a lot safer to do that and know how to come back from it, and it's also a lot easier, if necessary, if you need to *bring* someone back from it. If you add alcohol and drugs in, then it kind of locks you into a particular altered state of consciousness, and you really can't do all that much about it until the chemical wears off.

♦ *R/S: Yes, we are all soft machines, in a way. If you take a certain chemical, then it brings about a chemical reaction—*

♦ S: Yeah.

♦ *R/S: There are those who would argue that a lot of our culture has been created by individuals in drug-assisted states. Take, for example, Freud's letters, in which he said, "I just took some cocaine, and . . ." then relates some discovery or insight. Didn't Arthur Conan Doyle, or certainly Thomas de Quincey and Coleridge, get inspiration from taking laudanum or opium?*

♦ S: There's no denying that people can have breakthroughs with drugs or alcohol. But we also don't know what many of those artists might have done *without* the drugs and the alcohol. Many who ended up dying young might have lived on and produced a lot more if they hadn't used drugs and alcohol.

The practice of magic and the discipline of it can teach you how to open up a lot of those same states of consciousness *without* the drugs. Then again, we aren't telling people, "You should never drink," or, "you should never, ever in your life smoke a joint." We say, "Just not at our public rituals, please." What do you do? Most of us like to have a beer on a hot day, or a glass of wine with dinner, sometimes.

To really *learn* to open up altered states of consciousness, it's like learning to play the piano, again. You can sit there and bang around and have a lot of fun, but if you really want to learn how to do it, at a certain point you have to sit down and learn scales, and practice. The same is true of magic. You have to have some kind of regular practice of it. That really helps you in learning how to do it.

♦ *R/S: In your books, you have general discussions of pathways you might take: regular meditation, candle-burning ceremonies—things like that, right?*

♦ S: There's lots of that in *The Spiral Dance*, which is my first book. We have a brand-new book out called *The Twelve Wild Swans: Journey into the Realm of Magic, Healing and Action*. It has three whole pathways of study in it. One is around learning the basics of magic and the basic disciplines, and the art of changing consciousness at will. Another is around doing your inner work, and personal healing. The third is about how you take it out into the world and do political action, or practice teaching or organizing rituals for other people.

♦ *R/S: Reclaiming has affiliates not just in America but in—*
♦ S: Canada, England, Germany. There seems to be more and more. David and I did workshops in Norway, Spain . . . people we've trained are teaching in Switzerland and lots of other places.

♦ *R/S: How does European Paganism differ from American Paganism?*
♦ S: In Germany, where I've done a lot of work, Paganism always has to deal with the legacy of Hitler and the perception that Hitler was into a form of Paganism. Also, in America the feminist Pagans and the other Pagans have worked together a lot, and there is significant crossover—the lines aren't so clearly drawn anymore. But in Germany, feminist spirituality is still pretty much "Women Only." The men who are into Paganism are far fewer and further between, and are into very different things than the women. My partner and I have done German workshops together, and we find that the Germans tend to look at things more critically; they seem to need clearer definitions than we do. This makes for more separate groups, and clearer boundaries between groups.

In England, the Pagan movement is huge and growing all the time. A lot of their work centers around their sacred sites. During the past five years, every time I've visited sacred sites there I've found offerings—meaning that people are *using* the sites, doing rituals there. There's also a large scholarly Pagan movement whose associates host conferences, discussions, and read papers. But you should have been in Prague with all the Socialist Workers Party people! We were there doing some early training sessions.

♦ *R/S: Do you see differences between rituals in Europe and in the United States?*
♦ S: It's hard to describe exactly, because the energies of the earth feel different at every place on the earth. Each place has its own personality and character.

♦ *R/S: And the European groups are somewhat autonomous, but they must subscribe to some basic principles that Reclaiming has decided works—*
♦ S: We wrote "The Principles of Unity." Those overseas groups are autonomous, but if they're linked with Reclaiming, that means they support "The Principles of Unity." Otherwise they could be autonomous and be whatever they want to be.

♦ *R/S: Still, Reclaiming is appealing because it combines personal work, group ritual, and political activism—all integrated together—*
♦ S: Again, we came together when we were doing a lot of direct action around anti-nuclear protest in the early Eighties, and doing a lot of *ritual* around those actions, and also helping in very real ways to *organize* those actions. We've been involved in lots and lots of things over the years, as a community and as individuals. Many of us have been doing a lot of work around the anti-globalization issue. A lot of us who teach with Reclaiming also do non-violent training, direct-action training, and help to really organize some of these protests. For us, it's very important to bring the two together.

♦ *R/S: What else is there in life? You have the exterior political-social-ecological dimension linked to the interior*

Photo: Elizabeth Gorelik

religious-spiritual-creative dimension. Actually, do you use the word "religious"?
♦ S: Yeah, I do. Not in the sense of having a dogma, but it comes from a Latin root that really means "re-linking, making a connection." In that sense, I think we provide anything that any other religion provides, except, perhaps, a sense of sin.

♦ *R/S: I hate that—*
♦ S: And punishment.

♦ *R/S: And that horrible Christian guilt about sex, which is so life-destroying and life-denigrating—*
♦ S: Yes. **That's another thing you might get out of Paganism: it's a spiritual tradition that says, "Sex is good!"** [laughs]

♦ *R/S: Let's go back to the topic of the ecstatic state, taking the word "shaman" which is associated with Siberian shamans, among others. Allegedly they would wander off into the tundra and get visions and come back. Sometimes they might have been clinically mad individuals, at least part of the time, but they were tolerated and honored in the village because they're treading this fine line between madness and their ability to receive prophetic or insight-bringing visions for the benefit of the tribe or village—*
♦ S: You know, the thing is, I think there's a difference in the way a shaman functions in a traditional culture like that . . . and what a lot of people do now in the *name* of shamanism. It's a lot more than just "getting high to do a ritual."

If you were a shaman in a traditional culture, anything you took you would have either grown yourself, or gathered yourself—you would know where it came from, you would gather it under really strict ritual conditions. You'd have a *real relationship* with that plant, and the spirit or energy that's in that plant, and you'd take it under conditions that are really set out for you by your culture. And so there's a very strong—we'd say there's a very strong "container"—for that ecstatic experience.

In modern Western culture, we really don't have that same kind of container, and most of us don't have that kind of relationship with the plant world. And so, taking a substance to change your consciousness becomes a totally different thing. Really, in shamanism it's not the substance itself that's the real consciousness-changer, it's the *relationship* you have with the plant or the thing that substance comes from. And so, without that relationship, you're kind of missing the point if you're just getting the chemical reaction.

But in this world there are a lot of ways we can reach really deep, ecstatic, amazing states of consciousness *without* substances: using breathing, using visualizations, and using our understanding of how energy works and how to shift and shape it. Especially when you get a lot of people together. We find in our rituals that one person's consciousness affects others. And so you can reach a pretty amazing state just through meditation or through the dancing and the drumming. And we like to do that! [laughs] We think a ritual shouldn't just be boring, or just be about standing there repeating selected words—it's got to be about really raising some energy.

♦ *R/S: Overall, would you agree that you possibly can reach higher levels of ecstatic states, not so much in the public gatherings, but in the more private ones in which you really can drum for five hours straight, which you can't do at the public Spiral Dance—*

♦ S: For me, I think some of the deepest states I've reached have been in our witch camps, which are sort of in between . . . where you have a fairly large group of people together, maybe 50 or 100, but you stay together for a week. And you're out in the country and you can do a ritual and not have to get back in your car and drive across the city! And you have, like, days and days to build up to a state, and you have time afterwards to come back down from it.

♦ *R/S: And you're on private land; you don't have to go shopping for dinner at a store or otherwise return to the "real world." You've illustrated why people attend the more intensive gatherings on private land.*

You've been living an unorthodox Pagan life for 20-30 years, but you must have had to overcome a lot of resistance, at the least—

♦ S: Well there is, certainly, a lot of intolerance of Witchcraft out there, and a lot of prejudice. But it's not like somebody comes along and says, "You're a Witch; we're going to throw you in jail and burn you at the stake." It's more because you're a Witch and you stand for certain things, some people might just immediately dismiss you, and not bother to read your books or think about what you have to say. It's on a more *subtle* level. And the way that I've always dealt with it is to *just keep doing the work.*

In the new book, *The Twelve Wild Swans,* there's a fairy tale that we use as a theme. The heroine in the fairy tale has to weave shirts out of nettles to save her brothers who have been changed into swans. And all these things happen to her. She has a baby, the baby gets lost, she gets accused of eating the baby, she almost gets burned at the stake . . . and during the whole time all this is going on, she keeps on weaving those shirts.

For me, it's a story about staying focused on the work you're doing, and not getting caught up in thinking about what people think about you, what they're projecting on you . . . but just realizing that **all you have to do is keep doing your work,** because in the end it's your work that's going to speak, and answer those people.

♦ *R/S: Fakir Musafar also said to us, "You should ask Starhawk about using the title* **Modern Pagans,** *because she has experienced so much repression in her life, and has had so much to overcome. Starhawk never uses the word*

"Pagan" in any of her book titles—why don't you ask her about that? Because you could inadvertently bring down so much repression on people."

♦ S: I certainly use the word "Pagan" a lot. I think I just prefer to use a *metaphor* in a book title, rather than being blatant.

To me, I'm more amazed at the acceptance I've received than remaining focused on the repression. I don't feel like I've suffered horrible repression or attacks or anything. However, I live in San Francisco, a place that's pretty liberal and open. A lot of people have had worse problems, have lost jobs, have *whatever,* but—I never wanted to have a job in the first place! [laughs] I've been able to write and teach and travel and basically do the work of the goddess and do political work and still support myself for my entire adult life, so I can't complain! I've had a very fortunate life.

♦ *R/S: Why do you think Paganism is going to endure and grow?*

♦ S: It's a spirituality that's needed to help us make a transition into a saner way of living, and into a culture that reflects different values on every level. Not the values of profit and expediency, but the values of balance and diversity . . . the true sustaining energies of the earth! I think we need it.

The Internet has allowed the Pagan movement to grow tremendously, because it has provided a very safe way for people to connect with it. So a lot of Pagan groups are in transition. Reclaiming has had to deal with the problems of success. How do we get larger without becoming just a bureaucracy? How do we coordinate groups all over the U.S. and Europe without having a central hierarchy? How do we retain some of that exciting "edge" kind of feeling: of doing rituals in our own living room and making them up as we go along, and still have *connection* to tradition . . . and still preserve the richness of the experience

With Margot Adler at Pagan spiritual gathering in the '80s
Photo: Nemea Arborvitae

1984 West Kennet Long Barrow

and personal growth aspects of the rituals and other activities we were doing. Now it seems this is a time when the cycle has shifted again: a time to really start "taking it out into the world," and saying, "How do we actually use some of these tools to help bring about global economic justice and ecological sanity?"

There's also the aspect of the *stewardship of place.* I'm very involved with people in my country home, around community issues which are directly tied to some of the same issues we were struggling with around the World Bank and the I.M.F. They are issues of: How much power do corporations have? How much power do local people have, to control their own resources and the destiny of their communities?

It's a very powerful, political act for people to root themselves in a place and assume some responsibility for it. That's *one* true thing that Pagans really were: *they were the guardians of the land.* They were the people who knew the land, knew the trees, knew the earth, and knew when something was being done that shouldn't be done. And that can be the land, but it can also be your town, or your neighborhood in the city. It can be the block of the street where you live that you become responsible for . . . responsible for its well-being and its health, on *every* level . . . And that's a good start. ♦♦♦

after doing a ritual for twenty or thirty years? A lot of groups are facing those issues—Reclaiming is not the only one.

♦ *R/S: What would you like to see happen?*

♦ S: I'd like to see the movement continue to grow. I'd like to see lots of different variations of it springing up in many different places. I'd like to see more Pagans actually getting their hands dirty, as well as doing rituals about getting their hands dirty. On every level, I'd like to see more Pagans deeply involved in social and political activism, and see more political activists using resources in the Pagan community to help them sustain the work they're doing.

Reclaiming was really born out of direct action. With the W.T.O. protest in November 1999 and the April 2000 I.M.F. protest in Washington, D.C., there was a resurgence of direct action like we haven't seen in years. For me, that was very exciting. People were coming forward and taking their power, and standing up to some of the forces we *have* to stand up to— *and doing it with grace and humor.*

We had Pagan clusters at both of those actions. I was involved doing training and support, and I'm looking for ways to do more of that: to bring more activism into magical practice, and to bring more magic into activism.

There's a whole new generation of activists; most of the people involved are very young—in their twenties or younger. When I began my work in Pagan political activities, they were still in diapers.

Activism has always been ongoing; there has always been something we've been involved in, but it wasn't that kind of massive direct action. We were focusing more on the magical

Books by Starhawk

The Spiral Dance: A Rebirth of the Ancient Religion of the Great Goddess (1979)

Truth or Dare: Encounters With Power, Authority, and Mystery (1988)

Twelve Wild Swans: A Journey to the Realm of Magic, Healing, and Action: Rituals, Exercises, and Magical Training in the Reclaiming Tradition with Hilary Valentine (2001)

Circle Round: Raising Children in Goddess Traditions with Diane Baker, Anne Hill (2000)

The Pagan Book of Living and Dying: Practical Rituals, Prayers, Blessings, and Meditations on Crossing over with M. Macha NightMare (contributor), & the Reclaiming Collective, (1997)

The Fifth Sacred Thing (1993)

Dreaming the Dark: Magic, Sex, and Politics (1982)

Walking to Mercury (1997)

Magic, Vision, and Action: Changing Consciousness, Healing the Earth (audio cassette, 1990)

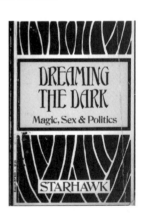

Madrone

Besides being Starhawk's assistant, Madrone produces the California Witch Camp as well as San Francisco's annual Spiral Dance, a public ritual and fund-raiser for Reclaiming. She was born in England and grew up in Australia, where she joined a theater group and appeared on Australian TV. Then she traveled the world as a spiritual seeker before moving to the San Francisco Bay Area in 1987. There she became sober with the help of a Twelve Step group, and became a part of Reclaiming.

Reclaiming organizes rituals, retreats, workshops, and publishes *Reclaiming Quarterly,* available at *www.reclaiming.org.,* or (415) 255-7623. In this conversation, Madrone discusses the organizational dynamics behind the Spiral Dance, her sex workshops, and an ecstatic experience. Interview by John Sulak; follow-up interview by V. Vale.

♦ *RE/SEARCH: Tell us about your involvement in the Spiral Dance—*

♦ MADRONE: Spiral Dance occurs around Halloween, when the veil between the living and the dead is the thinnest. I first got involved by building an altar to Pagan Celtic ancestors, when the Spiral Dance was still being held in the San Francisco Women's Building, which only holds 300 people. There were so many people waiting outside to buy tickets that I thought, "This place is too small." The next year, we took Spiral Dance to the Hall of Flowers in Golden Gate Park, but it was still too small. So the following year I took Spiral Dance to Fort Mason's Herbst Pavilion, which can hold 2,500 people.

♦ *R/S: How is the Spiral Dance organized?*

♦ M: A small group of people, or organizing *cell,* does most of the decision-making regarding the content of each year's ritual. We work by collective consensus, not majority vote. The planning cell, which varies each year, usually consists of about ten people. The production side—organizing the tech people, altar-builders, printing tickets, creating flyers and press releases—is mostly done by me. I'm paid a nominal fee for being the producer who directs the production team. We also have about a hundred volunteers who prepare food, build altars, and do whatever else needs to be done. There are altars to fire, earth, wind, and air; to our ancestors, a Burning Times altar, a fairy altar, a headwaters altar—there are so many that we have an "altar coordinator" now.

We have a 30-member chorus, an eight-piece band, and about six sound and tech people. Then we have the Dragons—the Reclaiming word for security—and the Graces, or ritual ushers. There are front-of-house staff, including the front-of-house manager—another paid position. She arrives at two in the afternoon and stays until two in the morning and doesn't get to do any of the ritual—which is why it's a paid position.

Recently we had a woman named Laura decorate the front

of house, hanging the veils through which people pass in transition into sacred space. To sum up, about 200 people make the Spiral Dance happen. In the years I've been involved, the event has expanded from 300 to over 2,000 people attending from all over America.

The Spiral Dance is not only a ritual but a production that requires professional sound crews, musicians, a chorus and choral director. Many professional artists, dancers and performers are involved. Yet Spiral Dance is a place where someone who has never spoken in front of a large group can stand up and do an invocation. Every year different priestesses and priests participate in grounding and casting the circle; there's no one "leader" leading the ritual.

♦ *R/S: How is Reclaiming structured?*

♦ M: Reclaiming is set up as cells, as I had mentioned—groups of people who work on projects. For example, the newsletter cell produces the *Reclaiming Quarterly,* which has become a glossy magazine. Sometimes we have cells for special projects; we organized one for Starhawk's recent workbook, *Twelve Wild Swans.* We have a cell organized by a woman who takes Goddess tradition into women's prisons. We have cells for teachers; a Witch Camp cell. And from each of these cells is a representative who can approach what we call "the Wheel." The Wheel is responsible for making financial decisions for Reclaiming as a whole—by consensus, of course.

When we were dissolving the original Reclaiming collective, it took two years of consensus meetings to come up with the idea of having organizing cells. Besides the cells I've already mentioned, we've added the e-cell, which handles e-mail and our Web site. Other cells include a community-building cell which puts on events that *aren't* rituals, to help newcomers come into the Craft, or into Reclaiming traditions specifically.

Each cell has different requirements for joining. For the ritual planning cell you need to take the Reclaiming core classes:

Elements of Magic for Beginners, Rites of Passage, and the Iron Pentacle—and to have attended at least a year of rituals. The Samhain cell consists of people who have been to at least one Spiral Dance and have taken Reclaiming classes. Dragons and Graces also need to have attended at least one Spiral Dance. However, there are lots of really fun positions that require no prior experience, such as altar-building, ticket-taking, and clean-up which is *very* important!

♦ *R/S: Reclaiming events are so varied; a recent one criticized genetic modification (GM) of our food plants—*

♦ M: And a recent Spiral Dance theme centered on our vision of the future: What's our vision, and how can we make life different? Have you read *The Fifth Sacred Thing?* It's a novel Starhawk published that's set 70 years in the future. There's been a war, and San Francisco is an isolated city that lives a utopian, non-violent, collective-consensus, feminist life. All the concrete has been pulled up to make gardens, and people move around the city on gondolas. The only vehicle that travels the Bay Bridge is the grain train that brings grain and vegetables from the East Bay. It's a very interesting book, and I'm hoping these aren't true premonitions in her writing, because this would be a really *intense* society.

At Spiral Dance, we've had acrobats flying through the air on ropes, and exotic fire and sword dancers. Sometimes we get accused of sponsoring a circus, but there's nothing wrong with a beautiful, thrilling performance. Is this a performance? Yes, it's a performance within ritual. It's inspiring to watch beautiful invocations; Pagan aesthetics shouldn't be limited by the word "spiritual."

♦ *R/S: How does Reclaiming make decisions?*

♦ M: Reclaiming is committed to *feminist process,* which means collective, consensus decision making. First of all, we don't use this as a *creativity* tool; consensus is only used for solving problems. With consensus, we always have a facilitator or "vibes watcher" present to notice if the energy's lagging, or if somebody's becoming annoyed and not getting a chance to speak. All of us try hard not to interrupt. We keep thrashing around in the process until every single person is in agreement. But any individual can block a decision if they have a good argument. However, it's rare when that happens, because Reclaiming does have a mission statement plus its principles of unity. And to be part of Reclaiming, you have to be familiar with both of these.

So at a meeting, someone gives a proposal, then everybody has a chance to voice their concerns. If you have clarity questions, you can ask those. Basically, we go through a few steps of process and then ask, "Do we have consensus?" Then we all twinkle our fingers. If it's a really difficult problem, it can take days.

Reclaiming's notion is that it's really disempowering to vote, because if you're against something, the majority rules. Yet that which is popular is not always just or correct. That's why it's so important that each person have a voice. We also thwart the rise of charismatic autocrats by frequently changing our "leaders"—especially at larger public events like Spiral Dance. Nevertheless, there are definitely power struggles within Reclaiming—it's scary how easily you can enjoy wielding power!

In the outside world, people think they need to *take* power from so-called "powerful" people to become powerful themselves. But really, every individual has power from within, which Starhawk talks about in *Truth Or Dare,* which is all about power dynamics. She discusses "power over," which is domination and repression, versus "power with" which is where we're equal. Then there's "power from within," which we all have. And a common mistake is to think that to become powerful, you have to take power from someone else. But really, there's enough for everybody.

Once people realize that everyone can take leadership, then it may be possible to have a more feminist, calm, spiritual community. But unfortunately, we're raised in a patriarchal, hierarchical, authoritarian society—especially in the United States, which is very much a "me"-centered culture obsessed with financial success. So I think that Reclaiming has all the faults of the world within its structure, but we're conscious enough to be looking at ways of undoing those kinds of patterns . . . undoing hierarchy.

♦ *R/S: What's your concept of feminism?*

♦ M: I think of the feminist movement as people who are committed to loving the earth as the Mother, treating all life as sacred, and definitely honoring women as being powerful contributors to our society, as well as treating *all* human beings with the same equal value and respect. The feminist movement also means making a political commitment to undoing racism, looking at ways of undoing sexism (and all the different "isms"), social injustice, and all of the environmental problems we face. And feminist spirituality is about honoring the Great Mother, who has many names: Gaea, Brigid, Isis, Diana, Astarte, Hecate, Venus, Keridwen . . .

♦ *R/S: Tell us about your teaching—*

♦ M: I started teaching eight years ago. Reclaiming has a policy that all teaching is done by pairs, to minimize the authoritarian tendency. While teaching, I usually wear a small pentacle which symbolizes motivation, determination, inspiration, liberation, and illumination. If you could have all of these working at once, you'd be unstoppable!

Over the past eight years I've taught mostly Reclaiming classes, but for the past five years I've also been teaching sexual empowerment classes. In Pagan sacred space, we look at the ways we've been hurt sexually.

We work on being able to be naked in front of people and not feel hideously ugly and horrible—especially women with body-hatred issues. After all, the Goddess *is* our body—we are part of her and she is part of us. For us to hate our bodies and be taught to hate our bodies, is one of the greatest sins against humanity!

Men have also been oppressed sexually. Being taught to be strong, manly, to not cry and not show feelings, is as oppressive as women being taught that they're second-class.

My sex workshops can sometimes get *loud,* with people wailing, crying and carrying on. If I did this at home, my neighbors would think I was killing people!

At my women's empowerment weekend, I teach processes for transformation and lessons that help people empower their sexual selves. Usually there's no genital contact, although in the weekend workshop we do erotic work on the second day—but it takes a whole day getting to that.

For the basic sexual empowerment/healing class, I screen people over the phone. (There are some people I'm not willing to work with, such as people with deep emotional disturbances.) Then I ask the participants to bring food to share so we can have a "naked lunch" together, bring an item for the altar, a journal, a pen, a towel and other necessities. We work naked all day. I encourage people not to just sit and look at each other, but to make an effort to meet and talk with the people they feel *least* drawn to, and break down some of their boundaries.

We create sacred space together and do verbal check-ins. We build the altar together, with each person making a contribution. We create *prayers of intent,* asking, "Why am I doing this? What do I hope to get out of this? What is it I actually hope to change?" In the morning we write a prayer to the Goddess and put it on the altar so it becomes a magical working throughout the day. Every person's intent is there on the altar.

After this we do ritual undressing, which can be fun. I break people into groups of three with at least one man and one woman in every group. People can put their hand up if they don't feel comfortable in their group and I'll move them—no questions asked. Sometimes people determine how they want their clothes taken off. For example, I might say, "I want you to chase me around the room and tear my clothes off." [laughs]

It's really fun watching everyone get naked. A couple of times I had two men in my group kneel at my feet with candles. While I slowly removed my clothes, they said, "Madrone, you are so beautiful." They kissed my fat belly while saying, "Thou art Goddess" in a reverent tone of voice. It was great; very empowering. I felt really beautiful.

People dream up all kinds of funny ideas. Some people hide behind a towel to undress. Then we all form a circle, naked, and I invite people to look at one another. They're all looking at each other's faces, and I say, "Don't stop at the heads—check out the breasts, the chests, the cocks and the yonis," and everybody laughs uncomfortably. We allow our gaze to wander over the entire body, because it's not something you often do. I have us turn around and bend over so you get a between-the-legs view as well, just for a bit of fun and humor.

I do a lot of talking about intentional and unintentional touch: how to set boundaries, including how to say "No." You might say, "I'd like you to take my clothes off and massage my butt for me." If I didn't feel comfortable doing that, I would say, "Thank you—what else would you like?" That would mean, "I can't immediately give you that because of the way I'm in my body right now, which has nothing to do with *you.*" Then someone else might say, "Oh, I'll massage your butt—no problem!" Our intention is to create ritual without invading people's boundaries.

Also, at the sexual empowerment workshops, I ask people to put down a "grounding cord," which is a psychic energy line that goes from the first chakra down into the center of the earth. It's for letting go of bad memories and experiences you need to let go of—flushing them down the toilet, so to speak.

We do a wounding circle, which is hard to describe. Each person gets to come into the center and state a way in which they've been sexually hurt. Anyone who's had a similar experience steps in, and we take a heart breath—you breathe in through the sex chakra and out through the heart. You take a moment to see who has stepped into the circle with you, see who your allies are, and then you step back. Each person gets to step in and talk about how they've been hurt, and often that's pretty intense, emotionally.

We do various blindfold exercises around touch, intentional touch, and giving people 100% focus, learning how to really be present. There are some exercises in the workshop that are quite erotic, with people rolling on top of each other and kissing passionately. But it's all about safe sex and safety; I try to keep genital contact out of it. I tell people that if there's someone they really want to have fun sex with, *then make a date!* At lunchtime we have a big vegetarian feast. The whole day lasts about nine hours, and even though it's a rollicking fun time, it's exhausting.

I call this class "The Magic of Sexual Empowerment." It needs to become a weekend workshop at a hot spring where we can stay overnight together. Annie Sprinkle did a "Sluts and Goddesses" workshop, where on Saturday night all of us dressed up as sluts or goddesses and fed each other chocolate fondue. It would be good to have some kind of erotic celebration like that at the end of my weekend workshop.

I've also led *yoni massage* workshops just for women.

♦ *R/S: Have there been any problems?*

♦ M: Yes, there are all kinds of problems—more so with men. Sometimes I'll say to the men, "If you're here to examine why you haven't been in

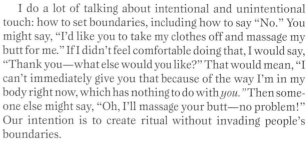

a relationship for awhile, and how you can make changes around that, you'll probably be happier. But if you come here looking for your dream girl, you might not find her." A few men have felt disappointed that some women in the group were gay. Also, they had to work with other men, and this was really hard for them. I say, "This is not about having sex. This is about changing your oppressive sexual patterns inside sacred space with the help of the Goddess. We all have different emotional patterns and histories that influence the way we deal with sex. There are many different ways of dealing with sexual healing, and this is just a jump-start."

At the end of the day, we review our prayers of intent and raise a cone of power so that our prayers of intent go out into the universe. People leave behind the written prayers and I burn them. I think that if you free the sexual self, the creative self becomes more free.

♦ *R/S:* **What do you like most about Reclaiming?**
♦ M: The name Reclaiming stems from our right to call ourselves Witches—reclaiming the words "Witch," "feminist," "earth-based spirituality," "queer," "faggot"—all words that have been socially taboo within our society.

The reason I'm most drawn to Reclaiming is because all of our rituals and events are clean and sober. We ask people not to bring drugs or alcohol—that way we support those who are trying to live their life that way. I consider myself sober—not clean and sober—because every few years I might partake in recreational drugs such as hallucinogens. And once a year I attend an annual Twelve-Step meeting to pick up my "chip"—that's an award they give for every year you've stayed sober. Walking down the aisle knowing I've lasted more than twelve years without a drink is a small, empowering ritual for me! (I began drinking heavily at the age of sixteen, and quit in 1987.)

One of Reclaiming's suggestions is to experience at least three other traditions' rituals every year, just to keep everything in perspective. I think it's great to go off and do another tradition's ritual periodically. People need to understand that different lifestyles aren't bad. I still see that "Us and Them" mentality everywhere, yet I've had some really great times with the "Them's."

This year I went to a Buddhist ritual about channeling divine love. I woke up at two o'clock in the morning and my room appeared filled with orange light. I'm blinking and rubbing my eyes, thinking I'm imagining it. There's a low, beautiful hum, this orange light, and I'm feeling so much love. I'm wondering, "Where is this coming from?" and then realized

it was coming from my own heart. My heart had been opened to some kind of divine love.

♦ *R/S:* **What** about *Pagan group support of ecstatic states? Supposedly these enable one to "break through" to a different level of consciousness, where transcendent insights appear—*
♦ M: First of all, while I do public rituals with Reclaiming, I also attend lots of other traditions' rituals, because this helps me keep an open mind. There are a lot of people in Reclaiming who don't like my ideas on sexuality, because I move within the radical sex community. I used to go to play parties and Queen of Heaven parties. I never understood SM at all until I started going to SM play parties.

But I experienced one of my most ecstatic moments of "spiritual enlightenment" at an SM party, when I had my heart chakra pierced. The piercer did a circle of temporary piercings around my heart with one central piercing, then bound them all together and pulled on them. (Historically, a lot of my wounding and pain has been in the heart chakra.) As she kept pulling on them I thought, "I don't like this; it's uncomfortable." Then I stopped fighting it and thought, "Just let go." And I discovered this was about surrender—surrendering all of this *stuff:* the should's and ought's about what's good and bad—of all of my oppression.

All of a sudden I got swept backwards into some unknown place. I felt my heart chakra go "*Mmmm*" and burst open! Then the piercer pulled the needles out—in a rough way, so they would bleed. I was sitting there naked from the waist up and my heart was bleeding and I had the most ecstatic, euphoric feeling I've ever felt in my life! It felt like the ultimate bleeding heart, and here it was literally bleeding, pouring down into my hands. It was like all the years of heart-oppression and all the years of broken hearts just poured out of me. I actually felt ecstatic for days after.

After that I've really been intrigued by the whole SM community's reaching of ecstatic states. I used to really scoff at it and be judgmental. Now I say, "*Never say never!* Never judge until you have really good information!"

♦ *R/S:* **Madrone is a character in Starhawk's novel, The Fifth Sacred Thing.** *Is that where you got your name?*
♦ M: No. In Reclaiming, our process of initiation involves asking for initiation from people you feel you have a lot to learn from. Over the next year-and-a-day you try to complete the challenges those people give you. Initiation includes a ritual of death and rebirth—I can't give too many details—but there is one part where you die, are reborn, and get a new name. About five years ago I was initiated, and the name "Madrone" just came to me.

♦ R/S: How does Starhawk deal with fame?

♦ M: Because of her writing, she's been famous since she was 25 years old. Personally, I regard her as one of the kindest, most gracious and generous people I know. She has turned from teaching goddess workshops to doing more overtly political work—unfortunately, it doesn't pay. At the W.T.O. she taught non-violence training: how to support each other, how to have affinity groups if people get arrested, and what to do if arrested. She also taught various tactics to use with the police if they're harassing someone or singling people out. She's com-

mitted to non-violence, and I think she's a leader who actually walks her talk.

The beautiful thing about Starhawk is she lives collectively. She drives a ten-year-old car. For years I had heard rumors that she arrives in a limousine and stays in a hotel suite, but in reality she stays in a hotel room with ten other people and arrives in a beat-up Toyota Corolla. Personally, I think she deserves the word "leader"—one whose leadership is based on compassion, non-violence, generosity, bigness of heart, and forgiveness. A person can become a leader when a group of people look to them for answers and guidance.

It's tricky when you *are* famous. Again, in this hierarchical, patriarchal society, we cut leaders down until they don't want to lead anymore. The question is, are humans "naturally" hierarchical? I see throughout recorded history humans fighting humans, humans dominating humans, plus a lot of greed-and-vengeance cycles.

Again, in the real world, most people have bosses and chiefs in charge; it's definitely about "power over." And this is why I'm so drawn to Reclaiming: because there has to be a *new way.* There has to be a way for the person who cleans the office to be as empowered as the person in charge of the office. Because each person *is* essential; we just have different work. ♦♦♦

RECLAIMING PRINCIPLES OF UNITY

"My law is love unto all beings …"— The Charge of The Goddess

The values of the Reclaiming tradition stem from our understanding that the Earth is alive and all of life is sacred and interconnected. We see the Goddess as immanent in the Earth's cycles of birth, growth, death, decay and regeneration. Our practice arises from a deep, spiritual commitment to the Earth, to healing and to the linking of magic with political action.

Each of us embodies the divine. Our ultimate spiritual authority is within and we need no other person to interpret the sacred to us. We foster the questioning attitude, and honor intellectual, spiritual and creative freedom.

We are an evolving, dynamic tradition and proudly call ourselves Witches. Honoring both Goddess and God, we work with female and male images of divinity, always remembering that their essence is a mystery which goes beyond form. Our community rituals are participatory and ecstatic, celebrating the cycles of the seasons and our lives, and raising energy for personal, collective, and Earth healing.

We know that everyone can do the life-changing, world-renewing work of magic, the art of changing consciousness at will. We strive to teach and practice in ways that foster personal and collective empowerment, to model shared power and to open leadership roles to all. We make decisions by consensus, and balance individual autonomy with social responsibility.

Our tradition honors the wild, and calls for service to the Earth and the community. We value peace and practice non-violence, in keeping with the Rede, "Harm none, and do what you will." We work for all forms of justice: environmental, social, political, racial, gender, and economic. Our feminism includes a radical analysis of power, seeing all systems of oppression as interrelated, rooted in structures of domination and control.

We welcome all genders, all races, all ages and sexual orientations and all those differences of life situation, background, and ability that increase our diversity. We strive to make our public rituals and events accessible and safe. We try to balance the need to be justly compensated for our labor with our commitment to make our work available to people of all economic levels.

All living beings are worthy of respect. All are supported by the sacred elements of air, fire, water and Earth. We work to create and sustain communities and cultures that embody our values, that can help to heal the wounds of the Earth and her peoples, and that can sustain us and nurture future generations.

Opposite left: 1997 at Burning Man, Black Rock Desert; Opposite right: London, England, age 5
Above left: Geeland, Australia, age 13; above right: Witchcamp 2000

Diana Paxson

Science fiction/fantasy author Diana Paxson is co-founder of The Society for Creative Anachronism (S.C.A.), Dark Moon Circle, the Fellowship of the Spiral Path, the Heathen kindred, Hrafnar (*hrafnar.org*) , and has led in the recovery of the Northern Oracular tradition of Seidh. She is currently serving as Steerswoman of the Troth, an international Asatru organization. She worked with acclaimed writer Marion Zimmer Bradley, author of *The Mists of Avalon*. Diana has an M.A. in Comparative Literature, is an accomplished storyteller and teacher, and lives with her extended family in "Grayhaven," a large house in the Berkeley hills. Her newest book is *Priestess of Avalon* (a collaboration with Marion Zimmer Bradley). Interview by John Sulak.

♦ *RE/SEARCH: Tell us about your home, Grayhaven.*

♦ DIANA PAXSON: We've lived in the house since 1971. My husband and brother-in-law had been profoundly affected by reading Robert Heinlein's *Stranger in a Strange Land* at an impressionable age, and that's where the idea of living in an extended family came from. We named our house "Grayhaven" because the family members had a variety of last names, and it seemed simpler just to give the house a name of its own.

The house has three-and-a-half floors. Over the years various friends and relations have lived with us, most of whom are still part of the family. There's a living room large enough to waltz in, and every New Year's Eve we remove the furniture, wax the floor, and people dance most of the night. We can host forty people for a ritual—the normal limitation on a Pagan group, which is the size of an apartment living room, doesn't apply! And we host weddings from time to time.

I have altars in almost every room. I realized some time ago that if I invited the god/desses in I would be more likely to keep the house clean! The kitchen has goddesses in the four corners for the four directions, plus a shrine for female ancestors. The kitchen is the temple of the goddesses and grandmothers. In a sense, the whole house is a temple.

♦ *R/S: The Society for Creative Anachronism (S.C.A.) and the similarly-themed Renaissance Faires have attracted many Pagans over the years—*

♦ DP: In the early days, people who attended the S.C.A. fell into three basic groups: 1) those who had no particular religion and didn't want one, 2) those who were still some kind of Christian, with varying degrees of fervor, and 3) Pagans. Most of the Pagans were "solitaries" practicing by themselves because in the Sixties, it was very hard to find a group—the British Wiccan traditions hadn't reached the West Coast yet. But there were a lot of people who honored various old gods, primarily Norse and Celtic. They had private altars and felt a reverence for Nature.

Eventually, some of the people who met through the S.C.A. decided to get together for religious rituals as well. It being the Sixties, this took place within the larger context of, "We don't like the world we grew up in, or the society and religion we were given. The civil rights movement changed society, so

maybe we can change religion—or at least create a new one." That's exactly what we did.

♦ *R/S: You worked with the S.C.A. member and writer Marion Zimmer Bradley. Readers of* **The Mists of Avalon** *might be surprised that she was a Pagan in real life—*

♦ DP: Marion had been interested in Occultism and British esoteric magical tradition since she was a teenager. She formed "The Aquarian Order of the Restoration" (A.O.R.) which aimed at restoring the balance between the masculine and the feminine in spirituality. Marion required everyone to take responsibility for one of the seasonal rituals. At that time I thought all I would ever be good for in a magical working would be to make sure the candles didn't fall over! But when Marion required me to write a ritual, I discovered I could. My mother had named me after a Greek goddess, so from an early age I had read about my namesake. I had worked with mythological images and archetypes in college and graduate school, so when I started writing ritual, I already had a vocabulary and background. The fact that I could write ritual was extremely satisfying.

♦ *R/S: You also created an all-female coven with her—*

♦ DP: In 1978, a 19-year-old woman who was living with us and who had been on her own for awhile asked if we could have a coming-of-age ritual for her. We remembered our own puberty experiences, which ranged from really awful (those who started their periods with no education and thought they were dying) to anti-climactic. After some discussion we put together a ceremony involving a ritual bath—Marion had a hot tub by this time—and three women took the parts of the three aspects of the Goddess.

Most of the women at that ritual were also in the A.O.R., or in various Wiccan groups. Partly because we were a women-only group working solely with the Goddess, we contacted a different flavor of energy. It was so exhilarating that we thought, "Wow—let's keep doing this!" So the women in that original ritual started meeting on the dark moon, because several of them already had *full* moon ceremonies they went to with other groups. And that became our Dark Moon Circle. It started in 1978 and is still meeting today—which is something of a record! [laughs]

At that time Marion was writing *The Mists of Avalon,* her version of the King Arthur legend. Her depiction of the priestesses was based in part on our work in Dark Moon Circle. Her great contribution to the Arthurian tradition was to tell the story completely from the point of view of the female characters. When *Mists* appeared in 1983, it became a major best-seller—and no one was more surprised than Marion! She was already well-known within the science fiction community, but this book reached a mainstream audience.

Dark Moon Circle was riding that cultural tide of feminist spirituality. And when *Mists* became famous, everybody in the world expected Marion to be Morgaine, the book's heroine, and to be their own personal guru. This was more than anybody could have coped with, and she became increasingly reclusive. Her health started to fail, and by the end of the Eighties she was able to do very little.

For a long time, Marion had wanted to write the book that became *The Forest House,* about British Druids in the first century. It was based on Bellini's opera, *Norma.* Because I knew British history as well as being familiar with the magical background of Avalon, she asked me to become her invisible collaborator. When *The Forest House* was a success, we wrote *Lady of Avalon.*

The most recent book in the series is *Priestess of Avalon,* which connects the British legend of Helena and the historical Emperor Constantine to Avalon. They lived during the era when official Paganism gave way to official Christianity. The question as to why Christianity superseded Paganism is one that haunts modern Pagans. **In many ways, contemporary Paganism is in the same situation as early Christianity. It was mostly an urban religion, people tended to be relatively closeted**, and there was a lot of fighting between factions. However, even with all the fighting between Pagan factions that I've seen, the early Christians still had them beat!

Marginalized groups tend to project their hostility onto each other rather than the outside world which is their real enemy—but which it's not safe to attack. You see that in early Christianity and in contemporary Paganism as well. But now there's this major shift from "We have to hide in people's living rooms and hope no one notices us" to "Here we are, out in the open." Which is what happened when Constantine [Roman emperor, 306–337] made Christianity the official state religion.

♦ *R/S: How much of the Avalon books is based on history?*

♦ DP: It's frustrating for Celtic scholars to read *The Mists of Avalon* because the Celts didn't have the kind of religion that Marion portrayed. She wrote psychological, esoteric and archetypal truth, not historical truth. Mainly she was writing about the conflict between the old Goddess religion of the Priestesses of Avalon and the incoming patriarchal Christianity. Naturally, her protagonist Morgaine is very upset

about this. At the end, Morgaine realizes that a lot of the spirituality of the Goddess has been transferred to the figure of Mary, and that the Goddess is going to survive—even if people do not realize that's who they're honoring. With medieval Christianity that's pretty much what happened.

♦ *R/S: Are many fantasy writers Pagans?*

♦ DP: There's Marion, myself, and maybe a few more. Many writers in their personal life are agnostic or some kind of Christian—consciously at least—but when they let the unconscious go they may invent absolutely wonderful Pagan theology. Anyone who studies mythology and ancient cultures and has any sensitivity will start pulling in kinds of mythic material, but it's not necessarily the result of learning or practice. This is an important distinction.

It's perfectly possible to read a lot of fantasy literature and find good insights you can use in a ritual. What you won't get is much information on *how* to do it, because the authors don't know. They're great at describing spiritual experiences, but not good at describing how you get there. I'm gradually moving toward writing more non-fiction, because it would be nice to be able to come right out and say something directly, rather than obliquely.

♦ *R/S: You and Marion Zimmer Bradley also started the Fellowship of the Spiral Path, which is still going strong today—*

♦ DP: The first form of the organization was the "Center for Non-Traditional Religion," formed to host Dark Moon Circle and all the other groups that were meeting in her garage. When Marion decided to withdraw from Pagan practice, the incorporation was transferred to "Spiral," so that we could continue consecrating clergy and receive tax-deductible donations.

"The Fellowship of the Spiral Path" is a legally recognized religious corporation in the State of California. We do distinguish, however, between the role played by ordained clergy and the ability to at as a priest or priestess in one's own circle. However, besides ritual and magical skills, a Pagan minister needs organizational and pastoral counseling skills, so we started developing training for that. You didn't necessarily

THE SOCIETY FOR CREATIVE ANACHRONISM (S.C.A.)

While still a graduate student, I invited over some friends for a medieval sword-and-shield tournament in my backyard. From that first event the Society for Creative Anachronism took form as an organization to recreate the Middle Ages not as they were, but as they should have been.

From the beginning it was about participation—to attend, you had to wear a costume. You couldn't go out and buy one—although now you can, because there are people making their living producing them.

In the S.C.A. people can achieve status by fighting well, by excellence in the arts, or by service. Some people have done incredibly wonderful work in jewelry, embroidery, spinning, cooking and carving—you name it. If it's a medieval craft, somebody in the S.C.A. has done it—including horsemanship, armor-making, and falcony.

There's a major event every summer in Western Pennsylvania that regularly attracts 10,000 people. They hold battles, and host all kinds of arts and crafts. Now, over thirty years later, the S.C.A. is an international organization with 50,000 members in a number of "kingdoms."

need this to act as a priest or priestess, but you needed it if you were going to be in a public role. It requires an oath whereby, karmically, you're basically stating, "I am now fair game. If someone needs a priest or a priestess, I'm available."

At the time, I knew that in some ways this was a really stupid thing to do, because once you have made that commitment, you give up your right to say "No." Marion and I were consecrated in the same ceremony. At first I worried about validity, because we had had to put the training program together ourselves, but when I got involved in the larger Pagan community and began meeting people like Starhawk and Margot Adler, I discovered that many leaders of the contemporary Pagan movement had had to bootstrap themselves up as well, which made me feel much better.

♦ *R/S: How did you get involved in Norse Paganism?*

♦ DP: I became interested in trying to recover the techniques of the shamanic practices of the North. Viking culture was not a shamanic culture *per se,* but a lot of the skills and techniques are the same. Oracular Seidh (pronounced SAY-TH) is one of the best recorded religious/magical practices of the north. It's the Northern equivalent of the Delphic Oracle, but instead of having people make a pilgrimage to a sacred site where the Oracle lives, the Oracle with her assistants would make a circuit around the different communities. When she arrived, the people of the community would build an elevated platform where she could sit. A song would be sung to some of the spirits, and she would then move into a trance state where she could answer questions.

My hope was that we could train a group of people to perform the same service for the Pagan community. So I put together elements that I had found in various Norse materials, interpreted them in the light of shamanic (and other kinds of) work, and started trying it all out. And it worked. The group, which we named "Hrafnar," eventually turned into a regular heathen kindred, and the Seidh group, which is now called "Seidhjallr," has been doing the oracular seidh regularly in the Bay Area for ten years. Every year people come back with more questions, so obviously we're doing something for somebody.

I have also performed seidh at festivals in other parts of the country, and taught workshops on it in various parts of the U.S. and in Europe. Seidh uses our natural abilities to journey within and to open up to intuitive knowledge. A related practice is god-possession, which is found in cultures all over the world, most vividly in the African diasporic traditions. The same psychological mechanism involved leads to dissociation and dissociated personalities. The difference is, if you do it in a religious context under a disciplined situation for particular purposes, then it enriches your life instead of destroying it. The mechanism may be the same, but the *context and application* transform something that could be disintegrating into an enriching type of practice.

♦ *R/S: How did you discover Pagan groups ascribing to Norse traditions?*

♦ DP: At a Midwest Wiccan festival I noticed a booth with runes all over it. The dealers had brought some great home-brewed mead, and after a day of meetings, drinking a horn of that seemed like a good idea. [laughs] It turned out they were Asatru, involved with a Nordic organization called the Troth, which was committed to being non-racist and open to everybody. This was the first Norse organization I'd heard of that might actually be safe to join!

"Asatru" means the faith of the "Aesir," which means the gods. In a wedding ceremony people say "I pledge thee my troth," an ancient British word related to truth, or being true. Another word for this religion is "Heathen," which is a Germanic word for "Pagan." Pagans are people of the heath who are still in the country practicing the old ways, as opposed to city people who have become Christians. Some people call this the Northern Way.

The main problem Pagans and Wiccans have to deal with is a commonly held assumption, "Oh, aren't you all Satanists?" **Pagans have to patiently explain, "No, Satanism is actually a *Christian* heresy, and Wiccans do not believe in Satan, much less worship him."** Just as many Christian saints adopted the iconography and attributes of various Pagan gods, likewise Satan picked up the iconography of some of the Pagan gods—in particular Pan, who provided the goat's horns and the rest of it. Pan, being a nature or fertility deity, represented a lot of what early Christianity was upset with—they had a real problem with sex.

Similarly, Asatru and Heathenism has to deal with the Nazi and Neo-Nazi problem. During the late 19th and early 20th centuries, European nations were striving to find a national

PAGANISM IN ICELAND

A thousand years ago, Icelanders voted to officially become Christian, otherwise a civil war might have occurred. Some Icelanders today think, "Maybe we didn't make the right decision—let's backtrack!" Iceland has

already given official state recognition and support to Asatru. Icelanders have never stopped working with land spirits; they detour roads around rocks where elves are believed to live ...

Top left: with husband Donald Studebaker (who writes pagan material as Pyrocanthus); Inset L: At Viking Symposium with cut-out; R: 2000 at Thingvellir, Iceland identity by reclaiming ancient history. Composers were orchestrating music based on folk themes, and people in general were studying ancient national mythology. The Germans in particular began getting back to the land, celebrating the spirits of the land, and hiking a lot. That wasn't bad. However, a nationalistic religion is a great way to unite people. So when Hitler came to power, he began using a lot of that imagery to rebuild German identity, appropriating symbols common to the Netherlands, Anglo-Saxon England and the Scandinavian countries.

There's nothing inherently Nazi about Germanic culture, but what Hitler did was take a few things, pervert their meaning, and put any scholar who didn't agree with him into the concentration camps. There were rune masters in the camps. If you actually examine the iconography of Nazi Germany, most of it is of Imperial Roman origin. Those rows of men marching with eagle staffs are Roman; the monumental neo-classical architecture is Roman. Hitler went back to the Holy Roman Empire and Imperial Rome for inspiration—not heathen Germany, which was the opposite of that. What Hitler did was a perversion and an aberration—abhorrent to people who work with Germanic deities.

1968 with son Ian at SCA event

Unfortunately, some Asatru groups *are* racist. Most of them are not public. Taking pride in one's own cultural background without excluding others can be difficult. I am very interested in recovering "Native European" religion.

A few years ago there was a United Nations Day celebration here, and the local interfaith community had a Native American in charge of putting on an event. They called me to represent the Europeans, saying, "She's a Heathen Priestess—she does what we do, only European." That was exactly what I was trying to get across—talking about ancestors, spirits of the land, and so forth. We have European traditions and they work well. But things become complicated because there are back-to-their-roots groups that don't encourage members who are not of European ancestry.

Personally, I've found that when the gods are calling, they'll call anybody who will listen, and they don't care what your ancestry is. So in Hrafnar we have people from all kinds of backgrounds, just as people of pure European background have become Tibetan Lamas. All that really matters is if there is a psychological affinity.

There are two basic elements of religion: 1) the earth we're living on, and 2) the culture. Western culture has tended to forget the former. The old medieval way of celebrating Christianity remembered it, with many seasonal festivals celebrated by the church. When you are on the move you lose your ancestral connection to the land—you can't go to the churchyard where your ancestors are buried. But if you live on land for a while and worship there, you can bind yourself to it. In Tilden Park, Berkeley, there's a cave just big enough to sit inside which has become known as the "Goddess cave." People meditate and leave offerings there. Gradually, places are becoming consecrated as people become aware of them as holy.

If you look closely at the Icelandic sagas, it appears that people worked with land-spirits and their ancestors more consistently than they did with the gods, although there were some who had their own temples for a patron deity. In some respects, this is true of heathens in Scandinavia today.

I think we can avoid some of the confusion about what one is worshipping by recognizing that there are levels of discourse. At one level you interface with the land, and at another with your culture. Depending on what you're doing, it is equally correct to say that a deity is neither male nor female, or to talk about the Goddess, or to talk about Athena or Freya or whoever, or to talk about the particular myth or spirit that goes with a spring.

♦ *R/S: Doesn't the Norse pantheon emphasize gods more than goddesses?*

♦ DP: Nineteenth-century Greek and Norse mythology books were written by people who could only see the gods, and didn't know what to say about the goddesses. Yet in the North, women had a higher status and more rights than they did anywhere else in Europe until the modern period—much more than they had under Christianity. For example, women could divorce their husbands. From the earliest times women were considered more spiritually sensitive, and both men and women practiced magic equally. The Norse goddesses are extremely powerful and participate in group deliberations—Odin learns more wisdom from female figures than from anybody else.

♦ *R/S: Tell us about Asatru rituals and how they differ from Wicca—*

♦ DP: Asatru has an uneasy relationship with Wicca, stemming from misunderstandings on both sides. Some people practice "Wiccatru," using Norse deities in a Wiccan format. This makes some Asatru unhappy, but I don't think the gods care! Most of the Norse Kindreds (Asatru groups are called Kindreds) meet once a month. Asatru ritual seems to have attracted more people of Protestant Germanic background, whereas Wicca gets more people from ceremonial traditions such as Catholicism and Judaism.

Asatru is very concerned with morality and ethical principles, and although Wicca is ethical, it doesn't worry about this as much. Wicca has the three-fold law and "Do what you will, but harm none." That's about all the general agreement you can get across the traditions. **Many heathens find it useful to list "the Nine Noble Virtues" as a statement of ethics. These are: Courage, Truth, Honor, Fidelity, Discipline, Hospitality, Industriousness, Self-Reliance, and Steadfastness.**

Then there are people who have developed their own ethical system. Unlike with Christian religions, there is no "One True Way."

♦ *R/S: Where did Asatru rituals originate?*

♦ DP: As far as we know, making toasts seems to have always been a part of Indo-European religious practices. Plato's *Symposium*, a Greek drinking party where philosophy was discussed, seems to have the same origin. At a wedding, the ceremonial toasts are really magical acts, even though most wedding guests don't regard them as such. Many cultural rituals are done out of some *need* without the participants knowing why. Whereas Pagans or Heathens know exactly what they're for and how to focus the energy.

Toasting, in Asatru, signifies passing the horn of communion between the community and the gods. You pass the horn, and you are in sacred space. Any oaths or promises you make bind you to the spiritual realm. Probably the one format that everybody in Asatru follows is the Sumble, in which you raise the horn and make a prayer, a boast or a promise. Many groups send the horn around once for people to honor the gods, once for the heroes, and once for whatever purpose is desired. Another form of ritual is called the Blot, which derives from the same etymological root as "blessing." This is a ceremonial honoring of a particular deity. The horn may be passed, and offerings made.

♦ *R/S: So Asatru rituals consist of sitting around drinking—*

♦ DP: But you could say the same thing about Christianity! The Asatru Sumble, like the Christian Mass, is built structurally around a ceremonial meal. That's the most widely accepted format, just as most Wiccan ceremonies involve cakes and wine. Usually something else is involved, such as a magical working. At Hrafnar, we sing in honor of the god/desses while the horn is going around.

♦ *R/S: Asatru members seem to be more "martial" than other Pagans—*

♦ DP: I would say that Asatru, or the Northern tradition, probably gives more honor to warriors and warrior deities than Paganism in general. This does not necessarily mean Asatru members are more aggressive; they may just be more willing to defend themselves. Each of the major Norse gods is a warrior in a different way, and many of the goddesses have warrior aspects as well. They're all capable of fighting, but that doesn't mean they're going to go out and be aggressive about it.

♦ *R/S: All mythologies have warrior gods and goddesses. Why do Asatru pay more attention to theirs than do other Neo-Pagan traditions?*

♦ DP: There has been a tendency in general Neo-Paganism to suppress and ignore that aspect in mythologies. But if you actually examine the Celts, they have just as much war and fighting in their mythology as the Norse—they were head-hunters, for heaven's sake! And they had female warriors all over the place. So the difference is not so much in the actual culture and mythology, but in the willingness of people to admit it.

Remember, there's a huge range of diversity among Heathens, Pagans and Wiccans. Only a few people have gone deeply into their religions, understanding the good points, the difficult points, and the balances between them. Most people possess very superficial understanding—yet they're the ones who come up with the most accusations! Anyone who has been involved in the Pagan community for a while realizes that just because Pagans believe in peace, that does not mean they're always peaceful.

Asatru is a tradition which recognizes that *conflict happens.* Just as the Japanese warrior traditions spent a lot of time teaching people how to control that aggressive energy, the traditions of the North help people learn how to control or channel it. Which is not to say that little explosions don't occur in the Asatru community from time to time. But we at least have some models and techniques for trying to act with honor and control our violent impulses. It's a matter of dealing with this by *recognizing* it, rather than repressing it and trying to pretend it doesn't exist.

You can learn a lot from the Greek plays, which have a wonderful way of dealing with issues on both the human experiential level and the theoretical level. In *The Bacchae,* Dionysus wanders around doing what he will, while the chorus comments, "If you repress things, they will break out in a worse way." The Greeks recognized that by giving things names, honoring them, and granting them a place and space, you had a safety valve integrated into your social structure.

♦ *R/S: How do you view the future of Paganism?*

♦ DP: We're seeing Paganism mature. When I first got into Paganism, any woman over forty who walked into the group was an instant Wise Woman, because we didn't have any. Now we have the graying of Paganism, with sages and wise women who have been around for twenty or thirty years.

Paganism is an idea whose time has come. Other religions can do some of the things that Paganism can do. But the connection to the earth, which I think is absolutely crucial to our survival, may be the great contribution from Paganism to the world's religious awareness. I'm not saying everybody should become Pagan, but I think there are a lot more people in the world who can agree with this statement: "The earth is sacred. The earth has spirit. We are part of this continuum of consciousness, not separated from it. Anything we do to the earth, we do to ourselves. Pay attention!" ♦♦♦

A Basic Heathen Reading List from Diana L. Paxson

The Elder Edda (Hollander translation)

Edda (the Younger, or *"Prose" Edda),* Anthony Faulkes, translator.

H.R. Ellis-Davidson: *anything,* esp. *Gods & Myths of the Viking Age; Gods and Myths of Northern Europe*

Kveldulf Gundarsson, *Teutonic Magic;* and *Teutonic Religion*

Freya Aswynn, *Northern Myth and Magic*

Edred Thorsson, *Futhark*

ed. Kveldulf Gundarsson, *Our Troth; Rheingold; Attila's Treasure*

Poul Anderson: *The Broken Sword; Hrolf Krakisaga; The Merman's Children; War of the Gods; Mother of Kings*

Diana L. Paxson: *Wotan's Children* trilogy: *The Wolf and the Raven; The Dragons of the Rhine; The Lord of Horses*

Recommended Websites

thetroth.org, hrafnar.org, aswnn.co.uk/ebooks.html

Clockwise from top left: Playing harp at festival   Photo: WilVon Dauster;

Margot Adler

In 1979 Margot Adler's *Drawing Down the Moon* was published, which noticeably catalyzed the Modern Pagan movement. Today she can be heard on the NPR shows "All Things Considered" and "Morning Edition." She also hosts a syndicated legal debate radio show called "Justice Talking," which focuses on constitutional issues—see *www.npr.org* and *www.justicetalking.org*. Interviews by John Sulak and V. Vale.

◆ *RE/SEARCH: Why are people drawn to Paganism?*

◆ MARGOT ADLER: One reason is a *search for roots*. Just as Alex Haley wrote the book *Roots* about looking for his ancestors in Africa, I think that the truth—*the harsh truth*, particularly about people in this country—is that all of us have lost our traditions. We either lost them because we were black and they were stolen from us when we came over in slavery. Or we were Native American and we were forced into colonization and Christian beliefs. Or, if we were White Europeans, most of our great-grandparents came over here to escape *everything* in the old cultures—sometimes for very good reasons. A lot of it was authoritarian and oppressive to women. So they came over to this land and *threw out* every tradition they possibly could, and Americanized very quickly.

Most people in this culture have a whitebread tradition. They don't remember the songs, the stories, the dances, the lullabies or the rites of passage and rituals. These were things that all Europeans had three hundred years ago. There were reasons why they came over here and threw that stuff away. But there is something very powerful about re-creating, in modern form, with intellectual integrity and a sense of freedom, new traditions that have songs and stories and rites of passage and ways of dealing with community and healing.

There is a huge search for that. No matter who we are, whether we're black or white or Native American, we come *bereft*. **We come to the table lacking a passionate ecstatic tradition that lets us, to be blunt, get off!** And I don't mean in terms of drugs or something. Why should the holy rollers have the only ecstatic tradition? Most of us are rooting around in the ashes for joyful, ecstatic traditions that we can live and practice at the same time that we can live our normal lives—dancing around a bonfire until dawn and yet still be able to get up the next morning and go to work as a doctor or lawyer or computer programmer.

Our culture dichotomizes everything. You're either black or white, male or female. You're either involved in your head or your heart. We tend to *split* everything. It's either the body or the mind, dark or light. What most Pagans are trying to do is to come to a sense of the *whole*, to reunite all those splits and dichotomies and create a vibrant, rich culture full of dance and song and ecstasy and life. But also, a culture that's in the modern world and is connected to democracy and liberty and all the things that we treasure as modern civilized beings. That's the contemporary Pagan experiment.

◆ *R/S: There are some Pagans who don't consider themselves to be religious at all—*

◆ MA: You do not need to *believe* in anything to be a Pagan, because it is a non-creed-based spirituality. If you think about Native American or Australian Aboriginal spirituality, even though there are many beliefs and deities, most of those religions are based on what people *do*, not what people believe. So rituals are set up in such a way as to say, "What do we do to celebrate our connection with the earth?" It's not based on what you "believe."

Paganism is a religion of atmosphere. It's not based *on the word!* It's not based on literal scripture. It's not a religion of *the book*. Christianity, Judaism and Islam are based on books. Paganism is much more metaphorical. You do not have to take anything literally. Some people do, and some people don't. You can be an atheist and be a Pagan, or you can believe in some kind of afterlife. I am pretty much of an agnostic about it myself.

There is no conflict between Paganism and science since there is no scripture to take literally, it's completely at home with change. So there is no problem with any scientific knowledge or theory. It has what someone described as "an open metaphysics"—it's totally *adaptable* to changes in knowledge and the way we think. Again, it doesn't have any hard creed or rules.

◆ *R/S: How would you say that Paganism is perceived in the media these days?*

◆ MA: There has been an improvement. It's a lot better than it was ten years ago. You still have to contend with the Hollywood-ization of Witchcraft, Paganism, etc. But at the same time that all those old stereotypes exist, there's a *huge* movement of all kinds of groups that embrace what we might call an earth spirituality. And that's happening even within some of the mainstream churches, or at least the liberal denominations. There are a huge number of Pagans within Unitarian Universalism, which historically was tied to the Transcendentalists, Emerson and Thoreau.

Reporters who come into it on an assignment and don't know anything about it use the old stereotypes. Twenty years ago you *only* got articles about Wicca on Halloween. But now you get articles about Wicca and Paganism on the solstices and Beltane and other times of the year. Most of the articles have been generally positive. It's treated with much more respect.

The real problem is that there is a tendency by the reporters to assume that Paganism is *silly*. So it's not that Witchcraft or Wicca is considered to be *evil*, although some people still confuse it with Satanism. It's just that they think that it's something that silly teenagers do.

♦ *R/S: They don't recognize it as being a* **real religion.** *Could you explain why it is a real religion?*

♦ MA: It deals with the things that every religion deals with, which is our relationship to ultimate reality, our connection to the cosmos and to all creation. **All religions deal with the larger questions of life, death and regeneration.**

Paganism is, in fact, the oldest religion. All of our ancestors, going way way, back, were Pagans. If you're from Ireland, you only have to go back to the 12th century. If you're Jewish you probably have to go back thousands of years. But the first religions of our own ancestors were about our relationship to the moon and the stars, figuring out how the crops grow and how to get into a right relationship with Nature. Paganism was the original religion of the land and of all people.

Every anthropologist and classicist has always understood this. But because there were religious wars and certain people won and certain people lost, it has been very hard, particularly in a Christian culture, to make people understand the larger aspects of Pagan religions.

♦ *R/S: What do you think the attraction of Paganism is for teens?*

♦ MA: I think the Pagan teen phenomenon has to do with television, and the popularity of certain teen shows, plus movies like *The Craft*—which was one of the worst movies ever made! Teenagers always want something rebellious and something new. Witchcraft seems hip and cool and interesting.

The fact is that most Pagan groups won't take teenagers—they're afraid of repercussions from unsympathetic parents. So in fact most teenagers just find like-minded friends, because there are very few groups that teens can enter until they're 18.

♦ *R/S: When you wrote Drawing Down the Moon, there wasn't a lot of Pagan activism. But now there is, and it's growing rapidly. What do you think of that?*

♦ MA: When Starhawk and I originally wrote our books [*The Spiral Dance* and *Drawing Down the Moon*], which both came out on the same day on opposite coasts, we had a dream about a certain kind of Paganism that included a lot of activism in it. But that kind of Paganism didn't exist. Now it does. We've often joked that maybe those books helped bring it about. [laughs]

Not all Pagans are activists. Not all Pagans are political. But there is a stream within Paganism that is very pro-environmentalist and gets involved in certain kinds of activism like anti-nuclear stuff and anti-W.T.O. demonstrations. It's been very interesting to watch as an outsider. The activism that I was involved with in the Sixties was more political, like the civil rights movement, the anti-Vietnam war movement, and feminism to some lesser degree. But I was not much of an activist when I got involved in Paganism. It is a natural fit, but it's not necessarily a fit for everyone.

♦ *R/S: Is Paganism an anti-authoritarian religion?*

♦ MA: Yes. **There is an anarchistic—in the best sense—strain that goes through the Modern Pagan movement.** People want a religion in which they are participants, not observers. And many of the religions that people have grown up with in this culture separated people from participation. They had to sit in pews and listen to sermons. Paganism is a religion without the middle person. The link to the divine is not mediated by a priest or a rabbi or someone else.

Paganism is participatory. It's creative. People write their own rituals for their needs at the moment—"What do we need to do to celebrate right now? What do we need to do to grieve? What do we need to do to heal this rift in our community? What do we need to do to heal this person's physical or psychological illness? What do we need to do to help this woman go through menopause? What kind of celebration can we do to show her that turning 60 is a beautiful thing?"

A lot of the rituals of the modern Pagan movement are very creative and are based on looking at our lives and saying, "How can we make life into a celebratory affair?" So it's self-made religion to some extent. Pagans look at traditions, and research them, but then write their own rituals based on what they've found.

♦ *R/S: You grew up in New York City . . . What's it like being a Pagan in New York City?*

♦ MA: It's a wonderful place to be a Pagan, although the community of Pagans in New York City leaves a little to be desired. There is a lot of Nature here—people don't realize it. Central Park is one of the best birding sites during migration in the United States. Thousands of birds funnel through there, and you can go out in the morning and see a hundred different species.

I walk to work through Central Park a lot, and walking is where I do my best meditating and thinking. It's a *ritual* for me.

Also, let's face it—where did all the Nature movements grow up? They grew up in the cities. Often people who live in the country take nature for granted because it is all around them constantly. If you think about the novels of D.H. Lawrence or other English novels where nature is vivid, they were often written by people who come from London. They saw what they were *missing.* Because in the country, people didn't realize that Nature was important because they had it all around them. [laughs]

Contemporary Paganism arose in places like St. Louis and Chicago and San Francisco, and near university towns like Madison, Wisconsin, where people read books. It was a very bookish phenomenon. People attracted to it were people who were readers and who like odd ideas and odd books.

♦ *R/S: What's the Pagan community like in NYC?*

♦ MA: It's complicated. There is a group called New Moon New York that has some large ecumenical gatherings. They do a beautiful Beltane ritual in Central Park every year and about 400 people come.

But in general most Paganism in New York City is very private. It's a lot of different groups, little groves and little covens. One reason is that around 20 years ago there was an occult shop in New York that was very, very prominent. And the person who ran it, who is now dead, was a complicated guy. There were a lot of antagonisms between him and other groups. As a result, the community didn't coalesce.

The East coast is a lot more uptight than the West coast. People are a lot more into doing stuff by themselves.

♦ **R/S: What would you say about the rest of the country and the world? Is Paganism becoming more public?**

♦ MA: I'm not sure that it's ever going to become a major religion. That's because you have to have a certain kind of strength and sense of self to be a Pagan. **Paganism does not give you The Answer.** It doesn't claim there is one truth, or that you're gonna get it all solved by just believing in this or that. That means that you have to be comfortable with living with confusion, multiplicity, and the idea that there are many truths and many answers. That's not so easy for a lot of people. They want an answer.

That means that contemporary Paganism is going to be a minority religion for a very long time. On the other hand I do see some important trends. Now the movement is older. People have families and are confronting issues that we never thought about before, like death. When people are young they generally think they are immortal. We thought we were immortal.

I think the women's, feminist, Goddess spirituality aspect of Paganism is growing up in a big way. A lot of women were attracted to it because they needed to feel strong. It almost worked as a kind of therapy for them. And I think that part of it is over, because that's no longer nearly as necessary. Many women have come into their own strength now.

We're seeing a maturing of Paganism both by women and men. The religion is getting more willing to deal with problems that other religions deal with, like alcoholism. Pagans are beginning to grapple with those issues. And Pagans are setting up their own seminaries and teaching traditions. People are beginning to want real training. If you are a Pagan clergy, what does that mean? In what way are you like all clergy? In what way are you different? There are a lot of struggles and tensions about "What is Paganism going to become in the future?"

♦ **R/S: How has Pagan ritual changed since you first did the research for Drawing Down the Moon?**

♦ MA: What we have witnessed in the last 25 years is the growth of good ritual. When I started out in Wicca in 1971, rituals were—excuse me for saying this—piss poor! They were really, really bad. People would stand in a circle and play something like Carl Orff's *Carmina Burana* on the record player, and they would kind of stomp around.

Let's face it, if you come from a white-bread culture where there is no dance and

there is no song, and the only people who are doing really good dance and song and chant are people who are trained for it in the theater, you're going to have really bad rituals.

Over the last 25 years a lot of people began getting really good at it. So now you have ecstatic dancing around a bonfire for hours, and incredibly beautiful rituals that are done with masks, beautiful music, and incredible movement—there is great ritual work being done. Thousands of people know the same chants and the rituals, and people are getting very adept at doing this. They are understanding how energy and movement and breath works. They've learned about timing and what things you should do differently if you're indoors or outdoors. There is a *ritual technology* that people are learning. And they've become much better at it than they were.

♦ **R/S: People are approaching ritual as an art form—**

♦ MA: It *is* an art form, but it's a sacred art form. Remember that art originally was part of sacred reality, but we've lost that connection. For hundreds and hundreds of years art has been disconnected from religion in most cases. We're relearning that connection.

♦ **R/S: Right; I've read that in primitive societies the word "sacred" and "art" don't exist, because their entire lives are sacred and artistic . . . Paganism seems to be providing a safe setting where all ages can mingle and relate to each other—**

♦ MA: Right; our society is *so* stratified. When the contemporary Pagan movement started in the Sixties and Seventies, a lot of it was young people, although there was always an openness to all ages. People realized that in indigenous religions there's a sense of respect for elders that our own culture doesn't have.

A lot of the women who got into Paganism got into Goddess spirituality. They started examining how women's lives were treated, and how only young, nubile, prettified women who are on the covers of *Playboy* and *Penthouse* were considered as the ideal. **In the Modern Pagan Goddess Spirituality movement, a lot of the ritual effort went into reclaiming all the different periods of women's lives.** So you have, for example, *croning ceremonies* when a woman turns mid-fifties or as she enters old age. You have rituals for menopause and rituals for menarche (for a woman's coming of age when she gets her period), and so forth.

Indigenous cultures all have rituals for women's and men's coming of age. In our culture there is none, except for the Bar

Mitzvah in Judaism and Confirmation in Catholicism. We really don't have a rite of passage into different ages.

Also when people started looking into Goddesses, they weren't just looking at Diana, the young maiden, they were looking into the Mother Goddess and Hecate, the Hag. There was a sense of looking at life as a *continuum*. As the Pagan movement began to get older and more mature, suddenly people started having kids and families. When I think about Paganism at the very beginning, there was really no talk about *death* or even *aging* until people began to experience it themselves. Now I think the exciting part about the Pagan movement is that it really does cover all people—it *is* a place where all ages meet. There is a sense of respect—for youth, for the elderly, and for all ages.

♦ *R/S: We need that—*
♦ MA: Absolutely. In our culture a lot of people past the age of fifty were being told, "No, you're too old. You can't have a job, you can't do this work." And in many different ways people started rebelling against that. You see these people retire and then have new careers doing all kinds of new work: writing books, becoming musicians—doing the work of their heart, doing the work of their *real* heart for the *first time.* So I think that Paganism fits in with this.

♦ *R/S: Can you say more about how our society stratifies us—*
♦ MA: There's advertising for kids, teens, and young adults. I was in a laundromat and I looked at a book that's used by people who do advertising. This was a 600-page resource book for people who need photos, so it included everything. There were weddings, funerals, people on sailboats, people in schools, people in the country, people in the city—thousands of photographs in all. And as I looked through it, I realized that there were maybe *eight* images of **women over the age of forty-five. They become, in our culture, invisible. I think that the whole move to earth-based spirituality counters this**, and celebrates the fact that there is birth, growth, decay, death, regeneration, and birth again. We're all part of this living cycle, and therefore *all* facets of that cycle are to be celebrated as sacred and beautiful.

♦ *R/S: A lot of us are seeking a different kind of wholeness— one that embraces TIME with its cycles of Nature and the seasons, not just things—*
♦ MA: Absolutely.

Right: 1955 with mother, Freydo;
Opposite page: 1949 NYC; Photos: Hella Hammid

♦ *R/S: Is there such a thing as Pagan aesthetics?*
♦ MA: *Oh boy.* I really don't know. There's a lot of Pagan art and Pagan music, certainly, in the world—both old and new. If you go to the Michigan Women's Music Festival, where over six thousand women gather on land, you'll see all these crafts people and artisans and art work and pictures. But I don't really know if there's a "Pagan aesthetic." I really don't know how to answer that question. Things that embody Nature are clearly going to be closer to a Pagan aesthetic, but . . . this reminds me of college students debating Postmodernism . . . which, as you know, is all a bunch of garbage! [laughs]

Clearly, within Paganism there is a lot of experimentation. So, for example, you did this book *Modern Primitives*—and a whole lot of people within Paganism have been experimenting with tattooing or piercing. Whereas I look at piercing and think, "Slavery!"—it has been very hard for me to get beyond the image of bondage. But **there are many people within the Pagan community that get into tattooing and piercing.**

There really is a *diversity* within the Pagan movement. There are people who sort of look like Sixties Hippies, or Leather Biker types, or even corporate executives. One of the more wonderful things about the Pagan movement is how it embraces a lot of different folks.

♦ *R/S: Actually, in our society aesthetics function to exclude people, whereas Paganism tries to be as inclusive and non-hierarchical as possible . . . Do you travel with any items to help keep you centered?*
♦ MA: First of all, I don't travel that much. But when I go and give workshops at various places, I definitely take several Goddess statues with me. Usually I take some symbol of earth-air-fire-water, and set up a tiny—not a real, whole—altar, but just a few little objects. I may take things to set up an altar just for a specific workshop. Usually I bring musical instruments like rattles, drums or bells. My workshops are filled with chanting and singing. I have been involved in singing and chanting since I was a child. I was a voice student at the High School of Music and Art, and when I was a kid, I dreamed of being a minstrel. Today, I spread Pagan chants and rounds and songs as far and wide as possible.

♦ *R/S: Can you talk about Paganism and children?*
♦ MA: Personally, I don't believe in forcing *any* religion upon a child. It's there if they want to sample it, and if they don't, they don't have to. I'm in a mixed family (I'm a practicing Pagan, but my husband is more of a quantum physics, scientist-oriented person)—it's not as if we're a Pagan practicing family. I've taken my son Alex to a couple of festivals—the Rites of Spring in Massachusetts and so forth, but I don't have him attend a lot of gatherings—he hasn't expressed a great desire to do so. If he does, I'll take him, and if he doesn't, I won't.

If something like setting up a Pagan altar comes naturally, that's perfectly fine. We're talking about a religion that is very much based on non-proselytizing, that people come to out of experience, and because it gives a name to something they've felt all their lives. It's not something you convert to, or adopt out of some kind of conversion and throwing out your old beliefs. It's something you adopt because it feels like what you always felt was right. You don't want to push it on people. If people really want it, they'll find it.

But it's perfectly fine to take children to the Maypole or the Pagan Eostar Egg celebration—kids love ritual. I've taken my kid to Mayday or Beltane festivals because there's nothing more wonderful than dancing around the Maypole.

♦ *R/S: Is Pagan culture as thorny as the area of Pagan aesthetics?*

♦ MA: No, I think there is a growing Pagan culture. The festival phenomena has certainly led to people around the country knowing the same songs, the same ideas, some of the same rituals, and some of the same phrases. There are basic ideas that most people involved in contemporary Paganism agree with, such as: the world itself is sacred. And that **the gods (whatever you want to call them: god, goddess, the gods) are part of us, and they are in us as well as outside of us. They're not above, and we're not below; we're all part of an interconnected web of vital sacred reality.**

I think those ideas have spread to a large, large group of people who are calling themselves many different things. Some are calling themselves Pagans or Witches or Druids; some are earth-based spirituality people, and some are Unitarian Universalists who are into the earth. Some say they are studying shamanism. Some describe themselves as involved in Nature Spirituality. Paganism is a minority movement, but there is a growing consensus among a lot of people that many of the above things fit them.

♦ *R/S: When you go to bookstores, are you fairly open to non-Pagan input?*

♦ MA: Very often I'm reading science fiction. **I'm not necessarily looking for Pagan fare in a bookstore, I'm looking for interesting ideas!** In fact, the Pagan movement evolved partly because people in small towns all over America began to get a hold of interesting books during the 1950's and decided, "Well, let's get out of this boring sterile environment we're in and do something imaginative." Some of these people had college degrees, but they weren't necessarily professors or intellectuals—they were people who were well read. And they liked odd and stimulating ideas—they liked working with them, thinking about them, and so forth.

The Church of All Worlds was started by a group of people in St. Louis, Missouri in the late Sixties. It included Oberon who's now with Morning Glory in the Ravenhearts. He and his friends were college students sitting around in St. Louis, Missouri in the late Sixties. They had been reading Robert Heinlein's *Stranger in a Strange Land,* Abraham Maslow (the self-actualizing psychologist), and Ayn Rand—forgive 'em! They put these three together in some kind of bizarre brew and called it The Church of All Worlds. They were just beginning to think about earth-based spirituality and the notion that all human beings come from a single cell. They had simply come across some really provocative ideas in some books and said, "Let's create an organization that deals with these ideas."

So a lot of the contemporary Pagan movement came out of looking at *ideas,* looking through science fiction. People came in who were medievalists—the Society of Creative Anachronism. All kinds of people like that came in. Books played a key role in this movement. Now, as the movement

becomes more mainstream, you have *The Mists of Avalon* becoming a best-seller, and the book becoming a big TNT movie. **Books played a very key role in the Pagan movement, despite the fact that this is a movement which emphasizes experience, feeling, and heart. Nevertheless, there's a lot of thought and thinking that went on here.**

♦ *R/S: And this is not a religion of the book—*

♦ MA: Exactly. Other very interesting books include Ernest Callenbach's *Ecotopia,* which has a lot of powerful statements about the environment. Then there's all the Goddess books—books by Marija Gimbutas, and all the Feminist books on Goddess Spirituality.

♦ *R/S: Some people say Gimbutas has been discredited—*

♦ MA: And some people disagree. For me, Ursula LeGuin was very powerful—*The Left Hand of Darkness* and *The Dispossessed*—those were two books that had wonderfully alternative views about the future and the way we should construct society.

A book called *The Sea Priestess* by Dion Fortune hit me really hard when I started out into Wicca. It was a novel about a woman who becomes a priestess of the Goddess. And Apuleius's *Golden Ass,* an ancient book written in the Second Century, has an incredible vision of the rites of the Goddess Isis. It's been a long time since I've thought about those books—

♦ *R/S: —but they were incandescent to you. You know, I have a library of about 15,000 books—*

♦ MA: Me too! I have walls and walls and walls of books. Come to New York and you'll find many people like that!

♦ *R/S: Can you sum up what Paganism can do for people—*

♦ MA: Paganism can help heal the wounds that our culture created. It looks at human beings as part of sacred reality—not above, not below, but totally connected with all life and creation. It basically says that we are sacred. And that means the body is sacred, the mind is sacred, sexuality is sacred—it's all part of the earth. And **you don't have to die to get the good stuff.** There is no split between spiritual and material. In other words, the *earth* is the domain of the sacred. The sacred is in this land, in the waters, in the trees, in all of life. It's in you and in me and we are vibrantly connected with it all. In fact, whatever "God" or "Goddess" is, it's not *above* us. It is part of us.

Obviously we don't always reach up to the highest part of that—it's a great struggle in life to even *approach* the highest part of that. But what is revolutionary about Paganism is that it says, "At least in potential, we are the gods."

There is an old quote from the first *Whole Earth Catalogue* which I've never forgotten: "We are as gods, and might as well get good at it." And if we could do that, and be that, then we would light up the world! In fact, we could create a world of peace and plenty and love. And on some level, that's what the Pagan movement is all about. ♦♦♦

Recommended Books

The Dispossessed; The Left Hand of Darkness Ursula LeGuin
Dreaming the Dark, The Spiral Dance Starhawk
Triumph of the Moon Ronald Hutton
The Golden Ass Apuleius

Patricia Monaghan

Patricia Monaghan, Ph.D., is a solitary nature mystic, poet, Quaker, and the author of *The New Book of Goddesses and Heroines, Wild Girls,* and *Magical Gardens.* She teaches at a Catholic university in the Midwest. Currently she is writing *The Red-Haired Girl on the Bog: A Celtic Spiritual Geography,* and a novel about St. Augustine's mistress.

Interviews by John Sulak & V. Vale.

♦ *RE/SEARCH: Tell us about your teaching—*
♦ PATRICIA MONAGHAN: Someone once advised me to teach what I love, and never teach what I'm fanatical about. So I teach interdisciplinary science and literature, which I love—not Goddess studies, which I'm fanatic about. My classes include "Chaos and Creativity" (one of my favorites), "Uncertainty Principle and Hermeneutics" (a complicated way of saying we explore the role of the observer in contemporary science and literary theory), and science writing. I was a science reporter and wrote about alternative energy sources before earning an interdisciplinary doctorate.

One of my favorite classes is a travel-study tour to Alaska, examining nature and culture (indigenous world views *versus* capitalism). Right now I'm planning a class on the literature of the prairies, to be combined with a prairie restoration effort near Joliet, Illinois. Meanwhile, as a hobby I research and write on eco-spirituality and Goddess mythology; I've written entries on "Gaia" and "Chaos" for *The Encyclopedia of Nature Religions.* To me, science, mythology and religion are all ways of describing the universe. However, Paganism is not considered a religion in academia.

♦ *R/S: Why not?*
♦ PM: Because most academics define "religion" very narrowly as hierarchical and usually monotheistic, whereas Paganism is decentralized and polytheistic. A recent book on comparative religion excluded Native American religions and Hinduism, which has many more adherents than Jainism [a 6th century B.C. Indian religion teaching liberation of the soul by right knowledge-faith-conduct]—which *was* included. And Shinto, Shamanism, and Paganism need not apply! An online community called Nature Religions Scholars, which is part of the American Academy of Religion (AAR), is working to redress this shortsightedness.

Did you know that all goddesses are Pagan—it took me about twenty years of religious study to notice this! There has *never* been a monotheist goddess religion; all monotheisms are based on gods only. *Wherever* you have a goddess you go into polytheism, which is immediately Pagan.

♦ *R/S: Must Paganism get academic recognition?*

♦ PM: If basic texts exclude Paganism, that means one of the main ways people find out about a religion is shut down. Many people are drawn to Paganism, not because there's a Pagan Church Box Luncheon in their neighborhood, but because they read something about it. I recently talked to a New Age/Occult bookstore owner who said that half of her customers are 15-year-old girls seeking an alternative spirituality.

♦ *R/S: What's your job title?*
♦ PM: Although I don't yet have tenure, I'm described as "Resident Faculty." I'm lucky to be working at an experimental college where the associate dean writes on gay men's spirituality, and another faculty member is writing a novel in which the Egyptian goddess Hathor is reincarnated today. Because my department is interdisciplinary, we have a psychologist onboard who is a performance poet, and an economist who writes fiction.

But when I was teaching at another small Catholic college in the early '90s, I was interviewed by a local newspaper for an article on Goddesses. By the time the school had opened that morning, the phone system had almost broken down. People, claiming to be alumni, were threatening to cut off their contributions and demanding that I be fired. But the school stood up to the firestorm, and I spoke personally to anyone who called my office—these were scary, angry people. I wasn't fired.

♦ *R/S: How do you think your Pagan consciousness evolved?*
♦ PM: I remember as a child trying to strip away what I saw as veils between myself and the air, the light, and the trees. I was feeling my way into a spiritual connection with nature. Eventually this led to a dangerous depression, when as a teenager I felt not only "weird" by comparison to other teenagers (*don't we all?*), but positively evil, because we had a local priest who fired-and-brimstoned constantly about "the passions of the flesh." (Several years ago, the diocese admitted that he had been engaging in such passions with unwilling altar boys, but that's another story.)

At one point I became convinced I was possessed by demons, and at church would look around and try to determine who the other evil people were. Then I started encountering literature that showed me that other people had experienced similar mystical states. Rimbaud became my personal savior: "A flower spoke its name to me." I knew what he meant.

When I was a little girl, my family lived in New York, then moved into progressively wilder spaces, through Colorado to Alaska, where they still live. I spent the better part of my life near true wilderness. For a year I lived alone in a cabin 80 miles outside Fairbanks, chopping my own wood, hauling my own water, and writing poetry. This was a touchstone experience. Everyday life in Alaska brings one vividly in touch with nature—especially when it's fifty below!

In Alaska, I attended the "Wheel of the Year" with a group of women that still meets after some 30 years. Basically, we invented our own rituals out of whatever we could learn about modern Paganism. We had no high priestess or initiation; we didn't know any other Pagans and had no sense of being connected with anything but the seasons and the earth.

Our initial rituals were pretty inventive. I remember boating across the Chena to a sandy island where we danced, yes, naked under the midnight sun. Where we were, that was a truly stupid idea—I think the dinner bell was heard by every mosquito in Alaska! We also cooked a whole pig. I had never seen a Pagan ritual before, so this was an amazing event for me.

But after that, we retreated to more modest and mostly mosquito-free rituals at various members' homes. We pretty much invented each ritual afresh, staying in tune with the seasons. To celebrate Samhain [Halloween] one year, we were outdoors chanting around a massive spruce tree while the temperature was 30 below—meanwhile, the aurora borealis [Northern Lights] was bursting out gloriously above us. Did you know there are also Southern Lights—identical mirror images happening simultaneously on the opposite side of the world—the South Pole? And nobody knows why, although some people think it might be caused by the Solar Wind. Isn't that stunning?

Another time, we created a funeral service for the drowned child of one of our group, ending by releasing balloons into the summer sky. Those rituals stay with me, as do the deep friendships formed over so many years. We were quite creative ritualists, paying attention to the earth and celebrating the seasonal dance of life. That, to me, is what Paganism is about—not some initiation by a specific person or group purporting to possess some "occult" or secret knowledge.

♦ *R/S: You're Irish—can you talk about Irish Paganism?*
♦ PM: I've known American Pagans who have traveled to Ireland and reported that there are no Pagans there. However, very few Irish are likely to follow rules set forth by an Englishman (say, Gerald Gardner, the father of the Wiccan revival fifty years ago). The Irish may speak English, but Irish English has certain peculiarities—for example, there's no word for "No"—so today's Irish native may appear devilishly indirect to Americans.

Q: "Is it true that the Irish always answer a question with another question?" A: "Now who told you that?"

In any case, because I was not looking for orthodox Wiccans, I found Paganism close to the surface in Ireland. Sometimes it looks suspiciously like Catholicism. But Irish Catholicism is grafted onto a Pagan root-stock—holy wells dedicated to Saint Bridget were once previously dedicated to the Celtic goddess Brigit. I visit holy wells every time I'm in Ireland, like the well at Liscannor near the Hag's Head, Ceann na Cailleach, that looks out from the cliffs over the Atlantic. I know specific fairy trees and stone circles and decorated caverns. And I know lots of people who honor the spirits of those places and can tell me great stories about them.

♦ *R/S: What does a Pagan do at a holy well?*
♦ PM: The Brigit Vat in Liscannor is a holy well far in the west near the Cliffs of Moher. You walk in spirals up and down a steep rocky hill, then enter the well-house. The well is actually *within* the hill, so you walk through a long, dark corridor to the flowing stream. You make an offering (others have left feathers, letters for help, coins) and then drink the well water. The event is solitary, as are many of the holy well rituals I know. But on one Imbolc I attended, there were mobs of people. At dawn I gathered up water from Brigit's well and brought it to my friend Jessie's dying dog, who had not moved for three days, and she rose *instantly* and was fine for six weeks! The locals considered that a miracle.

In Ireland, the early 20th century "Celtic Twilight" literary movement involving William B. Yeats (who was in the Golden Dawn), the fantasy writer Lord Dunsany, James Stephens (author of *The Crock of Gold),* and others marked a Pagan revival that focused attention on the loss of Celtic culture, and fed into the desire for independence and freedom. This was a kind of Pagan activism—but different from Starhawk's.

Many of the people involved were nationalists, and they saw the loss of Celtic culture as connected to the political oppression of the Irish. They also saw a connection between the loss of spirituality and political disempowerment. It was a kind of indigenous-religion movement rather like Native Americans have today, that survived through the bards, literature, and sacred sites. Yeats is a good example, because his work is deeply encoded with mythology, history and mysticism.

♦ *R/S: You recently returned from Ireland where you helped "relight the Bealtaine Fires"—*
♦ PM: Bealtaine (spelled "Beltane" in America) is May 1, and is one of the four great Celtic feasts. It's celebrated all over America by Wiccans today. In Ireland it was traditionally celebrated with fires on the significant 32 hilltops. This was one of the major unifying events of the Celtic people. The king would light the first fire, and then fires on surrounding hills would be lit until finally the whole island would be lit up. In the parable of the arrival of Christianity that's taught to every Irish schoolchild, everyone's waiting for the king to light the fire when *boom,* off on another hilltop a fire is ignited by St. Patrick. All the Druids run over, whereupon Patrick holds up a shamrock and causes their instant conversion.

The Bealtaine fires have not been celebrated for about 1,500 years. So for Irish Pagans, it was very significant to reinitiate them. The central fire is at Uisneach, the hill of Eriu herself—Eriu is the Goddess for whom Ireland is named.

♦ *R/S: Whose idea was it to re-light them?*
♦ PM: A group of people initiated a project called "Fire Eye." It started in Connemara, the wild beautiful land on Galway's west coast. My dear friend who died recently, Barbara Callan, was involved from the start. She was a beautiful singer who wrote traditional-style melodies with Irish language lyrics to the Goddess. Barbara's husband, Dave Hogan, a musician and ecologist, and Garry Jones, an Australian musician, are at the heart of Fire Eye, which is an entirely volunteer group of people all over Ireland dedicated to reviving the great festival of the Oenach, the yearly assembly of the tribes.

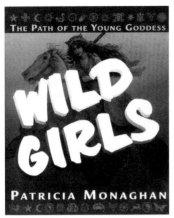

About 200 people gathered this year beneath the hill at the crossroads that marks the center of Ireland, drumming and chanting. Because the foot-and-mouth disease epidemic [spring 2001] had shut down all but the most necessary traffic, only four of us had been selected to ascend to the top of the hill: a shaman from Ulster; a pregnant woman from Leinster; a man from Galway, Connaught, who made the fire with flintstones; and me, representing Munster (where my father's family is from) and the diaspora. We represented all the parts of Ireland. We were conveyed up there in a wild truck ride by the farmer who owns the hill. He also had established the fire sites and gathered the shrub to be burned.

On the hilltop, two great bonfires blazed forth, symbolizing the eyes of Eriu opening to the springtime. In ancient days, every other major hilltop would have blazed in response. This time, because of the threatened epidemic, the dozens of answering fires in Ireland were in backyards rather than on hilltops. And around the world, literally hundreds of answering fires were lit. As many as 10,000 people around the world celebrated with us at places like Vermont, Chartres cathedral, and Macchu Picchu. They included prayers for the health of the animals, because Bealtaine involves such prayers. We felt a palpable connection to a world community of people joining in response to Ireland's effort to rekindle an awareness of spiritual connection to the land.

One of my favorite memories concerns the farmer and his assistant watching the fire and having a completely "farmer"-like conversation: "driving the beasts between the fires might kill lice, and besides, you have to burn the brush off at this time of year anyway—good idea, don't you think?" They wrapped their agricultural awareness around the event and grounded it in a way that made it *far* from a New Agey thing.

In addition to the fire-lighting, people read poetry, played music, and gave lectures on mythic subjects. Before the pre-fire-lighting ritual, Dave Hogan gave a gorgeous speech about the suppression of the Goddess in Ireland, and how she was being brought back. It was scholarly, spiritual, and yet off-the-cuff, all at once. Perhaps 70 people attended from "beyond," the lovely word for "outside Ireland" that old folks still use. The word also refers to the enchanted isles where the fairies live.

♦ **R/S: Do you maintain an altar at home?**

♦ PM: I'm not sure a visitor to my home would be able to tell the altars from the interesting arrangements of souvenirs, but I can! I build altars all the time for all sorts of intentions. On my desktop is an altar for every book I write—as my eyes drift from the computer screen I am refreshed with appropriate imagery.

I'm writing about the goddesses of the herds (e.g., Hathor, Bo Finne)—they look after the welfare of the animals. So my altar has an image of a cow from last year's "Chicago Cows On Parade" exhibit, a "Cow Egg" (a ceramic egg with black-and-white cowhide pattern), and a shamanic ivory from Alaska of a salmon turning into a woman. For my novel about St. Augustine's mistress I have the "A" volume of the *Catholic Encyclopedia,* surmounted by a statue of the Carthaginian goddess Tanith, along with a nut to represent Augustine's mother Monica—a nutty woman if ever there was.

♦ **R/S: Tell us about Augustine [A.D. 354-430]—**

♦ PM: Augustine is the man who invented the concept of Original Sin, as well as the concept of the celibate priesthood. He saw sex as this horrible affliction—which didn't keep him from f—-ing his way across North Africa. He was black, although he's gotten bleached over the years—you never see paintings of a black St. Augustine. He really was the devil—no, don't say that, because it's dualism and I don't believe in dualism. He introduced a combination of intense brilliance and psychopathological illness into Western mainstream culture.

As a young person, Augustine was a follower of the Persian sage Mani, the founder of Manichaeanism, which is extremely dualistic: all of life is divided into either light or dark. Before that, Christianity was far less dualistic; some people argue it was a very diverse collection of communistic cults. Celtic Christianity was much more holistic, but it was driven out by this anti-sex, anti-body, dualistic, revisionist version: "We are spirits *trapped* in a body." A good part of the reason we loathe and devalue the earth so much is because of dualistic thinking which holds that the body is "bad"; it's where our soul *temporarily* resides before it goes back up to heaven. All that "up and down" stuff is very theologically dangerous! Look at how it's applied to our body, where the head is overvalued because it's more up! Our head is not separated from our body—*hello!* It should not be—not if we plan to live a whole and healthy life.

♦ **R/S: Speaking of divisions between the soul and the body, what's your opinion on "angels"?**

♦ PM: Angels allow people to be kind of New Agey without actually having to leave Christianity. They want to embrace new thought, but also don't want to leave where they've been. Angels are *safe;* they're sort of like fairies, but not exactly. You can even have feminine angels and thus have a goddess-like energy concept, without really stepping outside the mainstream. Angels, goddesses, gods—I feel they're all just metaphors, really.

♦ **R/S: Sometimes it's easy to forget that. And maybe angels are a Christian co-optation of the "fairy" archetype, although personally, I find both concepts somewhat trifling—like, How many angels can dance on the head of a pin? Who cares … Let's return to your altars—**

♦ PM: I've described just the book altars. I have at least one altar in every room. An altar to me is just a *space dedicated to an intention* decorated with objects redolent of that intention. I have multiple intentions—hence, multiple altars.

I add to (rarely subtract from) my standing altars, but I have dedicated my front hallway to seasonal altars that I change every six weeks

at the holidays. Currently my spring altar is up, which includes my ceramic and stone egg collection, my photos of spring flowers, and many papier-mache bunnies. My friends entertain themselves by placing the bunnies in—uh, *provocative* (not to say salacious) positions. I have had some strange stares from delivery people when the spring altar is up.

♦ *R/S: You mentioned Rimbaud—*

♦ PM: One of my great unpublished lapel buttons is "I Got This Way by Reading." Probably most people attending any given Pagan event would qualify to wear one! For me at age 19, it was the French Symbolist poet Arthur Rimbaud who first reflected my own spirituality. He burst like a comet upon the French literary world in the mid-1800s: a sixteen-year-old boy from the provinces who overturned French poetry, wrote like a fiend (and an angel) for three years, and then stopped writing poetry at the age of 19. In three years he completely changed French poetry. He was very intense, surreal, spiritual—but not in the conventional way, more mystical. He ran off with a much older male poet, Paul Verlaine—he stole him from his wife. They got into a big fight in Brussels and Verlaine shot him. There's a lot more to his story, of course.

Normally Rimbaud is perceived as basically very instinctual, but I think he was much more intellectual than previously thought. **Rimbaud's whole poetic project was to argue against dualism and express the *unity* of mind and body, spirit and matter, where "thinking" and "being" are *not* separate.**

I had a classic education. Edmund Spenser got a lot of "The Faerie Queene" from his Irish servants; that poem is dense with Celtic and folkloric motifs. I first met the Fairy Mistress, Leannan Sidhe, in the almost oppressively opulent poem by Keats, "La Belle Dame Sans Merci." The Romantic movement in particular sought the alternative vision we now call Paganism—in reaction to the increasing urbanization and industrialization of Europe.

I think that a lot of people find alternative spirituality through books. Fantasy literature, like the books of J.R.R. Tolkien, has shown people visions of alternative ways to live. There is a new genre of visionary fiction that is neither fantasy nor science-fiction, but reveals ways of seeing the world from a non-capitalist and often woman-honoring perspective—such as my favorite, Elizabeth Cunningham, who writes fabulous visionary novels such as *Return of the Goddess* and *The Wild Mother. Visionaryfiction.com* has lists of these books. Marion Zimmer Bradley's *The Mists of Avalon* is pivotal in many people's pantheons. A new writer I like is Juliet Marliett. Also I like Alexis Masters, who wrote a trilogy, *The Guilana Legacy,* about Aphrodite being reborn.

In these days of corporate conglomeration, we have to fight to keep alternative visions available. I feel quite passionately about the freedom of the press, and keeping libraries out of the clutches of the right wing. **To me, reading was—and is—a way of feeling that I'm not alone. To find my inner experiences reflected in someone else's words has always been the most thrilling experience I can have as a reader.** When I taught in the inner city, I became vividly aware how infrequently my students had ever had that *primary* reading experience: finding their own secret thoughts spoken by a stranger.

I wonder if younger people are finding similar sustenance. Maybe I'm turning into a fossil, but to me the intensely private experience of reading—say, outdoors, on a warm summer evening, with fireflies beginning to flicker in the garden—is very sensuous . . . much more so than surfing the Web.

♦ *R/S: What about Paganism in the arts?*

♦ PM: Throughout Western history, artists have mined Paganism for material for their work: Pablo Picasso, Gustave Moreau, neo-classical painters with Greco-Roman themes, etc. Sometimes the work is disguised as mythic or mythological. Of course, many non-European and tribal peoples have kept on creating Pagan art, as in the great tradition of African Ashanti ancestor figures, or the Lithuanian *daina* or goddess songs.

♦ *R/S: You've written extensively about women and goddesses. What are your thoughts about* **men** *and goddesses—*

♦ PM: **I like to remind people that there is no known historical evidence of a monotheistic goddess religion.** All monotheisms are male-centered—every single one. Thus, if history repeats itself, we are unlikely to create (or recreate, or revive) a goddess religion that excludes men the way that monotheisms exclude women.

Goddesses have gods, and they have baby goddesses and gods—thus goddess religions become polytheistic, not dualistic. And polytheism is not just the opposite of monotheism, it is a different system of thought entirely. Monotheisms lead to dualism, because everything "not god" somehow becomes also "not sacred," which in turn leads to the concept of "evil." But polytheism is vastly more complicated, not either/or. Furthermore, polytheism tends to be decentralized, so there may be a temple in which a woman is priestess, and down the road a temple with a man as priest. And there's no pope to tell them to stop it.

Thus I think that goddess religion embraces men—not to say that all goddess women embrace men! But theologically the religion is inclusive. I wouldn't venture to say what I think men have to gain from the goddess; that's for men to say. I can say what I hope: that we can all learn to appreciate and revere what is different from us, as well as what is the same. ♦♦♦

Recommended Websites

Girls' spirituality site: *www.altogether.com/wildgirls/*
Relighting the Beltaine Fire website *www.fire-eye.org.*
American Academy of Religion (AAR) includes Nature Religions Scholars, *www.natrel-l@uscolo.edu*

Recommended Books

"Some Favorite Books Reinforcing the Pagan"—P.M.

Marija Gimbutas *The Language of the Goddess*
Carol Christ *Odyssey with the Goddess*
Jane Ellen Harrison *Prolegomena to the Study of Greek Religion*
Normandi Ellis *Dreams of Isis*
Serinity Jones *An Anthology of Sacred Texts By and About Women*
Eric Neumann *The Great Mother*
Ginette Paris *Pagan Meditations*
Riane Eisler *The Chalice and the Blade*
China Galland *Longing for Darkness*
Miriam Robbins Dexter *Whence the Goddesses*
Raphael Patai *The Hebrew Goddess*
Gerda Lerner *The Creation of Feminist Consciousness*
Mary Condren *The Serpent and the Goddess*
Caitlin Matthews *Sophia*
Joanna Hubbs *Mother Russia*
Janet McCrickard *Eclipse of the Sun*

Diane di Prima

Diane di Prima has had a long career as a poet, writer, publisher, teacher, Occultist, Pagan, Zen practitioner and Tibetan Buddhist. Her 34 books include *Memoirs of a Beatnik, Pieces of a Song: Selected Poems,* and most recently, *Recollections of My Life As A Woman.* She lives in San Francisco with Sheppard Powell, and studies with Lama Tharchin. Interview by V. Vale.

♦ *RE/SEARCH: You're well-known as a Beat poet, writer and teacher. Are you comfortable appearing in the context of* **Modern Pagans?**

♦ DIANE: I was thinking about that. Definitely there is the element in my belief system of Paganism, but basically I'm a Tibetan Buddhist. But I have incorporated Pagan practices into my life since around 1963—I wrote about this in my autobiography, *Recollections of My Life As A Woman.* I invited twelve people over for my first Winter Solstice celebration at my house in New York, including Merce Cunningham and Cecil Taylor. I had done a lot of research on ritual in James Frazer's *Golden Bough*—in 1961 I had bought for myself the 12-volume set of hardbacks which in those days didn't cost much—about $45.

We did different kinds of ceremonies. I had an orange that was completely covered with cloves—like people hang in closets, I guess. It represented the sun, and I put it in the fire—we had a fireplace. The first year we didn't have birch, but each year thereafter we would burn white birch logs. Everybody got a little scroll on which they wrote the things they wanted to get rid of with the old year. Then they tied it up with a ribbon and put it in the fire. We did more things like that—all except Merce. We were describing it as "Write down your demons" and Merce said that he *had* no demons and immediately went home—very telling about that man, isn't it?!

We stayed up all night until the sun came up. We lit candles and stayed up to help the sun come back, because it is the longest night of the year. Every year since then the solstice has always been celebrated by me in one way or the other. Until maybe the late 70's I would stay up that night. As I got older I didn't do that, but I leave candles burning in the window sill on solstice night, and I do a ritual, although it has changed over the years.

So the solstices and equinoxes had an importance for me from early on, and I think that although it was buried under miles of agnosticism and philosophy in my parents' house, my mother would always say, "It's the longest night of the year,"

with great awe and amazement. So something had come down to her that she wasn't quite articulating.

I remember being shown how the sun illuminates the planets. Someone stuck a pencil through an orange, shined a flashlight beam in the dark on it, and rotated the orange, showing how the light would change as the planet revolved around the sun. It was like how Galileo or Giordano Bruno might have interpreted the universe. So I have a root in some kind of Paganism like that which was also very deep in my grandmother's Catholicism. There was a day when you ate no salt, a day when you ate no bread—St. Lucy or Santa Lucia's day which is celebrated in Northern Europe, too, when Swedish women wear crowns of candles. The saint of light, Lucia, *lux,* Lucy— she was a very important figure in my grandmother's world. Although nobody said, "This is Pagan," there was a basic interest and awe in the things of the turning of the seasons and being on the planet, that were handed to me from way back.

When I was in high school, eight women in our writing group did a lot of experimenting with the paranormal—telepathy, trance, and seance. That all went away when I became just a writer and dropped out of college, but it came back with a big bang when I was about 31 and started to fool around with Tarot cards, and would have *lucid dreams.* I was living in New Mexico. In the afternoons when it was hot I would stare at one card and go to sleep. When I awoke I would always have had a dream about that card. It didn't seem remarkable or strange— I didn't have to *work* at it—it just happened.

Tibetan Buddhism is concerned with, at the least, the 31 major star systems that have *Dzogchen.* It's not based in the material facts of life. It's my main belief system, *within* which Paganism fits quite comfortably as regards how you deal with *this* earth and being on it.

In Tibetan Buddhism, there is *relative truth* and *absolute truth.* Relative truth is about here, where we are, daily life, and the appearances of things. Absolute truth is about the emptiness (which *isn't* empty) and the constant creative principle in that, which they call the *dharmakaya.* They fit comfortably together. In the same way, Tibetan Buddhism fits together with my Paganism and other kinds of ritual magic (I'm not talking about Judaic Kabalism; I'm talking about Kabalistic magic which grew out of the Renaissance, transmitted by Cornelius Agrippa and others). It's a seamless fit with no problems. So I have my Tibetan Buddhist practice, but if my daughter has a question, I will go to the Tarot cards.

♦ *R/S: Paganism is definitely earth-based and grounded in very real practices in this world, but you overlay it with this other theory, if I can call it that, from Tibetan Buddhism, which is more concerned with causality, multiple dimensions of reality, and other cosmic theorizings. You can't necessarily prove it scientifically—*

♦ D: No, but you can prove it experientially. It's not easy—you don't just go off and prove it, like in a laboratory. You have to do the groundwork, then find a teacher, then get pointing-out instruction, and actual experience of *in-dwelling, void, creative principle,* that is also the same as *vast, timeless, and spaceless creative principle.* So you can't prove it scientifically, but you can prove it experientially. I'm reminded sometimes, when I am practicing, of that line in the *Book of the Law* by Crowley, "Certainty, not faith, while in life."

♦ *R/S: "Certainty, not faith, while in life"?*

♦ D: It's from the *Book of the Law*—another aspect of magic. So the Pagan movement is wonderful and I am still continuing its practices, but I hardly think about them—they're just ingrained in my life. "Have you picked up the candles for the solstice?" Or, "Are you going to have time tomorrow for us to do something for Eve of May?" You know? I have a meditation room in the house which is wonderful, because I can roll out of bed, sleepy or sick, and do my practice, then come back to my daily life, because that room is not used for anything else.

I also have a magical altar in the healing room where Sheppard does his healing work (that's his livelihood), and where I do occasional guided visualizations with my students, or a Tarot reading. And the magical altar is—how can I say—a landing place and a launching pad for spirits and energies and businesses of this world. It has an arrangement of things that represent the *four elements,* so I have, using the Tarot model, a cup, a disc, a sword, and a wand. And **for the three principles from Alchemy, I have a vial of mercury, a big chunk of sulfur from Sicily, and a big crystal of solidified salt.**

So Mercury, Sulfur, and Salt are the three principles of Alchemy. I integrate this with the Zodiac, too. All this is part of what I used to teach when I taught "Structures and Magic" at our magic school, the San Francisco Institute of Magical and Healing Arts, which has been defunct since 1992.

For me, I started with just the simple notions I could get in Frazer's *Golden Bough* about the solstices and equinoxes and cross-quarter days and how they used to be celebrated. The whole set of volumes is indexed, so you can find information about the practices of islands in the South Pacific in one volume, and information about Greece in another—with the index, you can find what you want. Then I would shamelessly make my own synthesis of what I wanted from all that, to use as a basic form, a ritual.

Solstices are easy. Equinoxes are more subtle, because you have that simple slight turning toward the light or toward the dark at that point. The cross-quarter days are wonderful—I was going to say *divine* in terms of earthly things—they're earthly deities. So something comes up every six weeks that you try to at least commemorate in some little way, even if you're very busy. I have this shrine downstairs that is the earth magic shrine set up for that, having the elements and the principles of alchemy. Salt is that which remains after the transformation, the dross is that which remains after the mercury flies away (unless you catch it and use it), and sulfur is what is consumed from the burning. Those three principles work in the four elements—here I'm going by Paracelsus. Even if you only have half an hour, you can go down and commemorate the occasion in some way.

♦*R/S: Do you actually believe you can cross over to the land of the spirits of the dead—*

♦ D: Well, have you never met a ghost?

♦ *R/S: No.*

♦ D: *Oh.* I have. I'm not sure what part of a being does that. I believe in reincarnation. But I think there is a shell or some part of the *persona* that maybe hangs around, and it hangs around more if it's remembered more. I honor people who do a lot for ceremonies like the Day of the Dead, but I don't tend to do a lot of that. But after I do the Winter Solstice, I do a ceremony of cleansing the whole house, and then cleansing it again with sage and salt and so on and blessing each room, driving out any bad energy from the old year, and blessing it and calling in new energy, room by room.

You can do this systematically. As you go through each room you're lighting candles. You start around the time the sun goes down, so by the time you're done the whole house is lit *only* in candle-light. You sweep the bad energy towards the door or doors, depending how many entry ways you have. When you get there you toss out a handful of dried beans or lentils to feed the dead, because that's what Pythagoras said fed the dead. You bless them. In the old days when I did it thoroughly, my kids would go out and paint a sign on the door—traditionally you would put an occult sign on the door to seal it against the bad energy from the past.

Every place in the world has the same rituals, really. After everything's done I've always added a casting of the *I Ching* for the New Year. What I do now in the last ten years as I got older and more people were going— especially since the AIDS epidemic in the last twenty years—I then go into the shrine room, in the candle light, and one by one I say goodbye to all the people who died since the last Winter Solstice. I name them and I talk to them out loud, and I thank them for what they brought to my life. Sometimes I cry, or apol-

circa 1938

ogize for not having gotten back to them in time, or whatever, because **we always have those feelings of something left undone when someone dies.**

♦ *R/S: Right.*

♦ D: I do all that, and try to put some closure on every person I lost that year, and look at everything full in the face. Sometimes it's short, and sometimes it takes a long time. I'm not worrying about whether ghosts are there, or crossing barriers or anything, I'm just talking and blessing people, partly for my own closure, and to look at what the year has brought in the way of endings and loss. Then we can look forward to the next year.

I always consult the *I Ching,* some time between Winter Solstice and Epiphany (to go to another religion), but within the two weeks after solstice. Sometimes, right at solstice is a little too soon for the *Ching* to know what's up—it gives you a muddy transitional reading. So I wait a little longer.

♦ *R/S: Is Epiphany an observance from Catholicism?*

♦ D: Yes. Epiphany is the 6th of January. It's when the wise men found the child. It's an alchemical holiday, too, in that they brought basically Mercury, Sulfur, and Salt—Myrrh being the faculty of grieving for what's left behind; Gold being the essence of Sulfur, the finished transformational product; and Frankincense being the principle of Mercury, or the flying away—although it is solar; people juggle those around in different ways. The Three Wise Men are seen as the Three Principles in Alchemy.

I've been collecting pictures and paintings of The Three Wise Men for years—all the different concepts of the wise men. And the child of course is the alchemical stone, or the principle of renewal or eternal life. In the old days, in the part of Italy that my family came from, Epiphany was when you gave gifts to the children. *Not* on Christmas, but on the day the wise men gave gifts to the child. And each child was seen as the renewing principle. Every child is the Christ child in that sense, and that was the kind of Pagan Catholicism that my grandmother had. No one else in the family had that kind of religion. My grandfather on that side was an atheist and an anarchist; his wife was the one who had the Pagan Catholicism. My parents were, as they sadly said, agnostics.

On the other side of the family, I didn't know the grandparents that well. My father's father was a wonderful storyteller of the Catholic stories, but I didn't get to know him well. So I had a mix in my life. The grandfather who was an atheist and an anarchist was also a great reader of Giordano Bruno, whom he saw as a political rebel. But Giordano Bruno is also a great magician. His books are hard to come by; I have a few. He taught a lot of inner work, transformational work through visualization—Frances Yates's *The Art of Memory* touches on this. He was a great magician. So now that we've confused all the different traditions—

R/S: No, you haven't. Earlier, were you making reference to strega, an Italian tradition?

♦ D: No, the term *strega* is used in a more pejorative way to refer to a malevolent witch who is casting spells, the way most people think of witches. The Catholicism of my grandmother really didn't take sin seriously—that's why I say it was terribly Pagan. She would say, "The Virgin Mary is a woman—*she'll* explain it to God!" about people screwing and that kind of stuff.

♦ *R/S: Earlier, you mentioned having seen a spirit or ghost—can you tell us a personal story? I realize you're describing your experience; you're not saying this is real for everyone—*

♦ D: Well, I'm not a relativist. I think that what's real *is* real, but we all see different parts of it. We can only see what we see. I'm not saying I see everything or more than others; the parts I can see are the parts that I *can* see. But no, I don't think I want to do that. There are so *many* instances and they are so different from each other that I wouldn't even know how to start. You know what Blake said towards the end of his life, when they brought him news of one of his friends dying, "I can no longer think about death as anything other than walking from one room into another."

♦ *R/S: That's nice. So looking back, you've lived a life of Paganism in practice, without being labeled a Pagan. I think anyone who has been in a so-called "underground" always rejects the label applied to them. Like, my friend Philip Lamantia rejected the label "Beatnik" for himself—*

♦ D: Yeah, I don't like being called Beat. Not because I didn't have work that would definitely be called Beat, but because it's such a small percentage of all of my work. It's like being frozen in one moment—someone takes a photo of you in 1958 and that's how you're supposed to be for the rest of your life. That's silly. We didn't call ourselves Beats, *Life* Magazine called us Beats! Then after a while, it stuck. There *were* some people who kept writing Beat writing—maybe Allen Ginsberg was one. But most of us wrote many different kinds of writing— and Allen, too. He wrote Sapphics (in Sappho's meter), he wrote blues—not all of it was Beat. Labels come from somewhere else—usually after the fact. That's why they don't work.

♦ *R/S: They're used to market products—*

♦ D: Yeah. I guess in Europe people like to have movements and label them. Didn't the Surrealists call themselves the Surrealists? They had a whole book of manifestos—very boring. I love Surrealism but I can't read those manifestos—

♦ *R/S: But don't you apply some of the Surrealist principles contained in Bréton's* **Manifestos of Surrealism** *to your own inspiration process?*

♦ D: Of course. I consider some of them my foremothers and forefathers, especially the women painters like Remedios Varo.

♦ *R/S: It's great to hear of your Surrealist affinities, as well as your affinity for the so-called "Occult." Surrealism and the Occult are appraised in such a reductionist manner by most Americans—all they know are the labels—*

♦ D: It's just dopey. [laughs] We're in a kind of stupid society— forgive me for saying so—we're really in a very Dumb Age. **Anybody who could take seriously the value of profit as a serious motivation for living—?! They act as if they have a moral imperative—God says, "Make money." It's so weird.** And the whole world is following behind it at this point. It's so stupid because it makes this tunnel vision. People can't see— it's like they all have glaucoma, and they have no peripheral vision—they can't see anything that's right under their noses, or off to the side somewhere.

They kill their children really, in a way, by denying all forms of the supernatural and the non-material, because kids *live* with all that. They talk to non-existent beings (maybe they're existent, who knows?) from the time they're little. When my oldest daughter Jeanne was about five, she loved Egypt. Together we would look at big art books checked out from the library. We'd be looking at painted sarcophagi or mummy cases and she would say, "On this part here they tell about the person's family, and over here they tell all the things he did that were important." She was *five years old* and she knew things I didn't know. We deny that about our kids—we destroy access to everything they have that we don't. That's part of the stupidity of the time.

The first time I took my daughter Dominique to the Metropolitan Museum of Art (NYC), we were in the Egyptian section and she spotted one of those necklace collars made out of blue faience glaze. She said, "That's *my* necklace! What is it doing there—I want my necklace!" She would scare me all the time. She would say things like, "I'm really glad I went to the zoo and saw the rhinoceros so I can tell my grandchildren it wasn't a myth." Under five years old and saying that . . .

♦ *R/S: That's scary—*

♦ D: It was scary. It was sad-making, too . . . it made me really sad.

♦ *R/S: Tell us why you're drawn to Tibetan Buddhism—*

♦ D: I started out as a Zen Buddhist. I met Shunryu Suzuki in 1962—that's described in *Recollections of My Life as a Woman*—my meeting him was quite fortuitous. And as soon as I met him, he was the first person I'd ever met that I trusted—I was a *New Yorker* . . .

♦ *R/S: Right, you don't trust anyone—*

♦ D: No, and I'd had a kind of very vicious upbringing. Whatever he did, I tried to understand what was in his mind that was so open—it didn't have little nooks and crannies of manipulation and fabrication in it. He was just *there,* he was just present. What he did was sit, so I got instruction and I started to sit. I used to write to his student Dick Baker and tell him how my meditation was going. He would tell Suzuki, and sometimes I would get instruction back and sometimes not. That went on until I moved to San Francisco in 1967. I came to S.F. for two reasons: to do political work with the Diggers (I started delivering their free food right away, that was my job), and to sit with Suzuki. Those were the two sides of the coin for me then.

I did Zen long before I had met Chögyam Trungpa, whom I met the year he came to this country. He went straight away to Tassajara, where I was for the summer, to meet Suzuki. That was in 1970. In 1974 Trungpa started Naropa Institute, and Allen invited me to come teach there—Allen was by that time a student of Trungpa's. I was like, "*Ehh* . . . I don't know." But Suzuki, before he died in December of '71, had said that Trungpa was like his son. He left one of his two Zen staffs (they have those teaching staffs that they carry) to Dick Baker and the other one to Trungpa. So I felt, "If he's my teacher's son, I should help him."

So in 1974 I went and taught classes and started going to all of Trungpa's lectures; he lectured twice a week. I taught at Naropa in '74, '75, '76—those were big teaching years for Trungpa. I continued to go to Naropa every other year until

At Dan Entin's Studio, February 1968

recently when I stopped in 1997. So I put in my time there teaching summer writing school. Trungpa and I became quite close. Suzuki was dead, and the Zen Center—well, after one interview with Dick Baker I knew it was too bureaucratic for me, so I started sitting on my own. For meditation instruction or guidance when something seemed a little *off,* I had Kitagiri Roshi in Minneapolis, if I was on the road, and sometimes Kobun Chino Roshi if he came around. They had both been at the Zen Center with Suzuki.

So I was catching instruction on the fly. When I started going to Naropa I would have a formal meditation interview with Trungpa every summer. He was helping me, but I was still practicing Zen—I was still committed to Suzuki's teaching. I practiced Zen until '83. Around '81 I started to do both healing work and trance visualization work for clients—people who felt they had a shadow in their life that was wrong, and so on. And in doing the visualization work, a few times I ran into *forces* (that's what I call them—I don't know what they were) that were *way* bigger than what I had been asked by my client to deal with. I would just put up a shield wall and call on larger forces to take care of them and go about my business. But I was aware that some of this work was kind of like Frodo in Tolkien's *Hobbit:* "If you shine a stronger flashlight, it's going to notice you!" So I started to wish I had a *sangha,* or other people I could sit with, just to ground myself after doing that kind of work.

I decided to ask Trungpa to be my teacher, because I knew that Tibetan Buddhism openly embraces the whole Western magical view. So I had an interview with Trungpa in '83. I wasn't teaching that year, but I flew out to Naropa in Boulder and stayed at Allen's house. Both Sheppard and I had interviews, and we asked Trungpa to be our teacher. I told him I was doing all this Western magic, and that sometimes I needed *backup.* I said, "I'm not prepared to give up Western practices and Western philosophy for the East." **In my mind we're involved in a process that is going to take 500 years to amalgamate all these things.** We're bridge-makers, but we're barely at the beginning of the bridge!

I think I actually said, "I'm not prepared to give up Paracelsus for Padmasambhava." And he laughed and said, "*No* problem." He told me he wanted me to have instruction in a practice which is pretty well known now, called "Taking and Sending," *Tonglen,* from one of his students. He told me to write him and stay in touch if anything came up—any questions or problems with my magical work or anything—so the switch was a quite natural one. I'd practiced Zen for 21 years, and I've practiced Tibetan Buddhism for 18 years. I was receiving instruction in Tibetan View from 1974, so the switchover was quite natural. I *love* Tibetan practice.

In my last interview with Suzuki before he died, my last formal *dokusan,* he said, "Now is the time for you to find your own practice." Boy, that's scary when your teacher is dying. He said,

Sheppard Powell Photo: V. Vale

"It is *not* Zen Center practice." He also said, "Now is the time for you to start living your own life"—which I thought I had always been doing! He said, "Not your children's lives, not some man's life." It's taking me a long time to disentangle from my children's lives—I have five of them!

♦ *R/S: You overlay Paganism, which deals with earth reality and spirituality, with Tibetan theory which concerns other planes of existence or reality—*

♦ D: You know, if we had only *this* plane, I would rather be dead. I mean—the material world is beautiful and wonderful, but if this was all there was (and I was at the despair that I reached in my teens)—well, you can see to the bottom of it all the time, and it was never enough. But with *dharma* there's always enough. There's always more than you can see. It's deeper and it's fuller and it's faster. I love this earth, but if this is all there was, it wouldn't be worth it.

Blake talked about us being in a golden cage, with the stars being our inspiration—like we're in a prison of *materiality.* Matter is great, but it's only the tip of the iceberg—literally! [laughs] **If this was *it*, and it was *only* Paganism, I would long ago have probably—not killed myself, but I probably wouldn't still be here**, because my energy for it, my taste for it, would have gone long, long ago—probably in my forties.

♦ *R/S: So Tibetan Buddhism cosmology—*

♦ D: They use the word "View"; they don't always capitalize it, but that means their cosmology. I've always had this feeling since I was a little kid: If this was *it,* gawd—who would want it?! At the bottom of my saying that the culture is *stupid,* there's a real horror.

♦ *R/S: Apparently you put the two together and it's ultimately a deeper or more satisfying philosophy or view with which you can cope with living—*

♦ D: I put the two together. In Tibetan Buddhism, *they* have Paganism—if you were Tibetan. But I don't know *their* Paganism, and I don't need to learn another whole system of how to deal with the earth. I have a good one, you see, which was in place long before I became a Tibetan Buddhist, but not long before I had the view that this place would not be *enough.*

♦ *R/S: Tibetan Buddhist cosmology involves other dimensions, planes, and worlds—*

♦ D: Yes—of course. That's so *obvious;* it's like the nose on someone's face that our world isn't all of it.

♦ *R/S: You're deeply interested in the big questions that are almost unanswerable—the whys: where did this universe come from, and why?*

♦ D: I think everyone starts out like that. I remember as a little kid wondering about how amazing it was that *anything* existed. I think kids know that—that these questions are there.

That's what I mean when I say that we sell kids short in this culture. **If classes for nine-year-olds had discussions of "Isn't it amazing that things exist?" I don't think you'd have any trouble teaching those kids anything.** But they don't give them credit, or any context.

You know what keeps coming into my head, even though it's not *exactly* related: there's a great Zen story about Bodhidharma, the guy who went from India to bring Zen to China. He was summoned to teach the Emperor. The Emperor asked him, "What is the word of the Holy Truth?" And Bodhidharma said, "Vastness—no holiness." I think that's a *key* to how I see the *Dharma* taking root in America. *We* understand vastness, and it's a step from understanding vastness to understanding emptiness. You see what I'm saying? **Emptiness is not empty, but full and creative.** But to say "vastness—no holiness" takes this out of that pious place. Then there's only one more step to see what is *really* vast. Like that game that kids play, "Well, if the universe ends there, what's outside it?" I think that children just naturally play mind-expanding games—a practice of psychedelia, in a way. All cultures probably do this.

♦ *R/S: There's a scientific explanation for emptiness: the theory that matter doesn't exist, only energy. On the level of the atom, with electrons spinning around a nucleus, there are no particles—*

♦ D: Of course. Hindus knew this forever and called it *maya*—illusion. *Lila,* the dance or play of *maya,* is what makes the world.

♦ *R/S: And the magic show uses DNA to accomplish its deed, in the incredible way that DNA works to create our world—*

♦ D: Yes. It's wondrous. And *wonder* is one of the vitamins that we seem to be *real short of* in America. We could use a lot of it, because it would fix us up good. We would have more respect for children, for madmen, for each other, for death, for birth—we would have a bigger capacity for everything; for pleasure and for joy! Wonder—we need bottles of Wonder on the shelves of all the health food stores! [laughs]♦♦♦

Below right: Recollections of My Life As a Woman book cover

RECOMMENDED BOOKS

Tibetan Book of Living & Dying
Chagdud Rinpoche *Gates to Buddhist Practice*
Chogyam Trungpa *Journey Without Goal, Myth of Freedom, Cutting Through Spiritual Materialism*

Rowan Fairgrove

Rowan Fairgrove has been a Wiccan for over 30 years and is an initiated elder in the NROOGD and Gardnerian traditions. She created one of the first interfaith websites, as well as *www.conjure.com,* an early Wiccan site. Since 1996 she has participated in a cyber-coven. She also belongs to the Covenant of the Goddess. Interview by John Sulak; follow-up interview by V. Vale

♦ *RE/SEARCH: What's your official job title?*
♦ ROWAN FAIRGROVE: My business card reads "Research Librarian," ROWAN FAIRGROVE, and underneath it says "Technology Information Services Manager." I had the subtitle put there so I could talk to people at trade shows and not have them roll their eyes. People don't give librarians enough credit; you have to have a masters degree to be a librarian. The modern library degree requires much technology training. A lot of computer science reinvented the wheel that library science had *already* invented—especially anything to do with databases. They reinvented *thesauri,* for example.

♦ *R/S: Tell us about your online cyber-coven—*
♦ RF: We email each other a dozen times a day and *c.c.* everyone, so we're all following each other's lives—I probably know my coven-mates better than friends who live close to me! But I've only actually *met* one of these people in person—mostly I know them through electronic interactions.

♦ *R/S: How has the Internet helped Paganism?*
♦ RF: Pagan Web sites enable us to educate the rest of the world about who we are. People are learning that we're not something to fear. Our values about the earth and human responsibility are becoming more widespread. That can only be a good thing. Now you have high school kids wearing pentacles to school— I couldn't have imagined doing that when I was in high school. I got sent home for wearing pants!

♦ *R/S: How do you know which Web sites to trust? There are "Pagan" Web sites set up by Fundamentalist Christians to deceive people and offer disinformation—*
♦ RF: You do it in the same way that you evaluate any information on the Internet. Does it come from a trusted source? Does it come from an organizational source or an individual source? Does what they're saying seem credible? Are they trying to convince you of something? Are they advocating that you send them money? Do they look like they're "power-over"? (you rarely get guru-like leaders in the Pagan community). Isaac Bonewits has a great list of "Cult Danger Signals" on his Website.

Fundamentally, the Internet is a medium of communication. In past generations there were elite groups of people who were able to spend their lives in conversation. In the Twenties you could go to Paris and sit in cafes having wonderful, illuminating discussions with fascinating people you met there. The Web offers the democratization of that, at least potentially. The fact that it's technologically different from sitting in a cafe or talking on the phone doesn't mean that it's qualitatively different. Millions of people are meeting in chat rooms, communicating, finding validation for what they do, and making new friends—especially those with non-mainstream interests. It's a very powerful experience when you discover you're not really alone—that's the biggest difference the Internet has made.

♦ *R/S: Is there such a thing as a "Technopagan"? Or for that matter, a "Technomuslim" or a "Technobaptist"?*
♦ RF: I don't know; maybe the Baptists *do* conduct services online. You'd have to ask them. Well, another "Technopagan" thing I do is, I read Tarot cards online for people. The other person has to find a deck; I tell them how to do the layout. They tell me what the layout is, and I lay it out on my end, and interpret it for them. Of course, I also do live readings in person. I did eleven readings recently in a benefit for Covenant of the Goddess.

♦ *R/S: Tell us about the Covenant of the Goddess (CoG)—*
♦ RF: It's an organization formed in 1975 to be an umbrella group similar to the Congregationalist Church, which is an organization of congregations—there's no top-down authority. In looking for a model to create a *legal* entity for Witches, a bunch of us created Covenant of the Goddess to be that entity which got IRS 501c3 status, so that the covens which became members would enjoy the legal protection afforded to members of other religions. Now we have covens and local councils, which would be regional sub-groups, all over the U.S.

One of the big things CoG does is interfaith work. We are a body that can represent Witches in a context where we're talking to members of other churches, like the Parliament of the World's Religions or the United Religions Initiative. We're part of the North American Interfaith Network, which is made up of Buddhists, Muslims, Hindus, Christians, Jews—and now, Witches. CoG is also involved with the Interfaith Center at the Presidio in San Francisco. I had quite a few friends at the 2001

Genoa, Italy (G–8) protest who were part of the interfaith contingent for debt relief. The media only reported riots, but there were religious people from around the world there whose concern is debt relief for poor nations.

I myself have been to the Parliament of the World's Religions, both in 1993 in Chicago and in 1999 in Capetown, South Africa. Also I attended the North American summit of the United Religions Initiative in Salt Lake City, 2001. Back in '76 CoG joined the Berkeley Area Interfaith Council, so this is one of the things CoG has worked on behalf of all Wiccans and Pagans. Did you know that there are still laws against Witches on the books of some countries? CoG is a step toward eradicating that persecution and oppression.

♦ *R/S: Can you discuss Paganism and Virtual Reality?*

Rowan Fairgrove below and top right

RF: Perhaps not as a magical experience, but **as a teaching tool, it is possible to create a virtual environment that shows the energy flows.** Let's assume that a coven is all wearing wearable computers with 3-D goggles, all seeing the same thing. Somebody has programmed it so that when they do the Pentacle of the West, it glows blue, and the Pentacle of the South glows red. In a training situation where you're teaching people how to visualize and "see" energy flows, a more experienced person can create this environment that shows the subtle energies in a visual way that everyone can *get*. Maybe that will help a person become more sensitive to the things that are a little harder to see. I've known somebody who has done this with their coven, but it's not common or normal yet.

A normal cyber-coven does two things. There are people who are geographically distant from each other that are working together, and they use the Internet to coordinate what they're going to do: "I'm going to take this piece of the ritual, you're going to take that piece of the ritual." Then when you *do* the ritual, you're sort of working on the astral plane together—you're doing a traditional ritual but you're not physically at the same location.

Then there's another situation where the computer is actually *in* the circle, and you're all typing your experiences: "Now I'm going to invoke the West with this invocation," where everybody else knows the actual words that are being said. One person says the words and the others are "there" in a way that they couldn't have been, say, on the telephone—nobody's going to put the telephone on for an hour ritual, whereas you can do that on the computer. So you're actually coordinating it

by typing it.

There was one example where somebody coordinated a ritual that took place over 72 hours. People could drop in and drop out, leaving comments about what they were doing. It built the energy as all these different people would drop in and share what they were doing for this ritual. Afterwards, the person who had coordinated the whole thing edited it, so there's a transcript of the 72-hour ritual available for whatever purpose. The person who created this ritual was in Finland, and having 72 hours allowed people from many time zones to coordinate their work.

So, the two ways a cyber-coven would operate: you would either use the cyber-ness just for coordination, or you would actually "do it" in real time with the computer.

♦ *R/S: Tell us the history of Paganism on the Internet—*

♦ RF: Before there was the World Wide Web, there was FIDO (particularly PODSnet) and there was (and is) Internet Relay Chat (IRC), which was in real-time: everybody logs into the same server, gets on the same channel, and everything that everyone types is written in threads. I first logged on back in 1982. There was a whole culture and etiquette that developed—for example, every time somebody new logs on, you don't have the fifty people who are already there saying "Hi." This IRC culture allows both shallow and deep conversation; people have fallen in love over IRC. Obviously people feel they can make true friendships and work with other people.

The people that I work with in my cyber-coven are *not* people that I met in the IRC context. We were all on the same mailing list for women Witches for about five years before we formed the coven. We're "elders"; we have a lot more background to offer each other than strangers who just get together.

Sometimes there are Pagan IRC channels and they'll say, "On Tuesday night we're going to do a ritual for such-and-such." Or, "On Tuesday night we're going to have a class on such-and-such a topic."

♦ *R/S: So in a class, everybody's logged on and in real time the teacher is typing out the class lesson for an hour—*

♦ RF: Yes, plus people can ask questions. It's real-time Q & A; everybody's there at the same time listening in. If you're on IRC there's also a *back channel* where you can talk to anybody else on the same channel by just addressing it to them, and only *they* will see it—that's like passing notes in class!

♦ *R/S: Can you give an example of a cyber-coven ritual?*

♦ RF: This isn't exactly a cyber-coven, but let me give this example. There was an *alt.* group, back when everybody used *Usenet* (which is still around, it's just not the big deal it once was). Before the Web there was an *alt.* group who over the years had become very good friends. One of them got sick, and there were enough people there with magical consciousness who decided to do an online ritual for this person. They're all familiar enough with ritual so they know that you go in and acknowledge each other, then somebody casts the circle, and somebody calls each of the elements. You're all there, and whoever gets to the first element says that. The next person goes, "Time for South," and does that. And on and on.

The *body* of the ritual is all the work that people have done for healing, and they're sharing it together as the community. You may have done your *own* work sitting at home with a candle, envisioning this person as well and sending them energy to help them get well, but now you're seeing the *synergy* of all of

the work that everybody in this close-knit community has done. When everybody's done, you close the space, say goodbye to the elements, close the circle, and everybody is out of the magical space. But what you've done is what most magic is about: you're taking the energy of a *group* and creating something bigger than any one person could create by themselves.

In the above ritual, one person might do something with a candle, while another person might charge a talisman to send to the person. Somebody else might visualize soothing water, or I might sit down and create *ascii* art (typewriter-like art) and send energy to people as *packets* along with my email. If your leg is injured, I will make a little ascii graphic of a leg, surround it with exclamation points and stars and energy, and put in words like "energy, strength, healing, wellness" and send it off to you with my intention and personal energy behind it. That's a cyber-spell I might do—I'm always sending energy to people over the Internet.

♦ *R/S: What does "ascii" mean?*

♦ RF: *Ascii* means plain text, the 256 characters that are shared by *all* computers. Microsoft *Word* uses more than 256 characters, so if you're using a PC and use "smart quotes," those smart quotes are higher-bit; they're not in the 256 characters. So if I, on a Mac, get your document, those smart quotes appear as meaningless characters because they're not an *ascii* element—they're not a universal letter.

Ascii Art in particular comes from the days when computers used punch cards and plotters, when all you had was one monospace font—you could only view *ascii* in Courier or Monaco or a font where every letter takes the same amount of space—an "i" takes the same amount of space as an "m." (In a modern, proportional-spacing font, the "i" is smaller—an "i" would be one unit, and an "m" would be five units.) In the old days you could use a typewriter with a plotter using a mono-space font to actually do drawings that you could send to somebody else. I'm talking about fifty lines of characters which combine to make a beautiful woman, or a rose, or a birthday cake. (**For awhile there was this whole ascii art movement; somebody even made Bambi in ascii art, all made up of normal typewriter letters.**) So, if I wished you "Happy Birthday," I would send you a birthday cake and the words "Happy Birthday."

♦ *R/S: In other words, images plus texts are more powerful and perhaps more magically effective than just words—*

♦ RF: For me, part of the fun comes from creating the image. If I were going to do something for you physically, I might sit down and sew you a little mojo bag. I'm doing the sewing, choosing the herbs and stones to put in it, embroidering your initials on it—*whatever*—which is what I did for a friend who was dying of cancer. If I'm doing a physical spell, there's all this *preparation.*

So when I'm composing an on-line spell, part of that means creating the image. It's not just typing, "I hope you're well soon, dear"—I'm putting in my intention and energy and working on this picture of an ankle (because you've broken your ankle) and

putting all my intentions around the picture of the ankle to send to you. And when I send it, I send it with this big *oomph* of energy, because I've created it with this *intention.* (Here, I'm wondering how this can be talked about without sounding like a wacko!)

I went on television doing *ascii art spells* for a program called "Tech Nation." The hosts were talking to "Techno Witches," and they watched me send my little ascii art email packets to someone. I can do work that way for people I've never seen—the email provides a physical link from me to the person. It's packets being sent over wires and wireless, and my energy is just one more packet that's along for the ride!

♦ *R/S: When you meet people, invisible energy gets transmitted—even an invisible molecular transfer can occur, such as when their perfume is received by your nostrils and processed by your brain—*

♦ RF: **Researchers did a study on people you have an instant antipathy for. If they measure your brain waves, *their* brain waves are really different from yours**, whereas people you have an instant liking for—their brain waves are similar to yours. There's a whole lot more going on in life than scientists have been able to "measure."

There's an *implicate* order and an *explicate* order to things—a hidden order behind the visible. An American physicist, David Bohm, explains it this way: You put a drop of ink in a jar of glycerine. If you move the jar so that the liquid swirls, first the ink swirls like water going down a drain. Then it becomes suspended enough so that you can't see it; the glycerine becomes clear. But if you turn it so it spins the other way, it all swirls down and becomes a drop of ink again! In other

1999 Selena Fox, Don Frew and Rowan Fairgrove in Capetown

words, the drop of ink still exists in the apparently clear glycerine—and by turning the jar upside-down you can recreate or reconstitute it. So, you can extrapolate an invisible or implicate order that exists *separate* from what we can actually see—which is the explicate order. This is a way to look at the subtle energies that are in existence. They may not be as easy to see as the ironing board across the room, but they're still here. ♦♦♦

NOTE: For more information on David Bohm, see
www.bizcharts.com/stoa del sol/plenum/plenum 3.htm

Greg Stafford

Greg Stafford is the author and publisher of fantasy role-playing games such as "Runequest," "Pendragon" and "Hero Wars," and publisher of "Call of Cthulhu." He is also President of the Board of Directors of the Cross Cultural Shamanism Network, which has been publishing *Shaman's Drum* magazine for 15 years. Interview by John Sulak; follow-up interview by V. Vale.

♦ *RE/SEARCH: Tell us about yourself—*
♦ GREG STAFFORD: I'm 52 years old, a father and husband, a shamanist ceremonial leader, and author and publisher of role-playing games. I'm in a Nature-oriented spiritual practice based on experiences, discovery and self-discovery, tolerance and respect.

♦ *R/S: Tell us about your spiritual history—*
♦ GS: As a kid, basically I felt doomed and haunted. When I was in first grade, I was followed in the streets by a spiritual entity the size of a truck. It was a frightening spider-like demon with feminine characteristics and a nasty disposition—I didn't realize until a few years ago that she was Kali. I also remember being plagued by visions of a nuclear war. I used to walk down the streets and imagine burned-out buildings in a nuclear wasteland. At the time, the media were frightening us with that "Duck and Cover" propaganda. I was pretty wild as an adolescent, feeling like I was going crazy from that.

Eventually I reached a point where I had to go on a *vision quest.* That's a ceremony derived from a Native American practice in which the individual is sent to a sacred place to sit for days and nights fasting, trying to understand the great mysteries. Native Americans did this as part of a coming-of-age ritual. So 27 years ago I went on a vision quest overseen by the Bear Tribe in Spokane, Washington. I was fortunate enough to get a vision which explained a lot of things which had troubled me, like that spider. For the first time my frightening visions, nice visions, deep desires, creativity, and artistic envisionings all began to make sense. Previously I had read books, been to rituals and performed ceremonies trying to figure it all out, but nothing was satisfying.

My vision quest basically revealed a path of things for me to do that led me to my present position. Since that time I have been on a Neo-Shamanic path toward spiritual understanding. **I believe there is an *invisible world* that consists of anything and everything we don't know.** It's where the mystery of everything resides. Parts of it can speak to us, instruct us. As we go through life, we learn a bit more all the time and the mystery diminishes. But nobody will ever be able to learn everything.

As a kid I used to ask, "Why am I here?" Now I realize that I am here to serve as a co-creator of the world that is yet to come. That's enough for me—that's plenty. I have experienced the truth of this in a deep and meaningful way, and have performed ceremonies to help other people realize this.

Personally, I don't call myself a shaman, but I do practices that are called shamanistic. Basically, this means the conscious use of trance state in a spiritual practice. Dancing, drumming, singing, meditating, journeying and rituals of many types often aim to induce this state. Shamanism *demands* a personal experience and interaction with the spirit world. Your personal experience is the ground on which you base your understanding—as opposed to books, or what other people tell you.

♦ *R/S: What are your Pagan practices?*
♦ GS: Regularly we do a monthly sweat lodge ceremony and an annual oak tree dance. A sweat lodge is a prayer meeting whose purpose is to get in touch with the great mysteries. Here I invoke space—the horizontal layer corresponding to the spirits of place, and time—the vertical, corresponding to my ancestors. The big yearly summer ritual I participate in is an Oak Tree Ceremony. We set up a sacred circle, ask the Deity to be awakened in the tree in the center, and enter into a 10-12 hour trance dance. We also pray for healing for each other, or for help when someone is in a crisis.

For regular annual celebrations I've depended on a local coven. But for celebrations, I'm eclectic—I'll use anything that works. **I've been to tremendous *Macumba* ceremonies, inspiring Unitarian services, Buddhist ceremonies that were transfiguring, and Wiccan rituals that brought ecstasy. I believe that most of these spiritual practices share a common root: our human body and experience.** I think Yoga is the science of this experience. It looks like a lot of Neo-

Pagan practices are based on re-interpreted Tantric-Buddhist-Hindu practices. So many of us have a practice to ground ourselves and root down into the earth and then raise energy through our spine, our chakras, and so on. This is an ancient Tantric practice that was imported into Europe around 1900.

♦ *R/S: You seem careful not to say "Indian" or "Native American practices," but most of your ceremonies sound like Indian practices—*

♦ GS: I am not an Indian and thus cannot do Native American medicine. What I do are core human practices. Nonetheless, even though these core practices are universal there is always a local component of spiritual interaction. I spent decades before finding teachers, and I got permission from spirits themselves to call on them, mostly while in the desert, fasting. If I am vision questing in Death Valley, the life forms there are part of the experience. This continent imposes its presence on us.

♦ *R/S: You mentioned the Celts—*

♦ GS: My ancestors were Celtic, and I have learned from them—they even used sweat lodges. "Celtic" is greatly romanticized and misunderstood. If you say "Native American" (of North America) you're talking about hundreds of different cultures and a huge number of variants. The same is true of Celts—basically they were everybody north of the Greco-Roman Mediterranean world.

I think that the pre-Celtic people who raised Stonehenge and the standing stones of Europe, and the later farming immigrants were illuminated by sages who were basically teaching Tantric, Yogic practices. Whether you call it Shamanism, Paganism, Tantra, Yoga, or consciousness raising, all of these are gateways toward the great mystery. And everyone has a personal relationship with the great mystery.

♦ *R/S: What's your view of monotheism?*

♦ GS: Monotheism is intolerant; it always says, "There is only one spiritual practice that is 'the truth,' and we know what it is." Monotheism inspires fanaticism. I just have difficulty dealing with a fundamentalist mind set. **I have no more patience with Pagan fundamentalists than with Christian or Islamic fundamentalists—they *all* bother me. I think the *scientific* fundamentalism that pervades our society is an illness**. Scientific fundamentalism is the thing that keeps us from being Pagan. **The worship of "progress" is a real problem—it's like a demonic force in our society, because people are not content with *what is*.** The drive toward progress means that soon we'll pave over *all* the earth in America, so that the only thing you'll have to be careful about is lane changing, instead of poison oak! *That* is what's driving NAFTA and antiballistic missile shields. We don't need that; we need more thoughtfulness and living in the moment.

♦ *R/S: What's the connection between Paganism and role-playing games?*

♦ GS: Our experience is important, and we are hard-wired for some experiences. Allegedly, for thousands of generations humans lived as groups of hunter-gatherers interacting with Nature. In those days it was 15 people chasing down deer. We don't do that anymore, but we're still hard-wired for that group oneness. So when six of us sit down to play these games, we enter into that ancient state of mind.

Role-playing games allow us to activate some of our hard wiring that is generally shunned, or even condemned, by a lot of mainstream spiritual practices. By activating these archetypes—these poetic images that are in our heads—into our *play,* they come to life in a "real" way in our life. People who have played some of these games have said, "You know, I never really realized before that we *are* part of Nature. I never really had a feeling for how important it is for us to *imagine.* I never had an idea how important it is for us to exercise our *heroic selves!*" People do this in role-playing games in a way that is modern, whereas in the old days it was just part of our everyday life.

Since *Modern Primitives* was your biggest hit, why didn't you ask all of the people you interviewed for *Modern Pagans* about their tattoos, piercings, and scarifications? My theory about book-buying is if someone picks it up off the shelf, the cover has to make them open up the book, and the pictures have to make them turn the page to move to the next one. Nobody's going to pick it up and *read* it!

♦ *R/S: Well, you have tattoos—do they relate to your Pagan philosophy?*

♦ GS: All of my tattoos are part of my practice. On my left shoulder down to the elbow is a tattoo expressing a portion of my personal Medicine Vision—that was made by Bill Salmon. I got it because it was imperative for me to express this in a *physical* way—to take the immaterial vision that I had and share it with the world. **The tattoo is a response to my otherwise secret, visionary life that allows it to come out into the open.**

At the top is an eagle with constellations on its wings and the sun in the center of its body. The sun's rays descend through the rest of the tattoo. Underneath the eagle is a pine tree—the tree of life—and beneath that is a Japanese spider demon, one of my protectors. She's sitting in the center of the web of all being, with a guitar in the center of her body like the hourglass on a black widow's abdomen. She is the Below, the Many and the Interrelatedness of all things. He is the Above, the One and the Unity of all things. From her the life forces rise through the tree, and from him it descends as light and lightning.

Many people get tattoos for ritual purposes, even though they don't realize it. I truly believe that tattoos speak to us from deep, deep inside. Even punks who go in and get some crap flash from off the wall of a tattoo studio—you know what, it's

not crap flash. It's a meaningful moment. They might say, "Oh, it's just fashion!" but even that has some meaning.

Below that is my charm bracelet, for travel. I travel a lot, and there have been times when something important has occurred, so I try to get a tattoo to permanently imprint that moment onto me, so I can remember and share it. This is when I was at Ayers Rock in Australia; this is from visiting Dublin; this one is from visiting Dinas Bran in Wales, and this is from San Francisco.

Tattoos mark moments. They are physical marks of permanent inner change. I have a few amateur tattoos—they're homemade with a pencil and needle. This small circle on my right calf is simple, but it's my initiation tattoo—it will forever remind me of my band of brothers that also have this tattoo; it's a marker of the permanent change we went through in this initiation. On my left leg is my personal mark: a backward "C" with a dot in the center that's sitting on top of an angular "R" shape.

This one here, of a round face with two "dot" eyes, deer antler, and sabre-tooth tiger teeth, is my deer hunting tattoo. I got it as part of my sacrifice to the deer spirit, praying for help on my hunt. It represents the union of opposites—I am the hunter *and* the hunted, the prey and the predator.

I'm very much concerned with Rites of Passage, so at one point I formed an organization with some men—they're "the men with whom I became a man." Basically we wanted to restart the rites of passage for ourselves. We still get together; this weekend we'll be doing a ritual for my youngest son, who just turned 18 and is leaving home. I'm also in another men's group

Greg Stafford (third from left) with his three children

where we do much the same thing—in October, we'll be going out on a Vision Quest for a new set of men.

♦ *R/S: You mentioned hunting; obviously you're not a vegetarian—*

♦ GS: A lot of people are distressed when I bring up hunting; they're so anti-gun. But the truth is, when the god/desses made the world, they included a component of "necessary cruelty" in our lives. In order for us to live, something else must die, whether it's plants, factory-raised cattle, or wild game. For a long time this distressed me enormously. Then **I undertook a sacred hunt ceremony, the purpose of which was to interact in a sacred manner with our food.** Doing this has truly instilled in me the concrete reality of the *circle of life.* We go out

and pray to the deer spirit, the lion spirit, to help us and be one with us, and to help give us that understanding that we are not separate from Nature. **We try to be one with** *both* **predator and prey.** People who eat factory food bought from a supermarket, and pretend that killing is not part of their life, are cut off from something important. For myself, it has injected a deep respect for life and death and an understanding.

♦ *R/S: Do you have children?*

♦ GS: Yes, three. My daughter, who lives in Arcata, is a total vegetarian. I tell people, "I can't tell you what it's like to have children. It's as different as having an orgasm. You have one and say, "Wow—everything's different now; *now* I see!" You can't explain it without having done it. It's an experience which you can't intellectualize at all. This mirrors my own Pagan efforts and what I think life is about: **I have learned that there are many things you cannot intellectualize.** So much of our modern culture is intellectualization which almost always *removes* us from the actual experience.

♦ *R/S: You've tested Shamanic waters; have you ever done a peyote ritual?*

♦ GS: I find much of the Peyote church to be very fundamentalist. Yes. We have some potent helper beings in certain medicine plants. I occasionally indulged in psychoactive drugs in the Sixties. Medicine rites are really different—not like "getting stoned" at all. It's hard work, and not my primary path now.

♦ *R/S: What do you think of the concept of linear time?*

♦ GS: The Hindu concept is far more comfortable to me, of cycles within cycles within cycles. The notion of progress is complex; I have a friend who just had his appendix removed, and he would be dead today without progress. We all want to feed our children and live in a healthy way, but somewhere along the road we get twisted—you get a vaccination for *this,* and it makes you susceptible to *that.* You look at the agricultural revolution, and in the old days people ate less variety, whereas we eat more variety and suffer from a host of new diseases that had never existed before. What are we trading?

♦ *R/S: Right. Paganism demands accountability and responsibility—*

♦ GS: Yes. Paganism requires your personal commitment, thought, and responsibility to whatever form of consciousness you develop. It doesn't allow us to hide behind a corporate mask, or a brand name, or anything. We learn that we are responsible, not just for ourselves and our family, but our community, and humanity at large—*whoops,* now we're responsible for the whole earth! ♦♦♦

Erik Davis

San Francisco author of *Techgnosis [techgnosis.com]*, Erik Davis writes, practices Yoga and walks in Golden Gate Park. Interview by V. Vale.

♦ *RE/SEARCH: Is "Technopagan" just a trendy buzzword, or does it have some validity?*

♦ ERIK DAVIS: Both Margot Adler's *Drawing Down the Moon* and T.C. Luhrmann's *Persuasions of the Witch's Craft* make the point that **a high proportion of the earliest Neo-Pagans came out of early computer culture. The development of the computer itself has always been shadowed by the development of computer games where the dominant imaginal space is an essentially magical universe** of wizards, occult powers, and spells—the world of heroic fantasy that comes through Tolkien and *Dungeons & Dragons*. In computer game design, programming *language* literally creates the world.

Now, the West Coast "Virtual Reality" vanguard, using computers, sophisticated interfaces, and sensory plug-ins, is really staging the possibility of a kind of magical world manipulated by the imagination and the will, which has a shared symbolic context in which people can explore *other possibilities*.

The most famous book introducing the idea of "cyberspace"—the idea of a *media otherworld*—is William Gibson's *Neuromancer*. But there is an earlier, little-known novella that was extremely influential in early hacker circles—*True Names* by Vernor Vinge. It's a great story about hacker anti-authoritarians who are creating encrypted code spaces that the government can't get into. They plug themselves into a reality machine through some kind of science-fiction interface, but the world itself is a *Dungeons & Dragons* world. The author explicitly discusses how magic was just a metaphor—but it's *the* metaphor that best fits this new environment.

In a virtual reality environment of the future I would be able to shape shift, and manifest icons and images at will. We're slowly moving toward that kind of three-dimensional, immersive, costume-wearing, role-playing world. The whole idea of computer-game role play overlaps a lot of Pagan practice—when Pagans cast a circle, enter and call down the divinities, essentially they're doing what people do in role-playing games. But instead of saying, "This is just a game," Pagans say, "This is a religious or spiritual practice."

♦ *R/S: Paganism is also reclaiming the role of poetry and metaphor in society—*

♦ ED: **Both role-playing computer games and Paganism are attempting to restore the power of metaphor—the power of images to change perception, create new feelings and new kinds of social connections.** One of the only things making money on the Internet (other than pornography) are these immersive, graphic, three-dimensional worlds like *EverQuest* or *Ultima Online*. These are essentially Tolkienesque, medieval, magical, pre-modern worlds—which also attract Pagans. Incidentally, Pagans were the first religionists to take full advantage of the Internet. If you went to "alt/religion/pagan" seven years ago, you would have found a huge amount of discussion compared to what other religions were generating.

Do you know what a *mud* is? It stands for multi-user dungeon or multi-user dimension. It's a text-based role-playing game system that was very popular in the late '80s and early- to mid-'90s. It allowed people to play *Dungeons & Dragons*-like games on the Internet.

One called **Divination Web was remarkable. People of a Pagan or magical persuasion could explore different symbol systems or worlds—you could enter into a Celtic space, an Egyptian space**—very mapped environments. These virtual environments enabled you to build associational maps of symbols, god/desses, and icons, and show how they interrelate. "The Tree of Life" was a particularly good example which enabled you to explore the power of symbols at your own pace, in a new way. Much of the process of the Occult involves working with symbols and establishing interrelationships to manipulate and produce perception and states of consciousness.

♦ *R/S: I'll say—the ad agencies are the best at that. Look at how they've got everyone trained to buy GAP clothes and speak in soundbites.*

♦ ED: Absolutely. The funny thing is, if you analyze a lot of ad rhetoric, you're gonna find magic. *Magic, Rhetoric, and Literacy* argues that magic is an extension of what in the ancient world was called rhetoric. And rhetoric is a different art than the pursuit of truth. Essentially, it's the *art of persuasion*—using language and images to persuade. So it involves metaphor, figures of speech, performance, symbols, images—the art of manipulating perception. **Some nebulous eros is always flowing through us**—both Paganism and advertising have to do with *eros energy*. Advertisers ask, "How can you stage a scenario to produce an act of consumption?" Pagans ask, "How can you stage a scenario to produce group transcendence, or a cone of power?"

In a way we totally live in a magical world. We walk down the street and are always being pushed and pulled by advertising—basically unaware of how much magic is going on all the time. Pagans bring to the surface the *truth* about a lot of things like this that are going on in an unconscious and frankly harmful fashion—not to mention aesthetically repugnant. There's a Pagan Rule of Three that's often quoted, but in advertising there's also a Rule of Three: you say something three times, and it's implanted in your memory. That's the way the human memory works. You'll see many examples of the Rule of Three if you really start analyzing television commercials.

♦ *R/S: Paganism aims for enhanced communication, and also shared ownership of land, as real estate prices skyrocket and rents become positively life-threatening—*

♦ ED: There's the idea of getting a plot of land, getting off the grid, minimizing consumption and reducing your relationship to the money economy. Of course, the people who are actually pulling that off are a minority.

Paganism is countercultural and anti-authoritarian, in an era when seemingly countercultural activities are spotlighted, in ads and corporate media "news articles," as acceptable to the status quo. Today the market is perfectly happy with any number of things that would have been utterly scandalous thirty years ago. **You have to conclude that the "real" anti-authoritarian activity is being hidden—especially anything involving true advances in consciousness. ♦♦♦**

Darryl Cherney

Darryl Cherney is an Earth First! organizer, topical singer/song-writer, a bard of the Church of All Worlds and all-around pagan troublemaker He co-founded the Headwaters Forest Campaign with activist/photographer Greg King in 1986. He has organized hundreds of rallies and events, and authored countless press releases on behalf of forest protection. Darryl joined with Judi Bari to create the Redwood Summer 1990 campaign and well as a timber worker-environmentalists alliance. The two of them were bombed in a car in Oakland, CA in 1990 while on an organizing drive to promote those causes and subsequently blamed by the FBI for bombing themselves. They went on to sue the FBI in federal court for violations of civil rights. He hosts an environmental talk show and a political music program on KMUD-FM community radio in Redway, California. In 1997 he created Environmentally Sound Promotions, a non-profit with the mission of "Music, Arts and Media for the Earth." He has produced eight albums of environmental music and spoken word both of his own works and others, including his latest CD, "White Tribal Music." He holds a M.S. in Urban Education (1977) from Fordham University. He can be contacted at Environmentally Sound Promotions, POB 2254, Redway CA 95560; website is *www.darrylcherney.com*. Interview by John Sulak.

♦ *RE/SEARCH: Can you talk about Pagans and activism—*
♦ DARRYL CHERNEY: **Just declaring yourself a Pagan in the year 2001, anywhere on the planet, is an act of activism in and of itself!** There is a long history of suppression of earth-centered spirituality, and I have my own theories as to how we humans diverted from our interconnection with the earth. I'll offer a brief history of the world from a Pagan perspective.

I think we began our possession and enslavement of the elements when we first harnessed fire. Actually, we were enslaving two elements; as far as I can tell the elements are always paired off—fire requires air. So we were both harnessing and enslaving fire and air. At that point, they became a *possession.*

When you light a campfire, there is only a certain amount of space around it. Immediately there arises a power dynamic as to who gets to sit closest to the fire. Fire also allowed humans to eat meat and grains—food that we could only eat after we had cooked it. Further, it enabled us to forge metals and create phenomenal and dangerous technologies. Mastery of fire allowed us to move to other climates and leave behind our original, native habitat, the equatorial belt around the earth. **Human beings are the only species on the planet that wear clothing**—every other animal on the earth is naked. The reason we wear clothing is because we're out of our native habitat!

Once we started moving out of the equatorial belt into areas with colder weather, we developed agriculture almost out of necessity. A lot of people think of the "farmer *versus* the city," but they're actually two sides of the same coin. Agriculture creates a sedentary civilization. During cold winters, doubtless the nomadic societies noticed that these cities had all this food in storage. As hunter-gatherers they decided to go help themselves. So the agrarian societies had to develop walled cities and stand-ing armies to defend their food supplies. Thus developed the warrior—the warrior, who once offered his life for the community devolved into the soldier who guards the food and kills for the protection of the community. The food supplies were also fostering population growth.

Through all this, the male supplanted the female as the life-giver and life-provider, developing a violent role in society that ultimately led to the patriarchy. City folks developed bigger and stronger weaponry, and [as seen with Akhnaton, 1379-1362 B.C.], the Egyptian civilization embraced monotheism and the worship of sky gods. **Monotheism, in general, reflects the male supplanting the female as the life-giver, as well as it reflects the monoculture**, where the same crops are grown—instead of a diversity of foods and animals as food supplies.

As the war against the nomadic Pagans increased over the millennia, the city dwellers decided they needed to wage not just a defensive but an *offensive* campaign. So they started cutting down the forests where the Pagans lived. This was easy—you can simply ring trees with a saw; you don't have to cut them down. Even worse, you can burn down the forests, as was common in 3,000-2,000 BC. This is documented in Jonathan Perlin's *A Forest's Journey,* a well-researched history of logging throughout recorded civilization. As soldiers had to go farther afield to attack potential invaders, they weren't sleeping with their female partners at night. So rape became the order of the day—part and parcel of warfare.

After humans harnessed the element of fire, it wasn't really long before they developed the nuclear bomb. **From the standpoint of geological time, we put ourselves on the brink of self-annihilation within a nano-moment in the history of the world.**

Photo: Gary Thompson courtesy New Settler Interview

The Bible itself gives a fantastic metaphor that describes this process. Satan (or Lucifer) was God's chosen angel, his favorite. Then Lucifer decided that he wanted to be autonomous, and essentially become an "independent contractor." Is that not the *exact role* that human beings—especially men—have taken on for themselves? We have decided to be creators, and supersede God. We have decided to reshape, if not destroy, "the Creation." *We are the living, breathing incarnation of the Satan metaphor!*

Obviously, we need to rectify this by understanding our original, true connection with the earth and the entire cosmos. Every single thing on our planet comes from the earth (with the exception of a few meteor scraps). For very pragmatic reasons, humans' early spirituality honored and worshipped the earth, understanding the interconnection between human beings and the earth.

♦ *R/S: What can we do, on a practical level?*

♦ DC: Earth First's slogan, "No compromise in defense of Mother Earth," implies that an ant can move an elephant if it gets a leverage or fulcrum point sufficiently far away. And we're ants trying to move an elephant— rather, a planet. So we have to get pretty far out there on the edge of the spectrum.

I firmly believe that **we're never going to truly live in harmony with the earth until we get rid of the Safeways of the world.** We can form our communes, utopias, and cooperative communities, yet almost instantly we can escape the frustrations of trying to get along with each other by going to the nearest Safeway or Wal-Mart . . . to the corporate teat for our nutritional requirements. We always have an escape valve that prevents us from working out disagreements with our fellow human beings.

But if we can't get rid of all the Safeways tomorrow, there are other stratagems. We can build smaller houses grouped in circles, not each one of us living on our own 40-acre parcel as happens in Humboldt County, California. This leaves the majority of the land wild and free for the animals to live in.

Young Darryl, 1968 Photo: Abraham Cherney

Those of us who call ourselves Pagans are trying to reconstruct a workable "Pagan" lifestyle and philosophy. Yet if you try to capture spirituality on the printed page, it becomes doctrine, dead words—*inflexible.* If you judge things by their results, the Bible, Koran, Book of Mormon and so on have promoted the practices of hatred, bigotry and the subjugation of women.

In a way, the written word has pretty much killed God! Some people think there is a huge, fundamental difference between religion and spirituality. To me, a religion is institutionalized spirituality . . . as opposed to spirituality itself, which is an *internal* source of self-guidance. Spirituality is what guides our spirit—isn't that obvious? *Spirituality, to me, is the way we live our lives.* And the primary spirituality that rules the United States now is *capitalism:* the love and worship of capital and profit.

In a way, there's no separation of church and state in America; it all depends on how you define "church." **The founding fathers developed the separation of church and state because the Inquisition was still a frightening memory.** They understood how much damage churches could do. . .

Spirituality will change as civilization changes. Einstein said that the problem with harnessing the atom was that we had developed technology without an accompanying spiritual evolution. We need to develop a spirituality to accommodate *exponential,* technological development!

However, we have become greedy, taking and taking from our planet rather than giving back. The true nature of sustainability, which is what environmentalism is all about, is that there needs to be equal give-and-take. But our industrial civilization has been based on constantly taking and wasting what we've been given. This is partially based on the fact that **we still have untamed survival instincts—we think we need more in order to live than we really do.**

Every animal, including the tiniest ant, has an astonishing survival instinct. An ant or a flea will fight for its life just as hard as a human being. Every being on the planet wants to live. Now, since humans have evolved into beings that are technology-dependent and know how to create things in a virtually god-like manner, we have been able to procreate in vast numbers, while exterminating most of the other species on earth. Our natural fear of death, which was originally connected to a simple need to survive, has become profoundly exaggerated.

This is all connected to the survival instinct. When we developed our doomsday technology, we forgot that we need a spirituality to *guide* this technology— not just parrot "Thou shalt not kill," or "Thou shalt not commit adultery." We need a spirituality that allows us to have a *relationship* with our technology, so we comprehend that every knife, fork, spoon, table, chair, car, and computer comes from the earth—and when we get rid of something, it goes back into the earth in a totally polluting form.

As an environmental activist and Pagan, I realize that we need an earth-centered spirituality that is completely connected with environmental protection. To me, environmental protection is synonymous with the spiritual regulation of our technology, because it is our technology that is causing the pollution. And technology is not benign. The gun lobby is classic in this way: "It's not the gun that kills, it's people that kill." Well, *hello!*—a gun is designed solely to kill. And the gun people prey, like **all human technology preys, upon another human instinct: a desire to get from point A to point B in the quickest possible way**—not like the river that winds and weaves through the contours of the landscape. In many ways, a human being feels that it has to get from point A to point B in the straightest line possible, and technology facilitates that. Yet I call this desire for efficiency, for expediency, "evil"—that which is against life. It's funny that in the English language, "evil" literally *is* the opposite of "live." To me evil means the anti-life force.

Thoughts are *things*—they are electrical impulses that travel through the brain. I have come up with the notion that thoughts have survival instincts. Native Americans will tell you that all things are alive. And everything that is alive has a survival instinct. So when you have a thought, it desires to live. And now we find ourselves inundated by mind-control religions which are the written doctrines and dogmas of a few crazed, lunatic men who jotted their thoughts down on paper and decided that this is something that every human being needs to believe, or else they'll "rot in hell."

Anything that is alive has survival instincts and propagation methodologies, including bad thoughts. They provide a lure or a bait to trick people. "Hey, you don't need that horse. Try this car." And even within the development of the automobile, there were sub-debates as to what kind of fuel should be used: "Should we use this organic fuel that will help keep the farmers alive, like ethanol? Or should we use fossil fuels that are a finite resource and will pollute the planet? Let's use the fossil fuel because we can make more money." All these notions are actually the result of thousands of years of bad thoughts—they're viruses, really—coming together, interbreeding, developing new technologies and more survival tricks.

We keep developing more labor-saving devices, but when you think about it, a labor-saving device puts people out of work! Everybody wants a labor-saving device, but nobody wants to be out of a job. So obviously, we don't really think things through to their conclusion.

You've got labor unions and the American work force in general wondering why there aren't more jobs left. We've exported an enormous number of jobs to third world countries which allow slave labor and children to supplant our labor force. We've also destroyed numerous jobs through the creation of technology. And the jobs that are left don't have any kind of physicality to them anymore, so we have become physically weak. We sit glued to computer screens, or find ourselves in repetitive-motion jobs. Then we're fed a diet of hormone-

laden, fattening food. From an outside viewpoint, humans are being weakened and fattened for the kill!

Technology has allowed us to live longer, but we don't know what we're living *for.* What do we do with these extra years? We don't even have any place to put our old people! In fact, we have gotten rid of our elders, just as we've gotten rid of oral traditions. **When we put our elders away in old folk's homes or leave them somewhere to die, it is the functional equivalent of burning libraries.**

What does evil, which is anti-life, want to do? It wants us to get rid of any knowledge that allows us to live on this planet in harmony with the earth. It wants us to forget the past, because the past is in fact the repository of knowledge required for survival. And **when you cut a plant off from its roots, as we cut ourselves off from our elders, that plant is going to die.**

♦ *R/S: Today the mass media continually encourages us to buy new things and discard old ones, even if they're not worn out—*

♦ DC: Consumerism governs many, if not all, aspects of our lives. The getting rid of the elders *equals* the burning of the libraries *equals* the notion that old is bad and new is good and you need to buy it.

One more point I want to make about the written word is that *the written word makes knowledge a commodity.* And think about all the knowledge that has been lost or destroyed because the written word supplanted oral tradition. We can see this now in the world of music. The live troubadour, the original newscaster, the bard, was replaced by the player piano, which was replaced by the 78, the LP, the CD, and soon something will replace the CD. Every time a new technology takes over, the ability to use the old technology gets phased out, meaning an attrition takes place, and information gets lost—

♦ *R/S: —or dies. Paganism seems to be more accepting of death as being part of the cycle of life—*

♦ DC: Absolutely. I was thinking just the other day about looking forward to death. You can't destroy energy. And what are our thoughts? What is our being, other than energy? So when we die, all that we are has to be transformed into something else—it has to "go" somewhere—perhaps to another plane of existence which is not visible to the naked eye or to a scientist's instruments.

Historically, the greatest warriors have been ones whose foundation is rooted in spirituality. If you're trying to save the earth because of scientific reasons—like, for example, current corporate/governmental practices will lead to floods, droughts and famines—that's all very well and good. But if that protection of the earth comes from a *spiritual* place, then it becomes all-consuming. And you become an earth warrior, not just an environmental activist.

Earth First!ers describe ourselves as a tribe of earth warriors willing to offer our lives for the greater good. Which is why we often find ourselves in extremely dangerous situations. Until the environmental movement becomes predominantly a spiritual movement, it will lack the ardor necessary to defend our great Earth Mother. Here, the Pagans are holding a great piece of the puzzle in their hands. Both the environmentalists and the Pagans are honoring the earth, but in completely different ways.

Environmentalists understand a lot about vegetarianism, factory farming, recycling and re-using. Yet I see Pagans eating

Photo: Dave Kirkman

hot dogs and drinking Coca-Colas out of styrofoam cups. Pagans understand the cycles of the earth, spiritual quests, and the use of ritual to develop an understanding of the earth, whereas a large percentage of environmentalists don't. Of course, it's not only environmentalists and Pagans that need to get together and teach other—also working families and labor unions.

♦ *R/S: What is your involvement with Earth First?*

♦ DC: I became aware of Paganism in 1983 when I was living in New York City. I actually believe that every single human being is a Pagan. I once read a quote, "**If you scratch the skin of a Christian, you'll find a Pagan.**" I awakened to my own Pagan nature through a relationship with a woman, Judy Zweiman, who was a Vegan as well as a Pagan, a musician, and an astrologer.

When I came to California in 1985, I discovered the *Earth First!* journal and bumper-stickers. I noticed that the newspaper was published on Pagan holidays. I also learned that Earth First! is not an organization but a movement. It doesn't have any written by-laws or "officers." It still has some of the trappings of an organization—it publishes a newspaper. However, it isn't *the* official newspaper—an affinity group puts it out.

Earth First! activists embrace the following three precepts:

1) Biocentrism: which means that we put the earth and life at the center of our concerns. The continuation of life on earth as we know it is our primary purpose for our activism. We're not interested in just saving a piece of land for a park, we're interested in protecting entire *ecosystems,* and in reconstructing and restoring the land to its natural state. We believe that the earth is here to share with the other species, that we are not something special, that we are just another animal on the planet. And we're not particularly happy with the way we've conducted ourselves.

2) No compromise in defense of Mother Earth. We believe that the earth is not ours to compromise. **Who gave us the earth? Excuse me—it's not ours to give away!** We can't even imagine compromise. We understand the nature of compromise because we grew up in an industrial civilization. We watched other people compromise and we learned what the word means. But, just as Native Americans did not initially understand the concept of private property, we don't understand the concept of compromise. The native peoples understood that the white man was killing them, annihilating them and seizing the land, but they knew, as we know, that one can't really "own" the land.

Humans set up governments that give you a piece of paper and then charge taxes and regulate the land. If you don't pay your taxes, they take it away. But how can you *own* a piece of land? Do you own every little ant that's on it? Do you own the deer that cross it? Do you own the water? Well, some people say that they do—then the people downstream don't get any water.

3) The third principle of Earth First! is *action.* Unlike the Sierra Club, we don't have memberships—we're not interested in taking your fifteen dollars so you can say you're one of us. You simply have to participate in an Earth First activity. *Then* you become an Earth First! activist, not an Earth First! *member.*

Earth First! was set up structurally to foster a philosophical way of conducting activism. One goal was to implement a new paradigm for protecting the earth. Historically, Earth First! has provided the environmental movement with bene-

1997 Photo: Diane Darling

fits that go far beyond our numbers.

For example, since we don't have rules or official leaders, anybody can become a spokesperson or a leader. By "leader" I mean a true leader: someone who *leads,* as opposed to somebody who is elected. Leaders can change on a daily basis. You can be the leader of a tree sit, a media interaction, or a particular hike. Earth First "leaders" function as catalysts that make real things happen.

From Earth First sprang the Southwest Center for Biodiversity, and the Rainforest Action Network, our biggest splinter group. Earth First! has a fair number of conscious Pagans in it, and at Pagan gatherings you always see more Earth First!ers than members of any other environmental groups. But a certain number of Earth First!ers and environmentalists in general don't acknowledge that spirituality is an essential ingredient of the human persona. And unless we address that aspect of humanity, we're never going to truly reach people.

In a sense, we have been turned off to being spiritual through the philosophy of Karl Marx, who said that religion was the opium of the masses, and whose ideas led to atheism becoming the official non-religion of communism. So-called liberal, progressive people were taught to shun religion, and not to impose their religion on others. Well, I certainly don't believe in imposing my religion on anybody, but **to deny my own spirituality is to deprive myself of a phenomenal amount of power.**

While I was addressing some working-class families in Ohio, I said, "You know, I had a spiritual revelation . . ." Suddenly everybody woke up! I said that in order to defeat the Maxxam Corporation, we also need to bring in the Native Americans, the working people and the unions to make our circle whole. I saw this from a spiritual perspective: that all the members of the family need to be in the circle.

This spiritual revelation hit me while I was driving late at night. I started working with a number of native peoples, and ultimately the Native American Coalition for the Headwaters was born. When the United Steel Workers went on strike, I saw an opportunity to bring in both working families and labor unions into this Headwaters campaign. I visited one of the locals for Kaiser Aluminum workers, they embraced me with open arms, and we brought the unions into our campaign. This is an example of true activism guided by spiritual insight.

♦ *R/S: How many demonstrations have you been involved in?*

♦ DC: Certainly hundreds.

♦ *R/S: How has Pagan spirituality played a part in those?*

♦ DC: The demonstrations I've organized have almost universally been based on insights and revelations touching upon what I call *political acupressure points.* Also important is understanding the waxing and waning of the political tides, and the cycles of the moon. Of course, timing is supremely important.

Each demonstration is different because we're story-telling through each one: telling the story of where the loggers live, the story of the company headquarters in San Francisco before they sold it to the Japanese. We're telling the story of the Board of Forestry and how the animals don't have any representation. We're telling the story of a corporate CEO who deserves to go to jail, and the story of a failed savings and loan. And each one of these demonstrations represents a chapter of living history.

♦ *R/S: Are Pagans involved in national politics?*

♦ DC: Pagans have gotten involved in national politics when it intrudes into our personal lives. In general, environmentalists and Pagans tend to be regional—or even microcosmic—in their focus. If a Pagan is part of a tribe and if a tribe is really a small extended family or village unit, then it goes against our essential grain to become "national." We don't even believe in nations to begin with!

To fight our enemy, especially on his own terms, is almost to *become* our enemy. That is one of the great dilemmas. Gandhi understood the power of non-violence. He knew how to use decentralization and local activism against the industrial juggernaut. I attended a conference whose main topic was violence *versus* nonviolence. One activist asked, "Don't we want to use all the tools in our toolbox?" I replied, "Personally, I believe that violence begets violence. As soon as you physically force somebody to adopt your way of thinking, or physically kill them to eliminate them, you have set up a paradigm in which ultimately you can justify killing anybody just because you disagree with them! Speaking of 'using every tool in the box,' why are we not using more magic?"

This activist had worked with many Native Americans and had been to their ceremonies, so he knew what I was talking about. I said, "Magic is so much more fun than violence, and frankly, I think it's much more effective. Magic is a tool that has been grossly under-utilized by the environmentalist activist community. Let's try it."

So what Paganism provides is magic and ceremony. And my own experiences with magic have often been very effective. For example, a group of us went to Houston to join steel workers striking against the Maxxam Corporation. We came up with a picket sign that said "Hold Maxxam accountable"—Morning Glory Ravenheart channeled the word "accountable"—and the striking steel workers made hundreds of copies of our picket sign.

♦ *R/S: Morning Glory once said that organizing Pagans is like trying to herd kittens—*

♦ DC: —more like mountain lions; to hell with the "kittens"! These mountain lions are nasty, and sometimes they swat at each other in a serious way.

There must be some way for the Goddess to reclaim her rightful seat on the throne in order for us to survive this impending and ongoing holocaust that threatens the survival of every living thing on the planet. I regard this period of time as a real privilege, because it offers us the potential to be the last generation to be able to fight for the survival of our own species and of Mother Earth herself.

As warriors we have been given, in a sense, the ultimate test. This is why all the great minds need to come together, and stop swatting at each other like a bunch of hissing mountain lions. This is why the Pagans and the environmentalists need to come together—we need to share our knowledge, and foster and continue *evolution.* Here's a joke: "Why do fundamentalists not believe in evolution?"

♦ *R/S: "I don't know—why not?"*

♦ DC: "Because it's not happening to them!"

Here I believe that the *real* battle Earth First! is fighting is the battle for evolution: to enable evolution to continue. And these other forces are trying to enforce a monoculture. They're trying to make every town a line-up of Wal-Marts, McDonalds and Starbucks . . . where every human wears the same Gap clothing and everybody has the same hair style. That's what *their* religion has come to stand for. That war of creationism *versus* evolutionism is a mirror image of what's happening in society. By trying to pave over the evolutionary process, by trying to create tree farms, huge industrial agribusinesses and seas of genetically-engineered soybeans, the creationists are attempting to take away the ability of Nature to evolve. And what evolution really means is to make things stronger, heartier, more lively, more fun, and more joyous. Why? Because diversity is where we get our strength. And Pagans are very strong in the diversity department.

It's amazing how diverse Pagans can be. Most Pagans don't say, "This is our religion"—instead, **we embrace what's good from each spirituality we find, and incorporate it.** I don't think there is such a thing as a Starhawk-ite. There are a few Crowley-ites, but even they are as diverse as any Pagan can possibly be.

Terence McKenna described Persia as a cross-pollination center for spiritualities; a great crossroads and meeting center where all the religions stole and borrowed from each other. Of course, Christianity ripped off the entire Pagan set of holidays, rituals, and belief systems and perverted them into a weirdness wherein the resurrection of Christ is celebrated by a bunny that lays eggs, and the birth of Christ is celebrated by a guy in a red

1997 with Bonnie Raitt Photo: Bill Burton

suit giving out presents under a tree! **Christianity is an artificial, sham religion established by a few charlatans to centralize power for their own greedy purposes and sadistic mind-sets.** Christianity, Judaism, Zoroastrianism, the Moslem faith and the Mormon faith are derived from books that historically have been proven to provoke people into practicing warfare, hatred, bigotry, and subjugation of women.

♦ *R/S: Is Paganism a way out of that?*

♦ DC: Paganism is a generic term, just like the word "beverage" can refer to an infinite number of drinks. I understand that Pagans were people who lived outside of cities, outside of the surveyed areas, just as "heathen" means the people who lived out on the heath. To me, **a Pagan is someone who honors both the female and the male equally, and lives in harmony with the earth.** And to do that, you have to consider your location, climate, period of history, the technology that is available, the resident eco-system, the neighboring animals and plants, the culture and traditions of your tribe or clan, your friends and family, the kind of work that is available, the methods of transportation, the kinds of food and clothing . . . Paganism has to be woven into every thread of every piece of clothing, and every strand of every basket—into every step that one takes.

Saying that you're religious and going to church once a week is like saying you're political and voting just once a year. **Spirituality is a moment-by-moment thing; it is always in the present. Every word you speak and every breath you take is a spiritual act. To me, that is the essence of being a Pagan.**

Another thing: John Trudell, an American Indian Movement activist and poet/performer says that the middle three letters of the word "believe" are "lie"! That's why I say I don't *believe* anything—I either *know* it, or I don't. So why do I know that magic works? Because I've seen it work over and over again. That's why I would hope that more people understood and were educated in the use of rituals and ceremonies for accomplishing goals.

To those people who are skeptics, I would say: 1) Pagans certainly believe in the Golden Rule as Jesus put it: "Do unto others as you would have them do unto you." This is another version of the Law of Karma: "Whatever you put out comes back at you." So, inherent in the Pagan mind-set is the idea that if we kill somebody through magic, it's the same as if we killed somebody physically. The repercussions, the internal hell that we would suffer on earth, would be no less. 2) If you think that magic can be done for evil, then you are acknowledging that magic *works!* . . .

If we look at the Inquisition, for example (which I think was probably the darkest period in the history of humanity), we will find men who, in the name of a hippie peace activist named Jesus, tortured women and men in dungeons with fire and much worse. And they were telling their victims that *they're* the ones possessed by Satan! I would contend that the *Christians,* the people who were propagating by force the so-called Christian "faith," were the practitioners of black magic. As a Catholic friend once put it, **"There isn't a Christian on the planet who didn't have an ancestor converted at the point of a sword."**

But the Inquisition has been very long-lasting and continues to this day. It continues with the persecution of Native Americans, and the persecution of native peoples from Africa to South America, to the Lapps, the Picts, the Polynesians, and

1997 with Woody Harrelson Photo: Bill Burton

on down the line. Hawaii is the only majority Pagan state in the Union, with Pele as the Fire Goddess of the volcanoes.

My point is: Pagans have been persecuted. And environmentalists have been subjected to increasing, profound violence. It wasn't just that **Judi Bari and I were bombed in a car and blamed by the F.B.I. for bombing ourselves. Other environmentalists have been attacked, killed, and threatened.** They've had their houses burned down. So the message has been historically entrenched: Keep your Paganism to yourself. Don't allow the Earth Mother to enter your faith, at least not in a public way.

As feminist doctrine, I think restoring the Earth Mother as a spiritual entity has to be part of the greater agenda. How can you have a guy alone in the sky? To take the Goddess away from the God is to leave the God alone and lonely—it's blasphemy! It's time for the Earth Mother to beat down the doors of the churches, the synagogues, the mosques, the temples and all the religious institutions, to rightfully reclaim her place on the throne. Why shouldn't we have Pagans with picket signs right outside the Catholic churches, saying, "Let the Earth Mother In!" "Goddess Now!" "God Needs a Girlfriend!"

Earth Mother was kicked out, or relegated to being a virgin, deprived of sexuality, deprived of an equal place, and perverted into an archetype which has made us all feel guilty about sex. This is why Paganism has also become somewhat synonymous with sexual experimentation and revolution: because the patriarchal, monotheistic religions have suppressed sexuality. And sexuality is probably *the* dominant force in our lives. Sexuality, which is directly related to survival, is something that's on most human beings' minds for a fair percentage of the day. It is a natural function, a natural bodily desire that every human being has.

So I believe that it is time for us to go public. Let's bring the cauldron to the doors of the White House, to the doors of the corporations. It's time for the Earth Mother to bang down the doors of the churches and reclaim her rightful seat! Let's let those who would persecute us know that not only are we not afraid, but that we are here, we are proud, and we have a guiding light to assist humanity's return to harmony with Nature.

♦ *R/S: Can you talk about what happened to you and Judi Bari?*

♦ DC: Judi Bari and I were romantic partners for two or three years in the late Eighties/early Nineties. We were, in a lot of respects, the Dynamic Duo for Earth First! in Northern California. We fed off of each other's radicalism. She was a former labor union organizer and an extremely creative person. She could draw, she could sing, she could play fiddle. She was a fantastic organizer. She wrote great press releases, had a huge mailing list, and was a dynamic public speaker, which a lot of people remember her for.

The fundamental difference between Judi Bari and I—and it was the source of many of our arguments—was that she, at least when I first met her, was what you might call an atheist. She thought that people who gathered in circles and sang to the Goddess were out of their minds. She would stay in the circle and pray along with the rest of us, but essentially she was a Red Diaper Baby trained in Marxist theory.

Here's why environmentalists need to understand some of the tenets of Pagan spirituality. After Judi and I were bombed in the car, I started asking myself, "Why didn't the Goddess warn me? How could I have gotten into that car and not have sensed, psychically, that there was a bomb in it?"

Both Judi and I were ultimately protected, in that Judi, who was sitting on a bomb, lived. Even though she was crippled for life, she should have been killed. She had ten fractures in her pelvis, her right leg was paralyzed, her coccyx and sacrum were permanently pulverized and dislocated. She was impaled on a car seat spring and she suffered intestinal damage. I was sitting two feet from the bomb and was barely scratched. I had two busted ear drums and a scratched cornea. I needed four stitches over my left eye, and that's it. So I knew that we had powerful forces looking over us.

But I wanted to know why we weren't warned, and I have two answers. The first is a very pragmatic answer: Judi and I were in the process of breaking up, and we were fighting. **And when you are fighting with your friends, it distracts you from protecting yourself against your enemies or adversaries.** Actually, I don't like to use the word "enemies," because I really see all humanity as one great big dysfunctional family, with archetypal internal battles going on.

However, something else occurred that I didn't learn about until a year after the bombing. Both Judi and the woman who had the premonition told me the same story. There was a woman named Gail who was a world-class black belt aikido instructor. She was a big woman with broad shoulders—*strong like a bull.* She taught martial arts to police officers and to men in the military. She was giving a women's self-defense class in Ukiah, where she lives, and Judi decided to take the course. Judi and I were both receiving death threats; we both knew there was a need to protect ourselves.

So while Judi was in the middle of the women's self-defense class, a week before we were blown up, Gail was telling the women that they should not assume a victim's stance when attacked by a man. She said, "Don't look like a victim." Then all of a sudden she fell into a trance, wheeled around and pointed

1991 with Judi Bari   Photo: ESP File

to Judi, saying: "Except for you, Judi. Don't pay attention to any of this. You have to stay away from your car. You have to ride in different cars. You can't drive a car, you need to look under cars, don't go near any cars." That was it.

If Judi and I hadn't been fighting, or, if Judi had been a person who took trances, spirituality or messages from the beyond with even an iota of seriousness, she would have shared that information with me. But she didn't, because she didn't subscribe to any kind of spiritual practice. Also, if we hadn't been arguing, she would have shared every moment of every day with me. And when I finally heard this story, I realized that in fact the Earth Mother herself had warned us, and instructed us to stay away from that car.

On the day Judi's car was bombed in Oakland, Judi and I were scheduled to drive to Santa Cruz, where we were to sing, give speeches and show some slides. When the bomb exploded, we had different experiences. Judi knew it was a bomb, because it went off right underneath her butt and ripped right through her. But I didn't know until a couple of kids came running down the street yelling, "It's a bomb! It's a bomb!" That's how I found out—from the spectators. But I knew right away that Judi was hurt badly, so I put all my force of will into keeping her awake and alive. I kept telling her, "I love you, I love you. You're gonna make it, you're gonna make it." Not just with the words, but with intent.

A couple of hours later the F.B.I walked into my hospital room and said, "We can tell this is your bomb. So why don't you just confess and make it easy on all of us and get it over with." I was shocked, but I was not surprised. Because I had knowledge of my forerunners: the American Indian Movement, the Black Panther Movement, the labor movement—all of whom had been suppressed by the F.B.I. As Pagan ancestors teach spirituality, my political ancestors and elders had taught me knowledge of political suppression.

At Highland Hospital in Oakland, Judi's hospital room became an interesting encampment for six weeks. She had never been a big fan of Pagan spirituality, but she had also never been a big fan of the American medical establishment run by the patriarchy. Because she was injured, very well-known, and under incredible oppression, a great number of people rose to the occasion to support us, including Starhawk and some well-known acupuncturists, acupressurists and healers. Many of them performed healing rituals and methodologies for Judi. Some would touch her, some would wave their hands over her, and others would hang crystals, goddesses and other doo-dads on strings above her head and her heart, right over that hospital bed.

During that time, Judi shifted toward opening up her heart and mind and soul to an awareness of "the Goddess." She never really became a dyed-in-the-wool Pagan—I don't think she could ever have been that. In a way Judi, rather than being spiritual, was a spirit herself. She didn't believe in the Goddess—she *was* the Goddess.

♦ R/S: What happened as a result of the F.B.I. claiming it was your bomb?

♦ DC: The F.B.I. came in and falsely accused us of carrying a bomb that accidentally went off. They accused us of blowing ourselves up! Whereas all the evidence pointed towards us being the target of an assassination attempt. For example, they claimed that the nails in the bomb matched some nails that were in the back of Judi's car. Now first of all, Judi was a professional carpenter and always carried nails, hammers, and various tools with her, so it wasn't unusual that she would have nails in the back of the car. However, the nails in the bomb were finishing nails, and the nails in the back of her car were roofing nails. Finishing nails are long and thin, whereas roofing nails are short and fat with a big head. The finishing nails didn't even have a head. Ray Charles could tell the difference between these two nails!

But the F.B.I. and the Oakland Police claimed that these nails matched. It wasn't a mistake, it was a lie. And recently the U.S. Court of Appeals ruled that it was obvious the F.B.I. was lying, and that we deserved to get a trial date so that a jury could decide whether or not our civil rights had been violated.

The civil rights that were violated were these: 1) Our First Amendment rights were violated. The F.B.I. knew we were innocent, and declared us guilty to suppress our freedom of speech … to suppress our ability to articulate our beliefs about saving the environment.

2) Our Fourth Amendment (illegal search and seizure) rights were violated. Our homes were searched, our property was seized, and we were falsely arrested.

The F.B.I., which is supposed to uphold the Constitution of the United States, has been denying our

1999 with Julia Butterfly Photo: Michael van Broekhoven

ability to get a fair trial by delaying the trial for as long as they can. One would like to think that in a government that guarantees civil rights, the government would allow a jury to decide whether our civil rights had been violated. But the F.B.I has nickel-and-dimed us with various delaying motions and Motions to Dismiss. They claim they have something called "qualified immunity," which basically says that a cop can do anything he wants to do as long as he *thinks* he is doing the right thing. So for our lawsuit to win, we have to prove what they were thinking. But we can, when our case eventually comes to trial in late 2001 or early 2002, hopefully.

♦ R/S: Besides Earth First activism, what else do you do?

♦ DC: I've started Environmentally Sound Productions (ESP), whose motto is "Music, Arts and Media for the Earth." We are a non-profit organization dedicated towards raising consciousness through music, arts and the media.

I also give workshops on the power of music. Music is the antidote to fear. For example, when armies are fighting wars, they may have drummers or bagpipers or buglers playing. When activists are being arrested, they sing songs to unify themselves and stave off fear. It's well-known that music can sometimes "cure" depression or inspire courage. **If fear is our greatest problem, then music is our greatest cure.** Music has always been used as a form of prayer in virtually all religions.

I would contend there isn't a single living thing on this earth that doesn't sing. In fact, nothing on this earth or cosmos is standing still. Every single thing vibrates, and all vibrations give off sound—whether or not humans can hear it. And that sound is called music.

One powerful way that environmentalists and Pagans can create a national movement is through music. So I think that environmentalists, as well as Pagans, have to look to music as both a tool and a tactic. *Music is the sugar coating on the truth pill.* If you sing a message to somebody, they're much more likely to be receptive to it. Music opens up the heart receptor chakra so the message can be heard. If you give a speech, it may bore somebody. If you yell a political slogan at somebody, they may be offended, ignore you or be apathetic. But if you sing the message, they're much more likely to listen.

Music is used to sell the products of the consumer culture. Even Hitler certainly knew the power of music. Whereas "our" side neglects music, yet it's a *tool* that is equal if not superior to the lawsuit, the protest, the grassroots campaign and the election. Music can be far more powerful than all those. In the Sixties, musicians provided a lot of the rocket fuel and spiritual leadership that opened America and the world to feminism, civil rights, Eastern philosophy, gay rights, getting back to the land, metaphysics, and so on.

In order for broad, powerful social change to occur again, there has to come about a spirit of cooperation, not competition. One of the things I love about Earth First campfires is that the musicians encourage each other to sing—as opposed to everyone waiting for the other guy to finish so they can sing their song. In the music world, musicians are taught that the measure of success is fame and money. Whereas a Pagan or an environmentalist often believes that your success is measured by how much you awaken greater consciousness and provide good times for your tribe.

[note: Judi Bari died March 2, 1997 at 6:45 A.M.] ♦♦♦

Darryl Recommends

WEBSITES:
www.judibari.org
www.jailhurwitz.com
www.humboldt1.com/~ncef/

BOOKS:
A Forest Journey by Jonathan Perlin
Food of the Gods by Terence McKenna
Earth First! Journal

Oak

Deborah "Oak" Cooper is a Pagan activist who earns her living as a therapist in the San Francisco Bay Area. In this interview she discusses activism, therapy, why she founded the Temple of Elvis [*templeofelvis.com*], and her participation in the Seattle W.T.O. protest [fall, 1999]. Interview by John Sulak.

♦ *RE/SEARCH: What's the difference between a Witch and a Pagan?*

♦ OAK: A Pagan is someone who believes the earth is sacred, and whose sensibilities are earth-centered. Pagan rituals are nature-based; they see the earth as sacred and deity. A witch is someone who subscribes to the above, as well as working with the energies of the earth and magic. I don't think all Pagans do magic. Witches work magic with our imagination and work with other realms of the invisible to create change, and to heal.

♦ *R/S: What is magic?*

♦ O: The old definition is "changing consciousness at will." For me, magic involves believing in the power of the imagination, knowing there's more to life than meets the eye . . . *plus* believing we can create change through working with that invisible realm. In other traditions, *prayer* is a form of magic—you focus your intent, and sometimes things change.

Personally, I work with *grounding*—just feeling how my breath connects me to the breath of all other beings on the planet. This involves feeling connected to the elements of life: earth, water, fire, and air. The elements are more powerful for me than the whole idea of deities, although if I'm doing magic, I *will* call certain deities and they are real to me.

♦ *R/S: How did you become a Pagan?*

♦ O: Like many people, I've probably been a Pagan all my life. I was raised Episcopalian, but I always envied my Catholic friends because they had little tchotchkes—rosaries, candles, medals, and relics. As a kid I made little altars.

I became a Pagan out of grief. In the Seventies I became a feminist, so of course I was totally against patriarchal religions—even Buddhism—forget it, it's a guy! But when I was 22, three people died on me within six months. And there was no religion to fall back on except feminism. Feminism wasn't exactly my *religion,* but it was my organizing principle. I sought healing on the coast of Oregon and took walks on the beach. And the ocean *was* healing. I made a moon calendar.

I was returning from my grandmother's funeral when I discovered the *Spiral Dance* and read it on the plane. I thought, "Oh—*this is it:* politics, Paganism, a sense of the earth as sacred, plus working collectively and in community with people." As

luck would have it, I ended up attending the same graduate school as Starhawk.

I moved to San Francisco the very week that the Reclaiming community was demonstrating to shut down the Diablo Canyon nuclear power plant. Anarchists, Pagans, Christians, and many others came together to blockade and do civil disobedience against nuclear weapons and nuclear power. For most of my friends, it was the first time they'd been arrested.

♦ *R/S: Did Diablo Canyon get shut down?*

♦ O: No. [laughs] But our demonstration seemed to slow down the construction of more nuclear power plants. Ideally, **I like to think that the best we can hope for is immediate and total revolution *this second!*** But I also am willing to go along with slowing things down, and trying to awaken the public to the fact that nuclear power has consequences.

Now almost every schoolkid thinks, "Nuclear Power Plants *equals* Bad!" Appealing to kids is very important. There's so much controversy now about the Harry Potter books, but they're right on—kids are growing up now thinking that magic and being a witch is cool. And my son's friends are jealous, because his mother is a witch—just like Harry Potter!

I think the image of the hero is dying. We hear about the President getting a blow job in the Oval Office, and how terrible John Lennon and Martin Luther King, Jr. were in their personal lives. But something's wrong with everybody. Maybe our sense of heroism is shifting toward the idea of "people working together *equals* heroic."

For me, feminism involved the idea of people working together. When I think about the civil rights movement, I think of Martin Luther King, but I also think of all those nameless people who rode the buses and sat in at segregated restaurants. I'm trying to educate my son that while we can admire individuals, what's truly admirable is groups of people getting together to create change.

In Pagan or Wicca gatherings, the very idea that we work in a circle changes our psychology. There isn't one person at a pulpit preaching to a passive crowd; rather, we're all interconnected and working to create energy together.

♦ *R/S: Where did you go to graduate school?*

♦ O: About twenty years ago I went to Antioch College to get a

Masters Degree in Feminist Therapy. Starhawk was there and Reclaiming was starting. I attended meetings, a Spiral Dance, demonstrations, and fell in with a mad crowd. I started to create magic and mischief, and I joined a coven with people who are still my friends.

Back then, the San Francisco community was small enough so you knew everybody who was a witch. Anti-nuclear and environmental activism were new; there was a lot of excitement in the air. The Pagan/Wicca community was new and we were all in love with each other. Since the mid-Nineties everything's expanded incredibly. At witch camps I used to yell, "Great Big Pagan World!" and everybody would laugh. Now it's come true.

♦ *R/S: Are you still involved in activism?*

♦ O: During the Eighties I became a therapist, so now I can't travel as much. I'm not as much of an "street" activist as I was in the Eighties. I went to the W.T.O. demonstration in Seattle, but mostly I'm doing healing work.

My husband is a full-time activist and the director of the Rainforest Action Network. So I'm surrounded by environmental activists and people who put their lives on the line. What I do is try to teach them magic so they have some protection from the elements when they go into dangerous territory. At our land in Sonoma, we give three-day intensive workshops on the elements of magic, and the protestors are using it.

♦ *R/S: Are any of the protestors Pagans?*

♦ O: They don't *identify* as Pagans, but they're a pretty Pagan bunch: they're connected to the earth, and they hold the earth as sacred. When they get these tools of magic, it's incredible to see what they can do. They are some of the most powerful magicians I've seen.

After the first workshop, two of them went to Washington, D.C. to do an action where they would scale the World Bank and drop a banner. The night before they did a ritual to empower the action, and despite the fact that it was totally impossible, they pulled it off. Even though there were security guards and police everywhere, an opportunity opened up. Harold, who went up the building, was supposed to go up with someone else, but he had an intuition that he might have to do it alone. He went up, and said that it felt like invisible hands were helping him climb up the building. Everything went smoothly; he got arrested and they let him go with a $25 fine. Mind you, a similar action had been done in Houston and the participants had been jailed and given enormous fines. Oh, and Harold got the banner back—that's unheard of!

At Lawrence Livermore Labs, near Berkeley, a coven wove a symbolic web across the gates, and the cops tried to drive through the web and got caught in it—their vehicles ground to a halt. When activists hear about this, they go, "Oh, this magic is a tool we can use!" It's effective and it works. There are dozens more stories like that— I think we'll see more and more people using magic in their activism.

Kelly, my husband, used to do a magic ritual before demonstrating at Home Depot. Recently, after years of refusal, Home Depot, the biggest retailer of wood in America, will no longer sell endangered wood. So I think we're going to see more activism with a spiritual side. It used to be you were either political or spiritual, but now the two worlds have fused. Witches don't consider the spiritual and the physical as separate. I accept the cycle of death and birth, and the idea that people are capable of incredible good but also have a shadow—and that both are needed.

♦ *R/S: Your husband is a witch, too—*

♦ O: Kelly was raised Irish Catholic. He is initiated and considers himself a priest. The funny thing is, his mother always wanted him to be a priest—and now he is one!

We're raising a little heathen son together named Casey. It's nice to be raising a child in a tradition where he doesn't have to get rid of the burden of patriarchal religion; working with magic comes very naturally to him. He was born into a circle of witches who worked magic as he was being born. He was turned the wrong way in the womb, and they sang and moved him. The doctors couldn't believe it!

Casey did his first ritual when he was five. We went to the zoo. The Indian elephant had lost its friend and was grieving. My child is totally into elephants, and he was really upset. He came home and said, "I want to do a ritual for Tinkerbell" [the elephant]. He put his elephant figures around a candle and sat quite seriously in front of it, saying, "I want a new friend for Tinkerbell."

To him, this is just how the world is. I try to educate him about different religions. We were talking about spring equinox and I explained Easter and Passover. When I said that some people didn't like it when Jesus said he was the son of God, Casey said, "Which god? What was his name?" I said, "There are people who really believe there's just one God and his name is God." Casey said, "That's *dumb*—you mean he doesn't even have a *name* like Ganesh or Mercury or Pan? He's just *God?*" He couldn't believe it.

Last year I took Casey to a church for a lesbian Lutheran wedding. When they offered the sacrament—the blood and body of Christ—Casey leaned over and said, "I'll eat the body, but I am *not* drinking the blood!" We had to have a big talk about why they do all of that. I explained, "What they do is really different from what we do. But we have to be polite and tolerate it."

Casey deals with a lot of culture clashes. We put him in a progressive private school where the teachers have had me lecture to kids about Wicca. Yesterday he asked me, "Why do kids on the street think it's bad to be gay?"

♦ *R/S: How has he reacted to the sexual openness among Pagan adults?*

Spiral Dance

Temple of Elvis at *www.templeofelvis.com*

♦ O: He takes it as a matter of course—it's the *grown-ups* who have problems. He talked about inviting his teacher to the Spiral Dance, but then asked, "Do you think I should tell her that sometimes people are naked?" I said, "I think she'll be able to handle it!"

Casey began asking me about sex because of animals. Last year he was asked to contribute to a kids' page in *Reclaiming Quarterly*. He called his contribution "The Nature of Sex." He drew all these pictures of animals having sex: cow sex, ladybug sex, elephant sex, beaver sex. It wasn't used because it might not have looked so good having a Pagan kid drawing sex pictures. So he wrote a letter, "Dear Reclaiming: Why didn't you print my pictures of animal sex? Do you have a problem with animal sex? Love, Casey." In the next issue they published his letter and printed one of his pictures.

Other parents at his school told me that he's the one who explained what sex is to the other kids. We're Pagans; we see sex as part of life and the life force. You treat it respectfully—it can create life! Sex is powerfully connected to the whole energy of the planet.

♦ **R/S: Why did you found the Temple of Elvis?**
♦ O: As a witch *and* a therapist, over time I've realized how important stories and myths are. I also love looking at pop culture and seeing what stories are popular now. What are the big stories being played out? What seizes our imagination? And I love humor—it's one of the most healing, powerful forces in our lives.

So I got into Elvis as a Pagan deity. The yearly anniversary of his death at Graceland is the biggest Pagan gathering in the United States! Memphis becomes overrun with Elvis worshippers; the streets in front of Graceland are thronged with people carrying candles; they hold a vigil all through the night. Likewise, Pagans celebrating Winter Solstice stay up all night holding a candlelight vigil for the Sun King. And who is the Sun King? Well, Elvis was on *Sun* records. He was a Capricorn, born around the Winter Solstice, and he died after Lammas. The wake for the Sun King happens at Graceland every year.

Look at the story of **Elvis: he crossed gender (he wore pink when nobody wore pink; he wore nail polish and eye shadow)** **and he crossed race (the white radio stations wouldn't play him because he sounded too black).** In the beginning he was like a big trickster god. I like the fact that the love of his life was his mother Gladys. In Goddess mythology, the Goddess's consort is both her son and her husband, and the Goddess gives birth to the son. The great god of the Celts, the Dagda, was a very generous god who had a huge cauldron of plenty. He was a very humorous god who also made fun of himself; his pants always hung below his fat buttocks. Likewise, Elvis was very generous and threw rings and scarves out to audiences. In concert he ripped his pants more than once—especially when he put on weight.

I've seen many writings correlating Elvis and Jesus, but I don't think he's very Jesus-like. I think it's good for us Pagans to reclaim him as ours, and not let the Christians take him over. Remember, he opened the sex chakra of White America—he was Dionysus! When you see him on those early television shows, he's incredible—he was a Pagan god, no doubt. Christians were calling his songs the devil's music, but it was the Horned God's music.

A friend helped me come up with an image of Cernunos, and I have my Temple of Elvis T-shirts and votive candles. Something about his story resonates with people; it recapitulates some very ancient themes.

♦ **R/S: What's your view on the Horned God?**
♦ O: The Horned God is that aspect of the god who is connected to the animal world: the rutting god, the sexual god, the stag. The Cernunos figure, which is very old, is a man with horns, like Pan. The whole concept of "The Devil" is a perversion derived from the Horned God of the Celts and the Greeks. In the Bible, there's no description of the devil as having horns and a tail. In monotheist or Christian religions, the animal nature of humans is considered "bad." What's great about Paganism is the acceptance of our animal nature.

For me, gender is still a confusing subject in itself, perhaps because I gave birth to a son. But it's also because some of the male deities have more *humor* than the female deities—and I like humorous gods. I think it's healthy to not take ourselves too seriously. If there's any Pagan liturgy it's "The Charge of the Goddess," which contains this thought, "Let there be mirth and reverence within you." And that's very important to me as a witch: I don't want any reverence I can't laugh about.

Paradox, which I think is funny, is also *key* to me. As long as you say, "Oh, I'm not this," then immediately the Goddess will make you exactly that. Paradox will always get you!

I think humor is part of "going deep"; it's *not* escaping from being deep. The Temple of Elvis is my reverent mirth. Fringe groups usually see themselves as outside the mainstream, and have this "purity" idea to not contaminate or dirty themselves with mainstream stories. But as a Pagan I wanna take those mainstream stories and make them *ours*. That's true subversion.
[Second Interview after W.T.O. Seattle 1999]
♦ O: I just came back from the gym. I'm one of those witches who talks all the time about how the earth is sacred and so is the human body, but I have a hard time actually *being* in my own body. I think a lot of us live so much in the imagination and the mind that we don't actually go out and get any exercise. In school I always dreaded P.E. and sports, but now that I'm in my forties I find that I really have to deal with exercising. So I joined a gym—that's hilarious—and decided to try to go the whole nine yards.

I got a personal trainer and at our first meeting he said, "Sorry, but I have a cold. It's funny; I just get it on Mondays." I said, "Your body's telling you something." We talked a lot more, and now he's on his way to calling himself a witch! He's studying alternative ways of healing such as *Reiki*. He says that if he can teach people how to change the size of their biceps, maybe they can start believing they can change the world. So he's the perfect personal trainer for me. It's a great big Pagan world!

He trained me for Seattle, giving me exercises to do. And I did them when I was incarcerated in the holding cell, too.

♦ *R/S: Let's talk about the Seattle W.T.O. demonstration—*

♦ O: A lot of that organically sprang out of the magical activism workshops I was giving. After spending all day teaching people concepts of magic, in the evening over dinner we would discuss ways of applying magic to actions in general and to Seattle in particular. We wanted to shine a light on the dark doings of the World Trade Organization.

We started out discussing the Harry Potter books, and the whole phenomenon of witches being popular again. We came up with a "Wake Up Muggles!" campaign. (Muggles are non-magical people in those books.) We wanted to challenge the *Multi-National Mugglearchy!* That was a magical working in that it was about bringing magic back into the world, and we knew it would appeal to the media.

We started emailing people in the Bay Area Pagan community that it was important to go demonstrate in Seattle. In addition to the Muggles campaign, we wanted to work magically with the elements of life to transform the idea of what fair trade and free trade is. Momentum started building. We had a benefit "Dinner with The Dead" at Samhain where we invoked the dead who had inspired us to be activists, and with whom we wanted to work in Seattle. We called them in and toasted them.

Toasting was a major part of the Seattle action. We knew that we wanted to work with the powers of fluidity and infu-

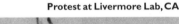

Protest at Livermore Lab, CA

Oak at the W.T.O. protest, 1999

sion. And then I got this great idea, in that "zone" between waking and sleeping where my best magical inspirations come from. My muse told me to go to Seattle, find a fancy bar in one of the hotels where the delegates were staying, and buy a round of drinks for the bar. Then, when everyone has their drink, stand up and toast the elements of life: give a toast to air, to fire, to water, and to earth. In other words, give beautiful poetic toasts to the beauty of this planet, and that we hold these things as sacred. And it happened! That "Dinner With The Dead" benefit had raised some real money, enabling us to do it. Delegates and trade ministers came and sat with the witches, and all of us ended up drinking together. We found common ground in our love for the planet.

♦ *R/S: Tell us more about that trip—*

♦ O: When I was in the San Francisco airport waiting for my plane, I looked around and saw activists from Rainforest Action Network, Ruckus Society, Amazon Watch, Greencore, Pesticide Action Network, and a lot of Reclaiming members. On the plane I met a lot of people.

On the first day in Seattle, a bunch of Pagans helped the Rainforest Action people make this enormous banner that appeared on the front page of newspapers all around the world. It depicted two arrows: one arrow for the W.T.O. going into Seattle, and another arrow for democracy going in the opposite direction. It got hung on this huge crane next to the freeway, and directly in front of the Space Needle. So if you were driving by, you saw this incredibly huge banner.

We worked on charging the banner with magic while working grommets into it. On Sunday, we did magical activism training. Monday, very early in the morning, I drove the climbers to the crane—it was like "Mission Impossible." A lot of magic went into making that happen safely, and everything went beautifully and smoothly. The activists got up and down safely. The construction workers using the crane asked the cops if they could keep the banner, because they loved it so much. Those same workers were going to be marching the next day. It was a totally positive, great experience.

The weather stayed clear—we had done a lot of magic with the elements so it wasn't dangerous for the climbers, and sure enough, the air was perfectly still. There was no rain. Just as the climbers got the banner into place, it started to drizzle, like, "I believe in magic, but this is ridiculous!" The timing was just too good—the rain got delayed until they were ready to come down!

Above: age 3; right: 4-H Club

Tuesday was the big march with 50,000 people. That was the day everything went crazy. There was the absolute, total wonderfulness of all these people from all walks of life—steel workers, teamsters, students, workers—all dressed up like sea turtles and witches, everybody marching together. It was an amazing feeling—people were dancing in the streets. The teamsters had a speaker system blaring out Aretha Franklin singing "Respect."

Then the tear gas, rubber bullets, and nastiness from the cops started. Somewhere in there a small contingent of people in black started to break windows. For some reason the cops did nothing to them—I was right there and the police were just watching them break windows and not doing *anything.* Meanwhile, right down the street, totally non-violent protesters were being teargassed. It was very strange.

My friend Fern and I were helping people who'd gotten teargassed, and we needed a scarf. So we decided to go into Nordstroms and buy one. Nordstroms is famous for their service, and when we told the saleswoman we needed a scarf she asked, "And what would that be for? Evening wear? Winter sports?" We replied, "That would be for tear gas." [laughs] She didn't miss a beat, saying, "My husband said it might get intense down here. I think you should go up to the children's department—they have smaller scarves that are cheaper and would probably do the trick." So we went and bought a scarf, wetted it and went back out into the street.

That night it got more insane. The police were going into other neighborhoods and teargassing. It was quite scary.

The next day was when I got arrested downtown and put in jail. The witches in jail really played a powerful role. That was quite incredible, to feel the power of magic. My husband Kelly, who works with activists all the time, keeps hearing from people that "If you have to go to jail, it's good to have a witch with you." We know good songs and we help to keep people's spirits up. We call in the elements of life, and people remember that they have earth, air, fire, and water in their bodies—even in an environment that is alienating and unnatural. That was really powerful. The women in the jail cell with me picked that right up. Anytime anybody would start to lose it, they would go, "Okay, ground. Call in the elements." And it would all be better. People were taking care of each other.

It was an incredible experience, because I saw the best part of human nature and the worst. There was so much brutality. We were repeatedly told that we didn't have any rights, we didn't have any rights. But we stayed really strong.

♦ *R/S: How did you end up being arrested?*

♦ O: On Wednesday they made this strange rule that you could go downtown if you were shopping. But if you weren't shopping, and if they thought you were a protester, you couldn't go. We all headed downtown. We got there just a few minutes after the police had just targeted a friend of ours with Ruckus. They had thrown him down and hit him; his head was bleeding. We'd heard that Starhawk had already been arrested. We were in the Westlake Park area wondering what to do. Tear gas canisters were rolling down the street, and then around the corner a contingent of people came running, and before we knew it we were totally surrounded by cops, riot police, and horses.

We tried to leave the park but were told by the police, "Stand against that wall and you won't be arrested." So we all went and stood against the wall. There were people sitting down who were being dragged away; I don't know what they were being arrested for. Many of us standing by the wall were singing as those sitting down were put on buses. All of a sudden the police charged the line of us who were standing against the wall. They threw down the guy next to me, so I grounded myself. I put roots down and branches up and said clearly to the policeman who lunged at me, "Don't hurt me. I'm non-violent." Then they arrested me.

It was my intention to go to Seattle and bear witness and

protest. I had no intention of getting arrested. I have a young son who was already upset that we were up there protesting—how do you explain being a political prisoner to a seven-year-old? I wouldn't have intentionally gotten arrested, but it happened.

The police never read me my rights or anything—they just put handcuffs on me. They threw all of us on a bus and drove us to a Naval yard. Nobody on that bus was emotionally prepared to be arrested, but here we were. We ended up staying on that bus for fifteen hours!

♦ *R/S: Did it have a bathroom?*

♦ O: No. There was a tiny hole in the floor in the middle of the bus that people were trying to pee through. Finally I tried to, but I ended up peeing all over my pants. And I remained in those pants another 14 hours; it was pretty bad.

Finally people were taken off the bus. Some were peppersprayed and treated quite violently. All of our possessions were taken from us. The police were quite vicious with me. I had been told by two different policemen that I would be able to keep my asthma inhaler, because I was noticeably wheezing after all the tear gas. But when the jail doctor asked me, "What's your name?"—well, none of us were giving our names as an act of solidarity; it was our right to remain silent. So he took my asthma inhaler, insisting I had no rights.

Eventually the jailers shackled us and sent us to another jail. The worse thing for me was that I was kept in a small, cold holding cell, in stinky pants, and I remained stinky for another ten hours. Finally they gave us "food." I took the food, which was a baloney sandwich, and used it as a pillow, and used the paper bag it came in as a mattress. It was pitiful.

Finally we got jail clothes and were locked up. I was there until Saturday. Being in jail was an incredible experience; people were getting really radicalized. The jailers think they can break your spirit, but they just make you stronger. The more brutality we saw, the stronger and the more determined we got.

Somewhere along the line in jail we started to hear that the W.T.O. was falling apart and ending in failure and disarray, and that we'd definitely won. We had shut them down! The whole experience is still emotionally confusing, because I saw so much violence and felt so brutalized by the whole jail experience, and yet we won. It's hard to reconcile those two. Paradox, I guess!

When I was released I turned in my jail clothes and they gave me my own clothes back. And my clothes smelled like tear gas, pepper spray, the vinegar that cuts the gas, sweat, boredom, fear, and the urine that had soaked my pants while trying to pee on the bus. But I was happy to put them back on. The smell of victory is not always a sweet one.

It was an amazing feeling when I finally walked out of the jail. It was 3:30 in the morning and I was thinking, "Jeez, how am I going to get back to my hotel?" I walked down to the corner and **there was this incredible block party happening with all these people waiting for us to get out of jail. There was food and drums and all this love.** These were people who had been waiting there to take care of us. It was this incredible outpouring of support and care. I walked into the arms of beautiful people who did not shrink from my stench, but embraced me warmly.

♦ *R/S: Do you think that the magic you did helped you "win"?*

♦ O: Yes; at the very least magic helped sustain people's morale. During the civil rights movement, Dr Martin Luther King was definitely a spiritual person, and Gandhi with his non-violence was very spiritual. So I think it's important to have some sort of connection to "spirit." I think that witchcraft, with its connection to the natural world, really helped. I believe that the elements of life *want* to work with us. When that huge banner got put up, everything felt just fabulous—as if the weather were totally paying attention to us. Even with the tear gas, it

seemed like there was enough drizzle in the air to mellow it out somewhat.

Because of what happened, it became visible to the rest of the world that the forces of greed are willing to clamp down without mercy on people who are just doing non-violent protest. We can't magically just stop those forces of greed—they don't pay attention and they're not even tuned in. They're nonsensical; they're willing to rape the earth. All the signs are telling us that the climate is changing, the ozone is vanishing, and we need to take care of the earth. And yet they're still willing to put their heads in the sand in order to make maximum profits right now.

We're just going to have to keep doing the magic and get more and more people to listen. And I think more and more people are. I deeply believe that by infusing magic and spirit into activism, we cannot fail. The elements of life want to work with us. And the more we work with the elements of life, we can turn the tide and create a world in which the earth, the air, the fire and the water are held as sacred. And if we hold the elements of life sacred, anything is possible. ♦♦♦

OAK'S READING LIST

Here are some basic books that have influenced and inspired me. I really don't tend to read much Pagan/Wiccan literature.

Women, Church and State by Matilda Joselyn Gage

Gage was a sister suffragette with Susan B. Anthony and Elizabeth Stanton. She researched the witch burnings and invoked the Goddess at gatherings of the first wave of feminism. She also was Frank Baum's mother in law. I feel a strong connection to Gage and sense her with me at every uprising.

Wizard of Oz by Frank Baum

The Oz books and the movie really influenced me as a child. Ozma of Oz and Glinda are positive glamorous witches. The story is about realizing your power is from within and that the Wizard is the fraud. This is a tale that challenges patriarchal thought. The Harry Potter books of the last century!

Revolution For the Hell of It by Abbie Hoffman

Abbie Hoffman and the Yippies! were role models for me as a youth. Working with symbol and a strong sense of humour, they were the witches of their day. All of Abbie's books belong on the shelf of any magical activist.

All poetry by Mary Oliver

Mary Oliver is a poet whose words capture the singing of this earth. She is a tonic for the soul.

Any articles or books by Michael Ventura. He examines and dissects pop culture, looking at the myths that are shaping our world.

Age 19 at Mayan ruins on Yucatan Peninsula

Thorn

Thorn Coyle was born Sept 24, 1965 and was raised in Whittier, California. She has been initiated by both Feri and Reclaiming people, and has taught at Witch camps across America. Currently she is studying religion and philosophy at San Francisco State University, with the eventual goal of attaining a Ph.D so she can be a Pagan Thealogian. In this interview she details how her theater training benefited her as a Pagan priestess. Thorn writes chants, poetry, and songs, and she plays drums. Her 2 CDs are available from *www.serpentinemusic.com.* Interview by John Sulak; follow-up interview by V. Vale

♦ *RE/SEARCH: Tell us about your involvement with Punk. You named your cat after Exene Cervenka—*
♦ THORN COYLE: When I was a little kid growing up in a Catholic working-class family in Whittier [Orange County, California], I was actually heavily influenced by the Hippies—their music and culture. But once I figured out that Punks were interested in politics, I became interested. At first, just the *names* of Punk bands were shocking to me: the Revolting Cocks; even the Sex Pistols! I think an early radicalizing influence on me was U2. I started walking around Whittier wearing 1950's thrift-store dresses with leather belts and chains all over them. My earliest Punk concerts were X, Iggy Pop, Oingo Boingo, and the English Beat, who plays ska.

My first consciously political act and prank was spray-painting "Reagan hates me!" all over the Republican headquarters in Whittier when I was 16, in 1981. In a year I went from being a nice Catholic girl who obeyed all the rules, to being a more Punk-like, politically-radical Witch. I've also been an anarchist for many years, now.

Sixteen was the pivotal age when everything changed in my life. That's when I started reading Harlan Ellison, the "Angry Young Man" at the time, and got into science-fiction. I started studying Witchcraft, began working for a newspaper, dropped out of high school, went to college, then dropped out of college two years later and moved up to San Francisco when I was 18. Then I started getting tattoos, got a motorcycle, worked in the stock market, and began belly dancing.

♦ *R/S: What did you get out of belly dancing?*
♦ TC: I used to say that "Belly dance saved my life!"—meaning, it saved me from being an intellectual. It got me into my body in ways that all my years of theater dancing never did. In tribal-style belly dance, the center of gravity is really low, which is quite different from most Western-style dance where the center of gravity is higher. It's very sensual; I consider it to be more in tune with the body and with nature.

Belly dance is very much about the power of women's bodies, the power of sex, the power of a woman to birth, and about women dancing with and for each other. And the more fat on your body, the better—you need something to shake around; if you're too skinny it's harder. So this dance is really designed for a "real" woman's form—it's very affirming and strengthening. It was very liberating for me.

Of course, I'm not talking about "Old School" cabaret-style belly dance, which is women dancing for men who then stuff dollar bills into their costumes. The Fat Chance Belly Dance troupe I was in, which was led by Carolina Nericcio, pioneered a tradition called "American Tribal Belly Dance." Our troupe was countercultural in the sense that most of us were tattooed, pierced, and artistic, but then it inspired people all over the U.S. to do this. So it has become a style and viable tradition of belly dance that never existed before.

♦ *R/S: Didn't the whole troupe get the same tattoo?*
♦ TC: Yes: the Tuareg Hand of Fatima that wards off the evil eye. One of the dancers also has a tattoo that says "Ghawazee." That signifies the name of a tribe of belly dancers, and it also means Warriors of the Heart or Warriors of Love—which also translates into "prostitute"! [laughs]

♦ *R/S: You also worked as an erotic dancer—*
♦ TC: That's true, and it was a fabulous learning experience for me. For four years I worked at The Lusty Lady, a woman-owned and operated peep show in the North Beach neighborhood of San Francisco. There is no customer contact; everything is behind glass. Mostly what I did was in a room with other women, and there were booths with windows going up and down, depending on how many quarters you put in.

That job came about as a result of a solo belly dancing gig that I had at a restaurant. One night the owner's husband got drunk and came on to me—the owner saw this and she fired me. I started to feel bad about myself, my body and the work I did—then my brain kicked in: "Wait a minute! You stopped believing that years ago, intellectually—where are these feelings coming from?" I realized that I'd changed the idea in my *head,* but hadn't changed it viscerally. I needed to do something about it, and that's when I made the decision to go audition at the Lusty Lady. I felt this was something I needed to work through, to affirm my sexuality and my power as a beautiful woman.

It was a great experience to be there dancing with other women—to be naked and powerful and realize that *I* was the one in the power position, not the man. (I recognize that in a world where women still have unequal economic advantage, this "power" position is relative.) This was about claiming the beauty and power of sexuality as a force in the world.

Most of the women I worked with were self-identified feminists. They included lesbians, bisexuals, college students, photographers and artists. This was an easy way for a woman to support herself and make money in a relatively non-degrading fashion. Some people said, "You were completely degraded." But I think that working in an office dealing with the sexism of a boss is *much* more degrading. Also, getting paid seven bucks an hour instead of twenty bucks an hour is much more degrading. Now I'm in a different place with my sexuality, and don't need to do that. But at that time, in my mid-twenties, I really needed to explore my sexuality as fully as possible.

♦ *R/S: So when did you first discover Paganism?*
♦ TC: When I was 13, a friend had a book on Witchcraft, and we would practice standing in the star position in our backyard. But we couldn't figure out how we could get a temple, whitewash the floor and paint a nine-foot pentagram on it! When I was 16 and went to college, a friend and I started attending free Witchcraft classes at The Olde Way Inn, a magic shop in Huntington Beach. That's how I met my first Witch! That shop got driven out of the community by some fundamentalist Christians.

♦ *R/S: How did you first feel about Wicca?*
♦ TC: I remember saying these words: "I feel like I've come home." Since then, I've studied other religions, including Catholicism—the study of religions will always be important to me, even though Wicca is now my primary religion. Catholicism, similar to Judaism, is a cultural indoctrination that shapes a person's world view. People who were raised Catholic, even though they rebel, are probably still being shaped by it—they're just reacting against it.

I'm writing a book about the similarities between Christianity and Paganism as well as Sufism. For three years I studied with the Mevlevi Whirling Dervishes, a Turkish order founded by Rumi, a 13th-century mystical poet. Both Wicca and Catholicism are heavily ritualized. Wicca celebrates the Triple Goddess: the Maiden, the Mother and the Crone. Similarly, Mary is a triple Goddess: the Virgin, the Mother, and the Mother of Tears (or Crone, when she's holding her dead son). Many of Mary's symbols—the pomegranate, wheat sheaves, the Star of the Sea—also belong to the Goddess.

At Easter, Catholics do a ceremony where the priest repeatedly plunges a giant Pascal candle in and out of a bowl of baptismal water. This is identical to the Wiccan Athame and the Cup: the joining together of the male and female principles. When I see a Priest doing this completely sexual act, I laugh: "Yeah, he's a Witch!" Catholicism has a ritual of transubstantiation whereby the eating of bread and wine is turned into the body and blood of the sacrificial God, similar to old Pagan stories involving the God who dies and feeds the people: the Stag King, the Corn King.

Humans all over the world put holidays around the solstices and the equinoxes, no matter what religion they are. So you can't really say, "The Christians stole this from the Pagans, and that from the Jews." Of course, there has been cultural imperialism. In Mexico, Catholicism incorporated some of the conquered Indians' religious symbology, to placate them. But Pagans themselves have also been conquering bastards with a violent, bloody history—witness the old Celtic tribes, the Norse, and the Romans.

When I was a teenager, I was more interested in what set us apart from each other, because I was angry and in reaction. These days I prefer to look for common ground.

♦ *R/S: Did anyone have a radicalizing influence on you?*
♦ TC: In high school, I had a teacher named Sister Sharon. She would show us films about what was happening in El Salvador—things like that. But it wasn't until much later that I heard about Dorothy Day and Daniel Berrigan—truly radical Catholics who have become my heroes. Dorothy Day founded the Catholic Worker movement, composed of Catholic anarchists who began feeding people in the Thirties. She was a suffragist and a truly radical woman. The last time she got arrested was with Cesar Chavez when she was 75.

♦ *R/S: What did you learn from the Sufi tradition?*
♦ TC: Sufis say, "Die before you die" . . . meaning, die to all the false parts of yourself that you hang on to, that keep you from joining with the divine.

♦ *R/S: At an early age you got into theater—why?*
♦ TC: I have seven older brothers and sisters. Our family always sang and danced at home, so I grew up with an impulse to perform. I sang in a folk group at church for Saturday Night Mass, and began performing in children's plays at the Whittier Junior Theater when I was eleven.

I did "Rumpelstiltskin," "Toad of Toad Hall" (from *The Wind in the Willows),* and "Oliver," the musical version of Oliver Twist. The first play I did with Whittier adult theater was "Wait Until Dark"—I played the little girl, Gloria. I did a number of musicals where I'd have to sing and dance. For the first time I found a place where I could be myself, with weird, interesting adults who understood me and took me under their wing. I hung out with them, and they saved me from the terrors of school. I was a loner nerd who read books a lot; I didn't fit in.

♦ *R/S: So your theater training helped you to later become a Pagan priestess—*
♦ TC: All my theater training *definitely* helps me. My voice is big; I can make my presence big if I need to. If we're working with some kind of myth or fairy tale as a form of ritual storytelling, I can take on different roles.

Theater puts you in a non-ordinary state of consciousness and reality; it bends reality. And ritual and magic are quite similar to that. So my body and my being have this ability to hold and transfer this power that can then slightly bend reality for that moment.

♦ *R/S: Part of an actor's training is to learn about costume, make-up, hairstyle, control of facial muscles, elocution, and the right gesture. How does this tie in with Pagan priestessing?*
♦ TC: Being a priestess draws together all of my disparate skills, which was quite a revelation to me. It draws together my strange intellect, all my theater and dance training, and fulfills the need I've had since a very small child to have a strong spiritual connection.

I had my first intense spiritual experience when I was seven, around the time of my First Communion. I was praying and suddenly I was surrounded by light. I could feel it and see it surrounding me, and knew that it was God—I was in the divine presence. This really affected me, and from that moment on I've been looking for that again.

♦ *R/S: But you haven't found it?*

♦ TC: I've found bits and pieces of it. I think those *big experiences* don't happen very often. This was a formative experience for me, obviously. It caused me to want direct contact, and that's one thing Paganism gives me. Paganism can give me direct contact with divinity, with Goddess—whatever we want to call it. This is sometimes called a "mystical experience." Most top-down hierarchical religions don't provide this.

♦ *R/S: How do you prepare for a Reclaiming ritual?*

♦ TC: Since Reclaiming is an anarchist tradition, we can do ritual in jeans and T-shirts, whereas in other traditions either you're naked or you wear special robes. However, people in Reclaiming enjoy the theatricality of dressing up. I definitely have a lot of ritual garb.

I have cloaks that I've hand-embroidered over the years. Anarchists have long consensus-process meetings, so I would sit and do my magical embroidery to keep myself from going crazy at these meetings. I've got special articles of clothing I've collected over the years: tunics, flowing skirts and pants, Renaissance-style corsets with velvet on them, things that I ordinarily would not wear on the street, where jeans and shirts are my basic uniform.

Putting on special clothing is definitely a first step into a special state of consciousness. I wear a lot more jewelry than usual. I have big silver wrist cuffs, amber and carnelian necklaces, strings of different-colored beads that hold prayers to the elements, to the different deities. This is a tradition that was passed to me from a priest, Donald Ingstrom, from Iowa (now he lives in Minneapolis). These necklaces are something you have to make yourself. You collect the beads, you decide what associations and meanings they have, and then you, with prayerful intentions, string them together. They can be used in meditation and prayer practice to help focus your intention.

♦ *R/S: Do you have a philosophy of color?*

♦ TC: Every color has a different vibration. Pagans and Wiccans use color to represent the basic elements of life: earth could be green, air yellow, fire red, and water blue. People have specific colors that they "vibrate" with; my favorite color happens to be Royal Blue. I feel best in it, it gives me energy, it helps me; it's a color I associate with myself. I have one magical tunic made of beautiful Royal Blue suede which I often wear for ritual purposes.

So putting on special garb is definitely part of bringing myself into a special state of consciousness. It would be similar to an ancient Israelite priest doing purification rituals before he approaches the tabernacle. I feel this helps you be more able to approach the divine, as you proceed along the continuum from the profane to the sacred, the ordinary to the non-ordinary.

In my tradition we say, "Everything should be sacred at all times and places; *all* acts are sacred acts." Nevertheless, I probably do more preparation for a structured ritual rather than an unstructured ritual.

♦ *R/S: What's an unstructured ritual?*

♦ TC: An example of an unstructured ritual is when I'm getting ready to leave the house. I connect with the earth, and breathe to center myself before I turn the doorknob. That's an everyday act that I can do in an instant.

But when I'm going to step inside a circle and lead a hundred people in a trance journey, I need more preparation—just like an actor needs preparation before entering the stage. I start breathing more deeply, I connect to the earth, I start to call on my inner divinity and my God-soul. If I'm going to be working with a particular story or particular deities, I call on them.

When I arrive at the circle and the different priests and priestesses start setting up what we call "sacred space" to bring us into what we call "non-ordinary time," we take certain steps. We do grounding, which is connecting with the earth, cleansing, casting the circle, invoking the elements, invoking the deities—all of these are steps into a non-ordinary state of being. So by the time we're ready to do the major working, we're most of the way there.

Then, if I'm acting as central priestess, I can step in and lead us the rest of the way into a trance journey or magical working.

♦ *R/S: Do you put on any special make-up?*

♦ TC: I'll powder my face and put on some lipstick, but I don't put on much make-up anymore. The only time I'll put on special make-up is if I'm doing what we call *aspecting,* which is a lighter form of trance possession than people do, say, in Voodoo. That is allowing deity to speak through me.

Sometimes aspecting can turn into full trance possession; it depends on how strongly the deity wants to speak. For a full trance journey I sometimes paint my face or parts of my body to further distance the everyday reality of "Thorn" from what's about to occur. In the past I've painted blue spirals all over my face, or used red body paint if the Red God was going to come through me—that sort of thing. Some priestesses use a lot more make-up; it's a personal choice.

I always take off my watch before ritual, because we're entering a space of no time. Also, I prefer to do ritual barefoot, so my feet have contact with ground. If this isn't possible, sometimes I wear special shoes. I also have thigh-high suede black boots that I like; they're very theatrical.

♦ *R/S: What other "props" do you use in ritual?*

♦ TC: I use an athame, a ritual knife that was crafted by a blacksmith I know. It fits my hand perfectly. It's sharp because my intention and my will have to be sharp. I also have a blade made out of an old fossil which I use if I'm working with what we call the *fey*—non-human entities with an aversion to steel. As a 21st-century person I think, "Of course that's ridiculous," but as a Witch who also enters into altered states of consciousness, I understand the feeling. [laughs]

There's a cognitive dissonance that any religious person in the 21st century has to manage. This means holding two realities simultaneously. We have an analytical, critical brain that says "That can't be true," while an intuitive, more primal and emotional part of us says, "That makes perfect sense." Part of what magic does is to help us access those more intuitive realms of knowledge we possess. Human beings are not solely rational, y'know.

♦ *R/S: Tell us about Witch Camp—*

♦ TC: In many ways it's participatory theater or performance art. At Witch Camps we do a lot of sacred drama, like take a fairy tale or myth, break it down, and do different rituals with the themes we've extracted. We also do ritual storytelling, with people enacting certain parts of a story to give it more meaning. During the old Russian tale of "Vasilisa and Baba Yaga," at a certain point the girl, Vasilisa, has to sort seeds and beans. We'll have people doing that to get a sense for what this task feels like.

Myths can be taken both as truth and as allegory, in the same way that gods and goddesses can be both unreal and real. Sometimes we feel them moving through us, yet our 21st-century brain says, "That's ridiculous; this god or goddess doesn't really exist." However, **a true skeptic is skeptical of science as well!**

♦R/S: Tell us about some of your other studies, apart from Reclaiming—

♦ TC: Besides being initiated in Reclaiming, I've also been initiated in the Feri tradition, which was originated by Victor and Cora Anderson. This incorporates lore from the Picts, Aboriginal tribes, Polynesian tribes; it's steeped in Celtic and Hawaiian traditions, with some African and Continental traditions thrown in as well. But it's not exactly eclectic. It emphasizes self-exploration uncovering what's hidden within the self and bringing it to light, or reclaiming it.

Feri's tools of reclaiming include the Iron and Pearl Pentacles. **The points of the Iron Pentacle are sex, pride, self, power and passion. Going up an octave, the Pearl Pentacle points are love, law, wisdom, liberty and knowledge.** A key Feri tenet, influenced by the Kahuna and Platonic Greek thought, is the notion of a triple soul: we have a younger self that stores and attracts life force and energy, a self that communicates, and our divine self. Or, more simply, we have our instinctive center, our intellectual center, and our deep psychic center.

♦ R/S: Tell us about Victor and Cora Anderson—

♦ TC: They're old-style shamanistic teachers. When you go to their home, Victor sits in his rocking chair and tells you stories as he appears to shape-shift from culture to culture—depending on the story, he could be any race and any age! Cora is a very psychic woman of Irish descent, from a coal-mining town. Visiting them is like seeing your grandparents, except you're kinda knocked to the floor by the time you leave.

When she was growing up, Cora had a relative who was an Herb Witch; he helped her learn natural Witchcraft and herb lore. Similarly, Victor grew up being taught by some *brujas* in New Mexico. **Together they developed the Feri ecstatic tradition in which, ideally, people are always open to the *poetry of the moment,*** getting direct inspiration from the work they're doing. This is in direct contrast to a tradition in which a teacher hands down knowledge that is "inviolate"; truth is always going to shift and change. So each Feri teacher teaches differently, and may even disagree with Victor and Cora.

In Feri, names hold power. **Certain cultures—for example, Arabic, Hindu or Hebrew—believe that *sounds* in**

Thorn belly dancing

themselves have power, aside from whatever the words might mean. Some Jews consider Hebrew a language for sacred text, so they only speak Yiddish aloud. Some Catholics believe that when you're hearing a chant in Latin, you're hearing the power of the tones themselves, above and beyond the meaning of the words. In one Feri workshop, we sat in groups of six while people chanted our names and spoke whatever images came up.

My own name "Thorn" came from my Reclaiming initiation, during a death-and-rebirth process where I was told to listen for my name—I heard "Thorn" loud and clear! At first I didn't like it; I asked, "Goddess, can't I be called something else?" But over the years I've gotten many lessons from that name—there's a poem by Rumi which says, "The rose's rarest essence lives in the thorn." Some Witches only use their magic names privately, or in their coven, but I felt I needed to hear it used in public, as a reminder of a lesson in perfectionism: you cannot have a rose without a thorn.

♦ *R/S: Your tattoos seem to empower you, right? Do they have magical significance?*

♦ TC: **My first tattoo came out of a trance.** At the time, whenever I would journey into trance to my place of power, a panther would be there as a guide to help me. Over and over it kept reappearing. So my first tattoo depicted that panther surrounded by fire and water, with the crescent moon above his head. It's on my shoulder blade.

I got a snake tattoo which symbolizes regeneration and life force. The snake is traveling through three wheat stalks; the Goddess Ceres is often shown with snakes and wheat in her hands. Grain goddesses are linked with snakes, probably because snakes were kept in the granary to keep the mice at bay. When my mom saw this tattoo, she asked, "That doesn't represent Satan, does it?" I said, "No, mom, why would it?" Actually, my mom's really great. I told her about my bisexuality and my Witchcraft when I was 23.

♦ *R/S: Can you talk about bisexuality in a Pagan context?*

♦ TC: Paganism celebrates sexuality as a part of the Life Force, and my bisexuality helps me as a priestess to channel energies that might be considered more "male." Some people might call me "twin-spirited," in that I have a lot of male and female within me, but it's all one to me. I have a great affinity for, and work a lot with, the gods, whereas a lot of women work strictly with goddesses—they can't relate to the gods.

For years, the way I would express my sexuality was I'd date men for a while, and then a woman—and vice versa. But I think that making a commitment to the Craft enabled me to make a commitment to another person. My partner and I had our wedding ceremony at a soup kitchen I volunteered at. Being married, and going through initiations, helped me become more

Fat Chance Belly Dance Troupe, Thorn in front, at the Carmanic Convergence, two years after the Harmonic Convergence.

because personally, if I have to teach something, I want more time to study and ponder what I've learned. But the Reclaiming people were trying to share knowledge as fast as possible: "You can do this, too."

Reclaiming classes aren't about listening to a lecture or being guided through an experience; students help co-create what happens. Each class is different. The emphasis is on passing on *tools* rather than exact dogmas or doctrines. This approach has its expansive and empowering possibilities, but it also has its limitations. There may well come a point where you need more guided teaching in order to grow.

♦ *R/S: Describe a class—*

♦ TC: For the basic "Elements of Magic" class, we assume people don't have any prior magical experience. The first night we talk about the powers of air, the East, the dawn, and inspiration and creativity. We may do a group visualization exercise, because one thing we do a lot of is trance journeying as a way of self-exploration. Trance journeys are a very old tradition that shamans of all cultures have done. If you were acting mentally ill, a Siberian shaman might go on a trance journey into your psychic landscape to try to figure out what was wrong with you.

So on "air" night, we teach how to visualize, because this is a first step into trance journeying. Hopefully people will get a kinetic, auditory and visual sense of a landscape. We might ask you to close your eyes and imagine an apple in front of you; notice the weight, its color and the way the light reflects off its skin. Then take that apple, bring it toward your face, notice how it feels in your hand and how it smells. Then take a bite, feel the juice, listen to the crunch, and savor the flavor. Once we've taken you through this trance visualization, we pass around some apple slices so you can compare your internal experience with an actual external experience. So, the tools for visualization and journeying into a different realm would be the first basic teaching we would give you.

A common misconception about Witches is that we use our tools to try to change the fabric of the natural world and control this or that. I find that mostly we use these tools for inner- or self-exploration and self-transformation. We're trying to become better, fuller, more well-rounded human beings and *then* act in the world, using our magic politically and environmentally.

♦ *R/S: What do you think of all these books telling how to cast spells?*

♦ TC: Much of magic is about opening up to the parts of ourselves that are *pre-verbal,* or that respond to *symbols* or *objects.* Some people say, "Why do you have to strike a match and light a candle? Why can't you just *think* about your problem?!" But there are parts of us that are beyond the reach of language.

Spells are physical prayers. They can help focus intention. I consider spells as lesser magic rather than greater magic. To me, spells are the least important part of our religion.

♦ *R/S: How is being initiated different from just taking a class?*

who I truly am; somehow my molecules became rearranged. I had found this person whom I felt was my partner, and I needed to make this commitment as a magical act in order to deepen my other commitments: to be a priestess, writer, scholar, activist, and whatever else I'm going to do with my life.

So **being married is good for me. It also means that while I still channel my sexual energy and life force in my work and in the world, it's done more effectively because I'm not always seeking that sexual partner who might be coming around the corner!**

♦ *R/S: Is your husband a Pagan?*

♦ TC: Jim is not a Pagan, but he's very respectful of my religion. He enjoys Wiccan ritual, but he's so psychically sensitive that often the energy gets too overwhelming for him. The last ritual he attended was a Solstice at the beach, but as soon as the circle was cast he had to leave, because the energy was too strong.

The reason we're partners is that our spiritual life is foremost for both of us. Awhile ago we both studied with a Gurdjieff group. Gurdjieff was a mystic philosopher and teacher, a rascal and holy man. He began teaching in Russia just before the Bolshevik revolution and died in France around 1950. Basically, he taught self-observation, and trying to wake up to yourself. He felt that most humans are automatons, and that we walk around like machines and are pretty much unconscious. His whole method, through movement, reading, observation, and different tasks, is about the process of trying to wake up one's self. However, I concluded that his system is too patriarchal.

♦ *R/S: Reclaiming was started by people trained in the Feri tradition, but it changed significantly—*

♦ TC: Right. Reclaiming also sprang from the anti-nuclear movement, which did rituals to close down a Diablo Canyon nuclear power plant, as well as anti-war demonstrations.

In the early days of Reclaiming, if you took a class you could then turn around and teach it. To me, that sounded horrifying,

♦ TC: First of all, Reclaiming is different from other Wiccan traditions in that no initiation is required for anything—you can teach or be a priestess without being initiated. It's not an initiation tradition, even though we have them. The first act you do is *self*-initiation; only *you* can dedicate your life to the work of the Goddess—no one else can do that for you.

In most other traditions, you study for a year and a day and receive one level of initiation, and then you're initiated into another level. Whereas Reclaiming initiation is strictly about what *you* need and where you are in your path. But if you want focused, intensive work on your self, with a few people to help challenge you and deepen your work, you can choose that, and it marks a personal rite of passage.

♦ *R/S: Is the trance state an important Pagan goal? It may not be for everyone, especially in this urban, concrete environment—*

♦ TC: As Neo-Pagans, we always strive to be connected to the natural earth—even in an urban environment. Wicca is based on an agricultural calendar. As I'm not a farmer, when I go through the wheel of the year I feel I am mapping the seasons of my soul.

What a trance journey does is it helps me take steps into my unconscious and discover things about myself that my logical consciousness can't access. In a non-ordinary state of consciousness I can journey into this interior landscape, which often looks like a physical place. I can get help there; there might be beings who guide me; even the physical layout of this interior space can provide insight. So I return with knowledge about myself that I didn't have before.

Sometimes a whole group of people will drop down into non-ordinary consciousness and try to work out a problem. And since we're working on a deeper, more intuitive level, different information will surface than if we're just sitting around talking in a regular room.

♦ *R/S: Why did you work in the stock market; in the belly of the beast—*

♦ TC: —the heart of Moloch, with his child sacrifices. As an anarchist, I wanted to see for myself what it was like on the inside of the engine of capitalism. The day I started work, the owner of the company walked in at 6 A.M. and hit the ceiling—the first thing he saw was the back of my head, and I had a bright blue mohawk with checkerboards shaved around my head. Immediately I got called into the director's office, and was told I had to wear a scarf or hat. But I refused, saying, "This is discrimination; *you* hired me. I have a right to look however I want. I'm not interfacing with the public, so your image is not going to be damaged. I can do whatever I want." And they relented: "Okay."

♦ *R/S: Subtly, you implied you'd sue them—*

♦ TC: [laughs] I said to my manager, who was an African-American, "This is just discrimination." He understood. The place was full of rampant sexism, so I started calling people on it all the time—I was this angry young woman stomping around the floor of the Pacific Stock Exchange causing trouble in my gold motorcycle boots.

It got to the point where I would approach a trading pit and people would stop talking; they'd probably been saying something they shouldn't have. Then my company hired this efficiency expert whom I hated. I went to talk to a couple of traders and said, "Hey, how about hiring me as a personal assistant?" So I ended up having my own business, being a personal assistant to three market-makers (people who trade with their own money).

Once, when the market was going crazy, one of the men I was working for yelled at me, "Go buy me some Krugerrands!" I looked at him and said, "No." He said, "What?!" I said, "No." His face got really red and his mouth got really tiny; he threw down his trading tickets, left the pit and went and bought them himself. Everyone knew that I had refused to buy them because of the *apartheid* policies in South Africa. One of the African-American traders came up and thanked me, but he was the only one; everyone else thought I was crazy.

I tried to have as many discussions with people about politics and corporate responsibility as I could. I'd say, "How can you trade with this Afrikaaner corporation that does business in South Africa?" and people's response would be, "Business knows no political boundaries. Capitalism should stay out of politics" (whereas we know that capitalism and corporations *run* politics). The stock market is a skewed, bizarre world—a heart attack waiting to happen. **Basically I learned that our whole economic system is based on gambling . . . which is rather frightening.**

Recently, an activist friend said to me, "We want to do this action regarding the Free Trade Agreement of the Americas, trying to tie in corporate involvement that is basically taking away more and more rights from working people. It's an *arrestable* action. Do you want to be involved?" I said, "Sure!" It turned out to be on the floor of the Pacific Stock Exchange, and I ended up being the police liaison. A bunch of people dressed up as Robin Hood and Maid Marian vaulted over the turnstiles, got past the guards and entered the options floor. It was fun. Eleven people got arrested.

♦ *R/S: The other night at Reclaiming's solstice celebration at the beach, there were a lot of "sky-clad" people who had just plunged and "purified" themselves in the ocean. Suddenly a policeman showed up, and you immediately ran over to talk to him—*

♦ TC: Policemen like it when they have an identified person to talk to—it makes them feel *safe*. They're used to a hierarchical chain of command, and so, if they can equate you with a person who has some "authority" in a situation, they'll be much more comfortable dealing with the whole group. You have to do this *right away* before they build up fear. The first thing you do is tell them your name and "title"—make up one if you have to. Ask them *their* name and title and start using them often.

♦ *R/S: Can you talk more about Pagan aesthetics—*

♦ TC: We're a pretty motley group; we're open to a lot of different styles of people. I can show up in a ritual in my tattoos and

Thorn while working at the stock market: "Psychologica I Portrait" by Brian Defer

Reading poetry at The Water Gallery in Los Angeles, age 16

leather bra and be next to a woman wearing "Marin Hippie" clothes: long, flowing, velvet, embroidered materials from India. Anything that reflects the artistic impulse is definitely part of the Pagan aesthetic.

The Renaissance and medieval part of the aesthetic comes in because Pagans have this romanticization about certain older times that seemingly "felt" more Pagan than now. The Arthurian times are romanticized, so people try to recapture this era where people may have had a greater connection to the earth and to magic.

The Punk aesthetic comes in because many of us are anarchists. We do believe in trying to work as non-hierarchically as possible, although natural hierarchies evolve, of course. Many of us are politically-involved activists. **We share the idea of doing things ourselves and not waiting for someone else to tell us what to do, or to sell something to us. A lot of us are anti-capitalist, anti-globalization, anti-corporate, and pro-earth, pro-people, pro-life-in-its-diversity.**

But the main thing is: Pagans like *stuff*—we're not Zen Buddhists. We celebrate the earth and our bodies, and we celebrate beauty in all its forms. If my body is something sacred to be celebrated, it makes sense that I would decorate it. And to me, that takes the form of sacred tattoos. To other people it might mean wearing beautiful velvet clothing. Our houses are full of decorations and tchotchkes; our pockets are full of sacred rocks. Pagans decorate their computers at their office jobs.

♦ *R/S: And with "stuff" comes commodification. It seems almost anything can be commodified—*

♦ TC: Wicca is being commodified. There's *Sabrina, the Teenage Witch* and *Charmed* on television. Today, on television, being a witch is considered hip, cool and cutting-edge; it's like being a lesbian was five years ago. (As a countercultural person, I don't believe in watching television.) But there's a cultural cognitive dissonance happening; even though it's kind of hip and popular to be a Witch, if you go to Wyoming or North Carolina and you're a teenager dressed in black or wear a pentacle to school, you're going to get in trouble—especially since

the "trenchcoat mafia" of Columbine. So on the one hand it's kinda cool to be a Witch, and on the other hand it's still frowned upon, feared, or laughed at.

I think that the "living culture" aspect of Paganism can never be commodified, just as the true Punk spirit could never be commodified, because it was always *about doing things yourself*, not buying things. The same is true with Wicca and Neo-Paganism: it's a living religion, it's a living culture. And you're always creating the experience!

♦ *R/S: It almost seems we're in a war over experience. The corporate powers want us to consume virtual experiences that they provide for us; they want us to be passive, consuming receptacles.*

♦ TC: So it's about each person's experience and the power of that. And experience is something that can't be taken from you and sold. It's about *living* culture. I think of when the Gap tried to buy Jello Biafra's song "Holiday in Cambodia" for their ad campaign—what a ridiculous idea: to think that you can take a Punk song and use it to sell khaki pants. It totally belies the Punk aesthetic and the power of Punk Rock, besides totally missing the point of the song "Holiday in Cambodia." There's something about the vitality of living culture that people create together that is so important to me and my friends—it's life itself. Our world is increasingly dominated by corporations and government hierarchies that institute systems of oppression rather than systems of liberation and equality. We hold vigils against wars, around death penalty issues, nuclear proliferation, and join with other movements that harmonize with Pagan vows to protect and nurture the earth. Sometimes this entails putting one's body on the line in front of a row of riot cops.

The idea of service to others as a spiritual practice is very important to me, too. For four years I lived in voluntary poverty in a community, Martin de Porres, that runs a soup kitchen in San Francisco. It feeds 200–600 people seven days a week. We treated hungry, poor and homeless people with respect—that's one thing they don't get in our culture. It's an intentional anarchist-Catholic Worker-style community of faith, although it's a community of many different faiths; we were Catholic nuns, Buddhists, Yoga practitioners, Jews and Witches all living together in a semi-anarchistic fashion.

Working there was a way to acknowledge that there's divinity in every human, that we need to take care of each other, and that we can't wait for governments and corporations to take care of people for us; we have to do it ourselves. So it's part of the anarchistic viewpoint that I appreciate about Paganism: that if I want something done, I need to do it myself. We also say, in my tradition, "Thou art Goddess, and thou art God." That is acknowledging that you have a spark of divinity inside of you, and it's not something separate out there. **There's a joke from a Pagan magazine where one Pagan says to the other, "Is nothing profane?"**

Paganism is also about reclaiming the sense of wonder you had as a child—before you "grew up" and became a skeptical, cynical adult. Children have that, and this gets trained out of us. Paganism is about reclaiming the sense that the world is alive, and that there is magic and divinity everywhere all around us. Divinity is not just "God on a throne." It's immanent divinity that enchants the whole world, and fills the whole world with life force, and beauty, and fun!♦♦♦

Thorn, age 33. Photo: Charles Gatewood
Inset: Thorn in High School

Some of Thorn's Body Adornment

- [necklace] Krishna and a Whirling Dervish fob.
- wedding ring: traditional Irish claddagh ring, symbolizes love, loyalty and friendship. A heart symbolizing love, held in two hands for friendship, and a crown on top symbolizing loyalty.
- rune ring made by an albino black magician in London, for health. He makes them in ritual space and sings the name of each rune as he pounds the silver. "I usually have more rings on"—TC
- Leonardo da Vinci watch is a human-in-pentacle form, the human as the star, the human that includes the five elements and the five senses.
- earrings: symbols of the goddess Inanna, bought at Pantheacon.
- necklace is a solar cross with the phases of the moon, so it represents the sun and the moon together, which Witches use to mark time and connect themselves with nature.
- labrette [lip] piercing with cobalt blue stone.
- tattoo: sacred heart. I was raised Catholic. A Catholic sacred heart would not be green, but Pagans often use the Hindu chakra system, and in the Hindu system the heart is green. Quote from Rumi: "Let the beauty we love be what we do. There are hundreds of ways to kneel and kiss the ground." To a Witch, the ground is sacred and the seat of divinity.
- tattoo: old Irish design, triskele, carved in stone at New Grange. One of the old monolithic solar clocks, where the sun comes in at Solstice and hits a certain spot. It also represents the Triple Goddess. Also it's my name; my last name is Coyle (coil). I've got the rune for "Thorn" around it, so this is my name, Thorn Coyle.
- tattoo: snake with Celtic knotwork. Behind it is wheat. Snakes and wheat are associated; the Roman Goddess Ceres is shown holding snakes. Snakes represent regeneration, and wheat represents the life force. So they're symbols of the moon, because the moon regenerates itself, and are also symbolic of the power of woman to regenerate every month with the moon cycles. Grain goddesses are also shown with snakes because snakes were kept in the granaries to eat the mice. So it's practical as well as mystical symbolism.

RECOMMENDED READING

This is a mixed bag of books I've loved and read, and books I use as reference only—sociology, anthropology, fiction, etc.—plus a few I've just gotten recently.—**Thorn**

Women of the Golden Dawn Mary K. Greer
The Rebirth of Witchcraft Doreen Valiente
The Sea Priestess Dion Fortune
Moon Magic Dion Fortune
Castings Ivo Dominguez, Jr.
The Pagan Book of Living and Dying M. Macha NightMare and Starhawk
Twelve Wild Swans Hilary Valentine and Starhawk
Dreaming the Dark Starhawk
The Spiral Dance Starhawk
Truth or Dare Starhawk
People of the Earth : the New Pagans Speak Out Ellen Evert Hopman and Lawrence Bond
Be a Goddess Francesca de Grandis
Cassell's Encyclopedia of Queer Myth, Symbol and Spirit
Ancient Ways Pauline Campanelli
The Holy Book of Women's Mysteries Z. Budapest
Thorns of the Blood Rose Victor Anderson*
Fifty Years in the Feri Tradition Cora Anderson*
Of Water and the Spirit Malidoma Patrice Somé
Drawing Down the Moon Margot Adler
The History of Magic Eliphas Levi
The Sacred and the Profane Mircea Eliade
Cosmos and History Mircea Eliade
Persuasions of the Witch's Craft: Ritual Magic in Contemporary England T. M. Luhrmann
The Pagan Religions of the Ancient British Isles Ronald Hutton
The Stations of the Sun Ronald Hutton
The Triumph of the Moon Ronald Hutton
Another Mother Tongue Judy Grahn
Witchcraft and the Gay Counterculture Arthur Evans
Real Magic Isaac Bonewits
The Encyclopedia of Celtic Wisdom Caitlin and John Matthews
The Politics of Women's Spirituality Charlene Spretnak
A Community of Witches: Contemporary Neo-Paganism and Witchcraft in the United States Helen A. Berger
Pagans and Christians: the Personal Spiritual Experience Gus di Zerega
Nature Religion in America: from the Algonkian Indians to the New Age Catherine L. Albanese
T.A.Z.: the Temporary Autonomous Zone, Ontological Anarchy, Poetic Terrorism Hakim Bey
Woman and Nature: the Roaring Inside Her Susan Griffin
Jambalaya Luisah Teish
The Mists of Avalon Marion Zimmer Bradley
Priestess of Avalon Marion Zimmer Bradley and Diana Paxson
Brisingamen Diana Paxson
The novels of Charles de Lint including : *Trader, A Place to Be Flying, Memory* and *Dream*. (Also, I like the German band Rammstein!)

*ordering info for Victor and Cora Anderson's books (the only place you can get them)
Cora Anderson, 1529 153rd St., San Leandro, CA 94578

Have you read Salvation on Sand Mountain? *It's an astounding book about that small Christian sect of snake handlers in Appalachia. This journalist got caught up with them and ended up handling snakes himself—it's a great book. It's amazing.*—TC

Isaac Bonewits

I saac Bonewits is a writer, lecturer, researcher and musician who has made an enormous amount of high-quality Pagan knowledge available on his website, *www.neopagan.net*, where his books and CDs are also available. When his book *Real Magic* appeared in the Seventies, it caused a sea change in the thinking of Occultists, Wiccans, Magicians and scholars. Pagan ethics are his forte. Interview by V. Vale.

♦ *RE/SEARCH: Weren't you the first person to receive a Ph.D in Magic?*

♦ ISAAC BONEWITS: If only I could find a way to market such exaggerations in regards to my academic degrees! Actually, I received a B.A.—the first degree of any sort granted by an accredited institution for studies in the field of the Occult. My diploma reads "Bachelor of Arts in Magic and Thaumaturgy" and it's from U.C. Berkeley.

♦ *R/S: What is thaumaturgy?*

♦ IB: It means wonder-working. Thaumaturgy, for example, involves ritual magic performed for the purpose of making it rain, or making the hunters more successful. Ultimately, it embraces things that people normally want to use magic for—of the practical, mundane variety. In comparison, theurgy, or theurgical ritual, involves the religious, mystical activity that people engage in to improve themselves.

♦ *R/S: Although—can we seriously say that creating a rain shower is mundane?*

♦ IB: Well, it is indicative only of the bizarre split our culture makes between the physical and the spiritual, the mundane and the sacred. Western Culture has been saturated in such Christian dualism for over 1,500 years. Any given ritual, spell, or act of magic will fall somewhere along that spectrum.

♦ *R/S: Yet we don't see people performing rituals to start their cars in the morning—*

♦ IB: Actually, talking to your car, motorcycle, or computer, is a very common psychological habit rooted in one of the basic laws of magic: *the law of personification.* There are people who swear that if they don't sweet-talk their computer, it won't function right.

However, 3,000 years ago all these things that today we might consider science were a part of the realm of magic—i.e., secret, esoteric knowledge. The day will come when almost everything we now think of as magic will be regarded as an aspect of science, art, or some other normal human activity.

Christian dualism—the idea that the universe can be divided into warring halves; black and white; good and evil; real and unreal—saturates mainstream science as well. This is largely because mainstream science was an outgrowth of Christian theology—as much as science distances itself historically from

this fact. There are a lot of secular humanists and professional skeptics who work very hard to cram the universe into either/or, yes/no answers. Unfortunately for them the universe remains far too complicated for such dualities. Very often there are no sharp and clear-cut dividing lines—the universe is *messy.*

♦ *R/S: Do you belong to a group?*

♦ IB: I belong to several Druid groups, and am the founder and Archdruid of ADF, the largest Neopagan Druid group in the country. I've also been initiated as a Wiccan priest, and was a member of the O.T.O., one of the major ceremonial magic organizations. I try not to let myself get painted into a corner!

I was also involved in NROOGD, the New Reformed Orthodox Order of the Golden Dawn, described as a sort of eclectic, do-it-yourself denomination of Wicca. When the feminist movement overlapped with the Wiccan movement, certain members of NROOGD founded Reclaiming, back in the Seventies.

♦ *R/S: Let's discuss the "shaman" concept—*

♦ IB: The best book on that is the original tome that made the word known to Western anthropologists: *Shamanism,* by Mircea Eliade. Essentially, what he describes is a person who is a tribal official, usually in a hunter-gatherer culture, whose primary job involves mediumship and astral travel on behalf of the tribe. Now that's a lot different from saying that anybody who does magic involving altered states of consciousness is a shaman, because in fact, *all* magic requires an altered state of consciousness.

There are a lot of people calling themselves shamans who are no such thing. The fact of the matter is: if you volunteer to be a shaman, you're not. Real shamans are *drafted.* They became shamans because they had a particular life experience that put them over the edge psychologically and psychically. And they survived to tell about it—so they then become a shaman.

A lot of the people who became shamans were what our world would call mentally disturbed. Sometimes they were gay, in communities that did not approve of that. Sometimes they were simply extremely psychic, and didn't have any other metaphor to use to describe what they were perceiving. Sometimes they were just smarter than everyone else in the tribe—*that* always gets you into trouble.

Regarding present-day "shamans"—take Michael Horner; his first book was really great. Then he realized he could make money on the New Age circuit, and started watering down what he had to say about shamanism. And then Lynn Andrews and company started coming in.

♦ *R/S: "Shaman" became a trendy buzz word—*

♦ IB: Exactly. For the same reason, I don't have much to do with crystals anymore. I have used various rocks and minerals as tools from time to time. But I never got into the fuzzy-minded, "Crystals are really alive—we just have to tune ourselves into their magical cosmic wavelength" *blah blah blah.* Older-era magicians would say that what mattered was the color, where you found it, and how it was consecrated, rather than the type of quartz it was. Almost anything can be used as a magical tool if it holds a particular psychological, cultural, or religious significance to you.

♦ *R/S: Have you read F. Bruce Lamb's* **The Wizard of the Upper Amazon?** *It's about a witch doctor, and how the magical or healing properties of plants were [allegedly] revealed in visions to people. Sometimes the preparations are quite arcane, involving a complicated boiling process which then transforms something poisonous into something useful.*

♦ IB: Today we would call these magical properties "botanical" properties. This includes Yage, Amanita Muscaria and wonderful things like that. Years ago I discovered why garlic is such a traditional herbal medicine for people who are sick—it contains sulfa drug analogs. It's an antibiotic.

♦ *R/S: Let's discuss the oldest source documents for Pagan thought—*

♦ IB: Apparently there's a new technology that may enable scientists to read the hundreds of old manuscripts that were discovered in a wealthy person's library in the ruins of Herculeum, adjacent to Pompeii when Vesuvius erupted. Pompeii seemingly was one big red light district, but Herculeum was a fairly normal trading town. Included are dozens of missing mystery documents that other Greek and Latin literature had referred to.

There is a more exciting rumor being circulated that archaeologists in Egypt, digging on the site of what used to be the library of Alexandria, had broken into a previously undiscovered sub-basement containing unknown documents, most of which are intact. This may possibly shed light on what Paganism was like in the Eastern Mediterranean before the arrival of Christianity. There may also be Gnostic materials on the early history of Christianity.

♦ *R/S: Have you investigated Shinto?*

♦ IB: Shinto is the name Westerners have given to the indigenous Paganism of Japan. Almost every Pagan religion includes an awareness of entities everywhere, and an attribution of spirit to natural phenomena—I believe the term is *kami* in Japanese. Every stream, every interesting stone and tree has its kami.

♦ *R/S: Weren't there once sacred groves where Pagan prostitutes were available?*

♦ IB: That was more common in Babylon and Sumeria than in the Greek and Roman areas. The Temples of Venus had their sacred prostitutes, but they would have described themselves more as priestesses, sexual therapists or healers—people who represented a Goddess or a God to someone in a fashion that was intimate and personal.

♦ *R/S: The healing power of sex . . . why not?*

♦ I.B. Sex can have a great deal of healing power. Does this mean it was never abused through becoming a commercial transaction? Of course not. Humans can abuse everything. The vast majority of writing about sex has been done by people who apparently felt that sex was dirty, nasty, and evil.

If there's one thing I've learned doing research, it's to ask 1) What are the author's prejudices? 2) Who is s/he writing this book for? 3) Who are they afraid to offend? This enables you to determine what filters affected the information they present.

♦ *R/S: On your site it says, "If you don't have a good sense of humor"—*

♦ IB: "—we discourage you from seeking positions of leadership."

♦ *R/S: Right! Can you illuminate us on the differences between Pagans, Wiccans, Druids, and—*

♦ IB: **Consider "Pagan" as the largest category, the umbrella. Within that you have the Paleopagans, the Mesopagans and the Neopagans.** As a category Paganism is equivalent to Monotheism, so Neopaganism could be likened to Christianity. Within Christianity, you have Catholics, Protestants, Eastern Orthodox, etc. Likewise, under the umbrella of *Neopaganism* you have Wiccans, Druids, Celtic Reconstructionists, and everybody else.

Thousands of Goddess worshippers who are part of the Feminist Spirituality movement may or may not consider themselves to be either Pagan or Wiccan. The problem is that "real" people don't fit into nice, neat categories. Let's say 80 % of the Neopagans are Wiccans and 10 % are Feminist Goddess worshippers from the women's spirituality movement. Out of the remaining 10 %, 5–6 % of the remainder may be Druids, and the rest are people who are reconstructing or reviving Neopagan religions based on other ethnic traditions, and/or are created out of whole cloth like the Church of All Worlds. You've got Egyptian Neopagans, Norse Neopagans, Greco-Roman Neopagans, etc.

♦ *R/S: I don't see any reference to Santería—*

♦ IB: Santería is mostly *Mesopagan.* It's a blending of different varieties of Christianity with different varieties of Paleopaganism. All those related African-based religions like Santeria, Macumba, Condomble are what I call Mesopagan. By and large, the overwhelming majority of Santerians are NOT part of the Neopagan community, and most of them have probably never even heard of people like us. In fact, to most people in the Santeria-Macumba-etc. community, the word "Witch" is a bad word meaning "magic user suspected of being bad." Nobody in history ever thought of Witchcraft as being a *good* thing until Gerald Gardner.

Ronald Hutton's *Triumph of the Moon* gives the absolute, final pounding of the nail into the coffin of fantasies about Wicca being a survival or revival of an underground faith from pre-Christian Britain. Hutton is a professional historian who spends 500 pages going through all the cultural, academic and historical *sources* of all the different ideas that Gardner blended together to create Wicca. He traces it back to the Romantic movement, the Freemasons, the Rosicrucians, the nostalgia for the countryside—all these social currents that were happening in the 1700s and 1800s, that created an intellectual milieu. And Hutton shows how these different strands of culture got woven together by Gardner. This is the one book that apologists for the antiquity of the Craft are going to have the most trouble with.

We have, in the Pagan community, *rabid fundamentalist Wiccans* who absolutely insist that Witchcraft was a Pagan underground religion going back to the Stone Age, and disavow all scholarship to the contrary. In their own way, these Pagans are just as desperate as the fundamentalist Christian apologists are!

♦ *R/S: That reminds me—what's the Pagan position on abortion?*

♦ IB: That's one of many topics where if you ask a half-dozen Pagans, you'll get twenty opinions. Paganism is still very much in a ferment, which is a good thing—it hasn't fossilized yet! As for the topic of abortion, I have a very firm and clear-cut position, which I will explain the very next time I'm pregnant!

♦ *R/S: It's a woman's right to choose.*

♦ IB: Actually, I'm trying to go to one level beyond that: the opinions of *men* on the topic, whether they're religious leaders or not, are irrelevant.

♦ *R/S: Let's discuss sex. You seem to have a rational treatment of more-than-monogamous relationships on your Web site—*

♦ IB: Polyamory. It's not for everybody, but for those for whom it is, it fits perfectly well with Pagan theology, or *Polytheology* as I call it. Dossie Easton and Catherine Liszt's *The Ethical Slut* and Deborah Anapol's *Love Without Limits* are the classic polyamory texts—there have been so few texts that it doesn't take much to be a classic! I think both books kind of tiptoed around the religion question. But since they were controversial enough, maybe they decided they didn't want to add yet another layer of controversy.

♦ *R/S: The invention of terms like polyamory or polytheology give the illusion that consciousness is progressing—*

♦ IB: They do. I'm a firm believer in mimetic engineering. A meme is a fundamental unit of concept (or word or image) in the same way that a gene is a fundamental unit of heredity. Mimetic engineering is the art of creating and combining memes in creative ways to cause fundamental changes in culture. And this is what all authors try to do—and all other artists, to a certain extent. But to those of us who coin a lot of vocabulary, it's even more important.

♦ *R/S: Language must continually aim for more precision and less dogma—*

♦ IB: I've always considered that precision of phrase is really important, if for no other reason than I really hate to offend somebody *accidentally*. I have no objection to offending people—there are some people in the world who *should* be offended, because they themselves are offensive.

The vocabulary that people agree to use to discuss a problem all by itself defines the universe of discourse within which the discussion can take place. That's why the troops in the dualistic division of the topic of abortion each insist on their vocabulary: Is it pro-life or anti-abortion? Is it pro-choice or anti-life? Which of those pairs of language you use already conditions the sorts of conclusions that people are capable of coming to.

On my Web site, I talk a lot about the topic of Christian dualism. It may seem somewhat obsessive, until you realize that this is a fundamental meme of Western culture for the last 1500 years, and has saturated Western culture to such an extent that it's the water that the fish are swimming around in—they can't even see it. Many seemingly insoluble problems, whether in terms of logic or social activity, exist because of the dualistic water all the fish are swimming in. They can't see that they have limited themselves in terms of the possibilities of solutions.

♦ *R/S: The mechanism of the dualism is one of the best arguments lawyers use: "It's either this or that," when in reality there could be a hundred possibilities.*

♦ IB: Not only is it either this or that, it's either *this* or "that which happens to be the extreme opposite of this." Only the extreme opposites exist! If you have a situation where you disagree with one extreme, you therefore must be in favor of the opposite extreme.

♦ *R/S: I don't know if you've read William Burroughs, but—*

♦ IB: Not for a few years, but he was quite the mimetic engineer himself. By the time people were using the phraseology, he wasn't being discussed all that much. But he worked very hard on trying to create new ideas and new ways of combining ideas. He had a technique of making tape recordings and then chopping them up and splicing them almost randomly, like sound or word collages. The very idea of using word collage ensures a different way of handling the memes. He did that with cut-up newspaper columns.

♦ *R/S: Years ago, he seemed to be in a war against the fallacy of the Either/Or syllogism: "Either something is* **this**, *Or it's* **that**"—

♦ IB: *The war against the Either/Or.* One way to describe the distinction between the Neopagan world view and the previous mainstream Western world view is: the previous world view is Either/Or, and the Neopagan world view tends to be Both/And.

I'm not a brilliant philosopher in terms of having done really deep thinking about this, but I just accept that dualism is a dumb idea. Unfortunately, most mainstream culture hasn't yet gotten to the point where it agrees with that.

♦ *R/S: Were the pre-Socratic philosophers, with their wonderful aphorisms, Pagan?*

♦ IB: Of course; they were Paleopagans, actually. Paleopaganism means Paganism before it was affected by monotheism, or Paganism when it was still a polytheistic, Nature-based religion. And that includes 99.9% of all the human beings who have ever lived. Humans have been around for a million years, and monotheism has only been around for about 3,000 years.

♦ *R/S: Is there such a thing as Pagan Nietzsche-ism?*

♦ IB: Well, Nietzsche himself could be considered a type of Mesopagan. He did have a lot of polytheistic ideas. And he was reacting emotionally to the Christian-saturated culture around him. But Nietzsche is one of these writers who has forever gotten a bad rap because of abysmal translations into other languages, and the fact that various people with axes to grind picked and chose from what he had to say, and ignored the rest.

♦ *R/S: He's identified with Hitler . . . Was Hitler a Pagan?*

♦ IB: Hitler might have had leanings toward Mesopaganism, but he considered himself to be a good Catholic. He considered what he was doing with the Jews as completely in keeping with Catholic doctrine, and in point of fact the Catholic church did almost nothing whatsoever to interfere with it—something the church has been very evasive about admitting. The Catholic church has constantly talked about the pseudo-Germanic-Mesopaganism that Goebbels and company put together to inspire the masses, and have said little or nothing about the 1,500 years of virulent anti-Semitism that the church had practiced in Europe that provided the *bedrock* for Hitler to build his concentration camps.

If there hadn't been centuries of Christian anti-Semitism, there would have been no holocaust, because nobody would have cared. Well, there might have been a holocaust against the Gypsies, and the Theosophists, and the other groups of people they wiped out, but the big pogrom against the Jews would not have happened.

♦ *R/S: Theosophists got wiped out?*

♦ IB: Hitler rounded up and threw into concentration camps all the Theosophists, Rosicrucians, ceremonial magicians, astrologers, psychics, and anybody else like that he could get his hands on. If they weren't willing to help the Reich, they were enemies of the state. Hardly anybody ever writes about it. The entire spectrum of the occult community of Germany and its conquered territories—an entire generation—was wiped out. A book titled *Hitler's Astrologer* was about the German gentleman who did astrology for Hitler for awhile and then defected to England. He spent the rest of the war as an official British Army astrologer giving the allies advice as to what Hitler's astrologers back home were probably telling him.

Most of the Masons, Rosicrucians, and other groups have always been suspect to tyrannical governments, in large part because they've been associated for so long with revolutions. It's ironic that at one point, the ultra-right-wing reactionaries in France blamed the Masons for a supposed conspiracy that brought about the French Revolution. But later, the liberals in France said, "Yes, that's right—the Masons did lead the conspiracy and the revolution because they were all intellectuals fighting for human freedom *blah blah blah.*" So people on all sides of the political spectrum agreed that the Masons and other secret societies were responsible for massive changes in the political landscape of Europe. Whether that was true or not, it would certainly have been something that Hitler and his associates would have believed. Therefore they would have been hostile to Freemasons, Rosicrucians, Theosophists, and members of other secret societies. If it's secret and you don't control it, then it's a threat—that's the reasoning pattern there.

♦ *R/S: Let's change the topic a bit. The Surrealist group drew a Surrealist map of the world, and also tried to construct a pre-Surrealist history of the world of art, people and events that were Surrealist before the term was invented—an example being Hieronymus Bosch. Do Pagans do something similar? I've never read a Pagan appraisal of New Ireland, for example, which is near New Guinea—*

♦ IB: Frankly, I think the vast majority of American Neopagans are completely ignorant about Southern Hemisphere history. I doubt if one Neopagan in a thousand has ever heard of New Ireland. So the answer is No.

I've met a lot of Pagans who assume that Nova Scotia, for example, must have some secret Pagan activity going on, because it was settled so early by all these Celts from Scotland. But as far as I know, all those Celts from Scotland were good Christian men and women. There's no particular reason to believe they were any more Pagan than the ones who stayed home.

♦ *R/S: The Pagan community seems to be tolerant and politically liberal—*

♦ IB: I'm a liberal—the "L" word—and proud of it. "Liberal" used to mean *generous!*

♦ *R/S: Somebody who wanted equal rights for all.*

♦ IB: Exactly. And somebody who thought the rich people should share their wealth with the folks who helped make them rich. But thanks to half a century of Cold War and multi-millionaires who own large publishing empires, the word "liberal" is now mud.

Regarding dealing with the media, I constantly tell people, "It doesn't matter how nice the reporter is who interviewed you, because the city editor is going to rewrite their story, or the director or producer of the news program will cut and paste your interview to make you look like a fool." So if you're interviewed, you try to make it as difficult as possible for a hostile person to cut and paste your interview badly. You give them some nice soundbites, but be especially careful about making a joke that could be taken out of context. Because a hostile editor or producer *will* take it out of context and use it against you.

Years ago, when I was still living in Berkeley, California, a person claiming to be a documentary filmmaker wanted to interview me. Having been burned a couple times before, I asked, "Is this being produced for some Fundamentalist group that is anti-Occult?" He said, "Oh, no. We're doing this for the Boy Scouts and the Y.M.C.A. and secular organizations like that." So I agreed to be interviewed.

The U.C. Berkeley campus contains a grove of towering eucalyptus trees with a set of benches carved out of logs that have been there for decades. I didn't want these filmmakers in my house, because I've had them do weird things with my house decor before. So I said, "Let's do it outside in Nature; it's a beautiful day." While they were setting up the cameras and microphones, they asked me to do a soundcheck. I said, "Sure," and as a joke began reciting Lewis Carroll's "Jabberwocky": "Twas brillig and the slithy toves/Did gyre and gimble in the wave . . . " I did this very dramatically, and then they did the interview.

About a year later I heard about a film called *The Occult: Echoes from Darkness* and went to see it. Lo and behold, these filmmakers *were* Fundamentalist Christians doing a movie about the evils of the Occult. Near the beginning the camera pans on these dark, mysterious-looking trees—and boy, they had to use a lot of filters to make them look dark and mysterious, because it was a brilliant, sunshiny day! Beneath the darkened trees this voice was intoning, "Twas brillig and the slithy toves . . . " and it sounded just like a Satanic invocation! They took the interview they had done with me and cut it to give the worst possible slant on every single thing I said. I learned my lesson: you can never trust a conservative Christian interviewer to tell the truth.

♦ *R/S: Christian monotheism perfectly suits the corporate mind-set—*

♦ IB: The idea that money is its own justification goes all the way back to the Calvinists [c. 1540] and the so-called Protestant work ethic. Wealthy people are wealthy because God likes them better, and God likes them better because they're better people than the poor.

I read lots of editorials in various mainstream publications about how the collapse of the Soviet Union proved that Socialism was a failed economic theory. No it didn't! It proves that the particular type of Socialism they had in the Soviet Union hadn't worked very well. The type they've had in Scandinavia and in other parts of Europe seems to have worked quite nicely for a good long time— but you don't hear about this in American economic discussions. Europeans have a very low opinion of Americans. They believe that most of us are extremely ignorant, badly educated, provincial, and disgustingly Christian.

Personally, I'm a Fabian socialist. That was a British school of Socialism that essentially says, "Food, clothing, shelter" (and today we would add, "Utilities and access to the Internet") "should be covered by taxes. All the things that are necessary for a safe and fulfilling life should be paid for out of taxes. Anything else is a luxury and can be handled by Capitalism. But nobody should live or die because they don't have money." This is closer to the style of Socialism that you'll find in Scandinavia.

♦ *R/S: It's amazing how Americans allow billions to be spent on "defense"— but against whom?*

♦ IB: Again, since childhood they've been saturated with the "Us *versus* Them" mind-set. And now with all this blathering about "The United States is the only Super-Power left in the world!"—well, you know what the East used to call Super-Powers?—*empires!* Sure, we are indeed an imperialist empire and have been most of our history. What else is new? But we're still picking and choosing *when* we decide to go and fight for freedom. And by some bizarre, coincidence the only time we ever seem to send American troops off to fight for freedom somewhere is if there happens to be a financial benefit to wealthy Americans and corporations. The rest of the time we don't give a damn about democracy elsewhere in the world.

♦ *R/S: Right. I read that the reason America was giving Columbia $12 billion to fight the "drug war" was because they wanted oil rights there—*

♦ IB: Oil rights, rubber rights—there are lots of natural resources still locked up in the Amazon region and in other parts of South and Central America.

Most drug laws are rooted in Christian theology rather than rational social policy. The underlying idea is drugs are evil because they're pleasurable, and pleasure is evil. Also, drugs give you a different world view, and people with a different world view are harder to control. Frankly, I think we would probably have far less damage being done if we legalized every currently illegal drug in existence, let the addicts kill themselves, and take the profit out of it for both criminals and the government enforcement apparatus that has been built up in a parasitic dependence on it.

♦ *R/S: Right. Those drug-law enforcers have to keep their jobs, so if there aren't addicts, they have to create them.*

♦ IB: Do you know the story of how marijuana became illegal? It has to do with Prohibition. When Prohibition was canceled, suddenly alcohol was legal again. Harry J. Anslinger and his Prohibition agents were out of a job. Realizing this, they launched a campaign against marijuana, which at the time was mostly consumed by Blacks and Latinos. This was a way to keep his agency employed, keep his paycheck coming in, and it wouldn't hassle the rest of the middle-class culture very much.

They transformed something relatively harmless into this "evil menace to society."

With the founding of the Drug Enforcement Administration (DEA), one drug after another that had been legal for many years suddenly became illegal. Opium had been legal for a long time, and was the primary ingredient in many over-the-counter medications like Lydia Pinkham's which women took at "that time of the month." And frankly, if I had been a woman living in America during that time period, I would have tried to stay stoned as much as possible myself!

The point is that a Christian world view saturates so much of what is supposedly "secular" culture.

♦ *R/S: A top priority now is the dismantling of the corporate bill of rights—*

♦ *IB:* The very idea that a U.S. supreme court decided to give corporations the legal status of being *persons* is an outrage, an abortion of constitutional law that should never have been permitted, and should have been removed at the earliest opportunity. You never see any discussion of this in the press. Since when is a corporation a person, with rights to free speech, and assembly, and *whatnot?!*

♦ *R/S: Since that 1886 Supreme Court decision—*

♦ IB: Yeah. That in its day was just as egregious a miscarriage of justice as, let's say, the current President managing to get the Republicans on the Supreme Court to hand him the election . . . when they could have simply told the State of Florida to count everybody's votes over. You know: the best government that money can buy! [laughs]

I have an essay on my Web site called "Why Neopagans should still vote Green." In it I quote an African political leader discussing the election of G.W. Bush the way it would have been reported in an African country. And it is scathing. "The son of a former Prime Minister, himself a head of that country's secret police, in a province run by the candidate's brother . . ."

♦ **R/S: Let's discuss death. No one has ever come back from the dead—**

♦ IB: The Christians claim their guy did, but there are a dozen ways a Resurrection could have been faked. Christian theologians rarely discuss this, since it's a lot quicker to simply kill the people raising the objections. [laughs] By and large, Christian theology is built on a foundation of might—and might makes right, of course. The fact that Christianity has survived as long as it has is in large part due to the political, economic and military power that the Church had to silence opposition. If bringing up a really good question is liable to get you killed, you don't bring up really good questions.

♦ **R/S: Are there any Pagan Ten Commandments?**

♦ IB: No, we're far more likely to have "Thou Shalt's" than "Thou Shalt Not's."

♦ **R/S: I think that one Pagan rule handles a lot of situations: "As long as ye harm none, do what thou wilt."**

♦ IB: Well, actually that's not a very good rule…because it's too bloody vague. First of all, what constitutes "harm" is really tricky to define. There are people who consider it to be "harm" whenever anybody thwarts something *they* want to do! "Harm none" makes good P.R., but doesn't make very good theology. I give a workshop about Pagan morality and ethics. The "harm none" rule falls apart as soon as you demand details. If you give a child who's dying medical attention when his parents don't want you to, have you harmed someone?

Let's say you organize a labor union to strike. You think this is perfectly ethical, but the factory owner will probably claim he is being harmed by your activity. What if you're a Pagan tattooist—are you harming someone when you give them a tattoo? Are you harming someone when you engage in completely consensual S&M?

This rule is probably a modification of Aleister Crowley's famous "Do what thou wilt" rule—which referred to following your *true* will or cosmic destiny, not a whim of the moment. And I have known people who had a whim of iron! So, that's my challenge to the first rule of Pagan ethics.

Then there's the idea that whatever you do comes back to you karmically three times stronger—therefore, Pagans would never cast curses. Well, the judgment of the karma of something is extremely complicated, and changes dramatically from situation to situation and person to person. Also, if karma really *did* work that way, all the nice people we know would be happy, healthy and wealthy, and all the nasty people we've met would have died horrible deaths long ago.

The last major ethical principle is that it's always unethical to cast a spell on somebody without their permission. But there are plenty of situations where people do things to other people without their permission, especially if it's "for their own good." (Isn't that what people always say?!)

But sometimes you really *are* doing it for their own good. Let's say that you're a brain surgeon leading a team of doctors in a complex operation on somebody knocked unconscious in a motorcycle accident. That operation is not going to work unless the person in charge has power OVER the rest of the medical team, and furthermore, the victim probably didn't give permission for the operation to take place.

♦ **R/S: Nevertheless, in a way the members of that team of surgeons gave permission to one doctor to be the leader. And I still think a lot of people don't apply the Golden Rule—**

♦ IB: Well, the Golden Rule doesn't work well, either. Maybe you should treat other people the way *they* want to be treated—not the way that you would like to be treated in their place. Because you and they may not have the same preferences. What's that old joke? "Beat me, beat me!" said the masochist. "No," said the sadist. The Golden Rule doesn't always work, either. Every situation has to be judged on its own.

The past century has seen the rise of situational ethics. Situational ethics is based on changes from situation to situation, rather than having one grand and glorious principle that always applies. In other words, it's not *monothesis-ism* again. Monothesis-ism is the idea that there's always one best answer to any question. Well, the universe can count higher than one—in fact, the universe is darn good at counting up to infinity.

If you go on the Internet and conduct a search on situational ethics, you'll find plenty. The universe changes from moment to moment, and there are no easy answers that fit every problem. That's okay, because the world never asks easy questions!

Paganism is much heavier on ritual than it is on theology. Our theology is often an afterthought. We get certain psychological and spiritual benefit from certain rituals, and then we try to explain why. The Samhain rituals are certainly meaningful and helpful to many people—myself included. I have remembered friends and loved ones who have passed on and have found it very comforting to be there with other people acknowledging that, "Yes, people die. Life changes. We miss them when they're gone." Regarding reincarnation, I have certainly run into as much evidence for reincarnation as for going off to a Happy Hunting Ground.

One issue in the Pagan community is that it's mostly white. When black people show up with an interest in being Wiccan or Neopagan, they're almost always welcomed with open arms. I think Black Americans interested in being polytheists already have a broad range of available religions to choose from: Santeria, Voudoun, Macumba, Condomble. Likewise, for Asians, Confucianism, Taoism, and Shinto are polytheistic religions available to them, whereas Whites have lost theirs.

♦ **R/S: Most people consider themselves atheists or agnostics—**

♦ IB: However, atheism and agnosticism all too often are still part and parcel of the Christian dualist world view. What's the "God" you don't believe in? Well, it's the one the Christians defined: the *Omnipotent* this and the *Infinite* that. That's the precise deity that the atheists don't believe in. This is why it's so ironic that the Secular Humanist movement, which prides itself on its rationality, is really just another version of Fundamentalist Dualism. There's a page on my Web site titled "The Evolution of Dualism"—tie that in with my essay on "Scientism" and you'll see what I mean.

My father used to be a Fundamentalist Agnostic—someone who just doesn't know, and you don't either! That sort of makes sense. There's also the idea of Deism: yeah, there was this Supreme Being—but so what? Deism basically is the clockwork universe theory—the idea that yeah, there was a Supreme Being who set the universe up and running, and then has had no further interest in it and can therefore be ignored. This was extremely popular among the intelligentsia of the 1700s, and was the theological position of most of the Founding Fathers.

A chart on my Web site graphically explains how dualism moved from Zoroastrianism, through medieval Christianity and Islam, and into Scientism—today's worship of mainstream western science—its fundamentalists—are the ones who practice Scientism . . . or *Scientolatry.*

♦ *R/S: Tell us about the everyday life of a "magician," as you've been described. Do magicians ever need aspirin?*

♦ IB: Oh, yes! Most headaches have a psychosomatic component and are susceptible to mental techniques such as meditation, self-hypnosis, and so forth. But there are times when I have to dig out the aspirin just like everybody else. We get tired, we get cranky, we get hungry, horny—we experience and express the full gamut of human emotions.

♦ *R/S: So you get colds and flus like everybody else?*

♦ IB: Magic is one of those things that gives you an edge in certain situations. It's not a panacea. It won't solve all your problems or prevent life from ever handing you lemons. Sometimes it just helps you figure out a really good lemonade recipe!

But life has ups and downs. My biggest downer, since you were asking about my health earlier, happened in 1989–1990 when I became one of 10–12,000 people to get the "Tryptophan disease."

A Japanese pharmaceutical company that was a division of a big petrochemical company called Showa Denko decided to make changes in how it manufactured its vitamin supplements. L-tryptophan is a natural amino acid, one of the building blocks that humans make protein out of. It's found in cow's milk and turkey meat. Heating up milk or turkey releases tryptophan which acts as an anti-depressant and a mild sedative. This is why people get sleepy after Thanksgiving dinner, and after drinking hot milk at night.

In 1989 Showa Denko decided they could improve their profit margins by lowering their standards from the human medicine filtration levels to the animal filtration levels. Simultaneously, they purchased a new brand of genetically-engineered bacteria for the production of the tryptophan. Ultimately, the new modified bacteria produced not only higher concentrations of tryptophan, but higher concentrations of a previously unknown poison as well. They sent a shipment to Germany, where their equivalent of the American F.D.A. tested some of the product and prohibited its sale in that country.

Knowing that the U.S. F.D.A *didn't* test imported vitamin and nutritional supplement products, Showa Denko shipped their tryptophan to the U.S. As a result, thousands consumed this product, including people with depression and insomnia, muscle-builders, and others who were health-conscious. **This was feasibly the first genetic engineering catastrophe in the history of the United States.** The poison killed a few hundred people within the first months, and put another 12,000 of us (we'll never know the exact number) into metabolic tailspin. It made us incredibly miserable. There were a couple of years when my body was in so much pain I could hardly move. This was a multi-systemic disease that attacked the muscular, nervous, hormonal, and possibly the skeletal systems. There weren't enough people affected for it to be profitable to research a cure. Only those diseases with high numbers of sick or dying warrant the pharmaceuticals' concern. It's the profit motive.

Now I'm 70–80 % recovered. Provided I give myself a lot of time to rest I can function. I can't hold down a 9–5 job because there are very few jobs that are willing to let you stop every two hours and take a 20-minute catnap. I got blindsided by this disease; it's Nature's way of telling me I'm not separate from everybody else—

♦ *R/S: Despite your superior knowledge of magic—*

♦ IB: Well, having a superior knowledge of art will not necessarily make you an artist. And healing oneself is one of the hardest forms of magic. There have been a few people like Buddha that I might consider to have been enlightened, but I'm certainly not one of them. People get into more trouble claiming they're enlightened then they ever do admitting that they're not and trying to improve.

In fact, I've never sought after enlightenment. Most systems that focus on enlightenment take the individual far from this world. At this point in human history, it's a lot more important to clean up our external mess than worrying about our enlightenment. The damage to our planet has been following an exponential curve for the last 200 years, and it's darn near vertical now! We may well have an environmental collapse within the next twenty to thirty years. Besides corporate polluters, military types as well as ignorant, uncaring types are doing the same, too. People in small towns dump their sewage into rivers, saying, "Why shouldn't we? The river is right there."

♦ *R/S: I read in the* **New York Times** *that each year over 200 billion gallons of industrial/urban waste are poured into the Pacific Ocean—*

♦ IB: That sounds about right. "It would be too expensive to do anything else with it. If we raised prices to cover the costs of clean-up, our customers wouldn't buy our products anymore. So therefore we've decided that it's just not cost-effective to clean-up our pollution. Besides, it would lower our stockholders' profits." That's the way people and businesses think.

♦ *R/S: Last weekend I saw this little bit of woods in San Francisco and took a walk. Cigarette butts, crushed beer cans and junk food packaging were everywhere.*

♦ IB: People still have not gotten the concept that *litter is pollution.* All this is related to the Christian world view. That idiot James Watt (Reagan's Secretary of the Interior) said, "We don't need to save the environment. Jesus is coming and the world's about to end, so why bother?"

♦ *R/S: And his job was to protect the environment—*

♦ IB: When Republicans are in charge, they generally enlist foxes to guard their favorite hen houses. G.W. Bush put the governor of one of the most polluted states, Christine Whitman of New Jersey, in charge of the Environmental Protection Agency (EPA). As governor she fought tooth-and-nail against every environmental effort that happened in the state .

I make it a point to read the ravings of the religious right on a regular basis. It's the old saying, "Know your enemy." And I try to regularly read at least one periodical from an area or subculture I know nothing about, because you need to know there are other world views out there. Sometimes you can get things out of a golfing magazine!

I also belong to organizations that keep track of the Religious Right. On my Web site, at the end of my essay titled "Understanding the Religious Right," I have links to the ACLU, Americans United for Separation of Church and State, People for the American Way, the Institute for First Amendment Studies—these are groups that keep track of what the Religious Right is doing. They email me newsletters.

♦ *R/S: Let's discuss the aesthetics behind Pagan clothing—*

♦ IB: I think a lot of people attending Pagan events wear loose, flowing and vaguely Renaissance-looking clothing because they *want* to get away from the mind-set they have to be in 9–5 Monday through Friday.

When Gerald Gardner created Wicca, one reason he wanted people to be skyclad (naked) was because England is absolutely obsessed with social class, which is partly communicated with clothing. He wanted his Witches to not be paying attention to social class distinctions when they were in the circle worshipping or doing magic.

♦ *R/S: What movies do you like?*

♦ IB: I don't go to horror movies because I'm not an adrenalin junkie—that's really what horror movies are about. I go to science-fiction movies because I'm interested in stretching my imagination. I had read *Jurassic Park* before I saw the film. In the book, a chaos scientist/philosopher discusses the fact that you can't put a perfect system together, because chaos always wins out. And when you're doing experiments with really dangerous things, it's a bad idea to think you can control everything perfectly, because sooner or later your bad, dangerous thing will get loose.

♦ *R/S: That's what's outrageous about the GM corn disaster. Couldn't those "scientists" have predicted that the GM seeds would fly all over the planet—*

♦ IB: **I'm really concerned about something called the Terminator gene—I suggest you search the web for "Terminator gene."** Monsanto, and the other big chemical company that owns half of the seed companies in America, have developed new hybrid forms of major food plants like rice, corn, and soy that are sterile in the second generation. Every year farmers have to go back to the seed company to buy new seeds, rather than saving seeds from the previous year's crop.

That is, to begin with, an obvious, nasty capitalist trick to force people to keep coming back to you. But worse than that, if those genes get carried by pollination and start spreading among the plant populations of the planet, within three years there won't be many plants anymore, because the gene makes the seeds sterile. And these idiots are planting this stuff outdoors all over the planet!

If there's any one thing that's going to destroy this planet, **it's corporate greed.** Not that other forms of "evil" aren't just as willing to destroy things for personal profit, but most of them aren't as *efficient* and *effective* as corporate greed. I'm a lot more worried about that than I am about genetically modified corn. The corporate mind-set is: *"Nothing can possibly go wrong…go wrong…go wrong…"* This is why I say Pagans tend to be cautious technophiles. We love our computers, but we also know that science and technology are never as neutral as they claim to be.

♦ *R/S: Do you have shrines in your house, dedicated to—*

♦ IB: —different pantheons. I have a Hindu shrine, a Celtic shrine, and so forth. To a great extent, the reason is because if you decorated a room in French Provincial style, you wouldn't stick Chinese or African objects in the middle of it, probably because the aesthetic patterns that trigger responses in the brain are different in those cultures. If you mix them up, you may wind up getting very confused. This is one area of my life where I do get conservative: I tend to be cautious about mixing elements from different cultures. You don't stick curry in the middle of an apple pie recipe,

Every culture defines "reality" for its citizens. Some of them do it overtly and some of them do it covertly. I believe our culture very consciously defines "reality" for people—*that's* a large part of what Madison Avenue, and politics, is all about. The idea that Third [political] Parties are irrelevant has been the official "party line" of the mass media for a hundred years! We've been conditioned to think that there are only *two choices*—well, that's a world view from a culture that has been thoroughly dominated by Christian Dualism.

♦ *R/S: Now, we're heading into the future with Paganism, the postmodern religion that's also a culture—*

♦ IB: **Religion is always culture, and vice versa.** These days, people are far less inclined to define themselves with an organized religion. Many "Pagans" say, "I'm a solitary practitioner. Yes, I worship the Goddess and the Gods, and I do some of the things that I read in books about Paganism, but I don't belong to any specific tradition or denomination." And there are lots of Jews who light the candles on Friday night but never go to synagogues. The organized religious church structures of our culture have failed the people miserably, and have shown themselves to be so corrupted that people no longer trust them.

♦ *R/S: Is your son growing up Pagan?*

♦ IB: My son was born March 24, 1990 and just turned eleven—going on fifteen. He's definitely a Pagan; he requested a Pentagram to wear to school! There's no doubt about it … ♦♦♦

On the Web:

Witchvox.com is possibly the largest Pagan community site. Druid sites, i.e., A.D.F. and Keltria have high scholarship quality. *Congressional Record* is online now!

Recommended books:

Alvin Toffler *Third Wave* and *Megatrends*: well worth reading, even though the author is a rabid secular humanist and seems to consider religion evil and stupid.

Robert Anton Wilson—he's the one who gave me the phrase "tunnel reality." That's what you live in when all you can see is constricted in a narrow circle in front of you.
Cosmic Trigger series (Vol. 1-2-3)
Prometheus Rising series
Illuminatus trilogy
Schrödinger's Cat series (not as much fun as the *Illuminatus* trilogy and in many ways just a rewrite of the same material)

Bobcat

Emma Restall Orr is a British Druid known as "Bobcat." She was one of the chief orchestrators of Pagan gatherings at Stonehenge, and is the author of *Spirits of the Sacred Grove*. The British Druid Order's Web site is *www.druidery.co.uk*, and Bobcat's site is *www.nemeton.demon.co.uk*. Interview by V. Vale.

♦ **RE/SEARCH: How did you begin to research your Pagan roots or affinities?**
♦ EMMA: There are a number of reasons why I became involved in Druidry. Some people are born interested in religion, and gradually that interest develops; and some people will never be interested, but I don't think it's a choice that we make. For me there has always been that interest in the reason *why,* in what is *beyond,* and in why my reality is different from the reality of people who don't see or feel spirits, and who don't have an animistic vision of the world—that the whole world is *alive.*

My parents are both naturalists. My father is an ornithologist living in Venezuela where he studies birds in all their glory, painting them exquisitely. My mother is a botanist and a registrar at the Royal Horticultural Society in England. She travels the world, and registers and catalogs strange and wonderful plants.

I was brought up in wild places: South America, the Far East and around Europe, exploring and trekking as my parents went on scientific expeditions. They were religious in a way; their spirituality was inside them—it wasn't expressed. I was brought up with a very clear view that nature was everything, nature was all-important—and perhaps more than anything, nature could not be tamed. Nature was not merely a resource to be "used up."

When I published *Spirits of the Sacred Grove,* I considered what my parents might think of the book. Both of them separately told me, "You've said what I've always wanted to say but never had the words." That book is my personal view of Druidry; my own perspective of the world viewed through my Druidic practice and understanding of the teachings I've been given.

Another central reason for my involvement was that I suffered from a hyper-sensitivity disorder—I was in a lot of pain for much of my childhood. It sent me wild in my early teens, and by my mid-teens I had attempted suicide a number of times, because I couldn't cope with it. That brought me to the edge of death, and led me to understand death and pain. Ultimately, I became deeply involved in some very strange practices as I explored healing: different ways of using energy, and using pain for transcendence—you talked about this in your *Modern Primitives* book.

In my late teens, I met some very strange people—ex-war veterans and other folks who showed me very dark places as I explored the pain inside my body instead of killing myself. As I went through that journey and came through on the other side, I hit the wall and had to make a choice: to live or die.

I was given a condition by spirits around me: "Well, if you choose to live, then you have to do it properly this time. We're not going to mess around with you anymore." I chose to live, and took a very clear, disciplined healing path from that time—I was about twenty-one. I also fell in love with a Scotsman, married him, and made a commitment to come to England and stay. I needed to explore the spiritualities of this land—having been brought up in the rain forests, with Native Indians in Venezuela, been with Maya folk in Central America, and the indigenous traditions of the Shinto—the really grounded, earth-based nature religions in Japan and China.

♦ **R/S: You lived in Japan and China, too?**
♦ E: Yes. I lived in Japan from the age of 15 to 18, and came to England when I was 18. I wanted to find out what the indigenous tradition of this country was; it didn't make sense to search for another one from another land. And exploring every avenue I could find, I came across Druidry when I was 20 or 21 and started to study that.

♦ **R/S: How did you discover Druidry?**
♦ E: I saw a small ad in a glossy alternative healing/culture magazine. It said something like, "Modern Druidry: if you're interested in studying the old tradition of Druidry, get in touch." And I did. It was a small mail order business, which is now the biggest in the world—it's grown in the past 16 years. The people ran a plain and basic correspondence course; it didn't tell much. It took me awhile to get involved. But I found teachers, I studied books, and eventually found people whom I felt could teach me face-to-face. *That's* the most effective way of learning: to apprentice to someone . . . to learn within a sacred space from a teacher you respect.

♦ **R/S: What are the most ancient written sources for Druidry?**

♦ E: Inscriptions—I know, that doesn't sound like much. In Britain, inscriptions were found on ancient Roman prayer plates and other objects in burial sites. Archaeologists have discovered debris of Roman villages and temples with inscriptions to local British gods. The Romans knew that they had to honor the local gods, if those gods were to allow them to thrive and rule in that land. *That's* how we know the names of the oldest British gods: from the Roman inscriptions. It's only a couple of words or a few sentences here or there, but these actually say an enormous amount just in a few words: the name of the god, what that god is, where that god is . . . The next source is the classical writers, the main one being Julius Caesar. Coming through Gaul and into Britain, he writes clearly, giving us a good deal of information about Druid beliefs and practices, about their training, philosophy, and social role. Writing as a superhero describing a war, he has a biased view of what the British and Druids were like. But you can take that into account and extrapolate.

There are other classical Roman and Greek writers writing from 1,600 to 2,500 years ago. Yes, there are gaps. Then we have medieval literature, which includes Celtic stories such as the Irish Book of Invasions, and Welsh poetry. These describe what the Druids did, most importantly giving us the mythologies that are so much a part of modern Druidry. Some of this was oral traditions, old stories, written down by Christians, so we have to take that into account. Just as we remove Caesar's pomposity, so we remove the Christian "purity"—we make it a little dirtier around the edges, and see what's really underneath!

We have all the archeological sources: ancient sacred sites, stone circles, piled rocks, tomb shrines, groves, digs, offerings, burials. Even though we make assumptions about what was done, this doesn't "invalidate" our practices which involve *personal* relationship to the land and the site. These sources give off clues, like words in a poem, that we can put together to create something bigger, richer, deeper.

On top of that, we look at the modern world's surviving tribal cultures, and they help us to understand more about the reality of what our ancestors were. We look at traditions which have not been destroyed, and tribal traditions which still have their religion. Far more important is to understand Druidry to be an animistic religion rooted in the earth. It's not about what someone else wrote, or about history and other people's thoughts, it's about our *own* personal relationship with the power of nature.

There's no human sacrifice left in the tradition now; there's virtually no blood sacrifice in terms of animal sacrifice. The fact that Druidry is an oral tradition means that we're not stuck to interpreting "scripture." That's the power and the beauty of it: it has to be appropriate and relevant to every new day. The modern tradition is incredibly contemporary, but has ancient roots. We're not trying to go back to what it was; instead, we honor its roots, and celebrate, revere, and practice in a way that is absolutely modern.

♦ *R/S: Admittedly, since there's so little written, it's hard to tell what it was way back when, anyway—*
♦ E: Exactly.
♦ *R/S: But at least you're not trying to pretend that there's some unbroken chain of transmission of knowledge—*
♦ E: There's a book written by John Matthews called *The Druid Sourcebook.* And there's a *Bardic Source Book,* which is a brick of a book. Both are good resources if you wish to explore what does exist in terms of history, written knowledge and understanding. There are a few Druids who claim an unbroken line way back to even Atlantis, but that's too much! It's mad. All the little bits and pieces of knowledge are fascinating, but I don't think it's necessary to have an unbroken line. For me, the unbroken line is the fact that these islands are still here, and that there are still people here—that's as unbroken as it gets.
♦ *R/S: The genetic code persists—*
♦ E: That's right.
♦ *R/S: Can you tell us more about Shinto—*
♦ E: Perhaps this is just a personal view: Shinto is closer to Druidry than any other indigenous tradition I've encountered. For me, Shinto is about the beauty of the tiny moment—the

eternal beauty of the tiny moment, and how those tiny moments extend forever through our genetic line, through our ancestors. Those stories of our ancestors are actually beautiful moments that still linger in our own blood, in our own minds, in our own souls, that we hold as treasure from our ancestors. For me, that kind of description is Shinto and Druidry completely together. The honoring of the blood, not as celebration but as contemplation—ecstatic contemplation in that kind of Japanese and English way, which is dignified, elegant, polite and slightly reserved, but actually enormous, hugely wild—just endless seas and wild winds. . .

♦ *R/S: In Shinto, don't people pay tribute to (if not exactly worship) a local spring that nourishes them, or to a beautiful nearby tree or rock that provides inspiration?*
♦ E: Absolutely. I live a ten minute walk from a spring, in a tiny village in the middle of the English countryside. It's very quiet, and there are old buildings around. Every other day or so I walk through the meadows to a spring which is in a glade of trees. I go as often as I can, taking flowers and bread and seeds. Sometimes I take beautiful stones there. I make prayers to the water and watch the water come out of the earth; it's like a vulva of life blood from the womb of the earth.

To me this local spring is *far* more sacred than Stonehenge—incomparably more sacred. Someone else down another road will feel the same way about *their* spring. Springs are the life blood of the community; without a spring, a village might not exist. Three thousand years ago, my village would never have emerged out of the tribal settlings without that spring. And that water comes out of the earth, out of the mud, and goes down through a brook and into a river all the way down to the Thames and then out into the North Sea, 300 miles away.

In Kyoto, Japan

♦ *R/S: Regularly honoring that spring is Paganism in practice. What do you think of the term "Pagan"?*

♦ E: To me "Pagan" is a beautiful word from the Latin *Pagus,* meaning the village, the community. It's about finding the law in nature, instead of in government or in some pompous ruler, which is what "civilization" does. And that nature is your locality, your community of trees and stones and sky and clouds and mud and the plants that grow and the springs and the animals. Many animals and plants have been killed off by this monstrosity known as **"civilization"—this disease that disconnects us from the law/lore of nature, allowing us to use, abuse, consume, to live without** *relationships,* **without reverence, without respect.**

♦ *R/S: Is there much Pagan political activism in England?*

E: In my memory, as someone who grew up through the Seventies and Eighties, political activism was stirred up by Maggie Thatcher. She wasn't even a matriarch, she was a patriarch. And she and the Conservative government after her had policies which were detrimental to the lowest layers of community in this country. In the last four years, the country has changed enormously because we've had a Labor government. It's not a left-wing socialist government, it's actually a centrist government. But it's considerably more "left" than the governments you've had in America. Even so, it has softened the mood in Britain enormously.

The political activism in this country now is global, it's about the W.T.O., global selfishness, global consumerism, and corporate monsters. Protest is very much on a global level. We had riots in Britain last year but not this year; at the May Day riots in London, the organizations which were hit were mainly American: Levi's, Starbucks, McDonalds, and the Gap.

An organization here called *Reclaim the Streets* started out many years ago as a free, peaceful carnival-protest. People would literally take over a street so that cars couldn't enter; they staged carnival parades and had music, dancing and wild drumming. But a hard-core faction emerged which is anarchist-violent, and this made things a bit tricky, because then government started coming down very hard.

But at the same time, protests make people listen. So this May Day, thousands of police in London and bigger cities were out expecting riots, and they didn't happen—because people aren't willing to get out and fight without a good reason. Because the police showed up, we got lots of news coverage of environmentalists and anti-consumerists talking on the radio and TV in anticipation of these riots. And the riots weren't necessary because everyone was *talking,* everyone was listening, everyone was thinking.

♦ *R/S: The intellectual ferment, the questioning, can have important repercussions . . . On another topic, the* **Wall Street Journal,** *a business paper that most "artists" never read, reported that the number of vegetarians in America has doubled in the past five years—*

♦ E: Wow—that's amazing! The number of vegetarians in England has gone up enormously, especially with the foot-and-mouth and Mad Cow outbreaks. People are wondering what in hell is going on. Even if it's ignorance that's making them stop eating meat; even if they think, "It's dangerous to eat meat which comes out of foot-and-mouth diseased animals" (which is ludicrous); nevertheless, they're realizing that it's dangerous to eat intensely farmed meat, anyway.

I haven't done a lot of front-line activism recently, partly because I have a ten-year-old son. If I were to lose my liberty, that would affect him. So instead, I've been working with the media, getting the word out, talking with lawyers and developers and trying to act as a *bridge,* getting ideas about Paganism and environmentalism out there in a way that is accessible and, to use a horrible word, "acceptable."

In other words, I try to couch Pagan philosophy in such a way so that I reach people. People need to feel and understand how Paganism might be relevant to them, even if they're living a non-spiritual, non-religious way of life. I want people to pause and think, "I get it. This is a beautiful tree, it's not necessary to cut it down. Let's not." Or, "Wait a minute, do we really need to buy a new car?"

In Britain, Pagans get more abuse from secular society than from any other religion. Secularism is stronger than any other religion in this country. We don't get evangelical Christians ranting at us—besides, they're not a political power here. And ranting or screaming in a "counterculture" way basically makes your message non-accessible. I try to talk to people in a way that they can understand, using their language. I'm a cat, you see—I sneak in and talk to people and suddenly they might realize that I'm talking about something which they previously had thought was much too odd to even contemplate.

At Stonehenge

♦ *R/S: That's more like real communication, rather than trying to inflict your "will" on somebody else, like a fascist—*

♦ E: Environmental anarchists can still be fascists if they impose their will. In Druidry everything is based on good relationship, and this relationship is based on good communication and respect.

♦ *R/S: Tell us how you were able to facilitate Pagan gatherings at Stonehenge, which is such a beautiful archetype—*

♦ E: That's the most extraordinary thing about Stonehenge: on a global level, it's an archetypal sacred site. Somebody in America made a Stonehenge model out of old cars—Cadillacs, I think—in New England. There's also a Stonehenge model made of concrete on the Columbia River gorge, near the Oregon/Washington border. It was built as a World War I memorial, and Pagans use it for ceremony.

I visited it, and this was very much a learning experience for me, because beforehand I was slightly cynical about it, thinking, "This is made of concrete, set on a tarmac; there can't be any magic here." We drummed for 45 minutes before we could feel any energy resonate . . . but then it was extraordinary: the power of the grief, the honoring of the dead . . . it made me wake up and stop being narrow-minded! We get rather complacent in Britain, with so much of our ancient heritage accessible. There is power in all kinds of places; **a site doesn't have to be 4,000 years old. It's about *intention*.**

Now about Stonehenge: there were gatherings there from the Sixties through the early Eighties. They kept getting bigger and bigger until they became enormous free festivals in the hippie fashion. In the mid-eighties they were closed down because of drugs and violence. Even though most of the celebrants were hippies and gentle folk having a great time dancing and drumming, these festivals also attracted "Brew Crew" types who drink strong beer out of tin cans, get stoned out of their heads and cause damage to local property. This minority included some drug dealers and violent types. A couple of people were killed at festivals, so the authorities closed down Stonehenge to the public. Also, this happened during Margaret Thatcher's reign; she stomped on anything that was fun. What made it harder for the free festival hippies was that one Druid Order still had access to the center circle of Stonehenge to do their rites, and to watch their rituals without access for everyone exacerbated the problem. It became an elitist thing.

In the early Nineties I began working actively in the Druid community. A couple contacted me who wanted to get married at Stonehenge. They had requested permission and had been told, "No, we don't allow weddings at Stonehenge." Somehow they found me and asked for help. So I phoned up English Heritage, made an appointment and sat down and spoke with the new manager, who was a woman. We chatted, like women do, about our children, about gardening, about how to lose a bit of weight, and about how I could marry this couple at Stonehenge. And she gave me permission.

It's about relationship: one-to-one relationship, real relationship. She had never met a Druid who wasn't a protesting, screaming hippie, and she didn't know that "we" existed . . . that mainstream, ordinary, gentle people existed in the Druid community, who weren't angry ex-hippies with acid flashbacks. And I became involved with the Stonehenge access committee. We started gaining access to do ritual, mostly after-hours when there weren't tourists around. Yes, we had to pay, but much less than the tourists pay. Which is only fair, really: it costs a huge amount to maintain Stonehenge and to keep it safe.

Stonehenge is a strange place. On every full moon, kids show up from the local towns, stoned out of their heads, drinking, and they jump the fences and fight the security guards. They're not Pagans, they're not anarchists, they're not *anything*. They're just drawn to the power of the place. Folks even bring hammers and try to chip off souvenirs in the middle of the night. Stonehenge does strange things to people.

So about seven years ago, when my relationship with English Heritage had grown clear and strong, we started to encourage other Druids and Pagan groups to get involved. Many were under the impression that English Heritage was intolerant of our religious tradition and had closed the temple completely to any possibility of old rituals. This was emphati-

cally not the case, and we began to work with others to make that known. Before long, various Druid orders began doing rituals there again.

Now almost anybody can get special access from English Heritage. The summer solstice, however, is still somewhat problematic. This is when you have a perfect alignment, where the sun rises over the horizon, hits the heel stone, passes over the slaughter stone, in through the trilathons, and hits the altar stone in the middle of the circle. It's extraordinary when this happens.

Some of the hippie protestors still maintain, "We should have FREE access—no money paid—for us, because we represent THE PEOPLE of Britain!" But they don't; they represent a small number of crazy hippies. Nevertheless, we conceded, "Okay, you don't actually represent the people of Britain, but we understand what you're saying." So we extended invitations to the access meeting to Druid groups, Pagan organizations, New Age groups, other religious organizations, archeological groups—you name it, if you wanted to send a representative, you could.

The access meetings became enormous, monstrous affairs where people took minutes, fought over chocolate biscuits and drank tea in a terribly English way for hours and hours, with everyone having their say and nothing getting done. But slowly things *did* get done. Four years ago we were able to announce, "If you want to attend Stonehenge on the 21st of June at dawn to see the alignment, all you have to do is ask for a ticket, and it's free." They couldn't all fit on June 21st, so the tickets were spread over three days. There were still protestors at Stonehenge who didn't want tickets at all, so there was still security.

Last year's event was an open free-for-all, with about 8,000 people attending. A local landowner offered parking, and we organized toilet facilities, cafes, and even some free food. It was pouring rain all night, and thick clouds obscured the sunrise. Some of the drum groups were extraordinary. There were moments that were wonderful, with wild drumming, trance and dance that was marvelous in the rain and the mist—and crazy, too. Yet as a Druid priestess, it was very difficult for me to watch people dancing on the stones in shoes, which destroy the lichen or scratch the stones. And the stones are not safe or solid; there's always a fear that they'll fall. Also many people were banging tent pegs into ground that is an archaeologically sensitive site. To me this is sacred ground; you don't pound tent pegs into a neolithic site. So overall, this event was difficult for me as a priestess.

By eight in the morning the sun came out from behind a thick cloud; it was still pouring rain. Everyone was gone, except for Pagans and Druids who wandered around picking up all the trash. There were needles, dog feces, bottles and cigarette butts everywhere, and candle wax on the stones. After that I delegated my role to another member of my Druidic order, because I found this experience too painful.

This year, I heard that a good time was had by those who had gone for the power of the rave—a total of 14,000 attended. There were 5 arrests—all drug dealers, but overall the event went peacefully. I'm glad that the place is open on this strange and potent day, open to anyone who can cope with the crowds. Again, for those who wish to celebrate the festival in a sacred manner with serenity, there are other days . . .

♦ *R/S: In the absence of literacy and written calendars, how did early Pagans know when the solstice would occur?*

♦ E: It wasn't the solstice they celebrated, it was mid-summer. If you watch the sunrise every day, it breaks the horizon a little further to the north east, further and further. But if on the third day it is rising in the same place, you know for sure that you've reached the climax of the solar year. The next day, sunrise starts heading south again along the horizon. The tide of the year has turned.

That's why our Druid group celebrates around the 24th or 25th, and the beautiful solar alignment at Stonehenge works just as well then. On that day last year we had majestic clear skies, the sun rose, and the alignment was exquisite. Without the crowds, there was serenity and peace. Everyone watched, and then the drums began, prayers were made for the sun, a bard started playing the harp, and beautiful, powerful, community ritual happened. But it was sacred, it was ceremony, it wasn't "people power."

Yet I think that people power is important. It's important that such an extraordinary, archetypal sacred place is open to the people—especially for kids to go and play in. We have to work out how this can happen. Just one day a year is okay, as long as the site isn't damaged through ignorance, irreverence, or even just the weight of numbers.

So that's the story, and that's the part I played. As a mainstream-appearing Pagan, I was trusted by English Heritage as well as the police. Basically, the Pagan community began being trusted as normal people, not anarchists.

The funny thing is, one day I'm out in the meadow dressed in my "wild" clothes with mud on my face, doing blood ritual and dancing naked around the fire, or the next day I'm in a pinstriped suit talking to English Heritage. *That's* understanding and communication! I think we need to be able to do both; personally, I couldn't do one without the other. Balance is my soul.

The Druid works toward **finding the balance between the wild and the wise—**which I think is wonderful. Wild and wise: that's what we hope to be. We can hold the wild without needing to tame it. That includes our own wild soul. We can scream and get naked and uninhibited and find ecstasy and trance and sexuality and music and relationship with geo-eroticism and the whole universe, while at the same time we can read and understand and explore and study and work with other people in different languages, as well as different *cultural* languages.

♦ *R/S: Let's talk about the daily life of a Pagan. Do you have altars in your house?*

♦ E: In every room. I have my most private altar, which is to the darker gods I work with, the gods of entropy, death, and the innermost parts—what I call the "womb of creation"—tucked away in my bedroom. I have my altar to the earth and sanctuary and the natural world, and altars to fertility. I have a big water altar in the bathroom, and an altar to abundance—the gods of vegetation—in the kitchen. I have altars to different gods, including a beautiful Buddha which has a gorgeous serenity. And I have a little Mayan corn god that comes from my childhood.

♦ *R/S: These different altars remind you how diverse the world's mythologies are, and also how the whole world is linked together—*

♦ E: Also, there are very few people who have a bloodline that

Rose Wedding

goes back forever in one culture and locality. Most of us are mixtures. It's important to honor all of our ancestry, wherever it comes from.

♦ *R/S: Right; in the middle of the Gobi desert, some tombs were discovered that contained bodies with red hair—*

♦ E: That's amazing.

♦ *R/S: Do you believe in reincarnation?*

♦ E: Absolutely. I have a very strong sense that we just meander through different incarnations. I think our soul creates our bodies, then undergoes the process of entropy and creativity again. But I have no need to believe in reincarnation in any one, dogmatic way. We probably all have different ideas about how it happens, just as we see the world in different ways.

♦ *R/S: What's your take on Dualism and Monotheism? Both concepts saturate our language so much that they're invisible, like the water that fish swim in—*

♦ E: And out of that comes good and bad, you and me, right and wrong—all the prejudices and intolerance and pedantry.

I think Druidry is about honoring diversity, the honoring of individuality without individualism—"individualism" being the selfishness of needing to compete at the expense of others, running with the scarcity myth, without faith, without community. So, it means honoring the individual, and individuality, and idiosyncrasy, uniqueness . . . but within the power of community.

For me, Druidry is based on finding inspiration through sacred relationship, through inspired relationship, breathing that in, absorbing that, and converting that into creativity: conscious, active, sacred creativity of living well, living life fully, living life beautifully and ecstatically, while understanding that solitary study is integral within that. I think that each relationship is unique, and so our inspiration is unique; the source of it is unique. (And each of us, because we're different, translates that inspiration into completely unique creativity.)

So in Druidry, tolerance is built in. Sometimes I say, "There is no tolerance in Druidry and Paganism, because we don't *need* tolerance." There's nothing that *requires* tolerance, because there is an honoring of individuality. Perhaps this has something to do with there being no all-compassionate deity in Paganism. There is no god or goddess who loves unconditionally, and forgives our misdoings. There is simply Nature, just Nature, life in its many forms, weaving together its various concentrations of power. Where there is an ever-loving and forgiving god, we can let go some need to be especially alert to our actions, letting go some level of personal responsibility. Paganism doesn't allow that. In that way it is a far more grounded real and mundane religious tradition than any monotheism.

So for me Druidry is, yes, a religion. Many people find that the word "religion" has too many bad associations. It seems wrapped up in monotheism, in "mono-goddery"—

♦ *R/S: —and hierarchy, too. In America, "religion" usually means a white male on an elevated podium talking down to a flock of followers sitting in linear rows of pews—*

♦ E: —back to feudalism. But, personally, I love the word "religion." To me it's about community. It's not about having to hide within yourself, or following a codified social dogma. Also, religion implies deity. For me, as a priestess of my tradition, deity is important. I'm an animist in an animistic tradition, but beyond that, I acknowledge deity, and for me religion is a quest for deity, whereas spirituality is just the honoring of spirit within ourselves and around ourselves. So the word "religion" is important to me.

♦ *R/S: The right words are very important—*

♦ E: It's important to be clear about our definitions of words. One of the constraints of our culture has been that we don't have a sufficient richness of language for the sacred. Maybe our understanding of the word "sacred" has been limited by the dominance of monotheism in the West. Whereas I think that the Japanese language has more of a built-in consideration of the sacred, as well as the beautiful.

I think that part of my role now is to enlarge the language of the sacred within the English tongue. I think that's really important: to coin words, and to wrap them up in the richness of poetry, and to give them new associations. You don't even need to create new words, although sometimes we do, of course.

To "reclaim" words sounds political—it sounds like I'm fighting something. Maybe I should say: to redefine and to reuse words, to really expand their original meanings. As we expand our language, we expand the possibilities of our thinking . . . of how we can abstract and conceive and give birth to the new.

But in terms of language and labels, to some extent I agree with you entirely. The idea of false classifying is very limiting. But at the same time, for me the word "Druid" is almost a *prayer* to my ancestors (of that tradition). As an invocation of my total potentiality "Druid" has no limits. This may sound like a contradiction in terms, but it isn't!

♦ *R/S: Let's discuss Pagan fashion, which seems to be mainly "hippie"—*

♦ E: I'm 36, so I'm a little young to have been a hippie. I suppose that the generation above, folks over 40, carry on through. There are two strands of Pagan aesthetics or Pagan fashion in Britain. There are people who tend to be more Bohemian Hippie. They wear deep, rich velvet colors and Robin Hood fashions; a lot of the men wear cloaks and *tights* (just kidding!), sporting long hair and facial hair. The other strand is more Gothic, more of the urban community than the rural community. There's a big difference in Britain between the rural and urban Pagan communities. The Gothic is slightly more romantic, darker and more punky, with more body piercing and maybe heading into the edges of the SM communities (or the pop edges of SM—obviously, there's an overlap).

All fashion or style is to some extent about belonging. I feel as if I'm an outsider myself, and perhaps always have been, living in so many different countries, cultures, and communities. I'm more into leather than hemp, but that may be a reflection of me being an international middle-class girl. I'm not sure I have that sense of needing to belong to one group, so much as seeking a way of being comfortable everywhere.

♦ *R/S: We're talking about fashion or style reinforcing hierarchy—*

♦ E: Regarding hierarchy, there seem to be hierarchies within *any* group, even though they're often unacknowledged and unstated. There are natural leaders and natural followers; people who are well-trained and educated, and people who are looking for teachers. If it's stated and overt, I don't think that's healthy. But if the issue is evaded and hidden, that's not healthy either. But I think it is natural, to some extent.

Many times, maybe it's that the teachers have been in the tradition long enough to perfect their outfits! They've had years to refine their identity within the tradition . . . to find the jewelry whose symbolism appeals to them, or the materials with gorgeous textures and pleasing shades of color. One of my great heroes is David Bowie, who's not a Pagan hero at all. But he's a hero of mine because he moves from one identity to another, while always remaining David Bowie. I think that to some extent I do that. I play the same, I'm in the same game, I'm always in the same religion, but I have different faces. I love that.

It's not about evading who you are, **it's about honoring the diversity within ourselves and being honest about that, instead of having to be one person.** One day I'll wear blue jeans and look like a normal person, and the next day I'll wear tiger-velvet jeans and big stomping boots. The next day I'll wear leather, then I'll wear my pin-striped suit, then I'll be in feathers and fur and be dancing around a fire in the wild. So I think it's about exploring who we are, and to some extent that exploration takes place in the realm of fashion, which can go to the pop culture edges.

I performed a wedding a few weeks ago, and the daughter of the bride was about fourteen. She was dressed in classic Gothic Pagan, with dark purple lipstick, black spiked hair, Cleopatra eye make-up, and masses and masses of jewelry. She was learning her way; she was finding her way into the tradition, and one of the first things she could do well was to dress the part. Maybe the next thing she would learn is how to read the Tarot cards or how to make ceremony. But her first perfection was her clothes—one step at a time.

With family

So much of life is about our creativity. Our body is our creativity, so we serve it well. We look after our body, we don't abuse it with drugs and whatever else. And our clothes, our make-up, our hair-style, is our creativity, so we do that well, too. Just as the way we talk, or the way we make our music, or whatever else we do with our creativity and our work is *important*. **We honor our gods and those who inspire us by striving to be beautiful, brilliant, creative, stylized ... you know what I mean.**

But I don't think it's healthy to make outsiders feel like outsiders if they're not "dressed the part."

♦ *R/S: Can you talk about the challenge of Pagan-raising?*

♦ E: Pagan child-raising? My ten-year-old son is sitting here playing a computer game. I'm just about to yell at him because he's done his time for the day. [laughs] **For many reasons, I home-educate my son. Some of those reasons are: I consider having children to be a personal responsibility, and I don't think it's a responsibility that we can delegate.** I can do this, partly because I have the opportunity, but I do this also out of choice. I could go out and earn money, but I don't. I choose to have very little money, because my priorities are my religion and my child.

I think that because Paganism is about individuality, to raise my son within a Pagan context or household isn't in any way to brainwash him into any monotheism. There's no monotheism, there's no "one way." So it's to honor his own individuality. Therefore I don't feel that I'm *limiting* him by raising him Pagan.

He has been in ritual with me since the day he was born. There are obviously rituals he doesn't come to: blood rites and wild crazy celebrations, but he's been falling asleep by the fireside at rituals from the beginning. I think this has taught him the power and importance of sacred space, of silence, and of individual creativity, because a lot of Druid ritual is about poetry and stories and different individuals' expression of their own creativity and their own inspiration.

I didn't send my son to school, because I don't think it honors his individuality. Even if it's secular, it's still based on monotheistic ethics—they creep in there. And some of the best schools are Church of England schools, just as in Ireland the best schools are Catholic. You can't get away from that; if you want a good school, you end up dealing with Christianity—certainly in the country; in the cities it's slightly different.

I also didn't want him to be brought up in a consumerist culture—**part of my religion is being anti-consumerist.** In a culture where he's competing with other children in order to gain favor, well—that's part of the daily "bully" culture of schooling.

♦ *R/S: Right, with status codes based in corporate-dictated consumerism, like who has the most Pokemon toys—*

♦ E: —Or the latest football T-shirts, the biggest Nikes. I didn't want that. My feeling is: when you send your child to school, you lose influence—the child spends 8 hours a day within a powerful consumerist society. Sure, he'll have to live in it eventually, but not through those tender years when he's learning values. So **I decided I would educate him at home until he had some strong Pagan values: environmentalism, non-consumerism, cooperation rather than competitiveness**...

I've found that I enjoy doing this; we have a good time and we're good friends. He'll probably go to college when he's 15 or 16, when he's an individual and strong enough, and secure enough in himself, to deal with the fact that he's not like other people. But, he's a *Trekkie*—he loves *Star Trek!* We bought a TV two years ago; we had no TV until then. And he was a *Star Trek*

Handfasting

expert within months—the whole thing.

So, it's important that he knows some popular culture, and obviously he can talk his way out of *Star Trek* arguments with any kid. So part of my responsibility is giving him latitude to develop his own strength. So I allow in popular culture which is kind of innocuous, like *Star Trek.* I mean, that program may have some underlying political kind of agenda, but he's old enough to deal with that.

Also, I'm Vegan [strict vegetarian; no dairy]—very difficult with a leather fetish! And I brought my son up to be Vegan, too—for me, that's part of education. **We don't shed blood unnecessarily.** It's not "Thou shalt not kill," it's "If you don't need to kill, you don't" (and also, "you don't get someone to kill for you"). If you *need* to, you do it—that's fine. But if you don't need to, you don't.

Those are the kinds of ethics I brought him up with, which I think are important. But again, it's about *individuality*.

♦ *R/S: What kind of Pagan books would you let him read?*

♦ E: *Harry Potter* is great. I know *Harry Potter* is a wild, mad, commercial phantasmagoria in America. In England it's so British, it's so English, so it doesn't quite have that trendy effect. It's like Arthur Ransom; it's like *Winnie the Pooh.* It's not like Walt Disney's *Winnie the Pooh* with an American accent, it's like A.A. Milne, like Christopher Robin—it's totally English. And it's about magic, and we love it. *Harry Potter* is good.

♦ *R/S: Anybody else?*

♦ E: I would NOT let him read Silver Ravenwolf—that's one of the few people I would ban from the house!

♦ *R/S: Her* **Teen Witch** *book has a big emphasis on spells—*

E: It's competition. To do that kind of spell work is to gain status. So it's about competing. It's about giving yourself witchcraft tools in order to be *better* than other people, and it's to get things for yourself. It's totally counter to the ethics of Paganism.

♦ *R/S: But on the other hand, she has sold hundreds of thousands of* **Teen Witch** *books, and at least she has exposed all those kids to a non-Christian, non-monotheist, alternative way of thinking about religion or philosophy—*

♦ E: That's true. But it would be nice if it were slightly different. I would write it so it's more based on developing the child's imagination, in the context of allowing the child to deepen their relationship with nature. And as you deepen your relationship with nature, you feel the power of joy and belonging. (That sounds a bit soft!)

I'd write it so you feel the strength and the power of who you are and where you are in time and space. The beauty of being a part—fully integrated, within where you are, so you appreciate the beauty of your environment. And from that, learn how to be creative. And understand that creativity is about freeing your soul in terms of poetry, writing, art, music, but it's also about freeing your soul in terms of exploring what you really want. And I think one of the issues she doesn't deal with, which I think is crucial, is that we are not taught to learn or to explore what we want. **One of the things that is screwing people up worse than anything else is not knowing what we want.** Over and over we go running after some object we think will appease our scarcity crisis, comfort our aloneness, get it, and then realize we don't want it.

Children and adolescents are searching for understanding—a sense of self-identity and place in society and in the world. So to guide them to explore how they can feel themselves more strongly integrated into the environment as people of Nature, and to get creative, to find out what they want, and to be creative in finding it, and making a way of doing that . . . *that's* what I would do.

♦ *R/S: How would you treat ritual? Bypass it for later?*

♦ E: No, no. Ritual is beautiful . . . because it's about *dancing your prayers*. It's about freeing your soul to express the beauty of your creativity. It's about learning how to make a relationship with the moon and the sky and the clouds . . . calling prayers. Calling prayers of honor—that's ritual. Creating a beautiful temple—that's ritual. Beautifying space. And creating temples which are utterly temporary.

So, go to the fields or the back room or wherever you need to be—your park in the city—and create something exquisite. And then, leaving just traces of energy or traces of beauty, you move on. It's about creating beautiful sacred places, exploring your creativity in words and movement, and releasing inhibition, so that even the shyest little kid or young adolescent boy finds a way of speaking honorable words, and giving respect to wisdom and beauty.

♦ *R/S: A punk parent told me, "We have a rule in our house: we don't allow any Disney videos, because they're so consumeris-*

tic and filled with subsidiary product marketing." This may be treading on the territory of censorship, but how do you keep your kids from watching those fast-edited **MTV-style** *videos that are full of sex and violence—*

♦ E: I think it's about honoring the child's ability to understand, and giving the child a big picture—giving as much information as can be understood. At the age of three, four or five you can start conceptualizing the variety of what's out there, and assigning value. However, it's only in adolescence when you really start to see the future and the past clearly, and are able to conceive of what's going to happen, and to anticipate clearly. But—just to say to a child, "You can't have this video!"—I don't think that's fair, because the child may see it everywhere around.

Take the example of *Winnie the Pooh* by A.A. Milne—the book. I can sit here with my son and read it and do all the silly voices and crawl on the floor and draw pictures. These beautiful and event-filled words evoke the rich imagination of our own creativity. I like to *read* the book because it makes us be creative within ourselves—rather than watch the video which demands much less of our imaginations.

In general, to just say No doesn't work. You need to give the whole picture, the whole story: "This is why I don't want you to buy Gap clothes. Look, these are the little children—the slaves in the factories that make Gap clothes."

♦ *R/S: On the Internet I saw an interview with an Indonesian factory worker who was getting paid 35 cents an hour to make Gap clothes—*

♦ E: Also, you can tell your child, "This is how much food you can buy for that amount of money." In other words, try to give the whole picture. It doesn't have to be gory or traumatizing.

I really think that we don't give children enough responsibility or credit. We don't respect how bright they can be, how extraordinary they can be. And then I think we should allow them to make decisions. And yes—sometimes we do bulls--- them, or manipulate them slightly out of expediency or impatience. But usually we don't have to do that, especially when they get older. You have to explain: "This is the deal. This is what I'm willing to accept. This is *why* I don't want to accept that. Do you see what I mean?"

♦ *R/S: Yes, give choices, and get children actively involved in the thinking process, the evaluating process—*

♦ E: And to do that takes time—you have to *slow down* to do that. And that's okay. Say, "All right, it's going to take us an hour to work out what video you're going to watch. So let's take an hour, because it's an important process." Now, I don't want my son exposed to [violent modern horror movies]. But a lot of cartoons *we* watched as kids contain things that are horrific. We have to be aware of *our* natural prejudices and biases.

♦ *R/S: Kids seem to learn early on the difference between "pretend" and "real" violence—*

♦ E: I think so.

♦ *R/S: Are you a single parent?*

♦ E: No. It would be really hard to be a single parent, because you don't have the options of *time*. Time is so important to me. I think we live too fast—

♦ *R/S: Right, one of the major pathological characteristics of our era is that time goes by much too quickly—*

♦ E: We run around, we drive everywhere, but . . . people complain because they can't get from one side of the country to the other soon enough. But I keep thinking, "If we were going on horseback, it would take us five days. So it's not a problem ♦♦♦

RECOMMENDED CHILDREN'S BOOKS
—by John Sulak, V. Vale

Winnie the Pooh ♦ **Animalia** ♦ All Margaret Wise Brown books ♦ **Stuart Little** ♦ Charlotte's Web ♦ **Witch Next Door** ♦ The Celts ♦ Witch Who Lost Her Shadow ♦ **Charlie and the Chocolate Factory** ♦ **Pagan Kid's Activity Book** ♦ Owl Moon ♦ **The Earthsea Trilogy** ♦ Dark Is Rising ♦ **Wise Child** ♦ The Woman Who Fell from the Sky ♦ Have Spacesuit, Will Travel ♦ **Earth, Fire, Water, Air** ♦ Winter Solstice ♦ **Brother Eagle, Sister Sky** ♦ Tree in the Ancient Forest ♦ **Coyote and the Magic Words** ♦ Missing Piece ♦ **Secret Garden** ♦ Walk to the Great Mystery ♦ **Velveteen Rabbit** ♦ Cupid and Psyche ♦ **Well-Wishers** ♦ East of the Sun and West of the Moon ♦ **Black Cauldron** ♦ **Forgotten Beasts Of Eld** ♦ Frog & Toad series by Arnold Loeb ♦ Giving Thanks: A Native American Good Morning♦ **The Patchwork Quilt** ♦ **Carrie Hepple's Garden** ♦ The Talking EarthRain Forest Secrets ♦ **Start Exploring Bulfinch's Mythology** ♦

Pete Jennings

Born in 1953, Pete Jennings recently retired as President of the U.K. Pagan Federation, publisher of *Pagan Dawn* magazine (*paganfed.org*). He's a musician with three albums to his credit, and a teacher, counselor, radio host, tour guide and author—his latest book being *Pagan Paths*. Pete's website is *www.gippeswic.demon.co.uk*. Interview by V. Vale.

♦ *RE/SEARCH: Since widespread literacy is relatively recent, and Gutenberg's movable-type printing press was only invented 550 years ago, how much written Pagan source material exists?*

♦ PETE JENNINGS: My own tradition, which is Northern, was written about by Tacitus in his work *Germania* around the first century A.D. He described the process of casting runes: Germanic tribes cutting pieces of wood from fruiting trees, marking them, casting them onto loincloths, etc. Although he didn't see this firsthand, he was regularly talking to people who did. **You can somewhat tell what Heathens did by the laws the Catholic church enacted: people mustn't dress up in animal skins or wear masks**; if they do, there's a three-year penance. Two hundred years later people are still doing this, even though the whole country was supposedly converted. So people are obviously still clinging to earlier practices.

The Prudence Jones-Nigel Pennick book, *The History of Pagan Europe,* describes some countries going from Pagan to Christian, back to Pagan, back to Christian, because of different kings coming in, or changing military alliances. They're doing whatever's expedient at the time.

I live in East Anglia, the lumpy bit on the Eastern side of England, and the last Pagan king was a man called Dredweld. He was invited to form an alliance with the king of Kent on condition he turn Christian, so he said, "All right, baptize me." Then he went home to his palace and set up a Christian altar alongside his Pagan one. He was buried at Sutton Hoo, the most spectacular Pagan ship burial in the whole of Europe. (**This fantastic Pagan burial, with masses of gold and treasure, is now in the British Museum.**) But his son turned Christian, and within a generation all Pagan worship was gone.

June 12, 2001 we celebrated the 50th anniversary of the repeal of the Witchcraft Act, 1951. I think it was repealed because of pressure from the Spiritualist church, which was very active in the Forties, particularly before World War II. Also, in 1951 nobody believed there were witches anymore! Of course, the moment they repealed it, along came Gerald B. Gardner, the father of modern witchcraft, who had already

published a fictional book on witchcraft. His books started the modern Witch movement, which then spread out. So how wrong could they be?!

♦ *R/S: What about the Gaia theory?*

♦ PJ: The author modified that theory later on, but by then it had taken on a life of its own. Basically it's **animism: everything has a life force. Personally, I can see there's a life force in people, animals and plants, but I'm not so sure about rocks.** What's more important is how you view your deities. Some people just believe in a god and a goddess, claiming that all the other gods and goddesses are just *aspects* of them. Others say, "No, there are fifty gods and fifty goddesses." Another might say, "They're all aspects of a higher force that is beyond gender, beyond understanding."

I'm a trained psychotherapist; I've spent time looking at *archetypes,* the unconscious and so on. Some people think Odin was a real person; a fantastic warrior-chief or magician. After he died, people spun ever-greater tales about him. You can see that process going on today with Princess Diana. Within weeks of her death, people were crediting her with performing miracles, which nobody had done while she was alive. At that point, a lot of people *needed* a divine feminine figure. If people read the newspapers about this a hundred years from now, they'd probably speculate about the existence of a late 20th-century Diana cult—

♦ *R/S: —and her tomb would be revered as a goddess site. England in particular has a lot of Pagan sites—*

♦ PJ: You're never far from a burial mound! There are a lot of holy wells around the country dedicated to various Pagan entities. **When Christian priests appeared they didn't stop people going to Pagan wells, they renamed them after Christian saints, using names that sounded similar**, like St. Helen instead of Ellen of the Wells. In terms of needing an archetype, this is an example of a need being fulfilled in one way or another.

There was a time that whenever a new burial mound was discovered, it was added to a master map. About fifteen years ago, the map-makers stopped doing this; at the rate they were being found, soon it would be impossible to read the map! You can find these sites in local town archives, but not on master maps anymore.

♦ *R/S: That sounds like a worthy Web site project to keep up-to-date. How many Pagans live in in the U.K.?*

♦ PJ: A Newcastle University estimate a few years ago was 100,000. At the moment, a census is being taken. We had asked for a tick box that said "Pagan." They said No, but promised they'd count all the people who wrote "Pagan" in the "Other" blank. In a year's time we might have a better idea. **The same study estimating there were 100,000 Pagans in the U.K. also reckoned there were about 80,000 Buddhists.** Interestingly, most people in the U.K. know one Buddhist, so by inference they know 1.25 Pagans—but may not know they're Pagans!

Pagans range from activists to those who are just vaguely Pagan—they don't do anything about it, and don't belong to any organization or subscribe to a magazine. The Church of England counts as members people who attend church every Sunday, and others who were baptized but never go to church.

♦ *R/S: Are there huge caravans of people in England regularly going to rock formations like Stonehenge and conducting rituals?*

♦ PJ: Stonehenge was a focus for that until people started using it for giant rock festivals. The authorities shut it down for awhile, but now Pagans have made arrangements to have access. Small groups go to local stone circles. There's only one stone circle in the whole of East Anglia, perhaps because there's no stone locally available. There are large areas that don't have stone circles or outcroppings, and areas with so many that people are blasé about them!

♦ *R/S: Wow. . . Do you have a day job?*

♦ PJ: I'm a community support worker in the area of learning disabilities. I'm a radio presenter for BBC Radio Suffolks doing a weekly folk music show. I also run ghost tours around my home town of Ipswich, telling stories about different historic places and the ghosts associated with them—people pay me good money to be frightened senseless! I also write books, and lecture.

I recently retired as President of the Pagan Federation after serving three years, which is a normal tenure. The job is very demanding; **the Pagan Federation is run almost entirely by volunteers; now it has 5,000 members in twenty countries.** It takes a day or two a week, on top of having the proverbial day job, plus having a family life and so on. I'm back to working on a local basis. I'm an honorary life member, which means I retain a place on the council, so I can stand in the corner muttering, "They didn't do that in my time. These youngsters nowadays—!"

♦ *R/S: How often do you do rituals?*

♦ PJ: Not as often as I used to. I moved away from Ipswich several years ago to be with my partner out in the country, in a small village in Essex. Consequently I don't have a local working group. Particularly at solstices, I might get together with people, either of my Northern tradition, or in mixed-traditions gatherings of Druids, Gardnerian witches, Shamans—all kinds.

Also **I run a *moot*: a monthly meeting for Pagans, which takes place in a bar, a room in back of a pub, or a person's house.** A moot can be just a general discussion group, or feature a formal talk, a conference, or even a ritual. For many people, a moot is their first contact with other Pagans.

♦ *R/S: Do you observe the full moon every month?*

♦ PJ: Occasionally I'll do a full moon or new moon or no-moon-at-all ritual, but nowadays, I'll only do a ritual if I *feel* like doing a ritual! It seems crazy to me to *have* to do one, especially if you have no goal you're working toward. If you have a local group, it's fine to have a regular time to meet, like at a full moon. But, if one were a wise woman or a cunning man several hundred years ago in England, you wouldn't wait until the next full moon to do something if somebody broke their leg and needed your attention. **I believe in doing a ritual when it's needed; not wait for some special golden hour.** This is just my personal view, and it probably will be offensive to some people.

♦ *R/S: Is the most important get-together time Samhain, or May Day?*

PJ: For me, May Day is very special. I've been involved in folk music since I was eleven years old, and to me, May Day is when my Pagan side meets my folk side. For many years, I used to dress like a bush and be the Green Man for the Morris Dancers on May Day morning. However, since I moved away into the country, I had to give this up.

On the East Coast of England, the sun comes up around 6 in the morning, so one has to get up quite early for the Morris Dancers. They usually have an arrangement with a local cafe, so when they've finished dancing they can go have a great breakfast. If May Day falls in the middle of the week, sometimes people will have their own private celebration, then get together with their friends on the weekend when it's more convenient. That's *practical* Paganism, rather than staunch Traditionalism where someone says, "We only celebrate May Day (Beltane) on the exact day."

Actually, **there are ultra-orthodox Traditionalists who celebrate May Day on the "old" day or May 11, because in 1752 there was a calendar change which cut 11 days from the calendar.** This applies to all the festival days, so there's "old" Samhain, "old" Beltane, etc. I suppose the advantage of this is: if you celebrate "old" Samhain and want to use Stonehenge as your gathering place, there will likely be fewer people wanting to use it, too.

A lot of people in the countryside aren't Pagans, but like Pagans believe you should only plant a certain crop during a waxing moon, and only harvest it during a waning moon—basically because they feel it works. Certainly there are cycles when the sap is rising and when it's not. Personally, I love to sit in a nice garden, but I *detest* gardening. I'll happily cook the

Pete Jennings, right.

Pete and Sue's Handfasting

meals or clean the house, but my partner does the gardening.

♦ *R/S: Why do you call her your partner rather than your wife?*

♦ PJ: We've been hand-fasted for eight years now, but we're not married within English law because only a Church of England wedding is recognized. (In America, a Pagan wedding is considered legal.) England doesn't even recognize Catholic or Methodist marriages; you can get married there, but a state registrar has to be present. So these churches often get their priests or ministers to qualify as state registrars.

Years ago I went to a Sikh wedding which lasts a week—at the end of which, the couple had to trundle down to the registrar's office to get their marriage recognized by the state. Pagans find this offensive; either have them all recognized, or none. There *is* institutionalized religious bias; England is officially a Christian country, and there are Christian teachings within the schools. If you're in the army, you're expected to attend church parades.

In the States it's different; I've heard of one army base where there's more Wiccans than there are Christians. I heard about a U.S. army base in Germany where a dozen Wiccans petitioned for a place to meet; by U.S. law, if a dozen or more members of a religion seek a place to meet, it has to be provided. There are still U.S. army bases here in England, you know.

♦ *R/S: U.S. imperialism yet prevails!*

♦ PJ: England doesn't have separation of Church and State; certain bishops or archbishops sit in the House of Lords. I'm not necessarily against people just because they're members of another religion, but here, it's obviously not exactly a level playing field. Perhaps there'll be a separation with the accession of Prince Charles, who is dating a divorcee, Camille Parker Bowles. Since whoever becomes the King of England automatically becomes the head of the Church of England, it's obviously "wrong" that the head of the Church of England be going out with a divorced woman, so the Church of England may protest, but—they've got a lot to lose. Charles has said that he would like to be styled as the "defender of the faiths" [plural] as opposed to the "defender of the faith." Good man!

The Church of England is the biggest institutional landowner in the U.K. But their attendance is down; they're becoming less and less relevant to the people. Terry Waite, who was held hostage in Beirut for a couple years, said after his lib-

eration [*London Times,* January 25, 2001]: "I think the Church of England is finished—dead. I think it will be dis-established and probably join with the free churches and the Methodists."

♦ *R/S: At Samhain, Pagans deal publicly with death, a taboo subject—*

♦ PJ: It is the last great taboo, isn't it? Everybody talks about sex now; it's all over TV. But death—no. Personally, I've written my own funeral service, which is quite a liberating thing to do. I've specified what music I want played. Hopefully this won't speed up the process! But at least I'll get what I want. I'd recommend this to anybody, regardless of religion. My service is in the Norse tradition, with messages for friends and loved ones.

♦ *R/S: You could make a recording of your voice to be played—*

♦ PJ: I thought of that, but that's a bit spooky. A friend who's a bit of a practical joker thought of having a fake coffin, and in the middle of the service somebody leaps out, giving one last scare to his friends! Then the real coffin appears. But . . . I've made out my will, of course, and made up a list of friends I've wanted to be notified, with all their contact information—that's very important. I used to be an insurance agent back in the Seventies, and saw all this misery that occurred when people didn't leave wills and instructions behind.

I've also officiated at funerals—conducted the whole service. In the U.K. we have an organization called Life Rights (*www.liferights.org*) who will put you in contact with somebody local to officiate at a funeral or baby-naming or whatever's required. People told me that my funeral services felt really personal—unlike professional mortuary personnel who use the same words every time and just change the names.

In England we're getting more "Green" burial sites now, where instead of erecting a tombstone you plant a tree. You use a biodegradable cardboard coffin or willow basket to bury the dead in, generally in a nice location—there's one locally that overlooks a river. Anybody who's into being more environmentally-friendly—not just Pagans—can see value in this. Plus, you don't have to pay thousands of dollars to a funeral director. Within English law you can be buried in your back yard, as long as you don't affect the water table and notify the local council. People are starting to implement any funeral service they want—which is great.

But nobody wants to die, right? Sure, I'd like to live as long as I can.

♦ *R/S: At least Pagans implement more of a cyclical time sense in their social gatherings, rather than a linear one which the Christians emphasize—at the end of which, Jesus will come!*

♦ PJ: Their Bible says that "Man will have dominion over the earth," whereas Pagans feel they have to go with the earth's flow, more, and respect the earth. You can't worship the goddess of a waterfall today, and pollute the waterfall tomorrow, can you?!

In America, as far as Pagans go, there seems to be more of a focus on celebrating Sowen (death), whereas really, Paganism is more about celebrating life. The *one* festival a year that celebrates death is the one that gets the most publicity. According to the Celtic wheel of the year there are eight festivals, and only one of them is about death. Well, Christianity has several celebrations, yet the one everyone knows is Christmas—

♦ *R/S: It's the perfect religion for a consumeristic, capital-*

istic, corporate and imperialist mind-set—

♦ PJ: Yes. The other day somebody asked me, "What's this about the Mystery Religions—is it a dark and deadly secret?" I was trying to explain the difference between a secret and a mystery. **A secret I could tell you, and then you would know. But you can't explain a mystery in words—you can only experience it.** If you look at something like the Spiral Dance cynically from the outside, or get told how it's a fantastic release and experience, you might think, "What are these people on?!" Until you do it for yourself, and experience it . . . *then* you know what it's all about. Then you realize how impossible it is to describe it effectively to somebody else. You can give them the mechanics of it, but you can't give them the feeling.

Until I was fourteen I used to take Holy Communion in the Anglican church: the bread and the wine. Now, that's a holy mystery too, and I respect that as well. You're told that this glass of wine is blood, and this funny wafer is the body of Christ, and you take it, and it's supposed to be a great religious experience. Having done that for three years, I can say that was a good religious experience—I still respect Christianity as a valid path.

♦ *R/S: Christianity offends me, with its authoritarianism and hierarchy.*

♦ PJ: The hierarchy offends me; **the bigoted attitudes of some Christians offend me, but I think they would also have offended Jesus!** All religions can be subverted, and Paganism isn't immune to that either. That doesn't mean that the core values of them are wrong. You look at most religions and they all basically say, in different ways, "Be nice to each other." Who can argue with that? (Other than a Satanist, or sadist.)

I buy into the thinking that there are many different paths to the same light; we see in different ways. I happen to think that *my* way is the way that's right for me—but it might not suit anybody else in the world. But I'm not trying to convert anyone else to my path.

Pagans are unique; we don't try to convert people, we don't try to proselytize. Ironically, we continue to grow, even though we don't try to convert people. We grow without advertising. To actually find your way into the Pagan community in the U.K. is difficult. Yet our numbers grow organically year by year, while other religions decay. The Church of England is going down the drain, but the Charismatics are growing—they seem to have a much more modern attitude, in many ways.

I have a boy of 18 and a daughter who's 19, and my daughter is the youngest person attending a certain theological college; she intends to be a pastor one day. And I'm proud of her. I'm glad she's got a spiritual life, rather than having no spiritual life at all. She belongs to a Pentecostal church, and we have some lively discussions. We disagree on a lot of issues, but that's not a problem. She comes and visits during holiday breaks; how many 19-year-olds do that?!

I've got a daughter-in-law who's Hindu (by my step-son, from my partner) and that's interesting. **Hindus are Pagans**, anyway. I met with the world secretary of the World Hindu Organization, and the second sentence he said was, "We regard ourselves as

Pagans. We have many nature gods and goddesses." Good start! One of their problems, actually, is size—their membership is in the millions. Their children are getting Westernized and losing their traditional values—that's a big concern.

How do Pagans deal with young people? That's a big problem. For years, the Pagan Federation said, "Don't deal with anybody until they're eighteen." This was more for the protection of the members, who didn't want to get attacked by the newspapers for "corrupting minors" and "abducting your daughters." But things have changed. Kids today are aware of Paganism. One article on Paganism in a certain British teenage magazine printed the Pagan Federation's address and it generated a thousand letters addressed to us! Then we had the problem: what do you do with them? Do you ignore them? Do you tell them to "Bug off!" until they're eighteen?

Some of those thousand inquiries were fairly banal: "Can you teach me how to turn my geography teacher into a frog?" But a large number were quite serious, indicating an interest in ecological issues and seeing Paganism as a way of accommodating that, which their other religions didn't.

There was a big explosion of interest in witchcraft and Paganism in the late Sixties/early Seventies by people eighteen to twenty years old. Now they have kids, and they're wondering, "What do we tell our kids now?" Do we say, "Go to bed, because Mommy and Daddy have friends coming over to celebrate this wonderful religion that you can't have any part of"?

The other thing is: If you turn youngsters away and say, "You don't want to know, until you're eighteen," well, kids today are taught to question and be inquisitive. It's not like my parents' generation, who would say, "It's right, because I told you so." So, if they don't get an answer from a responsible organization that they've approached, like the Pagan Federation or the Covenant of the Goddess in the U.S.A., they'll go elsewhere. And on the Web they can find a million Web sites and a thousand Chat sites, and we can't guarantee

Age 15

that every one of those is going to be honest and ethical. If they don't get an ethical response from us, they can end up in the clutches of people we wish they hadn't met. So I think Paganism has to grow up a bit and say, "We've got to deal with this."

The U.K. Pagan Federation has debated this issue considerably, and made some changes. Now they'll send information out to youngsters, along with a parental consent form. They're also channeling information through an organization called Minor Arcana (for teenagers, set up by teenagers, with Pagan parents involved). But this is definitely something the Pagan community has to come to grips with.

♦ *R/S: Especially with huge sales of Harry Potter and* **Teen Witch** *books to hundreds of thousands of teenagers—*

♦ PJ: —*Sabrina the Teen-Age Witch, Buffy the Vampire Slayer.* If you look at the Top Ten books children like to read, probably seven of them have magic in them, whether it's Harry Potter or C.S. Lewis's *The Lion, the Witch, and the Wardrobe,* or *Lord of the Rings.* Both *Lord of the Rings* and the first Harry Potter book are coming out as films this year, which will boost up interest in Paganism even further. We're actually going to have a mass outing from our Pagan moot to the opening night of the Harry Potter film. We'll go dressed up; it will be fun. We'll buy a block of tickets in advance.

There's a whole generation of kids now who have been brought up with ecology and environmental issues. Most of them will probably grow up to be consumers like their parents, but a percentage of them won't be throwing wrappers on the ground, or eating at McDonalds. Right now we have foot-and-mouth disease in this country—why? Because of intensive factory farming methods where animals are transported all over the country to end up in giant abattoirs (slaughterhouses).

In the old days, the local farmer would take his two local cows to the local abattoir to be slaughtered, and their meat would be sold to local people. Well, the local farmer is no more; in his place is some huge conglomerate that sells its cows to an abattoir on the other side of the country, with the meat being shipped all over the country. That's crazy. But **things will only change if financial pressure is brought to bear.** You can do it at the government level: "We'll put a tax on anything that's not environmentally friendly," or people will have to exert their buying power: "I'm not going to shop at that multinational supermarket; I'll only buy locally-produced vegetables and meat from the farmer's market instead."

♦ *R/S: In the Bay Area, Niman Ranch produces meat without antibiotics or hormones. They charge a bit more. And they're quite successful—*

♦ PJ: Not only are they doing this for ethical reasons, but they may actually find out this is more profitable. So if you can make it more profitable, people will get into it. As long as you get them to do the right thing, I suppose it doesn't really matter *why* they're doing it! [laughs]

Finally people are becoming aware of the dangers of G.M. [genetically-modified] foods. **A smaller supermarket near here posts a sign, "All food sold here is G.M. free." And their profits are up!** They probably did this purely for the profit motive, but it worked; apparently they're giving the public what it wants.

As Pagans are such a small group, it's difficult to change things by ourselves. But if we can influence larger organizations and movements, that's the way to do it. I always encourage Pagans not to set up separate environmental organizations, but to join already-existing ones like Greenpeace or Friends of the Earth, and work within them, because that stands a better chance of success, and they don't have to reinvent the wheel.

♦ *R/S: You mentioned a book,* **A History of Pagan Europe**—

♦ PJ: —by Prudence Jones and Nigel Pennick, published by Routledge. Prudence Jones took over again as President of the Pagan Federation, although she was its President many years ago. It's a well-referenced academic work. I'd recommend that one and Ronald Hutton's *The Triumph of the Moon: A History of Modern Pagan Witchcraft.* It gives the in's and out's of it. He's a professor of history at the University of Bristol. I'd recommend anything by Ronald Hutton, although I don't always agree with him. His *The Stations of the Sun: A History of the Ritual Year in Britain,* is an excellent read as well.

Basically, **Ronald Hutton has debunked a lot of Pagan myths and shot the sacred cows. This was needed.**

♦ *R/S: You seem to have a tolerant, eclectic attitude—*

♦ PJ: Oh, no—when I ran the Pagan Federation I was a benevolent despot; that seemed the most effective way to run an organization. Remember, I'm Northern Tradition. When I run a Pagan conference, it's easier if one person makes the decisions, as long as they know how to delegate. Yes, listen to advice and consult with people, but at the end of the day, have one person be responsible for decision-making. I have to admit that I was a sales manager for Coca-Cola for 14 years; in 1986 I was the U.K. Rep of the Year!

Pete as the Green Man, wearing a Green Man mask

♦ *R/S: You can take what you learned from branding and marketing and apply it to furthering Paganism—*

♦ PJ: Oh, yes! Also, I've spent nearly twenty years working in radio stations, ten years writing newspaper columns freelance, plus management training, plus five years of psychological training . . . it's very nice training for a media officer in learning how to manipulate the press.

In the U.K., the press is not as negative toward Paganism as they used to be. One tabloid, the *News of the World,* is the equivalent of the U.S. *National Enquirer.* But 95% of the U.K. press is either positive or neutral toward Paganism. That's the result of thirty years of campaigning by people like the Pagan Federation…challenging them every time they get it wrong, patting them on the head every time they get it right, getting to know the right people, and feeding them information so they've got good, positive material before they write up a story. Nowadays, somebody on a newspaper can call the Pagan Federation media phone number: "You want a Druid who lives in Cornwall? Give us five minutes and we'll find you one."

I went around the country training Pagans in media techniques, even taking them into radio studios and training them. If you're going to deal with the media, you've got to do it professionally. My hobby-horse with the Pagan Federation is my insistence that "Yes, we have to be professional." We might be an organization of all volunteers, but that doesn't mean we can't work professionally.

When Paganism was a cozy tea-club with twenty people who all knew each other, you could run things by the seat of your pants. If the magazine gets published 3 weeks late, well—the kid was sick. If a conference starts an hour late, well, it's okay because we all know each other. But the Pagan Federation's magazine, *Pagan Dawn,* goes out to 10,000 people now. People are paying good money for it, and they expect professional standards. If they write you a letter, they expect a response in a couple of weeks, not a couple of years—which used to happen in the old days.

For the first time in its near-thirty year history, the Pagan Foundation recently took on a part-time paid administrator. A very important stage. Nobody had the spare time to do that amount of administration—nobody in their right mind would take on that job as a volunteer, and would you want somebody who wasn't in their right mind?! So they had to bite the bullet and do it. Regarding magazine distribution, we used to have a dozen people sitting at a table stuffing magazines into envelopes, but when you're printing 7,000 *Pagan Dawns* you can't do that anymore—not if you're getting them out on time.

Basically, one of my goals as President was to professionalize the Pagan Federation . . . without alienating the grass-roots members. The Pagan Federation still doesn't have an office; it's run from people's kitchen tables. In one group I met, there's a guy who, every three months, addresses and sends out about 200 newsletters to local members. They never have to ask him; he always turns up and does it. One day I said, "Thank you very much; you've done a really good job." He seemed a bit uncouth; he said, "*Look.* I don't read much. I can't do all this ritual *malarkey.* But this is my way of serving my goddess, and don't you bleedin' thank me for it, mister. Don't you patronize me." I apologized to him, because what he said was completely right, and in no uncertain terms.

♦ *R/S: You've been wrestling with problems like the ethics of growth—*

♦ PJ: Well, if you get a large group of people coming in who are all used to having a hierarchical leader, they'll expect one in Paganism, too. Fortunately, I'm not wrestling with these problems so much anymore—I'm retired. Actually, I do get consulted. It's terrible to be consulted as an "elder statesman" when you're only 47. I got approached to join another Pagan group as an elder and I said, "I wouldn't join an organization that had me as an elder!" Similarly with the idea of "honorable membership"—I thought there should be such a thing as dishonorable members . . .

♦ *R/S: Give your thoughts on Pagan aesthetics or fashion—*

♦ PJ: There was a period within U.K. Paganism that was dominated by what we called "cloak-flappers": everyone was turning up in a cloak, trying to look dark and mysterious, wearing 18-inch ankhs or pentagrams. Nowadays people like that tend to be sniggered at. You still get one or two, of course.

A few centuries ago, there was a time when if you were suspected of being a witch, people would chuck you into the village pond. If you sank, you were innocent, and if you floated, you were a witch. Either way you died, of course. If people did this today, they would have to reverse this, because most Pagans, including myself sadly, wear so much jewelry they'd sink anyway! Personally, my hands are covered with rings.

Apart from fashions in clothes, there are fashions in *paths.* If you read the Pagan magazines, you see that one year it's shamanism, the next year it's Native American sweat-lodges, and the next year it's Northern tradition. Things do seem to happen in trends: "What's the flavor of the month?" "Chaos magic." Conference billings telling who's talking about what can indicate what the latest trend is, although sometimes it's just somebody flogging their latest book. I would like to think that eventually people see through the more banal books, like *One Hundred Spells for Fourteen-Year-Old Girls,* although . . .

Actually, banal books have their purpose. When I was about twelve or thirteen, I read all the Dennis Wheatley occult novels—unmitigated crap! At the time I was reading anything that was considered horror, but then I started reading more "serious" books. A lot of people are coming to Paganism because they saw films like *The Craft* or the *Blair Witch Project.* Perhaps one in ten delves a little deeper and then actually gets full-swing into it, even though the original attraction was banal in itself.

The same thing happened with the blues. Most people will just listen to Eric Clapton, but one in ten will notice when he says, "I got this song off an old Leadbelly record," and go listen to some of Leadbelly's records, or Robert Johnson's. So I think banal things have their value.

♦ *R/S: Have you ever investigated Egyptian polytheism?*

♦ PJ: The one good thing about the Egyptian path is: it's got huge historical resources. You can read out complete invocations from their *Book of the Dead.* You can find a translated Egyptian text and actually do a complete ceremony, pretty close to exactly as how they had done it, saying exactly the same words—which is really *something,* compared to most Pagan paths where so much has been lost. You could find an Egyptology group if you started looking.

♦ *R/S: What are some other advantages of Paganism?*

♦ PJ: Pagans don't have the concept of sin, whereas most other religions speak about that. Pagans have right and wrong, but it's very different. Take a couple going to bed together before they're married—that's against quite a few religions. Whereas Pagans would say that's fine. As long as neither is being coerced into it or being abused, there won't be an unwanted baby, and they both respect each other—it's okay. Which means: if you haven't got that sense of guilt, then you're free to enjoy yourself much more.

Have you ever been in a British tea shop with lots of cream cakes? Very often you see these oversize ladies sitting there, going, "We'll have a cream cake, shall we?" Part of their enjoyment derives from the feeling they're doing something naughty. If I waved a magic wand and said, "It's *okay* to enjoy cream cakes, as long as you don't indulge in it 24/7," would they actually enjoy them as much? Without that sense of naughtiness, I think not.

♦ *R/S: It was Slavoj Zizek who pointed out that any law actually depends upon its transgression, and if there were*

The Bunkas, Pete Jenning's folk-rock band

no more transgressions, it would disintegrate.

♦ PJ: Many Pagans seem to have developed the quality of playfulness, a childlike quality of wonder: "Doesn't that tree look lovely with the raindrops sparkling on it?" You don't have to be a Pagan to appreciate things like that.

Recently I went to the top of a hillside with some friends to have a little ritual. We joined hands, sang a little song, had a little prayer and that was about the extent of it—it was nothing grand or intense. At the end, somebody, instead of walking down the hill, rolled. And before we knew it, three-quarters of us were rolling down the hill, laughing and giggling, which is what children would do. Some people who weren't Pagans were walking up the hill looking up at us like, "The inmates have escaped—shall we ring for the men in the white coats to take them away?"

But that rolling down the hill afterwards was as much a religious celebration as the holding hands and the chanting on the hilltop. It had that feeling of freedom, of enjoying the hillside, the fact that we're all free to do these things and who the hell cares? I don't care if people do think I'm a bloody idiot; I'm going down to roll down this hill and get grass stains on my clothes anyway.

♦ *R/S: There is a soft taboo against rolling down a hill like that—*

♦ PJ: Right—enjoying your body bumping against the earth. We can supply profound meanings about being in contact with the earth afterwards! We're putting ourselves in an altered state of consciousness; we probably *are* dizzy at the bottom of the hill. But that's not what it was about originally; it was, "Let's have fun; let's roll down the hill instead of walking down as staid, sensible adults would do."

♦ *R/S: Another key fact is: you're among people with whom you feel free to do that. Johan Huizinga's* **Homo Ludens** *argues the importance of "play" as a crucial dimension of what constitutes being "human"—*

♦ PJ: Very often you'll see a young couple in the first flush of love and think, "What is it that makes them glow—apart from having very good sex?" It's very often the playfulness—like, they'll have a pillow fight or tickle each other. This doesn't necessarily always lead to a sex act; maybe it's, "I'm going to hide your book so you'll talk to me!" Unfortunately, people lose that over time, and relationships go stale and so on.

♦ *R/S: We have to work to maintain that conscious element of play in our relationships—*

♦ PJ: Or spontaneity: "When would you like me to be spontaneous?" [laughs] Once, when I hadn't been with my partner very long, I said, "You know, I really feel like flying a kite!" She said, "You're mad!" But she humored me and we went and did it.

♦ *R/S: At a Reclaiming ritual, everyone was asked to get down on all fours and go "Meow! Meow!" at each other. I just couldn't do this, so I withdrew from the sacred circle. But everyone else seemed to be enjoying themselves—*

♦ PJ: It's good to join in, but it's also good if you don't join in, because if you're doing it even though you're uncomfortable, you're going to bugger up the feeling of the thing and put negativity into it. At a Pagan event, I'd say that nobody is going to reprimand you for not joining in—

♦ *R/S: I didn't feel any censorship. But we all have our "personal space" and confrontation issues to deal with.*

♦ PJ: Judging from what I see in magazines, American Paganism seems a lot more politically correct than British Paganism. Like, "Use fruit juice instead of alcohol in the wine cup, in case somebody present is *in recovery*." Whereas in England that wouldn't be a consideration; there would be a cup of wine there. People feel, "If you don't want to drink it, you don't have to—just pass it along."

My own Northern Tradition has never been very politically correct, anyway. It involves meat-eating, for a start, and drinking mead or alcohol . . . There's a backlash against political correctness, of course. Like many things, p.c.-ness started with good intentions, and made people think twice about what they say and imply. Inevitably, something like that gets hijacked by extremists and made into a laughingstock—just as with feminism, when people began rewriting the language into "herstory"—

♦ *R/S: —and all the other neologisms that make you wince, like Ebonics. Using "she" everywhere, instead of "he."*

PJ: Pagans spend quite a lot of time analyzing words: breaking them down by their roots. People start wondering where words come from; they get curious about the etymology of words. Pagans often get into history because they want to know where their tradition comes from. Sometimes they join re-enactment societies or Renaissance Faires, which never caught on in the U.K.

♦ *R/S: Socially, Paganism seems to offer the most freedom with the least authoritarianism—*

♦ PJ: *Hmmm.* It does give me responsibilities. I enjoy organizing events, writing, traveling about and doing lectures. But you've got a responsibility to not let people down during any of those.

♦ *R/S: Do you have altars all over your house?*

♦ PJ: Yes, my partner and I have three. The things on an altar function as visual reminders of who I am and what I'm doing and so on. Sometimes I use them to conduct a full ritual. Other times I'll cart an altar out to the garden and give the neighbors a thrill. Fortunately, I have understanding neighbors—and high fences.

I think some people who get attracted to Paganism because they've read about the "nude rites" must get awfully disappointed when they discover what it's really all about. We don't have sacred groves with sacred prostitutes; that didn't happen in England—maybe around Greece and Rome . . . *whoops*—lost another fifty converts there!

Very few groups practice ritual skyclad (unclothed); they tend to be very few and far between. And the few groups who are skyclad tend to be very prim and proper, just like at a nudist camp—because they feel they have to prove themselves. Consequently, they're very asexual or nonsexual. Being skyclad is also not part of my Northern tradition, besides.

The problem is: outside of Paganism, people equate nudity with sex. It's hard to persuade journalists or reporters that people getting together without clothes aren't being on top of each other and fornicating. In the early days, nudist camps were accused of immorality: "If they're naked, they must all be bonking away." Today, they're laughed at; nobody accuses them of anything. Or they're accepted as something quaint—out of the past—and slightly eccentric.

I wonder if Pagans would have had much of a skyclad tradition if Gerald Gardner hadn't been a nudist himself. He belonged to a nudist club, and in fact had a witches' cottage moved next door to the club where he was a member, for handy access. When he was in Malaya, he studied the local natives and wrote a standard book on the Kris, a curvy-bladed knife. Now, how much of this influenced his use of the knife within ritual? Because it's alleged that traditional, hereditary groups didn't use any metal within a ritual space—they might have had a wooden or stone knife. So, perhaps his academic interest in knives led us down the path of people waving knives and swords about!

Take something like circle dancing—both the early Christians as well as Pagan religions used it. As the church evolved, it discarded the dance; particularly when it built structures with pews in them—you couldn't do circle dancing anymore. It's funny, the Charismatic Christians have taken the seats out of the churches and do circle dancing again—it's now gone full circle, literally.

Take something like Christmas carols. The word "carol" means to dance, and the objective used to be to dance and sing at the same time. If you look at carols, some of them aren't terribly Christian in their content, especially a carol like "The Holly and the Ivy." Try working out which are the Christian bits and which are the Pagan ones!

Another word used for caroling is to wassail, and that word comes from Anglo-Saxon and Norse tradition. It used to mean "Be hale" or "Be healthy." You'd pass a wassail cup around the room, drink some of its contents, toast the rest of the room "Wassail!" and pass the cup along. This is another example of Paganism taking you along the etymology trail.

♦ *R/S: How can somebody benefit from investigating Paganism?*

♦ PJ: I do class Paganism as a religion, I don't go along with the thinking that it's a Craft or a spiritual path, not a religion. I get out of Paganism a sense of belonging to my landscape, my tribe, my family, my surroundings, and so on. It gives me a sense of purpose, and provides an ethical framework to live within. It gives me joy and it gives me tears. It gives me a lot of questions all the time, which means you live far nearer to the edge.

I've gone on record as saying that I love my path, but I wouldn't wish it on anybody! It might be terrible for some people. It's hard being a Pagan. It constantly challenges your way of living—and if it doesn't, you'd better worry! If you belong to any religion that doesn't challenge you, then what's the point? ♦ ♦ ♦

A DIABETIC'S ADVICE

I have a sugar problem. How do you know if you're diabetic? Ask two questions: Do you get thirsty a lot? Do you get tired a lot? If you answer Yes to both of those, get your urine tested. Or, if you occasionally get a dizzy spell and you haven't been drinking, then … Or, if you feel slightly drunk but you're not, particularly if it's coming up meal time and you're a bit late. If you know anyone who's diabetic, just ask for one of their test kits: pee on it and see what color it turns. Thus you avoid paying a hefty medical bill. With that happy thought, I leave you to stuff your face with dessert!

Handfast

RECOMMENDED BOOKS

Isaac Bonewits' *Real Magic*. Probably had the most influence on my thinking. I read that twenty years ago and I still go back and re-read it. I look at his Web site, *neopagan.net*, regularly. He's an original thinker.

Nigel Pennick and Prudence Jones—anything.

Vivian Crowley—anything.

Jan Fries' *HellRuna: a Manual of Rune Magick*, & *Visual Magic: A Manual of Freestyle Shamanism*—those are two amazing books.

Freya Aswynn's *Leaves of Yggdrasil: A Synthesis of Runes, Gods, Magic, Feminine Mysteries, and Folklore*. Northern tradition, and very outspoken.

Ronald Hutton—anything. He's *Tops* for me.

Golden Dawn books—anything.

Doreen Valiente's *An ABC of Witchcraft, Past and Present; Charge of the Goddess*.

Philip Heselton: *Wiccan Roots: Gerald Gardner and the Modern Witchcraft Revival*. Well-referenced; a lot of Pagan writing isn't.

Margaret Murray's *The Witch-Cults of Europe*—faulty, heavily discredited. She only published the bits of research which supported her theory, and censored all the references that disagreed with it. That book had fairly huge circulation and was widely quoted by academics for years. She had academic credentials, which most authors didn't. She also wrote the foreword for one of Gerald Gardner's books, which gave *him* credibility. And she almost single-handedly destroyed the English Folklore Society. She was well-respected until people started carefully investigating her sources. But she still has her devotees, because many people read one book and don't read any more.

James Frazer's *Golden Bough*. He provides basic information about practices and beliefs from around the world.

Don Frew & Anna Korn

A nna Korn has an M.A. in Biology and works as a research laboratory scientist for the U.S.D.A. Don Frew has traveled around the world researching and documenting the origins and history of the Craft. They are both Elders in several Craft traditions, and currently are Priestess and Priest of a Gardnerian coven in Berkeley, California. Interview with Anna Korn and Don Frew by John Sulak; follow-up interview by V. Vale.

♦ *RE/SEARCH: Why did you choose Gardnerian Wicca?*
♦ ANNA KORN: I had been involved in a number of different traditions, including some fairly eclectic groups. But I've always been interested in history, and the Gardnerian tradition has a body of lore that wasn't made up on the spur of the moment—not to say that's not a viable option, too.
♦ DON FREW: I was a religious studies and anthropology major. I wanted a sense of history, and felt that the Gardnerian tradition had depth. So I connected with a local teacher of Gardnerian Craft and got initiated.
♦ AK: The Gardnerian mode of operating is more ritually or textually defined and often more ceremonially elaborate than what many other traditions do, but like other traditions of Witchcraft, we call the powers of the quarters, we draw a circle, we consecrate the elements, we invoke the God and Goddess, perhaps do some magical work, and have a sacred feast.
♦ DF: If you didn't know the history, you might think that Gardnerian rituals are similar to those of other groups. However, our texts and ritual actions are older than those of most groups, and have many layers of meaning built into them. On the one hand, some people would say that's restrictive. On the other hand, tradition gives a certain sense of comfort. In some groups, you just go into a quarter and call whatever comes from your heart... there's spontaneity built into the structure—
♦ AK: —and sometimes it's wonderful and sometimes it's lame! [laughs]
♦ DF: What feels different is the sense of history permeating our script; I think our ritual feels more grounded. I like to think we are tapping into something that is more deeply rooted. I can be in a circle with a Gardnerian from another country and we can work together the first time we meet. I met a Nigerian who belonged to a coven Gerald had founded many years ago in Africa. We compared notes, and found much in common.

Also, we can trace by lineage. **If I meet another Gardnerian, we can figure out how we're connected: "Oh, my great-great-grand initiator was your grand initiator." There's a sense of being part of an extended international family.**

♦ *R/S: What are the different degrees of initiation?*
♦ DF: Gardnerian Craft has three degrees of initiation.
♦ AK: In the old days, before the huge growth of the Pagan movement, people were initiated and only afterward began their training in a Gardnerian circle.
♦ DF: You couldn't see a circle, you couldn't see the tools, you couldn't do anything until you were initiated. The first ritual you attended was your initiation—which involved a considerable leap of trust, I would imagine—
♦ AK: —on both sides. Nowadays, most circles maintain an outer court for a year and a day. During that period, we use teachings modeled on the inner court circle, but without the secret words and gestures. This way people can become familiar with the basics of being in a circle.
♦ DF: A First Degree is a member of the group who knows how to do all the various things to participate in the group. A Second Degree is an elder of the coven—you can rely on them to take over the circle if you need them to. They can teach—
♦ AK: —in fact, they're expected to.
♦ DF: The Third Degree is the coven leader.
♦ AK: In the Bay Area, various leaders of Gardnerian covens are invited to attend quarterly Elders' gatherings to discuss topics of common interest—
♦ DF: —ranging from coven dynamics to the comparative study of texts.
♦ AK: Sometimes we compare curricula for training people. What has become popular lately in the Witchcraft community at large is what Starhawk calls "ensemble Witchcraft." People meet in a class, and form magical bonds, do workings together, perhaps even travel together to a festival or other gathering. But this isn't quite the same as a coven, which is very tight-knit.

There are also thousands of "solitaries" out there. Many people work as "floaters"—sometimes they're solitary, other times they get together with a few friends to discuss topics of mutual interest or attend a coven ceremony.
♦ DF: Sometimes we open up our Sabbats to solitaries or members of other covens.
♦ AK: Some Gardnerian covens are more reclusive and secretive

1998 Don Frew and Anna Korn at Temple of Venus, Sumatar Harabesi, Turkey

than we are. However, our lunar rites are just for the coven members.

♦ *R/S: Contrast the Gardnerian ritual with other groups' rituals—*

♦ AK: Our circle casting and calling the quarters is the same each time. Some people say, "That sounds boring—I like variety; I don't want to do the same circle twice." Those people aren't likely to be happy in a Gardnerian setting. But I find that if you tap into the same source over and over, you get a hypnotic sense of being opened up and getting to a deeper level. For coven work, I think this is important, because you're melding the energies of a specific group of people. If you do something different each time, you won't achieve the same focus.

When I was studying **in my first Gardnerian circle we had a rule: if we did a particular magical working, we didn't discuss or critique it for at least 24 hours, because that tends to sap the energy that's been put into the spell.** Now some of the more eclectic circles are starting to adopt rules like that. Also, when eclectic groups hit a snag and some difference arises, sometimes the entire group just explodes or dissolves. Groups that have a more traditional basis, with laws or practices that have been handed down, tend to last longer. Another consideration: Gardnerian groups tend to be run by a married or committed couple, and that can provide a more stable basis.

♦ *R/S: Explain how a group is "run" by a couple?*

♦ DF: When I talk about the Third Degrees, or Coven leaders— yes, Anna and I are the High Priest and Priestess of a coven, but our coven operates basically by consensus. We all get together and make decisions together. We don't dictate. So while we have traditional forms, in practice operations are a lot more egalitarian—

♦ AK: —although some covens that call themselves Gardnerian have a more hierarchical structure.

♦ *R/S: Do Gardnerians do ritual skyclad [naked]?*

♦ DF: In America, people assume that naked *equals* sex. But if they've ever stayed at a nudist colony, they would know this is definitely not the case. Seeing somebody stark naked does not necessarily make them more attractive. [laughs] But to answer your question, most Gardnerians work that way.

♦ *R/S: What about scourging? [ritual flogging]*

♦ AK: Scourging is a traditional part of the Gardnerian tradition, for both trance induction and purification.

♦ DF: The Gardnerian tradition is secret, initiatory, and imparted on different levels. All the tools and ritual steps have symbolic meaning. In some cases additional symbolic meanings are revealed over time. The scourge is one of the most symbol-laden of the tools and is sometimes associated with the Goddess Hekate. I would hasten to point out that ritual scourging is a symbolic act and is never intended to cause pain.

♦ *R/S: Can you talk about the Great Rite?*

♦ DF: Many Craft practices—not just Gardnerian—hold the idea that all aspects of life are sacred, and many are sacramental. A sexual relationship between committed people who have a loving relationship should be considered a sacrament, and made holy. The concept of the Great Rite—sacred sex between the God and the Goddess—is a pretty common idea.

♦ AK: These type of questions come up a lot, along with the

idea that Gardnerians are humorless and very hide-bound.

♦ DF: We're the butt of a lot of jokes, unfortunately.

♦ *R/S: Describe the original members of Gardner's coven—*

♦ AK: There were quite a few Bohemian, forward-thinking people, many of whom later emigrated—which helped spread the Craft. Some were ex-Colonials who had lived in places like Southeast Asia and Africa, where they had seen practices outside the canon of Christianity. Also, Gardner's base of operations, before he became a public Witch and purchased the Museum, was a nudist colony. So many members of his coven were already predisposed towards nudism.

♦ DF: Regarding the issue of the "historical validity" of our coven, a lot of people used to believe that Craft ritual practices descended in an unbroken chain from prehistoric days. Then the pendulum swung and Witches took the attitude of "Okay, we made it all up twenty years ago, and we're still making it up. But it doesn't matter—everything's fine." Now the pendulum is swinging back to the center and we're trying to find the middle ground. A popular concept of antiquity of the Craft involves the romantic idea of an ancient Celtic group, often women, being persecuted by the Inquisition. But that's basically a fantasy, and lacks documentation.

When many people talk about the history of the Craft, their attitude is: "Why do all this speculating, when we have so little to work with?" But with Gardnerian Craft that's just not true. Between the different versions of the Books of Shadows, Gardner's personal magical notebooks, and the correspondence between people involved in the middle of the century, we've got thousands of pages of documents. We'll probably spend most of our lives studying this material. If anything, there's so much that it's hard to wade through. People have this idea that the Craft is just about speculating in the wind. But it's exactly the opposite.

♦ *R/S: Describe Pagan life in Berkeley—*

♦ DF: There aren't just different Craft traditions in Berkeley, but also different types of Neopaganism. When people are not just exposed to, but have to live with, many different traditions every day, this fosters tolerance. People here are often initiates of more than one group. Someone might go to a Santeria bembé one night, a Gardnerian coven the next, and a Druid ceremony the night after. Our community here has been relatively peaceful for a long time.

In many other parts of the country, where there are only a few manifestations of Paganism, things can get more factional. You're more likely to get a situation where you're either in this group or that group, and people from different groups don't talk to each other. Plurality has really helped us be an open community here in Northern California.

♦ AK: In other parts of the country there tends to be a bit more suspicion. People may not be familiar with another group's practices—that can give rise to rumors or factionalism.

♦ DF: **Here, anybody who gets involved in the community learns, "Paganism is incredibly diverse."** That encourages a lot more positive interaction. Also, in Berkeley we don't have to be as closeted as in other parts of the country where, if you're exposed as a Witch, you could lose your job, custody of your children, and have rocks thrown through your windows. In that kind of atmosphere people are more closed and suspicious, because it's a necessary survival practice.

♦ *R/S: What are Pagan festivals in the Midwest like?*

♦ AK: I've observed that in the Midwest, people have a greater need for Weather Working. Here, where we have little summer rainfall to interrupt our festivals, people are generally less practiced and not as skillful. Also, since we are prone to droughts, we have ethical quandaries about whether it's right to change the weather. [laughs] In the Midwest, Pagans frequently divert storm fronts away from a festival site. Also, most Midwesterners are more integrated into the mainstream during their everyday life—consequently, they really cut loose when they come to a festival. People on the West Coast tend to be in a more alternate lifestyle all the time, so they don't seem to change as much or get as wild at festivals.

♦ DF: We went to a Pagan festival in Michigan. A friend picked us up at the Chicago airport; he had just gotten off work and was wearing a business suit. He drove us directly to the festival. A half hour later he was stark naked, painted blue, and covered with gold glitter! It was an incredible shift from a very straight, normal, mundane, everyday life.

♦ AK: A lot of anthropologists and sociologists who have been studying the Craft appear to think that festival culture is the entirety of Paganism.

♦ DF: There has been a tendency for outsiders to write about Pagans very superficially. If you're coming in from the outside, you only make contact with the most surface aspects. Sometimes journalists miss the point: in one interview I pointed out how refreshing it was that Paganism had both female and male clergy in positions of spiritual leadership, and that not many groups offered that. This got reduced in the published article to "Frew joined the Craft to meet dominant women." [laughs]

We're going through a demographic shift. The Craft started in the U.S. mostly with people either coming from England or learning from people from England, or reading books by people from England and trying to replicate the practices described. The basis was British Traditional style. Gradually, with the rise of the feminist movement and political activism, groups began forming that were eclectic.

Now, with the Internet making information so available, hundreds of people who may never have had personal contact with another Witch are self-identifying as Witches.

♦ AK: They've learned everything they know about Witches or Pagans from a few books and/or the Internet. But there's no way that can make up for personal contact and the kind of training you can get from a dedicated, focused group.

♦ DF: Eventually there's a shakeout: people move on to something else, or deepen their own practice and make contact with others. **If you've seen the movie The Craft or watched the TV show Charmed, you'd get the impression that Paganism is basically for teenagers.** While there are vast numbers of teenage Pagans now, there are thousands of us who have been in it for decades. But that's not the impression the public gets.

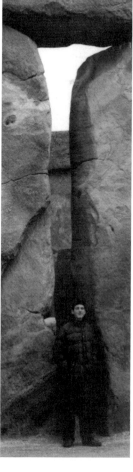

The Craft has grown over time in jumps linked to popular culture. The first one in America was sparked by the environmental movement. Perhaps the next jump was caused by the Joseph Campbell specials with Bill Moyers, then the publication of *Mists of Avalon,* followed by the collapse of the New Age movement. Each time, the number of Witches in the US nearly doubled. The current jump has been sparked by pop culture like the movie *The Craft* and the TV show *Charmed.* And each time, people say, "This book/show/movie is interesting, but what do I do now?" Basically, people get exposed to the idea that "I can have a personal spiritual experience that doesn't take place in a church."

♦ AK: If people get to know any Witches personally, even if they do not get involved in the Craft, they might think, "Well, it wasn't my path, but they're nice people." So myths associating Witches with evil get shattered.

I think that the experience of being a seeker, and testing notions you read against your own personal standards of truth, is a really important stage in life. Unfortunately, there aren't enough teachers or advisors for the numbers of seekers.

Teenagers have a very special problem. For very real legal reasons, most Pagan groups won't offer them much support—especially if the kids' parents are of some other religion and are opposed to Paganism.

♦ DF: The Covenant of the Goddess (CoG) website has my review of the movie *The Craft.* I said that the biggest problem with the movie, which I thought was relatively harmless, was that now thousands of teenagers will want to get involved in Paganism. And I used to get emails from teenagers complaining, "What's wrong with that?" I would reply, "I understand—I was a teenager myself when I became a Pagan. But it's a very serious legal problem." Especially since most of the teenagers emailing me explicitly say, "My parents don't know about this; I have to hide it from them." Or, "My parents don't approve." That means I run the risk of being charged with "contributing to the delinquency of a minor." So we usually take a hands-off approach with minors—unless we have the consent of the parents.

♦ AK: Most Pagan clergy recognize there is a need out there, but in many ways their hands are tied.

♦ *R/S: Books can be a teenager's first introduction to Paganism—*

♦ AK: And **a lot of "Witchcraft" books contain spells that nowadays would be considered at least borderline unethical: attempting to interfere in someone else's free will.** Not just with love spells, but attempting to change the way people feel about you, or forcing someone to give you a job—whatever. I think most people have to learn the hard way how spells work, and they learn this by having a spell backfire. Then they realize, "So *that's* why we're not supposed to interfere in somebody else's free will!" [laughs]

♦ DF: People need to know there are groups they can contact, so they don't get their whole impression of the Craft from a superficial book. If they read something and think, "I want to know more"— that's great. But I'm afraid people will look at one

1975 Don age 15 at Stonehenge, England; opposite: Anna Korn

of the many superficial, popular books on Craft flooding the market these days and think, "Is that all there is? What a crock!" Then they won't investigate further.

♦ **R/S: *You're involved in interfaith community work—***
♦ DF: I've served nine terms on the National Board of the Covenant of the Goddess in the last 16 years—five of those as National Public Information Officer. As part of that job, I first attended the Berkeley Area Interfaith Council in 1985. I walked in the door and found myself facing a divided room—Christians, Jews, Buddhists, etc. on one side; Scientologists, Hari Krishnas, etc. on the other. Thanks to the previous involvement of another CoG member, Glenn Turner, years before, I was immediately welcomed like a long-lost friend into the more "conventional" side of the room with pleasant sounds of "How's Glenn?" and "It's been so long—good to have your group back with us." In many other parts of the country, a Witch might not have been so welcome.

However, the story of Pagans in interfaith starts long before that. In 1893 the World's Fair in Chicago sponsored "The Parliament of the World's Religions," where representatives from the world's religions got together and talked. At the time, Native Americans weren't taken seriously as a religious group and weren't invited. There was also an ulterior motive at work; many of the Christian groups thought, "If we get all these groups together in one place, then the obvious superiority of Christianity will be demonstrated, and our work in evangelizing the world will be that much easier."

Lo and behold, the 1893 Parliament marked the entry point of Hinduism and Buddhism into the United States—most American interest in these Eastern religions dates from that time. Shortly thereafter, the National Council of Churches formed in response. As 1993, the hundred year anniversary, loomed, people organized the second Parliament of the World's Religions, which took place in 1993, again in Chicago. There were 7,500 people representing almost every religion on Earth.

The event lasted nine days in one big hotel. The first address was given by Dr. Gerald Barney, who had prepared the Global 2000 report on the environment for then-President Jimmy Carter. Basically he said, "**There's this much arable land on the planet, and it can feed this many people. This is how the population is growing, and this is how quickly the arable land is being destroyed. Basically, if this keeps on happening, then about 2020 the whole world will begin to die.**" He laid a lot of the blame at the feet of the Western monotheistic traditions, saying, "We need to find new faiths, with new ideas on how to re-sacralize nature." And there we were.

I was there as a representative of the Covenant of the Goddess, accompanied by my co-Public Information Officer that year, Michael Thorn, and our then-First Officer, Phyllis Curott. CoG had a hospitality suite, literature to give out, and was attending the press briefing every morning. We had gone there figuring, "We'll probably be a minor player in the background, but at least we'll be there." Suddenly, after Dr. Barney's speech, we were in the spotlight. CoG was one of three Wiccan groups sponsoring the Parliament—the others being Circle and EarthSpirit. All totaled, there were about 100 Witches at the event. All of us suddenly found our workshops and talks filled to overflowing. The Parliament organizers had to keep moving us to larger rooms. Our Full Moon ritual in a nearby park, planned for 50 people, drew 500 plus the media.

At an event called "The Assembly of Religious and Spiritual Leaders," a document titled "Towards a Global Ethic: An Initial Declaration" was presented. Basically it said that while we may disagree about particular behaviors, we hold certain core values in common. And based on those core values, we actually have a lot more common ground between religions than we might think. CoG's representative in the Assembly, Deborah Ann Light, signed the Declaration just after Cardinal Giaoa, the Papal nuncio from the Vatican. [The text of the Global Ethic can be found online at the Council for a Parliament of the World's Religions website at *http://www.cpwr.org/calldocs/EthicTOC.html*]

This document declared the sacredness of the Earth and our responsibility for all living beings. Suddenly, all the mainstream religions were coming around to ideas that we as Pagans had held sacred for years! By the end of the Parliament, academics were saying, "In 1893 the country was introduced to Hinduism and Buddhism. In 1993 the country was introduced to Paganism." Certain press people, mostly from other countries, were calling the Parliament "The Coming Out party for the Neopagans." We didn't get much publicity in the American news media because **the American press took the position: "All these religions met and everybody got along—that's not news!"** But the world press treated the 1993 Parliament as one of the most important meetings of the 20th century.

As result of that 1993 Parliament, there is now a growing interfaith movement all over the world, with groups springing up everywhere dedicated to interfaith communication and cooperation. The organizers realized, "This is too important; we have to do it again." So in 1999, another Parliament convened in Cape Town, South Africa. The Pagan groups Circle, EarthSpirit, and Covenant of the Goddess were all represented there. This time, I was invited to join the Assembly of Religious Leaders (now renamed "the Parliament Assembly"), which includes the Dalai Lama and the Pope's representative. In other words, Pagans were finally getting mainstream recognition as a religion.

This Assembly had 250 religious representatives plus 150 "participant observers" from groups like the Red Cross, the World Bank, etc. We worked on the Global Ethic statement from '93 and asked, "How can we make these principles a reality? What do all the different guiding institutions in the world—like education, science, and media—need to do to put these principles into practice?" The Assembly not only endorsed a new document, called "A Call to Our Guiding Institutions" (online at *http://www.cpwr.org/calldoc.html*), but guided us through a process whereby everybody there created "interfaith service projects," through which religions could work together to address world problems like hunger, deforestation, AIDS, illiteracy, etc. By the end of the Assembly, we had come up with 300 service projects, and had networked with people who could make them happen.

I proposed "The Lost and Endangered Religions Project," which came out of a visit to Turkey in 1998. Anna and I had visited a Yezidi community in Eastern Turkey, inquiring about scriptures and texts, and were told that, four generations ago, their sacred texts had been lost. It turned out they had been collected by a Western anthropologist in the 19th century. I located these texts, xeroxed them and sent copies to the Yezidi village, thus restoring their scriptures to them.

That got me wondering. How many times have anthropologists, sociologists, and professors of religion collected data in the field in the form of texts, songs, dances, or recordings of rituals, gone home, written their papers, and then put everything into an archive where it lay forgotten? In the meantime, the material collected may have been lost in the culture from which it was originally collected—like the scripture of those Yezidi villagers. What could we do to restore this information back to the original cultures?

The "Lost and Endangered Religions Project" could network existing databases of ethnographic information and sort everything by source—whatever tribe or culture it came from—then go back to those people and say, "This is what exists in archives. What do you need? Does anybody remember the birthing song any more? If not, we have a recording of it." And this doesn't have to just be tribal—it can be any group, any religion. Essentially, the project would attempt to build a bridge between academia and religious groups. Of course, the

Anna Korn at work

main focus would be indigenous and tribal groups, because they're the most endangered.

[The Lost and Endangered Religions Project (LERP) has a website at *http://www.crseo.ucsb.edu/~frew/private/lerp/* or email me at *LostRelig@aol.com*]

By the end of the 1999 Parliament, the administrators of three different collections of such data in different parts of the world had signed up to make their databases available, and we got an offer of initial funding. So, just as 1993 was the birth of the global interfaith movement, I think 1999 was the birth of the global interfaith service movement. In 1993 we showed we could come together in peace, and in 1999 we showed that we could work together for peace. And Pagans are part of this! **Ten**

years ago Pagans were a far fringe group; now we are at the heart of religious organizing to make the world a better place. This campaign is going on all over the world, but American media are largely ignoring it. There were over 400 media representatives at this event, but almost all were from Europe, Asia and South America. I talked about the insights Paganism offers, particularly the focus on recognizing the sacredness of the natural world, and the audience loved it.

In summary, finally there is a growing awareness that Paganism represents a valid way of being religious. And while Pagans don't believe in proselytizing, we can freely share our insights. Because nothing is more important than rebuilding our relationship with the Earth and recovering our most primal cultural heritage.

♦ *R/S: Ronald Hutton's* **Triumph of the Moon** *has received a lot of acclaim recently by various Pagans—*

♦ DF: Well, we have our differences, but we're in correspondence, working on where our differences are, with an eye toward writing something jointly in the future. In my opinion, he didn't have sufficient access to a lot of the documentary material surviving in North American archives, but he DID have greater access to surviving witnesses in England. However, I'd probably give more credence to a contemporary document—like a diary entry made the same day—than to a witness's recollection of an event decades later. Ideally, you have to use the two together; witnesses can give context to a document.

♦ *R/S: What do you think is the importance of* **Triumph of the Moon?**

♦ DF: It explains, in some depth, the Occult subculture of early twentieth century England, which was the milieu out of which the Craft movement arose. In fact, there were many groups interested in Naturism and mythology (if not Paganism) at that time, so it's not surprising that a modern Craft movement would arise out of this ferment of people exchanging ideas and meeting each other.

There have been many theories as to how the Craft arose, each one the "latest"; until it gets superseded. There was Aidan Kelly's *Crafting the Art of Magic* (now out-of-print) which basically says that "Gardner made it all up." Then the Woodcraft and KibboKift theory was popularized in *Gnosis* magazine: that the Craft came out of British boy-scouting groups at the time. The latest theory is Hutton's, who argues that it came out of a group of people that were all part of the Occult and Romantic subculture of the first half of the 20th century. My own view is that all those theories have significant problems.

One of the factors influencing current investigations into Craft origins is the fact that most of the living witnesses are in England, while many of the most important historical documents are in North America. Another thing: the Craft "scene" in America is very different from England—and, consequently, academic studies of the Craft have been affected by these differences.

For example, the book *Persuasions of the Witch's Craft,* by Tanya Luhrman, is an academic study of occult groups: "Why do ordinary people believe in this?" She examines different occult groups, including Craft groups in England. It's fascinating, but many of her conclusions just do not apply to North America. Occult groups in England seem more focused on, "Let's learn how they did it in the past so we can do it that way," whereas occult groups in North America go, "Let's learn how they did it in the past so we can incorporate that into something more oriented towards the future."

Obviously, the American approach is far more experimental, whereas the British approach tends to be more "looking backwards through trance work." Also, the political scenes are very different. In England the more traditional (Gardnerian and Alexandrian) groups tend to dominate because they've been around much longer—they're a much larger percentage of the Craft community. In the U.S., the Gardnerian and related groups, while older, are just one part of a much larger scene; they don't have the same kind of standing in the community as they do in the U.K. and Canada.

1999 Altar for New Year's Eve Wiccan service at Interfaith Center in the Presidio, San Francisco

♦ **R/S: Who purchased Gerald Gardner's archive?**

♦ DF: When Gardner died, he willed his museum on the Isle of Man to his last priestess, Monique Wilson, and her husband. They fell on hard times. Around 1975 they pulled out texts that they recognized as Books of Shadows [i.e., occult source texts containing rituals] and they sold the rest to Ripley's (of "Believe-it-or-Not" fame). Ripley's sold the cases of amulets and "lucky charms"—little things Gardner had collected on his travels—to A&B Trading Company, and some of them can probably be found on eBay. The splashier items like swords ended up in Ripley's museums and were on display, but most of the books and papers ended up in storage. At one point a lot was on display in Atlanta. The head of the Atlanta lodge of the O.T.O. [Crowleyite group] saw a charter from Crowley granting Gardner the right to found an O.T.O. lodge, and he purchased it.

At some point, Ripley's split the documents and books they had, and 2/3 ended up in Toronto, Canada, and 1/3 in Orlando, Florida. The Wiccan Church of Canada in Toronto purchased the material Ripley's had there, including Gardner's large occult library and a pile of documents including correspondence, notebooks, and private papers. Only later did they discover there was a second collection in Orlando, Florida.

Most of the significant occult books ended up in Toronto, while the Orlando collection contains more popular fiction. The primary item of import that ended up in Toronto was *ye Bok of ye Art Magical* [commonly referred to as the BAM] which is the oldest known Book of Shadows. It had fallen into the back of a filing cabinet and had been lost there since around 1950. When it happened, Gardner was reportedly very upset. Clearly this was the book he was using when he joined the original Craft group. So the earliest versions of various texts are in that very historical document, such as the "Charge of the Goddess." There have been hand-copied transcripts made from this book, but nothing compares to using color photographs of the pages (as we do) which show the various different forms of handwriting, spellings (or misspellings), and inks—all which can indicate different authors.

Between the two archives, there are 18 handwritten notebooks of Gardner's. They're all in his tiny, crabbed handwriting, and none of it has been transcribed. The correspondence has a lot to say about the relationships between various individuals. There is almost too much to study—not the other way around! And for various reasons, I've concluded that there's no solid evidence that Gardner ever wrote any ritual at all. He may have copied from one ritual and added to another ritual, but there's no proof of any actual composition or authorship of an ordinal or unique ritual.

Then there's the view that perhaps the group he joined made up all the ritual. Proving that Gardner didn't write it doesn't necessarily prove that it's ancient. My own belief is that a core of his material does go back to late antiquity, but that the current form of the rituals is no older than 150 years.

♦ **R/S: What are the oldest "source" texts for the Craft?**

♦ DF: The single oldest existing text is *ye Bok of ye Art Magical.* It appears to date from when Gardner joined the group in the New Forest, 1939, and he's writing down what they're telling him. The real question is, How much older than that is it?

There is another, parallel lineage of Craft called Central Valley Wicca [California]. Their oldest book was brought over from England in the '60s. We can compare that with *ye Bok of ye Art Magical* and demonstrate that they must have been copied from a common, hand-written source text, because: 1) there's too much overlap in significant passages for them to be independent of each other, and: 2) each contains significant omissions that make it impossible for one to be a copy of the other. So there must be an earlier book out there from which they were both copied.

♦ **R/S: Do you have more to say about Ronald Hutton?**

♦ DF: Hutton's earlier book, *The Pagan Religions of the Ancient British Isles,* was one of the first to examine the history of ancient Paganism in England. It pretty much established the idea that modern Craft is not ancient Celtic religion—in fact, **the more we learn, the more diverse Celtic religion appears to have been; it's virtually impossible to generalize about it,** let alone describe any one body of beliefs and practices as "Celtic Religion." This was a very important step forward in our understanding of Craft origins. And his current book, *Triumph of the Moon,* is important for providing the cultural context of the early Craft movement.

Another important book is Philip Heselton's *Wiccan Roots,* to which Hutton wrote the introduction. Heselton looked at material like old wills and deeds and deduced all sorts of information about the people in the group that Gardner joined. I think this is one of the most important books of Craft history in the last 20 years.

♦ **R/S: What's your perspective on Crowley?**

♦ DF: In modern Occultism in the U.S., Crowley people (such as the O.T.O.) and "popular" Witches tend to be two completely

1999 Simonstown, South Africa

different groups. The Crowley people are perceived by the Witches as very Satanic or dark, and the Witches are often not taken very seriously by the Crowley people. In traditional Craft such as in England, with initiations and things handed down, there's more overlap, with people practicing both. Whereas in the U.S. popular Witchcraft tends to rebel against the more "ceremonial" approach of the O.T.O.

Even so, there seems to be an uneasy relationship, because there is definitely an influence by Crowley on early Craft. For instance, the person who purchased the O.T.O. charter that Crowley gave to Gardner said: "Now I have the O.T.O. charter; does this mean I'm now the head of all the Witches?!" I've had O.T.O. people tell me, "I should have complete access to your Book of Shadows, because I'm an O.T.O. member of such-and-such degree, therefore your material is all really mine"—and that has not endeared them to me! And Witches who are focused on Wicca being ancient, shamanic, Celtic Craft don't want to see any connection with Crowley at all.

In Gardner's first book, *Witchcraft Today,* he says, "Clearly the rituals are very modern." Meaning that they have to date from after the time of mass literacy, which isn't all that long. He asks, "If these things are modern creations, who could have had a hand in them?" Then he says, "The only man I can think of who could have invented the rites was the late Aleister Crowley. When I met him he was most interested to hear I was a member [of the Witch-cult], and said he had been inside when he was very young, but would not say whether he had rewritten anything or not." So there's Gardner himself implying that some of the writing was by Crowley. The question is: To what extent did Crowley write material for the group? Did he pick up phrases from the group and use them in his own work? But because of the "bad boy" image of Crowley, a lot of Witches don't want to "go there" and examine the evidence.

I think Crowley was a brilliant magician, and his books on magic are fantastic. But when he gets into "Thelema" and is "the prophet of the New Aeon," he loses me. He also was Hell-bent on dissipating himself as rapidly as possible with as many drugs as possible. That's also not an image that people want to associate with the Craft—both for public relations reasons, and also because that isn't Craft. Craft isn't about burning yourself out with drugs as quickly as possible.

♦ *R/S: You said earlier that the "Charge of the Goddess" predates Doreen Valiente—*

♦ DF: Oh yes, the earliest version is in *ye Bok of ye Art Magical.* No one knows who wrote it but it must have been after 1919, because it definitely incorporates material first published by Crowley then. In *ye Bok of ye Art Magical,* there's the "Charge," a commentary on the "Charge," and a commentary on the commentary—all copied in Gardner's handwriting, yet clearly not composed by him.

Now, in *The Rebirth of Witchcraft,* Doreen recounts that she recognized some of the material as by Crowley. Doreen rewrote the Charge into a rhymed version, then rewrote that into prose —which is the version most people have encountered; either that, or Starhawk's version, which is based on Doreen's. But, Doreen's is a rewrite of the earlier one from the BAM.

Aidan Kelly's *Crafting the Art of Magic* included some transcripts from *ye Bok of ye Art Magical,* but they had serious, significant errors. The Canadian journal *Ethnologies* did a special issue on Wicca about a year ago [1998] that contains some of my writings on this. And on-line, Kelly has acknowledged some of the errors he made.

♦ *R/S: What's your position on "The Burning Times"?*

♦ DF: Most of the Craft elders I know would debunk that. There are a number of good, critical evaluations out there. **The figure of "nine million Witches/women burned" is obviously absurd.** The "nine million" figure can be traced to a single source, Matilda Jocelyn Gage's *Women, Church and State,* an early feminist work. She produced this number out of thin air, and it got picked up by Mary Daly in her *Gyn/Ecology,* and then got repeated everywhere. But there's no substance to it at all. Yes, there was a "Burning Times," i.e. a period in which being a Witch was a capital offense. Many people, both men and women, were tortured and killed under horrible circumstances. But they were not all "Witches"—the net was cast far wider than that.

There was a time when the Goddess Religion movement and the Craft movement were a lot closer together, but increasingly they're separating. The view that "in the old days everybody worshipped the Goddess and everything was peaceful and wonderful" and "we have an unbroken line of descent down into modern Craft" . . . we in the Craft dumped that over 20 years ago, saying, "It doesn't matter; what matters is what's valuable today."

But the Goddess movement still clings to what is sometimes called a "Gimbutista" [lampooning Marija Gimbutas] outlook. But those with a more informed, skeptical view of history question her theory that the world was once covered with matriarchal sites. **There's a very simple way to analyze her views: just continually ask yourself, "How do you know that?"**

If you unearth a small, hand-sized statuette of a woman with large breasts and a prominent vulva, well, how do you know it's a fertility goddess? How do you even know they had gods or goddesses in that culture at all? Lots of cultures don't have gods and goddesses. Was the statue found by the hearth or out in the yard? Maybe it was a child's toy. If it WAS a goddess figure, maybe they made earth goddess figures in stone, which survives, and hunting god figures in wood or antler, which doesn't, giving a skewed picture of their beliefs. Many explanations are possible.

One example Gimbutas cited in *The Civilization of the Goddess* involved the burial of a man with a head wound, with a woman buried next to him. She says something like, "Obviously, the man was killed in combat and when he was buried, the woman was killed to follow him, like the Indian practice of suttee." But how does she know? Maybe she died years earlier from disease and the grave was reopened to bury her husband with her. Or when she died, HE was killed with a blow to the head to follow HER into the afterlife. Or they both died in the same raid, but her damage was all soft-tissue, not leaving marks on her skeleton. How do you really *know?* It's all speculation.

Marija Gimbutas made a lot of statements that have no support. More reasonable people would say, "Here's what we found, and here are some possible explanations" instead of presenting it as, "This explanation is the only possible answer."

One of the reasons I'm opposed to the "in the ancient days everybody worshipped the goddess and was peaceful" idea is that I think it's disempowering. I think you cannot posit such a Golden Age without asking, "Why isn't it still there?" You have to say, "It fell; it fell to the evil, nomad male invaders." Meaning, "It's a system that, whenever it experiences outside pressure, it will fail to survive." What kind of system is that to hold up as an example?! Personally, I'd rather go, "It looks like pretty much everywhere has been a patriarchy. Isn't it great that we're moving beyond that? We are learning the error of that; we are learning how to value everybody and incorporate all these voices into a more egalitarian, balanced view." Isn't that a much better picture of the future?

There are articles that say, "The problem is not patriarchy; the problem is having a monolithic view. There's every reason to think that any culture that is wholly Goddess-focused would have just as many abuses—albeit of a different type—than anything that is fully God-focused." So, I think that balance is the name of the game—

♦ *R/S: And that's hard to achieve . . . Why should anyone join, say, your Gardnerian coven? It definitely seems to involve some kind of "hierarchy," which many Pagans have issues with—*

♦ DF: A coven is embedded in a tradition and feels a responsibility to the tradition. A coven does not have an exclusive claim on truth, or the only access to truth. If anyone is dictatorial toward you, then vote with your feet! Join another group, or start your own. No one can validly say you're wrong, or that you're not going to succeed in your spiritual path. The coven might say that what you're doing is not in accord with a particular tradition— but so what? Go to another.

There was a book that came out in the eighties—can't remember the title—that described the Craft as a counter-cult, because there was no mechanism enforcing conformity. If anything, there's a constant force in the other direction. The Craft has a concept called "hiving"—which means that if a group of people can't agree enough to work together, then they should split up and start new groups. We empower a force to encourage constant growth and change.

♦ *R/S: So where does the shape of the modern Craft come from?*

♦ DF: At any given point in the history of an occult tradition, it is shaped by two factors: where it actually comes from and where its current practitioners THINK it comes from. The former is the clay the group has to work with; the latter is the shape they form that clay into. Currently, for the Craft movement in the US and UK, that shape is Celtic. Since there is precious little in the way of written pre-Christian Celtic history, there has been a tendency to look for inspiration to living cultures that seem similar. A majority of these are shamanic, so shamanism has become an important shaping force on contemporary Craft.

♦ *R/S: That reminds me: what are the oldest written sources for Pagan theory and ritual?*

♦ DF: Well, the oldest Pagan texts in the West are myths, like Gilgamesh. But if you're talking about texts ABOUT Paganism, then late Neoplatonic theurgy and late Classical material provide some of the earliest material—we're referring to the writings of Porphyry, Iamblichus and Proclus, among others. In their search for the most ancient sources of Pagan "theory" or history, most Pagans today don't look at Neoplatonism. When modern Pagans look for their Pagan ancestors, they pretty much restrict their search to tribal peoples living in the woods of Western Europe. The Neoplatonic theurgists, on the other hand,

1999 Good Hope Center, Capetown

were highly educated, urban, intellectual Pagans—the end products of a Pagan academic system spanning over two thousand years. There's an Arabic connection here as well; one I've written about at some length in an article called: "Harran: Last Refuge of Classical Paganism." [see appendix]. I am also in the process of organizing a symposium on this at UC Berkeley for Spring 2002.

Julian (called "the Apostate"), the last Pagan Emperor of Rome, was a Neoplatonist. In his attempt to revitalize Paganism in the Roman Empire, he asked his friend, the

1988 at Ring of Brodgar, Orkney Islands, Scotland

philosopher Sallustius, to prepare a sort of "catechism" of Paganism. Titled *On the Gods and the World,* this is a marvelous book of Pagan theology and it is usually overlooked by modern Pagans. It is filled with wonderful pithy statements. Speaking of myths, for example, Sallustius says, "Now these things never happened, but always are." In fact, Gerald Gardner commended the teaching of Sallustius for "its startling modernity—it might have been spoken yesterday. Further, it might have been spoken at a witch meeting, at any time, as a general statement of their creed." So, Gardner himself said that this Neoplatonic "catechism" described the beliefs of the witch group he joined. In the terms I used before, if Celtic shamanism is the shape of modern Craft, then late Neoplatonic theurgy is the clay out of which it has been shaped.

Another early source of "Pagan" theological writing is the Hermetica, said to be the teachings of Hermes Trismegistos and recorded in Hellenistic Egypt c. 2nd century CE. Get the Copenhaver translation from Cambridge; the other 4-volume set available (the Scott translation) contains much corrupt source material, although Scott's introduction and notes are great.

There are often problems with such written Pagan "source" material, a major one being that most were translated decades ago by Christians, who when they encountered phrases like "the divine" translated it as "God." Greek and Latin are both gendered languages with masculine as the default, so any gender-neutral concept would have been indicated by a gendered term, so we have what was probably "Parent" in the original getting translated as "Father." This kind of patriarchal language can be very off-putting to modern Pagans.

Of course, there are a lot of non-Western Pagan texts that are much older—the Mahabharata; the Bhagavad-Gita; the Vedas; Upanishads—they're all Pagan texts.

♦R/S: Some people think that "God" is something that humans can't really conceive of—

♦DF: In Neoplatonism, there's the idea that the ultimate Divine is beyond gender—a "One" beyond human conception. This concept is found in Gardnerian Craft and called "Dryghton." It's also a thoroughly Pagan concept. The conflict in late antiquity was NOT "one God *versus* many Gods"—monotheism

versus polytheism; that was a rhetorical device used in Christian propaganda. The real conflict was between the monotheism of the Christians and the monism of the Pagans. The Christians said there was only one God and his name was YHVH, so all other gods were false. The Pagans said there was ultimately only one Divine Unity (which they sometimes called "God"), so it necessarily had to encompass and embrace all gods and all faiths. It was a conflict of exclusivity vs. inclusivity. **The fact that non-dualism is at the heart of the Western Pagan tradition has been obscured or lost, because we Pagans have let the Christians of late antiquity define the terms of the argument!**

Related to this, one issue which many Pagans aren't clear on is Transcendence ("beyond the material world") versus immanence ("within the material world"). Many Pagans, adopting a Christian usage misunderstand transcendence to mean "not immanent," but neither "transcendence" nor "Immanence" necessarily excludes the other—Deity can be both immanent and transcendent. But because of buying into Christian rhetoric, many Pagans talk only in terms of immanence—again, we're letting the terms be defined by the Christian dualists.

♦R/S: Can you explain the concept of Pantheism?

♦DF: Basically, Pantheism is the idea that the Divine *is* the material universe. Most Pagans I know are actually "pan*en*theists," they just haven't heard the term before. Panentheism argues that the Divine is manifest as the material universe, but is also more than that. Almost all Pagans believe both in accepting our physical bodies as ourselves, but at the same time in a reincarnation that says that something transcends the death of that body. The old Hermetic dictum of "As above, so below" would certainly argue that, in this as in all things, is a reflection of the Divine.

♦R/S: How old is the Wiccan Rede [ethic]?

♦DF: The earliest known appearance of the Rede as: "An it harm none, do what you will" was in the Gardnerian tradition and was written by Doreen Valiente. She, in turn, based it on the following, passed along by Gardner: "[Witches] are inclined to the morality of the legendary Good King Pausol, 'Do what you like so long as you harm no one.' [The Meaning of Witchcraft] The passage to which Gardner refers can be found in a story by Pierre Louys called "The Adventures of King Pausol" [1901], a story about a utopian kingdom whose monarch has reduced all laws to two:

"I. Do no wrong to thy neighbor.

II. Observing this, do as thou pleasest."

—that's the first written appearance, as far as I know. Misinformed assumptions about the Rede being copied from Crowley has resulted in an occasional drift to "An it harm none, do what thou wilt," but this was not the original wording. The "Do what thou wilt" part is much older than both anyway, and can be found in Rabelais.

♦R/S: Let's Discuss the Wiccan Rule of Three—paraphrased, "Any curse you cast comes back to you threefold"—

◆DF: I prefer to put it as: "Do unto others as they would have you do unto them"—it's much less self-centered. While the Rule of Three is not found in the earliest Gardnerian material, there IS something a lot closer to the Golden Rule: "As you receive good, you are equally bound to return good, three-fold." I think that's a lot more positive.

◆*R/S: We're discussing Pagan ethics—*

◆DF: When it comes to Pagan ethics and magical workings you have to be very careful, and very precise. Let's take an intent like "Let's work to stop the logging of old-growth redwoods!" If that's the sole focus of your working, you open the door for many possible ways in which the goal could come about, ranging from a Board of Directors deciding to donate the land to a park (Great!) to some corporate headquarters burning down, incidentally killing the late night janitorial staff (Disaster!). Many folks try to avoid the latter by including a caveat in their spell like ". . . for the greatest good for all concerned." In my opinion, such a hobbled spell is completely useless. All the folks employed by the companies cutting those redwoods certainly don't think that saving them is for THEIR "greatest good." Truly effective magic for social or political change requires a much more focused and targeted approach, the ethics of which are a matter of some debate.

◆*R/S: Let's change topics. Do you believe in spirits, angels, fairies?*

◆DF: For years humans have interacted with entities lacking physical bodies—from spirits to ghosts to Gods to fairies to ancestor spirits. There are many names for different categories of spirits. Arguably, while the entities are real, the names are constructs and the same being may be called by a different name in a different circumstance or culture. Few Witches refer to angels, because "angel" as it is used today is a Christian concept, even though it comes from a Greek word for "spirits of light." This is another complex matter involving a lot of etymological discussion. Oddly enough, the word "devil" comes from the Sanskrit "deva," also meaning "being of light." The Christian word "demon" derives from the Greek "daimon" or Latin "daemon," which was a sort of generic term for spirits. The modern, diminutive, cutesy fairies of Hallmark cards bear little resemblance to the forebears in English folklore. In the Middle Ages, fairies were dangerous; there are many folktales of children being kidnapped, people being kidnapped, people going to dinner with fairies and when they emerge it's fifty years later and everyone they know is dead. In the old days, folks entering a forest at night would pray that they didn't meet a fairy.

◆*R/S: Speaking of fairies, what do you know about the Feri tradition?*

◆DF: Let me hand this off to a Feri initiate—

◆ANNA KORN: Victor and Cora Anderson grafted together material from a variety of sources, including traditional root-doctor curing from the American South, pre-Gardnerian Wiccan sources, Huna, theosophical teachings, and their own contacts with spirits and past-life beings. Victor tells of his membership in a coven early in the last century that was very shamanic in focus.

Although initiates share a body of lore at initiation, there's very little published. Feris are very secretive, so naturally there's the lure of the unknown—a mystique. Gwydion Pendderwen and Starhawk both trained with Victor. Victor, who is legally blind, sees very clearly in the Other World. He is widely read in the spiritual traditions of many cultures world-wide. He writes poetry and has oracular gifts; if he's been studying Tibetan Buddhism, for instance, then that will often flavor his inspirations. He's in the poetic realm. Similarly, if you read Robert Graves, you read for inspiration, not historical accuracy.

◆*R/S: What do you think of all the "teen witch" books coming out—*

◆DF: Many of the books today reinforce the notion of Witchcraft as being all about spells. I find in them very questionable ethics, sloppy language, and sloppy history. For example in *Teen Witch,* Alex Sanders is mentioned, but his last name is misspelled "Saunders." Starhawk is described as having followers called "Starhawkians"—but nobody I know has ever heard that term used. The goddess Diana is invoked as the "daughter of Aradia," but anyone who has actually read the early Craft book "Aradia" would know that there is a lengthy myth all about how Diana gave birth TO Aradia! There are references to "God" and using "Holy Water" in spells—is she trying to confuse people? If you want a good introductory book on practical magic, try *True Magic* by Amber K.

Popular books on spells give teens the idea that magic is about gross displays of power, when actually it depends on wisdom, understanding, and subtlety. A lot of magic is about overcoming momentum—you can think of the world as a big ball rolling down a big trough. It's going to take a lot of energy to shove that ball out of the trough into the path you want it to take. But with careful observation and magical understanding, you can figure out just when a small push in just the right direction will send that ball rolling down a new trough. Isaac Bonewits discussed this in *Real Magic*—find the small change, the linchpin, that can give big results. That's where you focus your magical effort.

Let's say you're going head to head against a corporation determined to log old-growth redwoods. In a way a corporation can be viewed as a magical enterprise: sometimes, hundreds of people are all doing visualization and focusing their energy toward the goal of making the corporation succeed. So if you go head-to-head against that, you have a lot of momentum to overcome! But if you can determine that the decision as to whether or not to cut those redwoods is going to happen on such-and-such a day by such-and-such a person, you can focus your efforts on reaching that person and trying to change their mind—that might be a lot simpler.

◆*R/S: What do you think of shamanic practices involving peyote, etc?*

◆DF: Nowadays, people talk about "entheogens," substances that manifest divinity, and focus on a natural pharmacopeia which encompasses plants from the Amazon, so-called Witches' ointments, psilocybin mushrooms, whatever they took during the Eleusinian Mysteries, etc. Terence McKenna has written a lot about this; Alexander Shulgin wrote his *Pihkal* which was banned in the U.K. (allegedly, drug manufacturing trade secrets were revealed), and Jonathan Ott has written *Pharmacotheon.* While there may be insights to be gained by pharmacopeia-sparked experiences, I personally don't use any substances—I've learned how to reach altered states without drugs. They can open doors, but after that, you should be able to go through on your own. With regard to drugs—and experimental sex, too, for that matter—*harm* may be the issue here. "An it harm none, do what you will." If nobody's being harmed, then what's the problem? ◆◆◆

Pre-4th Century
Paganism & Polytheism practiced — Christianity Illegal

Christianity Legal — 4th Century A.D. — Paganism Illegal

Gerald Gardner (1884-1964)   1891-1930   Travels Malaysia, Ceylon, visits archeological digs & gains interest in exotic cultures, nature, and dieties of the Earth.

1900: moves to Ceylon, circa 1908 moves to Borneo, and in 1911 to Singapore

1920's: becomes a Mason in Johoro
1923: begins work for British Civil Service in Johoro

1919-39: "Charge of the Goddess" is written
1936: 1st book published: "Kris & Other Malay Weapons"

1930-1950

1936: retires from Civil Service, travels his way back to the U.K. until 1939, visits Egypt, Cypress

1939: Back in the U.K., initiated into a coven, publishes "A Goddess Arrives" (Pagan themed novel)

May 1947: Meets Alistair Crowley

1951: Witchcraft Act of 1735 is replaced by Fraudulent Mediums Act, making witchcraft more difficult to prosecute

1950 - present

MVSEVM

Publishes non-fiction: "Witchcraft Today" (1954) "The Meaning of Witchcraft" (1959)

1953-54: Purchases and begins to run Museum on the Isle of Man

1954/56: new version of "Charge of the Goddess" written by Doreen Valiente

Modern Pagans

A nudist for health and enjoyment, paves the way for "Skyclad Witches"

Goddess   Horned God   CRE'01

Gerald Gardner
His Life and Influences

GARDNERIAN WICCA:

Witchcraft was against the law in England until 1951, when the last of the Witchcraft Acts was repealed. Subsequently Gerald Gardner (1884-1964) published two books: Witchcraft Today (1954) and The Meaning of Witchcraft (1959), and became the resident Witch at The Museum of Witchcraft and Magic in Castletown on the Isle of Man. In his books Gardner discussed topics such as celebrating the seasonal sabbats; the Wiccan Rede; covens as led by a priest and a priestess; casting a circle to do ritual; working skyclad (naked); raising energy through sexual magic (including "The Great Rite"); and ritual scourging. Today, people continue to be initiated into the tradition that now bears his name.

♦ ANNA KORN: Gerald Gardner was a plantation manager who was employed in British colonial outposts like Ceylon and Malaysia. As part of the Customs Service, he helped regulate the traffic in opium. Gardner was interested in, but rather skeptical of, subjects like Spiritualism. He read widely in occult books, conducted his own experiments in psychic abilities, and was a member of the Masons. An active amateur archeologist, he wrote a book on the Malay ritual knife, the kris, entitled *Kris and other Malay Weapons*. When he retired in 1936, he visited archaeological digs in the Middle East and didn't settle in England until 1939. There he met a group of Witches who initiated him into their coven. For the rest of his life he promoted Witchcraft, sometimes in a flamboyant way in the press.

♦ DON FREW: The group Gardner joined included members who had split from the older Theosophical Society, some of whom had learned ritual from another local coven. But when Gardner started asking harder questions, he was often stymied. Consequently his books are full of, "This is what so-and-so says, but this is what *I* think." He freely incorporates information from Margaret Murray's *Witch-*

Cult of Western Europe and other sources in his reconstruction of the origins of the Craft. Doreen Valiente added additional material from Celtic sources into the material that came to be called "Gardnerian Craft"—

♦ AK: Probably every Witchcraft group in the world uses the "Charge of the Goddess," which in its presently-recognized form was written by Doreen Valiente.

♦ DF: Doreen based hers on an earlier version she got from Gerald and his people. Actually, Gardner's group didn't call themselves "Gardnerian"—that was originally a derogatory term implying, "You're not really an *ancient* Witch; you're descended from Gardner." But over time "Gardnerian" became acceptable. However, the material used by the Gardnerian tradition pre-dates Gardner—he was just the reporter. Through his commentary and Doreen's modifications and additions, it got reshaped to be the basis of the Craft today.

Almost all of modern Craft celebrates four Sabbats, the cross-quarter days: Beltane, Lammas, Halloween and Imbolc (also known as Candlemas or Brigit). Then Gardner went away on a trip to the Middle East. Gardner returned to find his group celebrating *eight* Sabbats [adding the solstices and equinoxes]. He said, "Fine!"

♦ AK: The Wheel of the Year with eight Sabbats was slowly adopted from 1957 through the Sixties.

♦ DF: To say, "In the Fifties, Celtic material was grafted in," doesn't mean that the Celtic material is "wrong." Throughout history, people have always been writing their own material and re-interpreting it. And in the future the Craft will need new manifestations, because at the core of any nature religion is the recognition that nature changes. Still, some people equate history with validity: "This practice is older—therefore it's more valid." We don't support that. ♦♦♦

Some of the EARLIEST Written Sources for PAGANISM

Sources on Late Neoplatonic Theurgy including Hekate & the Chaldean Oracles, Hermes & the Hermetica, the Emperor Julian, Harran, the end of classical Paganism, and other related subjects. Here are some texts that I have found both accessible and informative. The list is by no means comprehensive, but offers introductory material on a wide-range of related subjects. Contact me if you have any questions: DHF3 @ aol.com

LATE CLASSICAL MAGIC & RELIGION
Ankarloo, Bengt, and Clark, Stuart, eds., *Witchcraft and Magic in Europe: Ancient Greece and Rome* (Part of a series. Good source book.)
Armstrong, A.H., ed., *Classical Mediterranean Spirituality: Egyptian/Greek/Roman* (Excellent collection of essays covering Classical spirituality, including Neoplatonism.)
Faraone, Christopher, ed., *Magika Hiera* (Excellent anthology on ancient Greek magic & religion.)
Godwin, David, *Light in Extension: Greek Magic from Homer to Modern Times* (An attempt to update classical magical systems for modern practice.)
Graf, Fritz, *Magic in the Ancient World* (One of the leading figures in the field.)
Luck, Georg, *Arcana Mundi: Magic and the Occult in the Greek and Roman Worlds* (Good anthology on Classical magic, including theurgy, as presented in original texts.)
Martin, Luther, *Hellenistic Religions: An Introduction* (Good intro to the background and context.)
Meyer, Marvin, ed., *Ancient Magic & Ritual Power* (part of very good anthology!)
Reale, Giovanni, *The Schools of the Imperial Age* (*A History of Ancient Philosophy, vol. IV*) (Good systematic survey of Hermetic, Chaldean, and Neoplatonic authors, philosophy, and theurgy.)
Ritner, Robert Kriech, *The Mechanics of Ancient Egyptian Magical Practice* (Too early for our period, but the definitive work on the subject and useful for comparison with later systems.)
Rollins, Alden, *Rome in the Fourth Century A.D.: An Annotated Bibliography with Historical Overview* (Where to go next.)
Turcan, Robert, *The Cults of the Roman Empire* (Excellent overview of mystery cults in the late Empire.)

LATE CLASSICAL MAGIC & RELIGION
(Papyri Graecae Magicae)
Flowers, Stephen Edred, *Hermetic Magic: The Postmodern Magical Papyrus of Abaris* (Dicey history, but good portrayal of the mindset of a late antique magician. The "Papyrus of Abaris" is a creation of Flowers'.)
Stewart, Randall, and Morell, Kenneth, trans., "The Oracles of Astrampsychus," in Hansen, William, ed., *Anthology of Ancient Greek Popular Literature* (A 2nd Cent. CE fortune-telling text.)
Meyer, Marvin, W., and Smith, Richard, *Ancient Christian Magic: Coptic Texts of Ritual Power* (Includes a lot of non-Christian material.)

ORPHISM & ORPHIC HYMNS
Athanassakis, Apostolos N., *The Orphic Hymns: Text, Translation and Notes*
Guthrie, W.K.C., *Orpheus and Greek Religion: A Study of the Orphic Movement*
West, M.L., *The Orphic Poems*

PYTHAGOREANISM, NEO-PYTHAGOREANISM, & NUMBER MAGIC
Barry, Kieron, *The Greek Qabalah: Alphabetic Mysticism and Numerology in the Ancient World*
Burkert, Walter, *Lore and Science in Ancient Pythagoreanism*
Godwin, Joscelyn, *The Mystery of the Seven Vowels: in Theory and Practice* (Good discussion of the basic element of late antique magic and theurgy.)
Guthrie, Kenneth Sylvan, ed., *The Pythagorean Sourcebook and Library* (Excellent collection of source texts!)

Kingsley, Peter, *Ancient Philosophy, Mystery, and Magic: Empedocles and the Pythagorean Tradition* (Revolutionary re-evaluation of the work of Empedocles, the role of magic in the birth of philosophy, and its influence down into the Arab world. Highly recommended.)
Levin, Flora R, tr., *The Manual of Harmonics* (of Nicomachus the Pythagorean)
O'Meara, Dominic J., *Pythagoras Revived: Mathematics and Philosophy in Late Antiquity*
Morgan, Morris Hicky, trans., *Vitruvius: The Ten Books on Architecture* (Probably more Dionysian than Pythagorean, it still contains much useful information on classical conceptions of number and proportion.)
Shaw, Gregory, "Eros and Arithmos: Pythagorean Theurgy in Iamblichus and Plotinus," in *Ancient Philosophy*, Spring 1999, Vol. XIX No. 1 (Excellent article using Pythagorean concepts to reconcile Iamblichus and Plotinus.)
Waterfield, Robin, tr., *The Theology of Arithmetic* (attrib. to Iamblichus)

CHALDEAN ORACLES
Majercik, R.T., *The Chaldean Oracles (Religions in the Graeco-Roman World, Volume 5)* (The only edition of these texts in print in English.)

CHALDEAN ORACLES (Hekate)
Johnston, Sarah Iles, *Hekate Soteira: A Study of Hekate's Roles in the Chaldean Oracles and Related Literature* (Hekate's role in theurgy.)
Ronan, Stephen, ed., *The Goddess Hekate* (Good collection of previously published material plus Ronan's essay on Hekate in the Chaldean Oracles.) Also, *Hekate's Iynx: An Ancient Theurgical Tool*
Von Rudolf, Robert, *Hekate in Ancient Greek Religion* (Mostly too early for our period, it includes some late antique material as well.)

HERMETICA & HERMES TRISMEGISTOS
Cicero, Chic & Tabitha, eds., *The Golden Dawn Journal, Book III: The Art of Hermes* (There are several very good essays in this collection, including those by Stoltz, Forrest, Tyson, Oz, and Webster.)
Copenhaver, Brian P., trans. and ed., *Hermetica*, Cambridge University Press, 1992 (The single best edition of the Hermetica in English.)
Faivre, Antoine, *The Eternal Hermes* (Survey of Hermes Trismegistos from antiquity to the Renaissance.)
Fowden, Garth, *The Egyptian Hermes: A Historical Approach to the Late Pagan Mind* (Hermes Trismegistos in the theurgy of the Hermetica and of Neoplatonism.)
Hauck, Dennis William, *The Emerald Tablet: Alchemy for Personal Transformation* (Quirky, but basically good overview of Hermeticism for the casual reader.)
Kingsley, Peter, "Poimandres: The Etmology of the Name and the Origins of the Hermetica," in *Journal of The Warburg and Courtauld Institutes*, Vol. 56, The Warburg Institute, London, 1993 (Proves an Egyptian origin for the Hermetica.)
Mahe, Jean-Pierre, "Preliminary Remarks on the Demotic Book of Thoth and the Greek Hermetica," in *Vigiliae Christianae: A Review of Christian Life and Language*, Vol. L, E.J. Brill, Leiden, 1996 (The only comments available in English on this newly discovered Hermetic text.)
Mead, G.R.S., *Thrice Greatest Hermes* (Dated and more than a bit slanted towards Theosophy, but an unparalleled collection of lore.)
Salaman, Clement; van Oyen, Dorine; Wharton, William D.; and Mahe, Jean-Pierre, *The Way of Hermes: New Translations of The Corpus Hermeticum and The Definitions of Hermes Trismegistus to Asclepius* (The only English translation of the latter text, recently discovered in Armenian manuscript.)
Scott, Walter, ed. & trans., *Hermetica: Introduction, Texts and Translation* (The English translation is no longer considered reliable, but Scott's notes and comments are considered invaluable.)
van den Broek, Roelof, and Hanegraaff, Wouter J., eds., *Gnosis and Hermeticism: From Antiquity to Modern Times* (Very good for understanding the differences and similarities.)
Waegeman, Maryse, *Amulet and Alphabet: Magical Amulets in the First Book of Cyranides* (The Cyranides was one of the so-called technical, i.e. magical, Hermetica. This is the only English translation of which I am aware. It includes magical correspondences between plants, birds, fish, and stones.)

MITHRAISM
Clauss, Manfred, *The Roman Cult of Mithras: The God and His Mysteries*, tr. by Richard Gordon (Good summary of current scholarship on this subject.)
Jackson, Howard M., *The Lion Becomes Man: The Gnostic Leontomorphic Creator and the Platonic Tradition* (On the origins of the lion-headed god.)
Ulansey, David, *The Origins of the Mithraic Mysteries: Cosmology & Salvation in the Ancient World* (Revolutionary work on the subject.)

NEOPLATONISM
Hornum, Michael, *On the Availability of the One*
Luck, Georg, *Theurgy and Forms of Worship in Neoplatonism*, in Neusner, Jacob, et al., ed., *Religion, Science, and Magic: In Concert and Conflict* (Switch the names and terms from Roman to Celtic and these folks sound Gardnerian!)
Dillon, John, *The Middle Platonists: 80 B.C. to A.D. 220* (The precursors to the Neoplatonists. This book has useful sections on Neopythagoreanism, the Chaldean Oracles, the Hermetica, and more.)
Nock, Arthur Darby, ed. & trans., *Sallustius: Concerning the Gods and the Universe* (A Neoplatonic catechism.)
Peters, F.E., *Greek Philosophical Terms: A Historical Lexicon* (Useful reference, with English-Greek dictionary.)
Wallis, R.T., *Neoplatonism* (Absolutely the best single work on Neoplatonism. Heavy going at times, but well worth the study.) Also, ed., *Neoplatonism and Gnosticism* (Good collection of relevant essays.)
Wright, Wilmer C., trans. *Philostratus and Eunapius: Lives of the Sophists* (Two books in one; the Eunapius has biographies of many Neoplatonists.)

NEOPLATONISM (Plotinus)
Armstrong, A.H., trans., *Plotinus*, (7 vols.), (Loeb Classical Library #440-445 & 468) (Best translation of the Enneads available in English.)
Gerson, Lloyd P., ed., *The Cambridge Companion to Plotinus*
Hadot, Pierre, *Plotinus or The Simplicity of Vision* (Very good introduction to Plotinus from the perspective of a personal spiritual path.)
O'Meara, Dominic J., *Plotinus: An Introduction to the Enneads* (Introduction to Plotinus from a theoretical perspective.)
MacKenna, Stephen, trans, *Plotinus: the Enneads* (The most readily available edition of the Enneads.)

NEOPLATONISM (Porphyry)
Hoffmann, R. Joseph, *Porphyry's Against the Christians: The Literary Remains* (Porphyry's original work was in 14 volumes and was considered by Christians to be the most dangerous book on Earth. All copies were collected and destroyed. This book is a collection of quotations and citations from Christian authors. The tone is so strident that I believe that Porphyry's words must have been altered by his opponents. Even so, this is an important work.)
Smith, Andrew, *Porphyry's Place in the Neoplatonic Tradition: A Study in Post-Plotinian Neoplatonism* (The second half of the book is on theurgy and Iamblichus.)
Zimmern, Alice, trans., *Porphyry's Letter to His Wife Marcella* (The Introduction by David Fideler is a great, concise, intro to Neoplatonism.)

NEOPLATONISM (Iamblichus)
Blumenthal, H.J., and Clark, E.G., eds. *The Divine Iamblichus: Philosopher and Man of the Gods* (Papers collected from a conference in 1990.)
Dillon, John, tr., *Iamblichii Chalcidensis in Platonis Dialogos Commentariorum Fragmenta*; Also, with Hershbell, Jackson, *Iamblichus: On the Pythagorean Way of Life*
Ronan, Stephen, ed., *Iamblichus of Chalcis* (Taylor's and Wilder's translations in parallel columns, plus "On the Sacred Art" and "On the Signs of Divine Possession" by Proclus.)
Shaw, Gregory, *Theurgy and the Soul: The Neoplatonism of Iamblichus*, (Excellent book on these subjects! Highly recommended!)
Taylor, Thomas, trans., *Iamblichus: On the Mysteries* (Dated language, but one of the few English translations in print.)

NEOPLATONISM (Proclus)
Guthrie, Kenneth S., trans., *The Life of Proclus* (Biography.)
Siorvanes, Lucas, *Proclus: Neo-Platonic Philosophy and Science*

continued next page

NEOPLATONISM (Damascius & Simplicius)
Athanassiadi, Polymnia, "Persecution and Response in Late Paganism: The Evidence of Damascius," in *The Journal of Hellenic Studies*, Volume CXIII
——————, trans., *Damascius: The Philosophical History*, Apamea Cultural Association, Athens, 1999 (The only English translation of this work by the last head of the Academy, who went to Harran.)
Hadot, Ilsetraut, "The Life and Work of Simplicius in Greek and Arabic Sources," in Sorabji, Richard, ed., *Aristotle Transformed: The Ancient Commentators and Their Influence* (Another Neoplatonist who went to Harran.)

JULIAN
Athanassiadi, Polymnia, *Julian: An Intellectual Biography* (Biography.)
Browning, Robert, *The Emperor Julian* (Biography.)
Smith, Rowland, *Julian's Gods: Religion and philosophy in the thought and action of Julian the Apostate*, Routledge, New York NY, 1995
Nock, Arthur Darby, ed. and trans., *Sallustius: Concerning the Gods and the Universe* (Most recent English translation of this work, commissioned by Julian to be a popular catechism of Neoplatonism.)
Taylor, Thomas, trans., *The Arguments of the Emperor Julian Against the Christians* (Hilarious rhetoric by the well-educated, thoroughly Pagan, Emperor of the known world against those upstart, country-bumpkin Christians!)
Vidal, Gore, *Julian* (Biographical novel and a good read!)

THE LAST DAYS OF CLASSICAL PAGANISM
Athanassiadi, Polymnia, and Frede, Michael, eds., *Pagan Monotheism in Late Antiquity* (Excellent and eye-opening! Must-read!)
Bowersock, G.W., Brown, Peter and Grabar, Oleg, eds., *Late Antiquity: A Guide to the Postclassical World* (Encyclopedic and comprehensive.)
Chuvin, Pierre, *A Chronicle of the Last Pagans* (The last days of classical Paganism.)
MacMullen, Ramsay, *Christianity & Paganism in the Fourth to Eighth Centuries* (One of those "Everything you know is wrong" kind of books. A must-read!)
Momigliano, Arnaldo, ed., *The Conflict Between Paganism and Christianity in the Fourth Century*
Smith, John Holland, *The Death of Classical Paganism* (A history of this period by a scholar who professes to be sympathetic to the Pagans. Refreshing and eye opening!)
Smith, Jonathan Z., *Drudgery Divine: On the Comparison of Early Christianities and the Religions of Late Antiquity* (Very good expose of Christian bias in the study of the religions of Late Antiquity.)
Valantasis, Richard, ed., *Religions of Late Antiquity in Practice*

CLASSICAL "SURVIVAL" IN LATER EUROPE
Baigent, Michael, and Leigh, Richard, *The Elixir and the Stone: Unlocking the Ancient Mysteries of the Occult* (Popular book by controversial authors of *Holy Blood, Holy Grail* is nevertheless a good history of the influence of Hermeticism down to the present day.)
Hankins, James, *Plato in the Italian Renaissance*
Maguire, Henry, ed., *Byzantine Magic* (Anthology.)
Merkel, Ingrid, and Debus, Allen G., eds., *Hermeticism and the Renaissance: Intellectual History and the Occult in Early Modern Europe*

CLASSICAL "SURVIVAL" IN ISLAM
(Note: This part of the Bibliography is a bit more extensive, as it hopes to be fairly comprehensive about this little-known area.)
Affifi, A.E., "The Influence of Hermetic Literature on Moslem Thought," in *Bulletin of the School of Oriental and African Studies*, Vol. XIII, pp. 840-855, (no other data available), 1951
Arberry, A. J., *Revelation and Reason in Islam*
Bowersock, G.W., *Hellenism in Late Antiquity*
Fowden, Garth, *Empire to Commonwealth: Consequences of monotheism in late antiquity*
Gutas, Dimitri, *Greek Thought, Arabic Culture: The Graeco-Arabic Translation Movement in Baghdad and Early Abbasid Society (2nd-4th/8th-10th centuries*
Kraemer, Joel L., *Humanism in the Renaissance of Islam: The Cultural Revival During the Buyid Age*; also *Philosophy in the Renaissance of Islam: Abu Sulayman al-Sijistani and His Circle* (Both include many mentions of Harran and the Sabians in connection with Classical learning.)
Morewedge, Parviz, ed., *Neoplatonism and Islamic Thought*
Nasr, Seyyed Hossein, "A Panorama of Classical Islamic Intellectual Life" and "Hermes and Hermetic Writings in the Islamic World," in Nasr, Seyyed Hossein, *Islamic Life and Thought*; also *Science & Civilization in Islam*; also *The Islamic Intellectual Tradition in Persia* (Discusses the influence of Hermeticism and Neoplatonism.)
Netton, Ian Richard, *Allah Transcendent: Studies in the Structure and Semiotics of Islamic Philosophy, Theology and Cosmology* (How Hermeticism and Neoplatonism shaped the Muslim conception of the Divine.) Also, *Al-Farabi and His School* (A Muslim philosopher influenced by Neoplatonism.)
Nicholson, R.A., *Literary History of the Arabs* (Lengthy history of intellectual thought and philosophy in Islam.)
OiLeary, De Lacy, *Islamic Thought and its Place in History* (Chapter 1 is The Syriac Version of Hellenism.)
Qadir, C.A., *Philosophy and Science in the Islamic World* (Includes Classical influence and mystical schools.)
Rosenthal, Franz, *The Classical Heritage in Islam*
Schacht, Joseph, ed., *The Legacy of Islam* (Discusses the role of Islam in transmitting Classical thought to the West.)
Smith, Margaret, *Studies in Early Mysticism in the Near and Middle East* (Influence of Neoplatonism.)
Walker, Paul E., *Early Philosophical Shiism: The Ismaili Neoplatonism of Abu Yaiqub al-Sijistani*

CLASSICAL "SURVIVAL" IN ISLAM
(Harran & the Sabians)
Ball, Warwick, *Rome in the East: The Transformation of an Empire* (Comprehensive account of Roman influence on the Middle East and vice-versa. Very good!)
Chwolson, D., *Die Ssabier und der Ssabismus (2 vols.)* (The standard classic on the Sabians. While dated, it is still an amazing collection of source texts.)
Corbin, Henry, *Temple and Contemplation* (The chapter on Sabian Temple and Ismailism is very interesting.); also *History of Islamic Philosophy* (Lots of info on the Sabians, Hermeticism, Neoplatonism, etc.)
Drijvers, H.J.W., *Cults and Beliefs at Edessa*
Green, Tamara, *The City of the Moon God: The Religious Traditions of Harran (Religions in the Graeco-Roman World*, Volume 114) (Excellent book on the survival of classical Paganism in Syria.)
Gunduz, Sinasi, *The Knowledge of Life: The Origins and Early History of the Mandaeans and Their Relation to the Sabians of the Qurían and to the Harranians*, (Journal of Semitic Studies Supplement 3)
Kurkcuoglu, A. Cihat, *Harran: The Mysterious City of History*
Lloyd, Seton, and Brice, William, "Harran," in *Anatolian Studies*, Vol. I, pp. 77-111
Peters, Francis, "Hermes and Harran: The Roots of Arabic-Islamic Occultism," in Mazzaoui, Michel M. and Moreen, Vera B., eds., *Intellectual Studies on Islam: Essays Written in Honor of Martin B. Dickson*
Prag, Kay, "The 1959 Deep Sounding at Harran in Turkey," in *Levant: Journal of the British School of Archaeology in Jerusalem*, Vol. II, pp. 63-94
Rice, D.S., "Medieval Harran: Studies on its Topography and Monuments," in *Anatolian Studies*, Vol. II, pp. 36-84
Ross, Steven, K., *Roman Edessa: Politics and Culture on the Eastern Fringes of the Roman Empire* (Includes important info on the inscriptions at Sumatar Harabesi.)
Saunders, J.J., *A History of Medieval Islam* (The place of Harran in the history of the Crusades.)
Segal, Judah Benzion, "Pagan Syriac Monuments in the Vilayet of Urfa," in *Anatolian Studies*, Vol. III, pp. 97-119 (The only published study of Sumatar Harabesi.); also "The Sabian Mysteries: The Planet Cult of Ancient Harran," in Bacon, Edward, ed., *Vanished Civilizations of the Ancient World; also Edessa:* "The Blessed City," Oxford University Press, Oxford, 1970
Springett, Bernard H., *Secret Sects of Syria and the Lebanon: A Consideration of Their Origin, Creeds, and Religious Ceremonies, and Their Connection With and Influence Upon Modern Freemasonry* (An odd book connecting Freemasonry and the Sabians.)
Stark, Freya, *Rome on the Euphrates: The Story of a Frontier* (Good, first person description of Roman remains in Mesopotamia, including Harran.)

CLASSICAL "SURVIVAL" IN ISLAM
(Harran & the Sabians: Contemporary Sources)
al-Andalusi, Saíid, *Science in the Medieval World.* (11th cent. CE. Discusses the Sabians, and Roman pagans as Sabian.)
al-Biruni, *The Chronology of Ancient Nations*, trans. & ed. by C. Edward Sachau (discusses Harranian festival dates.)
Broadhurst, Roland J.C., tr., *The Travels of Ibn Jubayr: A Medieval Spanish Muslim visits Makkah, Madinah, Egypt, cities of the Middle East, and Sicily* (12th cent. CE. A first-person description of Harran shortly before its fall.)
Brock, Sebastian P., "A Syriac Collection of Prophecies of the Pagan Philosophers," in *Orientalia Lovaniensia Periodica*, Vol. 14, pp 203-246; also, "Some Syriac Excerpts from Greek Collections of Pagan Prophecies," in *Vigiliae Christianae: A review of early christian life and language*, Vol. 38, pp. 77-90 (c. 600 CE. Both of these address texts attributed to Baba the Harranian.)
al-Nadim, Abu ël-Faraj Muhammad ibn Ishaq, *The Fihrist: A 10th Century AD Survey of Islamic Culture*, trans. and ed. by Bayard Dodge (10th cent. CE. One of the lengthiest discussions of the Harranians by a contemporary.)
Ibn Khaldun, *The Muqaddimah: An Introduction to History (3 vols.)*, trans. by Franz Rosenthal (14th cent. CE. Volume 2 includes a discussion of Sabians.)
Ibn Wahshiyya, *L'Agriculture Nabatenne (2 vols.)*, trans. and ed. by Toufic Fahd (10th cent. CE French translation of the Nabatean Agriculture, primary source on Harranian religion.)
Levey, Martin, tr. and ed., *Medieval Arabic Toxicology: The Book on Poisons of Ibn Wahshiya and Its Relation to early Indian and Greek Texts* (10th cent. CE. One of the few surviving magical writings by a Harranian.)
Maimonides, Moses, *The Guide for the Perplexed* (12th cent. CE. Lengthy discussion of the Sabeans and their beliefs.)
von Hammer-Purgstall, Joseph, tr., *Ancient Alphabets and Hieroglyphic Characters Explained* (translation of Ibn Wahshiya's "The long desired Knowledge of occult Alphabets attained.") (10th cent. CE. One of the few surviving magical writings by a Harranian.)

CLASSICAL "SURVIVAL" IN ISLAM
(Harran & the Sabians: The Ihkwan al-Safa (Brethren of Purity) & the Ghayat al-Hakim (Picatrix)
Nasr, Seyyed Hossein, *Islamic Science: An Illustrated Study* (Discusses the Ghayat al-Hakim.); also, *An Introduction to Islamic Cosmological Doctrines* (Discusses both the Ghayat al-Hakim and the Rasaiil Ikhwan al-Safa.)
Netton, Ian Richard, *Muslim Neoplatonists: An Introduction to the Thought of the Brethren of Purity* (Aka the Ikhwan al-Safa.)
Pingree, David, "Some of the Sources of the Ghayat al-Hakim," in *Journal of the Warburg and Courtauld Institutes*, Volume 43; also, ed., *Picatrix: The Latin version of the Ghayat Al-Hakim* (The *Picatrix* is an important source for Harranian ritual. While this edition is in Latin, the introduction is in English.)
Widengren, Geo, "The Pure Brethren and the Philosophical Structure of Their System," in Welch, Alford T. and Cachia, Pierre, eds., *Islam: Past Influence and Present Challenge*

CLASSICAL "SURVIVAL" IN ISLAM
(Harran & the Sabians: The Ishraqqiyah (Illuminationist School)
Nasr, Seyyed Hossein, *Three Muslim Sages: Avicenna & Suhrawardi & Ibn Arabi* (on Avicenna and Suhrawardi.)
Razavi, Mehdi Amin, *Suhrawardi and the School of Illumination*
al-Suhrawardi, Hazrat Shabuddin Yahya, *The Shape of Light (Hayakal Al-Nur); also, The Philosophy of Illumination* (English translations of 12th cent. CE texts.)
Walbridge, John, *The Science of Mystic Lights. The Leaven of the Ancients: Suhrawardi & the Heritage of the Greeks.*
Ziai, Hossein, *Knowledge and Illumination: A Study of Suhrawardiís Hikmat al-Ishraq*

WEBSITES

Websites with Frew's online articles:
http://dmoz.org/Society/Religion_and_Spirituality/Esoteric_and_Occult/Personalities/Frew,_Donald_H./
Interfaith Websites:
* Council for a Parliament of the World's Religions:
http://www.cpwr.org
* United Religions Initiative:
http://www.uri.org

Sam Skraeling - IOWASKA

Sam Skraeling is the female guitarist/vocalist for Iowaska, a U.K punk/psychedelia/Pagan band with members formerly in the Skraelings and Amebix. In the early '80s, Sam was involved in Anarchy & Peace, a U.K. collective, and has been a Pagan cultural activist for years. Iowaska happily plays benefits for environmental and political protests. Sam is also a painter. For more information, search for "iowaska" on *google.com* or *surfwax.com*. For their new CD, *Vine of Souls,* see *www.alternativetentacles.com*. Interview by V. Vale.

♦ SAM SKRAELING: The first three women to be hanged for Witchcraft in England in the 16th century came from the area our band is based in—Essex, on the east coast. In 555 A.D. when St. Augustus sent a Christian posse to Christianize England, Essex was the last Pagan holdout 'til the 8th Century.

One of our songs is called "Modranicht," meaning "Mother's Night" after an ancient festival celebrating the mother and the mother goddess—the women of the tribe as life-givers. Gifts were exchanged. We learn this from the 7th-century writer Bede, who described the Pagans of his time. *Modranicht* (December 24) became Jesus Christ's birthday.

Unlike the west country which contains Stonehenge and the Avebury rings [stone circles], Essex was ignored by archaeologists. There were stone circles, but long ago they were robbed to make buildings. But there are a lot of longbarrows (ancient Pagan burial sites) which, in my opinion, symbolized re-entering the womb. There's a dark, long passage into the earth, opening into a big, swollen room. I think this symbolically represented taking the soul back to Mother Earth.

♦ RE/SEARCH: *That's a great metaphor.*

♦ S: Essex has also yielded a number of small statues of women with big breasts and rounded tummies. For a university course, I began research into women land-holding here. After the Norman conquest, women were no longer allowed to own property. But I found that previously there were 48 Saxon women landholders who were major powers in society. If Harold had won the Battle of Hastings, maybe women wouldn't have had to wait until the 20th century for emancipation!

A 1985 archeological dig in Essex uncovered a settlement of wooden Saxon buildings once belonging to Odin the Dane. [Through research I determined this was "Berewic," described in the *Domesday* book.] A horse's skull with full gold bridle was found, Pagan burial urns, and a great broadsword amazingly decorated with stones, silver and gold, which had been bent into a *circle.* This site lies practically at our doorstep. Oddly enough, a friend belongs to a rune guild which often does "workings" here, calling upon Odin and Freya. What a mad coincidence—at the same *site* they were calling upon the same Norse deities as Pagans had done a thousand years earlier!

Actually, Paganism is very intertwined in our culture. I'm interested in archeology and history, and when I was in San Francisco's Haight-Ashbury district I saw a number of streets named after Freemason lodges. A lot of old names, or street names, give you clues as to what was there originally.

♦ *R/S: What about Paganism appeals to you?*

♦ S: Taking control of your life. When the free festival movement in England got big in the late Eighties, I lived in a van on the road. I went to Stonehenge and saw a police cordon seven miles long—imagine what that cost?! What really scares "authority" is lots and lots of people with open minds and an *idea* getting together to change things.

Religions like Christianity are about you not wanting to accept responsibility for your own life—you can say, "The Devil made me do it." These days, people are born and sent to school, school tells them what to do, then they go to work, the boss tells them what to do, the boss gives them three weeks' holiday, they take a package holiday where the holiday rep tells them where to go. Most of these people, when they actually have a day where no one's telling them what to do, say they're bored! They literally have no more mental capacity anymore to take responsibility for their own lives. Their religion reflects this non-responsibility. I think what Paganism does—and this is the reason why it scares people—is, it's total responsibility for your own life. **What you do in your actions, you are totally responsible for. That is the fundamental basis of the Pagan religion.** And this is why I'm vegetarian—I couldn't look an animal in the eye and then hit it over the head!

Many are Pagans without calling themselves as such. For centuries people around Essex would bury a cake in a field—they felt that if Mother Earth is going to give them a whole field full of crops, the least they can do is bake her a cake! As for people who think they have no spiritual side, you could ask them, "How many times have you thought about somebody, and the phone rings and it's *them?*" There are many powers and forces that are yet unaccounted for. I feel that the basic philosophy of being totally responsible for yourself *is* Paganism, even if the person who believes this doesn't call themselves "Pagan." This relates to D-I-Y punk—what counts is what you actually *DO* yourself. You don't have to put on a robe and tote out a bell, book and candle—you can practice Paganism naked if you want! You can do it anywhere, anytime, any place. I can understand that some people feel a need for theatrics, but I personally feel that the real truth behind it, and what's real, is just *you*—your belief, and you being "real" inside. That's real Paganism.

Paganism is about people taking back empowerment, acknowledging that there are phenomena that can't be

explained in terms of molecular biology and science. A lot of disinformation about Paganism comes from corporate media—they want to make it farcical and unbelievable, just like the way they reported about crop circles in Britain. In England there have been a lot of symbols appearing in corn crops, like fractals and *ad infinitum* circles, paisley shapes, etc. For example, one farmer went to bed and the next morning 400 perfect circles could be seen in his cornfield from the air—they weren't there the night before. All the stalks had been bent 45 inches up from the ground at a 45-degree angle. This couldn't have been done in that time by actual people on the ground. Yet—just like Paganism—none of this gets any serious consideration in the media. ♦♦♦

Sam & Tara Webster

Sam & Tara Webster each have 20 years of magical practice. They write and conduct workshops. Tara is a licensed clinical social worker and works as a psychotherapist, while Sam works as a project manager for a software firm. Interview by John Sulak; follow-up interview by V. Vale.

♦ **RE/SEARCH: Why do you think you're attracted to Paganism?**

♦ TARA WEBSTER: When I was a child, I used to love to play witch. I would call myself a witch and pretend to cast spells and talk to other beings. My mother was very supportive, calling me her "little witch." She's always been a very magical person.

My family is Irish. My great-grandmother came to America from Ireland, and raised her daughter in a very "accepting of psychic phenomena" way. That in turn was passed down to my mom and me. Magical and weird ways of thinking have always been normal in my family.

I've been a practicing Pagan, formally, for about 20 years. I'm also a professional psychotherapist and a licensed clinical social worker with a masters degree. A lot of my magical work is focused on personal transformation and healing.

♦ SAM WEBSTER: I have a masters degree in Divinity from Starr King School for the Ministry, which is part of the Graduate Theological Union in Berkeley, California. I'm an adept of the Golden Dawn, a Sovereign of the Chthonic Ouranian Ordo Templi Orientus, and have been a Pagan about as long as Tara. Like many Pagans I make my living with computers. And I serve my community as a priest of the god Hermes.

♦ **R/S: Who is Hermes?**

♦ SW: Originally a Mycenaean Greek deity, he became one of the gods in the Olympic pantheon. He is principally known for his messenger service but is also known as a trickster god. On the day he was born he invented the lyre, stole Apollo's cattle, and made fire by inventing the fire drill. He is known as the master and teacher of languages, mathematics, the sciences and all of the arts. Basically, he represents the impulse to take what we're given by nature and extend it through technology. He's the little boy who followed the Neolithic woman scattering seeds and said, "Why don't we take a stick, dig a furrow and put the seeds under the soil so the birds can't get them?" That's the Hermes intelligence, and that's whom I serve.

Originally Thoth, the Egyptian scribe god, was my patron when I started doing magic. I felt that he was showing me how things actually worked—as opposed to the way they were described in books. While I was studying at the Seminary in Berkeley he introduced me to Hermes, who is much more human.

♦ **R/S: Tara, what deities do you work with?**

♦ TW: Hekate, who migrated from Anatolia to the Greek pantheon, and is a guide between the world of life and the underworld (the world of death). Birth and death are sacred to her. She represents working with transition—it can be psychological or physical. Anytime anything is shedding its old way and moving into a new way—that's her realm.

She's a crossroads goddess, and one of her main symbols is the junction where three roads meet. Mythologically, that's where she's present: helping travelers make choices. She won't tell people what choice to make, but will point out different paths available to them. The ancient Greeks put food out at crossroads to honor her. Another one of her symbols is a key, to make the transition through a door easier. She helps people get to where they need to go. Keys are sacred to her.

Sam and I are probably ideally suited to be magical partners; Hermes and Hekate are said to be consorts. As far as we know, Hekate weaved a karmic spell to bring us together. Our relationship is founded on creativity; we've known each other 13 years and have been married for 12.

♦ **R/S: How did you find out about Hekate?**

♦ TW: When I was working with a circular tarot deck called the Mother Peace deck, the accompanying book discussed the crone card as the goddess Hekate. After doing research, I started invoking her and doing meditations with her. Then she started showing up much more often in my life.

♦ **R/S: The two of you have created wonderful rituals—**

♦ SW: Ritual always involves *transformation through communication.* In Western society, the Protestant reformation brought about a revulsion against ritual—not surprising, since the dominant ritual culture of the Roman Catholic Church had become very corrupt, peddling indulgences and the like: "No matter *what* you've done, for a price you can get into heaven!"

Ritual had been cheapened and degraded; it had ossified and hadn't changed to serve the needs of the day. **In living ritual societies, however old and formalized the rituals are, the "masters" know how to adjust the ritual to serve the reality of the moment:** "Okay, today we don't have blue flowers, so we'll use yellow ones. But it'll all be fine—don't worry."

I was raised Roman Catholic, so I had a ritual sensibility. But early on I started questioning the church's rigidity. What I immediately liked about the Pagan community was that people had the freedom to not only use old rituals, but to continually create new ones.

A major purpose of ritual is to enable us to transform ourselves, especially when "who we are" no longer works. Who we are is an adaptation to the last set of challenges we've been given, but the reality is that life moves on and we receive new sets of challenges. Whether it's making the transition from child to adult, or from winter to spring, periodically there awaits a whole new set of duties.

Ritual helps us more quickly adapt to become who we have to become. It's about drawing the line, killing off the old self, creating the new self, and stepping across the line into that new self and new life. And to the extent we do each of those well, we create powerful, effective, transformative, renewing rituals.

How do we do that? This led me to the discipline called Ritual Studies.

In 1906 Arnold Van Gnepp coined the term "rite of passage" to identify the transformation from one state to another state. He compared it to moving from one room to another room, with a passageway in between. There is a threshold you must cross to get from where you were, to where you're going to be. This appears to be *the* basic ritual pattern, and everything else is a variation on that scheme. For the past ten years Tara and I have composed rituals for all kinds of people—especially established groups where we know everybody involved. And we all sit down together and by consensus design a ritual.

♦ TW: Those rituals are the kind that serve people. But Sam and I also do solo practice. Deity-oriented magic, which is a devotional between the practitioner and the deity, is a very personal relationship which is usually private. Frequently the deity will disclose particular lessons somebody really needs to learn, and answer questions. The deity gives me tasks, guides me, and tells me what I need to do for my own growth. Not to sound too New Age-y, but they tell us what to do on the earth plane.

♦ SW: It's a collaborative relationship.

♦ TW: Exactly. I don't see them as great beings that I supplicate; I see them as partners in a powerful working relationship. They need *us* and the tools we can offer, just as much as we need them.

There are certain people who have an affinity for a style of magic, where you communicate with the deities. You remain completely and consciously aware the whole time—you don't lose your memory or go anywhere. You're just sharing your consciousness with the deity's presence.

I've struggled with questions like, "What *are* these deities that I work with? Where did these words emerging in my consciousness come from? Is this a power from myself that I project outwardly and have a 'relationship' with? Or is there in fact an independent, separate entity that I communicate with?" Those are tough questions. It really doesn't matter where it's coming from, so long as I take responsibility for its effects.

♦ *R/S: How were the deities originally worshipped?*

♦ SW: In Mesopotamian culture, the temple was where all the metal tools, grain, and records were stored. It was the hospital, the administrative center—basically the center of the community. When the community became attacked by the horse peoples, they had to develop a warrior group to protect themselves. The epic of *Gilgamesh* is about that transitional period when a warlord arises. There's tension between the palace and the temple for the latter period of that culture.

Now, our economic system is entirely different; we're not an agrarian or pastoral society. In those days, you needed to monitor the sun's cycle to know when to plant or harvest. But moving quickly to the present: when I worked in Hollywood, what was important in my life was the production cycle of the film industry. You work hard during the summer, rest a bit and then search for your next job—in spirit, it's the same thing. I don't have to cut down the grain fields and kill half of my lambs to have enough provisions for the winter, but fundamentally the same cyclical challenge exists.

We do a Mesopotamian temple-culture reconstructionist ritual for the first crescent of the moon. When the moon was not visible, that signified that Ishtar/Inanna was visiting her sister in the underworld, so the temple was sealed for those three nights. That was when the staff took a break. When the moon returned, they staged a big party: "We're so glad you made it back—here, have some food and drink! Let us again receive your blessing!"

♦ TW: Then it's time to recommit, and rededicate ourselves and our energy to the next moon cycle's work. One month the focus might be on service to the deity, the next month about service to others. Ishtar/Inanna are very powerful when it comes to sexual healing and sacred sexuality, so when we do the "first crescent of the moon" ritual, that's a chance for sex workers and sexual healers to receive nurturing and then re-commit themselves to that work.

♦ *R/S: Is this ritual about sexual healing, or sexual pleasure and celebration?*

♦ TW: Both. There are three kinds of rituals: celebratory, devotional and magical. Celebration is simply for celebration and enjoyment. Devotional is for giving the gods and goddesses their due, to help them gain strength and a stronger presence in this world. Magical rituals are for taking the power we can generate within ourselves and directing that toward a specific goal.

Paganism views sexuality as a sacrament. It can be used as a mode of worship, celebration, or to generate magical energy to achieve a goal. It could be energy generated for spell work. Unlike some other religions, sexuality is valued positively.

♦ *R/S: How long have you done the crescent moon ritual?*

♦ TW: Nine years. We also do a very old Greek ritual where we make offerings to Hermes and Hekate. At the dark of the moon, travelers often had a hard time finding their way. At the heketerions or herms—stone markers on roads—they would leave offerings of food for the deities, and receive directions and guidance which helped them find their way.

Nowadays we have a room set up with altars and a temple space where we do invocations, make offerings, and pour ale for Hermes and wine for Hekate. Everybody in attendance has an opportunity to ask for something they want to happen that month, as well as honor and celebrate the deity. Then we do an oracle reading with Tarot which I call "The Dark Moon Report." Everybody pulls three Tarot cards—that's a way of receiving symbolic guidance from the Goddess and the God.

♦ *R/S: What about people who need professional help?*

♦ SW: We may suggest they find a good therapist. On the other hand, psychotherapy doesn't have all the tools. One of the great powers of ritual is that it actually helps people transform.

♦ TW: Psychotherapy works on the basis of language. A psychotherapist addresses the conscious and unconscious mind using words and metaphors that work on a certain level. But for some people, "talking therapy" doesn't speak to a deeper part of the brain. Ritual works with metaphoric and archetypal symbols that circumvent the verbal defenses our minds put up to protect us from the pain of the issues we cling to. **Ritual work can bypass the defenses that keep us from being able to heal! The same defenses that protect our pain also keep us from being able to access it, release it, and heal it.**

As a psychotherapist I've worked with people for years, and have watched them try various anti-depressant medications and not make much progress. But I've seen people cured of life-long depression using ritual. I believe you can get value from both practices.

Many ancient myths are about people learning how to take their own power and create boundaries. Adolescents grow into adulthood by setting boundaries, cutting ties that are unhealthy for them, and making choices. Rituals of rites-of-passage affirm people's ability to do that. Our culture, on the other hand, actually *creates* co-dependent situations by roping us into feeling that we always have to get approval.

♦ SW: Psychotherapy or ritual is about hacking somebody's code—the very code of their existence, the rules and symbols by which they operate. Inherent in everyone is a deep, powerful symbol system which their own psyche hooks into and activates. My task as a ritualist is to uncover this system and language and weave it into a ritual that will achieve a transformation—from where someone is, to where they want to go.

Once people learn basic ritual structures and patterns that work, and have the opportunity to fail enough times gracefully, they'll hit upon what constitutes "success." Ritual is intuitive, aesthetically driven, and is an art form. To make it really *zing* takes artistic ability and experience.

♦ TW: I take my inspiration from natural processes on the planet. For example, the process of childbirth provides a powerful lesson in how to use pain to grow, and how pain and life are intertwined. In this case, pain actually brings something wonderful into the world. We can take that as a model for handling emotional pain, for instance, and valorize it as beneficial: "While I'm going through this painful process, I'm experiencing an internal rebirth of my psyche."

♦ SW: The notion of studying "Nature" is so important that it's overlooked in its obviousness. Historically, most monotheist doctrines portrayed nature as irrational and "fallen"; you'd want to study reason and scripture, but not "Nature"—it was too red, bloody, tooth-and-claw—just nasty.

However, a few people inherited the Egyptian perspective and viewed Nature and the human mind as a manifestation of the divine mind; i.e., humans are operators in the world for the divine mind. This Hermetic movement started over 2,000 years ago and is the basis for most of Western magic, thanks to the preservation efforts of Witches and magicians through the ages. It advocates that Nature is already the embodiment of the good, therefore we should study it. It turns us away from the anthropocentric view of the world—the Biblical idea that nature is here for us to *use*. Instead, **Nature is regarded as the ultimate technology which has taken billions of years to develop.** It has endured more trial and

error than we ever could. So if I want to learn something, I'll first ask, "Hasn't nature solved this kind of problem first? Let me see what she has already come up with."

♦ TW: You can study ritual for 60 years and still have more to learn. As humans, we do rituals every day—brushing our teeth is a ritual that marks a transitional point in the morning.

Rituals bring meaning to people's lives. Creating an altar of meaningful objects can help people pass through perplexing times; it can help ground and center them and connect them to nature. Get a shell, a feather, a rock and a candle and you have the four elements. They're on your table, and you can call on them. You light a candle and your consciousness changes—that's magic, that's ritual. Just sitting with those objects, looking at them and thinking about where the shell came from, and meditating on the ocean that gave birth to it and all of life on the planet . . . somehow your mind begins to deepen and open, you relax, and you start to shift into a state of consciousness that, if you were hooked up to a biofeedback machine, would probably consist of alpha-level brain waves. That's magic!

You don't necessarily have to read a lot of books, study with a coven and undergo elaborate training. Ritual is available here and now to all of us, and our intuition has a lot to teach us, too. We need to be suspicious of anyone who says, "You must find an all-knowing authority to help you access this." I think it *helps* to have people to guide and teach you, and offer information and wisdom. But so much of it is already within ourselves—that's one of the most powerful ideas of Paganism. However, not all traditions agree with this.

When I teach someone magic, I'll give them basic information about doing a Pagan ritual and what the elements mean. But really, I'm listening for how they process the world, what's meaningful for them, and what the symbols are that they work with. I'm helping them access their own wisdom. **That's what it's all about: helping people access their own wisdom**—i.e., empowering them to come into their own.

♦ SW: Which is what the Hermetic tradition means by, "Our minds are already part of the divine mind." It's already there; you just have to learn how to listen. The *techniques* are about learning how to calm down enough to be able to listen to the inherent wisdom within ourselves that has always been and will always be. If we continue to delve down to that level, we can access that wisdom, understanding, and guidance throughout our lives.

♦ **R/S: *Where do the deities fit into all of this?***

♦ TW: Not everybody who works with magic and ritual is going to feel comfortable working with the external polytheistic pantheon that so many Pagans subscribe to. Instead of calling some being named Hekate, they may just go into their back yard, put their hands on the soil and connect to the nearest tree, feeling the power and the energy right there. That *immediate pantheism* can transmit power, intuition and information, just as when I sit at my altar, call Hekate and hear her talk to me.

♦ SW: It's all about seeking access to, for lack of a better term, the Great Divine. Gods and goddesses like Hermes, Hekate, Ishtar and Inanna have very distinct personalities, whereas Egyptian deities are more like the principles of nature. Some beings function like masks you can wear—you learn to look at the world through their eyes. And this brings us to the two principal approaches to deity work.

The standard Western, Judaic, Christian and Islamic

approach is dualistic: you worship, supplicate and ask for a blessing from an Other. This is very powerful, and we do it regularly. Yet it's not the only way. To a Hindu who had studied the *Vedas* and the *Upanishads,* the divine is already within. Part of working with deities involves *becoming* deity.

There are techniques whereby we shed our human selves. In Pueblo culture, the Kachina initiation ceremony involves putting on the mask of the god and looking out through the god's eyes. Buddhism regards this as a kind of ultimate practice—something that will take you to complete enlightenment, because this is how you learn to transform the world into the divine realm. Everyone around you and everything around you becomes deity—your cats become divine creatures! The whole world becomes alive and rich with symbolism and meaning. It can utterly transform a life.

♦ *R/S: Can this "transformation into deity" be done in larger groups?*

♦ SW: Yes. At a recent Pagan festival, two of our priestesses (one of whom was Tara) donned the deity forms of Ishtar and Inanna and participated in a ritual with 150 Pagans. And people had the opportunity to worship them as beings holding that goddess form. This kind of large-scale ritual is about *embodying archetypes.* It's not about cognitive verbal instruction: "This is who she is, and here's what this action means." Rather, these are *symbolic* actions which impact people at a deeper level.

♦ *R/S: What recent rites of passage have you assisted?*

♦ TW: Last month we were in a wedding ceremony where the couple asked Sam and I to each hold a particular deity they wanted to "charge" their wedding with. At some point we felt they needed to be whisked away and nurtured and pampered—

♦ SW: The bride and groom were far too busy making everything happen to do that for themselves.

♦ TW: Right. So we blindfolded the bride and brought her before a room, asking questions like, "You are standing before a threshold; what are you letting go of as you move into this new phase of your life? What are you moving towards, and what does this mean to you?" We brought her into the room and gave her a simple ritual bath. We were singing and drumming while bathing her; we had beautiful flowers and fragrant oils and performed a body blessing upon her, and gave her a massage. Then we sat in a circle and told stories about what it meant to be married. We listened to her talk. We gave her gifts and pampered her. And at the end, she was ready.

It was very gentle. Some initiation/threshold rituals can be brutal and challenging, where you feel your guts are being ripped out. But this was very sweet and nurturing.

♦ SW: It needed to be. The groom had just had a nasty fight with his father on the rehearsal night. He thought he would just try to calm down after this nasty interchange. But when his bride got whisked out of the room, I said, "You didn't think we were going to leave you alone?" I asked him to trust us, and we blindfolded him and led him to the other end of the hotel. Then we anointed him with earth, reminded him just how much of a threshold he was walking across, and bathed, oiled and massaged him for an extended period of time. The men present reflected on their different states of marriage, opening their hearts to him. The others didn't even know about the conflict he'd just had with his father, but we all knew we needed to do something to help him prepare.

This wasn't elaborate or a big deal—we just used the resources at hand. We came with no preparation; the ladies were much better prepared for theirs. The men gathered, talked about it, quickly worked out a simple pattern and made it happen. Basically, we helped him put aside the past and prepare for moving forward. As part of the separation aspect, we trimmed his pubic hair: "This is the setting aside of all those old sexual relationships and partnerships that didn't work. Now you're entering into something new. Be prepared to receive your bride, and now just rest." And it worked for him; he needed nurturing from the warmth and hearts of other men. And from there, he was ready to get married.

You can be your own priest or priestess. In this case, we had an advantage in that a number of us had already worked ritual together, so we were comfortable with that. For example, nudity wasn't an issue, so stripping the groom and putting him in the shower was, again, not problematic. Homophilia and homophobia aren't an issue with us; we, as a community have that advantage. But, with allowances for other people's needs and values, somebody else could compose something similar.

I attended two other weddings last month, including a traditional bachelor party with a stripper for the groom. The girl engaged in a play situation with him, and yet even she understood that this was a threshold. That was rather touching: she said that he was "kissing his single life good-bye."

♦ TW: Ritual is one of the ways whereby we give more meaning to our lives, access who we are, and are able to be more fully "present" in our lives. Putting ritual in the context of Paganism means living more closely in tune with the cycles of nature.

♦ SW: **Ritual is, at the very least, a human birthright—it is your right/rite! Not having it, I believe, creates long-term mental illness in Western society.** Ritual is something that we have to reawaken. The Pagan/magical community is one of the last places in Western society where there is a living ritual tradition.

But I want the ritual methodology to spread out to anyone else who wants to use it. Because the truth is: the cultural overlay and symbol set that a person uses is entirely dependent on the person using it. It could be Christian, Islamic, Native American, Goth, derived from J.R.R. Tolkien, or just be something entirely made up!

What truly matters is that people use symbols that are meaningful to *them,* having them transform their life. Because all too often, people get stuck and they suffer. On this point, I'm with the Buddhist program: the core purpose of Buddhism is to relieve suffering, and first we must acknowledge that suffering exists. For warriors, there is no greater opponent than suffering itself.

But, I'm an engineer because I like to construct things; I figure we can work on our problems and solve them—build a way out of them. The big goal is to defeat suffering ultimately and permanently. This may a few billion more lifetimes! But I don't know of a more worthy task to do with a life than to serve that end.

♦ *R/S: What do you think are the most important "source" materials for Pagans?*

♦ SW: There are tons of books, in a certain sense, and not many, in another. The books of theology, theory and philosophy have been preserved. The books of technique/technology have mostly not been preserved for two reasons: 1) that tends to be taught mouth-to-ear, so a lot of it never gets written down, 2) when it gets written down, those are the books that get burned first!

Magic is an art of mixed value in society. When it is "legitimate"—permitted by the state and society—its practices tend to get incorporated as religion or as civil ritual, which you have in the Roman state. Then you have illegitimate or illicit ritual and magic, which sometimes is tolerated, and sometimes is hunted down and exterminated—the so-called witch burnings of the 14th century are a good example of that. **Even today in Africa people are picked out as being negative magic users and are killed.** And they're called witches, although they could simply be old people who somebody thought threw a hex on them. *That's* why "tech" is not very available.

In addition to the *Picatrix,* the ancient "ur-grimoire" or the Western magickal tradition, what we have as sources for "tech" include breakthrough works like Ficino's *How To Live Your Life By the Heavens* and Agrippa's three books of *Occult Philosophy.* More modernly we find the books by Eliphas Levi, the Golden Dawn, and Aleister Crowley. Those are the big pulses of "tech" being poured out into the world. Most of what we have comes from there—at least within the core hermetic Neo-Platonic stream.

Then we have all the other cultures with their more "native" types of religions which are essentially drawing on shamanic foundations. But they're usually coming up with the same tech, because ultimately we're all, as it were, dealing with the same hardware or *wetware*—the same set of problems and the same set of tools. So even though the maps vary a bit, the methods are pretty much the same worldwide.

I'm reading Iamblichus who, in his own modest, eternalist manner, is describing the same reasons for doing "deity yoga" as the Dalai Lama gives. Union with the deity is one of the fundamental techniques of magic and religion. So, *tech is tech,* as I like to put it.

♦ *R/S: And tech is also the most threatening—*

♦ SW: Because it's the means by which you can actually DO the stuff the philosophers talk about. Basically Iamblichus was saying to the other philosophers, "We have to DO the work; we can't just talk about it." By doing so we resanctify the world and actually complete the process of creation of the world through perfecting ourselves.

There's a split between the magical community and the Wiccan or Pagan community. **In the magical community you can't get around Crowley; he's just there.** I'm not really Crowleyan, but I am "Thelemic" in my approach—which is a philosophy that he scribbled down in some bizarre poetry.

There are different strategies along the spiritual path. Christianity, at least in theory, focuses on *love,* and Buddhism to some extent, on *compassion* but also emptiness and meditation. In Thelema, we focus on will . . . that is, the fundamental question of will and ethics: *What do I do?*

♦ TW: "Thelema" is the Greek word for will.

♦ SW: We mean the creative will. Crowley outlined an approach to using the will in a magical setting in the *Book of the Law.* Intertwined with notions from Egyptian "theology," Yoga, Buddhism, and a few other schools, he described the crystallization of a technique and an attitude that is incredibly powerful. (I happen to be fond of it, myself.)

♦ *R/S: Can you connect Paganism to Egyptology—particularly the legacy of R.A. and Isha Schwaller de Lubicz?*

♦ SW: Even the academics are recognizing that the whole hermetic corpus, the hermetic texts, include restatements of the Egyptian mode of worship. By including Egyptian cultic practices, Iamblichus was attempting to restore meaning and power into his philosophy. Allegedly, the Egyptians had the purest, most original, *old* way of doing things that embodied the divine nature on Earth, thus making Earth holy with people living in harmony.

Egyptian religious or magical practice got re-introduced into the Western psyche through the Golden Dawn, who used it as the basis for a lot of their work. They used Egyptian god forms, colors, images, etc—and this shows up in Crowley's *Book of the Law.* One might call this the Thelemic restatement of the Egyptian *gnosis,* because it definitely draws on Egypt while creating something new. There's an "Egyptian" group in Southern California, and a Bast [Egyptian cat-deity] group in the Bay Area. Many Thelemic folk use Egyptian modes of worship, including me.

But R.A. Schwaller . . . he's known to be a numerologist by the academics. Amongst scientists and chemists, he's known as an alchemist. He may have been the last person to produce the blues and reds in the stained glass of the Chartres cathedral. This is his fundamental claim to fame and it's no mean feat—*nobody* has been able to do it except him. It has to do with the way the pigment moves throughout the glass. Apparently it's an alchemical process which, if you don't do the work within your own being or psyche, you can't get it to happen in the material realm. And he presented a theory and methodology for this, rooted in an apprehension of the Egyptian *gnosis.*

Schwaller de Lubicz was one of the first to demonstrate that the Egyptians were clear on the proportions of humanity as reflective of the cosmos [*The Temple of Man*]. This was sometimes thought to be a Greek notion, but de Lubicz demonstrated that the initiatory temple at Luxor was built on the basis of the human form: "I think the Egyptians built these walls crooked on purpose." He had workers take up the floor panels to uncover the double axis down below—the perfect dimensions to show *Phi,* which is the mathematical constant that governs biological growth and spirals. That was just heart-stopping to me. Of course, when some British saw this, they said, "What's with these Egyptians? They can't build anything square!"

Basically, the path we're traveling is a spiritual process. We're putting on god forms, invoking deities, and conjuring spirits so as to temper our souls and make them more whole. There's a sense in which our experience of the world is incomplete and unfinished. So by conjuring up "sets" of things—and the "set-ness" is very important—we then begin to apprehend the whole of existence as a unity, and get an inkling of what it's like to live in that divine experience.

The *neters,* the deities of Egypt, the elemental principles, the planetary principles, the supernal principles that are invoked in Kabalah—all of these have as their initiatory purpose to make

Photo this page: Bruce Folck

the aspirant whole. By following this path, we become whole, hale, healthy and happy in the world; we continue our inherent cosmogonic function as agents of the creator in creation, continuing creation. It's not like we have nothing here to do! And the only way we can do this is by fulfilling our own process of self-development and then getting to work.

Those are the two first phases of magical practice: first, as a *neophyte*—one who figures out how to put the whole together, and then as an *adept*—one who begins to wield that whole so as to understand the world and eventually attain mastery. That's the salvation of the magical way.

♦ *R/S: Why aren't Pagans more influenced by the Egyptian heritage? These are some of the oldest rituals and invocations, preserved quite precisely—*

♦ SW: Well, there's a big legacy in India and China, too. There's also the Aboriginal tradition, which may go back tens of thousands of years. In Australia, people have started tape-recording the old stories as fast as possible, or writing them down; the culture is quickly being destroyed. In China, the Taoist stream goes back thousands of years—legendarily, Taoist magicians had the ability to perform astonishing feats (change the weather, climb

ropes up into the heavens), along with the fakirs in India and North Africa. And The *I Ching* is at least a couple thousand years old.

♦ TW: We use the *I Ching* all the time.

♦ *R/S: What about Tantra?*

♦ SW: The problem with Tantra is, unless you've broken the hold of *form* on your being, it's only going to make things worse! All magic is fundamentally based on the

principle that you have to be able to *handle* the attractive nature of form and not get immersed in it. Normally we get attached to it, we hang onto it. It's like picking up rocks on a seashore—you pick up more and more, and after awhile you can't carry anymore . . . instead of just picking up one, enjoying it, then putting it down and going on to the next one.

In trying to blend sexuality with spirituality, people tend to get obsessed with the sex and not move on to the spirituality which involves the sex fully. There's this strange dynamic around the body and materiality where, as long as you don't clutch after it, you can have it. But the second you start clutching after it, it becomes a real problem.

Tantric sex is a method of practice, and it takes learning to view the world from that perspective, plus having a partner to share the total practice with. Sex and transcendence—that's a whole book in itself. That point where everything in the universe makes sense to you—that's called omniscient Buddhahood.

♦ *R/S: Do you use oracular technologies such as the Tarot, numerology, the runes system—*

♦ SW: I don't use runes as a mode of divination. But the Tarot is integral. Kabalistic style numerology is unfortunately in my brains and blood; I can't get away from it. Astrology is intertwined with all of that. I learned the *I Ching* relatively early on, and it's really good for decision-making, so I find that it's still a useful technique.

♦ *R/S: Even trashy pop-culture books on numerology still seem to "work"—*

♦ SW: All whole systems map to other whole systems. As long as you've got some sort of [cohesive, structural] basis for your divinatory system, it's going to work. The question is, Can you get the kind of answers you're looking for? Different systems work better for different situations. Astrology tells you *when* to do things. Tarot tells you what's going on. The *I Ching* basically tells you which to choose.

♦ *R/S: Tara, what are your thoughts on Pagan aesthetics?*

♦ TW: The Pagan aesthetic is about adorning the body in such a way as to reveal the magickal self. It lets us reveal our personal symbols. It induces trance in both the adorned and the onlooker. Individual Pagans do this in different ways.

Some people do it through body modification, and others simply through clothing. For ritual, some covens will wear the same kind of robe with a belt that shows a different color, depending on one's level of initiation. Others will dress in special garb that is unique to each. Still others may be in what we call normal clothes. Nudity is common among Pagans; we call it "skyclad." As an aesthetic choice, nudity can symbolize being wide open, revealing the self fully in love and trust. It can also mean pure comfort in one's body. My personal aesthetic involves clothing that accentuates the movements of Middle Eastern dance. As a Bellydancer, one of my primary ways of worship and celebration is through dance. So, essentially, the Pagan aesthetic creates a way to contact and invoke the deeper magical self.

♦ SW: I tend to wear a black shirt and black pants that are comfortable and loose. Maybe I'll put on some ornaments. It's functional.

♦ TW: There's a phenomenal amount of support—not only tolerance of, but *celebration* of—diversity in the Pagan community. People are encouraged to express themselves visually in ways that are unique. Clothing can help bring us into a different state of brain activity, literally moving into slower alpha wave production. This also helps put us in touch with our child-like nature. Both children and Pagans like to dress up; perhaps Pagans are trying to reclaim that part of the magical mind that gets lost as children mature into adults.

♦ *R/S: Even in ritual, humor seems to be okay—*

♦ SW: It's not only okay, it's *essential*. I have a harder time hanging out with the Buddhists because they're not poking fun at themselves. The Pagans will evoke the high and mighty and holy and snigger at themselves at the same time, and I *trust* that so much more!

♦ *R/S: Does music have an important role to you? What do you think it really means, beyond entertainment?*

♦ TW: For me, it goes back to what helps contact and evoke the deeper self, the magical self. Musical rhythms can induce trance states and evoke different emotions. Music evokes an emotional state, and magic works on emotional energy—being able to raise emotional energy to a really high peak, combine it with mental energy, and then shoot it into the universe—that's what magic is all about. Songs, rhythms, and melodies can evoke different flavors of emotional energy, thereby shaping the work you're doing.

♦ SW: *Incantation* is the principle whereby music creates flow and changes of consciousness. It could be spoken, verbal, non-verbal like instrumental music—it could run the gamut. The classical musicians of the Renaissance used the music of their day. The Orphic hymns go back a good 2,000 years.

I learned some of the basic Golden Dawn conjurations in ceremonial magic to the Who's *Quadrophenia* album, because it happened to have the right dramatic flow. A lot of kids are learning processes and invocations—not necessarily knowing that they are such—by getting lost in a song. The example of singing along with the stereo cranked up to the max, and being transported by it, is the very concept of invocation or incantation. Once you learn that fundamental technique, and learn how to focus it on the things that actually count, then you can cause transformation in your life. This is hardwired into the base nature of the universe. All it takes is hitting the right notes!

♦ TW: I'm a Bellydancer, so I'm very tuned into music—specifically Middle Eastern music. Sam dabbles in music more than I—

♦ SW: —"dabbles" is definitely the right word. I pick out a melody on a bamboo flute and I can hold a rhythm for a little while on my drum, but we have friends in our coven who are a rock'n'roll band. Sharon Knight and her husband Winter have a rock band called Pandemonaeon whose music aims to create tribal and magical transformation. What *we* do is: we sit around thinking about such things. Meanwhile, the musicians are off in ecstasy, playing . . .

♦ *R/S: Does Paganism embrace the Surrealist discoveries of automatic writing, and the use of the cut-up method (as discovered by William Burroughs and Brion Gysin) as a way of divination—*

♦ SW: Automatic writing has been entwined with the Western magical tradition at least since the Spiritualist movement—sometimes antagonistically, sometimes positively.

♦ TW: We sure do a lot of it. It is a way to access the wisdom of both our own unconscious minds and the external beings we work with.

♦ SW: Many of the women we know, and some of the men, do this. It's a way of getting the deities to talk to you in such a way that it doesn't vanish as soon as it's said. Austin Osman Spare, in the first half of the last century, did automatic drawing that was stupendous, incredible art on the level of Beardsley. But he pissed off the wrong people when he was young, and became black-listed. Spare was part of a new wave of magical practitioners who were talking intimately about the ontological level of practice. He understood the twisty-turny, reflective nature of *karma* at a level not generally found in Western expression. This attitude, both philosophically and in practice, can also be found in a 12th-century Nyingma lama named Longchenpa.

♦ *R/S: It seems you're taking an overview of the world's culture, trying to encompass it into your own synthesis—*

♦ SW: Well, we're the inheritors of all culture. Every time new input arrives from the East, Western magic seems to be spurred into further development—sometimes embracing and sometimes denying. Usually new books get written and we learn more. I'm someone who wants to take appropriate input from *anywhere* and weave it into my practice. I'm mostly seeking the truth, you might say, and I try to just take the pieces that seem truthful. So for me, the focus is on technology—the method—of doing magic and evolving the self.

Part of what I'm trying to do is to understand, Where did we come from? How did we get here? And what are we, now that we're here? That's why I'm so interested in history—particularly the history of what I consider to be my spiritual ancestors. There's so much more to learn.♦♦♦

Photo: Bruce Folck

RITUAL OUTLINE

OPENING

Select a place where you will not be interrupted. You may wish to decorate the place and build an altar as a group—it's fun! When ready, gather in a circle…

Refuge/grounding To get started, ground and center. You can send your attention/energy down into the planet below and draw up the energy of the earth into your body for grounding and stability. Then send your attention up into the heavens and draw down that energy. Alternatively, ask for help from deities, spirits and guides by sounding "ah" from the heart. Sound 'ah' again, imagining all those sources of help. Sound 'ah' a third time. This starts the ritual on a level more fundamental than the intellect, and sets apart the time of the ritual from ordinary time.

Cast circle, Draw Circle Have someone walk around the circle with a blade, broom, wand or staff. Consecrate with water or salt water, flame or incense, or other means, singularly or together, in serial or at the same time.

Invoke Quarters Mark the North, South, East, West quarters with a gesture and signs such as pentagrams, hexagrams, equal-armed crosses (sometimes in circles), triscalions, etc. Some also invoke the center as a fifth principal. Often these calls will mention the purpose of the ritual.

Invocation of Deity(s) and/or Principal of Aspiration Invoke that deity or deities or those principals, forces or qualities that are harmonious with the ritual's intent. Let the feeling grow in intensity until you can say "He/She/It is here." This is where you clearly express the purpose of the ritual.

MAIN ACTION

Ritual follows the pattern of drama: set-up, tension building, climax and release.

Invoke the various parts of the story "Purify" the persons or objects to be used in the ritual. 'Consecrate' them by designating their meaning and purpose in the ritual. 'Anoint' them, which is to charge them with emotional intensity.

Bring them into relationship with each other and establish dramatic tension Have the prepared persons or objects interact in accord with the story you are telling. Encourage the rising intensity of feelings around the conflict, crisis, challenge, or change the ritual is intended to deal with.

Work dramatic tension to climax and resolution (raise and drop cone) Build the energy to a climax and convulsive release through voice, dance, or other means. At the peak release the energy towards its goal.

CLOSING

To conclude, undo the set-up. Thank Powers invoked during ritual and bid them farewell. Thank Deities/Principals invoked during ritual and bid them farewell. Thank Quarters invoked during ritual and bid them farewell. Do the same for the quarters each in turn. Some do this in the opposite order in which they were called.

Uncast Circle Undraw the circle by marking it in the opposite direction from which it was drawn with main tool(s) used.

Distribute Merit Dedicate the benefit of that work to the aid of all beings by gathering the good done into a mass at the center of the circle and together hurling it up into the heavens to rain down on all beings. Or use a verse such as: "May the benefit of this act and all acts, be dedicated unto the Complete Liberation and Supreme Enlightenment of all beings, everywhere, pervading space and time! May the benefits of practice, mine and others come to fruition, ultimately and immediately and I remain in the State of Presence. Ah…"

AFTERWARDS

Sharing a meal, or at least a small amount of food and drink, will help your body ground after ritual. It is also a good way to enjoy the community spirit that comes at the end of this work.

SOME RECOMMENDED BOOKS

Beyer, Stephen *The Cult of Tara*

Bianchi, Ugo. (ed.) *Mysteria Mithrae*

Blofeld, John *The Tantric Mysticism of Tibet*

Bremmer, Jan *The Early Greek Concept of the Soul*

Burkert, Walter *Lore and Science in Ancient Pythagoreanism*

Colquhoun, Ithell *Sword of Wisdom*

Conze, Edward *Buddhism: Its Essence and Development*

Culianu, I.P. *Psychanodia*

Couliano, Ioan P. *Out of this World*

Cozort, Daniel *Highest Yoga Tantra*

Crowley, Aleister *Magick, in Theory and Practice; 777 and other Qabalistic Writings of A. Crowley; The Holy Books of Thelema*

Csikszentmihalyi, Mihaly *Flow, the psychology of optimal experience*

Deikman, Arthur J. *The Observing Self*

Eliade, Mircea, ed. *Encyclopedia of Religion, The Forge and the Crucible, The Sacred and the Profane, The Myth of the Eternal Return, Rites and Symbols of Initiation, The Quest, History and Meaning in Religion, Shamanism*

Ellwood, Robert S. *The Feast of Kingship, Accession Ceremonies in Ancient Japan*

Ficino, Marsilio *The Book of Life*

Fortune, Dion *The Mystical Qabalah*

Frazer, J.G. "Adonis, Attis, Osiris," "The Dying God" (from *The Golden Bough*)

Galland, China *Longing for Darkness*

Gilbert, R.A., ed. *The Magical Mason*

Goffman, Erving *The Presentation of Self in Everyday Life; Stigma*

Grimes, Ronald L. *Beginnings in Ritual Studies*

Gruenwald, Ithamar *Apocalyptic and Merkavah Mysticism; From Apocalypticism to Gnosticism*

Guenther, Herbert, tr. *The Creative Vision; The Matrix of Mystery*

Guthrie, W.K.C. *Orpheus and Greek Religion*

Havens, Norman, tr. *Matsuri: Festival and Rite in Japanese Life*

Idel, Moshe *Kabbalah, New Perspectives*

Jensen, A.E. *Myth and Cult Among Primitive Peoples*

Jung, C.G. and C. Kerenyi *Essays on a Science of Mythology*

Kaplan, Aryeh, tr. *Sepher Yetzerah; The Bahir*

Kendall, Laurel *The Life and Hard Times of a Korean Shaman*

Knight, Gareth *A Practical Guide to Qabalistic Symbolism*

Levi, Eliphas *Transcendental Magick*

Longchen Rabjam *The Practice of Dzogchen*

Mathers, S.L. MacGregor, tr. *The Kabbalah Unveiled*

Matt, Daniel, tr. *Zohar*

McIntosh, Christopher *Eliphas Lévi and the French Occult Revival*

McLean, Adam *The Alchemical Mandala*

Mead, George *On Social Psychology*

Menninger, Karl *Number Words and Number Symbols*

Meyer, M.W. (ed.) *The Ancient Mysteries*

Moore, Thomas *The Planets Within, The Astrological Psychology of Marsilio Ficino*

Mylonas, G.E. *Eleusis and the Eleusinian Mysteries*

Ngawang, Dhargyey, Geshey *Tibetan Tradition of Mental Development*

Obeyeskere, Gananat *Medusa's Hair*

Orsi, Robert Anthony. *The Madonna of 115th Street*

Papus, (Dr. Gérard Encausse) *Qabalah, Secret Tradition of the West*

Phillip, J.A. *Pythagoras and Early Pythagoreanism*

Philippi, Donald. L. *Norito, A Translation of the Ancient Japanese Ritual Prayers*

Regardie, Israel, ed. *The Golden Dawn; The Middle Pillar; Tree of Life*

Rudolph, Kurt *Gnosis*

Sax, William S. *Mountain Goddess*

Scholem, Gershom *Kabbalah; Major Trends in Jewish Mysticism*

Seltzer, Robert M. *Jewish People, Jewish Thought*

Shaw, Miranda *Passionate Enlightenment*

Sherburne, Donald W., ed. *A Key to Whitehead's 'Process and Reality'*

Strauss, Levé *The Naked Man*

Tishby, Isaiah *The Wisdom of the Zohar*

Tsong-ka-pa *Deity Yoga*

Turner, Victor *Dramas, Fields, and Metaphors; Process, Performance & Pilgrimage; The Ritual Process; Image and Pilgrimage in Christian Culture; From Ritual to Theater*

Ulansey, David *The Origins of the Mithraic Mysteries*

Van Den Broek & Vermaseren, eds. *Studies in Gnosticism and Hellenistic Religion*

Van Gennep, Arnold *The Rites of Passage*

Waite, A.E. *The Holy Kabbalah*

Wolkstein, D. & S. N. Kramer *Inanna Queen of Heaven and Earth*

Yates, Frances *Giordano Bruno and the Hermetic Tradition; The Rosicruician Enlightenment*

COLOR SCALES

3 scale This scale is based on the fundamental 3 colors that all humans acknowledge. (For instance, there are parts of Africa that only have words for these 3 colors) Magic users also use these 3 colors to designate the 3 major strategies of Magick: Power, Compassion, Wisdom, and are the 3 great schools of magickal practice.

BLACK ~ Wisdom
WHITE ~ Compassion
RED ~ Power

5 scale This scale is the 'active' color set in the realm of the elements, the foundation of magickal practice. Each element corresponds to an aspect of a human being.

YELLOW ~ Air ~ Mind
RED ~ Fire ~ Will or Spirit
BLUE ~ Water ~ Emotion and Intuition
GREEN ~ Earth ~ Body
WHITE/BLACK ~ Spirit/Space ~ Soul or Self

7 Scale "This is one version of the Scale of the Planets, called the 'King Scale.' This is the domain of human experience, the various masks we wear in our lives."

RED ~ Mars ~ Motivation and activity
ORANGE ~ Sol ~ Illumination and energy
YELLOW ~ Mercury ~ Communication and commerce
GREEN ~ Venus ~ Romance and artistic creativity
BLUE ~ Moon ~ Growth, spirituality and change
INDIGO ~ Saturn ~ Life & Death, endurance and wealth
VIOLET ~ Jupiter ~ Rulership and lawgiving

Matthew Fox

Matthew Fox is a former Catholic Dominican priest, the author of 24 books and President of the University of Creation Spirituality/Naropa West. His Techno-Cosmic Masses usually include directional altars for the four sacred elements, the calling in of the Goddess and the God, Native American drummers, and rave DJs. His Website is *www.creationspirituality.org.* Interview by John Sulak.

♦ *RE/SEARCH: You were formerly known as Father Fox—what happened?*

♦ MF: I was a Catholic priest for thirty years and then I got my pink slip from the Pope. His letter said that 1) I was a "feminist theologian," which is anathema, 2) I don't condemn homosexuals, and 3) I associated too closely with Pagans. This was really about power and control; **I had become a casualty of a theological downsizing from the world's oldest and biggest multinational.**

Some young ravers from Northern England were bringing rave into church liturgies in the Anglican Church. I asked, "How can I help?" They said, "If you were an Anglican priest, you could run interference for us." So I talked to Bishop Swing in San Francisco about becoming an Episcopal priest. He took me in with the express intention of developing liturgies based on dance, postmodern language and the rave experience. For the last four years we've been holding Techno-Cosmic Masses.

What I like about the rave movement, dancing, and what I call the "pre-modern" or Pagan world is that you pray by dancing. You go into an altered state through dance, drumming and ceremony. You plunge headfirst into the darkness engendered by the elements—the sky and so forth. I have attended many Native American ceremonies including Sun dances and consider their way of praying as much more profound. It's about the lower chakras, and that's where European education and religion have been off the mark for centuries. Descartes argued that the soul resides in the pineal gland (at the top of the head) and that disregards six out of the seven chakras! That's why people today find church boring—especially the new generation; they're not there because they're not committed to Descartes! [laughs]

The word "Pagan" derives from the Latin word "Paganus" which literally means "a country person." It's interesting that the word "Pagan" has received such invective over the years. Those who have fled from their lower chakras, and no longer comprehend their relation to the earth, project their unconscious hatred onto what they label as "Paganism." A part of society is making scapegoats out of Pagans, and what is that about? It's about the flight from earthiness, matter, the body and its flesh.

One thing we have to do is quit blaming evil on flesh. Because now, with the new cosmology, we can understand that, first of all, **flesh is apparently rare in the universe. It's a special gift to have flesh.** Our flesh is light . . . slow moving light. Physicist David Bohm says it's frozen light.

For every particle of flesh-embodied light in the universe, there are a billion particles of unembodied light. In other words, having flesh, having light as flesh, is a great privilege and responsibility—it's not a pain in the ass! [laughs] It's not the reason why we choose evil. As Aquinas says, "The body doesn't sin, the soul does." Meaning that our choices are the key.

Paul [of the Bible] who said, "Flesh and blood shall not enter the kingdom of heaven" tainted the whole Christian message. Jesus never said anything like that. Jesus was Jewish. Paul, while a Jew, was educated by the Greeks, and that's where he got his suspicion of flesh. Plato had a dualistic attitude, saying, "Your soul is trapped in your body like a bird in a cage. And I can hardly wait to die, because then the bird will be free to sing." What madness! And this self-hating delusion, like a toxin or virus, has entered Christian theology . . . first with Paul and even more intensely with Saint Augustine in the fourth Century. St. Augustine was a Manichean who really hated matter.

♦ *R/S: Tell us about your books—*

♦ MF: I've written a number of books trying to bring back "creation spirituality" to the West. It's the oldest tradition in the Bible: the religion of many indigenous peoples, including Native Americans and Celts.

I work with a lot of scientists who view creation in terms of fifteen billion years of history. That cosmology and sense of scale is very important: how can we relate to and celebrate that by our rituals? **I've also been working with Meister Eckhart, Aquinas and Hildegard of Bingen, who are all creation- or earth-centered mystics.** Hildegard was a 12th century Abbess—a painter, musician, healer and genius. Aquinas was a 13th-century Dominican theologian who was condemned three times before being canonized as a saint. He worked with Pagans (e.g., Aristotle) and said, "revelation has been made to many Pagans." And "the old Pagan virtues were from God." Of course, that really shook up 13th-century fundamentalists.

Meister Eckhart (1260–1327) was also a Dominican. He was condemned by the Pope a week after he died, and his work has never really been in the mainstream. But it's very much about the earth and about justice, and is very prophetic. He made statements like, "Every creature is a word of God and a book about God." In other words, the word of God is not just in human books, it's in every creature. This whole tradition of creation spirituality, which includes Francis of Assisi [1182-1226], is what I've been involved in for over thirty years.

This is why I am attracted to Hildegard, Eckhart and Francis: they resisted the "hatred of the body" position that is at the core not only of organized religion's demise, but of the demise of the earth. The ecological crisis is obviously related to a corporate civilization that doesn't even think about its kinship and intimacy with forests, the soil and other species.

Again, that's where the new cosmology can help us realize that, in fact, the atoms of your body and mine are the same as the atoms of galaxies and stars great distances from here. We share the basic matter with all other beings. Sixty percent of our bodies are hydrogen atoms, which means they originate from the original fireball fourteen billion years ago. This is exciting news! This makes us all kin again, and interdependent with all of the other beings. This is what we should be celebrating as a species. And I honor those drawn to Paganism today for recognizing the importance of this.

♦ *R/S: Let's talk more about The Body. One of the big reasons people become Pagans is because they want a religion that celebrates sex. They're tired of all the guilt inflicted upon them by the monotheistic religions—*

♦ MF: Frankly, **a lot of my work is about re-framing our sexual experience as mystical experience.** People in an urban culture are deprived of seeing the stars at night and hearing the animal kingdom talk to us. Human love is one of the few experiences of nature still remaining in our lives.

In my earliest books I was deconstructing the pessimism surrounding sexuality. Again, Augustine was the dominant Christian theologian feeling extreme guilt about his sexuality—if anyone ever needed Freud it was him, but unfortunately he was born 1500 years too early! [laughs] From then on the Christian church has been carrying that guilt. We have reduced sexuality to morality, a list of Do's and Don'ts that view sexuality as a problem instead of one of the powers we possess . . . through which we experience harmony, love, ecstasy, communion and the divine.

Obviously, there are great responsibilities that accompany sexuality, especially with today's diseases and population boom. Birth control is another issue I had with the Catholic Church: Jesus didn't discuss birth control, but Augustine did. He said that sex gets legitimized by having children—therefore you should never interfere with the process of having children—which means no birth control! And that's what the present Pope is still running on: a 4th century teaching. It's pitiful, really.

The Bible contains Solomon's "The Song of Songs," a beautiful series of poems celebrating sensual love as an experience of the divine. It's a great mystical work, and one of the greatest works on sexuality as a mystical experience. Unfortunately, for centuries Christian theologians have been trying to clean up that book. [laughs] They claim, "This is really just a *metaphor* about Jesus loving the soul, and God loving Jesus, and God loving the church."

The "Song of Songs" refers to lovers coming "out from the wilderness," and wilderness, in the Hebrew scriptures, is the place where you encounter the divine. To position our human love in the wilderness is really wonderful, because that's where human passion is allowed its voice: in a location where both wildness and the divine co-exist. In other words, the divine is invoked not just in contemplation but also in the wilderness. And they go together nicely.

♦ *R/S: Do you think Paganism and Christianity can work together?*

♦ MF: They have to; we haven't any choice. As a species we are in deep, deep trouble. Lester Brown of the World Watch Institute said that we have eleven years [!] left to change our ways as a species. His organization collects data from around the world on the scientific health of the planet, and **at the rate ecological devastation is occurring, in eleven years we will not be able to undo the damage we're inflicting.** And you can see this damage everywhere; species are becoming extinct at a catastrophic rate. The biggest issue today is long-term species survival, and things are getting down to the wire.

What can we do? I think we have to call upon all the wisdom we can synthesize from Paganism, Judaism, Buddhism, Sufism, Christianity, et al. Eckhart says that God is a great underground river that no one can damn up or stop. So I see divinity as a river, but with many wells tapping off it. There is a Pagan well, a Sufi well, and so forth. We have to go down those wells and tap the wisdom beneath. The fact is that the spirit, or "God," moves in infinite ways.

I know that **I've survived spiritually because of Native American spiritual practices such as sweat lodges and dances.** The Techno-Cosmic Masses as well as the rave movement have that spirit where dance is supremely important.

We have to work together to contribute to a universal ecological consciousness, thereby creating an environmental revolution. We have to shift from an anthropocentric mode of being, which focuses our entire economic system around consumerism and advertising, to a sense of reverence, gratitude and awe that is earth-centered. This is the essence of the sacred, and where healthy Paganism, healthy Buddhism and healthy Christianity can all find common ground: in the struggle to save the earth. It's about our children's children, and the long-term survival of our species.

I was recently in the Philippines, which like many Third World Countries is in dire straits ecologically. Their forests are being clear-cut and sold to the Japanese and Chinese, and as a result they're losing their topsoil —consequently there are a lot more floods and heat spells. The Philippines once had more coral than any other place in the world, and now 98 % of it is dead. A Catholic Sister asked the rain forest Indians there, "What is the biggest mistake Western missionaries have made?" They thought that was a good question, and went away for three days to obtain a tribal consensus. Upon their return they said, "You Westerners! You put God in a little white house, and the rest of creation you treat however you like!"

The missionaries doing the most destruction today are not in religion, they're in global, corporate capitalism which has the same mentality as a religion. Our so-called secular culture has picked up some of the worst elements of toxic religion.

The concept of Original Sin says that, in and of yourself, you haven't got what it takes. So that sets you up for consumerism: you've got to find some outside salvation to buy your way out of the situation. And I think hell, like heaven (if you will) is something we create on this earth in our lifetime.

Pagan spiritualities can help bring back the sense of celebration, and that's a key doctrine and practice. One of the great affronts to capitalism is the idea that we're here not to be anal-retentive savers of our wealth, but to let it go. We're here to party, to celebrate. So celebration is very subversive; that's one reason we don't do it very well in Western culture. Marija Gimbutas, the feminist archaeologist, said, "The essence of the Goddess civilization was the celebration of life." And that's so important! Without the celebration of life, you're set up for the addictions of consumerism. You're out there shopping. Rabbi Heschel said, "If you forfeit your sense of awe, then the universe becomes a marketplace for you."

So **the whole universe can be turned into a shopping mall—that's how people in our culture think.** We have to replace that attitude with one of cosmic awe. And I expect Pagans to not only be fellow journeyers in this, but to be leaders.

♦ *R/S: Over the centuries Christianity has transformed Pagan gods and goddesses into saints, changed Pagan holy days into Christian holidays, and built churches over Pagan temples and sacred lands. Any comments?*

♦ MF: It's first of all a great compliment to Pagan wisdom. In medieval Christianity, Mary was the Goddess. The cathedral at Chartres was built on a sacred well hosting Goddess worship. In a 125-year period there were 500 temples the size of Chartres Cathedral built in Europe—each one dedicated to Mary. That's an absolute sociological phenomenon; the last time the Goddess roared into Western civilization was in the 12th century. The time we're living in now, the return of the Goddess, is the nearest parallel to that era.

The 12th century was a very exciting time that gave birth to universities. **"University" originally meant a place where you could find a place in the universe.** Today, it means a place to go find your place in the man-made work world, which is much duller than the universe.

The Black Madonna is Isis, and she's very visible at Chartres and many other medieval cathedrals in France. Isis means "throne," and that's what cathedral means. The cathedral was invented in the 12th century, when young people were flocking to cities as the serf/feudal system was breaking down. So at the same time you have the Goddess, the birth of the university, and the birth of the cathedral.

The word "cathedral" has been co-opted by male clerics as the throne where the male Bishop sits, but originally it meant the throne where the Goddess sits, ruling the universe with compassion and justice for the poor.

♦ *R/S: Have you been to Chartres?*

♦ MF: Many times. It was a sacred place for the Druids, at the center of the wheat fields of France amidst the tradition of the goddess of the grain and fertility. When you drive down the highway toward Chartres you literally see it rising out of the wheat fields. It's still a very powerful place.

Underneath the 12th century cathedral is a subterranean church dating back to the ninth century. And in the basement of that is the well, which dates back to the 4th century or earlier.

♦ *R/S: You've stood by the well?*

♦ MF: Numerous times. Again, **here's the idea of divinity coming from below—not above! That's a very important, feminist notion, and has to do with our lower chakras.** The idea that

divinity has to come from above because God is in the sky is one-sided; the fact is, divinity comes from below, too.

Hildegard of Bingen painted a picture where the Christ is coming from below, out of the ground like a snake in a Hopi Kiva. It's very exciting. She, by the way, was into snakes. She says the snake got a bad "rap" in the book of Genesis, and that the snake was the wisest of creatures. In her paintings she often depicts a snake as the frame.

♦ *R/S: Can you talk about Starhawk?*

♦ MF: The fact that Starhawk was on our faculty and I refused to let her go kept the Vatican awake at night. Working with Starhawk has been a special blessing because she combines the celebrative dimension of Paganism with the prophetic struggle for social justice of her Jewish tradition.

Frederick Turner's *Beyond Geography* gives a history of America from the point of view of Native Americans. His theory is that Europeans at the time of Columbus had already repressed the sensuous in their religion and souls. So when they landed here and saw people living very closely with nature, this repressed sensuousness came up as projection. Europeans called them "savages" and said they needed "redemption." This notion legitimized and gave impetus to the horrible destruction of the indigenous people here.

You can also talk about slavery along these lines, too. Slavery is not just a religious issue but an economic one—both feed each other. **There have been horrible deeds done in the name of religion, and we need rituals to grieve over this.** Grief work is so important today, yet we don't have those rituals in our culture, churches and synagogues. Racism and Paganphobia both should be grieved through ritual and apologized for, and we should be grieving and doing this together.

Paganism can drill down to the deeper bedrock of grief by the very nature of its individual, bodily, participatory involvement in ritual. More than an internal architecture of speaker/audience, we need rituals that involve the body in movement, engage in grounding exercises, and tap the founts of joy through group song, chant, chorus and dance.

Without access to all of our chakras, we're denied whole solutions to our problems. We need song and dance to deal, ultimately, with our inevitable fate: death. Without dance, we can't really deal with death. And we need to deal with death in order to live fully. We need spaces to let our creativity flow. ♦♦♦

Raelyn Gallina

An early piercing pioneer, Raelyn Gallina is also a brander, scarification practitioner and jewelry maker. She was featured in *Modern Primitives*. Raelyn follows the Santería tradition, and can be contacted at 584 Castro #142, S.F. 94114. Interview by John Sulak.

♦ *RE/SEARCH: Why do you consider Santería to be a Pagan religion?*
♦ RAELYN GALLINA: To me, the term "Paganism" means those traditions and religions that are earth-based—those that interact with the forces of nature in its raw and more refined forms. SANTERÍA is the syncretized blending of the West African/Yoruban-originated tradition of Orisha worship with Catholicism. ORISHAS are anthropomorphized forces of nature—African gods and goddesses who preside over forces or aspects of nature and human nature.

For example, we have Oshun, the river Orisha. Civilizations evolved faster near rivers: living was easier, freeing up time to develop skills like weaving and pottery-making—in fact, all the arts. So Oshun is identified with the arts, relationships, love— the things that make life worth living. But just as the river can flood, with death and destruction following, flooding also brings fertility to the land. So Orisha, as forces of nature, can both heal and destroy.

Yemaya is the Orisha of the oceans, and since all life sprang from the oceans, she represents motherhood in all of its manifestations.

Over the centuries Orisha worship has managed to stay alive. When it crossed the ocean and syncretized with Catholicism, it hid behind the Catholic Saints. It might have changed and substituted a few things, but it pretty much preserved its essential integrity and power.

We have BEMBÉS—celebratory drum ceremonies for initiations and other rituals in which deities come down and possess their priest and priestesses—they're "the real deal, Lucille." And if you start calling on forces that are very powerful—and some forces are very chaotic if you haven't put the proper protections in place or done the right invocations, or if you don't have the right people doing the right things—well, this can be harmless, or it can open the way for forces to come and play with your head!

Santería has very sophisticated means of divination and the power to transform and transmute energy and matter. I've seen cancer disappear because of the work that was done in between trips to the doctor.
♦ *R/S: Tell us more about the origins of Santería—*

♦ RG: Orisha worship came from West Africa, Yoruba land, preserved by a divinatory sect. During the slave trade, when Africans were taken across the Atlantic to the new world, wherever they encountered Catholicism in Cuba, Puerto Rico, the Caribbean, Brazil, they would, in order to keep their religion alive, look at the Saints and say, "Oh, Santa Barbara—that's obviously Shango . . . Okay! And Our Lady of Merced, that's Obatala!" That's how their Orishas could hide.

While the Catholic Church was celebrating their high holidays, Saint's Feast days and masses, the Africans were going, "Yes, we're saying the prayers, but we're drumming and singing to Shango instead of Saint Barbara." Under the surface, they were keeping their ancient tradition alive. In America, the last vestiges of this are manifested, *maybe,* by Southern Baptists who can be "touched by the spirit" and testify. What I practice is called LUCUMI, and it's the line that came through Cuba. But there are lines that went through Brazil and other countries.
♦ *R/S: So the religion of Orisha worship has been alive in Africa all this time—*
♦ RG: Yes, although it's dying out there, because in order to get an education you have to be either Christian or Muslim. But it's extremely active in Cuba, the Caribbean, Brazil, and large urban centers like Miami, New York, L.A., S.F. and Chicago. It's spreading.
♦ *R/S: How about Haiti? What's the connection between Santería and "Voodoo"?*
♦ RG: Voodoo, or Voudoun, shares some of the same African roots as Santería, but is mixed with French Catholicism, so their practitioners' prayers are in French patois. Voodoo has nothing to do with Hollywood zombies; it's about a lifetime of service to the spirits. Voudoun means spirit.
♦ *R/S: Earlier, you mentioned spirit possession—*
♦ RG: When you have a BEMBÉ, and everyone is singing and dancing and the energy is heating up, an Orisha may come and possess a priest or priestess. They become a *channel,* and you then have *deities in the flesh* interacting with people and giving guidance.
♦ *R/S: Santería has been closed to outsiders—*
♦ RG: One of the reasons is that we deal with animal sacrifice, which a lot of people have issues with. **Even though most**

Americans eat burgers from McDonald's, they don't give a second thought to the fact that their burger was once a living cow. People have a problem with the idea of killing chickens and goats as sacrifices to heal or help people. Some Santería practitioners in Miami took their beliefs to the Supreme Court, saying, "This is our religion. This is no different from Kosher meat. If you can allow a Rabbi with a special knife in ritual circumstances to kill animals, what's the difference? We do the same thing."

A few people were trying to stamp out the sale of live animals in the San Francisco Asian community a few years ago. The Santería community got up in arms and joined forces. Because why should these protesters be able to tell the whole Asian population of this city that they can't give a chicken to their ancestors at New Years? You'd have a revolt! It got dropped.

Who deals with killing their own food now? Not a whole lot of people. Up until fifty years ago, you didn't go to Safeway and get your pristine, plastic-wrapped, nondescript meat with no icky stuff anywhere. Our modern times are *really nice!* But our great-grandparents were killing chickens and cows and nobody gave it a second thought. People who grouse about "animal sacrifice" are being hypocritical, and I highly doubt that they're all vegetarians. *We* conduct our sacrifices within strict ritual practices, and with the proper songs and incantations—wholly unlike how chickens and cattle are slaughtered today in a neither humane nor kind way.

♦ *R/S: You seem to respect the animals—*
♦ RG: Absolutely, because an animal may save your life. **Hey, if it came down to me having cancer or the chicken going, the chicken is gonna go—I'm staying!** And that animal deserves my respect and gratitude.

When someone is initiated into priesthood, it's called making OCHA. During the OCHA a person can receive up to nine different Orisha, and each Orisha gets their four-legged animal and their feathered animal. Certain parts are removed and cooked in a very specific way for the Orisha, and the rest of the meat is cooked for the people. Sometimes 200 people, including family and friends, show up for the BEMBÉ the day after the initiation. There's African drumming, call-and-response singing and dancing specific to the Orisha. Everyone eats what was sacrificed the day before.

I was initiated 14 years ago in October, 1987; in fact when *Modern Primitives* came out, I was an IYAWO—a newly-initiated novice. I had to dress in white from head to toe for a year and seven days. I couldn't have my picture taken; I was like a baby—a newborn. I went through an intense purification process; I had to be inside by sunset. There are a lot of precautions taken to protect the newborn. Also, the Orisha that was put into your head is newborn.

I got into Santería because in 1984 I had five Lesbian friends die. They were young, 25 to 32 years old. They died from different causes: an overdose, an accident, leukemia,

1964 Carmelite in a Fife-and-Drum Marching Corps Photo: Mom

cancer . . . **it was so intense and so deeply troubling that these young, young women—friends of mine—had died in that short amount of time. Even though I feel like I've always been a spiritual seeker, I went searching anew for some way of dealing with their deaths.**

At the time I had a friend who was just getting involved with Luisah Teish's House. She had been initiated and was just starting to form her House. I started attending different events that were open to non-initiates. I noticed that if I asked, "What can I do for this or that," she'd say, "Try doing this." And every time it *worked.* I thought, "Holy s—-!" I mean, I grew up Italian Catholic in Massachusetts, and since then I'd been searching, really trying to find things that actually worked. Like, "Give me proof!"

♦ *R/S: So this brought better results than a magickal ritual, or prayer?*
♦ RG: Better than anything I'd ever seen to that point. I felt like there had been a hook going out and I had gotten reeled in. I felt this pull that was so intense, and thought, "All right . . . *fine.* I'm volunteering." So I entered her house and got my ELEKES, which are these bead necklaces with a set of six different strands of beads that represent six different Orishas. They're sanctified, washed with special solutions—they're empowered. You go through a whole purification ceremony and you receive them.

I did that, and a while later I got my WARRIORS—that's the second step in the tradition. Receiving your warriors helps to bring stability, protection and grounding. Basically, if there are fights to be fought, they're going to do it for you or help you *do* it. They're very real.

This is an experiential and oral tradition—there aren't a whole lot of reputable books out there. However, once you experience some of the rituals and have interactions with Orishas, once you participate and have the *bodily* experiences where something really affects you, then it affects your way of thinking.

Besides the Orisha worship we also deal with EGUN, or the dead: our ancestors, our guides, our elevated spiritual dead. I've seen people, once they start dealing with the dead, say, "Ohmigawd, I'm not alone! I'll never be alone again in this life. I may have *felt* alone, but I now know, in my *body,* that I'm not alone." That can change somebody's life permanently.

At one point right before I made OCHA, things were really hard. So finally I said to Oya, the Orisha I'm initiated to, "Listen, mi Madre, I'm trying to do everything I can, but obviously it's just not working. I need to turn this over to you. I need to know: Is this what you want? Give me a sign!" The next time I was at the House I joined, my arms were raised, words were coming out of my mouth—and the house started shaking! I thought, "Okay, okay—I got it."

The Orisha I'm initiated to is Oya, who rules the winds of change and transformation, from a breeze to a hurricane. Again, Orishas can be really gentle or really destructive, and she has the power of both. Oya was like the first feminist. She's a warrior; she owns masks and disguises. She also owns the dead, so the whole spirit world is her playground. Her place is at the gate of cemeteries, where she is kind of like Charon, the ferryman at the River Styx. She's not death itself. But once you're dead, she'll get you where you need to go. She's also the market woman.

She has many different faces—they all do. Every House has its own flavor, depending on what Orisha rules. Houses of OBATALA could be more quiet, where respect is really the main emphasis. A House of OSHUN might be into parties, dancing, singing, music and all the arts. Oya rules change and transformation.

Spirits come through and possess different people. Sometimes they're old Creole spirits, and they're smoking cigars, drinking rum, and giving advice and cleaning people off—it's really cool. But if someone shows up and says she's your Aunt Bess, you may react, "Well, I don't have an Aunt Bess—who the hell are you?" You have to *verify*. And that's where elders come in—people who are experienced and who have the "second sight"—who know what to do to make sure something is okay.

♦ R/S: How can a person determine if this is the path for them?

♦ RG: The first thing to do is consult—get a reading by a reputable, experienced priest or priestess. And you're never certain about what may come up in a reading—hidden problems may surface. A person might say, "I just lost my job and need another one," and the Orisha may say, "The most important thing is your health—you need to go to a doctor and get checked out. In the meantime, get a cleaning with this." With a cowrie shell reading (and this is one of the things I love about this tradition), you're told, "Here are these problems and we're gonna see if we can fix them." You don't get left with your problem; you get a prescription. You can

At San Francisco Gay Parade 2000   Photo: V. Vale

rest assured that if you do what you're told, then that work on your part will put the energies in motion to transform that problem.

My deities that I've seen and trusted have all proven their abilities. Through divination my deities give me direct help. The problems that are harder to solve are where the person has to change herself. Like, someone gets told, "You know, you have some habits here—things you do over and over again—that are bordering on abuse. You need to change those habits." Well, if they're long-term habits, that could be very hard. But I've seen this tradition help many people.

♦ R/S: You're still supporting yourself by practicing the same profession when you were interviewed for Modern Primitives—

♦ RG: Yes, I'm a full-time piercer, scarification artist, brander and jeweler. I actually get to use some of the tools I've gotten from Santería. For example, I have pierced many women who were victims of incest, abuse, or rape. They may want to get their clitoral hood pierced, or their nipple pierced—some body part that has been degraded . . . a location where they basically had their sexuality taken away from them, where because of abuse they haven't been comfortable with their body and how they look. And in order to reclaim that, they'll want to do a piercing and maybe a little ritual around that.

Where I live and work is a House of Oya, who rules change and transformation. When someone walks through the door consciously seeking transformation of their abused sexuality, of their body image, Oya lends powers to accomplish that. When you bleed, whether it's by piercing or scarification, your blood is the greatest sacrifice you can give. A person's intention and desire at the time they're bleeding is really important and in fact *key* to them getting what they want.

♦R/S: When Modern Primitives debuted, the body modifications you were doing were underground. Now they're mainstream—

♦ RG: Oh yeah—overkill! [laughs] In order to make a *statement,* this generation of people wanting to be pierced has had to go much further. So what I'm seeing are people that look like display racks. They've lost the aesthetic they may have started out with; somewhere along the line they forgot to look in the mirror. I see the loss of aesthetic sensibility in an attempt to elicit shock value. It's overkill. I see kids being disfigured.

The turning point arrived when you could turn on your *MTV* and see some rock star with a pierced nipple, or open up *Vogue* magazine and see some supermodel with a pierced navel. Then your teenyboppers and everybody wanted it; it became a commodity. When that happened, it was over as far as underground community-building goes. **Now you can have all the tattoos and piercings and cuttings in common and have nothing in common!"** ♦♦♦

Genesis P-Orridge

Performance artist, musician, writer, and visual artist Genesis P-Orridge has had a career since the Seventies with mail art, Coum Transmissions, Throbbing Gristle, Psychic Television and various group projects.

In 1981 he founded Thee Temple Ov Psychick Youth as a global experimental ritual magick network. Currently he performs with Thee Majesty and other musicians, puts on art exhibitions, lectures, and travels. He also collaborates with Miss Jacqui, his partner of the past seven years; the two live in the New York area where they amuse themselves deciphering words such as "sully," "bulbous," and "besmirch."

For decades Genesis has studied metaphysical and Pagan traditions such as Thelemic Magick, Wicca, Tibetan Buddhist, Native American, Agori and Yoruba traditions, and is now an initiated Priest of Eshu Eleggua. He credits Brion Gysin for much inspiration. His website is *genesisporridge.com*. Interview in San Francisco by V. Vale.

♦ *RE/SEARCH: Tell us some reasons why Paganism is applicable to people's lives. One motivation for me was the quotation, "Monotheism is Imperialism in religion"*—
♦ GPO: I always thought of Paganism as being a form of anti-establishment activity, basically. My entire life has been about goading, prodding, and exposing the pus-filled underbelly of the established social status quo. I've always seen it as my natural prey and target. I feel like that is why I was sent here, merely to be a thorn in the side of the great big sow of capitalism.

But having said that, for me it's something I crusaded about a long time ago, and created various small tribal experiments to see if my theories were valid or not. At this point, for me it's so simplistic. There is submission to the status quo—to the hallucination that we're told is "reality" (and we're told that by mass media, advertising, and pseudo-politicians—there are no *real* politicians anymore, just dolls that walk around, mannequins that spout bumper stickers). Or, there's **the only activity worthwhile in this world: trying to unveil mysteries, and lead pleasurable, sensual, stimulating, and dangerous lives. There's no other reason to be here.**

The status quo quite clearly is a feudal system. It perpetrates monotheism because it suits those in power. If you have a system where there is one almighty, all-seeing, angry God, and you have a tyrant who's a king or a president or whatever title they give themselves, who is also all-seeing, all powerful and angry, then all aspects of authority use the concept of punishment as the motive for agreeing with them or serving them. That's the only motive. There is no other motive in organized religion in society—it's all based on punishment.

Once you reject that and say, "I don't see any point in being here just to be threatened with punishment, just to agree with

someone who is obnoxious and vile," then you begin looking for what predates those systems—Paganism, for example.. One *naturally* begins to ask, "Was there another story? Was there another way that the universe, the planet, was viewed?" And as soon as you go back through *Western* society to Greece and Rome, you find Polytheism, with lots of different divinities. They have the characteristics of people: they get jealous, they squabble, they argue, they have affairs, they have illegitimate children. They even breed outside of their own species, they mate with other forms, people, and even with creatures. There are mid-way creatures and strange mutants called fairies or demons or Pan-like creatures. There's a great big huge vibrant metaphor for how it really feels to be alive.

Utilizing those parables and those allegories, one can immediately make sense of one's *own* situation. If they really look, most people conclude, "At the very least this is like good psychotherapy. I can see a story here that tells me if I behave this way, these might be the consequences. Or if I behave *that* way I ought to be ridiculed, because this is a really stupid way to behave, and eventually some consequence will happen that I won't like."

So most of the so-called Pagan religions are about behavior and consequence—and that's a very healthy way to live one's life: to be aware of consequence. Most people do not think about consequence, hence they will throw things down in the street and assume it's someone else's business to clean up the environment—*someone else* will take care of it. And that's the other downside of the authority pyramid: people no longer have responsibility for the consequences of their actions, because Big Daddy will look after them, and Big Daddy will sort it out, and Big Daddy will punish those who did the wrong thing—and it's never *you*. One is always encouraged to think that *you will be the lucky one*.

One idea Miss Jacqui brought up to me is that **reincarnation is a great belief system even if it's *not* true, because if you *believe* you're coming back, you would like to have a tidy, sensible and balanced place to come back to.** But if you think you're going to heaven and never coming back, you don't *care* what happens after you're gone. So in terms of caretaking the planet and the environment for those who come next, reincarnation is a great system for being responsible. If it *is* true, you will come back and things will be improved—or at least stable. If it's not true, then those who come after you—your children (which are a form of reincarnation anyway) or other people's children will have a more balanced, tidy, and positive environment, too. So you're in a win-win situation with reincarnation. And that's considered to be a Pagan system, too.

So as soon as you go *pre*-Judeo/Christian/Muslim *paramilitary* power, you actually get far more sophisticated systems. It's interesting: those things called "Pagan" or "primitive" are always far more sophisticated, because they were necessary for absolute survival and to maintain the healthiest possible organism—social organism—that one could have. And there's a lot of tolerance. There are hermaphrodites, there are rebels, and there are questions in those systems, always. If you go to the Yoruba belief system that I'm involved with, Eshu (which is my deity) is the *trickster,* and interest-

Genesis with Miss Jacqui in Nepal. Photo: Carl Abrahamsson

ingly the only Orisha that knows the location of God. That's why you always pray to and offer gifts to Eshu first in any ceremony, because without his help you cannot communicate with or even *get to* the divine.

There's a nice story about Eshu, who wears red and black, a bit like a harlequin or court jester, in sections. His face is half red and half black, and he's walking along a path toward the village. There's a farmer on one side tilling his fields, and a farmer on the other side. On one side the farmer looks up and says "Eshu, that's a blessing!" The other guy looks up, sees Eshu and says, "Oh, it's Eshu— that's a real blessing!" They meet later in the village and one says, "Did you see Eshu today? He was beautiful—such a beautiful black face." The other guy goes, "No no no—he had a red face." The first one goes, "He did not!" And the other one goes, "Yes he did!" They start to argue

and fight, and it goes on. In that story you see the basic problem that occurs as soon as people become "fundamental" and believe in one thing only: it *always* causes friction, even with someone who is looking at the same thing.

The whole idea is that there is fluidity, and nothing is fixed. Those are important points. I would argue that if people want to begin to comprehend the psychology of the state of being alive, then they have to go to the oldest models—simply because those are the ones that grew from being closest to the source of life. And contrary to popular theme, we're *not* getting more intelligent; we're just becoming better at making machines to convince ourselves of what we already know. And that's the whole problem with technology—it's the same thing as these pyramid structures of authority. **We worship technology in and of itself, and let the technology tell us what to do. And guess what, the technology can punish us too**—with biochemical weapons and nuclear weapons. We built the same system with technology that we have with the Judeo-Christian monotheistic system. It starts off at the bottom apparently being about service, manufacture, and consuming, and it goes to the top where it's about annihilation. It's exactly the same system.

So you have to go pre-technology, too. You have to go back to a place where you can actually consider the idea of just living in balance to survive, and interacting with others to maintain balance and tolerance. Because without that you won't survive. **Just because you have beautiful huge buildings and all this "tech" stuff, the basic human condition has not altered.** As soon as you travel away from the West and go to the so-called Third World countries (whatever that means), you will see that there are still people with buffalos trying to grow enough rice to feed themselves and their family, and share with someone else to get what else they need. Most people still live in that original Pagan state, in terms of their day-to-day life. And they still have to have some sort of a practical relationship with survival and nature-based systems and phenomena. If there's a flood, they all starve. If there's a drought, they die. Our world picture does not consider these really simple, basic facts. We've become so arrogant in the West—and again, arrogance comes from the same authority system where those at the top are somehow superhuman, and we are all less than human. Hence the blue blood idea of aristocracy, in which the leaders are the spokes-people of God. They are the interface with God, and that's why they have the power and you can't challenge it.

♦ *R/S: You've been developing the analogy of the pyramid model for society, which maintains hierarchy, hegemony, and the world as it is now. Some people have called it soft fascism. It's definitely corporate rule—to a great extent corporations are more important than governments, although it's more complex than that. Underlying this is an invisible foundation of dualism, or Either/Or, which aids and abets the control process—*

♦ GPO: Either/or—I can't remember how many times I've said that my enemy is the Either/Or, Black-White, Good-Bad universe. That just is *not* how this dimension of the universe works. That is the most callous and damaging way of viewing things that has ever evolved. **The whole dualistic system is ultimately the enemy—there's no question of that**. That's why improvisation and creation is so important in every possi-

Genesis in solo COUM action, circa 1975

passed on from cell to cell, as far back as the slime mold before we even became clusters; this can be accessed by all beings, and that *that* is the real story that is unfolding; not individuals telling us there is something else going on.

One of my feelings right now is that human bodies are actually like a coral reef—a cluster of inter-reliant cells, single cell structures like a huge city, and the ones that are skin, suit the ones that are bone, etc. But the basic point of all of them is to carry around the consciousness. And the consciousness is built from the DNA of all the cells; it serves all the rest of these cells. The cities, societies, and belief systems, to be the most effective and the most healthy, should reflect that too.

If that's the case—if the case is that there is a whole other story, then in a sense we're almost arbitrarily allowing the single-cell clusters that maintain memory to keep replicating. So in fact, **human beings in and of themselves are far less important than the replication of the DNA. And that's a very different way of looking at things, than thinking human beings are Super Beings that have inherited the right to bully, cajole, and annihilate all in their path.** That's not what we're doing—we're actually just clusters of stuff, carrying around someone else's memories, which is the slime mold from the beginning of time. For all we know *that's* actually God! If you travel back far enough through the strata, you'll get back to the stuff in the soup. And it's probably laughing at us right now, because we're acting so self-important.

These ways of thinking and speculating—whether or not they're accurate doesn't really matter. The thing is that they *liberate;* they liberate one's behavior and one's way of dealing with things, and they tend to breed compassion and kindness, too. Because **when you're no longer so self-important, you start to *listen*, and you start to *touch* more gently in every sense.** And I think this came to me because of absolutely abandoning Either/Or, Good/Bad, Male/Female, and Physical/Non-physical—I actually just opened up and said, "What's my feeling? What's actually happening?" I was aided and abetted by going back to pre-history and trying to *listen* to the evidence, rather than read books about it.

In Britain, I used to go around and take photos of stone circles and stone carvings. One day I was staring at all these different things carved in stone, in circles and patterns, and I said, "These are cell structures—cells dividing—and they've got nuclei and these atomic structures." But mainly they were cell structures, like single cell structures and amoebas and spirals and it was all basically microbiology. I thought, "How the hell would [the ancients] know this, and why are they building these monuments to single cell structures? Suppose that's what they *are* doing?"

Then the whole idea intruded, of "as above, so below; the smallest is the same as the largest"—a very ancient idea. And it fits: everything is a mirror to everything else, no matter how small you get, no matter how large you get—it's all absolutely and uncannily a mirror of itself. If that's the case, then it's one huge or minute non-physical reflection of itself. Which means we aren't important and we don't really exist in the true sense of the word. We are merely blessed with a *sense* of existence!

When you go to those [ancient Pagan sites], you start to marvel at the preciseness of the so-called Heathen, Pagan, ignorant, uncivilized people. There is something miraculous about the knowledge that is contained in these very beautiful, time-

ble sense. That's such a given. How could anybody believe that they know the so-called fixed "truth"?

One of the things I realized a long time ago is that everything everybody says is true. Even when they try to lie, there is within that a truth about their attitude. And when one actually starts to step back and assume that every single person is telling the truth, and everything that is happening, and every object around you is actually telling you a story, you start having a great deal more respect, and you start listening a lot harder to the dynamics and resonance of every moment. And that's part of the process of *waking up*. **One of the only reasons that consciousness exists is to feed itself.** The consciousness in a sense is the ultimate organism—we're fragments of the original consciousness, or fragments of the only consciousness.

We're feeding ourselves by experience. If we limit experience, and if we try to artificially define it, then we are ultimately crippling God in a sense, or crippling the divine in ourselves and in the potential of all of us. I would suggest that everybody find every possible creation myth and put them all together. They will notice a lot of similarities, and certain differences. But what's remarkable is the number of similarities between people who were apparently not in contact. And what that suggests at the very least, is that one can access a pool of consciousness—whether it be a DNA memory bank that's less structures. And how much of what we're making now is going to be as remarkable as Stonehenge? And Stonehenge is not necessarily the best—there are many other amazing, beautiful sites in Britain. There are thousands, literally.

And interestingly, recently some archaeologists decided that to build Stonehenge and other sites required a very organized society that was much more populous than they had imagined. They always used to think there were a few villages with people living in dung, wandering around in sheepskins. But **to move the rocks from Wales to where they are in Somerset required a lot of different communities collaborating for that single purpose over hundreds of years!** Certainly that means generations of people, because people died young then.

So we're talking about many generations of people working together to do something we still can't do, with their tools. Different kingdoms, different tribes, all decided to agree

Genetic Paganism? Genesis age 4 with an early stone circle he created

together to do this one task. And then people started to wonder: "Hang on, then—this was a very sophisticated society." The spiritual, metaphysical, and metaphorical health of the entire nation would seem to have been involved with this symbol that was being built. It was that important.

Likewise Egypt and the Mayans: why did everybody collaborate to such an extent to build these abstractions that *we're* still trying to make sense of . . . these incredibly precise abstractions? The archaeologists also decided that stone circles moved out from Britain to Europe, not the other way around.

Once you start to explore these different pathways, you become a lot more respectful and humble about the idea of what is or is not "sophisticated," or what is or is not a usable map. Really, that's all we're looking for is maps—maps to navigate this strange mystery.

♦ *R/S: I think that in the West we operate on the model of the human as the pinnacle of civilization—that pyramid model again. The result is that we're no longer integrated with our environment. We've killed off many of the other animal and plant species which we should have been respecting. Part of this is the complete absence of integration of what we used to call the "sacred" into everyday, daily life.*

♦ GPO: Absolutely. **One of the most exciting effects of going to Katmandu the first time was to see the devotions or the appreciation of the sacred. Everything was devotion**—it's even in the poems that all is devotional. That's something that has been lost. But over there it's matter of fact—it's the same as eating, breathing, and washing. Everybody is constantly aware of being in some form of relationship with something sacred and/or divine. And whether those are just archetypes that serve the purposes of balanced relationship with everything else, or whether it's the best way to maintain a healthy personality in the widest sense, doesn't really matter.

I just loved Nepal—you'd go down a street and there would be someone sacrificing a goat to Kali on the way to work. There would be these rich wives in their perfect clothes and jewelry and they're going to a little shrine and they'd be bringing bells and rice and doing a benediction. Some Tibetan would be going along with a prayer wheel intoning *om mani padmi hum* and wasn't even worth glancing at. The locals just wandered past because that's how it is.

Of course one is doing that, because of course one is constantly aware of one's blessing for being alive and the transience of being alive. Even as a trick, an awareness of something larger and Other is actually very healthy—even if it's just a way to trick oneself into making sense of things. I felt more relaxed and more sane than I've ever felt. Because I thought this is how I always thought it should be.

This is basically living your poetry. This is being an artist or being creative—to me it's a 24-hour-a-day lifetime's work. Ultimately I'm what Miss Jacqui said—I'm a lifestyle artist. That sounds really corny; it's probably the worst word. But it's about living, it's an attitude of life.

As far as I'm concerned, **anything that an artist made or created is just** *stuff*—**luxury stuff. That's the detritus of the** *process* **of living a creative life.** And really, a creative life is the nearest we have to a holy life. That's what I think I got from Kerouac, is that life is a holy venture.

The holy fool, the trickster, the seeker after truth, the mystic—it's a gift, it's a blessing. The creativity when one actually acts it out is a *calling,* just the same as being a doctor or a priest once was. As such, at the very least we are the holy fools and should be given respect. At best we're there to cleanse and purify the water of life. In a way, we're *living* for everyone else; it's one of our jobs to cleanse for everyone else.

Once I would say I was a Pagan, but I would say it as a provocation. It was a less commonly used word back in the '70s. But I would say that to utilize any model that is about inclusion and integration is always a good first step. In terms of breaking one's previous imprints and starting to build new ones, or giving ourselves the freedom to choose new ones . . . You know, I'm on holiday!

♦ *R/S: We're always on holiday and we're always working at the same time, and we're always playing and working at the same time—*

♦ GPO: That's true. When I was getting out of school in 1968, I went to my friend Peter's house for dinner. His mother asked me, "So what are you going to do now, having left school?" I said, "I'm going on holiday for the rest of my life." She threw me out of the house! At which point I thought, "Hmmm . . . I must have struck on something here!"

It was an instinctive response. The idea of a holiday was that one was going to try to build a soul and be creative and make daydreams come true and interrelate with others, and explore experience and pleasure. Supposedly it's your own time where you do the things that you want and you like and for the reasons *you* choose. So I was precisely drawn to use the word *holiday*—which of course is "holy day," originally. And that fits again with the whole concept that creativity is a holy calling.

♦ **R/S: You struck an ax at the foundation of the slave-hier-archy society—one in which work is the holy good, or where the profit motive is the highest possible aspiration.**

Your 15 minutes just became eternity

♦ GPO: Well, there is a certain blessing to being British because that's very clearly defined—that pyramid structure has been in place for over a thousand years now, with the ruler, king or queen, and then the aristocrats, all blue-blood, which means of God rather than of human, and then, if you like, the middle-class which is the management ,the collaborators. And then the serfs, the slaves, the working class.

♦ **R/S: It almost does seem like Us versus Them. Us, the slaves, versus the ruling class.**

♦ GPO: Absolutely—ever since Roman times, Greek times— mainly Roman times, which is the real foundation of so-called Western civilization. You have the Caesars. The Greeks were a bit more interesting in that they were also philosophers and abstract mathematicians. We have a lot to be thankful for—for their way of viewing things, and their Polytheism. Plus their idea that things don't begin and end in a particular place. There are those who are raising sheep and there are those people who go all the way through up to having love affairs with Goddesses and Gods.

So it is actually a bit like I was describing before—it goes from the void all the way through to the most solid and all the way back down to the void again. It's a very different way of viewing the world, which is that everything is integrated and inter-related and interdependent—in a very good way. That's what gives balance and sense and compassion and justice. As soon as you stop, as soon as you try to put boundaries and say there is either this or that, there is either a God or a human, there is either the material life or death. . . once you start to put these fences around and make a little box, instead of it being this invisible wash that goes all the way from before-time all the way to after-time, this infinitely expanding possibility—then you start to create these incredibly *violent* perceptions of reasons to exist, and vested interests and self-interests. The idea of superiority against inferiority and so on—notions which aren't really there at all—which have no concrete existence.

But **that is the key to most problems—the belief that human beings are so *special*.** You hear people say "the end of the world," and what they mean is *us killing ourselves off.* And I've always thought that was the ultimate arrogance—that we

assume that because our particular version of physical bodies might get wiped out, that the whole world ends. Unless of course it *is* literally *maya* and it only exists because we all perceive it— then that would be true.

But if we actually thought it was *maya,* and that was the reason for saying that, we would have a very different attitude, too, and we would go back to the [non-materialist views of the] Orient and the Far East. So the fact that we are so obsessed with the control of *material* things and material substances suggests that we have inherited a very unsophisticated view of the world.

The idea of "Original Sin" is probably the worst meme and invention, ever—that we are innately incapable of improvement. That is such a despairing view of being alive, and that is the basic one that we inherit, especially from Christianity. That's such a devastatingly hopeless idea. But I'm sure it was put into place *because* it cripples people's expectations—it cripples their potential for growth in every possible way. And it distracts them from what is really spiritual, which is metaphysics. **Philosophy is one of the most joyful things there is.** Speculation and philosophy and conversation and listening— I just adore traveling the world and watching what goes on, watching the way that these strange little creatures run around and do stuff, so brave—and musing about it.

♦ **R/S: One of the things I like about the Pagan viewpoint is the emphasis on the cyclical nature of the seasons, and the**

Bottom right: In Nepal   Photo: Carl Abrahamsson; Top left photo: Miss Jackie

After studying with Brion Gysin for 10 years, I met the Agori Baba through my spiritual brother Tri Lochan in Kathmandu, Nepal, 1991–92. I was tapped on my right shoulder by an intense, dread-locked figure with a big smile who said, "Come with me." He took us to the cave where a fire burned, which allegedly has burned continuously for over a thousand years. There was an incredible altar with deities, offerings, knickknacks and ritual objects. The path of the Agori is the "Path of No Distinction"—meaning that everything is equal, everything is beautiful, everything is ugly, everything is the same to eat—the same to have tantric sex with. Our scales of worth and value are an illusion that traps us. In 1991, only seven agoris were following this path. The cause of much unhappiness and friction is the concept of righteousness, being correct, valuing one thing, one way, one idea above others. This path of non-prejudiced, non-judgmental perception and positive humility I have tried to integrate into my daily vision of the mystery of being alive.—*Genesis P-Orridge*

Left to right: Pagalananda Nath Agori Baba, GPO, Tri Lochan   Photo: Carl Abrahamsson

way the earth interacts with the seasons. This is different from the linear Christian viewpoint—that we're all just biding our time here on this planet until Jesus comes and whisks us away to where we will play harps in heaven all day. There's no sex there, because we all get transformed into angels who have no sexual organs or bodies.

You know, ten years ago you were encouraging raves, which are like huge public ecstasy celebrations—
♦ GPO: We used to call them "Technopagan." Just like what happened with tattoos and piercing, the same thing happened with raves. It was people reclaiming their heritage, rediscovering their ancient roots, finally taking a step away from their inherited systems. Why? Ultimately because people are absolutely repulsed by hypocrisy (or, they want to be *consumed* by hypocrisy—I think those are the choices people make).

If you *are* absolutely repulsed by hypocrisy, you start to look for something that *feels* like it makes more sense. It doesn't have to be verbalized or articulated or rational. And we're still seeing the fruits of Surrealism and Dada and Jung. **We're still very *larval* at the moment in terms of the changes that are happening to us as beings.** These convulsions in culture are symptomatic of something much deeper, which is that the lineage, the heritage, the metaphysical and spiritual connectivity of people was ripped from our earlier consciousness by the Judeo-Christian-Muslim monotheistic tyrants.

From the moment that stupid little bit of desert at the end of the Mediterranean decided it was egocentric enough to claim direct contact with God, we've been in a war against slavery in different forms, really. We haven't had any encouragement to be in synch with and in love with nature and the environment and the seasons and each other—in extended families, not just nuclear ones. All the truly healthy and joyful things about being here are being ripped from us by violence.
♦ *R/S: It's the triumph of monotheism, monoculture—*
♦ GPO: —which ultimately serves economic power and political power.
♦ *R/S: Again, that quote by James Breasted opened up so much: "Monotheism is Imperialism in religion." That just nailed it. What is Imperialism? It incarnates authoritarianism and hierarchy. That's something else that people attending illegal raves were rebelling against—*
♦ GPO: Right. But they were also experiencing the equivalent

of *bembé.* When you start to travel, as I have been blessed to do, you can meet, especially in Nepal, these holy men. You see how people live lives that have devotion included in different forms, every single day, 24-7. And the same with some of the African Yoruba religions, and so on. Then you realize that we are tremendously, intellectually, spiritually, and emotionally crippled. You might say to a holy man, "Oh, I took this acid and I saw these other dimensions, and the void." They look at you like you're pathetically naive: "Of course it's like that. Of course there's *nothing here.* Of course there are no particles. Why are you telling me this? We knew that from the beginning."

So **we've been disenfranchised from basic information that allows an empathetic relationship with apparently being alive.** And when that happens, you have fear and paranoia moving in, because one's heart (whatever that is—the metaphor of heart *equals* one's soul—that's probably the real reason why we're here—to build souls) is disturbed and distressed. Because it can feel something is missing, something has been removed, something taken away, and whenever one tries to go towards that which feels like *soul* or *heart,* one is blocked by bureaucracy, violence, fundamentalism, and intimidation. So most people surrender to fear in exchange for what they think is a peaceful life.

We've had 2000 years of a very, very repressive system, and that's imprinted in our bodies, it's imprinted in our architecture—in everything. But I think a lot of people are rebelling now, more than is imagined.
♦ *R/S: And they're reclaiming their lost Pagan heritage—*
♦ GPO: It's actually quite a relief when you get to the point where you realize **the only real reason to do *anything* is in order to have some form of spiritual or ecstatic experience or reconnection.** If you look at this more from the point of view that ultimately life is a holy experience in its widest sense, then everything takes on a much more optimistic slant.
♦ *R/S: And we definitely need more optimism—*
♦ GPO: I'm innately optimistic, surprisingly. I just think this is actually a wonderful experiment or a mathematical accident. For all we know somebody in the future came up with the mathematical equation for creation which created creation, which would then go through the loop back to the point where they created themselves—who knows. Given that it's *all* a mystery, you might as well explore the mystery to the fullest!♦♦♦

YORUBA PRIMER

by Miss Jacqui

Miss Jacqui Breyer is a photographer, choreographer and aesthetic nutritionist for the "Troubadours of the Worlds" performance group, Thee Majesty. She collaborates with Genesis P-Orridge on art exhibitions, works as a healer, and is a Priestess of Oshun.

1 Yoruba is a form of earth-based magick: it uses material/concrete objects as symbols of the divine essence that created them, the emphasis not being on the physical object. Along with these symbols, this divine power that the Yoruba call ACHÉ is accessed through the use of ritual, faith, prayer, dance, song and sacrifice.

2 Those who practice the Yoruba religion may use it as a means to assist in achieving a balanced character, one of a practitioner's highest goals. As one's divine consciousness develops, behavior mirrors the divine.

3 THE ORISHA: There are numerous Orisha. Some of the most important/most often propitiated are called The Seven African Powers.

1 OBATALA is the arch-divinity of the Yoruba, representing spiritual purity and the creator of the human form. In Santería, he is syncretized with the Catholic "God the Father."

2 ESHU is an extremely powerful messenger divinity who acts as an intermediary between humans and Orisha, and between the Orisha themselves (similar to Hermes in this respect). He is always propitiated first. Sometimes identified as the Devil—not because Eshu is evil, but rather because he's a trickster beyond good and evil, with the role of presenting humans with challenges and temptations, testing their character, and offering opportunities for one to choose one's own path.

3 OSHUN: Goddess of the river, divinity of fertility and feminine power. Represents the things that make life "sweet", such as love, beauty, the spark that ignites physical passion or creative passion, and the uniquely human ability to dream of perfection.

4 OGUN: God of iron, one of the "divine hunters." The divinity of clearing paths. Together with OCHOSI, another Orisha hunter, they represent, among other things, the shortest path to one's spiritual evolution.

5 YEMOJA: Goddess of the ocean and matriarch of the Orisha. She represents nurturing and protective energy.

6 OYA: Goddess of the wind, storms, hurricanes. Guardian of the cemetery. Upon superficial observation she may be misunderstood as the deity of death, but actually represents the cycle of life, as all things must die in order for new life to generate. In this respect she is similar to Kali.

7 SHANGO: a strong and masculine warrior. Identified with drumming and music, dance, lightning, and diplomacy. An extremely competent strategist in war, although war need not necessarily imply violence or physical combat.

The BEMBÉ is a communal gathering where the Orisha are revered. Typically celebrated using drums and song to invoke the divinities. Animal sacrifice is not generally a part of this ceremony. Most often, sacrifice is in the form of water, rum, herbs and tobacco, fruit, flowers, food, candles, prayers and incense. Sacrifice may be used for different purposes—for example, to give thanks or to remove suffering or negativity.

ANCESTOR WORSHIP is an important part of the Yoruba tradition. Ancestors are recognized for their wisdom accumulated and passed on through culture, ritual, and intuitive wisdom passed along through one's bloodline/DNA. The Yoruba believe that they reincarnate through their own bloodline. Children are considered a great blessing and grandchildren help to ensure one's return.

DIVINATION: the Yoruba use several methods. Some are:

1 The DILOGUN: cowrie shell divination sacred to the Orisha. All initiated priest/esses may use this method.

2 IFA: a form of divination used by a high priest/ess (babalawo). This method is believed to represent the voice of God.

3 OBI: simple divination using coconut shells to answer yes or no questions.

RECOMMENDED BOOKS   Philip John Neimark *The Way of the Orisha*. Julio Garcia Cortez *The Osha: Secrets of the Yoruba-Lucumi-Santería Religion in the United States & The Americas*. Ocha'ni Lele *The Secrets of Afro-Cuban Divination*. Raul Canizares *Santería African Spirits in American & Cuban Santería*. Migene Gonzalez Wippler *Santería: The Religion*. Michael Talbot *The Holographic Universe*. Maya Deren *Divine Horsemen* (not Yoruba/Santería, but in my opinion gives the deepest, most emotional description of these divine archetypes. Illuminating book!) Howard Bloom *The Lucifer Principle*. Timothy Wyllie *Dolphins, ET's and Angels*. James Hillman *The Soul's Code*. Brion Gysin *Here To Go*. Antonin Artaud *The Peyote Dance*. Julian Jaynes *The Origins of Consciousness in the Breakdown of the Bicameral Mind*.

RECOMMENDED WEBSITE: *www.orishareligion.com*

Miss Jacqui with Naga Babas, Nepal, October 2000.

Neo-Paganism:
An Old Religion for a New Age
by Oberon Ravenheart

Neo-Pagan religions are many and diverse. They range from the sublimely artistic Paradisal vision and reconstruction of old Pagan Mysteries of Feraferia to the astrological divination and ancient Egyptian religion of the Church of the Eternal Source; and from the Wiccan-oriented myth and ritual of the Pagan Way to the transpersonal psychology, science-fiction mythology and deep ecology of the Church of All Worlds. All of Neo-Pagan religious traditions now in existence, and most of the countless sects of Witchcraft, hold certain values in common. It is these values which relate them to Paganism in the older sense.

One of the key values of Neo-Paganism is its insistence on personal responsibility. The Church of All Worlds expresses this in the phrase, "Thou art God/dess," implying total personal freedom and individual responsibility on the part of every one. Paganism has no concept of "original sin," hence has no need of saviors. Neo-Pagans do not expect divine retribution for breaking social taboos. Rather, concepts of "sin" and "atonement" are restated in the framework of ecological awareness and karma. If our actions are discordant and in opposition to the evolutionary flow of Life, we suffer the ecological consequences, in much the same way, and for exactly the same reasons, as diseased cells in the body are attacked by the antibodies and other natural defenses. Whatever energy we put out returns to us multiplied threefold. Love returns love; hate returns hate. Robert Ingersoll observed: "In Nature there are neither rewards nor punishments; there are consequences." Total responsibility (hence total freedom) rests in our hands.

As in the Old Religion, Neo-Pagans conceptualize Divinity as manifest in the processes of Nature. In a literal sense, Mother Nature, Mother Earth, is "Goddess," and She has been recognized as such since time immemorial. Thus ecology is seen as the supreme religious study:

"Nature is Divinity made manifest ... It is creativity, continuity, balance, beauty and truth of life.

"Everything we encounter in the Biosphere is a part of Nature, and ecology reveals the pattern of that is-ness, the natural relationships among all these things and the Organic Unity of all of them as a Biospheric Whole. Thus ecology shows the pattern of man's proper and creative involvement with Nature, that Nature which encompasses his own life and on proper relation to which his survival and development depend.

"Of all man's secular studies, ecology comes closest to bringing him to the threshold of religious relationship to his world. Ecology not only confirms the wonders of form and function that other secular studies have revealed, but it brings these into organic union with each other as one dynamic, living Whole; and it points out the conditions for the well-being of both this overall Unity and the parts that comprise it.

"An intense realization of these conditions, and of one's own immediate role in their sustainment and development, brings one to the threshold of religious awe. To worship Nature, therefore, is to venerate and commune with Divinity as the dynamically organic perfection of the whole." (Council of Themis, from Green Egg #43)

Neo-Paganism is a recent mutation of the Old Religion which had its earliest emergence during the European Renaissance with the rediscovery of the ancient Greek philosophers via Arabian texts. However, this was also the time of the Burnings, and the budding Neo-Pagan emergence was suppressed until the late 1700s, when it found expression in the Romantic Period of art, music and literature, especially in Germany.

This Romantic flowering of Neo-Paganism, notably the element known as the Bavarian Illuminati (whose mottos were "eternal flower power" and "eternal serpent power"), greatly appealed to a visiting American named Benjamin Franklin. Upon his return to the colonies it became a major spiritual force in the post-Revolutionary America of the 1780s, where its influence continued to shape the new nation through the presidencies of the Adams family. It was Monroe and the War of 1812 that managed to suppress this movement for a time, but it re-emerged 60 years later in the form of the Transcendentalist Movement, exemplified in the poetry and writings of Whitman, Thoreau and Emerson, and the commune movement in the 1840s.

The Civil War, Reconstruction, the conquest of the West and the Gold Rush drained the Nature-oriented spiritual energy from the people of America for another 60 years, but it blossomed again through Art Nouveau in the 1900s. Then came the World Wars, the Depression, McCarthyism. Sixty more years had to pass before the gathering impact of Eastern religious philosophy, especially Zen, and existentialism gave birth to the "hip underground" counterculture of the Beatniks. Experimentation with drugs, sexuality, music, poetry, communal living and alternative lifestyles paved the way for the Hippie phenomenon of the 1960s, which curiously resurrected the old Illuminati motto of "flower power." The seeds of Neo-Paganism which had lain dormant for three generations took root in fertile soil and emerged once more into the light, to be joined in the '70s by the heirs of Wicca, the last vestiges of the Old Religion of Europe.

The New Religion is still very much Paganism, for its inspiration and orientation is based, as were its predecessors', upon an understanding of the relationship of Humanity with the larger perspective of Life, Nature and the Universe. Fred Adams of Feraferia coined the term "eco-psychic" to describe the type of awareness that permeates this new religion.

Revealed religions, especially of the monotheistic variety, tend to see man as a special creation, exalted above all Nature, the epitome of God's handiwork. Thus the Biblical injunction to Man to "have dominion over all the Earth" is not seen by Judeo-Christians as outrageously presumptuous; nor is God's destruction of all life on Earth in the legend of the Deluge seen as insane, immoral ecocide. Both God and Man are considered to have a "divine right" to desecrate the Earth at their pleasure. This is in direct opposition to the view of Paganism, which sees humanity's duty not to conquer Nature, but to live in harmony and stewardship with Her.

Every revealed religion claims to have its own direct pipeline to the Divinity and its own essential precepts derived from direct, uncontestable revelation. Neo-Pagans, on the other hand, have outgrown egotistical, temperamental gods and expect no intervention from some Big Daddy in the Sky to solve the problems of our times. Instead, we look to Nature (through the clear glass of ecology) for inspiration and direction, and to ourselves as the instruments for all that needs to be done. Thou art God/dess! ◆◆◆

The Ravenhearts

An outstanding example of extended-family living is provided by the six individuals who have chosen to adopt the last name of "Ravenheart": Oberon Zell, Morning Glory, Liza Gabriel, Wolf, Wynter, and John. Sharing a small ranch with several buildings 75 miles north of San Francisco, the Ravenhearts support themselves by designing and producing Pagan ceramics and statuary which they market from their website, *www.mythicimages.com*. The Ravenhearts also travel and teach workshops, give rituals, regularly host celebrations, and in general catalyze and inspire the growing Pagan community. Oberon was the original publisher of *Green Egg* magazine. Interviews by John Sulak & V. Vale.

Women L to R: Wynter, Liza, Morning Glory; men L to R: Wolf, Oberon

Morning Glory

Morning Glory in the Ravenheart family sculpture studio

(Interview with Morning Glory Ravenheart by John Sulak)

♦ **RE/SEARCH: Tell us about your childhood—**

♦ MORNING GLORY: I was born in 1948, right after the war ended. I had a pretty happy childhood, except that I was very different from my parents—I always felt like a changeling. In terms of religion or spirituality, I took what was available, which was mostly Fundamentalist Christianity, but it never quite fit me. It was like borrowing someone else's clothes; they bulged in places I didn't, and vice versa. I always would ask questions that the ministers didn't have any answers for, and often made them feel quite uncomfortable.

My mom seemed like a doormat. Whatever my dad did was okay with her—it *had* to be, because periodically he would beat her and threaten to kill us both. That kind of behavior shaped me. I would argue right back and start to debate my dad, putting him down when I felt he was wrong. I acted as though I were his equal, and he hated that—we got into huge fights. I can remember a time when he held a knife to my throat and threatened to kill me, and I tried to bite his hand. He looked into my eyes and saw his same spirit blazing right back at him, and he couldn't snuff that out.

But paradoxically, I never stopped loving my father. My father was my window and door into the natural world—he was an agnostic naturalist who loved nature and introduced me to its wonders. In spite of his craziness, he imparted that gift to me.

My mother gave me a real love and appreciation for the spiritual world. She was an incredibly nurturing, loving parent. If it weren't for her, I would not be the person I am today at all. She taught me and gave me unconditional love. Hers grew out of devout Christianity and I took it in a different direction, but we still share in common a belief in unconditional love and a reverence for life.

What I did not get from my mother was *fear*—I rejected her whole fear component. I think that saved my life, because if I had been fearful, my father might very well have killed me.

♦ **R/S: What church did your family attend?**

♦ MG: I grew up in a fundamentalist Pentecostal church called the Assembly of God. They practiced a form of ecstatic Christianity, with baptism in the name of the Holy Spirit and congregation members speaking in tongues. I was fully involved to the point where I went to the minister and said,

"Look, I'm concerned, because my father beats my mom and beats me. Where is God's will in this? What is our recourse?"

Back then, there weren't any battered women's shelters. Previously I had gone to a psychiatrist to try to get family counseling help, but he had told my parents that I was crazy and needed electroshock therapy. When I went to the minister, he told me that it's a woman's duty to surrender to the will of her husband, and that if my dad killed my mom, she'd get a crown in heaven some day!

This happened when I was 13. Right after that I had an opportunity to visit my aunt in New Orleans and attend Mardi Gras. It was so exciting that I exclaimed, "Wow—*that's* my religion!" I glimpsed another universe! After that, I knew I was not suited to be a Christian.

♦ **R/S: When did you discover Paganism?**

♦ MG: When I was 17 I discovered Sybil Leek's *Diary of a Witch* and everything clicked into place. The book told how the "old religion" had been suppressed by the Romans and Christianity; it described a Horned God and his consort the Goddess. I realized that I was a witch. Unfortunately, her book also said, "If you're not born a hereditary English witch, you don't get to be one." I thought, "What do you mean—that's what I *am!*" I felt I'd been offered this perfect gift, and then it had been snatched away.

That same summer—my junior year of high school during the early Sixties—I discovered LSD. I had a friend who was a folk singer, and he introduced me to the whole Bob Dylan/Joan Baez folk-singing circuit in Los Angeles and Venice. I traveled around with him, went to all these clubs and wild parties, and had a wonderful time.

♦ **R/S: How did you support yourself?**

♦ MG: I was also working full-time at a hospital, doing emergency room services, EKGs, phlebotomy and laboratory work, as well as grungy tasks like washing test-tubes. I was in the midst of life and death attending to a lot of people when they died, and this experience really made me want to understand the passages between the two worlds.

Based on my reading, I decided that what I needed was an initiation. I went to Big Sur, lived off the land for a week, and then fasted. Then I took a major LSD trip, and at its peak I climbed thirty feet up the side of a waterfall and dove into the pool of water at the bottom. The person who dove off that waterfall was a girl named Diana, and the person who climbed out of that pool was a woman named Morning Glory. I took that name and have been Morning Glory ever since. And that was my initiation. I told everybody it was under the jurisdiction of an English witch, because otherwise it wouldn't have been legitimate!

♦ **R/S: Were you still living with your parents?**

♦ MG: Yes, but I was about to graduate. I wanted to join a hippie commune, so after graduation I packed up a suitcase, took my boa constrictor and started driving to Oregon. This was at the height of the Vietnam War. I had been heavily involved in the anti-war movement, working at the Peace Center, and recognized somebody hitch-hiking along the side of the road. I picked him up. He'd been in the military and almost went to Vietnam, but at the last minute he convinced them he was too weird, and they discharged him from the service. To celebrate he was headed for San Francisco, and I gave him a ride to Big Sur.

When we got there I offered to share my sleeping bag with him, because he didn't have one. But the deal was, if he wanted to do that, he had to help keep my boa constrictor warm. That's how I met my first husband! [laughs]

After being together for several years we decided to have a child. But even though our relationship was always open, it began to feel very limiting. I was teaching, traveling, and writing articles for local newspapers on witchcraft, and I really wanted to share my spiritual vision with the world. I had tried to start a coven in Eugene, Oregon and was known as the town witch. I gave lots of interviews, and lectured high school students in honors classes. My husband was more of a quiet, retiring, Buddhism-oriented person. Eventually, our lives began to diverge.

In 1972 I had a precognitive dream that I would meet a man who would lead me into a new life. In 1973 I hitchhiked to a Pagan gathering in Minnesota and met Oberon, who was then known as Tim Zell. Almost instantly we felt a total psychic melding; we were so in love we could barely speak. But I've always had the ability to step back from my feelings, pause, and take a deep breath. I looked at him and said, "You know, this is amazing and wonderful and I love you so much I can't even think straight. But I can think straight enough to be honest with you. I need you to understand that as much as I love you, I can never be in a monogamous relationship—it's just not my nature. I want to be free to have other lovers, and you're free to do that as well. **I'll give you my whole heart and soul, but I cannot give you monogamy. That's just who and what I am.**"

Oberon looked at me like he'd found the Holy Grail: "Ah, the goddess has appeared in my life! She has finally come through for me." **From that point on we were soul-mates— there was no question about it. He had the missing pieces I needed, and I had the missing pieces he needed.** We entered into an incredible partnership that has been the most amazing adventure of both of our lives; for over 25 years we've been a dynamic duo. And we did it based on an inclusive, rather than an exclusive, relationship.

It did take us years to sort things out; I had another husband, Gary; and Oberon and I were in a triad relationship for ten years with another woman we considered our wife. I introduced the other woman to Gary, and they hit it off, got married, became our neighbors. We still have fun times together. But after ten years Oberon and I broke up our relationship with the other woman over irreconcilable differences. He and I then continued our own adventure.

Then I was introduced to another amazing man with whom I connected and bonded—that's Wolf. He was living in Houston, Texas. I started courting him and we formed this powerful, passionate relationship. I said to Oberon, "Look, we've done it your way. We've had the two women/one man situation for ten years. Let's see if I can't find you a co-husband here; let's try two husbands." And he said, "I'm game—good luck!" Oberon has always gotten along better with women than men. But Wolf and I had this powerful sex-magic going,

Morning Glory

this dark, kinky energy with a lot of juice. Oberon said, "Do you guys ever talk about anything other than sex?" I said, "I'm going to visit him; I'll let you know."

When I walked into Wolf's room, it looked just like Oberon's room! He had the same Star Trek toys, the same library, the same Klingon athames. I went, "Ohmigod—these guys are gonna be great friends. They have everything in common." Sure enough—when Wolf came to visit, the two of them spent hours sharing all kinds of common interests: *Batman, Star Trek, Star Wars*—they really hit it off. Wolf decided to take the plunge and move to California to be with us. It was difficult and painful for him because he was divorced and had to leave behind his daughter from a previous marriage.

Four years ago the three of us were handfasted [married], and we formed the nucleus of a new group. Oberon had also met Liza at a gathering on the East Coast and he brought her in. Liza does amazing seminars that are like four-day slumber parties. They're all about touching and feeling and breaking down the walls between people, going into places of deep intimacy and bonding. She brings spirit and sex together in a very practical, tangible, hands-on way. **She creates temporary safe environments where groups of people can go about the process of communicating soul-to-soul with other naked, living, joyful beings.**

Earlier in the year, right in our midst there had appeared a young woman who had grown up near us. She had wanted to be part of the Church of All Worlds, but her mom had kept her from us.

She showed up on our front doorstep and demanded to be apprenticed to me, and we totally clicked. We talked late into the night and really fell in love; I realized she was the woman I had been looking for my whole life, the same way that Oberon was the man.

Wolf and I have a wonderful partnership, but it's a bit different. We're lovers, partners, business partners, and just plain co-conspirators. But Wolf and I don't have that special soul relationship I have with Oberon, and I knew he would be looking for a woman to have that with. So I introduced Wynter to Wolf at Beltane four years ago, and they fell in love. Meanwhile, Oberon had his other Significant Other, Liza; and Wolf and Wynter were my Significant Others. We all got together.

In a way it was an odd kind of a hodgepodge, because Liza, Oberon and I share a lot of background history, while Wolf, Liza and Wynter don't—although Wynter shares some interests with Liza. In other words, we don't share everything in common. But Wolf and Wynter have that soul-mate connection that Oberon and I have.

So **that's how we built our family . . . organically. It's messy and quarrelsome because we all do things differently.** It was Liza's idea that we should all move in together. She put a lot of energy into finding the means so that our family business could be the supporting foundation.

♦ *R/S: Where did the name "Ravenheart" come from?*

◆ MG: We were creating a family out of five very different people, but it was an extremely painful process. We lived together for two years in a beautiful but isolated environment, built up a business, and established our family on top of a pressure-cooker situation. **Some of us had to go through intense changes and make sacrifices to make this family happen. We had to put aside our ideas of "the way things ought to be" in order to allow what was actually destined to occur.**

Originally we thought we were going to have a group marriage, but that's not what happened—we realized we were a *family*. At the time we were doing a lot of shadow work. Some of us are into classical, witchy, stirring-the-cauldron, dark magic. Some of us are into kinky SM. Some of us are into mysterious, veiled-dancing types of spiritual practices. But we all have this love affair with the dark side, and at the time, that was the one thing all of us could identify with.

All of a sudden we were visited by a plethora of ravens—were they migrating? Everywhere we looked there were ravens! We went, "Whoa; what's going on? Maybe this is a message." So we started investigating their mythological significance. I knew the raven was the North American trickster bird, but then I discovered he is a conveyer of magic. Raven walks between the worlds; he is the shadow, and the messenger that carries the magic from where it's conceived to where it needs to be manifested. If tricks and humor are part of him, it's because he's a communicator. **Humor is a kind of lubrication for communication, especially of weightier matters—sometimes you have to play tricks and amuse people to get your point across.** So we spent some time learning what Raven had to teach us.

While we were doing that, Liza was also working on transferring and translating the sex-and-spirit work she was doing on the East Coast to a system on the West Coast. She was doing a lot of heart chakra work, and said, "Whatever name we choose has to be about the heart, because that's what we're about— **we're a bunch of hopeless romantics who have ended up together. We're as different as can possibly be, yet we share a place of love.** And love is the only universal solvent that will dissolve our boundaries and allow us to manifest our dreams and our hearts' desires together." So she stood for the infinite possibilities of the heart, and together we symbolized the infinite possibilities of darkness. Meanwhile, all these ravens were going, "Caw! Caw!"

Finally I had an epiphany. I said, "I understand what it is—we are *Ravenhearts*. We're about communicating the secrets of love and darkness; being able to transmit and translate the mysteries of the heart to the world."

Morning Glory with "Living Unicorn"

◆ *R/S: How did the family all end up working together?*

◆ MG: My life work has involved teaching Goddess history and Goddess lore. I travel around the world telling fabulous tales of the mythology, lore and practice of the ancient Goddess religion. I teach at schools, seminar centers and Pagan gatherings using my collection of over 200 images of goddesses from around the world and throughout history. If the image is in the form of a sculpture, then people can hold the Goddess in their hands, and when I describe her and tell her story, they can feel that which speaks to them.

Oberon, an incredible Renaissance man, began making me new goddess sculptures that were museum-quality reproductions. He made goddesses from the Stone Age, the Bronze Age, Crete and Czechoslovakia. I wanted world-spanning imagery, so that all races and ages of history would be represented.

I never made enough money giving lectures to support myself, but when I turned 40, I realized I could supplement my "Goddess Historian" income by selling reproductions of Goddess statues at my lectures. A friend who is another crazy genius helped find methods whereby we could create molds that could reproduce Oberon's originals. Later on, I also began creating originals. Initially, we created our "Mythic Images" business based on three or four pieces. Now we have dozens of products.

Originally, I was a one-man band; I made everything and got help wherever I could. I hired local teenagers—that's how I got Wynter into my life. She came to work for me and right away there was a major difference—she was not just a worker-for-hire. As she began shaping sculptures with her hands, her goal became to make her own goddesses. She apprenticed to Oberon and developed her artistic talents. Now some of our hottest-selling items are Wynter's creations.

So, our business and family grew together around each other. Wolf became the business manager we desperately needed; he made it all work in the real world by having computer and managerial skills. Oberon is my inspiration, helping me attain wild, crazy, wonderful visions. But Wolf teaches me discipline to finish what needs to be done. [laughs]

◆ *R/S: Didn't you coin the word "polyamory"?*

◆ MG: "Non-monogamy" is a popular notion among Pagans. In the Sixties there were a lot of people working on utopian communities and engaging in active social experimentation. They weren't necessarily Pagans; their focus was more on the sociological aspect rather than on religion and mysticism. But nobody had a word for polyamory; they were defining themselves by negatives!

I said to Oberon, "We need a better defining word for our multiple relationships." **Claude Steiner had coined "omnigamy," which has to be the ugliest word I've ever heard in my life—sorry, Claude.** What does it mean: "marrying everybody?" Another term being bandied about was "polyfidelity" [which sounds like high fidelity]. But the idea needed to be about *loving,* not marrying, and there was no one word that embraced it all. Finally I realized, "This is about love and having many lovers. This is really about people who have many lovers and many loving relationships."

I'm a person who loves words, and in fact I've pursued linguistic studies. I grew up with a classical education and, besides taking four years of Latin, have studied a little Greek on my own. I've always been interested in paleontology, and have worked in the medical profession, so I understood a lot of medical terminology in Greek and Latin. I started playing with

Greek and Latin roots and came up with "poly," which was already being used in "polyfidelity." But "fidelity," the notion of being faithful, always smacked to me of moral preaching. Besides, I wanted a term that was more about love. So I took the Latin root for love, "amor" ("amour" is the French twist on that) and the Greek root "poly" (meaning many), put the two together, and created the word "polyamory."

Here's a word, an umbrella term, that describes what we're doing, I said. The movement was already there, but finally it had a word it could rally around. It was no longer defining itself by what it wasn't. **Polyamory is now listed in dictionaries; there are books about it; and it's listed on the Web. The word has spread all over the world.** The reason is because it is difficult to do something you have no word for. Some people are doing things they have no word for, defining the ineffable, but by and large they will remain isolated in their own universe until they find a word that other people can congregate around. This process works like salt crystals that coalesce around a single seed-crystal. **The word "polyamory" is the seed-crystal, and the movement is collecting around that. Because if you can think it and say it, then you can actually BE it.** Adrienne Rich once said, "Whatever is unnamed, undepicted in images, whatever is misnamed as something else, made difficult to come by, whatever is buried in the memory by the collapse of meaning under an inadequate or lying language—this will become, not merely unspoken but unspeakable." What I stand for is *creating possibilities*. We do that with words; the word gives a sound, and the sound launches the reality.

The goddess Saraswati created all that we see and recognize as the universe. She was hatched from a cosmic egg in the void. Initially she stood up and sang a single note, and her pure tone vibrated everything into being. The universe, out of chaos, began pulsing into its evolutionary order. Each of us, when we come up with a vision and name it, are Saraswati, recreating her act of creation. Each of us are gods and goddesses capable of creation by that act of naming a thing that has no name.

The other word I want to share is a very important word in the polyamory universe: it means the opposite of jealousy. The concept of jealousy permeates our whole world—you can't listen to the radio, hear an opera, see a play, or watch television without having this world view of jealousy, limitation and "You're mine and nobody else can have you" in your face. We live in a world in which love is a commodity to be hoarded. But love is not something you want to keep in a cage—unless that's your "kink" and is truly what you want. Unless lovers beg really hard, you don't put them in cages. Love and its affiliated notions deserve to have wings and fly free. Sexuality is not a thing to be is kept under lock and key, only let out on a leash.

People have strong feelings about the word "jealousy." They say, "I can't love a lot of people," or "I wouldn't let my partner love somebody else because that would make me jealous.

But what if you don't feel that way? What if you see two people you love walking along together, laughing and happy, and they smile and wave to you while you're doing what you have to do. They're going off to have a wonderful time and you watch the bounce in their step and the light in their eyes, and you feel warm and happy. That's a spark you don't have to blow on; that's a happiness he's giving to her that you don't have to give her—something *you* don't have to do. You don't have to

work at making somebody happy in ways that perhaps you're not even suited to: "I don't have to go to that movie I don't want to see, because *he's* taking her instead. I can stay here and work on my sculpture, or read a book,

Photo: Charles Gatewood

or go out to a concert with somebody else. Her needs will be met by him. Oh, thank you so much—you're saving me from a movie I didn't want to see!" [laughs]

The moment you have those thoughts, which stem from a purely polyamorous experience, the word that was coined to describe that feeling is "compersion" (pronounced "come-Persian." (By the way, I didn't coin that word; it came from a utopian group called Kerista.) **COMPERSION is the opposite of jealousy.** When you see two people together that you love, loving each other, then their love kindles the love in your heart. And you smile, laugh, and heave a sigh of relief that they're having such a wonderful time. That is compersion.

This is a wonderful, beautiful word: *come…purr…* [laughs] Compersion is a dirty little word around the edges, too, because it can also signify that voyeuristic thrill you get from watching people you love do naughty things together. Compersion is a big word. It can go from a kind of hot, sexy, "watching people get it on" juicy thrill to a completely platonic reaction where you see your children all playing together and they're not fighting—they're making each other happy. They're playing quietly and harmoniously. That is also compersion.

People say, "You can only love one person," but to me that's nonsense. Any mother or father who has more than one child realizes that you can love all of your children. You may love them in different ways, but you can love them equally powerfully—you would rip your heart out and sacrifice it for them in an instant, because they're your children, and you love them.

What's the difference between having one husband, and then having a second husband and loving him, too? You would give your life for either one. You love them both with all of your heart. Adding sex doesn't have to change the equation.

Some men feel, "If I had to listen to my wife making love with another man, I'd die!" You know what, buddy? You wouldn't. You'd just hear those noises, and you'd go through some changes. But if you really let yourself listen to her joy, if you really let yourself hear those sounds, and imagine her face, the way it is when she makes those noises for you, you'd realize that "Somebody else is making somebody I love happy." Why is this not a good thing?

We have to give ourselves permission to make each other happy. Oberon and I are so much alike that we're like stereo. But you know what—he doesn't like chocolate! And there are many things he *likes* that I can't stand. So why should we make each other suffer, when we can delight each other by going off and sharing those things with other people?

Last night Oberon and I went to a concert and had a rip-roaring, wonderful time. But if Oberon had forced Liza to go with him, she wouldn't have—she doesn't particularly care for those musicians. Instead, Liza was off with someone else doing something they wanted to bond around.

Next weekend Wolf, Wynter and I are going to a Chieftains concert, but we're not going to drag Oberon, because they play largely instrumental music and he's tone-deaf—that would be a waste of a concert ticket. So the three of us will go and have a wonderful time listening to music we love. But does this mean I don't love Oberon? Or that I'm being unfaithful to my husband of 25 years because I'm having a desire fulfilled that he wouldn't enjoy? No, that's ridiculous. But no human being can meet all of your needs.

Whenever anybody hears about polyamory, they always say, "Oh, that would never work." And I go, "What do you _mean_ that would never work? Does monogamy work?" Think about all the monogamous people who get divorced—they go back to the same paradigm and get married again to yet another monogamous person and try to make that person meet all their needs—sometimes over and over.

The American family is in so much trouble that Congress is trying to pass Congressional Acts to save it. That's why I think polyamory is part of the wave of the future—it's a way of re-visioning the family. And **polyamory is not _opposed_ to monogamy. I am upset that the word I coined has been codified or defined in dictionaries as being "in opposition to monogamy"—nothing could be further from the truth!**

We used to consider homosexual or bisexual people as failed heterosexuals; we now know that they are just _different_. Poly people usually start out thinking of themselves as failed monogamists, whereas it's _time_ we started claiming our space as "something completely different!" We need to define ourselves sexually and then get together with our own kind. This creates a win-win scenario: monogamous people no longer have to have their hearts broken by cheating partners who are really poly people stuck in a choiceless paradigm. Polyamory is about supporting monogamy, not opposing it.

♦ _R/S: Are there any rules?_

♦ MG: Our first rule is: _Be excellent to each other!_ We want to do things in an ethical fashion, where people are not bruised, battered, and wounded by love. But we also want to maximize freedom. A second rule is _Honesty:_ you have to tell the people you want to date that you are polyamorous, and make sure they are also—no cheating!

But really, I think the only way anything works is if you make it up yourself. And that's what Pagans are doing with religion—making it all up. We're inventing it. People may need to customize their relationships, because there isn't a "one size fits all" model that works. That's what both polyamory and Paganism offer: _alternatives,_ so people can chop and channel their relationships, families, religions and lifestyles until the people involved are comfortable. People are more likely to feel whole and completed if they had a hand in creating something,

and this feeling comes from within. Religion isn't a thing that gets grafted on from without; your religion should be something that grows from within to meet your individual needs.

Not all Pagans are polyamorous—no way! But tolerance for different tribal customs is part of the Pagan ethic. Pagan families come in all different categories.

I like to make up new endings for romances, because the problem with most stories is that the ending is too predictable. There's nothing wrong with "and they all lived happily ever after." But why does the "all" have to be only two?

So let's find a family model that has room for all people's sexual, romantic and child-rearing needs. One thing I want to see happen in the Ravenheart family is that we'll have the child-rearing space and the erotic sexual space—and these will not be in the same buildings! The kids need to be able to wreck the place, leave toys all over and be in a safe, happy, messy environment. I also want to have an absolutely wonderful space with a dungeon, giant bedrooms, trapezes, and closets full of sexy lingerie, whips, chains and who knows what.

People need to find ways of envisioning what's possible and work hard to manifest that. They have to be willing to adhere to the discipline involved in asking hard questions: "We've got a lot of great ideas—now how can we make this happen?" And you aren't going to make it happen by trying to move people back into a 1950's mold—or a Bronze Age mold, for that matter. We have to create something that has never been created before.

We need to have families that are composed of moms and kids, dads and uncles, and more. We need families in which people are related by blood, by love, and by whatever else people need to create their vision of utopia. Because **everybody is entitled to their own happy ending, and the only way to get that happy ending is to write it yourself.**

♦ _R/S: Why are Pagans drawn to polytheism?_

♦ MG: Because it takes many aspects of the Divine to reflect the many aspects of humanity and the rest of Nature as well. **Additionally, there is this great hunger for the archetype of "the god as _lover._"** Christians go around proclaiming that "Jesus loves you"; nuns become the brides of Christ, and there are many women who are completely fixated on Jesus. But Jesus was a celibate—did you know that?! Yet many women in Christian culture take this unsuitable archetype and try to mold it into something that will suit their needs.

I think it's great to have a balanced idea of a _hero_ as a lover, and a _god_ as a lover—one who is skilled at manifesting love for the world. The Greeks had Eros, the god of love; the East Indians have Kama, the god of love. In Sumer and Greece, there were temples to the goddess of love where anyone could come and worship sexually. The Hindus also had Krishna, the lover-god who satisfied a thousand milkmaids in one night.

One reason there are no gods considered to be lovers in the sexual sense is because of the advent of monotheism and

Morning Glory at Eleusis, Greece

monogamy. If you have a monotheistic god, you can't have a goddess! Monotheism has no goddesses—therefore god has no sex. And sex is often demonized in monotheistic religions, whereas polytheism can always provide a deity to work with, regardless of your gender, sexual preference—fill in the blank.

I feel we need to come up with better mythologies. In Africa, the hero Shango is both a warrior *and* lover *par excellence*. Whereas heroism in Western culture is usually about war, not sex—in fact, heroes often have tragic sex lives. Hercules is the classic example of that.

It's time for religion to come forth into the world of political genocide, globalism, and corporate environmental destruction. Why did the religious patriarchs of the Serbian nation not speak out against what was being done to the ethnic Albanians in Bosnia? Why did they go still swinging their incense and blessing their friggin' troops as they went out on their campaigns of genocide? Why is the Catholic church able to prevent the use of condoms so effectively in parts of Africa where AIDS is spreading all over? If the church had supported the use of condoms, there might not be ten million orphans in Africa right now. The whole continent is being devastated by a plague.

Religions claim to be the guardians of morality, but the truth is, they mirror the dominant imperialist, corporate mindset. **Traditional churches are still operating out of a "Conquer the Earth" imperative.** One of the most important doctrines of the future is a reverence for birth control and population control. Malthus was right; if we don't control our population voluntarily, then Nature will do it for us by war, plague or famine. We have a choice, and in order to practice that choice we have to go against what mainstream religions teach.

I choose to recycle—**I consider recycling to be a religious duty! I don't get any immediate direct benefit, but I do this for my children and for the future. I planted hundreds of trees 20 years ago, and now there is a forest instead of a clear-cut area. That is religion in action** as far as I'm concerned. Most religions cut us off from our Mother the Earth—not Paganism. That tree over there *is* directly connected into the dirt. I can pick up a handful of that dirt and touch my Mother's flesh with my own flesh, and know that I'm just as surely one with that dirt and that tree as all other beings on this planet.

I think humans have been stuck in a kind of nationalism for a long time. **We are naturally tribal beings, yet tribalism can be both good and bad.** Some tribes embrace a wonderful multicultural diversity within themselves, but are utterly bigoted and opposed to the tribe over the hill. So they engage in endless conflict and warfare.

It's time we get beyond *that* kind of tribalism and attain more of an awareness that we're all connected. The more we're aware of the earth and its dirt, the more we'll notice that we don't see any lines or boundaries. We don't see differences except between organisms, and you need *all* the organisms to survive. Trees breathe out oxygen which you breathe in; you breathe out carbon dioxide and the trees breathe that in. That's a kind of Tantric love-making between plants and animals! We eat plants and in the end they eat us. This is part of a beautiful and terrible cycle of birth and death and re-birth. It's gritty, dirty and bloody—terrifying for many people, so they try to impose human ideas of sanitizing things. But ultimately, Nature is a messy business.

We are destroying divinity as we reduce the number of species on this planet, and the number of species is vanishing at an alarmingly rapid rate. And when a species is gone, it's gone forever. What happens if all the tigers are dead? "Tiger" will vanish, and a thousand years from now there will be no Tiger. What will our children think? They will not have knowledge and conversation with that god that is the great "Tiger"—it will just be a word or picture. There are other species disappearing from the rain forest at a dizzying rate, and we will never learn what they have to offer us. When we don't learn from our environment, we stunt our growth and do ourselves harm.

Fundamentally, we need to learn to recognize divinity everywhere, and the only way we can do that is by recognizing divinity in ourselves. We have to look in the mirror and see our own divinity—see the God and Goddess within us. It's absolutely necessary to grow into our own divinity—find the necessary beings, teachers, role models and guides to carry us forward to become what you potentially are. Because if we can't recognize our own divinity and say "Thou art God" or "Thou art Goddess" to your own flesh, we can't begin to extend that same love and harmony to others.

In Greece at Eleusis, Pagan site

You can't love others without first loving yourself. **The recognition of your own divinity is where change starts; the next step is coming into harmony with other divinities.** When we shine with the stars, we don't need to fill our emptiness with excess and destroy the rest of Nature as a result of our empty greed. We don't need to be addicted to status-based culture—**the best things in life are often not *things*.** It's all about saying both No and Yes to create real boundaries, for an ecologically positive life. I'm dreaming of a time when our movement comes of age and we create enough gods and goddesses that mix freedom with responsibility. Again, we need a new mythology.

Pagans need to learn how to work smarter, and focus more on how we want to manifest our visions, because being a god or goddess doesn't mean you don't have to work for it! It only means that you have a really good idea of what's worthwhile working for. So many people are working very hard for somebody else. How about working for the god or goddess within you? Work hard for that divinity to manifest. And think about what the world could be, if we all did that . . .◆◆◆

Oberon

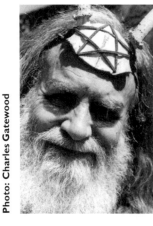

Photo: Charles Gatewood

Oberon Zell Ravenheart is an artist, writer, and founder of The Church of All Worlds, inspired by the science-fiction novel *Stranger in a Strange Land*. As the original editor/publisher of *Green Egg* magazine he helped disseminate Pagan ideas and concepts. Today he is the master sculptor for Mythic Images, the Ravenheart family business (*www.mythicimages.com*). He has been doing ritual at sacred sites and Pagan gatherings for almost 40 years. Interview by John Sulak; follow-up interview by V. Vale.

♦ *RE/SEARCH: Can you explain the "Gaia Thesis"—*

♦ OBERON RAVENHEART: The Gaia Thesis is very simple: all of life on Earth is one single organism. We're a continuity. Something like four billion years ago, all of life began with a single cell that came into being at that time. Whether it came from outer space or emerged spontaneously, we may never know until we go out there and see what else is in the universe.

But **the thesis is that all life on earth, all of the DNA, is descended from one original cell, just like each of us—you, me, all of us—are descended from a single fertilized cell. Which means that all life on Earth is a single organism. All the species are like different systems in a body.** Each living being here is like a cell in the body of Gaia, Mother Earth. Everybody, in all Pagan cultures, has always known this. She is the Mother of All Mothers.

In the future Paganism may expand in many directions, but one common myth—that we're all part of the living system of Gaia—will hold it all together. That will be the one universal constant. That means we are all interconnected, and we are all brothers and sisters with all the species.

♦ *R/S: How did you come up with this thesis?*

♦ OR: 1970 was a very important year for me: the first Earth Day took place, and a total eclipse of the sun occurred in the Midwest where I was living. That was the year I first took LSD, read Robert Graves's *The White Goddess,* and started taking Witchcraft lessons. It was the year that the Church of All Worlds, which I helped found, first had a public temple. 1970 was an intense, fomenting year when all this creativity percolated and flowered.

Previous to this, I had spent my life pursuing the studies of biology, natural history, evolution, and paleontology. It all came together on the first weekend of September, 1970. The friend who had turned me on to *The White Goddess* had a brother who was an attorney with a very nice house. The brother went away for a weekend and left him in charge of the house.

I came over and we "tripped" on LSD. In the night I went into the backyard and lay stark naked on my back on the trampoline, looking up at the stars. I felt like I was floating up into space. Astronomy being one of my interests, I know all the constellations, so I was tracing the stars with my hand, drawing trails and connecting the dots.

I made the Star Trek's Vulcan "Live Long and Prosper!" sign, and as I moved my fingers apart it looked like a cell dividing. And that single image: of a cell dividing against the background of the stars, opened up a gateway in my mind. Suddenly I went flying down a wormhole of consciousness through the continuity of cellular division or mitosis, receding further and further back. It felt like I was running a film backwards, until I was back to that first cell that was the beginning of my identity.

But I didn't stop there. I continued on backward through all the cells that coalesced to form my parents. I kept going through this reverse coalescence back through geological time until I reached that first original, primal cell that begat all life on earth, and which we are all descended from. It was like all of us were condensed into that single cell, the Big Bang of biological evolution.

Then the film ran back the other way. That cell kept dividing and all forms of life derived from it. Different species emerged, and I saw whole families of life open up, evolving through the different lineages. I traced the first protoplasm through all its different DNA divisions. As life from that first cell spread out across the planet, my consciousness rose from the planet and started looking down on the whole Earth below me.

The previous year the first photographs of the Earth had been taken from space by the Apollo astronauts returning from the moon. So I rose above the Earth and saw life spreading across the planet. I saw all this flowering and germination as one vast, single organism. And it was absolutely identical to the way my own body had grown from that first single cell.

I looked down and at that point the mythology of Gaia overlaid itself upon this entire planetary organism. I suddenly saw the Earth in a whole new light. I saw this living Being, instead of just a planet full of separate beings. At this point it was like Mother Earth opened her eyes and smiled at me, saying, "Now you know me." My response immediately was, "I shall ever serve you." And I have—from that moment forward.

This wasn't a vision, it was a revelation—I felt this in the deepest part of my soul. Thirty years later, it is still hard to speak of this without choking up, because it really was the most profound experience of my life. I wrote about this experience in the *Green Egg* magazine, and set about finding more information, background and scientific details. I did research into genetics, DNA, cosmogony, cosmology, nucleotides and the nature of amino acids found in meteorites. This was three years before James Lovelock wrote his *Gaia Hypothesis,* which essentially advocated the idea that all life on Earth is descended from a single cell. That has now become a basic theory.

Lovelock was an atmospheric biochemist helping NASA create sensors for the probes they were developing to detect life on other planets. He said the Earth looked like a single living organism, because the atmosphere resembles the shell that a snail exudes to maintain and protect itself. He got this idea from studying those same photographs of the Earth I saw. But he saw it from the outside looking in, and I saw it from the inside looking out.

My experience was both scientific and religious; I think there has been an artificial demarcation between the two since the founding of the London Royal Academy of Science in 1660.

The founders set out to invent categories, and some subjects were classified as science while others were shunted into categories such as religion, mysticism and superstition. Astronomy was divided from astrology, and chemistry from alchemy. Essentially this was all done so that "science" could have a territory it could claim to explore on its own—one that was grounded in experimental, so-called "objective" procedures. The world of subjective experience, dreams, visions, and artistic ideas was put elsewhere.

When evaluating phenomena, it's hard to draw a line as to whether something is "scientifically verifiable" or in the realm of the "spiritual" or "mystical." **To me, everything can be experienced *both* scientifically *and* spiritually.** In high school I had been a science brat; I got a scholarship from the high school science fair to go to college, back in the days when Russia's Sputnik galvanized America's participation in the space race.

To me, it's all about learning to know the universe: to know who we are, where we are, how we got here, where we come from and where we're going. Lovelock called his discussion of all this the Gaia

1971 Oberon at CAW meeting, St. Louis

Hypothesis. "Hypothesis," a word that's used in science a lot, essentially refers to a theory you're going to test: "I've got this *hypothesis.*" But there's no difference between that and saying, "I've got this idea, or myth, or story."

Many scientists will admit they got some profound revolutionary theory in a dream, or while washing the dishes, or that it came to them out of the blue. An example is the legendary story of Newton watching an apple fall from a tree, then developing his whole theory of gravity. This is the way ideas come to people.

All of our lives are stories; we live in a realm of stories. This is the most unique thing about us as humans: **we are makers of stories, which means we are makers of myth, which means we are makers of science. It's all the same, and I don't see any way to draw a hard and fast line between them**. However, that line has been drawn in a very rigid way by people who call themselves "scientists." You're a scientist if you're working on a grant. But it used to be that characters tinkering in their backyard could be scientists, just as much as somebody working in a big university laboratory. James Lovelock was one of those backyard scientists—he's just a British eccentric.

"The Gaia thesis"—*thesis* being a slightly different word from *hypothesis*—galvanized and united the Pagan community in the early Seventies. It became a unifying story and myth. Joseph Campbell said, "The only myth worth talking about in the immediate future is one that talks about the planet"—the idea being that we need a unifying myth. Right now the dominant myth of monotheism reinforces a competitive world in which each group believes they have the "One True Way," and that everybody else is wrong. Historically, this has led to Holy

Wars, Inquisitions, the extermination of ethnic cultures around the globe and the oppression of women and people of color—terrible deeds.

The Gaia thesis, which is globally unifying and comprehensive, is *the* fundamental myth in Pagan culture. I've been all over the world, and have engaged in rituals and talked with native shamans from many different cultures, and the most universal myth in the world is that of Mother Earth/Mother Nature—*everybody* knows about Her. They may not know about Jesus or Zeus or Hades or Persephone or Krishna, but they know about Mother Earth. **The Gaia thesis is the first unifying myth waiting to be universally adopted: the notion that we are all children of the same Mother.** Everything that's wrong with our modern culture can be traced to our forgetting of this fundamental notion.

♦ *R/S: So a new unifying myth might say—*

♦ OR: "Once upon a time we were united by an understanding that we were all children of the same Mother. Something happened and we lost that connection. Now we are seeking to find it again, and when we do, we will once again be able to live as a family."

We can't continue living as if we're not all connected—we can no longer afford that. It used to be you could live your whole life for generations and not have any contact with the people in the next valley. They spoke a different language and you would have no communication with them at all. There are over 300 language groups in the islands of New Guinea. People have been there for 40,000 years and each valley has evolved separately. Neighbors can't talk to each other. They had to wait for the development of a common language, which only happened quite recently.

Having a common language and mythology is a great key to being united. This has profound implications for ourselves and our future. Part of the great Pagan mission is to bring the whole family back together again. I recall a Hopi prophecy which says, "Once upon a time all the races were united. Then we separated and spread across the Earth. Someday the time will come when the four races shall return and reunite." And their symbol of that reunion is the cross in the circle, representing the Earth and the four directions.

♦ *R/S: How were you introduced to mythology?*

♦ OR: Every child everywhere knows who Mother Earth is. **When I was a kid, the first images I had of "Paganism" came from Disney nature movies**: "In the fall, Mother Nature paints the trees with brilliant colors." They never mentioned "God"—they talked about Mother Nature!

The first books I read contained Greek myths adapted for children—in fact, the myth of Hades and Persephone was the first myth I ever learned. Then I was exposed to fairy tales, which were all Pagan. Comic books and super-heroes whose powers and abilities are beyond those of mortal men are Pagan, basically. Science fiction also appealed to me, because it is future mythology. The advantage of science fiction is: it's mythology that hands *you* the power. Most myths describe a Golden Age lost long ago, such as Atlantis or Camelot or Eden, but they don't tell you how you can get there again. Whereas science fiction is not about a Golden Age long past—it's about one yet to come, if we have the wisdom to create it. Many science-fiction writings are basically maps on how we might go about creating a New Golden Age.

One of the greatest magicians of all time was Gene Roddenberry. In 1966 he was asked, "What did you have in mind when you created *Star Trek?*" He replied, "I'm trying to create a vision of the future so compelling that we will choose it over a nuclear holocaust." At that time—the Fifties and the early Sixties—the predominant myth of the future was one of nuclear apocalypse.

Creating a new myth of the future allows us to choose that future. Roddenberry's myth had a profound impact—think about all the things we take for granted that were first shown on *Star Trek!* That's the work I'm engaged in, in a sense. There are realms—the game of politics, corporate power, and wealth—where we don't necessarily have much power, because those games are created and run by other people. But a game we can all play is the game of magic and myth-making. One example of the power of myth is the Harry Potter books which are taking over the country—and in a very positive way! They're introducing young people to a world of magic, and contrasting it with a mundane world, the world of the "Muggles." The people opposed to magic are seen as dorks. **The Harry Potter books are very threatening; the fundamentalists are crusading against them. But the more they crusade, the more people will get interested in them.**

Paganism incorporates myths, legends and pantheons from all cultures. When I first started reading mythology in earnest, the only books available were Robert Graves's *The White Goddess* and Edith Hamilton's mythology books. Today we also have mythology from non-European countries such as India, China, and North and South America. All of it works together to give us a bigger picture, as we continue to expand our own mythological vision.

Gaia places our different traditions and backgrounds into a holistic unifying context. Instead of being seen as competing ideologies, they can be seen as different flowers growing in a garden. All mythologies can be viewed as part of one grand ecosystem, like the different species in a rain forest. Each tradition that everybody brings is like a different color thread in a tapestry. We are weaving a tapestry of multi-colors—if you have all the same color thread, you ain't got nothin'!

♦ *R/S: Regarding mythology, philosophy and religion, there's a great quotation: "Belief is the enemy of knowledge"—*

♦ OR: Right, and this isn't about belief, this is my *life*. It's who I am, what I do, and what I am about. I don't think about it in terms of belief.

I read a collection of letters written by Victorian children at the turn of the century. In one, a little girl was asked to define faith. And she said, **"Faith is believing something you know isn't true."** I try to always keep that in my mind, and speak from my experience and what's in my heart. I don't have to question or debate whether something is true; my myths don't

require validation. Myth is simply a place to come from, the story you tell, the story you live.

♦ *R/S: Some Pagans are political activists—*

♦ OR: Pagans are not escapists. **The contemporary Pagan movement arose in the Sixties out of people who were social activists, civil rights demonstrators and anti-war protestors.** Social issues and social conscience have always been important to Paganism, because the opposition has always been the forces of empire and oppression, dating back to the Roman times when Pagans were fighting against the expansion of the Roman empire that wanted to control everything. It's always been the Empire versus the Rebel Alliance, you know? [laughs]

Pagans have always been the rebel alliance. We've always been the tribal people on the fringes who had to combat the attempts to control everything—that control sickness that is part of the vision of "empire." So we're always championing the underdogs and celebrating diversity. Whatever the issues are: feminist issues, racial issues, social issues, justice issues—that's what we're about!

And of course, Paganism is the religion of Nature. We are a green religion. Just like we have green politics and green economy, we have green religion, and that's us. We're definitely tree sitters and tree huggers.

We had a strong Pagan contingent at the demonstrations in Seattle. The W.T.O. is an imperial type of force that tries to control everybody and eliminate the possibility of people having any say over their lives. **We definitely want to prevent the big corporations from running roughshod over people, polluting, paying slave wages, cutting down forests and jungle and all the rest of it.** We stand for the rights of the individuals and of the people. And what we oppose is imperial control that tries to impose a monopoly on the whole universe. It's always been that way.

♦ *R/S: You helped start the Church of All Worlds almost forty years ago—*

♦ OR: The whole idea was to create something that by its nature embraced diversity. Those of us who formed the very first "Water Brotherhood" were in college in the early Sixties. I wasn't aware of any Pagan groups then. Gerald Gardner had his witches' groups in England, but nobody here knew about them. There were also people doing research into Egyptian and Greek ideas, but nobody seemed to be in contact with each other; we were all out there seemingly alone.

I went to college in 1961. For years Robert Heinlein had been my favorite science-fiction author; his books were great lessons in what it means to be human, explored from every possible perspective. Each story was a lesson set in a different context, as well as a thrilling adventure—I read them all. A lot of them featured kids as heroes.

When I was 19, the hero of *Stranger in a Strange Land* was Valentine Michael Smith who, like me, was 19. He felt the same way I felt. When I was growing up, I felt I was a different species from everyone else around me. I used to wonder, "Who the hell am I?" At night I'd go in the backyard with a flashlight and signal the flying saucers to come and get me. I knew I was something else—but what? I kept wondering, "Who are my people?" *Stranger in a Strange Land* had that perspective; it looked at the world in the same way I did—from the outside in, like alien anthropologists exploring this strange Earth culture.

In college I gathered together a diverse group of friends who were geeks like me. There were foreign students and people with weird physiological characteristics. One guy was a Thalidomide baby whose hands were like flippers, another was a scrawny seven-foot-tall albino, and another was a Masai African exchange student who, growing up in Kenya, had had to kill a lion as part of a rite of passage in order to become a man. Another was a Hawaiian Wahini . . . our group had all the weirdos!

We talked about religion and having a church—the kind that put on plays and pageants. Those talks lay the foundation for today; the Church of All Worlds puts on a lot of mystery plays. In fact, **the theater is the best possible training you can have for Pagan priesthood.**

When *Stranger in a Strange Land* appeared, it contained the concept of the Church of All Worlds, which was based on diversity and a deeper level of bonding between people. My group of friends really felt a natural affinity for that idea, because none of us felt like we belonged to the families in which we had been born. But we *wanted* family; we wanted a tribe. The only way we could get this was to come up with different criteria. To refute the old saying that "blood is thicker than water," we created a family in which *water is thicker than blood.* The sharing of water became a stronger bond to us than the blood relationships that formed the basis of families prior to us.

That's how the Church of All Worlds began: we read *Stranger* and we shared water. Sharing water and saying "Water shared is life shared" is the fundamental ritual of the book. **The book also introduced ritual nudity and priestesses—which by the way only exist in *Pagan* religions; no other religions have priestesses!** And that book introduced the idea of diversity, because all the people in the book came from different religious backgrounds, yet they didn't have to give up anything. They didn't have to forswear their own heritage; they simply integrated their backgrounds into something larger. There was a place for everyone.

♦ *R/S: Give us an example of a diverse ritual—*
♦ OR: In 1990 we helped create an Interfaith ritual that was done for the 20th anniversary of Earth Day in Ukiah, California. The local Methodist Church had called for an organizational meeting, but the only people they had invited were Christians. We showed up and offered to bring in people from other religious paths, and they agreed. So we brought in Indians, Tibetan Buddhists, Sufis and all kinds of people.

Then we had to come up with a ritual that worked for everybody. Nobody knew how to do that; they each had their own ideas. So we asked the Sufis, "Okay, let's start with you. What do you think is important in ritual?" It turned out that they like to dance in a circle. Then we asked some Native Americans and they said, "We like to call the four directions." So we had the Sufis cast a circle, and then the Indians called the four directions. And everybody responded, "That's really nice—very ecumenical."

Then we turned to the Christians and asked, "What do you think is important?" "We want to make prayers to God." We said, "Okay, each different religion will come in and pray to their deity." Everybody thought that was fine. So we're casting a circle, calling the four quarters, invoking the god and goddess . . . and then we went on. The Methodist youth group wanted to plant a tree, and we agreed.

We ended up doing a ceremony where everybody got to do what they wanted; everybody loved it. The final "Blessed Be" was pronounced by a Catholic priest doing the benediction—and it was a Pagan ritual! We felt this was a complete, perfect Pagan ritual from beginning to end, because it wove together everybody's ideas. That's the vision Heinlein gave us in *Stranger in a Strange Land:* What if we could create a religion that had a place for everybody?

♦ *R/S: But aren't there Pagans that abhor Christians?*
♦ OR: Some Pagans really resent the fact that there are people out there who not only burned untold numbers of us at the stake, but would enjoy doing so again if they could get away with it! But really, our conflict with Christians is not about Christianity. Most of us have a high respect for Jesus and other religious prophets. Paganism is a religion of diversity, and we embrace all wisdom from wherever it comes. I think that if Jesus showed up again, he'd probably be hanging out with *us.* He'd certainly be invited; no problem.

We only encounter conflict with people who feel their religion gives them a mandate to oppress and suppress everybody else: "Because *I* have the One Right and Only Way, that means I get to murder you, and destroy your life, and tear down your temple and your sacred groves." We would never do that, or tear down a Christian church. But Christian churches throughout Europe have been built on top of Pagan temples that they demolished just to put their churches in their place. We consider that to be sacrilege. Nevertheless, we wouldn't want to turn around and do it back to *them.* We don't want to burn them at the stake, persecute them, and launch holy wars and crusades against them. We want us all to get along.

It's like thousands of years ago there was a messy divorce between the Mother and the Father, and some of the kids went with the father and some went with the mother. We think it's time to bring the whole family back together again!

♦ *R/S: What do you think about Christian missionaries, who systematically decimated Pagan culture all over the planet?*
♦ OR: Yes, the whole Christian missionary program for the past 500 years has been to go out and "convert" the Pagans. We think that's terrible. We wouldn't want to do that and we never did. I think the missionary practice has been devastating.

Years ago I was in New Guinea living in a village that had a little abandoned church. It had been built with concrete blocks in a village where all the homes were grass huts. White people had come and taken away all their artifacts and art works and put them in museums in Europe and America. I've been to museums that had artifacts taken from the very village we stayed in. The people in the village had nothing.

But there was nobody in the church, because the missionary who had created it in the Forties had died long ago. We were sitting around on the beach eating fish and seafood with the villagers, sharing songs. We were singing them Grateful Dead songs, and they apologized, "Unfortunately, all of our traditional songs" [which went back 40,000 years] "have been lost because the missionaries forbade us to sing our own songs." And these are some of the oldest tribal people on the planet, akin to surviving Neanderthals—they and the Australian Aborigines are the oldest races still alive. They had lost all their cultural heritage because the missionaries had forbade them to sing their own songs and transmit their own stories.

So instead, the villagers sang us "Away in a Manger" and "Jesus Loves Me" in Sussarunga, which was their language. The missionary had simply translated these Christian songs into their language, and because of their short lifespan, 40,000 years of cultural heritage had been lost during the time he was there.

The villagers were sad about this, but they had no way to get their songs back because they didn't possess writing. They had no way to record their culture—it was gone forever. *This is a terrible crime!* It's not just a crime against those people—that little village of maybe a hundred people. It's a crime against all of humanity that we've lost a precious part of our heritage. It's like losing a species somewhere in the ocean or in the rain forest—we can't *do* that. **We need all of us, just like we need all the parts of our body—cutting off a finger here or a toe there is not okay.** It's not a matter of we can just go on without it. Every single species, every culture, is precious.

♦ *R/S: There are more primal reasons why people are attracted to Paganism, such as being more in tune with the seasons, the cycles of the moon and the crops. The holidays celebrated are not commercial fake ones—*

♦ OR: That's true. The celebration cycle of Paganism, what we call "the Wheel of the Year" or "the Sacred Round," is not about commemorating historical events or the birthday of some famous prophet. It's about the changes in the seasons, the equinoxes, the solstices, and May Day. These are ancient and universal festivals that are celebrated throughout the world by Pagan peoples everywhere. They simply commemorate Nature's cycles: when animals are born, when the geese return, when the first flowers bloom, and the best times to plant and harvest crops.

Oberon as Leonardo da Vinci

These are the times of celebration. The key astronomical alignments include the solstices, equinoxes and the cross-quarters that fall halfway between them. There are also the cycles of the moon: on a full moon, go out and celebrate! That's really basic: if there's enough light to go out at night, then do it—why not?

This sense of *cyclic* celebration marks a different attitude about our lives. It's not a linear time sense, where you begin with birth and march right through until you die and it's all over. It's a sense of being *part* of the cycle: in the fall the leaves fall from the trees, and in the spring the leaves come back, flowers bud and new life is born. And we partake of this.

Thus the concept of reincarnation is very much built into the Pagan world view in which everything gets recycled. Some people literally think that you die and you come back, born again. Others regard death as more like being part of the *recycling process,* where you return to the elements of Nature, and then, once again, the elements of Nature bring forth a new being that has your molecules in it somehow. The same elements just keep going around and around.

♦ *R/S: Right; I read that the amount of water in our world never changes—*

♦ OR: **The whole idea of "what goes around, comes around" is very much built into Pagan philosophy.** So the whole fear of death and the sense of final ending is really not a part of the Pagan world view. Death is just part of the cycle, just as birth is.

♦ *R/S: Paganism is one of the oldest religions on the planet, yet Modern Pagans embrace all the latest technology—*

OR: Some people think Pagans are Luddites who reject all technology, just because we like Nature and want to return to living in harmony with Nature. But that's not the case at all. Magicians have always been into the highest forms of technology available ... think of the legendary crystal balls, magic mirrors and far-seeing objects in legends. They resemble what we have today with computers and cellphones and TVs. The latest toys have always held a fascination for me.

Some of the great magicians of all time have been alchemists, astronomers and inventors, like Leonardo Da Vinci, Galileo, Archimedes, Paracelsus and Merlin. We definitely like our toys; we're definitely into the latest technology and we use it—

♦ *R/S: —and the Internet too—*

♦ OR: The Internet—boy, that's great! That's just the best, magical thing you can imagine. It puts you in touch with everybody ... we love it! The Internet may well be the vehicle and the medium for the coalescence of planetary consciousness. It may well be Gaia's neural network.

♦ *R/S: Any advice for people starting their own Pagan groups?*

♦ OR: The whole trick is to weave something together out of that which has already proven itself to be valuable, useful, meaningful and beautiful. And there is so much to choose from. Work with other people and other groups. Study. Go through at least a full year with some tradition and learn their whole cycle of the seasons. If you've been to a couple of events and they don't seem to be working for you, that's okay—go somewhere else! But when you find something which resonates with you, then get involved.

♦ *R/S: Was the Church of All Worlds started publicly?*

♦ OR: For the first few years after we read *Stranger in a Strange Land*, our group was more of a secret society. We were a Water Brotherhood and were very close. Gradually we grew, developed, explored and expanded. But around 1967 we started a conversation about our mission to change the world. We wanted to have a world that would be safe for people like us ... a world we could live in comfortably without being lynched.

Out of our conversations two different scenarios emerged. One was to continue to be a secret society and work behind the scenes in various revolutionary causes, and inject these ideas, shaping events. The other was to go public, with a public church that would be *out there.* And we never resolved this in terms of choosing one or the other—in typical anti-dualistic fashion, we decided to do it all!

We formed two groups: a secret society called the Atlan Foundation, and a public church. My water brother Lance

Sculpting a statue for Mythic Images

Christie, who was the first person I ever shared water with, became the main director for the Atlan Foundation. I can only speak of this now because it went public just a few years ago, after some 30 years of secrecy. The Foundation was involved in some very interesting experiments. They took lessons from Kurt Vonnegut's *Cats Cradle* and Robert Rimmer's *The Harrad Experiment*—especially the final chapter that talks about a secret group going to an underpopulated state in the Western U.S. and infiltrating governmental agencies. And this is what they did. They were responsible for some of the earliest marijuana reform laws for medical marijuana in the state of New Mexico, and other changes even I don't know about, because they were so *sub rosa*. Lance was the director of public health services for New Mexico.

I was chosen to direct the Church of All Worlds, because I seemed to have that kind of personality. Six months later, the C.A.W. received legal incorporation from the State and the Feds and we opened up our own coffee house. People started asking us to officiate at weddings and funerals—the church was off and running.

♦ *R/S: Modern Paganism started around the same time as the New Age movement, but there isn't much cross-over—why?*

♦ WOLF RAVENHEART: "Religion." New-Agers don't use that word—they don't like it. They'll use "spirituality," "inner peace" or "tranquility," but not the "R" word. They think of themselves rather as a "spiritual" movement. The difference may be hazy, but to them it's very distinct. "Religion" scares them.

♦ OR: That's a good point. There are other differences, too. The New Age movement seems to draw its inspiration from Eastern and Native American rather than European sources. It's like a bunch of Europeans who are Hindu and Native American wannabes . . . wannabes of *both* kinds of Indians. Also, the New Age movement seems to revolve around spiritual masters, gurus and other people they want to *follow* around. People in the Pagan community largely reject this concept as distasteful on some fundamental level.

Much New Age activity takes place in the form of very expensive workshops and yearly expositions that people pay big bucks to attend. It's not like they hang out together, or have camp-outs, or sit around the fire telling stories. Everything they do costs a lot of money! **Isaac Bonewits once stated that the main difference between Paganism and the New Age movement is one decimal point** . . . which is a very interesting and accurate figure. You can go to a Pagan festival for something like $50, but a New Age festival will be $500. A crystal which you pay a Pagan vendor fifty cents for would cost you five dollars at a New Age Expo.

♦ *R/S: Don't Pagan clergy make money giving workshops?*

♦ OR: That hasn't been the main path. For people who teach the New Age workshops, that's their livelihood. I have no objection to that, although there seems to be a contradiction involved: you're advertising how important your teachings are to change the world, yet the teachings are copyrighted and you mustn't tell anybody about them. Their knowledge costs you a lot of money; you have to take many workshops to get the point. Most Pagan teachers will tell you anything if you just *ask*.

But I don't want to couch this in the form of a put-down. Many people involved in New Age pursuits are genuine, sincere people who are searching, the same way we have been. **Many New Agers are looking for the same "enlightenment" we're looking for. But the people administering the programs are very competitive and market-oriented.**

♦ *R/S: Didn't you once take a vow of poverty?*

♦ OR: Yes I did, but that wasn't because I felt I was supposed to be poor! That was a matter of not wanting to have to pay taxes—that's what a vow of poverty is about. The Pope is on a vow of poverty, but he doesn't live in poverty. Jerry Falwell is on a vow of poverty. **A vow of poverty simply means that all the money you make goes to your church, which then supports you.** You simply don't pay taxes to the government out of it—that's the deal. I think this is a splendid idea, and I wish it had caught on more. Unfortunately, some groups tended to abuse that, and not support the people who were earning them their money.

I did this in the early days, and **all the money I would have paid in taxes went to supporting the *Green Egg* publication and the church. Wherever I worked, the employers wrote checks directly to the Church of All Worlds. It's a great system. This is why legal churches are so important**, why people go to the trouble of incorporating them, and why groups like the Moonies and the Scientologists, that aren't really religious, try so hard to incorporate and register as churches—because they have that tax advantage.

♦ *R/S: You've helped raise several Pagan children—*

♦ OR: My son Brian is 37; Morning Glory's daughter Gail just turned 30; and my stepson Zach is 24. They're still Pagans, although they don't necessarily all practice in the same way. Gail is somewhat non-religious. She keeps an altar and Pagan values are still important to her, but she has her own life, her own profession, and doesn't really involve herself in our life. My son Brian is not involved directly, although he still occasionally comes to festivals. Zach is very active as a Pagan. He grew up a bit later when there were more kids and more activities to be involved with.

The newer generations have increasingly gotten more involved. Now there's a group of kids who call themselves the

P.N.G.: Pagans Next Generation—

♦ *R/S: That's taken from Star Trek: The Next Generation—*

♦ OR: And they seem to have taken it into their own hands to raise the next generation of kids. They've moved through the church like a warthog through a boa constrictor, and now they're grown-ups! They're taking their power.

Wynter is part of that. For part of the time her mother pulled her out, but she came back as soon as she could. The P.N.G. all know each other and many are intimately connected, dating or being lovers or getting married to each other. They're a very tight group and always have been, once there were enough of them to reach critical mass.

Brian was, as far as I know, the first second-generation Pagan child. Groups that preceded us, like the Gardnerian witches in England, did not let their kids get involved; they kept their practices secret from their kids. Witchcraft itself didn't make itself available to its own next generation until the mid-Seventies.

Last year a Gallup poll of American teenagers revealed that 17% listed Witchcraft as a major interest. In high school, most of the really savvy, hip and cool kids are Pagans. A couple of years ago a dyed-in-the-wool Pagan daughter of a friend won a scholarship to a writer's conference in Los Angeles, which was attended by kids from all over California. When she returned, she reported that all of the other kids were Pagan—every single one! This was one of the first things they discovered about each other; they all showed up with their Pagan jewelry prominently displayed.

♦ *R/S: Won't Pagan kids rebel against their parents?*

♦ OR: That's a topic we discuss a lot. I've stayed up really late at night after rituals talking to kids around the campfire. Our teen kid-pack gave me a certificate declaring me an honorary kid—the feeling is that there is plenty in the *rest* of society to rebel against! They don't have much cause to rebel against their parents—except that maybe they would like to have a little more money.

Sometimes it almost seems like Pagans necessarily think it's a good idea to be poor. Most of us would like to have a lot more money than we have, just like anyone else. But the kind of work we do often doesn't pay very well. I was a damn good editor of an international magazine for many years, but it didn't pay. If I had worked for some slick magazine—well, I have a friend who did just that: he edited *Green Egg* for a couple of years, then went and got a job editing a computer magazine. Now he's making $80,000 a year.

But we want to work for *ourselves*. We want to do what we think is good and right. Wolf could be making ten times more if he were working for some corporation. But all of us choose to do what we do because this is where our heart is, and this is what we believe in. This is our way of trying to change the world. If we weren't doing this to make a living, we'd be doing it in our spare time.

♦ *R/S: You've said that the Ravenheart family is in some respects a very traditional American family—*

♦ OR: We are. At the turn of the century the traditional Victorian family consisted of a large household. There would invariably be a main couple and their kids, but there would also be in-laws, cousins, aunts, uncles and grandparents all living in the same place. The average American household back then included at least one live-in servant, or someone who wasn't even a relative but lived there as part of the family. The Addams family was your typical Victorian, American family.

This was what enabled people to survive the Great Depression. If it hadn't been for that, they would have been dead in the water. That all broke down after World War II. During World War II, the whole economy, including factories and industries, was focused on the war effort, and a lot of men got killed. When the war ended, the economy was completely different. All these factories were no longer needed, so they all retooled for peacetime.

The American manufacturers started making appliances and household goods. A whole new consumeristic way of life was devised, involving little nuclear family units and small identical houses cranked out of a factory. These houses were set up in rows. The developers went in and mowed down every tree over dozens of acres and built all these ticky-tacky boxes in neat linear rows, putting little fences and driveways between them.

They created these artificial neighborhoods that had never existed before. Nothing like that had ever been *imagined*. The houses were all identical, and each one had its own lawn mower, refrigerator, car and backyard barbecue pit. Previously, in a whole neighborhood there might be one lawn mower. But now everybody had to have their own, and they were all identical.

In order to sell this to people, the companies created a fictionalized ideal family, which is Mom and Dad and Buddy and Sis. If you look through magazines from the Forties and Fifties you will see these paintings, because they didn't have any photographs of this family. It was always the same family: the dad with his slicked-down hair and his pipe, mom with the same hairdo and apron, and the kids—all sitting around enjoying the wonderful life in the Modern Age. And it was completely fabricated.

Television shows like *Ozzie and Harriet*, *Leave it to Beaver*, *Father Knows Best* and *Donna Reed* were created to sell people the idea that this was the "normal" family. These were models that were set up for people to follow. These programs showed people how to "do" it, because nobody knew how to live like that. They created these TV families so you could watch and see how they dealt with things, and then you could do the same. It was the world of "Pleasantville."

Television, which had been invented decades before, overnight became available when the advertising agencies saw it as a great and highly effective way to sell products. Had it not been for commercials, TV would not have become institutionalized. Every family had to have their own TV set, and they glued themselves to the TV to see how they were supposed to live, and what products they had to buy to do it.

This broke the continuity of parents living with children, because now the houses were too small. Grandma and Grandpa had to go somewhere else. They put them in an old folks' home and they disappeared from the family. There was no room any more for Lurch. Uncle Fester was out on the street. Now it was just Gomez and Morticia and the kids—and there was only room for 2-3 kids, because they only had that

Church of All World's Precepts:

1. Be Excellent to Each Other!
2. Be Excellent to Yourself!
3. Honor Diversity!
4. Take Personal Responsibility!
5. Walk Your Talk!

many bedrooms in those houses. It was all a set-up. The soldiers came back from the war shell-shocked, and missed that whole period of learning from their parents.

But there is a place deep in our hearts where we yearn for something else. Because for all of our primate history—not just human history—we lived in family groups and clans like a troop of gorillas. Go see the Disney animated movie *Tarzan*—it's all about that. There is something deep inside us that yearns for the kind of family that has existed since the dawn of time, when your whole extended clan is around you. We Ravenhearts have recreated this in a new way, and across the land people are experimenting, creating communes and co-housing situations or finding compatible roommates.

People think of Pagans as being "radical," or being a new religion that is completely off-the-wall. Yet everything we embrace feels so deep and familiar to most people. A few years ago Tim Leary was at the Starwood Pagan festival. He looked out at the crowd of 1,500 people and said, "Wow! Now that I know what the word 'Pagan' actually means, I realize that I've always been a Pagan." Everybody cheered, because that's the way we all are.

The world, for some reason, still has very little idea as to what Paganism is about. People know about the Moonies and the Scientologists, but they don't seem to know what Pagans are. I find that baffling.

Yet at the deepest level, most people *already* understand what Paganism is about—most customs and holidays have Pagan origins, as well as most of the legends and stories we grew up with. The Greek myths are taught in school. If more people realized how much of our common knowledge and culture stems from Pagan sources, there might be a lot more Pagans out there.

♦ *R/S: How is the Ravenheart family structured?*
♦ OR: We talk in metaphors a lot. Are you familiar with "Dungeons & Dragons"? To win that game, the key is to build a really good team with great characters who integrate well because they cover a wide variety of functions or roles. Another model for us is Gene Roddenberry's *Starship* crew: a very diverse team of people who wouldn't necessarily get along under normal circumstances. On the original *Star Trek* there was constant bickering between McCoy and Spock, yet they were part of the same team. And both were absolutely essential. Roddenberry integrated the crew racially, and pioneered the notion of creating a very diverse team. That, to me, is the secret of the model we've been working with.

Life is not always easy; sometimes the differences between us are really a challenge to overcome. There are many ways in which we are not alike; we all have very strong personalities. We have our own missions and our own visions as to how life should be. But we are united by our commitment to the family—to being Ravenhearts. We're committed to being on this mission to go where no one has gone before, as it were.

I like to warn people that just because we can do this, doesn't necessarily mean this is something that everybody else, or anybody else, ought to try to do exactly the way we do it. Some of what we do is only possible because of the unique personalities we have together. Other people wanting to do something similar will undoubtedly have to work out different arrangements, based on who they are.

I've had people write to me: "I want to be just like you." And I write back, "No, you don't—you want to be just like you! Try to be just like you, don't try to be like me. Besides, you can't be just like me, because I have my own particular background and interests and peculiarities that make me who I am. And you have yours. Find out what they are, and be you."

♦ *R/S: What's the Ravenhearts' definition of love?*
♦ OR: In *Stranger in a Strange Land* Robert Heinlein said that "love is that condition wherein another person's happiness is essential to your own." So we put a lot of energy into trying to come up with ways to make sure that everybody is as happy as is as possible for them to be! We try to ensure that their needs are met and they feel fulfilled. If somebody is not happy about something—which happens quite a lot, sometimes—we really care, and try to do something about it.

♦ *R/S: Don't you have problems with jealousy?*
♦ OR: People would probably feel a lot more comfortable if I said, "Oh sure—just like everybody else." But I've never really had that problem; I've always been fundamentally polyamorous. Since I was a little kid, I've always had two girlfriends.

I think jealousy is deeply related to insecurity. And there are good reasons for people feeling insecure: people will leave people, people will dump people, people will betray people and do things like that. **Insecurity is not a condition that is not justified!** Many people have been raised in families where life was very precarious and love was very conditional. You had to do certain things or behave in certain ways in order to get love. And all this contributes to that feeling of insecurity.

I just don't have that. I'm secure in my personal identity, and not at all worried that the people I love are going to leave me. I'm not insecure about my relationship with Morning Glory. I'm not insecure about my ability to do what I do, or the friendships and relationships I have. I trust the people around me.

I *have* trusted people who have betrayed me completely, but it hasn't changed my basic attitude that it's still a good idea to do that—I just figured they were the wrong people. It isn't a bad idea to trust people, but it's essential to find people who are worthy of trust—*that's* very important!

If in the future somebody changes or goes in a different direction, I can handle that—I've handled it before. But that's not going to change my basic attitude. We come into a world where there are a lot of things we don't have any control over.

Oberon at Annwfn, Church of All Worlds' sacred land, on Beltane

We don't have any control, for instance, over how other people may treat us. But we have total control over how we treat *them*, and how we respond. So I can make commitments that are deep, profound and powerful, because I know that I can offer this and I will do these things. It doesn't really bother me so much whether somebody else does it. I'm not dependent on the behavior of someone else; my love is not conditional upon somebody's behavior. It's just simply there.

Although I don't really have a problem with jealousy, I can understand that it *could* happen if I were somehow placed in a situation where my relationships were precarious. Then I might be much more concerned. But so far that has seldom been the case.

I'm concerned that some people might think this is some kind of moralistic judgment. What often comes across is, "Well, I don't have this problem, and that makes me better than you. You wouldn't have it either if you were as good as I was." However, in many ways I'm significantly more screwed-up than lots of people—this just doesn't happen to be one of them!

♦ WOLF RAVENHEART: There are two kinds of jealousy: 1) personal jealousy, where you're going out with my girlfriend and I'm jealous of you. 2) situational jealousy—every football widow knows what that is. They're jealous of the fact that their husband is watching a football game, and doesn't have enough time for them.

People ask us how our relationship works and how it doesn't work. My favorite reply is, "The human capacity for love is infinite. Time and attention are not." You've only got so much time, and you have to break it up. You give some to this person, some to that, some to your work and some to yourself. Jealousy isn't always about a person; it can be a matter of: "I want your time and your attention."

♦ OR: I have three wives and a major girlfriend in my life right now. It's more a situation of them needing more from me than I have to offer, than me expecting more of others than they have to offer. It's very simple, really. My love of women is my religion. It's my love of the Goddess. The Goddess is everything: life, nature, all that lives, Mother Nature. There are lots of gods and goddesses, but when we talk about the Goddess, we're talking about Mother Nature, Mother Earth. She is life, the soul of life. She gives birth to all. To me, all women are avatars of the Goddess.

The Goddess is a manifestation of all that is female and all that I am drawn to. It's that polarity that draws me to it. It's a tropism; just as plants are drawn to sunlight, I'm drawn to the female. I'm drawn to the female in the abstract, in my heart, in my thoughts, my envisionings and my imagination. To me, being crazy about women is like bees being crazy about flowers—of course they are! That's what they're supposed to do. It's really fundamental to me; absolutely fundamental.

♦ *R/S: How can people be introduced to Pagan philosophy?*

♦ OR: Anybody who is new to Paganism, and who really wants to experience what's involved, I recommend that they plant a garden. Go and work in the Earth. Plant seeds and nurture them and watch them grow. Stop and watch the sunsets. Keep track of moon cycles and watch the moon go through its changes. Celebrate the turning of the seasons. Just notice and be a part of our greater world of wonderful magic going on all the time. I've dragged people out of stores, including shopkeepers, to look at sunsets they might not have seen!

The world is so full of such incredible beauty that it's enough to bring tears to your eyes. Throw yourself into it—live it! That's what I would say to anyone. Live your life as completely as possible, because that's what we're here for! ♦♦♦

OBERON'S THOUGHTS ON HIS SCULPTING

My mission is to be a catalyst for the coalescence of consciousness. At the moment, making statues is the major vehicle whereby I do that. These are altar figures; images that people use in their worship, religion, spirituality, and devotions. They're not *tchotchkes* or action figures to sit on people's shelves.

The Millennial Gaia, in particular, is a complete sermon in stone—even though she's not made of stone! But everything that I have to say about what is important to me: the world and life and the interrelationship of everything, is all in that figure. It's the culmination of thirty years of dreaming, visioning, teaching, and working with Gaia.

Photo: V. Vale

Wolf Dean Stiles Ravenheart is a game designer, motorcyclist, comic book collector, Technopagan and an aspiring science-fiction writer. He moved from Houston, Texas to Northern California to be part of the Ravenheart family, and is the manager of their family-owned business, Mythic Images, *www.mythicimages.com;*. 1-888-mythic1. Interview by John Sulak.

♦ *RE/SEARCH: Tell us about Eros—*
♦ WOLF RAVENHEART: Sure. Ever heard of something called "White Liberal Guilt"? It could be described as "white liberals who feel guilty for what their race has done to black people." Even though they personally have never owned a slave or persecuted a black person, they feel guilt because their class, their race, has done so.

Well, there is something similar for Pagan men that I refer to as "Pagan Patriarchal Guilt." The amount of harm done by the heavy-handed male-oriented society to this world is incomprehensible. Because of that, a lot of men feel guilty because they're men. They have never struck a woman or gone out and committed horrible crimes of patriarchy. But because men have done these things, they feel guilty for being men.

Have you heard the term "S.N.A.G." (Sensitive New Age Guy)? I kept running into all these men, Pagan men in particular, who were so sensitive that they were practically ineffectual. They had so much guilt that they were really disempowered and stuck in their powerlessness. Dealing with all these goddesses didn't help matters.

So I started talking to women—Pagan women in particular—about what they wanted. They didn't want to be pushed around, but neither did they particularly want men they could push around. **What a lot of women really wanted were peers. And in the Pagan mentality where every woman is a**

goddess, in order to be a peer to a goddess, you have to be a god. The only peer a goddess can know is a god.

Well, that's really hard for a lot of guys to deal with: "What do you mean I'm a god? Come on"—talk about having a God complex! Well, there are different kinds of gods: the omnipotent sky father who throws thunderbolts, as Yahweh, the Old Testament god did. Or there are gods like Hades and Kernunos—gods who were not held up as the "One High God" but who were part of the community, along with the goddesses.

So I started talking to men about "Eros Pride": the idea that they could be gods and manifest "god energy" in a constructive way. They don't have to be domineering Zeus sky-fathers—in fact, that's the kind of myth I was trying to direct men *away* from, directing them more into the communal.

Eros and Psyche is a beautiful and very important myth: a beautiful mortal woman, Psyche, falls in love with Eros, the god of beauty. Basically this is a tale about what you can do to reach a level of deity. Eros was the god of young male beauty and virility; the one who stirred the seas of chaos and created the world. In "The Theogony," Eros is the primal creative force that stimulates the great fertile womb of chaos which gives birth to everything. When he was relocated into Roman mythology he was reduced to Cupid, an infantilized cherub with no genitalia who flew around causing love, yet unable to take part in what he generated. This is a shame.

Sexuality has really been repressed in the last 2,000 years—probably because controlling sexuality is a way of controlling people. And Eros, being the god of male sexuality, has particularly been denigrated. Today both men and women fear male creative and sexual energy, yet in and of itself it's not something to be feared. Male sexuality is vitally important; the world would not exist without it. Fire can heat your home or burn down a village—but it's the same fire. Male sexuality is a very potent force, but like any other source of power, it can be easily abused.

There have been two victims of patriarchy: women who've been abused or had their lives or choices taken away from them, and men. Think about our society today: the media is full of stories about men going home, finding their wives in bed with their best friend, and shooting them both. But when you take the sexes and separate them that way—the men over here are the owners, and the women over there are the owned—you damage the women deeply.

But **by being the owners, the men are also damaged deeply. Because the set-up is: if women are the property or chattel, then men are always jealous of other men.** They're afraid that other men will come and take their women away from them. This condition isolates men and sets brother against brother, so that a man can't trust another man. This whole society is set up almost exclusively as competition between men: "I'm trying to do better than this man. I'm trying to be richer, more powerful, own more cars, more TVs, and have a prettier wife. And I'm worried that this other man might come and take it away from me."

This great fog of competition and jealousy has robbed men of their brothers, so that a man can't trust another man. Whereas women have always had their girlfriends: when they've been downtrodden, they've had this camaraderie of the oppressed. They could commiserate with each other.

♦ *R/S: At least until recently; now a lot of women are as competitive as men—*

♦ WR: **I watched my step-father die from patriarchy, die of the role that he was forced into by his society.** He thought his role was to be the bread-winner who goes out and supports the family. I watched him work himself to death, because he thought that this was what he was supposed to do. He never had any close friends or men he could hang out with and trust. By being a bad example, he taught me the most important lesson of my life: *giving up your dreams will kill you.* And he did it because he thought this was the responsible thing to do, and that it was expected of him.

The fact that I have a "brother" is one of the most important things in the world to me. This is a man that I trust completely. We're not actually related, but we did a blood brother ceremony. We went to high school and college together, and now he lives on the East Coast. We shared the same girlfriend when we were 20-23 years of age, and that was a lot of fun. He was a grad school student, holding down two full-time jobs, with no free time. The fact that I was willing to be his lover's lover gave her something to do, and was really appreciated by both him and her.

Paganism, with its broader focus on life, is much more accepting of variations on the nuclear family theme: dad, mom and 2.3 kids living in a tract home in the suburbs with a station wagon and a dog. That idea always seemed very rigid and unnatural to me. **I kept running into people who were going through serial monogamy**: having one lover for awhile, then meeting another person and dumping the first one, then meeting a third one, etc.

Personally, I never learned how *not* to be in love with anybody. I was madly in love with the first girlfriend I had in high school—so much that I walked around bumping into walls. I've got some pictures of her somewhere, and if I look at them, I get misty-eyed because this is a person that I still adore. I haven't seen her since I was 17 years old, and if I ran into her, I'd probably still be the same tongue-tied, impossibly shy 17-year-old I was then. The second lover I had was Maggie, my brother's lover, who is now his wife and the mother of his children. We had a great three-way going for a long time.

Years later, when we were living in different states, my brother had a three-way going with Morning Glory, and then he set me up with her. Morning Glory and I were lovers immediately. After having a long-distance relationship for two years, I came to California and eventually moved in with Morning Glory and Oberon. Things got serious enough that we decided to get married—so Oberon and I got married to the same woman.

♦ *R/S: Couldn't you have done this without being Pagan?*

♦ WR: Paganism just seems to provide a better, less judgmental framework. The whole concept of judgment: that some day you'll be dragged up in front of some moldy old guy in the sky who says, "Because you did these things, I'm going to punish you eternally" always seemed like a crock.

♦ *R/S: How do all of you work together in a business?*

♦ WR: Oberon, Morning Glory and Wynter are artists—that's what they do. When I met Oberon they were all doing this, but they weren't making any money. I'm not an artist—in my opinion I have no artistic ability whatsoever! I'm a technician. I can create posters and catalogs and do photography, graphic layout, and design. I felt it was very important to help artists make a living at their art. I have some experience in business management, and I sit at the computer. And they play in clay all day long or paint. They don't have to worry about things like, "Is there enough money to pay the rent? Is there gas in the car? Do we have medical insurance? Are the taxes paid?" That's what I do. They just have to worry about form, color, and magical significance. And I don't have to worry: "It's time to design a new mermaid, and what should it look like?"

♦ *R/S: When did you become a Pagan?*

♦ WR: I was born into a Southern Baptist family. They were really relaxed—they would take us to any church that happened to be nearby: Pentacostal, Methodist, Lutheran...At the age of eight I started feeling more and more that "something wasn't right." When I was fourteen, I went with a friend and his extremely religious family to a Church of God in Pensacola, Florida, and it got rubbed in my face that I really was not Christian.

When I was in college, I went to a Renaissance festival and met Oberon. At the time he just seemed like "this strange wizard with a unicorn." After college I began dating a woman who called herself a "Witch." She didn't call herself a Pagan; I don't think she had a clear idea of what the whole concept was. We had a very painful relationship that ended on a dark, cold November evening. I was leaving her house for the last time, feeling heartbroken, and for some reason I looked up at the sky and said out loud, "Gaia, cry for me, because I cannot cry for myself." *Right away* it started to rain softly, and the rain was so gentle it felt like tears falling on my face. Immediately I knew I was a Pagan!

♦ *R/S: How do you see the Ravenhearts now?*

♦ WR: The Ravenhearts are a family—a large family—and parts of us are a group marriage and parts are not. I'm married to both Morning Glory and Wynter, and I call them my wives. That indicates, to me at least, a sexual relationship. I don't call Oberon my husband, I call him my co-husband! That, to me, indicates a non-sexual relationship—more of a brotherhood. Currently we're six people: three men and three women. A new member, Jon, joined us recently.

Oberon once said that there is no way he could manage caring for these women without another husband. Morning Glory says that Oberon is her creative mentor. Apparently, I am her practical mentor, pushing her to be mindful of schedules and actually complete her tasks. In our family, if there is anything that needs to be done by a "husband," it doesn't necessarily have to be done by me . . . or Oberon. That's a really positive thing.

Sometimes Oberon and I go out together to see movies. We both collect toys and share a fascination with comic books as well as books on mythology and science. If we watch TV, we mainly watch the Discovery Channel. The women in our family are very disparate and have different needs, and Oberon and I each fulfill different needs. I had a monogamous marriage about twelve years ago, where every physical, sexual, emotional, intellectual and spiritual need that my partner had—if you didn't meet it, it went unmet. Whereas in this arrangement, I don't have to stress over: "Am I satisfying this woman sexually?" Or: "These women love to go horseback riding, and I don't." Because there are other members in the family that share those passions.

Morning Glory and Oberon are serious ritual magicians who put on rituals that shake the earth! I'm more of a shaman, going out alone into the woods. I don't orchestrate the big rituals or participate very much in them—Morning Glory has Oberon for that.

Oberon and I also enjoy having a "three-way" with Morning Glory. We don't do it that often, but when we do, it's hot! We set up special dates just to do that. Last night the three of us went to a concert together. Morning Glory loves to sit in the middle between her two husbands.

In the past I've gone out with Morning Glory and Wynter, each dressed to the nines—a beautiful woman on each arm! Other guys would look at me with daggers in their eyes: "He's got two women . . . and I don't have any!"

♦ *R/S: Paganism fulfills a need for meaningful ritual which is seriously absent in today's society. Tell us about a ritual you've participated in—*

♦ WR: In ancient Greece people would make a pilgrimage each year to Eleusis, where they would experience the Eleusinian Mysteries, which was about going down into the underworld and trying to convince Hades to let Persephone come back to earth. This year we staged a modern recreation of that ritual in which I played Hades. It was an intense, extremely magical mystery—in a way it was utterly terrifying. You are visiting the realm of death to talk to Hades, the dark god of the underworld—what questions would *you* ask him? **The Eleusinian Mysteries are about facing your own personal fears and examining yourself: "What is my legacy?** What am I going to leave behind? How have I changed the world by being in it?"

♦ *R/S: What's most important to you about Paganism?*

♦ WR: The idea of *immanent divinity:* God or divinity is everywhere, everything is sacred—therefore you think twice about throwing a cigarette butt on the ground! Whereas monotheism, the dominant religious paradigm which includes Christianity, Islam and Judaism, supports a power pyramid with God on top, then priests, then men, then women and children, then animals, plants and everything else. It's like this gigantic pyramid scheme, you know!

I don't think people understand the power of mythology, and how important myth is in ruling our lives. Robin Hood taking from the rich and giving to the poor, fighting oppression and tyranny, is a powerful myth. Stories like this shape our aspirations. People need to ask themselves, "What is your personal myth, and how does it affect how you live?" Many myths are toxic; if you buy into a bad myth, you can really doom yourself. If you imagine yourself as a modern-day Jim Morrison, you might have a bright, brilliant life and then quickly burn out and die. If you buy into that myth, you could harm yourself.

I have my own personal mythology which is a belief in who I am, where I've been, and where I'm going—the three most important things! My personal myth begins when the glaciers were receding from Europe in the Paleolithic age, and the setting is an old village somewhere in Europe. In my myth I was one of the great archetypal wolves of Europe. One day I ran into a little girl and, for whatever reason, chose not to eat her. Instead I escorted her back to her people. I sat on a hill, watched the villagers take the girl child into the village, and I died. Then I took the body of a human in the village so I could be near the little girl.

The little girl, in my mind, represents an archetype I call the Gaia Child who manifests her first blossoming of awareness of her own self, of her own divinity, of her own place in the universe. Now, I'm living in this village with many people for dozens of lifetimes, becoming familiar with the souls around me. **My theory is that when you die and want to take another body, you find those same souls who were in your village.** You're reborn as a child to those same people . . . all of your village comes back again and again . . .

Whether this has any basis in fact or not is unimportant; what matters is my belief that my friends now are all people I recognize from earlier lives. Oberon, Morning Glory, Wynter, Liza, and my brother are old souls. I've known them from a long time ago and have been with them many times. Maybe this is a total fantasy, or is based on real memories—I believe they're real, but I can't prove that.

I like the quotation that goes, "Do you remember the time when women ran wild and free in the forest and were never afraid? Well, if you don't remember such a time, make it up!"

Liza

Liza Gabriel Ravenheart, M.A., gives lectures and workshops, paints, is a singer-songwriter and community organizer. She is part of the Ravenheart family and its business, *www.mythicimages.com.* Interview by John Sulak.

♦ *RE/SEARCH: When did you first discover polyamory?*

♦ LR: When I was sixteen my best girlfriend and I read *Stranger in a Strange Land.* Then we met this guy and decided to share him, so we had a three-way relationship. I wasn't sexually active then, but our triad was very real for us. The man of that trio is still my friend. He's a Pagan and has been in an open marriage for twenty years. I occasionally hear from my old girlfriend.

♦ *R/S: How did you become involved here?*

♦ LR: Oberon and I did a workshop together and fell madly in love. I was living in Massachusetts, so I went to California for two weeks to visit him. He told me about Morning Glory. Morning Glory knew that I was a major love interest for Oberon, so she made a real effort to get to know me. She met me at the airport with a bouquet of roses, and we shared Thai food together. On the way home she played industrial rock on the car radio. I had a crash course in Morning Glory.

She and I had sex as part of getting to know each other—we wouldn't have sex with Oberon together until we had had sex by ourselves. Then Morning Glory, Oberon, and I took an acid trip as a vision quest about our lives. Finally Morning Glory said to Oberon, "I trust her to love you." In other words, she gave me her okay. At the time we couldn't "grok" the possibility of all of us living together, but I found and rented a property big enough for all of us, and invited everyone to live there. It has several buildings.

♦ *R/S: What's a typical Ravenheart day like?*

♦ LR: There's no such thing! We have a "make it up as you go along" lifestyle. [laughs] Imagine the variables in your life as an individual, and then multiply that by a factor of eight. On top of that you're dealing with unusually chaotic and mercurial people. I regard us as a group *family*—the term "group marriage" gives the impression we're all sexual partners. Actually, we experimented with that at first, but in reality not everyone is compatible as a sexual partner. We have what's called a "condom compact"—we don't use barriers with each other, but we do use condoms with everyone else.

We all share a major commitment in that we own a business together and maintain a property. Can you imagine how many toilets, gutters, and light bulbs there are here? Somehow we keep it all working without assigning tasks. I remember Morning Glory saying to me, "If you use that omelet pan, won't you please clean it *right away!*" When we first lived together we made lists and checked off tasks, but after awhile that ended. Somehow, things get done.

♦ *R/S: Don't you paint?*

♦ LR: I did a series of pictures I called "The Divine Female Infant." I have a song for her, too, called "The Girl Goddess Song." **Throughout history and diverse cultures you'll see divine male infants, but almost no divine female infants.** There are a few paintings of St. Elizabeth with Mary as a child, but that's pretty much it. In Hinduism, with all of its glory, grandeur and diversity, there is no image that I know of. So I set out to create images of her.

♦ *R/S: Tell us about your life before you became a Ravenheart—*

♦ LR: My practice centers around the sacredness of the body, group energy and group empathy. Before I met Oberon, I was living in a sacred erotic community called The Temple of the Trance Lucid Heart in Western Massachusetts. Our house had a large room that was a temple, with altars to the four directions. Four of us who lived there served as the hub of a tribe. We came together to worship our human bodies as sacred manifestations of divine beauty, mystery and love.

For several years I've been helping to build a national network of ecumenical sex-and-spirit organizations. These groups help give people an initiatory experience of what it's like to live in a community where sexuality and spirituality are

Liza doing ritual on Capital steps

honored and *inseparable*. We have two retreats a year, and every six weeks we have afternoon and evening meetings that last eight hours.

One of our rituals is called "The Conspiracy of Heart's Desire." We have a circular garden with a Celtic cross in the center. You take a heart-shaped piece of paper, write your heart's desire on it, and plant it in the garden. Then you walk around the circle three times. The more people that participate, the better the possibility of fulfilling as many heart's desires as possible.

My overall focus is on collective consciousness. I don't mean to dishonor people who have incredible, original insights, but **I think that consciousness is everywhere and that thoughts arise from the collective mind.** In *Stranger in a Strange Land* the Martian language was a transformative technology for changing what it meant to be a human being, and what it meant to function on many different levels, including sexuality, health, and telepathy. No one human being created Yoga, and no one human being will create this language either. I'm writing a book on this, and am implementing a website where people can network and add their contributions to this transformative and empathic way of communicating. Thus people of all traditions can come together to envision and build the best, freest, most beautiful future possible. That's my big project and my dream.♦♦♦

Wynter

Photo: Charles Gatewood

Wynter Rose Ravenheart is twenty years old and part of the six-member polyamorous Ravenheart family. She has eight snakes: a little rosy boa and seven Colombian red-tailed boas, including six-foot-long Rosy, eight-foot-long Rex and five babies. Wynter says, "They're so very cute—I love snakes!" Interview by John Sulak.

♦ WYNTER: I was raised by two hippies. For the first ten years of my life I was on the road a lot. I lived in an old Chevy van with my parents and two brothers, and there was a horse trailer behind it with two horses in it. We also had two dogs and a cat—we always had animals.

In between traveling we might settle down in a mobile home park for six months or so, but never for long. Mostly, we were traveling all over Northern California and Oregon. I've seen a lot of places and "lifestyles," and that contributes to my being polyamorous—I grew up "having a boyfriend in every town." In many ways I grew up really fast.

♦ **RE/SEARCH: What did your parents do for money?**

♦ W: They were on welfare. My dad did landscaping and other odd jobs to fill in the gaps, and my mom is an incredible artist who drew and sold pictures of horses and farmscapes. She also modeled nude on horseback. My mother was, at the time, an extreme survivalist—one of those "carry a gun, wear khaki pants" kind of people. She thought the end of the world could happen tomorrow, and that if martial law was instated we had to be ready to head for the hills. Now she works in computers.

♦ **R/S: How was the family van set up?**

♦ W: There was a king-size bed in the back and most of our belongings were stored underneath. A stove, cooler, and our kitchenware were on the left, and on the right were my mom's books. At night the dogs slept beneath the van. Usually my

mom, dad, and youngest brother Roy slept on the bed, and my brother Daniel and I were on the floor with our dog Gretchen keeping our feet warm. At night the horses would be tied between two trees so they could graze. We never stayed longer than two weeks at one place.

My dad is still basically a vagabond traveler—it makes him happy.

♦ **R/S: Describe your schooling—**

♦ W: We would move around remaining within a general school district until I had completed that school year. Usually I would walk to the nearest bus stop and catch the school bus. When I was nine, my parents got divorced. After that I lived with my dad in a trailer on land owned by a larger community of people. I didn't learn the meaning of the word privacy until my parents divorced. After that, my dad made sure I had my own space. That's why wherever I am, I always make a little corner mine. I need a place to recharge.

After the divorce, I went back and forth between my parents. When I was 13, I lived with my mom and went to school in Laytonville, California. In school I met another oddball-weirdo, and she introduced me to her parents, who were Pagan and members of the Church of All Worlds. I started getting into trouble with this young woman—just basic teenage girl stuff like going out, getting drunk, and staying out all night with boys. She and I went to a Brigid festival and had a lot of fun with other members of the Pagan Next Generation (PNG), a kids' group. At this particular Pagan gathering, by choice I lost my virginity. In my opinion it was the best place in the world to have done that—it wasn't like I was on the couch in the basement watching *Jeopardy.* And my first experience was really awesome. But my mom flipped out.

I was 14, going on 15. I ended up moving in with that young woman and her family for over a year. But the tribe viewed me as a troublemaker. So I went away and didn't have any contact with the Church of All Worlds for about two years.

After my 17th birthday I returned—at that point I had changed my physical appearance so much that nobody recognized me. I was a new person and had assumed a new name to go along with that. I had dyed my blondish/reddish curls black and returned as a Goth girl; I wore all black all the time.

I was introduced to Morning Glory by a friend. Morning Glory and I had a real hot connection, which we couldn't act on until I was 18. We had to wait six months to f--- each other wildly. But then she introduced me to Wolf.

I met Wolf at Beltane, which is the week before Mother's Day. Then Wolf and I went to my mom with a bouquet of roses and took her out to lunch, where he formally asked my mother's permission to be with me romantically. She asked him questions like, "What do you do for a living? Do you have any sexually-transmitted diseases?" right on down the line. She really grilled him. And he was as charming as he could be—and Wolf can be pretty charming. So he won her over.

I proceeded to learn about the Goddess and study magic with Morning Glory. I got involved with the family business and helped craft statues. I got my driver's license and a car—Morning Glory helped me get "reality" taken care of. She must have seen something in me, because she really helped me. Perhaps she wanted somebody who could be her apprentice, and I was eager to learn.

The first six months of my involvement with Morning

Glory, Wolf, and Oberon were really hard on me, because being underage, I didn't get to go to festivals like the "Loving More" polyamory conference. I spent a lot of time being sad, not knowing how I would fit into the family. I wondered, "What do I have to offer, anyway? I'm only 17-and-a-half."

It didn't help that in the third week of my relationship with Wolf, he accepted Oberon and Morning Glory's proposal of marriage. I was fairly new to the idea of polyamory; I had been promiscuous and had had many lovers, but it wasn't in a polyamorous context—I didn't understand the rules. Suddenly I was tossed in with the big boys and expected to float. And I did.

At first it was really hard for me emotionally. There were two possible outcomes: I could become emotionally stunted and f—-ed up, or prosper and grow and learn how to love, be in love, and enjoy watching my lover with other people. I had jealousy issues with Morning Glory. The man I was desperately in love with, and soul-mated with, was married to somebody else—*two* somebody else's! I dealt with it as best I could. I'm a survivor and do whatever is necessary to get to the other side of any problem or situation.

But it was really wonderful, too. I was taught to love my body and appreciate my beauty. I became obsessed with watching Oberon sculpt; he was working on Aphrodite and Eros at that time, and I knew that some day I would learn how to sculpt. I met wonderful people. Even though life was emotionally stressful, it was also mind-expanding and beautiful.

Oberon and Morning Glory are the King and Queen of Costumes, and we did some wonderful photo shoots by a nearby river—and swam in it, too. I also value the magic lessons I received, like how to cast a circle, and the herbal lore. Morning Glory and I would go to the city and spend three-day weekends in San Francisco. Morning Glory and Wolf were obsessed with taking me places and showing me things; we went to a lot of museums and historical places, and had a lot of fun.

♦ *R/S: You and Morning Glory also became lovers, right?*

♦ W: Yes, yes. On my 18th birthday we went to the roof of the house we were living in and screamed to everyone, "WE ARE HAVING SEX NOW—AND THERE IS NOTHING YOU CAN DO ABOUT IT!" And nobody was listening. That's how it works sometimes.

Soon after we became lovers we became wives—we were very sensible about it. [laughs] We decided to get married at a Summer Solstice festival, because everyone we wanted to invite would probably be there. We wrote the ritual the night before. Morning Glory is a High Priestess, so the next day she married us.

We cast a circle with our swords together, because we're both fencers, and made vows to each other. After that, we pierced each other's ears. We passed around almond cookies shaped like crescent moons, and had my brother Daniel and Aleese, his girlfriend at the time, hold our swords together while Morning Glory and I jumped over them.

♦ *R/S: Ho do you divide your time between Wolf and Morning Glory?*

♦ W: Wolf is my principal primary partner, and he comes first in all things—second only to me! [laughs] We shared a lot of triad experiences. On specific nights I slept with Morning Glory or Wolf—we tried to keep it fair as much as is emotionally possible.

My marriage to Morning Glory has always been considered as a *secondary* marriage—our relationship does not require a lot of everyday maintenance. However, that encourages bad habits, like saving all of your criticism until you're together, and then having a big fight on your date night—and not having enough of the juicy, good stuff together. Sometimes I would sleep with Wolf just so he wouldn't sleep with Morning Glory, and this kind of behavior affected my relationship with both of them. Another thing: Morning Glory had to go from being his primary partner—the only woman in his life—to being the secondary. And I was none too gentle about claiming my position and my emotional turf as primary partner with Wolf. After I turned 18, I learned to be more compassionate.

Initially, a lot of my problems stemmed from feeling as though I didn't have anything to offer, so I moved out for nine months and went to college. It was necessary to go away to find out who I could be. Now I'm a Ravenheart and every day I try to accomplish something and learn something new. I feel like I'm a functioning, working part of the family.

♦ *R/S: You have lovers outside of the family, too—*

♦ W: Oh yeah; everybody does, and we all get together as often as we can. That helps me gain perspective. The Ravenheart family is not all that I am. One being cannot fulfill all your needs, and neither can one group or organization. So timewise, life is *interesting* now! Occasionally I have a schedule conflict, but eight times out of ten my family comes first.

For clubbing and San Francisco events, I go visit my lovers there. As the youngest Ravenheart I'm given a lot of freedom, because everybody knows I need it—not just because I'm young, but because of who I am. I'm an air-sign: a fidgety, fluttery, here-there-everywhere kind of person. I try to go dancing every Monday night.

Also, I have serious family ties—my blood family and my chosen family are on an equal par. And family, to me, is the most important thing there is—*period*. I visit my mom and my brothers regularly. We've always been very close, because of how we grew up—we were all very close in the van!

Our whole family is artistic. My brother Daniel is an artist, my dad is an amazing portrait artist, and my brother Roy is more of a song-and-poetry type of artist.

♦ *R/S: How do you envision the future?*

♦ W: Ever since I was a little girl, I've always dreamed of having a 500-acre horse ranch with all the animals I've ever wanted, including a big white dog. Plus, I want a large ranch house. I picture Morning Glory, Oberon, and Liza still connected to that—maybe on the same property, but in different houses. I also picture my dad and mom having their own ten acres of land nearby.

My dad is an amazing horse trainer—he and my mother used to tame wild mustangs. So ideally, I would hire my dad to train my horses. My mom is an excellent animal keeper. So when I'm out traveling, doing my Pagan polyamorous "thing," she would be there to take care of the farm animals. And both my parents love that idea—they think it's fabulous! [laughs]

♦ *R/S: You want to bring your chosen family and your blood family together—*

♦ W: Yes, for the rest of my life. My most unrealistic fantasy is to have *all* of my friends and lovers living in houses and property next to me, so I can see them whenever I want to! ♦♦♦

Carol Queen

Photo: V. Vale

D r. Carol Queen is a well-known writer, columnist, lecturer and sexologist—see *www.carolqueen.com*. She lives in the San Francisco Bay Area with Dr. Robert Lawrence. Interview by John Sulak.

♦ *RE/SEARCH: You're a sexologist; can you discuss sex in a Pagan context—*

♦ CAROL QUEEN: Whether it's in a Pagan, Wiccan or sex-positive "alternative" context, people are hungry to hear sex spoken about positively. People don't *want* to be screwed up. People desire sexual comfort and joy; if their sex life is unsatisfactory, they aren't happy.

I'm deeply grounded in Pagan beliefs about who we are as humans and who we can be; I believe in the notion of divinity as a part of each one of us. People really want the message that sex can be a spiritually powerful and connective force. In this day and age, **most sex is not about procreation—it's about connecting,** and entering an *altered state* through sex. Even people who disdain anything "spiritual" desire that.

Women were always the ones who were supposed to say "No" to men; they were always supposed to be the upholders of the relationship. And now, a lot of people are looking to women leaders for better attitudes about sex. There has been a lot of discussion about male sexuality as *problematic.* I know that *I* was deeply entrenched in a feminism that didn't respect or care much where men were coming from sexually. Then I came to Paganism, with its image of the Goddess and the God uniting in equality—each bringing something equally important to the union. That actually kicked a lot of the sex-negative and male-phobic struts out from under me.

When I was still a lesbian, Paganism was what allowed me to "come out" as bisexual. The big image of the Goddess and the God in union, sacred, to be respected and honored got me to the place where I could say, "You know what? I want balance in my life—I want *erotic* balance in my life."

Not everybody is bisexual, but a lot of people might be open to this kind of erotic balance if it weren't for social forces: homophobia and "heterophobia." I always put quotation marks around heterophobia because it's *not* the kind of virulent, hate-based condition that homophobia is—but it still affects people's individual lives so they're afraid to explore what they might do and who they might be. **The ways that people are stopped from being Who They Might Be in this culture are legion.** It's not just about sex; it's about *assuming our full power.*

That's another appealing aspect of Paganism: it allows us to take our power seriously. **If we're all expressions of Goddess and God, then we have to take ourselves a little more seriously in the world!** Discovering Paganism was like discovering sex-positivity: "Click!—this is how I want the world to be! This explains things, and it doesn't explain them in a way that casts people as victims, with a negative, overarching understanding of who we are as people."

♦ *R/S: When did you first encounter Paganism?*

♦ CQ: In 1968, when I was 11 years old. My best friend and I saw an ad in the back of a magazine for a book titled *Potions and Spells of Witchcraft.* We both managed to convince our mothers to write checks to some obscure post office box somewhere—neither of us told our mothers what we were ordering. The books showed up, and we read them. I've never seen a copy of this book since, and I don't know who published it. In retrospect, the book didn't give me any awareness that there was an existing Wiccan community or a larger set of spiritual beliefs to Wicca. It contained a purported history of witchcraft: "We have come upon these ancient spells that grandmothers have handed down to granddaughters . . ." It was the Craft without the Goddess, without the God, without any of the religio-spiritual context that so many of us take very seriously now. There was no cultural or community link.

I practiced my spells dutifully. I have to say that as a 12-year-old in a place where I felt pretty powerless about everything, there was something very healing about having something ritualistic to do that was supposed to give me more power in the world. I don't remember whether anything I did had any effect. It was important to draw a circle and in a Crowley-ite way get in touch with my *will*—something little girls aren't supposed to have! And this book allowed me to secretly, surreptitiously say, "I want this! I want that!" It was kind of about wanting things or wanting changes in my social circumstances. I don't know if any love spells worked, but I think I made it snow once when I didn't want to go somewhere!

My best friend abandoned this practice a long time before I did, so at the age of 12, I was a solitary practitioner with no links to others. Gradually I abandoned all practice. It wasn't until I took a Women's Studies course in college that I encountered witches discussed as a persecuted minority, in a context establishing them as feminist martyrs and heroes. The notion was that a subcultural religion had been exterminated. I discovered contemporary feminist writing by authors such as Z. Budapest, and this helped me understand Wicca in the present. I began resuming my practices, although not in a spell-casting way; it was more about altar construction, meditation and thinking about the imagery. From Z. Budapest I went on to Starhawk, who gave me a much more co-sexual, egalitarian, all-embracing view: "Okay, here it is, laid out in a way that is bigger than spell-casting, but that also gives lots of tools for ritual."

Spell-casting today is more like prayer, and prayer means asking "God" for what you want, right? So, it's still this desire-based, will-based act. What contemporary Pagans need is the "liturgy," or ritual, that Paganism provides. I believe that this **ritual fulfills a need in people, one that exists on a different level than ordinary, conscious, day-to-day mental functioning.** There is a space which people try to access via sex or through drugs. There's a widespread desire to go beyond or transcend our mundane daily "reality."

Most people who affiliate with any of the branches of Neo-Paganism are open to other levels of awareness. In contrast, the Christian religion doesn't give ordinary people access to divinity, except through mediation—in terms of power it's totally top-heavy, especially the branch propping up the Pope. Christianity is not a spiritual choice for people who want to grow as much as they can, and be as empowered as they can in their lives.

♦ *R/S: Were you raised Christian?*

♦ CQ: My dad was a school teacher in a tiny Oregon town, and the principal told him, "You know, to keep up appearances in our conservative town you really should be taking your family to church every Sunday." My dad was gregarious anyway, so he went. He enjoyed chatting with people after the sermon, and my mother played the church piano, which gave her a creative outlet. I went to Sunday School but didn't like it, because of the stick-up-the-butt, conservative rural ladies who wouldn't let their kids be rowdy. Finally I said, "I don't want to go to church anymore." And my parents said, "You *have* to go to church, because we can't leave you at home alone." We compromised: they let me sit in the car. While my family was in church, I read all the volumes of Andrew Lang's fairy tales!

I gave myself an in-depth education on the myths of the Northern European peoples from whom I am descended. Looking back, from the age of 7 to 10 I read fairy tales; from 11 to 13 I read about Wicca and spell-casting; from 13 to 18 I was a vicious atheist; and from 18 until now I have engaged in a slow rediscovery and reclaiming of Wicca.

A turning point came when I read Margot Adler's *Drawing Down the Moon* **and learned that there was a contemporary community spread all over the country, with many facets.** I soon found a coven to celebrate with; I loved the fellowship but didn't like the personalities involved—it wasn't the right coven for me. But I needed to come out of my little hole and say, "Yes, this is who I am and this is what I want."

From a sexual-orientation perspective, I know all about "coming out": declaring publicly a former secret identity. I've come out as a bisexual, a lesbian, a leather fetishist, a sex worker—and that's what I was doing with this coven affiliation. I was no longer agnostic or atheist, but instead was believing in a Goddess and a God—not in the way most Christians say they believe in God, but rather feeling that there are huge spiritual metaphors for the whole wheel of life. I didn't believe that there was a Lady and a Lord sitting on a throne somewhere up in the sky; rather, I felt that the energies of these *archetypes* permeated everything on earth in a way that was deeply meaningful to me.

When most people delve into the depths of spiritual understanding and belief, their language fails them—I know mine does. There are *poetic* realities that help shape my understanding and my sense of self—that's what most people look for in a spiritual system, anyway.

I didn't feel the need to affiliate with another coven when I moved to San Francisco. I didn't find Starhawk and get in on Reclaiming. I set about locating the community space that would evolve into Queen of Heaven, which is the sex party my partner Robert and I have been facilitating for over ten years. I wanted to do AIDS work, so I came to San Francisco to study sexology and was immediately plunged into a cauldron of sex-positive discussion. **In the way that Wicca was a spiritual fit with me, sex-positivity was a cultural fit. I was exposed to ideas about sexuality that fulfilled needs in me I didn't know I had!**

Everybody wants sex to be okay, a pleasure, easy—we don't want it to be horrible. I had begun to be healed by the co-gendered Wicca pantheon, where it was finally okay for me to have my bisexuality. **Being attracted to men was not any worse than being attracted to women!** For ten years I had been on an emotionally painful see-saw over this issue. I should make it clear that this isn't a "Big Picture Spiritual Reason for Lesbians to be Bisexual"—I'm just talking about *my* path. My lesbian community affiliations didn't want me to explore the side of myself that was about erotic connection with men. But my sex-positivity community said, "That's perfectly splendid—of course, you want to explore that!"

I would never say that there is one path everybody should follow—*except* adhering to consensuality in the world. Both Paganism and sex-positive philosophy underscore respect for diversity, essentially saying, **"We really are all different, just as we are all similar."** This is a Zen conundrum—an ever-present contradiction that isn't going to get "resolved." We're all different, we're all individuals, and we're all together. We're the expression of the Life Force, with many similarities and differences.

For me, Pagan spirituality and a sex-positive philosophy are not different. Together they constitute a union, or a unitary foundation. They flow together like yin and yang, providing a support that helps me view the world. Together, they give me a lens with which to view the world, a belief system, a set of ethics, and a finely-tuned language. Sex-positive practices are not merely about a social contract outside my spiritual reality.

I don't believe we should separate sexuality into female and male energies. The notion that there are binary female and male energies in the universe is fine, but there is also a whole spectrum inside and outside the male/female yin-yang notion. Even though I embrace the idea of the God along with the Goddess, I don't believe there must always be a man and a woman in any sexual or spiritual context. Our energies meet, connect, and swirl around on a lot of different levels, and the notion that there are rigid ways to be is wrong. Rigidity, binary identities—those are all constructs to help us think we have a handle on the world, when life is really so much more complex!

♦ *R/S: Right—there's that dualism again, which thoroughly saturates our language. We've got to get rid of it.*

♦ CQ: Within Paganism, there is room for honoring all kinds of sexual exploration. I've never come upon a stronger, more meaningful, or more influential statement within Pagan culture than this line in "The Charge of the Goddess": *"All acts of love and pleasure are my rituals."* That's *not* what your garden-variety Christian is taught about sex and relationships! In the straight and conservative Christian-influenced world, a boy and a girl have to get married and procreate, and everything is so rigidly expressed. If your highest Divine Law sanctions "all acts of love and pleasure" as divine rituals, that means that in one fell swoop sexual diversity gets honored.

This isn't just a question of straight/gay, it means that people's solo sexual explorations and pleasures are honored. It means that groups being erotic together are honored. It means that if you get your pleasure by being tied up and flogged, that's honorable. It means that people in their gender and sexual diversity can grow into the differing individual entities that they are. Everything is honored, provided that "ye harm none."

That is all the direction most people need in matters of sex and relationships: to go ahead and pursue pleasures and loves without undue effect from outside, although, of course, we live in a culture where there are plenty of undue effects from the outside. There are still states with sodomy laws; there are still plenty of contexts where a person cannot reveal their sexual identity. It's not like we live in a fully realized utopia!

Outside of communities that have come together specifically around sex and sexual desire, like the gay men's bathhouse community and the leather community—places where people actually come to find sexual partners and be okay with that . . . outside of those communities, the most sexually open place I have found is the Pagan community. Here, people take these questions seriously and allow others the most space.

Who today is taught to put sex in the context of a ritual? For Pagans, sexuality is honored for itself—as a way to access holy energies and archetypes. This is a radical notion: sex can be a sacrament. And this is also an extremely powerful reason for people to come to Paganism in the first place. All of this is woven into my journey towards Paganism—especially the elevation and empowerment of the female . . . and the elevation and empowerment of the male in a different way than a sexist society wants. I'm not talking about the man in the gray flannel suit, but rather the Horned Lord with his cock high in the air.

But that's not who dances around *this* culture. There is a segment of the feminist community that feels as though heterosexuality is, by its nature, oppressive, and would like to say that all masculinity is about the penis imperative. But one of the problems with masculinity is that there isn't *more* penis honoring—truly! **We need true Pan energy, or Pan/dick energy, but there's not enough of it in our culture.** It's not rampant. So many men are so disempowered that if they have anything left, they're reduced to dicks and guns. But that's not the same thing as empowerment. Everyone needs to consider what kind of power we exercise in an ideal culture. **A sexually-empowered culture doesn't elevate one gender over the other—that's something to meditate on, think about, and learn from.** That needs to become one of our goals; we need to grow into that.

Our larger culture is Christian, or isn't Christian but isn't much of anything; it's sort of a secular American culture. I see people who either deny sexuality, or who are frantically attracted to it, without a sense of their own sacredness and their partner's sacredness. **If we could get to a place of understanding ourselves and each other as sacred, and understand that any sexual contact we have is, at the very least, an attempt to connect with another sacred being and have pleasure, then a lot of what plagues our society could just fall away!**

I'm not the first to say that if people had sexually-fulfilling lives, we would have less war, strife, power-motivated behavior and violence. This is a gift that Pagan spiritual understanding could give to everyone—that and the notion that we can be "elevated." I mean, what place does low self-esteem have in a person who truly believes that she is a Goddess?! It's not like we *don't* have to unravel any old images we're still saddled with from childhood. Paganism offers a cure for low self-esteem, if you and the people around you take it seriously.

These are places where we could really do an enormous amount of healing. People come to the Pagan community for healing, in a sense, as well as for community, comfort, and confirmation that their understanding of the world isn't crazy. How many of us have been called crazy, and have even been institutionalized, for ideas that within the Pagan community are perfectly acceptable? Alternate ways of experiencing the world are acceptable here.

♦ *R/S: Tell us about your Queen of Heaven parties—*

♦ CQ: Queen of Heaven happened because I chanced upon the world's first "Jack- and Jill-off" party when I came to San Francisco. The Jack- and Jill-off party had been preceded by the Jack-off parties, which have met on Monday nights for the past twenty years. Now that's surprising—I can barely wrap my mind around the notion of a sex party on a weeknight! I saw a flyer at the Sex Institute and went, figuring that if nothing else, it would be educational. And it was *very* educational. [laughs]

This was a co-ed safe sex party without any f—king—that was the rule. You had to masturbate, or do what you do with toys, hands or what-have-you. You had to put condoms on your sex toys, gloves on your hands and plastic wrap between tongues and pussies. And no one could f--k. In a culture that fundamentally believes that sex is about f--king (if you don't believe this, reread Bill Clinton's testimony about the Monica Lewinsky affair), then having a pansexual, no-f--- space is *radical.* And it allowed people of different orientations, who ordinarily wouldn't come together in an erotic way, to all be in one place and figure out ways to have a good time together. There were swingers, sexologists, gay men, dykes, leather people, heterosexuals—all together, doing a lot of things.

A fairly enormous change happened to me at that first party: for the first time in my life I had a multiple orgasm. I'd had plenty of sex before—good sex; I'd had plenty of lesbian sex and I'd masturbated a lot. But I'd never experienced a multiple orgasm. All of a sudden, in this diverse group of mostly strangers, there was enough going on that when I started, I didn't stop for quite a while. Some people might think that this was no big deal, but I thought it a *very* big deal! Not only that, my sexuality and my spirituality were already conjoined—enough so that it felt really transcendent. What does "transcendent" mean? You rise above the state you're in; you rise above your limitations. I rose above my sexual state, and it was amazing.

I felt I had inhabited a powerful spiritual space as well as an erotic space, and I wanted to find ways to acknowledge this in a more open way. That's where the Queen of Heaven came from—as an outgrowth of Jack and Jill-off parties.

♦ R/S: What is "Queen of Heaven"?

♦ CQ: Queen of Heaven is an on-going series of private parties. It's neither as closed as a coven nor as open as a public ritual, but it may be different in the future. It started from the Jack- and Jill-off structure. My partner Robert and I began to do our parties 11 years ago, but with a difference: we wanted to honor f—-ing. Because once everybody was comfortable together in a pansexual context, we didn't see any reason for them not to be f—-ing. We just wanted to make sure they practiced safe sex. In another time and place, latex would probably be irrelevant. But in our era, latex is extremely relevant, so it's *required*—partly so people don't have to announce that they're HIV-positive; everybody can just *do* it. That way, people get more empowered about using latex in their personal lives. People don't have to have "*The* Conversation" [about AIDS], and this minimizes the impulse to lie. We wanted a simple basic structure that allows people to come in, no matter who they are.

The "no matter who they are" part is important to me personally, since **I have a personal history of struggling with how diverse my sexuality is. I've been in communities that wanted me to be straighter or more lesbian than I really am.** So I prefer being surrounded by all types of people having many kinds of sex: "We're all okay together here. I'm okay the way I am. We're all expressing different facets of this jewel that is sexuality." I like that diversity—I find it very affirming as well as incredibly exciting.

♦ R/S: Is Queen of Heaven a sacred ritual?

♦ CQ: We cast a circle encompassing the whole social entity, and acknowledge the spirits of air, fire, water, earth and the center. Both the Goddess and the God are with us. We've done that from the very beginning.

People think that Queen of Heaven is named after me, when in actuality it's named after the Queen of Heaven! [laughs] The fact that my last name is Queen is simply a little in-joke. People say that *I'm* the Queen of Heaven, and I say, "No, I'm merely her earthly representative in this particular event." So I want to make it clear that I am not crowning myself Goddess. The notion of "thou art Goddess, thou art God" is very meaningful to me, and I accept that appellation as I want to give that appellation to others. But I think of myself as a *facilitator* rather than a high priestess. There is a certain priestess-like responsibility in choosing to do this to begin with, but my sense is that I want

everyone to feel elevated. Everyone should feel like they are an integral part of the ritual.

Non-Pagan people sometimes attend Queen of Heaven—it wasn't set up as a space for Pagans only, *per se.* It was set up as a Pagan space to create a sacred circle, within which sex could happen and people could be transformed. For me, casting the circle is sufficient to let every attendee feel the spiritual importance inherent in the event—whether they walk in the door believing it or not. I have heard from people who have attended various kinds of sex events that Queen of Heaven feels especially sweet and safe.

Most of the people are naked or wearing erotic clothing—whatever is erotic to *them.* Only in a few cases have people felt the ritual off-putting. By just going out to the periphery, people can have a less central experience if they want to. Or, they can get right in the middle of the circle and get *the energy.* A while ago I invited a Pagan woman to attend, and at the end of the ritual she was indignant: "My elders would have a fit that you did it that way!" I replied, "We didn't invite your elders to the party. And anybody who was an elder would probably *get it.*"

One time a pair of friends from the leather community brought two friends. When we began the ritual, the two guests got as far away as they could from the circle and started breathing hard, all scared and freaked out. It turned out they were Christians who'd thought that we were doing devil worship—but they were *Leather* Christians! I got a big laugh out of that. But at the same time, this reminded me that as Pagans, we are in the line of fire from assumptions made by people who are told lies by priests and ministers. Suddenly, I felt part of a long historical continuum that includes the burning of witches not so long ago.

Wicca is back. We've reinvented it; what we're practicing probably isn't like what the people who got burned at the stake were practicing. But those tortures and slaughters are still part of our history, because of how we've chosen to name ourselves.

So . . . if Christians think I might be a devil worshipper, I don't want to just laugh it off. But **the devil is a Christian god and a Christian invention—I wish they would get that! The devil is *not* a Pagan entity**, but a member of the Christian pantheon. The devil is *not* Pagan.

It was funny to experience these big rough, tough leather people screaming and running out of the room. It made me aware that we live in a funny world, where the different ways we understand spirituality and spiritual communities sometimes put us at odds with each other. But I've never had another experience like that, and we try to let people know in advance what we're going to do.

♦ R/S: How often do these parties occur?

♦ CQ: Quarterly, although we can never find space on the solstices and the equinoxes—it's really sad. We skew the year a bit in order to have spaces when we can get them.

♦ R/S: How many people attend?

Center Photo by Phyllis Christopher

♦ CQ: About 120. It's not a coven doing the Great Rite, although a couple of times two people chose to do that. The only time we ever said that condoms were optional was for a couple who were trying to conceive. We gave them a special Queen of Heaven dispensation because they were trying to enact the Great Rite in

order to conceive—who can argue with that?

♦ R/S: What is the Great Rite?

♦ CQ: It's a ritual within Wicca that can be done in other Pagan contexts. In it, the priestess and the priest have sex in the center of the circle, with the coven members around them. They draw the energies of the Goddess and God as a powerful point of spiritual focus for everyone. The part of the "Charge of the Goddess," where she says, "Sing, dance, make music and love all in my name"—they're making love in her name.

This is one of the profound things you can do together in a coven. The classic way to do it is right in the middle of the circle. There is some indication that a rite very similar to this was performed on a regular basis in some of the ancient Tantric temples—only in their spiritual context, they would call it something else. But its purpose was to raise energy, honor the erotic, and honor and make explicit the bond between the Goddess and the God.

In the cycle-of-the-year mythology within Wicca, the Goddess gives birth to the God, the God matures, he becomes her consort and erotic partner, and then he dies. And then they do it again. So the priest and priestess are making explicit that part of the myth cycle where the Goddess and the God get sexually connected. There is, at least theoretically, ancient precedent for this in the Goddess temples of the Fertile Crescent, in which the High Priestess of the temple crowned the new king by f—-ing him. It's the "Heiros Gamos," the sacred marriage. Contemporary Wicca has this space, which some Wiccans choose to do. But I'm sure many Wiccans have never been near a Great Rite.

Queen of Heaven allows for something like that—not as concentrated, but with everybody who's willing participating.

♦ R/S: So at a Queen of Heaven party with 120 people in attendance, you cast a circle, call the directions (North, South, East and West) and invite in the God and Goddess. Then what happens?

♦ CQ: The intent is not so much to do an act of magic, although you can argue that getting a whole bunch of people to have sex in a room is an act of magic! [laughs] It's a surprising departure from the way that most of us were raised. The point, though, is to marry the ancient form of the orgy, which has showed up at different times and places throughout history, with the Pagan conviction that all acts of love and pleasure are rituals of the Goddess. It makes a space in which people can have both erotic exploration and expression, and an explicitly spiritual honoring of it.

When she said that her elders would have had a fit, what that Pagan woman probably referred to is that we use the simplest

basic structure of Wicca: Pagan circle casting. But we don't do the remainder of the ritual that coven members would expect. I personally don't believe in the necessity for doing that, given that this ritual, in its relative simplicity, does what it sets out to do: affect people's hearts and spirits in this erotic space . . . permanently.

♦ R/S: Once the circle is cast, what happens next?

♦ CQ: Some people are watching. Some are masturbating. Some are f—-ing. Some are ogling each other. People do whatever they want, as long as whatever they do is safe sex, and as long as they don't just elect to walk up to somebody they haven't spoken to and start to do things to them. It's not about being a kid in a candy store, it's about asking and consent.

♦ R/S: Describe the physical space—

♦ CQ: Usually there's one big room with plenty of heat. Occasionally we have a place with multiple rooms, which changes the energy of the event. We have them either in sex clubs or in art galleries, inter-

estingly enough, because there are a couple of gallery owners who are sympathetic. You can say that this is art, just as easily as you can say this is a spiritual event. It's performance, certainly. It's extemporaneous. It doesn't have an audience, except for those participants who prefer to be voyeurs.

The idea is that it's a *private* space. It grows and its membership changes. People get invited by somebody who is already present; it's a community that grows organically. We assume that people will invite people who are "right"—and except for those Leather Christians, it has pretty much worked out! [laughs]

♦ R/S: So in ten years, that's the worst thing that has happened—

♦ CQ: That says something right there! We've thought about making this open to *anybody* who wants to show up. The Jack-and Jill-off parties actually tried that, and they had an interesting and difficult experience. More heterosexual men wanted to go than men of other orientations, and within a couple of years there were parties that consisted of 3 women and 80 men!

♦ R/S: What's the ratio at Queen of Heaven?

♦ CQ: It's about 50/50—if anything, there are more women than men. I attribute that to the "letting people invite who it's right for them to invite" decision. That was the only way we could think of to try to remedy this unbalanced situation. The fact is that plenty of women want to go to a safe erotic space. But the majority of women in this culture don't feel safe in a situation where there are a few of them and a lot of men, even if they *are* really safe there; it often won't feel that way to them. Yes, once in a while at the Jack- and Jill-off parties we'd get a woman whose idea of a good time was getting erotic attention from all the men in the room, and to her it felt perfect! But to the other women, it can feel frightening and overwhelming.

I'd like to develop a ritual and an entrance procedure that would help "newcomers" be together in comfort and safety. I'm always thinking, "What else can we *do?*" We've had groups ask us to oversee something like this for them, and it's hard to know what would be the perfect set of precepts and circumstances.

So I choose to believe that Queen of Heaven is presently, in some ways, a transitional learning cauldron: we're learning how to be in an erotic space in numbers. Most people don't know how to do that. Within our lifetime, the only sub-cultural group that has tried this is gay men in bathhouses and sex clubs.

There are plenty of swingers who have made great strides towards learning how to do this, but they are extremely heterosexually-focused. They've addressed the "equal numbers of men and women" problem like this: if you're a guy and you want to walk through the door, you have to bring a woman with you (hopefully, she *wants* to be there). It's not addressed organically. So, that's not quite what we want either. We want a space where queers feel just as welcome as heterosexuals—that's part of the whole point.

The hardest part about Queen of Heaven has been knowing who is ready to walk in the door. If we were a much smaller group, we could have a different way of processing people into the space. This is the hardest part of Queen of Heaven events; it's a major challenge. I really wish we could just have a temple and throw open the doors, but I don't think that this culture is ready for that yet! [laughs] I know the police would pay more attention to us if we did that, and so would the Christians. So it's just as well we operate on a smaller scale right now, incubating.

My partner Robert and I are facilitating a fairly complicated event. You have to put yourself in a position of service to do that. It's not like we get to go lie in the middle of the floor and have people "do" us—we have to change the toilet paper! We have to plunge the toilet, replace the paper towels. We have to squeeze out the sponge. People, when they romanticize orgies, don't think about that aspect. [laughs]

There's the part that we consider exciting and romantic, and then there's taking out the garbage. This has to happen in our psyches, in our cultures, everywhere.

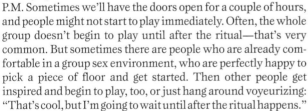

♦ **R/S: Does Queen of Heaven begin at the same time?**
CQ: The doors usually open at 7 or 8 P.M. Sometimes we'll have the doors open for a couple of hours, and people might not start to play immediately. Often, the whole group doesn't begin to play until after the ritual—that's very common. But sometimes there are people who are already comfortable in a group sex environment, who are perfectly happy to pick a piece of floor and get started. Then other people get inspired and begin to play, too, or just hang around voyeurizing: "That's cool, but I'm going to wait until after the ritual happens."

♦ **R/S: So at a certain point you lock the doors, and nobody can come in. How long does it go on after that?**
♦ CQ: After the ritual we usually go for at least three hours. Occasionally it's shorter or longer, but usually it's about three to three-and-a-half hours.

1964 San Francisco Zoo   Photo: Dad; 1990 in drag   Photo: Robert Lawrence

♦ **R/S: Do you close the circle at the end of the ritual?**
♦ CQ: We don't do that; we let the sacred space leave with people. I know that's controversial, but I believe that the circle is always open and is intact in each person as they leave. We haven't seen any ill effects.

This is the way that my earlier desire for coven and community wound up playing out. Queen of Heaven fills that space for me; it's a way that a lot of our dearest friends have come into our lives and gotten closer to us. Yet people have repeatedly attended whom we haven't gotten to know. In any group situation some people are shy and others gregarious. Some people sit quietly and meditatively and don't introduce themselves, while others really try to get to know one another and form friendships that way.

Personally, I always have a set of functions—whether it's greeting people at the door, making sure the food is set on the banquet table, or changing the toilet paper. This precludes me getting to know people very well—although often, that's how we make the first connection.

♦ **R/S: You have a buffet table at an orgy—**
♦ CQ: Almost every public sex space I know about, with the possible exception of bathhouses, has a food table—people have to eat, right? They get tired and they need replenishment. Sharing food is an ancient ritual that makes people feel comfortable and convivial; sharing of food is involved in rituals of all kinds. For the same reason, we have a buffet table at a wedding.

♦ **R/S: Potluck dinners are a church-social activity—**
♦ CQ: That's right. One of the oldest ritualistic acts humans have done, to see whether or not they're safe together, is to break bread together. If you're breaking bread together and eating, you don't have your hands on your sword. You're communing.

There is an explicitly sacred element in whom we decide to share food with. Those of us who grew up eating jello on TV trays with a screaming mom or dad are going to have to really stretch it to believe this. But there are ways in which food sharing becomes a universal ritual.

♦ **R/S: Eating is also sensual, and can be an erotic, too—**
♦ CQ: People use dining out for seduction and for cementing relationships. In the decade I've been affiliated with these group sex environments, I've observed that when people are first-timers, they're nervous. They don't know what to expect; they're scared. They may have body image issues and have never been explicit in any public context before. Sometimes people get brought by their lovers who think, "My friend is ready for this." But that isn't necessarily the case. So what do these people do? They go to the food table and hang out chatting with other people until they feel they're in a safe space.

There's another important aspect of food that rarely gets acknowledged. Food preparation is really alchemical and magical. Imagine what a big leap it was for primitive humans to start cooking with fire. And when you get right down to it, one of the things that

Pagans yearn for is a connection with those people who lived so close to the earth. Remember, **the earth is the source of all food, which is how we subsist.** Once we became able to change that food into wonderful dishes, it was an amazing cultural step—that was like art! When Pagans say, "May you never hunger," it's harkening back to the beginning. If you stop to think about those words in the present, they mean just as much as they ever did. Food is about a social contract; it's about good ways to live together as people, where we take care of each other.

♦ *R/S: You worked as a sacred prostitute or courtesan—*

♦ CQ: In the context of Goddess worship and Paganism, there is a history of the Priestess and the Goddess Temple playing an enormous role in conserving the ongoing health of the state—particularly in Middle Eastern antiquity. The priestesses of the temple were erotically available to worshippers, who would come to experience the Goddess by consorting with them—performing what we would now call sacred prostitution. They didn't necessarily receive the money for themselves; it went to the temple which took care of all the women. The people in the community could go there thinking: "It's important for me to connect with the Goddess, and I want to do this sexually through one of the priestesses."

There is a subculture of contemporary prostitutes, men as well as women, who have chosen to revive that understanding of the prostitution work they do. They're dedicated to the Goddess. They meet with a client in a sacred space, one where the client can experience not just a mundane sexual act but a sexual act with a context of spiritual significance. There is a spiritual significance that takes place in any sex act when you *acknowledge* it as such—that's the basis of sex magic, really. You don't have to do any special ritualized *anything;* you just have to say to your partner, "We are in sacred space now," or "We are honoring the Goddess with our action," or "We are going to raise energy together and use it to heal the world," or whatever you want to do to make that a magical experience.

Some prostitutes have said that the way they experience their work is through showing the face of the Goddess to the supplicant or client. Other prostitutes say, "The Goddess gives me strength; I am doing this erotic, powerful work in her image and in her name. And I am dedicating myself and the energy I raise with this client to the Goddess." In that case, the client may not know that is going on.

I think it's a little more common to take on that latter understanding: communing with the Goddess regardless of whether the client has any spiritual desire or understanding of the process. Many of us who understand ourselves this way will say this makes for a more respectful honoring; a finer connection with the client. It's pretty common for those who call themselves sacred prostitutes to honor the fact that someone is coming for sexual gratification. Regardless whether the client is present in a spiritual state of mind, I am honoring our interaction that way because I feel greater safety, a greater sense of respect and more space for it to be pleasurable—all those kinds of things.

In a way this is an internal point of view: if you are understanding yourself this way, experiencing yourself as an embodiment of the Goddess, or engaged in drawing down the spiritual and erotic strength of the Goddess, then the whole act of prostitution can be put in a less adulterated context than when it is mundane. It's another way of going into the culture's sex-negative garbage to pull out salvageable parts from situations we've been told aren't salvageable.

The thing that contemporary prostitutes have heard over and over again is that for every Xaviera Hollander (author of *The Happy Hooker*) who said she had a great time, we have "rescued prostitutes" who turn to a particular strain of feminism to explain why they had such an awful time because they were being exploited. And we have right-wing, anti-sex forces saying that prostitution is inherently a negative experience for everyone, especially for the prostitute. She is being used and isolated in a context in which she is both "selling her body" and "giving up her personhood" in this very essentialized way.

This is all such negative magic. I can't even begin to articulate what an evil influence it is on people who find themselves in some context within the sex industry, whether purveying or buying. In the first place, prostitutes don't sell their bodies—they rent their time, their sexual skill sets, their psychological and emotional skill sets.

People who pay for sexual pleasure probably seek that pleasurable altered state that sex brings. For whatever reasons, they don't want to, or can't experience that with their ongoing partner—or maybe they don't have one. So you can just twist the lens a bit and call what a customer wants an honorable desire—you could call it a *sacred* desire! And sacred prostitutes choose to employ that little flip of perspective, rather than that other direction of flip which says, "Sex is a weapon used by men against women to control them, *blah blah blah.*"

Prostitution has many ritualized ways in which safe space is created—emotional as well as actual. Safe space is created by the use of condoms. Often it's created in a context: "My friend is expecting a telephone call at the end of our session, and if they don't get one, they'll come here and intercede." This business of believing all prostitution consists of women selling their bodies and being turned into sexual slaves is somebody's very messed-up sexual fantasy. Most prostitutes live their lives in ways that incorporate structures of safety and well-being, at least to some degree. Of course, some people have more wherewithal to do that than others; it depends on many variables, from class and educational background to self-esteem issues.

The sacred prostitute wants to take that conventional basis for interchange and turn it into something more explicitly safe and honorable. Partly, she or he is doing it for her or his own safety—emotionally and spiritually as well as physically. Partly, they have a personal conviction that sex *is* sacred, and think that long ago this role may have been an honored part of the culture.

No one thinks that sacred prostitution will be an accepted part of the culture in which we live any time soon. But in our *alternative* sexual cultures, this is getting respect and attention. Pretty much, prostitutes are on the cutting edge of what's happening in the culture sexually. They're having sex with people who want to have sex, who need to have sex, and who might not understand any of these philosophical notions we've been talking about. For the most part, they're managing to do it in a way where they come out on the other side and can do it again. And eventually they can retire. **Funny, we rarely hear from people who had a good or decent time with prostitution!** So this is another way of trying to shore up sex workers' well-being, via the notion that what they do is truly important, honorable, and has spiritual significance.

I didn't go into prostitution and *then* discover the notion of sacred prostitution—I already knew about Pagan beliefs and reality when I went in. And from the very beginning, Paganism allowed me to understand the work and connections I had with clients as existing in a context of respect, and under the protection of the Goddess. This made an enormous difference in the experiences I had. In some cases I was able to convey and relate that sensibility to clients, too.

I did not take out a newspaper ad that said, "Sacred Prostitute! Come experience the beauty of the God and the Goddess in my arms!" I worked via the referral of a Madam who sent me guys listed in her little black book. It was up to *me* to get a sense of who they were, and explain, "This is the way I understand myself"—or not. If I didn't think they'd "get it," I didn't see any point in talking about it, but if I thought that a person had an opening around spiritual issues, I would sometimes talk explicitly. I often found people saying, "Wow, yeah—I feel there is something I'm searching for and desiring, and you could call it that."

There are probably as many different ways of understanding sacred prostitution as there are prostitutes who embrace that idea. It's not like we have a rule book or a liturgy. But there is a space, potentially, to develop that sacredness again.

Prostitution is heavily regulated by the State. We could argue that one of the reasons for this is that Christianity, long ago, had to seize power from the Goddess religion wherein prostitute-priestesses had a lot of power. All through the Christianized ages and Christianized countries, the laws worked to repress people who had wielded power previously—hence the origin of our laws against prostitution.

There's no question that prostitution's illegality as a "notorious crime of vice" is defined in explicitly Christianized language. I'll stick my neck out: there is something implicitly *Pagan* about all prostitution! Not all prostitutes will be able to relate to that, and probably lots of Pagans will go, "Wait a minute! What are you saying?" But **to some degree, one of the ways we understand "Pagan" is through searching for a way to live in a world that's hamstrung by Christian laws and rituals.** Christian belief systems have infiltrated not only our legal codes but our psychology—especially in the area of "insanity." Many common assumptions date back thousands of years to the clash between Christianity and non-Christian religious systems, and we still exist in the midst of that fallout.

The laws against sex for money totally partake of that clash, even though people today don't think twice about it. Prostitution is illegal because Western Culture doesn't want women to have this option for financial autonomy and strength, so identifying as a sacred prostitute can also be a *political statement!* It has to do with the long, very politicized war between our people and the Christian hierarchy that wants to stomp out us and our ways. They hate our more open sexuality, our devotion to the Goddess—everything we cherish. And their **Christian dogmas are codified in our country's laws.** That's why it's important to talk about these issues. Having an alternative spin on subjects we don't think twice about is very healthy.

I don't separate my spiritual understanding from political issues. There is supposed to be a separation of church and state in this country, but there is *not!* So I don't see any reason why I should separate *my* church and my state. I've lived as a persecuted sexual minority when I was a lesbian and when I was a prostitute, and I don't see any reason to keep quiet about this or say, "But this has nothing to do with my spiritual beliefs." I think it has *everything* to do with my spiritual beliefs.

My spiritual beliefs help give me strength and help focus me toward working for a different world. Not everyone sees their spirituality that way, but I do, and many other Pagans do, too. In some ways it's almost a coincidence that my lens is sexuality—I could be taking the same set of spiritual beliefs and directing my activism toward anti-poverty work, or Green Party work, or radical environmentalism. These are all places where Pagan people with strong feelings about making their world-view real are involved.

But my place to do this work is sex, and I do it in every way that I can. I write, I teach, I do sex work, I do movies, I throw sex parties. **Everything I do centers around sex—except when I'm antiquing or walking on a beach.** This is the way my path has manifested, in the same way that Julia Butterfly Hill had to climb the old-growth redwood tree and live there for two years. I think there's a spiritual or karmic reason I got here and am doing this work. I answered the call, rather than say, "Nah, I deny this." I *don't* deny it.

I'm in the middle of this sexual maelstrom and I might as well speak up whenever I have the opportunity—that's my job. I talk about it, write about it, think how it could be different, talk to other people about how it could be different. It's all linked, and underscored, by my belief that **sex could be, and *is*—when we let it be—one of the most powerful *spiritual* experiences we can ever have. ♦♦♦**

1975, Haight Street Photo: Will Roscoe

Photo: Nemea Arborvitae

Charles Gatewood

A world-class photographer who has captured subjects such as Bob Dylan and William S. Burroughs for publications like *Rolling Stone* and *Newsweek,* Charles Gatewood is also a published novelist, writer and the cinematographer/director of his own company, Flash Video. Currently residing in San Francisco, Charles has traveled the world in search of unusual images, rituals, festivals and sacred sites—all to satisfy his anthropologist's soul. His independently published books and videos are available from 415-267-7651, PO Box 410052, San Francisco CA 94141, or from his Website, *www.charlesgatewood.com.* Interview by John Sulak.

♦ *RE/SEARCH: You've been "alternative" for a long time; how did you start?*

♦ CHARLES GATEWOOD: I grew up in Missouri—the Ozarks—and came of age in the Fifties. I was especially drawn to the Beatniks because they were champions of personal liberation. Some of them, like Gary Snyder, were into Buddhism and other Eastern practices, and that was fascinating to a kid raised in the land of Southern Baptists. **The Beats were also very anti-authoritarian, which is definitely a Pagan trait.** And they were busy exploring art, poetry, literature, philosophy, writing and uncensored self-expression in general. In those days there was a lot of censorship, and the Beats were speaking out against it; **books by Henry Miller and William Burroughs and Allen Ginsberg were being banned. You could be jailed for writing, publishing or distributing "obscene" books.**

The Fifties was a very tight-assed, repressive time, with a huge emphasis on conformity and social control. Most people were totally brainwashed into thinking they had to dress conservatively and do everything Big Brother told them. The Beats said, "Screw that—we're going to live in our own poetic, visionary way, and travel and experience the world *directly,* not from television or advertisements."

I was a rebellious teen, and the Beat message made a *huge* impression on me—I grew a beard at 16 and blew everybody's mind! Shortly after, I hitchhiked from Missouri to Seattle and back—just like Kerouac. After college, I hitchhiked to New York and got jobs on two Norwegian ships and sailed around the world, because my Beat heroes had done things like that. When I had first told people my intentions, they'd laughed at me. But when I returned from my travels with wild stories and amazing experiences, they were forced to take me seriously.

So the Beat culture showed me that anyone can be a romantic visionary, and that the first thing you have to do is take charge of your own destiny. Starhawk calls this "power from within," as opposed to "power over." It was tremendously liberating: you didn't have to blindly obey your mother or your boss or the President of the United States. To quote Starhawk:

"The immanent conception of justice is not based on rules or authority, but upon integrity—integrity of self and integrity of relationships."

In the early Sixties, I witnessed my first civil rights and peace protests, and other human rights movements. When the Army tried to draft me and send me to Vietnam, I moved to Sweden for two years, because, as Cassius Clay said, *I didn't have any quarrel with the Vietnamese.*

In Sweden, I became an expatriate and an existentialist Beatnik-Hippie. **I sat reading books and essays like Norman Mailer's "The White Negro," which said you had to live as a super-aware outsider, on the edge.** I also read *The White Goddess* by Robert Graves—an important book about the history of poetic myth and rediscovery of the Goddess. Timothy Leary's work was also important to me. Leary wrote about turning on, tuning in, and dropping out—expanding your consciousness, opening up, and seeing through the lies and the bulls---. He advocated listening to your body, tuning into your unconscious, and exploring the dark sides of your psyche. Exploring your dark side—also called "Shadow Work"—is a central Pagan practice. Starhawk's *Dreaming The Dark,* which is my favorite book about Pagan politics and practices, explores the ramifications of this idea in fascinating detail.

♦ *R/S: Didn't you start visiting ancient Pagan sites in the Sixties?*

♦ CG: An anthropology teacher took my class to visit some Native American ceremonial mounds along the Mississippi. And some of my other university studies were in classical archeology. I saw pictures and descriptions of sacred sites in Europe, so naturally I wanted to see them in person. I got to walk around Stonehenge back when there was no fence around it; you could freely explore the standing stones. I visited Altamira in Northern Spain and saw the magical prehistoric cave paintings on the walls. I thought, "Wow, this isn't art as decoration, or art as status symbol—this is art as *magic.*"

I went twice to Delphi, Greece, where the famous Oracle had been—a magnificent site. I also visited the Parthenon, and the Palace of Minos at Knossus in Crete. A few years later, I hitchhiked across North Africa, from Morocco to Egypt. That trip took three months. **In Morocco magic is an essential part of everyday life. Everyone practices it. There are trance dancers, and trance music, and mystical brotherhoods**—it's intoxicating. All across North Africa there are perfectly preserved Roman ruins—in Libya there's a town called Leptis Magna, where you can still find Roman coins in the sand. In Egypt I visited Alexandria, climbed down into Tutankhamen's tomb, and studied the mummies at the Egyptian Museum in Cairo. You see pictures of these things in books, but you can't imagine the scale, or feel the *magic* of the actual sites. Imagine walking down an avenue of sphinxes a half-mile long! Also, in studying Egyptian philosophy, I learned about Polytheism—an important Pagan idea.

♦ *R/S: When you were in Morocco, did you see the Master Musicians of Jajouka?*

♦ CG: Ah—I have to backtrack. In the Seventies, I lived in Manhattan and worked as a professional photojournalist. I met a writer named Robert Palmer who wrote for *Rolling Stone.* Robert was a musician, a mystic, and a William Burroughs fan. I'd been taking photographs at Mardi Gras, which I now realize is a Dionysian festival. I was fascinated by the idea of huge numbers of people getting together, putting on masks, and being someone else—living their fantasies for a day. I took Robert Palmer to Mardi Gras and we did an article for *Rolling Stone.*

Rolling Stone liked my photographs. At the time, they were headquartered in San Francisco, so they asked me to be their New York photographer. Then Robert Palmer sold them the idea of interviewing William Burroughs, who was living in London. Robert took me along as the photographer. I got to spend a week with Burroughs and his friends.

Burroughs was living with Brion Gysin, who for many years had lived in Morocco. Brion had discovered the Master Musicians of Jajouka, and had opened a restaurant in Tangier so they would have a place to play. The Jajouka musicians would get blasted on kif (a marijuana/tobacco mixture) and play far-out trance music. **The Master Musicians and trance dancers, said Brion, were indeed practicing the ancient Rites of Pan, and their rituals go back into prehistory.** There are lots of references in later Roman history to similar rites, like Lupercalia, which in turn are the source for our own *carnival.* Suddenly all the dots began to be connected for me, and I sensed that ritual and trance were parts of an ancient, sacred human drama. Ritual activates parts of the body, mind and spirit that are not usually accessed during day-to-day activities. These rituals activate the *old mind* within us, so we can tap into our deeper selves.

♦ *R/S: When did you first become aware of the existence of altered or ecstatic states?*

♦ CG: My parents liked to get drunk and party—they were chasing ecstasy in their own way. In my early teens I went through a brief Christian phase, where I had visions of God in one form or another. These visions weren't exactly *transcendental*—I remember praying to a blinking radio antenna—but they were a kid's fantasy of transcendence, for sure. It wasn't until later, when I began seriously experimenting with sex and drugs, that I first tasted true ecstasy.

I also felt a strong, rising interest in the creative process. I wanted to be a visionary artist—yet I was struggling to find my medium. Then one day I met a fellow anthropology student

who was also a hugely gifted photographer. He showed me some amazing prints, and I thought, "Wow—maybe I could do *that!*" Finally I'd found a way to integrate my interest in social science and behavior with my need for artistic expression. Immediately I had a vision that my life's work could involve photographing behavior—especially unusual and strange behavior—in an artistic way. So I started doing exactly that, and now, almost forty years later, I'm still doing it.

♦ *R/S: Was this also a kind of spiritual path for you?*

♦ CG: Yes, indeed. When I began, I was a skeptic and considered myself an atheist, having totally rejected my Christian upbringing. In 1966 I moved to Manhattan, settled down, got married, and for a while had a fairly "normal" life working as a photojournalist. Time passed, and I published my first book, *Sidetripping,* and a book titled *Wall Street.* But then I became more and more interested in wild underground scenes, and began the work that was in my book *Forbidden Photographs.*

About this time—the late Seventies—my marriage broke up. I'd been drinking hard and doing lots of drugs. In the divorce papers, my wife testified, "He often spent his days and evenings taking—and posing for—photographs of an unpublishable nature." I was going deeper into the dark side, responding to the lure of the forbidden. I was also self-destructing.

One day I found myself in Woodstock, New York, teaching a workshop, and I looked around and said, "Yes—it's time to go back to the woods." Instinctively I knew that Nature would help me regain harmony and balance in my life. So I moved to Woodstock, bought a house, and lived in the woods for ten years. It was wonderful. As a child I'd spent countless hours playing in the woods, and *it all came back:* walking outside and seeing the stars and the moon, listening to the birds sing, and watching the afternoon sunlight dance through the trees.

I found a girlfriend who was a spiritual seeker, and we began meditating, trading massages, reading Krishnamurti and other sacred texts to each other by the fireplace. Suddenly spirituality made terrific sense! I began meditating and chanting with some Tibetan Buddhists who had established a monastery in Woodstock, and I took a great workshop in Sufi meditation with Pir Viliat Khan at the Omega Institute in Rhinebeck. I also quit alcohol, tobacco and hard drugs—I did a lot of Twelve Step work. It took a long time, but finally I turned my life around and regained my faith and balance.

♦ *R/S: How did you shift to a more Pagan orientation?*

♦ CG: Well, in the mid-Seventies I started photographing and videotaping all sorts of body modification. **Often, when I asked people about their tattoos, they would mention their totem animals, or various Goddess figures, or their chakras, or their spirit guides**, or say that their tattoos represented empowerment, reclaiming, and so on. Their answers were much deeper and more interesting than I'd expected, so I began to delve into Pagan ideas.

Also, I'd heard about a man named Fakir Musafar, and I knew I had to meet him. Roland Loomis was a modern guy who ran an advertising agency and drove a BMW and wore three-piece suits, but he had a secret life you could read about in scarce, hard-to-find magazines like *Piercing Fans International Quarterly (PFIQ).* In private, Fakir was performing elaborate rituals, leaving his body, hanging from flesh-hooks, experimenting with sensory deprivation and *all kinds* of body play. He was cutting, branding and piercing himself (and a few oth-

Charles Gatewood self-portrait, Greece

tant teachers. He's made me think about numerous topics that have made me better understand the Pagan world, and other radical communities. I moved to San Francisco to be closer to these communities, and I consider them my extended family. So my interests have completely changed my life: who I hang out with, where I go, what I think, what I do, what I wear, and how I express myself.

♦ *R/S: When did you first attend a public Pagan ritual?*

♦ CG: In the early Nineties, the writer and poet Michael Perkins took me to a Beltane ritual in Western Massachusetts. It was a big gathering of several hundred participants, and I felt I was "coming home"—as Pagans often say. After that I made a conscious effort to get more involved—to read more books, take more workshops, and attend more rituals. What I especially liked was the fact that Paganism isn't dogmatic—it's a religion of experience, of consciousness-changing practices. I also like the emphasis on community, and strengthening the bonds between conscious and responsible individuals.

ers), using pain as a vehicle to higher consciousness in the same way his ancestors had done. And I thought, "Wow— what's he tapping into? I've got to know more about this." Fakir's journey wasn't abstract and intellectual—it was intuitive and visceral. **Intense physical experiences were leading Fakir to new spiritual paths, where body play, Paganism, and ecstasy all fuse together.**

I finally met Fakir at Annie Sprinkle's New York apartment in 1980. The next year Fakir and I worked together on a feature film by Mark and Dan Jury titled *Dances Sacred and Profane,* in which Fakir not only explains but *demonstrates* his philosophy and practices. The climax of the film shows Fakir doing the Native American Sun Dance ritual. He performed a preliminary ritual at Devil's Tower in Wyoming—a sensational sacred site. Then **Fakir found a remote wooded area, consecrated a cottonwood tree, and suspended himself with flesh-hooks while he left his body and communicated with the Great White Spirit.** The footage was awesome, and when the film opened at San Francisco's Roxie Theater in 1985 there were lines around the block. Lots of people were interested in these rituals.

While working on that film, I introduced Fakir to Vale. Vale instantly understood that something important was happening. I showed him other pictures I'd been taking of Pagans, radical sex people and body modification enthusiasts, and Vale said, "Hey—we can do a whole book about this." That book, of course, was *Modern Primitives,* which came out in 1989. So far *Modern Primitives* has sold about 80,000 copies, and we figure over a million people have seen it and thought about the ideas and practices detailed in it. It really is a seminal book that has spread those ideas around the world, and it's certainly changed a lot of people's thinking and behavior.

Because of *Dances Sacred and Profane* and *Modern Primitives,* Fakir decided to come out of the closet. Now the whole world knows his work. Fakir is one of my most impor-

Later I took a workshop with Fakir entitled "Ecstatic Shamanism." It was a three-day series of lectures and show-and-tell about piercing, cutting, scarification, branding, sensory deprivation, S/M—all from a shamanic perspective. It was about deep learning from altered states, and it was fascinating and very moving. No cameras were allowed; I had to leave my camera at home and *participate.*

On the last day of the workshop, Fakir pierced us all and we did a ball dance. I had photographed piercings dozens of times, but I'd never been pierced myself. Fakir grabbed thick pinches of flesh, just above my nipples, and pierced me twice, with a big thick needle. It hurt like crazy, and I screamed! Then he pulled thread through the piercings and sewed two baseball-sized rubber balls on me.

All thirty members of the workshop were pierced—there were no voyeurs. It was a test, of sorts, and a total participatory experience. Afterward we danced to drumming and chanting, and got really high on our endorphins and adrenalin rush. It's one thing to be an observer; it's totally different being part of the action. I learned right away that I loved it, and that I was stronger than I thought.

♦ *R/S: Pagan rituals and body-modification practices are controversial—how can piercing one's penis, for example, be liberating?*

♦ CG: I hear Pagans describing epiphanies all the time, and I experience them myself—frequently. The real front-line players experience transcendental peaks, and physical and psychological spaces most people have never dreamed about. I call them astronauts of inner space. They're using ancient techniques of trance, ritual and pain to attain altered states of awareness, exploring inner spaces in order to learn and grow and feel like part of the whole.

Society often tells us that our bodies are inherently sinful. That's a very false message. Piercing one's genitals, for example, may be a way of affirming and reclaiming physical and sexual freedom. The act may serve to remind us that our bodies belong to us—not the church, nor the state, nor our parents. As **Fakir says, "It's your body—play with it."**

Pagan spiritual traditions call for individuals to explore paths that can be dark and dangerous. Many people deny their dark sides, yet we all have darkness in us. It's much healthier to explore and to integrate all that, instead of trying to repress those dark instincts. Rituals provide a safe and supportive way to further those explorations. I was nervous about participating in the ball dance, and found it painful at first. But afterward I felt exhilarated; I had a glow that lasted for days. I felt more alive, more aware, and more multi-dimensional. I found the ritual to be empowering, cathartic, and transformative.

♦ *R/S: Isn't some of this activity just a passing fad, a trend?*

♦ CG: Yes and no. Much of it is deeper. During a recent ritual, a man I know had a large footprint of a bear cut deeply into his back. The bear is his totem animal, and he wanted a big scar to mark his union with the bear's energy, and to commemorate the ritual. For others, body modification can be a rite of passage. In primitive cultures, when you reach a certain age, it is common for you to receive some hard physical experience as an initiation. Suddenly you're no longer a boy—you're a *Man*. It's been called "ritual wounding." Your body receives marks that show you've changed. You realize your vulnerabilities and your strengths, and feel a deep, strong bond with others involved in the ritual. And you're experiencing this directly, not watching it on television. That's important, because **we get so much of our so-called experience second-hand, from the media. After you participate in a good, deep ritual, television seems so silly!**

♦ *R/S: How about your private Pagan practices?*

♦ CG: I've done a lot of inner work. It's hard work trying to scrub away all our conditioning, so we can begin to think for ourselves. I've been fascinated with ideas about expanded consciousness since the Sixties. Starhawk defines magic as a function of consciousness, and I relate to it very much in that way. I see magic everywhere, every day. Everything is alive, connected, pulsing with life, wondrous.

My photography and video work is very much about magic. I try to be alert for those rare opportunities to make the occasion transcend itself and become more anticipated. You can verbally articulate some of those ways, but usually the **magic is ephemeral, and quite ineffable. Often it's** *unrepeatable.* You can't just read a book and follow instructions. You have to go in deep, play around, lose yourself, go off the map. I don't always know what I'm looking for. I suppose some photographers might follow a more analytical process, but my approach is very visceral and intuitive. Pictures come *through* me.

When I photograph candids, or pictures on the street, I try to put myself in a trance-like state of mind so I'm super-receptive and super-aware. I've been a photographer long enough to know how to see things that other people miss. I can see things coming together, just by being alert and *paying close attention.*

Lately I've been taking more explicitly erotic photographs. What fun! I'm doing creative work/play with my friends, in ways that really get my blood moving. There's nothing I'd rather be doing, no one else I'd rather be doing it with, and no place else I'd rather be doing it than San Francisco, here and now. I get very, very high doing this work. It's so exhilarating!

♦ *R/S: What are your thoughts on sacred sexuality?*

♦ CG: I indulge in it every chance I get. [laughs] The Pagan idea is to integrate all emotions and bodily acts and not divorce some of them as bad or dirty. Spirituality always has a physical context, and sex is a beautiful, natural thing. The body is not evil, and there's no such thing as original sin. What a ridiculous concept!

♦ *R/S: Describe Carol Queen's "Queen of Heaven" parties—*

♦ CG: Sure—they're really great. You walk in, check your clothes, and there are a hundred or more naked people, getting down. Everywhere you look, there are couples having sex, and kinky threesome and foursomes, and gays, and bi's and transsexuals—all having fun. And it's *wonderful*—like Jessie Helms's worst nightmare.

Sacred space is created, following the Pagan motto: "All acts of love and pleasure are my rituals." And no cameras are allowed—you *have* to participate!

♦ *R/S: How do contemporary Pagan sex parties compare to Sixties orgies?*

♦ CG: The participants are much more conscious and evolved, and there's usually no drinking or drugs. The first nude party I ever attended was in New York in 1966. There was no sex, just total nudity. There was some hugging and kissing and a little *horseplay*, but in those days it was radical enough just to be naked with a bunch of strangers—*I* found it tremendously exciting!

In ancient times, in Greece, there were Dionysian rituals—wild Pagan orgies—where people got drunk and stoned and went into trances and danced all night and got out of their heads and performed all kinds of erotic acts. **As Tim Leary said, "Sometimes you have to go out of your head to use your mind."** Here, the idea is that the "normal" brain filters out most incoming sensations like a reducing valve, so sometimes it's useful to open that valve and let it all rush in. Usually you have a good laugh at what a one-dimensional, mechanical robot you've become!

Another thing I like about Paganism is the playfulness. Usually there's a conscious effort to make jokes, to play, and not to take it all *too* seriously. Often people leading the ritual tell terrible jokes, or their pants fall down, or they prank one another. While this is serious sacred work, it's also *playful*. We don't want to get our spiritual egos all puffed up—that's been called "spiritual materialism." Goddess forbid!

That reminds me of a joke: What did the Holy Man say to the hot dog vendor?

♦ *R/S: I don't know—*

♦ CG: "Make me one with everything!" [laughs]

♦ *R/S: You're an artist—do you think there's such a thing as "Pagan aesthetics"?*

♦ CG: Well, art and creativity are essential aspects of Pagan practice. The first artists were the first conscious human beings, and the first art was probably sex—some early humans said, "Hey, it's richer and more meaningful if we do it like *this*." Most early artists were probably shamans and priests, and we have evidence that humans were decorating their bodies, painting on cave walls and making sculptural figurines thousands or millions of years ago. This early art was deeply magical—about birth, death, fertility, the hunt, the spirit world, etc—and it depicted deep and mysterious primal energies.

Most contemporary art has lost any dimension of "sacred content." Today's art is mostly commodity, propaganda, status symbol, or this week's clever illustration of academic theory. A Pagan artist I know refers to this postmodern, intellectual work as "dead art." In the Pagan world, art isn't something you see in a big museum for an hour on a Saturday afternoon (underwritten by IBM/Exxon/Mobil). Instead, art is *everywhere, all the time,* and is entirely integrated into your daily life.

Many Pagans are drawn to so-called "Primitive" art, like Hopi sand paintings, aboriginal dreamtime images, Huichol yarn paintings, African masks, mandalas, neolithic statuettes and sacred sites like Stonehenge and Delphi. The Western artists that I prefer include soulful, romantic visionaries like Blake, Gauguin, Van Gogh, Dali, Whitman, and Rimbaud. One contemporary painter I like is Alex Grey, whose "psychedelic" paintings are gloriously transcendental. Grey has also written and illustrated *The Mission of Art* (Shambhala), which deals specifically with the function of sacred art.

Of course, different Pagan groups have their own special objects and practices. Hippie Pagans love crystals and gemstones, Indian fabrics, playing and singing music (and creative states of cannabis intoxication). Feminist Pagans may favor sacred songs and chants about healing the planet, and figurines of the Earth Mother and the Minoan Snake Goddess. Pagan Goths mix mysterious black capes, veils and robes with spiked collars, sharp pointy daggers and tattoos of mythological beasts. Body-modification Pagans often have body piercing jewelry set with sacred stones, and elaborate tattoos illustrating totem animals and energy chakras. Techno Pagans use the drug Ecstasy and electronic trance music to attain divine union. Renaissance Faire Pagans dress with lots of theatrical frills and accessories, and love creative role play. And Radical Sex Pagans wear magical fetishes and amulets, ornamental S/M gear, phallic jewelry and faerie wings. The bottom line is: *it's all sacred!* ♦♦♦

Charles Gatewood Photo Gallery

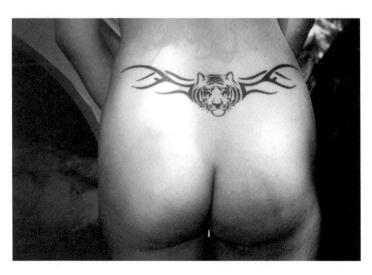

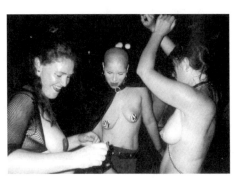

Dossie Easton

Since the early Sixties, Dossie Easton has participated in the psychedelic, hippie, and SM/lesbian undergrounds. Now she is a licensed therapist working with queer or sexual minority community members. She is the co-author, with Catherine A. Liszt, of the polyamory primer, *The Ethical Slut: A Guide to Infinite Sexual Possibilities.* Their other books are *The Topping Book: Getting Good at Being Bad; The Bottoming Book: How to Get Terrible Things Done to You by Wonderful People;* and *When Someone You Love Is Kinky,* all on Greenery Press, *www.greenerypress.com.* Interview by John Sulak.

"We want to set you free to invent the society you want to live in."

"One of the most valuable things we can learn from open sexual lifestyles is that our programming is changeable. Starting by questioning all the ways we have been told our sexuality ought to be, we can begin to edit and rewrite our old tapes."

♦ **RE/SEARCH: When did you become interested in Paganism?**

♦ DOSSIE EASTON: I became interested in Goddess worship and the Tarot in 1962 when I was 18 and living in Greenwich Village. I fell in among people whose whole focus was rediscovering the world's religions trying to *practice* them, not just do anthropological research. There was a tremendous feeling that there was this ancient wisdom from thousands of years ago just waiting to be rediscovered.

Previous to this, I was at Bryn Mawr, a small exclusive women's college on the East Coast. During Christmas break I met Timothy Leary and Dick Alpert (who later became Baba Ram Dass), as well as 26-year-old Robert Thurman, the first Westerner to be ordained by the Dalai Lama. He has written books about Tibetan Buddhism and has done translations for the Dalai Lama. After meeting these people who were doing wonderful things, I dropped out of Bryn Mawr and moved to Greenwich Village. This was just before Leary and Alpert got fired from their teaching positions at Harvard.

I'd already been introduced to marijuana. At that time everybody was reading Aldous Huxley's *The Doors of Perception,* and the concept of developing one's perception was on everyone's mind. I had grown up very non-expressive, pretending to be completely rational, and it was a wake-up call to smoke some pot and hear music and taste food in an intense way. Meeting Leary, Alpert and Thurman gave me a rationale and a *format* for something that was already happening inside me. So I went to New York, moved into the East Village, and set out to fulfill my goals of being both a psychedelic revolutionary and a slut!

♦ **R/S: Not many people were doing that in 1962—**

♦ DE: No, but I have an enormous drive to go after the truth, even at tremendous cost. I lived most of the first 25 years of my adult life in poverty because of this. It's only recently that I've become a professional and migrated to the middle class.

♦ **R/S: Were you influenced by the Beats?**

♦ DE: I had a boyfriend in Boston who was a beatnik, and I certainly identified as such when I first arrived in Greenwich Village. The word "beatnik" went out of fashion while I was there—I suppose I was a late, or baby, beatnik. There were people like Richie Havens performing in clubs on McDougall Street as part of a post-beatnik folk music culture. While we screamed about the hypocrisy of the mainstream culture, everybody worried about prostituting their art.

I met warlocks and people who were into science fiction, sword and sorcery, Goddess worship and the Tarot. That's when I learned about the Order of The Golden Dawn, Aleister Crowley, and Tibetan Buddhism. There was a Lama named Wen Wal who had established a Lamasery in Freewood Acres, New Jersey to keep Tibetan culture alive.

I also met Tom Waters, who later wrote about mentalism and stage mentalism: how it's done, what does it mean, how much is truly due to intuition, and how much is charlatanism. His girlfriend was about 4'10"—tiny, but very *pneumatic.* She always wore high heels and had big hair because she didn't like being short. Once they were doing some kind of bizarre ritual involving burning a black rose, with their living room draped in black. He was wearing black velvet robes, while she wasn't wearing much of anything. Some Jehovah's Witnesses knocked on the door. Tom surprised them by coming out in his robe and saying, "Oh, do come in!" They took one look at the room and went running down the stairs!

I started maintaining an altar. I happened across a Bible with the words of Christ written in red, and if you only look at what Christ was reputed to have said, it ain't bad! A lot of people think Christ was a Gnostic, and Gnostics have a sympathetic resonance with Pagan traditions. I consider myself a Gnostic as well.

I studied a lot of medieval sources, and fancied myself a psychedelic revolutionary searching for examples of mysticism:

St. John of the Cross, Saint Teresa of Avila who went into ecstatic trances and talked about the exquisite agony of being pierced by her Lord—real SM! I discovered that Thomas Aquinas, in his later years, wrote visionary essays and recanted all of his more logical writing, but the Catholic Church obscured this. Yes, the great logician of the Roman Catholic Church actually became a mystic.

I searched for mysticism everywhere: in Eastern religions, Hinduism, Buddhism. When I was 19 I was walking home from Greenwich Village and encountered Santería. I had been talking to a young man and suddenly he tried to forcibly drag me six blocks away to his apartment. I was yelling and hollering and a bunch of teenage kids, whose families were obviously from Puerto Rico, came running up to see what all the excitement was about. This young man panicked and ran away.

These kids couldn't have been more kind to me. They took me into their home and one of their grandmothers made me a cup of tea. She had a typical Santería altar in her house, although at the time I didn't know what it was. There was a Virgin Mary, a couple of Saints, a crucifix, a couple of carved African heads from Benin, and on top of it all was a green plastic Buddha with a red crystal in the center of his forehead. This is called a *syncretic altar*. Santería is a syncretic religion; you tell members that there is a new god or a new Saint and they go, "Oh great!," tuck it into the pantheon, and everything's just fine! They just keep incorporating everything. They don't think they're in competition with other religions.

It turned out that this family was connected to another family that ran a botanica. This was my first contact with an organized Pagan religion.

In California in 1967 a man named Ayin was teaching that "Paganism is a European oral tradition whose rituals we, as contemporary Pagans, can reinvent to serve our needs in the contemporary world. Let's not try to reproduce something from 5,000 years ago, let's learn as much as we can from the past and create new traditions for our time.

These folk were not into hierarchical structures. People took turns being High Priest or High Priestess—the person who organized the sabbat or celebration or new moon or whatever ritual was next. Subsequently, my own ritual practices have been very idiosyncratic.

I've been interested in Santería since the early Seventies; back then it was quite closed to Westerners and wisely so, I'm sure. Recently I've been researching queer mythology from the world's religions. Twenty years ago we began putting women back into mythology, and now we're looking for our queer ancestors. Did you know that Joan of Arc recanted her recantation? By the size of her armor, she was a big old butch woman who was larger than most of the men of her time. Transgender people claim her as a female-to-male ancestor. Of course, whenever there's a movie about her they cast somebody tiny and pixie-looking.

♦ *R/S: So you left New York and went to San Francisco—*

Dossie corseted. Photo: Fakir Musafar

♦ DE: —with flowers in my hair, as part of the great migration of 1967. There was a wonderful interview in *Life* magazine with a picture of a hippie girl in 1967—a flower child. And she's saying, "We believe that it's okay to have sex with somebody you love. And we believe that you ought to love everybody." [!]

I stayed in a huge two-story flat that had been rented by members of the Vietnam Veterans Against the War (VVAW). I connected with some people from the old League for Spiritual Discovery (L.S.D). On my first day in San Francisco, I went to Golden Gate Park and somebody gave me a vitamin C tablet with a blue dot of LSD on it. I went into the aquarium and was staring at the individual scales on a fish while some complete stranger next to me did the same thing. It was like, "Wow!" [laughs]

Everyone I knew was having a wonderful time. We got our clothes from the Free Store and gave clothes back to the Free Store, yet we were clothed more brilliantly than all the lilies of the field. I read that 1967 was the wealthiest year this country has ever known. We weren't aware how much of this wealth was dependent on the waste of munitions in Vietnam. A bomb is a perfect disposable item—you can only use it once and then you need another one (like a cigarette). You drop some bombs and then you have to drop some more bombs—the waste economy in action.

In 1968 I decided to have a baby. Joe, the person with whom I was having the baby, began having psychotic episodes and then became violent. I was six months pregnant when he threatened to murder me. I was forced to move and hide. Joe tried to burn down a house he thought I was staying in, but fortunately somebody had gotten me and the baby out of there before he arrived.

Then I attended a Ken Kesey Be-In at Big Sur—and Joe was there. He came after me with a knife, and a friend shoved me into a car while the owner stood there saying, "I don't want to get involved!" All these bikers came up and everyone formed a big circle. There were reporters taking pictures while I was locked in this car, completely hysterical. Joe was waving his knife and Kesey came up and calmly sat on the trunk, asking: "What's going on?"

Joe pointed at me and said, "My woman!"

Kesey said, "Well, you know, we don't connect to our women with knives. We save that for the lambs"—the Pranksters were roasting lambs in barbecue pits nearby. My ex started talking about Easter sacrificial lambs, and Kesey said, "*Oh . . . kay*" and talked the guy whose car it was into driving me out of there.

In retrospect, my daughter's father liberated me, in his own unfortunate way, because I got what I wanted and needed: a baby and no husband. The baby was what grounded me. I needed that grounding, and raising her was a wonderful experience. She's thirty now, and we're very close. If I had selected a man who had been less obviously oppressive and brutish, I might not have gotten the life I had. Raising a child was a wonderful

education for me.

Left to right: as infant with mom; age 1; age 5; age 17

I started getting queerer and queerer, and in 1974 began exploring SM. I was on the first board of directors of the Society of Janus, a seminal SM support group in San Francisco. The SM scene was very idealistic in a lot of ways, with a lot of focus on *communication* as being essential to SM. Both George Carlin and Lenny Bruce said that **if you can't talk about something, you can't think about it.** And if you can't think about it, you're helpless.

Fast forwarding: I moved to Santa Cruz for awhile, and now I live in West Marin. My daughter grew up. I went to graduate school and became a licensed therapist. I got involved with Black Leather Wings, the leather arm of the Radical Faerie group. That name comes from the grandfather of gay liberation in the Fifties, Harry Hay: "We must not forget our brothers with black leather wings"—meaning the SM people.

Today Pagan SM has expanded its practices, borrowing from Native American, Hindu and other cultures. We use body stress and piercing in a spiritual journey. I do ball dances, in which balls the size and weight of lemons are sewn to the skin. This is trance dancing as a visionary experience, and it really works. My most extreme experience involved lying under a frame and being pierced with sixty spears while people were drumming on the frame. It was incredible, felt wonderful, and inspired a vision quest in which I met an important ancestor guide, a gay man who had fought in Vietnam and died of AIDS.

My groups have done big SM rituals at large Pagan gatherings like Pantheacon, the Ancient Ways Festival and Women's Building events. I also write and act as priestess at large-scale performance rituals.

♦ *R/S: What makes Pagan SM different from conventional SM?*

♦ DE: There's more conscious ritual context. Usually when I call the four corners (North, South, East, West), I write something new for each ritual to engage the elements in a specific way. I make prayers to each of the directions, for whatever it is that I'm looking for. For example, for a Samhain ritual called "AIDS as a Labyrinth," which was presented at Ashkenaz in Berkeley a few years ago, I wrote invocations based on Elizabeth Kubler-Ross's 5 stages: anger, depression, denial, bargaining and acceptance. As we invoked the elements we traveled through the emotional processes of grief and death. This was one of the most powerful pieces of public ritual work I've ever done.

In SM there are Pagans, Buddhists, Santería practitioners, ecstatic Christians, even people who go to gospel churches—you can ignore the stuff about sex and sin and focus on your "direct perception" experience. Formerly, all of us SM folk did our spiritual practices in private. Gradually, some of us found each other and gathered together to do rituals like *sabbats* and new moons. Because I live in the country and hike in the hills, I make fetishes out of things I find—bones and feathers and shells. I do a lot of Nature magic.

W.B. Yeats said something wonderful in "Anima Mundi": that a person's life was like walking on the beach, and the experiences we have in our life are like what the tides bring to us. Symbols, he said, are like mirages, refractions in the air that allow us to experience something from a distant part of the ocean. I see ritual as walking a symbol path to access intuition, psychic perception, spiritual awareness, ecstatic states, and the knowledge that comes with them. Ecstatic states bring not only experiences of ecstasy but—when I come down from them—lessons to be learned. After the peak experience must come the *zazen:* the wisdom has to be incorporated into daily life. It's not enough to know something, you have to live it.

There is the Jungian notion of "Shadow" as that dark area that contains everything we banish from our awareness. And in the unconscious, which is kind of *underneath* the Shadow, there are archetypes—mother and father figures, pantheons of gods, and SM characters like Nurse Nasty! What we are doing in SM is reclaiming parts of ourselves that we have forbidden to our awareness, for whatever reasons. We're reclaiming our precious inner victim, our precious inner bully, or emotions like anger or fear or grief that we have forbidden ourselves to feel. By enacting our drama with another person, we bring a part of ourself out into open consciousness. This is a *profoundly* mind-opening experience that's perhaps a gateway to accessing buried archetypes, and beyond that, spiritual consciousness.

Once I went with a former lover to a Christian college bookstore. She was searching for *God, the Rod, and Your Child's Bod,* a horrible fundamentalist book about beating your children as a religious exercise. She was really turned on by the image of Little Susy on the footstool. I thought the employees were going to tar and feather us any minute, so I said, "This is really scary—we have to get out of here. Will you stop chortling over the books?!" When we got home she said, "Look, I know my fantasies have dirty roots." That stopped me in my tracks, and I realized, "How else can you grow flowers?"

♦ *R/S: Self-discovery is what Paganism and SM are about.*

♦ DE: You know, in many ways I'm not against Christ but against what people have *made* of Christianity. The notions of sin, damnation and Eternal Judgment have resulted in self-loathing and self-hatred, which facilitate sexual suppression. Wilhelm Reich, when he was lecturing to young Communists in Germany in 1936, said that without the suppression of sexuality and the imposition of anti-sexual morality, you cannot have an authoritarian government. He thought that people with a healthy grasp of their sexuality would not obey orders to operate death camps. It's funny that the term "free thinker" used to be synonymous with "screwing around." To my mind there's nothing like open sex and free thinking.

The majority of people have never seen anyone else have sex or make love. To see other people having sex is something we are deprived of. **It is an amazing experience to de-privatize sex.** It's very radical. It's a wonderful way to learn how to get beyond the shame, self-loathing and insecurities we've been taught in a sex-negative culture. Because when you see somebody whose body type is wrong (the way you imagine yours is, right?) being ecstatically turned on, having an orgasm, waving their legs in the air in some ridiculous position, that happy person is radiant—perfectly gorgeous.

An early part of my sex education involved seeing films of two women masturbating. Neither of them were people who would be cover girls on magazines, yet they were totally beautiful. You could see them transforming themselves as they got turned on. I was very moved and impressed by that.

If you explore public sex, you need to be really accepting of yourself—some people discover unexpected feelings and personal problems surfacing. Be easy with your expectations: go into that orgy room expecting to stay maybe an hour, and kind of look around. When you get comfortable in the space, you can explore further. De-privatizing sex makes a lot of the shame that people grew up with impossible—it dissolves it. When you're in that sexual environment where many people are having sex, you get to share in all the psychic energy and turn-on in the room.

A group sex environment for spiritual opening can be created by chanting, burning incense and building altars, so that all share in the ritual and reinforce each other in opening up spiritual consciousness. We try to create the right kind of environment for people to feel free. And we turn the heat way up, so people will *have* to take their clothes off. This, by the way, is the basic principle of running sex parties: you need to make the rooms too hot!

Sex is the only area where we are expected to know everything without learning from other people. On any other subject, you get to learn from other people who know how to do it—but not sex! So at public sex parties, there is an opportunity for tremendous learning. For some people, sex becomes an art form. In that sense, there is always a search for the next original expression. I don't want to imply that one has to keep getting further and further out in some physical sense—it can be a mistake when people try to do that. But there is a notion of "expansion of art." Monet didn't just paint those water lilies over and over again. His many paintings of that same

Ready for Ball Dance Photo: Steven Brown

patch of garden grew wilder and deeper as he developed his vision.

I like to do public sex where there's an opening ritual where a circle is cast, and sacred space is created that connects people together. This setting creates a tremendous opportunity for expansion and learning. If I see people doing something interesting that I don't know how to do, I can go ask them afterwards.

♦ *R/S: Do you ever enact the "Great Rite" where the High Priest has sex with the High Priestess while people watch?*

♦ DE: No I haven't. I suppose some people have. I had one lover who had a spectacular cock as well as extraordinary endurance, so we tended to produce some spectacular public f--ks—that was fun! But I like to think of public sex as an environment in which everyone is a star and can do something wonderful. Certainly, a part of it involves a challenge: there *is* a performance aspect in that people try a little harder. Which is a good thing if you like occasional marathon sex.

In a ritual sense, some sexual experiences are only possible with a large size group of people. For my 49th birthday, I gave a Black Leather Wings ritual party where I invited everyone to bring their inner children. I especially wanted to create a ritual for the Baby Goddess, because we have very few images of child goddesses in classical mythology—they're almost all of baby boys like Jesus or Krishna. But there are very few little girls, and almost no babies. I wanted to fill in this gap.

So I threw a ritual. People told me it was the scariest party invitation they had ever received. One woman showed with a tiny dress that she wore when she was delivered to her adoptive parents. Another woman played out a scene involving healing from her childhood. With sex, you can connect very powerfully to deep spaces inside yourself. If you want to do a healing ritual to reach a profoundly conflicted psychological space within yourself, so you can open the wounds and heal them, that's one of the purposes of SM and ritualized sex. You can access that conflict. It's difficult and frightening stuff, but it's there. And once we get there, we have access to that part of ourselves that got buried because it was too scary. Since we write the script, control the outcome, we can nurture that wounded part. We can love that part of ourselves, we can make that part safe. ♦♦♦

LaSara FireFox

L aSara FireFox has been a Pagan all her life. She grew up "living on the land," and as an infant attended gatherings of the Church of All Worlds. Her daughter is now a third-generation Pagan. Here she speaks frankly about her upbringing by radical feminist parents, how her Pagan path led her to the sex industry, and her activities today as a parent, poet, dancer and artist. LaSara writes for *Hip Mama* magazine and gives workshops as well as individual counseling. She is very active on the Internet, frequently sending out news and publicizing Pagan events. Interview by John Sulak.

♦ **RE/SEARCH: You're a second-generation Pagan—what are your earliest memories of Paganism?**
♦ LASARA FIREFOX: The term that I use for my early spiritual reality is "Organic Paganism." I grew up in a "Back to the Land" family at a place called Greenfield Ranch in Mendocino County, California. While both of my parents had a superstitious orientation, my mom had an intense relationship with the land and soil.

A lot of my early patterning around spirituality was a direct experience of living on the land. We were more at the mercy of the elements than most people are used to in this day and age. For example, we had to drive down a dirt road and through a river to get to town and back—there was no bridge. When we were coming home there were times when the river was too high, and the car or truck would stall in the river. We'd have to wade to the other side, run up the hill, and get a neighbor who had a winch to tow the vehicle out of the river.

We lived off the land as much as possible. We had a huge garden, milked our goats, and would spend the summers sleeping outside under the stars. As you go through these experiences, you gain a real context for life and death and the cycles that occur. With gardening, for example, you go through the cycle of planting, watching the plants grow, and then harvesting what you grew—which is amazing to a kid. You actually sustain yourself off the soil.

You also watch things die. We ate our animals, which forces you to accept the responsibility of taking another life. Going to Safeway and buying hamburger is devoid of any connection with the being that gave up its spirit so you could survive. When you raise animals from the time they're born, and then slaughter them, you're completely aware of what you're doing. Those experiences are something that a lot of people, especially in [modern] America, miss. They don't have a real context for what it means to live with the earth.

My earliest memories of Neo-Paganism probably date from when I was four years old, when some City Pagans moved up to Greenfield Ranch. I remember going for a hike to the top of a hill on a full moon, and seeing a bonfire across the valley. There were people dancing around it in a circle. It was miles across the valley, but we had a clear view.

Morning Glory and Oberon Zell (now Ravenheart) would come up to our house and hang out. In those days, if you went somewhere you would hike there, and that would take four hours. You'd hang out, stay the night, and then hike back the next day. It was a different reality. When people ask me where I'm from, I say, "A third world country called Greenfield Ranch."

I was home-schooled and I credit a lot to that. Oberon sometimes taught me history. He has a very different take on history than most people do. He would talk about what might have happened if the wind were blowing in a different direction during a certain battle. He taught me about the possibility of reality being completely different than we know it. I was educated along the lines of the current "Unschooling" movement—in child-led education in which the children are encouraged to pursue their own interests.

Mythology and cosmology were a constant part of my education. I was introduced to Greek gods and goddesses as well as Moses. We celebrated every holiday there was to celebrate, including both Christmas and Hanukkah. For Easter, we might go to the Passion Play or do a Pagan ritual. All this was very diverse. I'm Neo-Pagan for lack of a better term, but I usually describe myself as an "eclectic spiritualist" to those who ask.

We started going to Church of All Worlds events when I was a preteen. I remember the time my parents did the "Invocation of the West" by singing Forties songs. [laughs] One of them was: "By the sea/ By the sea/ By the beautiful sea/ You and me/ You and me/ Oh how happy we'll be."

My parents separated when I was 14. We had been involved with the Church of All Worlds, but we did not have a lot of time to spare away from our land. However, I remember cultivating my own interests in a sort of Celtic-oriented Paganism. I did spells and harvested mistletoe. I don't even know where I got the information, but I was very much into ritual from an early age.

Personal ritual is very important. There's only so much that group ritual can do for you—it's great, but the two serve different purposes. The magic that you do for yourself on a daily basis improves your life as you reach for enlightenment or whatever your goals are.

Small group ritual or magic-working gives a sense of continuity, and family and outside reality checks. The group or coven consists of the 2, 5, or 13 people that you hang out with. At times I find it really valuable to have people familiar enough with my personal processes and language, that can understand what I say. If I'm trying to B/S myself, they can help me through whatever is going on. Small group ritual is for going through the *deep s---*, the real process, whatever it is we have to go through to get to the next level of our spiritual development. That's where that can happen most easily.

Large group ritual can also have a transformative effect, but that's unusual unless the ritual is amazingly well-scripted. To me, large group ritual is much more about a sense of excitement, or something different, or being with people you don't know everything about. It's like a spiritual watering hole. At a large public group ritual you get the chance to be with a lot of people who think similarly to the way you do, and that can produce a sense of renewal. Large group ritual is about community-building and belonging to a *culture*.

Greenfield Ranch, Mendocino County, CA

♦ *R/S: Can you discuss Pagan sexuality—*

♦ LSF: That's an interesting and complicated topic. I'm a cerebrally-oriented person, but there is a side of me that is physically-oriented. I've always been fairly sexually aware. I remember starting to flirt with people when I was pretty young, probably from the time I was 11. I was aware of my power in that arena, and I think a lot of girls are—despite what adults think. As far as my Pagan sexuality goes, that's where the complication comes in, in that I was part of the Church of All Worlds before I hit puberty. When I hit puberty and flirted with people, that was okay. However, the closer I got to my 18th birthday, the more comments were made [by church members] like, "Oh, you're going to be 18 soon. I bet there's going to be a line a mile long," implying that people were expecting to have sex with me as soon as I reached that age. But I had started having sex when I was 16, and felt, "If I had wanted to have sex with any of you people, I would have done it by now."

At this point, the Pagan community has attained a multi-generational lineage. The question of taboo comes up: What are our taboos? What purpose do they serve, if any? Taboos are important; they do serve a purpose. Most of us know what those taboos are or should be.

If you know a girl from the time she's three and you're two decades older than her, just because she turns 18 doesn't mean it's open season. For me, the line between that and incest is not clear; it feels too close to home for me. Having to feel that you need to insulate yourself sexually while you're making the transition from teenager to adulthood is not right—I don't think we should have to feel that way. I think that there can be a more clear-cut line as to what constitutes an intergenerational relationship. I'm not saying that intergenerational relationships are, by definition, bad; I think that consent laws are off-base. In New Mexico the age of consent is 14, and I think that's fine. People know who they want to sleep with by the time they're 14. But if they don't, they need to take some time to figure it out.

I do think that older people, especially if there is any kind of familial overtone to the relationship, have a responsibility not to provoke a situation. If a young person comes up to someone and says, "I want to have a relationship with you," or "I want to sleep with you," or "I want to be initiated by you," or whatever, and they're really clear about what their desires are, and you talk it through and you get to an agreement, I think that's okay. But what's problematic is the assumption that because we're sexual people in a sexual culture, anything goes.

♦ *R/S: You're talking about the Pagan subculture—*

♦ LSF: Yes. In this subculture, the previous generation of Pagans (who are hitting "elder" status at this point) had an attitude towards sexuality that's really a holdover from the Sixties. In a sense, the Pagan subculture has gone through its own adolescence and suddenly has become multi-generational. There's a lot of confusion. Many younger women have felt there exists a certain aspect of sexual "predation," and I use the term loosely. I don't mean people who are stalking or raping people in the woods, I'm talking about just a pervasive feeling of being under sexual scrutiny. A lot of my female friends in the Pagan movement feel that at certain gatherings the sexual climate is . . . questionable. They think, "I'm coming here to hang out with people, not necessarily to hook up," yet sometimes a gathering can start to feel like a singles bar. A lot of people are there just to get happy, and there's nothing wrong with that . . . but not everyone is on that wavelength. Some of us are monogamous, married, have kids and don't want it any other way.

♦ *R/S: Is chauvinism a problem in the Pagan world?*

♦ LSF: Yes. We're a product of our environment, and we happen to live in a patriarchal culture. The fact of the matter is: you can't just exorcise that. You can't say, "I'm a Pagan, therefore I no longer have any of the issues that my culture of origin has with women and men in relationships." That's bulls---. We all have situations that set us off, and we start acting like our dads or moms, or our teachers in high school. We emulate our mentors, even after they're no longer our mentors because we've decided they're f---ed up . . . they are *still* integrated into our psyches.

I also think we have a lot of *shadow patriarchy* and subverted or underhanded misogyny in Paganism. Those things

Left: 2000 Aurora O'Greenfield, Bobby Cochran, LaSara, Solome O'Greenfield
Right: 1971 little LaSara and mom, Marilyn Motherbear Scott

I had my own guilt issues around sex, but I don't know where those feelings came from. My dad was kind of a predator; he came from a dysfunctional family. I was never sexually abused by him in a physical way, but I think there was a sexual overtone to him watching me reach puberty, that actually made me want to leave home. This happened to my older sister too, and she ended up leaving home at 16. When I was 14 I had this plan all hatched to leave, but my dad left first so I didn't have to. I was glad because I really didn't want to leave my mom with him; I felt protective of her and the rest of the kids. I didn't want to think that they were still having to deal with a raging alcoholic while I had gotten away.

Any residual anger I might have had around that situation probably tainted my experience of turning 18 and having a lot of older men lusting after me. I think my healing has come by being able to accept myself as a sexual being, and living in the arena of the sex industry. That has had a really good normalizing affect on me with regards to sexuality.

♦ *R/S: You grew up amidst adults who were polyamorous?*
♦ LSF: I think growing up around people who had more of an open reality about relationships was really positive. I knew there were more options than monogamy and the "Til death do us part" concept. The post-divorce generation has a real boon in that we know that many relationships aren't stable. Therefore, I think my generation might work harder at maintaining the relationships and the families that we do create. We know that nothing's going to work out by itself—you have to *work* for it. The key is realizing that we always have the freedom to say, "I don't want to be in this relationship." This didn't exist before people started getting divorced.

♦ *R/S: When did you start to regard sex as sacred?*
♦ LSF: I think there are a lot of different levels to the sacredness of sexuality. I don't think that all sex is sacred. Sacred sex is a conscious decision. One of the reasons sex is sacred is because of the procreational ability that sex has. I think that growing a child in your body is the closest to being God that humans get. Creating a life from your own flesh is amazing. It's an astonishing power that is the root of the sacredness of sexuality.

Another aspect of the sacredness of sex is summed up in this passage from Aleister Crowley's *The Book of the Law:* "I am divided for love's sake, for the chance of union." Conscious sex is an opportunity to experience union with "the other," and with the universe as a whole. That can be an intensely enlightening and renewing achievement.

Our culture will always be at a loss until we can somehow redeem sexuality. If we could do that, we would have far fewer problems with objectification and inappropriate sexual conduct. Sex is constantly used to alienate people, to put people down, and to make people feel inferior. John Whiteside Parsons, in *Freedom is a Two-Edged Sword*, observed that sex is both pedestal-ized and denigrated at the same time in our culture. I think that's totally accurate.

On the one hand, sex is like the Holy Grail and you see it everywhere; in an urban environment you can't walk out the door without seeing sex in advertisements. Yet the sexuality depicted in advertising is almost non-human: all the models are

exist—they don't just disappear. Again, we're still under the influence of the dominant culture.

Then there's the "newbie" syndrome. When somebody is new to the community, often they're like, "Ohmigod—you're all so great and I love you all!" Then, when you come out on the other side, you think, "What just happened to me?" A lot of people end up having issues around that where they feel, "Well, I was really wide open, and now I feel taken advantage of." I had a boyfriend who was raised in a Catholic family, and when he came into the Pagan community he went, "Ohmigod—you guys don't have any rules!" But there *are* rules; they're just different rules. You can't come into a situation not recognizing the rules and assume there aren't any. You have to come into a situation and say, "What are the rules here? What are appropriate guideposts? What kind of agreements have you come to as a subculture to keep yourselves safe and sane?"

♦ *R/S: What advice would you give to Pagan "newbies"?*
♦ LSF: You have to be careful with people that come in and are wide-eyed, taking it all in, and feeling like "they're finally home," which often happens when people get into a more free situation than they've been in before. Those kinds of transitions need to be handled with sensitivity.

First of all, your own spiritual development starts with *you.* It doesn't start with other people's ideas, but with your own soul and journey. That means paying attention to your heart, gut and head. Interacting with large groups can be a great way to experience the joy of being in that awareness. Basically, be *safe, sane, and consensual.*

♦ *R/S: Humans often grow up feeling shame about their bodies—*
♦ LSF: Growing up as a child in a hippie community, I grew up around a lot of nakedness, which is totally different than sexuality. If you grow up where it's normal to be naked, then "naked" doesn't have the connotation that our culture puts on it. Naked doesn't have anything to do with sexuality unless you make it. For me, it doesn't.

♦ *R/S: Did you ever have any guilt feelings about sex?*
♦ LSF: I remember seeing animals mate. I remember sex being part of normal reality. It was a non-issue. "The Talk" never happened. My mom was a Seventies-oriented radical feminist. Our cultural lies about sex—like, men want sex more than women. I've never met a man who wanted sex more than me!

illusions of a perfection that doesn't exist. They're air-brushed, skinny supermodels that represent a tiny percentage of the actual living, breathing population, and they have an android-like appearance! Those men and women are far from what we actually look like when we get out of bed in the morning. Our sexual awareness in America as a culture is so damaged—I get to see plenty of that working in the sex industry. At the same time, if you have a lot of sex—especially if you're a woman—you're a loose cannon . . . dangerous and unacceptable.

♦ *R/S: How is Paganism offering an alternative to this?*

♦ LSF: I have worked in the sex industry on and off for five years, in different categories of service jobs. Currently I model for adult-oriented and fine art photographers. I'm 5'3", and weigh anywhere from 140 to the 200 pounds I reached when I was pregnant. I was still modeling until a week before my daughter was born. Because of the whole Madonna-whore complex, you're either the Virgin Mother or you're the Whore of Babylon. So for me to be able to be a *mother-whore* was revolutionary!

When I became pregnant with my first daughter I was shocked at how drastically my interactions with men changed—just because I was pregnant. Previously I had never had a problem getting attention from men. Then, when I got pregnant and it started showing, it became extremely rare that any flirtation happened between me and a casual acquaintance, or just a guy on the street—unless it was totally me who was provoking the situation. It became more like, "Oh, can I get the door for you?" or "Would you like help carrying your groceries to the car?" Whenever I initiated a flirtation, guys were like, "Ohmigod, I can't believe this woman is flirting with me!"

1990 hitchhiking on the Autobahn, age 19

there's much more reverence for pregnant women, and that can include sexual attention.

♦ *R/S: Tell us about your family life now—*

♦ LSF: I'm a fast-living, wild woman. Having kids has been a real developmental process for me, because kids are so incredibly demanding. To raise them the way that I think is right takes an intense amount of energy, intention, and communication—with a certain amount of surrender to the process. The hardest thing about having kids is slowing down enough to be with infants. Their reality is so immediate; it's not like you can say, "Just a minute, I'll be there soon," and they will understand. I have two children. There are a lot of concerns around having more kids these days—**one American kid uses more resources than fifteen Third World kids!** It's crazy.

My children are growing up as third-generation Pagans, and it's amazing and scary—what if there were another witch hunt in this country! Just the fact that I'm a sex worker and a parent makes me suspect—plus, I'm a priestess in the Church of All Worlds. I may sound paranoid, but every day kids get taken away from parents for ridiculous reasons.

I feel that we need to be more open with our children about sex, about their bodies, about human interactions, and tell them that "happily ever after" is the biggest lie we were ever told. Children need to get more honesty. I'm very open with my kids about what I do for work, yet what happens if you send a five-year-old to school and somebody asks, "What do your parents do?" If the kid says, "Oh, my mom is a naked model," how is the school system going to react to *that?* Or, "My mom is a Pagan."

When your personal values and beliefs are diametrically opposed to the prevailing cultural values and beliefs, you just have to be careful.

My three-year-old daughter has a grasp on different deities, as much as can be absorbed by a small child. She can tell if a ritual is for Ganesh or Ra Hoor Khuit. She knows all sorts of words most people who are forty and straight don't know yet. I feel strongly that the way I'm raising my children is good, and hopefully it will have a positive long-term effect, even on a larger scale. By raising your children in an ethical, earth-based spirituality, you're helping to decide what the next generation of the world is going to be like. My hope is that we can raise our children in such a manner that the issues we're dealing with won't be issues in the next generation. ♦♦♦

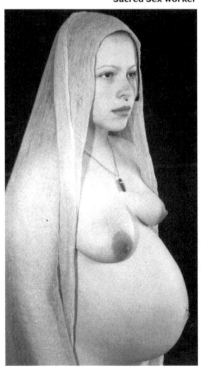

Sacred Sex worker

When I started modeling as a pregnant woman, I felt like I was breaking all the cultural rules. It was fun as well as an ego boost to be able to keep my sexual persona while being pregnant.

To demand that a woman drop her sexual persona when she becomes pregnant is almost cruel. It's like, "You're pregnant; you are no longer allowed to be a sexual being." Even after you have kids, a certain amount of that attitude lingers. This is finally becoming a vocal issue; women are saying, "Yes, I am a mother and I am still a sexual being." In the Pagan community

Anne Hill

Anne Hill is the co-author, with Starhawk and Diane Baker, of *Circle Round: Raising Children in the Goddess Tradition.* The book contains information on Pagan parenting including specific rituals that can be done for each of the Pagan holidays, with kids in attendance. Anne Hill also runs a Pagan music mail order business at *www.Serpentinemusic.com,* or call (707) 823-7425. Her book's website is *www.CircleRound.com.* Interview by John Sulak; follow-up interview by V. Vale.

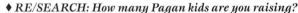

♦ *RE/SEARCH: How many Pagan kids are you raising?*

♦ ANNE HILL: Five—my own three children plus my niece and nephew. Their ages are 18, 17, 16, 14 and 8.

♦ *R/S: What's different about "Pagan" child-raising?*

♦ AH: We tend to look a lot more at *passages.* We look at things that happen to our children in terms of, "Would having some sort of ritual observance of this help them? Would it support their growth? Would it aid them in getting to the next place where they want to go in their life?" Specifically, in terms of "rites of passage," I think we really work to make sacred all the changes kids experience. Providing rituals is a great way to support children in their passage through adolescence. Some people feel the need to do blessing rituals for infants, too.

♦ *R/S: How do children respond to rituals?*

♦ AH: In my experience, their response has been overwhelmingly positive. At first some kids are reluctant because of all the attention they're getting; they might be a little nervous or embarrassed. Afterwards, I usually ask, "Well, what did you think about it? How did that help you?" Every single one has appeared grateful for that attention and recognition, so I'm pretty gung-ho about rite-of-passage rituals!

♦ *R/S: There are rituals for different ages—*

♦ AH: For our kids, we've done two rite-of-passage rituals. None of them have left home yet, so when they leave we may feel the need to do something.

The age of six marks a significant point: when a child leaves babyhood, and moves on. Children become concerned not just with their place in the family but also their place in the world. They begin dealing with mythologies, bigger thoughts. So at that point we've given all of our kids a ritual to observe this marker and to support them: "Yeah—you are getting big! Now you have all this knowledge; you are stepping into the realm of independence!" We celebrate that.

According to Jean Piaget [author of numerous child development books], the age of six to seven corresponds to the move from concrete to abstract thought. A friend of mine from Senegal said that in his tribe, people always had a ritual for children at about age six, welcoming them as "children of the *people*"—not so much as children of their parents, because they're getting socialized at that time.

They start making plans; what they do is not so random.

They really are thinking things abstractly. It's kind of thrilling to watch.

♦ *R/S: In your book, Circle Round, you give "sample" rituals, although you encourage parents and children to use their own imaginations—*

♦ AH: There has to be a balance point there. We also include explanations of various elements of rituals—it's very much a cut-and-paste, make-your-own, use this-if-it-suits-you type of thing. You can use the elements you feel the most affinity for.

With each child this rite-of-passage takes different forms, depending on the temperament of the kid. This is part of our "Pagan Pragmatism." [laughs] For my youngest daughter we decided to combine her ritual with our annual May Day party for which all of our friends and family gather each year. We knew that she would be carried along by the momentum of preparing for the May Day party, and it would make her ritual all that more special for her.

For my son, we designed a ritual that included a friend he'd known since birth. He wanted this connection with his really old friend. We've really tried to keep in mind what a child's needs are at the moment, avoiding "one size fits all" rituals.

♦ *R/S: Adolescence can bring troubling changes in children's lives. How do you deal with that?*

♦ AH: A ritual can be important, but for adolescents what is almost more important is how you interact with them *afterwards.* Can they really sense a change? Or, are they going to be left feeling, "Gee, they had this great ritual and party to make themselves feel better, but they're still treating me like a kid." This can be very tricky. You have to give kids challenges, because that's what adolescence is all about. Kids need to know they can overcome great odds and possible dangers.

When my nephew turned fifteen, we had a "coming-of-age ritual" for him that lasted all summer. He had come from a Muslim family, so rather than just stage a Pagan ritual, we needed to tailor something to meet his needs. First, he went on a three-week Outward Bound expedition where he busted his butt in the mountains, took on a variety of challenges, and made it through. Then he went to the desert and survived for a few days with my partner.

Finally, at the end, we had a ritual for him. But we didn't tell him beforehand; we wanted the element of surprise. My partner said, "Come on down to the barn with me; we're going to put a blindfold on you." And this really worked, because it was high drama.He didn't have time to think, "Oh gawd, they're having a ritual for me—I think I'll go downtown and elude them." He got taken by surprise and it turned out to be beautiful.

There are rite-of-passage rituals in many different cultures. Bar Mitzvahs, for example, recognize that a young man is entering manhood, taking responsibility for his community as well as for himself. He is honored by reading the Torah.

Personally, I feel really fortunate that we're raising our kids close to the Bay Area—as opposed to the backwoods of Wisconsin or Nebraska. For years, our kids have gotten connected to other really nice kids through seasonal rituals and public gatherings. We're friends with the parents and we all hang out together, so there's a genuine sense of community. That helps.

Our kids also have a lot of open-minded non-Pagan friends—that's part of the beauty of living in the Bay Area. They haven't encountered many situations where people openly discriminate against them. At school, one kid who was trying to convert everybody into being a Mormon asked my son, "What religion are you?" My son felt strong in his own beliefs, but didn't want to get into a big argument, so he didn't say, "I'm a Pagan!" That was his choice.

However, we've been carefully ecumenical and have never said that they *had* to be Pagan. Instead we say, "This is what we believe and what we like to do. Here's how we celebrate the circle of life and the wheel of the year. If you want to come along, it should be a lot of fun. But you get to decide."

At one point I was really encouraging our kids to go with their friends to a Jewish temple, or with their grandparents to a Christian church, just so they could "see if there's something there for you." The door is always open for them to do something else if they want. So far none have shown any inclination to be anything other but Pagan, but that may not always be the case.

♦ *R/S: What's an example of a ritual for 12-year-olds?*

♦ AH: We just had a ritual for my daughter, who turned 13. For girls, we do rituals when they get their menstrual cycle. For boys, there's a wide range, and we've found, with the boys we've been raising, that 15 has worked quite well. Anyway, for girls, our ritual is partly a "Women Only" thing. The ritual really started when she got her period. Then she gets to decide which women she wants to have with her during this whole "Women's Mysteries" part of the ritual; the other part involves community celebration. We called around and got all the women together and went out to the beach. One part of the ritual is really lovely: the mother and the daughter hold hands and take off running down the beach while the rest of the women remain in a circle, holding the circle there. They run and run and run until the mother can't run anymore, and then, you just gotta stop—you're out of breath. But the daughter still has energy to keep going. So she breaks the grip and runs on down the beach. And there's this moment when your heart is in your throat: it's so beautiful to see this young woman taking off down the beach—it's such a wonderful metaphor for going joyfully into her adulthood.

♦ *R/S: What else is different about Pagan parenting?*

♦ AH: I think the Pagan belief in reincarnation (actually, there are many different Pagan views on reincarnation) has some bearing on how we view our children. In other words, they have

wisdom that comes from places other than our genetic material, if you will. There's an emphasis on looking at where their innate wisdom is—who they are as "soul beings." Or, looking at the child as a whole, "This person is coming into this world; what do they need?" rather than, "We have to make them a cookie-cutter reproduction of ourselves." And that gives a broader perspective when looking at child-raising issues.

Many of us believe in ancestors or spirits, so attending to the guardian spirits of that child is important. And children love altars! I grew up Christian, and that interdiction that says "No graven images!" really messed up our concept of interior decorating! [laughs] Children have that sense of "Let's put the item with the powerful emanation in the middle. And then we'll decorate with feathers, shells, flowers, rocks, leaves . . ."

Like all parents, we try to teach justice. If we have a cake and there are two children, we say to one, "You can cut it up, but the other person gets to choose first." That really does encourage fairness.

♦ *R/S: To introduce theological or deity concepts, do you have to wait until around age twelve?*

♦ AH: I find that toddlers are such animists. You tell them that a rock is alive and they look at that rock and feel that rock, they empathize with that rock. They see that rock as more than just a little stone in the path. It's from those beginnings . . . you can talk about the spirits of the elements and it's very clear to young children what you're talking about. And they may start jumping ahead of you and saying, "You know, I was talking to the wind, and the wind told me . . ." And from there it's just a short jump to talking about deities—which are basically names for elemental powers, in a certain sense.

Every deity is part of the one great consciousness of the universe which we sometimes call "the Goddess." We use the terms "gods" and "goddesses" too, so at times our language can get unwieldy!

♦ *R/S: How do you teach children the difference between myth and reality?*

♦ AH: We deal with questions like this as part of our "age six" ritual. At that age, kids are starting to move beyond the Easter Bunny or Santa Claus—they're thinking, "Some of this isn't real. What do I believe? What do other people believe?" For years I've collected legends and myths of other cultures—there are some great picture books out there. We'll read them together and I'll say, "This is how the Iroquois explain the changing of the seasons," or "This is how the Goddess and the God were portrayed in Babylon or ancient Greece." This gives kids a real

sense of relativity. At that age, kids easily understand that different people can have very different explanations of the same phenomenon, and that all are equally valid.

♦ R/S: What do you do when a pet dies?

♦ AH: A corner of our yard is our pet graveyard, for our cats and the various dead birds we've found. We do a very simple burial ritual in which we say, "The body is going back to the earth, but the spirit is moving on to the spirit world." (Here, I think of the spirit world in terms of a world that is diffused in our world. I think James Hillman talks about "the invisibles"—they're among us. It's not a heavenly realm; it's an invisible realm.)

When our kids' grandmother died a couple of years ago, that was a major event. We scattered her ashes and said, "Her body is going to the earth, but her spirit is still alive." We tell our kids that there is a place called Summerland where your spirit goes back to the Isle of Apples, the Isle of Youth, to the arms of the Goddess—they're all metaphors for the place where your spirit is alive and part of everything. If you decide to come back into the world, you leave that place, enter a new body and start the whole cycle over again. This is pretty standard Celtic mythology.

♦ R/S: Do you actually believe that the spirit of the grandmother is alive?

♦ AH: In the instance of the grandmother, I believe that if our kids call on her, if they have a need to pray or seek guidance, she'll be right there. That's what I meant by "her spirit is still alive." In that invisible realm, we are able to call on those spirits when we need to. Pagans definitely have a different view of spirit, and of life.

♦ R/S: How do you deal with the issue of drugs?

♦ AH: We don't go to certain gatherings because we don't want our kids to be there. But we don't censor what they see or read. They know that some Pagans (and non-Pagans, for that matter) do drugs, and others don't. We say, "We don't do this, but this is why we think other people do." There's recreational drug use and there's ceremonial drug use. We also know people who are involved with the medical marijuana debate.

It all kind of boils down to: I think our kids' strongest influence is us. We keep an open mind about drugs. As kids become teenagers, the drug culture is right there; it's not something they have to go out and seek. [laughs] At the same time, the dangers of addiction are very real, and they are not limited to illegal drugs. Kids are very susceptible to the cultural message that drug use is cool, and it is difficult to counter this. We're very careful about what we model for them. We try to keep dialoging, keep the conversation open, and be as frank and honest as we can. Our main goal is to help them figure out what their own values are.

♦ R/S: How do you explain sex to your kids?

♦ AH: It's all a process of helping them find their own values. Our kids are growing up in a family whose parents (Ross and I) have been together for twenty years in a very stable setting. With that as a base of security, our kids can make their own judgments about people who live differently.

There are a few people in the Pagan community I don't want our kids to be around. Sometimes I might pull my daughter or niece aside and say, "You see that person there—if they give you any problems, let me know." I don't think we should just open the door wide and leave our children vulnerable to whatever experiences come their way—I want them to be prepared! I want them to know who's got a reputation as being a respectful person, and who they should stay away from.

♦ R/S: Is nudity at public rituals a problem?

♦ AH: Not for my kids. We actually think it's good for them to be around nudity, just so they're more comfortable in their own bodies. First of all, as a parent you have to be comfortable in your own body, and actually model that for your children. And getting to that point involves a lot of shadow work and personal work. For example, if I were really uncomfortable soaking in a public hot springs in the nude, but was telling my kid, "Your body is beautiful and you should be proud of it"—that would be a mixed message! I have to practice what I preach.

♦ R/S: What if you bring your children to a ritual and then want to enter a trance state—

♦ AH: When you take your kids to a ritual, no matter what age they are, part of your consciousness needs to always be focused on them. That's just goes with the territory. You can mitigate that by bringing somebody to take care of your kid. But a ritual is delicate and requires attentiveness—with your children present, you're probably not going to have a deep, sustained experience of trance. When I had little kids, I only took them to rituals where I felt they would be welcome.

Actually, there are some rituals where it's fine for kids to run around, and kids can bring a great energy to a gathering. But the bottom line is: parents always must take responsibility for their kids. My kids have been going to Pagan rituals since they were babies, and they're quite accustomed to them—but I still always keep an eye on them. I know I'm going there for community and connection with people, and some experience of "Turning the Wheel," depending on what season it is. But it's not comparable to a small intimate gathering with just my circle.

We call the eight seasonal rituals the "Wheel of the Year." If we're at a summer solstice ritual, part of the energy of our being there, creating this ceremony or ritual to mark that point, is: our effort actually helps turn the wheel to the next cycle. It's a pretty ancient concept which I think has wonderful poetic value: that we as humans can be co-creators.

♦ R/S: At what age are kids able to enter trance?

♦ AH: My daughter has been in an ecstatic trance since she was born—I'm waiting for her to get out of it! [laughs] It varies from kid to kid. Actually, it's hard for me to determine what kids get out of a ritual. Our family regularly attends the Spiral Dance and other large public rituals, and I see my son sneaking around and trying to get into doors marked "Do Not Enter." [laughs] I think, "Well, he's here with his friends taking in the scene and all the people, and he feels comfortable and is obviously having fun."

Once we attended a ritual at the beach. My son was outside the circle, letting other kids bury him in the sand. I thought, "Well, he's not really paying much attention to the ritual, but that's fine—he's having fun." But halfway through the ritual he came up to me with a mature, concerned look on his face and said, "You know, I don't know what it is, but I'm just not getting into this ritual the way I usually do." I looked at him and thought, "So much for my assumptions of what's going on with him!" But I really have no idea what his level of participation and consciousness is.

♦ R/S: Do you teach your children how to cast spells?

♦ AH: I tell them that spells are a lot like prayer—in fact, they are prayers. I'm not a big "Spell-casting Queen," but I have done spells with my kids; in one instance it was to help them find something really precious that they'd lost. Usually I ask, "What is the effect that you want?" I make sure they get their intention spelled out first: "You need help finding your special necklace? Let's take some Bergamot, which has a magnetizing influence. Let's light this particular colored candle." I may encourage them to speak to whatever guardian spirits they're working with. Basically I show them how to go about asking magically for what they want.

♦ *R/S: Do they always find what they're looking for?*

♦ AH: Sometimes it does work, sometimes it doesn't. When it doesn't, we have a discussion about the greater good, and why we don't always get what we want.

♦ *R/S: Did you see that movie "The Craft"?*

♦ AH: Yes, in 1996. People in the Pagan community were complaining about it. I took my 13-year-old nephew and my 11-year-old son to see it, because I wanted to see what a hack job Hollywood had done. Basically, if teenage girls can afford 52 matching pillar candles for every ritual they do, they've got way too much spending money! We were able to make fun of much of the film, and discuss what was true in their portrayal of Witches, and critique how various issues were dealt with. I hate suspenseful movies, so I don't know if I'll see "Blair Witch."

♦ *R/S: What do you think of the Harry Potter books?*

♦ AH: My daughters have each read every Harry Potter probably ten times. We are definitely a Harry Potter-friendly family! However, the concept of "Muggles"—people who are totally clueless—seems a bit unfair, because we're all part-Muggle; we're all clueless about *something*. But it doesn't mean we can't have magic in our lives, too. Yes, we talk a lot about the media, and try to analyze it.

♦ *R/S: Have you ever witnessed a fertility ritual?*

♦ AH: You bet! I went to the fertility ritual of two good friends who conceived right afterward. They had a lovely daughter who is now a good friend of my daughter's. I've seen fertility magic really work!

I also have a friend who did just about every fertility spell you can imagine, and kept having miscarriage after miscarriage. I've had friends who ended up adopting because they couldn't get pregnant. So what does it mean if for whatever reason the gods or the Goddess don't grant your wish? Fertility for women is an incredibly huge issue, and there's a lot to learn. If a woman can get past blaming herself or her body or whatever, she can learn a lot from thinking about this.

Before I had a child I was a student at U.C. Santa Cruz. I majored in Women's Studies and then got a teacher's credential. After about a year, I realized I wasn't really cut out to be a classroom teacher. But that experience taught me a lot about how children learn. I think I've brought a lot of that educator's perspective into mothering.

One of the most wonderful things about mothering is watching a child learn; it's totally thrilling. Suddenly an infant will be able to reach out and actually grasp what they're seeing in front of them. You get swept up: "Ohmigawd, using all those synapses between their eye and their brain and their hand, they've carved out this little channel so they can now grasp something!"

Learning exists on so many different levels. Once an infant can grasp your finger, that's just the beginning of being able to express their needs and desires, being able to feed themselves,

or otherwise get what they want. Their ability keeps on multiplying, infinitely.

Personally, I think the most challenging thing about being a mother is—and it doesn't have anything really to do with Paganism—is that it's an opportunity to work through my own childhood garbage. I can compare my own history when I was a kid, and reflect that my assumptions about how they're feeling are to some degree based on how *I* was feeling way back when. Sometimes the insights I get from my kids are so profound it takes me years to figure them all out!

Hopefully, Pagan children will have memories of rich rituals, and of sharing deep bonds with other Pagan friends. They grow up with the sense that "I can create my own altar, I have access to spirits that are helping me—my ancestors, the elements." Hopefully you have bonds with the community where there are people you consider elders that you can go to for help if you need it, or maybe even a circle you've grown up with since you were little. Having both the inner and community resources to help you through tough times—or to help you celebrate great joy—is a real advantage.

And so—best case scenario— my hope is that a child who was raised Pagan will as an adult have a sense of connection to the divinity within *everything*. That will affect everything: politics, relationships, choices in food and housing, their creativity and their work; *everything*. ♦♦♦

Top to bottom right: Anne Hill growing up

Serpentine Music

CIRCLE ROUND AND SING!
SONGS FOR FAMILY CELEBRATIONS IN THE GODDESS TRADITIONS

ANNE HILL

"These songs will bring the magic to life in your family circle."–Starhawk

♦ *RE/SEARCH: Describe Serpentine Music—*

♦ ANNE HILL: For the past eight years I've been a distributor of Pagan music. When I started, I could never have imagined how many bands and artists would be identifying as "Pagan." As the Pagan community has grown, so my business has grown by leaps and bounds.

I distribute music that speaks to Paganism, articulates what it is to be a Pagan, and reinforces our connection with each other, the earth, and with certain traditions. My goal is to get people to expand their horizons and open their ears to different music from a lot of different regions, not just the U.S.

What is Paganism going to become in this century? We don't really have any liturgy, we don't really have any leaders, but we do have a lot of music. So for us, music really is our liturgy.

♦ *R/S: How do you identify "Pagan music"?*

♦ AH: 1) music made by Pagan musicians; 2) music about Paganism, that has Pagan themes; 3) music that a lot of Pagans seem to like. A lot of Pagans are into Loreena McKennit, who has a Celtic style and sings about themes that many Pagans respond to. So by my definition, what she does is Pagan music. When choosing music, I try to keep in mind those three considerations.

♦ *R/S: On your Web site, one of the music categories is "Pagan Rock." This reminded me of "Christian Rock." [laughs] To me, these are mostly bands that aren't very original or interesting musically, but they sell records because of their religious lyrics. In the Eighties there was a Christian band named Stryper who had big hair and wore spandex. I doubt anybody would have listened to them if they hadn't done things like throw Bibles into the audience when they performed live. Are there "Pagan Rock Bands" like that?*

♦ AH: Yes—what can I say? Though I haven't yet heard of a big hair Pagan band throwing copies of the *Spiral Dance* into the audience. Some of this I end up selling because people like it and there's no other place they're going to find it. I started out as more of a purist: "I know what good music sounds like and that's what I want to sell." But at a certain point I had to concede, "If I'm in the business of selling music to all Pagans, I have to expand my boundaries a bit."

People often call me up and ask for recommendations. I ask, "What do you like, and what don't you like?" Then I can make suggestions. I try to be non-judgmental, because I don't consider my opinions to be the final word in music criticism. If people ask me what *my* favorite is, I might answer, "Oh, this band is really hot."

♦ *R/S: What do some of these bands sing about?*

♦ AH: There's a whole new cosmology being formulated that involves the notion of the entire cosmos being alive. Some Pagans are saying that the Big Bang theory is like the myth of the Star Goddess; the scientist Brian Swimme is proclaiming that

"Gravity is love; it's this force of attraction." As scientists are talking about theology and metaphysics in scientific terms, so musicians, who always have an ear for a juicy metaphor, are weaving that into interesting lyrics accompanied by joyful music. The whole new cosmology is becoming quite danceable! [laughs]

Music is magic. One of the ways I feel a connection with the universe is by playing or listening to music, and feeling that rhythm. When people join in, that's magic, because we're creating this energy in the form of a song. Music is a form of energy creation and energy generation that we really don't know that much about. We know when it feels good, but there's so much more to it.

Different musicians have different goals. One may be, "Let's get a dance band together and sing some songs about the sacredness of the earth." Another may be, "Let's sing songs about how Pagans have been persecuted; we can get really angry and have a hard-driving beat." Others may explore sound and chant as a way to connect to the spirit of a goddess or god. I've heard great examples of all three, and I've also heard music that really sucked!

There are a lot of great bands out there that generate incredible energy. Musicians are magicians, but sometimes they don't even know what they're doing!

♦ *R/S: You have a CD out of your own music—*

♦ AH: It's called *Circle Round and Sing,* and was created at the 1999 Winter Solstice full moon. It contains songs to help families with kids bring music into their celebrations. There are chants useful for raising energy levels; a chant for every season, a lot of celebratory music, and some nice singalong material.

Sometimes you go to a ritual and people start a chant to raise energy. And you think, "Oh no—not *that* chant again!" With this album I wanted to give people chants they could use, and maybe dress up some old chestnuts. Basically, I really wanted to give kids something to listen to that is life-affirming, and that might help them in constructing their own identity as Pagans.

BOOKS: There's a really great book on child development called **Natural Learning Rhythms.** It really goes through the stages of growth in a way that makes sense. They would say that a child from age 1-7 is in the "body being": they relate to things more with their body. Then from 7-12 it's more "emotional being": they're exploring their emotions, and they list all these skills and cognitive things that are being developed, plus things that really help that development, and things that really hinder that development. It's a really great system to work with. **Brian Swimme** has written several books including **The Universe Story.** Basically it's about giving us a new Story (with a capital "S") to live by. It incorporates new science of the past 15 years as to how exactly we came into being. It starts with the Big Bang and moves forward; it's a great book.♦♦♦

Joi Wolfwomyn

Joi Wolfwomyn was adopted, lived through the punk, Goth, Grateful Deadhead, Queer and Transgender subcultures, and is now affiliated with the Radical Faeries, an avant-garde Queer Pagan international disorganization with a strong presence in the Bay Area. A certified priest/ess, she lectures, gives workshops and ministers to the dead and dying. Joi is raising a teenage daughter in a shared Pagan household. Interviews by John Sulak and V. Vale.

♦ *RE/SEARCH: How did you get your name?*

♦ JOI WOLFWOMYN: The name Wolfwomyn came to me in a non-traditional vision quest when I was 17 and was living as part of a loosely centered radical feminist community. I was sitting by a fire in Northern California's Mendocino County when a large gray wolf walked out of the woods into the fire circle where I was doing an extended ritual. I thought, "There are no wolves in California." It walked into the circle and then just walked through me. I concluded this was the "vision" of my vision quest—mind you, the only drug I was on was sleep deprivation and fasting. So I took the name Wolfwomyn.

I lived with that name for four or five years while all around me in the Pagan and hippie communities people were christening themselves with names like "Wolf," "Eagle," "Lion," "Bear"—fine, upstanding, powerful totem creatures. It seemed more than a little pretentious, until I realized I had done the same thing. But I also was not going to discount the vision I'd had. However, I came to the point where I felt, "I don't want to be the noble wolf—the protector of the forest—all the time." And that's where my faerie name "Wolfie" came from. There are plenty of times I would rather be a puppy and be able to run around and goof off, so "Wolfie" became a way to not always have to do the "grown-up" role.

You don't meet that many Pagans whose names are Aardvark, Piranha or Snail. I do know a few Squirrels, and I know others who are squirrelly!

♦ *R/S: Tell us your background—*

♦ JW: I grew up bi-racial, fat and adopted by a conservative white family, so I always felt Other. My adoptive mother was a member of the Worldwide Church of God, a cult which was founded by a man named Herbert W. Armstrong. It taught that Jesus was the Savior, but that all of the Levitical and Pharisaical laws were still in effect. We weren't supposed to have friends or date outside the church. There were constant reminders from my adoptive family to "be grateful for the better chance you've gotten in life." I remember some relative saying, "Joi should go live in Hawaii—everyone there looks like her." I spent the first 16 years of my life trying to "pass" as white and normal.

Well, I failed miserably. Actually, I was an incorrigible, unholy brat (I still am, but keep it under control). **I've never taken to authority structures very well—which is why anarchism makes so much sense to me.** At the age of 14 I started coming to terms with the fact that I was a dyke, even though I didn't even know the word. I just sort of "lost it" and went into the medicine cabinet, washed down a bunch of sleeping pills with a bottle of whiskey and woke up two days later in the mental hospital. Apparently I had called my English teacher to apologize for not being in class anymore.

It was in psych ward that I finally found "my people." I was drawn to a man who was playing with a deck of cards unlike any deck of cards I'd ever seen before. It was the Aleister Crowley Thoth deck, the man's name was Chuck, and he changed my life. He was also a big ole screaming fag. I thought, "Wow—hey, you're cool!" He talked to me openly about sexuality and magic, telling me, "No, you're just really hyper-aware, and whether that's a psychic awareness or just being incredibly observant, it doesn't matter. It's still magical." He was the first person to discuss concepts of magic that weren't based on the Judeo-Christian Yahweh-God. Being with Chuck was an incredibly stunning experience that broke me out of the insulation that had clothed me my entire life.

I was locked in that hospital for nine months. While I was there I met my first girlfriend, a butch country girl who had been locked up because she was a dyke. Back then kids like me who were "different" routinely got locked up, beaten up or kicked out of school. One reason I'm willing to go public with my history is that, a long time ago, reading *Modern Primitives* sparked me to give myself permission to explore more of the things that I was drawn to. If, by sharing this, even one person feels, "Oh, maybe I'm not so bad, or crazy," then I've accomplished something.

In my opinion, conformity just *kills*. It does not make you happy. You must feel okay with who you really are. Just after I became a mom about fifteen years ago, I made a last-ditch attempt to pass as "normal," and it lasted about six months. Then I realized, "I'm not going to be a decent mother if I'm not happy with myself."

In this culture people are trained from birth to look for an external source to make them happy. The foundation of the $40 billion diet industry rests upon convincing people: "You're ugly, and there's something wrong with you, because your body doesn't fit this narrow little stereotype of what we call attractive." My coming out as a dyke and a witch and a pervert requires self-analysis that this culture doesn't encourage. Before you can announce to somebody, "Oh, I'm a witch," there is a certain amount of internal strength-building and self-knowledge that is necessary to attain.

There are lots of people who, for whatever reason, don't come out. I saw a show on MTV featuring a polyamorous family (one woman, two men and their kid) who came out as Pagan and as poly. Within three weeks the kid was taken away! That case is still in litigation to this day. As a parent, I started wondering who might try to take my kid away, especially when I began teaching sex and SM classes.

In Western culture, anyone who is too deviant gets locked up, yet many more spiritual cultures honor the mad ones, sometimes as shamans. They're said to have vision and to be able to see other worlds. If they become absolutely damaging and are not participating in the collective reality at all, then sometimes they're sent off to be hermits—but not out of disrespect or invalidation. But in this culture there's no place for mystics or shamans.

The dictionary definition of psychosis is "a sharply altered and different reality." But that's what we go for when we're doing ritual or taking psychedelics: we're altering our reality. The trick is finding a way to live within this sharply different reality, and still be able to connect and communicate within the larger collective reality. When I first entered the Pagan community, I was having some intense mystical experiences that I couldn't tell anybody about, mostly because I had no language or lexicon to describe the things in my head, but I managed to find other outsiders who understood. It took me some time to learn the languages of Paganism, so that I could communicate my experiences to other people. Now, even if the rest of the world thinks I'm crazy, I'm okay with that—because the rest of the world really *is* insane. **I look at global capitalism and transnational corporations and how much of the planet is being destroyed and workers exploited, and I think being crazy or depressed is a healthy reaction to that!**

From being in the madhouse, working with street people and individuals going through dementia, I've learned that once you stop letting yourself feel threatened by "Other" or by "different," then it's much easier to hear what they're trying to communicate. One of the big deterrents to understanding is fear: fear of Other, fear of different, fear of attack, fear of vulnerability. It's ingrained in us to be afraid of that which is different. So much anger, aggression and "us *versus* them" dualistic dynamic is based and rooted in fear. **My perception is that monotheism fuels this dynamic of fear of difference, through its reliance on dualism and the balance of manufactured rules of "good/evil."** For this reason, fear has become a really good signifier for me—it means that I should become more *aware* of something!

In Paganism, especially in the Radical Faeries, we learn from the permissions we give ourselves in magic, ritual, gatherings, or in sex. Additionally, I learn by giving myself permission to screw up sometimes: to do things wrong or to do things that don't work, and learn from that. (Just as long as I don't repeat the same mistake over and over again.)

It's important to give ourselves permission to be deviant, and to experience magic. One of the things I do is that I tend to throw glitter on people a lot. I think glitter is a very potent magical tool in this culture, where people are not supposed to wear glitter all over themselves, and sparkle. If you have someone close their eyes and then cover them in glitter, when they open their eyes they go, "Wow, I'm full of stars!" And that's what we all thought magic was like when we were little. The thing that is ultimately stomped out of us is sparkle. So I've made it one of my missions in the Pagan community to glitter everybody and everything.

For the past ten years I've been studying the Hindu mythos and spirituality as well as Tibetan Buddhism, while attempting to integrate these into Pagan practices. And our Western mindset has a *subject-object* viewpoint: "I am this; everything else is Other." **Our colonialist, capitalist, monotheist/dualist viewpoint supports the doctrine of hierarchy, which in turn supports oppressive government in which everything funnels up to one great removed, alienated power.** Whereas the Radical Faeries have been exploring and testing *subject-subject* consciousness, a concept used by Harry Hay, a man who has articulated much of my life. He's a 90-year-old San Franciscan who back in the Fifties helped found the Mattachine Society (the first Gay Rights organization), and also was an early Radical Faerie.

I remember when I was the wide-eyed novice going, "Okay, we're all standing in a circle holding hands and people are talking and I guess I'm supposed to feel something 'magical' now." From that I progressed, gradually. It wasn't until 1991 that I actually stepped into my priesthood, creating and manifesting my own rituals, and leading rituals for other people. My practices balance very conservative traditionalism and very anarchist-eclectic, sexual outlaw ideas.

One reason I've been studying other philosophies and playing with doing interfaith work is that for the past ten years I've been working with people who are dying, and I've had to confront and deal with a wide spectrum of religious beliefs. I've been creating memorial rituals, doing grief counseling, as well as actual caregiving and caretaking for people in the process of dying. *That* has been the primary focus of my private magical practice.

Also, I'm a mom. Ultimately we need to be bringing up children with a sense of self-responsibility. And **one of my big issues with monotheism as a *structure* is that it does not teach self-responsibility. The very structure itself of externalized deities, one that is good, and one that is tempting and bad, alleviates the whole need for self-responsibility.** It's either: the Good Deity did it, or the Bad Deity made me do it. This does not encourage the attitude of "I am choosing to do this; I am enacting my will; I take on all responsibility for the effects of enacting my will."

Rural homesteading with baby daughter, Chandra

Kids aren't raised with an emphasis on self-responsibility, partly because it's a real pain to raise kids that way! I have raised my 14-year-old daughter to be a good anarchist and question all authority figures and enact her will. It has been a difficult process because on the one hand it's "Yeah—go girl!" while on the other hand it's "But I'm the mommy—*that's* why!"

I believe this process makes for more responsible, and ultimately more self-reliant, children. Subcultures rely on interdependence for survival, whether they're the Dead's extended family, hippie communes or punk collectives. **Ultimately it's the subculture parents that are bringing about change. Punk moms are teaching their kids different lessons, like: "I'm not teaching you to conform!"** I know I've been doing that as a dyke mom.

My kid does some things partly to annoy me. I didn't tell her what she had to be, so fortunately she doesn't have to go to *major* extremes to differentiate herself from me. When I was growing up I thought, "I'm never going to do any *girl stuff* like crocheting and knitting!" Well, I'm 33 and don't have to rebel against my mother anymore, so I'm learning how to crochet and knit. Anytime anyone joins a new subculture or community, the first two years are like, "We rule! Everything else is not us!" The next step involves not being *reactive* like that—moving beyond being reactive and judgmental, something that more and more people are finally realizing.

♦ *R/S: You live in a collective household—*

♦ JW: There are seven of us living in a Queer Radical Faerie household we call the Chaos Cabaret. I've been here seven years; this is the longest I've lived anywhere. My daughter has been raised in the Queer community all her life, amidst Queer culture—art, music and language. Subcultures are defined by a common language and lexicon; that's how they differentiate themselves and identify each other.

We're all artists and most of us are drag queens. We refer to ourselves as a semi-collective, because we don't go "full collective" and share our incomes. Every month we add up the costs of maintaining the house and everybody pays an equal share. Our monthly house meetings are not just about business—we perceive ourselves as a chosen family, albeit without the lifetime commitment—it's more on an "I choose to make family with you right now" basis.

Our meetings are set up as magical circles, and we try to maintain this house as a safe house or oasis. Visitors can come and "ground" themselves if they're feeling overwhelmed—occasionally we do rescue- and crisis-intervention for people escaping abusive situations. We try to make this a place where magic can happen whenever it needs to, and that's an ongoing task.

When the house throws rituals, like at a full or dark moon, we create a space where magic can happen. We designate the back yard as a TAZ, or "temporary autonomous zone" where people can come and have whatever magical experience they need to have.

For five years I've helped organize the Queer Spirit Pagan Festival, defining Queer as "deviant"—deviant from the social as well as sexual norm. Because there is a big difference between "Gay" and "Queer"—lots of Gays are not particularly deviant. My friends and I have been exploring what makes Queer magic different. **People who come into Queer magical space and rituals remark, "This feels different—wow!" It's partly because our magic is based on androgyny, not male/female polarity.** Whereas in the greater Pagan community, the male-female, God-Goddess polarities invoked are more often the energy invoked.

I was ordained—I hate that word so I use the term "desecrated"—by a Pagan church known as The Fellowship of the Spiral Path. They've got 501c3 status, so I received a ministerial credential card which meant I could go into hospitals and hospices when I was doing caregiving. When I was desecrated, I was dedicated in service to the *Divine Androgynes*. During the training program, I examined different spiritual cultures in search of androgynous deities, or deities that moved beyond gender or played with gender.

I don't mean to state that Queer or androgyny-based magic is somehow *better* than polarity-based magic, I just maintain that all of these energy patterns are equally viable. Sometimes people ask, "How can you define faery?" Well, you can't! You can *describe* faeries, but my theory is that once something has been defined, it tends to stagnate or ossify—so I'm loathe to define almost anything! **Historically, Pagans, Witches, Queers, Perverts—*whatever*—have never been able to describe themselves; that has been done by the majority culture. And then it becomes much easier to write them out of history altogether.**

♦ *R/S: Can you discuss polyamory—*

♦ JW: I've had one attempt at a monogamous relationship in my life and it was an absolute disaster. Having grown up as the fat, ugly, weird kid I had many hang-ups, and my first issue was about having sex with other people in general. I went through the standard fat girl phase of "I think I'm ugly, but if you want to have sex with me I'll do that because then you'll hold me and I'll get some affection out of it for a while." It took time to get beyond that.

When I finally accepted the idea that people might actually like me for *me,* I thought, "That's cool—but do you mean I can only have *one?"* I felt that nobody is so simple or simplistic that one person can meet all their intimate needs—whether sexual or psychological or whatever. I've had a quad relationship with three other women; I've had a quad relationship with two men and another woman.

At this point there are people around the country I consider my lovers—that I see once a year or once every couple of years. But I define lovers and sex differently from most people. I consider one of my roommates in Chaos Cabaret House as a lover; we do magic and drag together and have tended the body of our best friend together. That's way more intimate than most sex!

The people that I do really intense rituals with are my lovers. To me, genitals are all fine and good, and everybody can mix and match their wobbly bits as much as they want. But for me, a sexual connection means something that engages *all* of me—not just the specific, isolated part of my body defined as "genitals," but something that requires my entire attention and presence. "Sexual" could mean sharing chocolate with somebody, or just walking through a rose garden holding hands while letting the scent overtake both of us. That to me is a very sexual experience.

Some people say, "Those aren't your lovers, because you're not having actual 'bang your crotch together' sex." But there are so many limitations put on sex, love and intimacy that are bogus. I'm one of the few people that enjoys having crushes and being in love with people, even if

they're not in love with me! Part of that is my Zen doctrine of "No attachments." That's why I have a lot of lovers who are fags. We're never going to have sex; the wobbly bits don't work for that. But I can sit and have this intense orgasmic experience just cuddling in their lap, or them cuddling in mine. We can gaze into each other's eyes. There's a faerie that I'm head-over-heels smitten with right now; I adore him. And I told him, "I think that I am really in love with you. This does not mean that I expect or want anything from you. But I just wanted to let you know that if you catch me looking at you all googly-eyed and sighing, that I really love you and I'm really happy with that. Don't worry about it."

I think that so many people get caught up in "I have this crush on someone that's unrequited, so I have to be miserable about it." Why be miserable when you don't have to be? It doesn't make any sense. Being in love is like eating really good chocolate. I like that little high I get from chocolate, and I get a little high from being in love in with people.

♦ *R/S: Weren't you in the Glamazon Warriors, a drag queen group—*

♦ JW: Yes. During one Gay Pride parade, my friend Ggreggg Taylor dressed up in his NAMBLA the Clown outfit, which was black Venetian hunting leathers with rainbow-colored rhinestones all over. He carried three dozen black balloons filled with glitter. The rest of us made pentacle spears with sharpened points. In the parade he marched a hundred yards ahead; we would follow later and pop the balloons with spears so glitter would explode over everybody.

I actually started using glitter in ritual with my partner Kalyn, because so many people were allergic to sage or oils. I've been to rituals where scented oil was splashed and immediately someone got a migraine because they're allergic. Splashing people with glitter makes a lot more sense, because nobody is allergic to glitter. Everybody has that four-year-old kid in the back of their brain who goes, "Magic! Sparkles!" Glitter makes visible what people thought magic looked like when they were about four years old.

There's new glitter on the market now that's non-toxic. You can get it at craft shops, or in bulk by the pound at *creativebeginnings.com.* For Gay Pride parade one of my housemates bought twelve pounds of glitter, because he has a geek job. We made enormous salt shakers and marched down Market Street glittering everybody—cops got extra; it looks good on their uniforms. Then we covered as much of Civic Center as we could, and still had three pounds of glitter left over.

♦ *R/S: How much does it cost?*

♦ JW: The microfine non-toxic is $35 a pound, and the holographic glitter is $45 a pound. You can use it for food decoration too—it's plastic, so it just goes right through your body. We have many jokes in our house about glittery sh--s!

♦ *R/S: Let's discuss death—*

♦ JW: Over the past ten years I've done a lot of work with the dying . . . dealing with death, doing grief counseling. I've handled many bodies, including the bodies of friends of mine.

A friend of mine named Crystal died. Those of us who were the Glamazon Warriors had been in the caregiving circle of Crystal when she died. In the drag queen pantheon we've created, she is the ascended Goddess of Glamour. She was very much into Egyptian magic, so my friend Goneaway and I ripped up 15 yards of black silk into strips, went into the mortuary and wrapped Crystal's body Egyptian-mummy style. Here was our best friend who was alive a day and a half ago—although not very. So we burned incense, rang bells and wrapped her body. On her chest we bound an owl feather and a peacock feather for wisdom and glamour. A lot of people sent things to be wrapped up with her: her teddy bear, glitter, coins to go over her eyes and mouth. Everybody had put something in there, including Crystal's parents who had known her as "Eric." This was an incredible bonding moment.

Before she had gotten sick, she had designed a copper death mask for herself much like the Egyptian masks on mummies. It was a copper skull with two tubes coming out it, and those came down and crossed over into a copper heart that was filled with her earrings, her favorite perfume, and really bad leaf, because that's what she smoked a lot of when she was sick. Goneaway and Cirus carved the eyes of Horus and runes into the outside of her casket.

The morticians were great. They had put her up on blocks so we could get the fabric under her. **They warned us, "Be careful you don't drop her head, because her mouth is glued shut. If you drop her head, the lip will give before the glue does"—meaning we might rip her face open. So of course we did drop her once.** That was a defining moment—when that happened, and her mouth didn't break open, it broke the tension and we laughed. But we were still able to maintain magical focus. The day after her death, the five of us went to the beach and did circle ritual there, including running naked and screaming into the ocean at 1 A.M. on New Year's Eve.

Just this past year an old, dear friend named Maudie died. This was the first time I have tended, bathed, and dressed a body alone. It was more intense because she had been autopsied—she had these whip stitches all up her chest and her body. She looked like a big rag doll. I just thought, "This is really strange."

So much of this culture is invested in avoiding death; people don't touch their friends when they're dead. It's like, "Okay, somebody else take it away and deal with it." If it's a casket funeral the attitude is, "Okay, we'll look at them after they've been made up and dressed to look like something they aren't. Then we'll close it, lock it, and seal it away in cement." Or, "We'll burn them and put them in this little sealed jar and never handle them again." And it's wrong—people should not disconnect. **Even though the Pagan community vocalizes about how "Death is just naturally part of the cycle," there is still avoidance, with people feeling guilty because they're hurt and upset. No—we still need to make death more of a part of our life.**

There has to be a way and a structure whereby we bring death back into everyday life. I've dealt with people who have been Pagan for thirty years, but when they die, that little seed that was planted by their monotheistic upbringing springs back to life: "Am I going to be judged on Judgment Day?"

People who weren't brought up with that "judgment" notion don't seem to go through that fear phase.

Ultimately I'd like to see our Western Culture accept death as a normal part of everything else—not have it be something that's hidden away, not talked about or dealt with. The death of my friend who had that autopsy was a kind of rite of passage for me. Previously there had been a co-priest in attendance whenever I had dealt with friends' bodies, but this was the first time I had gone into a room containing a dead body all by myself, dressed her in her ritual drag and done her ritual make-up. I veiled her face and then wheeled her out into the room where the wake was to take place. And not only her Pagan family but her "straight" family were there. Her partner brought their son up to her body and lifted the veil so that the boy knew that his mother was dead. It was not horrible; it just *was*. This was definitely something to grieve and be sad about—it wasn't, "No, you can't feel anything." It was also very much a feeling of "She's dead; her body is leaving us."

We packed all of her ritual tools, including her staff, wand and broom into her shroud. The crematorium was wonderful, because they didn't interfere and allowed us complete freedom to dress her body in full ritual garb and make-up before putting the body into the crematorium oven.

Each time I handle the bodies of my friends, I feel a power arising that's unlike other magical powers and energies—you feel fully yourself in that state of presence. This level of awareness is absolutely required to deal with the dead—especially dead that you know. **As part of the Faerie community, there were several years when I had ten or more people a year dying in my lap. And people wonder why I'm an extremist!**

It's a *gift* that I can go in and hold people when they die—not everybody can do that, although it would be nice. As word got around that I was willing and capable, strangers started calling me: "Hi, I'm dying. Would you come sit with me?" That has been interesting in and of itself.

I want to see people and the culture at large embrace death as part of life, instead of being afraid. People don't want to think about dying and not existing anymore. People have an ego need to perpetuate the individuality of self, whether it's manifested as "I'll go live in Heaven!" or "I'll be reincarnated!" But fundamentally, death happens and the world goes on.

Personally, **I don't buy the reincarnation theory, because that's still an ego perpetuation of the individual. A part of me thinks I'm having all my lives at once!** I believe that the evolution of humanity will go on. It's all just theory, and none of us really know. And it has to be *okay* to not really know.

The whole profit-making industry that's built up around death is insane. In Tibet, people staged open-air mountain top burials, and after the vultures picked the bones clean, you made ritual tools out of the bones. Some people think that's weird, but it makes total sense to me. I've made ritual objects out of the bones and hair of my pets, familiars and friends for the past ten years. I have wands with hair from dead friends woven into

them, and jars on my altar containing the ashes of friends.

My friend Daisy was a "rave" kid, and he wore these little bottles containing glass beads, stone chips and tiny objects in them. After he died, I took his ashes and made a bunch of little reliquary bottles, because that's what he wanted. I had to search all over for Mardi Gras supplies, plus little plastic babies, and crack them up with a hammer and mix them in with his ashes. I made these little bottles and gave them to all of his friends and his relatives.

As a graduate of a Pagan Seminary, I'm actually a credentialed priest in California. So I get to go in and handle the bodies. A couple of hospitals know me now; I've done rituals in more ICUs and hospital rooms than I care to think about. When my partner Kalyn died at Alta Bates, several of the nurses told me they really liked hearing my chanting coming from his room. They said it was soothing, and that everybody on that floor slept better.

♦ *R/S: Doesn't it feel strange: handling the body of your friends?*

♦ JW: It's always odd; I'll never say, "Yeah, I'm used to it." It's weird and strange, but somebody has to do it. Personally, I'd rather it was me doing what I *know* they wanted, rather than have some total stranger involved.

Occasionally I sit down and think, "This is not what I thought my life would be: handling dead bodies all the time!" But if I can do it, then it is what I should be doing, because not everybody can. Lots of people see a dead cat and flip out.

I've had many people die in my lap. That's how it started: I would hold people as they were dying and they would die in my lap. Over the past few years I've been called to attend a lot more people who have died, which meant I wasn't always part of their death. Maybe I last saw the person perfectly alive and now they're a stitched-up body— and *that's* strange.

I keep my focus by chanting a lot, because all these mysterious things happen. There is an energy field surrounding dead bodies that is intense; all this energy in the cellular structure of the body is evaporating. Most cultures assume that process takes at least three days.

At this point my life project is to open a Pagan cemetery. There are religious exemptions permitting cemeteries to do burials without embalming chemicals and a foot-thick cement box, which is the normal regulation—most Pagans would rather go back naked to the earth. You have to qualify for a religious exemption, which basically requires founding a church—that's a 501c3. So I'm basically founding the Church of the Androgyne. It will be a church for people who live their lives and worship deities outside of the polarized gender spectrum. The biggest regulation for cemeteries is that you can't be anywhere near a water table, which makes complete sense. I'm looking into Eastern Washington, New Mexico and possibly Tennessee—the latter two states already have home burial laws. Who knows? I've got a few more years of research to do before I really decide. Which is fine, because that will give me a chance to get an established church together beforehand. ♦♦♦

Jack Davis

Photo: V. Vale

J ack Davis is a member of the Radical Faeries, a group of queer men co-created in the late1970s by gay rights pioneer Harry Hay. Jack is also involved with Reclaiming, has a teaching certificate, a B.A. and M.A. in Art, and currently works at Good Vibrations, a worker-owned cooperative in San Francisco. Interview by John Sulak.

♦ *RE/SEARCH: Describe your childhood—*
♦ JACK DAVIS: I grew up in a really small town in Illinois where we had a house with a big lawn and a garden. I was constantly raking leaves, mowing lawns, working in the garden and shoveling snow, so I was always connected to the seasons and the earth. My grandfather lived with us, and he was a really good gardener and cook. I grew up eating food that we grew.

I was raised Catholic and was an altar boy—I was pretty devout. In college I stopped going to church—this was in the Sixties, the time of sexual liberation, the Vietnam war, when people were questioning authority. I joined a men's group and finally came out as a gay man. I also joined a collective that was trying to start a vegetarian restaurant—*that's* where I learned about the consensus process. The consensus process is a way of making decisions where you listen to everybody's concerns until you come to an agreement everyone can live with. The difference between that and voting is: when you vote, usually whoever has the most people wins. The minority either get stepped on or ignored.

Now I belong to Nomenus, a group of about 50 Radical Faeries who jointly own land in Wolf Creek, Oregon. Twice a year all of us get together over a long weekend and hash things out. We have two facilitators, an agenda, and a timekeeper. Again, we keep discussing a topic until everyone agrees. We sit in a circle so we can see everybody, and so no one person is in charge. A circle facilitates participation and the sharing of experience. We begin and end our meetings with a ritual that affirms our connection with the land.

At Wolf Creek there are four buildings—two of which we built—with electricity, running water and phones. We can accommodate a lot more people in the summer because there's plenty of room to camp. There are a few full-time caretakers—they care for the garden and live there. Visitors contribute to the household fund and help out with gardening or repairs—there's always something to do!

At Faerie gatherings it's always fun to see people you haven't seen for a while, and meet new people. There are regularly scheduled gatherings on Samhain, Winter Solstice, and Beltane. Every summer there's a week-long gathering in August or September attended by about 200 Faeries. Usually there's a big opening ritual at the beginning of the week that welcomes everyone to the gathering. During the day people

host circles on creative writing, sex magic, massage, ritual, and other topics. In the evenings after dinner there is usually a ritual or some sort of performance. When Faeries from the city get accustomed to the country, they gradually slow down, and it's great to see this happening. Eventually, as the week progresses, people's conversations seem to become more meaningful.

In the past, I've taught "phallic image" workshops with Keith Hennessy, an adventurous performance artist. These are for queer men, and we'd be naked the whole day. First we'd work on movement, with music and drumming. In the afternoon I would show students how to make penises out of scraps of fabric. We would meditate, do trance work, put the penises in a big pile and then talk about them. This all happened within a larger context of workshops honoring the male body in ritual or sacred space.

During that time, other gay men led workshops where men would take off their clothes and spend the whole night dancing naked, or they would be given a specific set of exercises or experiences to undergo. This was very different from going to a sex club where queer men don't talk to each other—they just have sex. We were guiding people through various experiences they wouldn't have any other way.

I remember when groups of gay men started doing sex ritual in the street during Halloween in the Castro, San Francisco's gay neighborhood. At the corner of 19th and Castro we'd have people playing drums, and at some point we'd announce, "Let's take our clothes off now!" Then we'd walk to 18th and Castro and form a huge circle of naked queer men, drumming and doing sex ritual—basically dancing and touching. There may have been a couple times when people were actually *being* sexual, but mostly we were raising this amazing energy by being naked, queer men in the street. We were doing Pagan street theater, honoring our queer ancestors and reclaiming our neighborhood. It was Halloween, the time when the veils between the worlds are thinnest. And I consider friends who had died recently as among my ancestors.

The land ownership happened because the Radical Faeries had been having big get-togethers for years. At some point someone said, "You know, we spend all this money to rent places for our gatherings—why don't we just pool our money and buy some land?" Someone else knew of some cheap land which had been a gay men's collective—and since it had a history which some of us knew, we bought it. That's how Nomenus was born.

♦ *R/S: Right, there needs to be a lot more Pagan land ownership. Tell us more about the Radical Faeries—*

♦ JD: I learned about the Radical Faeries when I was still living in Illinois. The first Faerie gathering took place in 1979 in Arizona, and the first gathering I attended was in Oregon in 1983. Radical Faeries tend to be gay men who are *not* in the gay mainstream, like me. As a kid growing up, I always felt unique. That feeling of isolation continued past childhood. Stonewall happened in 1969 and there was a kind of mainstreaming of gay culture, but again, Radical Faeries tend to be people who don't fit into *any* mainstream—gay or otherwise. When I went to my first Radical Faerie gathering, I saw all these other fags who didn't fit in, either. They were political, they did ritual, and they were funny. It felt like "coming home"—finding all these other weird people who not only did the same crazy things I did— they *appreciated* that I did them.

Many Radical Faeries do Wiccan ritual, but they're very anarchistic about how to do it. The distinction between Wiccans and Radical Faeries is that Radical Faeries are really good at raising energy, but they aren't always good at grounding it. Whereas I like ritual that has a clear beginning, middle, and end. If I'm leading a ritual, at the end I might say, "Okay, the planned part of the ritual is over." Then people may continue doing what they're doing—usually it's drumming, dancing, and singing.

I believe there are eight or ten other Radical Faerie groups who own land in the U.S. Short Mountain in Tennessee owned their land before we owned Wolf Creek.

♦ *R/S: Have the Radical Faeries changed as a result of AIDS?*

Halloween on Castro Street, San Francisco Photos: Jim James

♦ JD: Significantly, I never expected to be an elder at my age, but I am one now because a lot of Faeries my age or older have died. Also, a lot of Faeries who knew our history are just not around anymore. I've kept records and over a hundred of my friends have died—most of them Radical Faeries. Fortunately, there are new Faeries with new energy showing up. The younger generation has a bit more of an edge—they're more street-smart.

I've learned to confront death with a certain amount of humor. In San Francisco so many of my friends were dying that we Radical Faeries felt free to deal with death and memorials the way *we* wanted to. Some Radical Faeries started planning their memorial service before they died, saying, "I don't want a memorial—I want a party instead!" I led one memorial at a sex club which had a number of huge beds. We put two together, made an altar, stood around it in a circle and talked about the person who had died.

I had the very humbling experience of watching a friend die. About thirty of us were crowded into a hospital room, and we watched him take his last breath. It was amazing to realize that this spirit had just left this body. We could touch him, kiss him and say goodbye, and talk to his lover. This was an intense experience that not many people have.

♦ *R/S: Have you been to other queer Pagan camps?*

♦ JD: Recently some queer Witches from Reclaiming did our first queer witch camp in Vancouver. We set up two ritual experiences: one in the wild (for the wild side of being queer), and one indoors by a fireplace (to represent the home side). We divided people into two groups and at some point switched them so they could experience both "sides" of being queer in sacred space. We had an Oscar Wilde tea party, a poetry reading, and a Red Dragon dinner where everyone wore red and did ritual around the vitality of the community. My friend Patrick, who's a costumer, wore this fabulous red outfit with a red tiara that people were lusting after.

In Wicca people talk about the male energy and the female energy coming together and creating something. During our queer camp, we told people going into trance: "You're going to invite into yourself your own personal queer deity. Then you're going to dress as that queer deity." There were people of all genders there and they came up with some pretty amazing ideas—one person dressed as a monolith…a stone has no gender!

Paganism provides a place to showcase the theatrical—the trickster or creative god—including aspects that are more stereotypical of gay male culture. There's always the creative possibility of making up your own god. In fact, I've thought of doing a workshop for gay men where they create their own deities, starting with stereotypes of gay men: the actor/waiter, the artist, the caretaker, the leather daddy, the sex worker. Similarly, you could do a workshop in which you make up your own goddess. **One of the purposes of this exercise is to elicit help for whatever work you're doing—that's what a deity is for.** So you invent a deity that can provide the help you need. ♦♦♦

Jeff Rosenbaum

R osenbaum is the Executive Director of the Association for Consciousness Exploration, which for 20 years has produced the yearly Starwood Festival, a major Pagan gathering in New York (*www.rosencomet.com*). Interview by John Sulak.

♦ *RE/SEARCH: Describe the Starwood Festival—*

♦ JEFF ROSENBAUM: Starwood is a big college of alternative thinking and alternative spirituality that suddenly appears like a carnival or circus. The tents go up, it stays there for a week, and then *BOOM* it's gone, til next year.

We have 140 or more classes from 9:30 in the morning till 6:15 in the evening—sometimes as many as 12 at a time. You can learn about Druidism, Ceremonial Magic, Wicca, Tibetan Buddhism, and Native American Practices. We have classes on psychedelia and psychology, and different "movement systems" like tai chi, yoga and aikido. Past speakers have included Timothy Leary, quantum physicist Fred Allen Wolf, Paul Krassner, and Steven Gaskin, who created the Farm, the biggest hippie commune in America. It's all included in the cost of admission.

We try to bring in the "purist" forms of spiritual paths—real Africans teaching African culture, and real Native Americans teaching Native American ritual. Evenings include rituals from different cultures—a Voodoo ritual on Thursday, a Druid ritual on Friday, etc. Live music features everything from trance to jug bands to Pagan folk music. At midnight we set up an inflatable dome and have all night-raves. We want people from different lifestyles, backgrounds and world views to *party together* and find out the ways they're the same, rather than different. *It's important for people to learn not only how to live with each other, but celebrate each other.* Robert Anton Wilson said that the real evil done in the world is usually done by *good people's* crusade against badness—by people who are *rabid with righteousness* and *bristling with holiness.*

There's a huge bonfire ritual on the last night with over a hundred drummers—it's an amazing catharsis. Sometimes the flames are 75 feet high.

The local hardware store opens a store on site during the event. Members of the local volunteer fire department are on hand, and we have first aid stations. Most people camp out; they can bring food and cook it. We also have a food court where vendors offer everything from basic American breakfasts to gourmet cooking, including lobster. We're not roughing it! You can even order pizzas from a local pizza place which delivers on-site. Starwood is a complete village. People get their mail there.

♦ *R/S: What's your drug policy?*

♦ JR: We're concerned with *behavior,* not personal choice. If somebody is misbehaving, we don't care if they have drugs in their system or are sober—they have to leave. We have good neighbor rules: no littering, be considerate, and watch out for each other. If somebody's having a hard time pitching their tent, give them a hand.

A lot of families arrive; over a hundred kids attended the last festival. We have teenagers who have attended every year of their lives. There is kids' programming for all ages, including day care for toddlers. Sometimes there are rite-of-passage rituals. It's hardest dealing with teenagers; part of the reason is because they often can't or don't articulate what they want. We teach kids how to drum, use a didgeridoo—things like that.

I remember Margot Adler saying that before the festival movement, if you were interested in Paganism, it would be *years* before you could get to be part of a major ritual, or even witness one. At Starwood, in the space of six days you can be part of ten different rituals from different cultures, *and* attend classes where people explain what it is that you're experiencing.

A lot of people in the Pagan community were very uncomfortable with their birth religion. They felt that they were worshipping a god who didn't like them because they were gay, or a woman, or poor, or whatever. Now they have the opportunity to find a spirituality that fits comfortably with the life they want to lead. That's an amazing thing, and a very *freeing* thing.

DRUMS AT PAGAN FESTIVALS

There has been an evolution of drums at Pagan festivals. At first people played anything they could get their hands on—ornamental drums, bad bongos that were never intended for actual use, then congas. Then the dumbek (small, easy to carry) and the bodhran (a Celtic hoop drum) were really popular for a while. Every culture has a hoop drum—in the Middle East it's the tar, the Irish have the bodhran, Native Americans have the shamanic drum—all of which are usually played with a stick. In the Nineties, African drums like Ashikos and Djembes appeared; you see them everywhere now.

Top Photo of Jeff Rosenbaum: Rev. Ivan Stang; Photo top left: Craig Mitchell; bottom left: Diana Wood-Turman

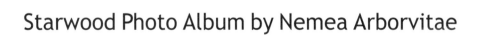

Starwood Photo Album by Nemea Arborvitae

Pagan Portraits

Laurie Lovekraft

Photo: Charles Gatewood

Former prom queen and star athlete Laurie Lovekraft has studied Wicca, Faery tradition, Thelema, and Buddhism, and has led numerous Pagan rituals over the past ten years. She has an M.A. in Anthropology, is a "visiting poet" in the Sonoma County (California) school system, manages a non-profit for children at risk, plays African drums, and sings in several Bay Area bands. She also rides a motorcycle while wearing thigh-high leather boots. Interview by John Sulak.

♦**RE/SEARCH: *You went from Prom Princess to Pagan Priestess—***

♦ LAURIE LOVEKRAFT: You never know who you're going to turn out to be. In high school I was a real conformist and a jock. I was pretty sheltered and didn't question authority much. I wasn't yet *awakened* to the fact that I was young and vital, and that these hidden doorways I'd read about in sci-fi and fantasy books actually existed. I was an avid reader.

What I learned from being a jock was discipline—and to be a priestess you also need discipline. You have to be able to stay up all night long for a ritual, or run up Solstice Hill wearing a backpack and carrying a gallon of water and a cauldron. You have to be able to haul your own provisions into a forest if you're doing a spell to save a forest. I learned discipline from sports and how to keep my body strong, and for that I'm grateful. Being a college athlete also paid for my schooling.

I went to the prom because that's what everyone did in my small east coast town. You know, the prom is just an American ritual and rite of passage! But when you're a priestess you put on lots of costumes, just like you do in the prom—it's *all* costumes! So the experience contributed to me being a darn good priestess.

Two years into college I discovered art classes and gave up my basketball scholarship. When kids start becoming nonconformist, you can always blame artists—free thinkers! Also, I heard Dr. Helen Caldicott speak about nuclear disarmament and the threat of nuclear winter (this was 1986). I became an activist on the spot. During my senior year of college, I discovered both feminism and Paganism through reading Betty Friedan's *The Feminine Mystique* and Starhawk's *Dreaming the Dark*. I started working with my first coven in Boston, attended a Witch camp, and through the years studied with different people. I've practiced Vipassana meditation, studied the work of Ramana Maharshi, and took a year-long Clairvoyant Training Program at the Berkeley Psychic Institute. Now I live in Sonoma County on three acres, teach classes about magic, and lead seasonal rituals at Ocean Song, a 350-acre farm and wilderness center. I'm also a founder of the Crescent Hellions.

♦ **R/S: *You work with herbs, but what's your position on psychedelics?***

♦ LL: Terence McKenna was a personal friend, so I have lots of opinions on psychedelics! Some of us see psychedelics as tools, or as *medicines.* That notion is derived from indigenous cultures all around the world. When there's a sickness of the soul or the community, you might take medicines to aid in accessing wisdom to help you live your life in a more complete way, or bring you or your community back into balance. Using plants this way is one of the "green mysteries." Use and misuse is really about personal responsibility. Psychedelics can be a crutch. You can have a dynamic ritual without anything stronger than chamomile tea! Ritual transcends reality, and it definitely can get you high—without a hangover.

Several years ago I took LSD and attended an all-night Samhain celebration—a time of year when many believe you can contact your beloved dead. This took place in the woods, with a huge bonfire. We did a ritual and descended into the underworld. I felt this huge surge through my body and started screaming—the ritual had tapped into a part of me that had a very deep wounding. Fortunately, this was a very safe space to do that. The whole experience was wonderful, but I wouldn't want to do it all the time. That was the last time I took LSD.

♦ **R/S: *How do you enter into a trance state?***

♦ LL: Intention. For example, I had been collaborating on a "Hekate" ritual for months, so I had a battery reserve of intention for what I wanted. I did some breath work, put on dramatic make-up and jewelry, took my drum to the ritual site and met my friends. I got into a very reflective, deeply quiet space and made room for the goddess to come through me, and it felt very powerful; I was charged for hours afterwards. I was dancing and singing and it was great! Music is a spiritual path for me. That ritual was a very successful encounter with the Dark Lady.

You know that you're in a dimension of magic when surprising things happen: when you're spontaneously speaking poetry, having visions, dancing for hours, or doing handstands—and you've never done handstands! Or you're speaking somebody's name and the phone rings and it's them calling from Kenya. Or the wind will pick up when you're invoking the East. Of course you can't *expect* this to happen, because then you're attached to the outcome of the ritual. Being a magical practitioner and priestess includes suspending belief and disbelief at will. You have to put aside your "lust for results." Magic definitely is beyond notions of good and evil.

♦ **R/S: *You've been described as a "kitchen witch"—***

♦ LL: A friend once said that "all women and cats are witches"—men can be too. My great-grandma was a kitchen witch; she emigrated from Eastern Europe and used folk remedies and herbal wisdom. Basically, a kitchen witch is a home remedy practitioner who isn't necessarily trained as a ritualist, and who perhaps hasn't read dozens of books on the Goddess. Grandma Libby would turn a cup upside-down when something was missing and the missing item would soon be found (the women of my family still do this).

At home, it's empowering for people to create their own personal altar (or altars) with candles, cloth, photos, or sacred objects. A kitchen witch knows how to make do with what's on hand. You don't need a $25 candle that's been specially anointed by His Highness the Head Honcho; it can be a candle in a jar with a picture of Inanna, Pan, or even Mother Mary taped to it. Add things to your altar that you find on a walk at the beach, or at Goodwill. I'm a thrift-store witch!

When I was traveling and studying music in India recently, I started having bad dreams in one of my hotel rooms. So I went down to the hotel kitchen, got some table salt and sprinkled it in all the corners, on the door sill, window ledges, around my bed and under my pillow. After that, I slept great! Salt and sage are good for purifying the energy in rooms.

♦ *R/S: You were a "good girl" in high school, but now you consider sex to be sacred—*

♦ LL: How can you *not* get into your sexual self when you're walking in the mud on a warm summer day in your garden? You're in your garden because you want to get into the actual—not metaphorical—earth. The world is a sensual place—especially a garden. Bodies are beautiful! All shapes and sizes. A woman or a man has a right to do what they want with their body, and decide who they want to display it to.

The thing I've learned most from being a priestess is *compassion.* Sometimes you hear folks in the counter-culture putting down "straight people"—but that's where I came from. I grew up eating Twinkies and Swanson's TV dinners; I had Barbie dolls; I went to the prom. Today, even though my politics are radical and my spirituality has strayed from the "Big 3" (Judaism, Christianity, Islam), I never want to lose track of where I came from. Because that means losing compassion for myself and others, and when you lose that, you become self-righteous, arrogant and cynical—just look at religious fundamentalists! You may think you're

better than others, but you're not. What Pagans are doing—reviving what some call the Old Religion—is just one more flavor, one more myth, one more strand in the "great weaving." We can't lose our tolerance, or all is lost.♦♦♦

Ivo Dominguez, Jr.

Ivo Dominguez, Jr. is a founder of the Assembly of the Sacred Wheel: *www.sacredwheel.org.* He is involved in implementing The New Alexandrian Library, a Pagan archive, resource center and meeting place for scholars and seekers. Interview by V. Vale.

♦ *RE/SEARCH: How can one set up a Pagan resource center?*

♦ IVO DOMINGUEZ: It's just a question of commitment. James T. Welsh, Nancy Stuart and myself started looking for land in 1988. We purchased 102.5 acres of wooded land and built the first house ourselves. The first year we rented a port-a-potty and nearly froze to death the first winter because basically our house was plywood with no insulation and drywall—we just huddled around a wood stove trying not to die. We had a big celebration for every little improvement, like when there was finally running water in the house.

We have a 16-year mortgage and mutually interlocking wills to make sure that if any of us dies, our money goes to the Assembly of The Sacred Wheel. Seven years later, Jim Dickenson and Mike Smith, joined us and also built a house like ours, with one very large great room for classes and rituals. We chose a property next to a state forests, and are trying to buy adjoining parcels of land.

At our annual retreat, people talk about what their vision is and what our collective vision is. One is to create an institution of longevity that's self-sus-

taining. Secondly, we want to be a resource for the evolution and development of magical communities in general. Our coven leadership is elected, with term limits. In covens, once a person reaches a certain level they usually go off and form their own coven. With us, we will hold meetings with her about this before we grant approval.

Another source of danger comes from people who start a coven and then think it *belongs* to them—it doesn't.

♦ *R/S: I love the notion of consensus, not voting.*

♦ ID: We started by voting, went to consensus, and now have a *hybrid system* whereby some decisions are done by votes, and some decisions are done by consensus, depending on what kind of decision that is. Anything related to *spirituality* is done by consensus. But the mundane planning of a conference, for example, is done differently. I'll give you an example why.

If you're a Delaware resident you can rent this beautiful hunting lodge for a weekend for only $150. As a favor and at their request I reserved this for the Mid-Atlantic Reclaiming people, and mailed in a check ten months before their weekend. Time passed, and I never heard from Reclaiming. When I finally got through to somebody, I was told, "The group decided it was not egalitarian to let the teachers have a retreat, so they canceled it."

Because they operate by consensus and nobody was clear as to who should have contacted me, Reclaiming had to have numerous discussions about who was going to reimburse me. I called them a few times to remind them. Well, it's been three years now and there's been no reimbursement. I finally let it go.

The point is, there are some things for which consensus is suited. But for practical matters like putting on a complex conference, where a hundred things can go wrong and solutions must be improvised on the spot, someone has to be the *manager*. The only thing our group requires is that the person submit reports showing where the money went. Making *everything* flow through consensus is, I think, as dangerous as making everything flow through the process of voting. I guess our perspective is: use the right tool for the right situation.

♦ *R/S: I'm sorry to hear that about Reclaiming. I love Reclaiming. Maybe there's more to the story—*

♦ ID: Don't get me wrong; I do too. We're *all* in the process of evolution as an anti-authoritarian Pagan community that prizes freedom above all. But I think it will take a very long time to develop all the "right" guidelines—ones that really work. Frankly, I really believe that we're not going to have any *real* Pagans for several more generations—until you have people that were raised by people that were raised by people that raised by people that were Pagans.

♦ *R/S: Let's discuss your New Alexandrian Library project—*

♦ ID: For some people, books are like a one night stand, whereas the books that I love I've read at least a dozen times and go back to them again and again. Our library project is about preservation. Because most publishing is corporate, and therefore profit-driven, many important resource books about magic and metaphysical thoughts have been out-of-print for years. We aim to preserve and make available not only scarce books but in-house magazines, ephemera, and small periodicals containing important articles that have never been anthologized and may vanish. People with material like this have started putting us in their wills.

Are you familiar with the Hermetic Brotherhood of Luxor? They predate the Golden Dawn and are a shaping force in modern Western magic. A friend who's in the Golden Dawn discovered a widow living in Pennsylvania who had in her attic all these Brotherhood papers her husband had collected. This is an example of the material that's out there, and needs to be in a library.

For historians, anthropologists and sociologists seeking to trace the history of ideas and social movements, our library may enable access to documents unavailable anywhere else. The Dewey Decimal classification system is fine, but it doesn't provide adequate cross-referencing for Pagan data, so we are working on making information searchable in many different ways. Some techies ask, "Why are you are even bothering with books? Why not get everything digitally?" The reality is that there is a value in having the original source material in its original format. Personally, I believe that the full meaning of a book isn't completely conveyed unless you can hold it in your hands.

Many Occult works were labors of love from small presses. From a purely magical perspective (and some people will snicker at this), you're closer to the energy of the author and/or the people that created that document if you handle the original. Another thing—hopefully our library will be a place where scholars and writers can meet and interact in a way that may produce an evolution of thought—results beyond what was originally envisioned.

Are you familiar with Kepler College?

♦ *R/S: Not at all.*

♦ ID: Kepler College, based in Seattle, is the only institution in the United States where you can get a legitimate B.S. or M.S. degree in Astrology. Some will argue, "Is this necessary?" It depends on who you are. Profit unfortunately plays a big role in our society—for example, there is a certain publishing company whose name begins with "L." They have published some good books, as well as a whole lot of books whose goal seems to be, "Let's make money on this year's fads. Let's target books at a group we can exploit—like teenagers." Certain books they will never publish because the audience for them is too small.

As far as Pagan history goes, there is no history of the evolution of Pagan ritual, or a comprehensive history of the development of Neo-Pagan thought and ideas. If somebody asks, "Explain the inter-relationships between the Neo-Pagan traditions and the Ceremonial Magic traditions," how many people could answer that? That kind of inter-linking of knowledge doesn't yet exist.

In addition, it's important that our library be inclusive of *all* magical traditions, including esoteric Christianity, mystical Judaism, ecstatic Sufism, Islam, and those of indigenous peoples. And of course you need all the "normal" reference books, because a world-class global outlook rests on a foundation of information from all disciplines, from all over the world.

Anyway, there are a lot of reasons to do the library. We hope that other people form libraries, too, because there need to be lots of libraries. Our goal is to match the standards of a well-equipped university library, with a high level of professionalism.

SOME RECOMMENDED BOOKS:

Lady Morganna Davies *Keepers of the Flame*—interviews with old-time witches that are pre-Starhawk.
Ursula K. LeGuin *Wizard of Earthsea* trilogy
Roger Zelazny *Lord of Light*—in this book I think he invented the term "aspecting."
Joscelyn Godwin, Christian Chanel, John P. Deveney *The Hermetic Brotherhood of Luxor*
Israel Regardie *What You Should Know About The Golden Dawn*
Murry Hope *The Psychology of Ritual*
Dolores Ashcroft-Nowicki *Highways of the Mind* ♦♦♦

Andras Arthen

Photo: Deirdre Pulgram Arthen

Andras Corban Arthen is the director of EarthSpirit, a non-profit pagan educational and service organization founded in 1980. As part of the Covenant of the Goddess, he represented pagan traditions at the United Nations Interfaith Conference in 1991, and the Parliament of the World's Religions in Chicago, 1993.

He is a poet, teacher, lecturer, storyteller, and musician. His CD (with Deirdre Pulgram Arthen) *We Believe* is available at *www.earthspirit.com*. He performs with Mother Tongue, EarthSpirit's ritual performance group. Andras lives with his extended family in Glenwood, a 135-acre Pagan conference center and nature preserve in the Berkshire hills of Western Massachusetts. Interview by John Sulak.

♦ *RE/Search: You consider yourself an agnostic—why?*

♦ ANDRAS ARTHEN: Reality is so complex, and humans are so limited. The whole notion of a human professing to know if there is or isn't a God/Goddess, or what reality is, or what the universe is truly about, really baffles me. How can anyone claim to have *certainty?* **How can anyone be sure of anything? So I'm fairly comfortable living with uncertainty.**

As Pagans reclaiming an Indo-European tradition (my particular tradition is Scottish), we occasionally get asked, "Are you white supremacists?" I reply that it's not a matter of race, it's culture. It's true that European Americans are responsible for a lot of the racism and destruction of indigenous cultures all over the world. Yet **it's important for the old ancestral traditions of Europe to be revived and stand side by side with the cultures of Native Americans, Africans and indigenous peoples all over the world.** It's really an act of healing, reminding us that our not-so-distant ancestors had a very different way of life from ours—one that was much more in harmony with Nature. Part of our work involves negating the modern Euro-American idea that Nature is separate from humans—something to be *transcended.*

In modern times, some people claim Witchcraft is an ancient religion, but there's no evidence of that. Druidism had priesthoods. Witches functioned as seers, midwives, herbalists, and tribal healers—somewhat akin to what we call a "shaman" today. And just as they might be respected for the benefits they bring, they could also be feared for the harm they could potentially do if you crossed them.

As Christianity spread throughout Europe, the church progressively took over the more beneficial roles associated with the witch, leaving behind the harm she could potentially do. The church capitalized on that by portraying the witch as someone who was evil because she or he was *not a Christian* but was holding on to the old traditions. Part of this was an attack on the power of women. But it was more that Christianity wanted to control *everything.*

A monotheistic religion like Christianity carries with it *totalitarianism,* because if you believe you have the "one true faith," you are compelled to *force* people to agree with you. Christianity was overwhelmingly patriarchal, so there was no power role for women in it. In the early days of the Christian era, when some of the Celtic and Germanic chieftains had converted to Christianity, there were laws passed that forbade not only the practice of Witchcraft but also the veneration of Pagan deities, the lighting of bonfires, certain kinds of dance—anything that could be construed as "the old Pagan ways."

I make a distinction between "Witchcraft" and "Wicca." "Wicca" is a hybrid Pagan religion that developed in the 1950s. As the modern pagan movement spread in the 1960s, the Wiccan texts and rituals popularized by Gerald Gardner and others were the most accessible. Many pagans, without knowing it, are using materials that came from people like Gardner. Whereas "Witchcraft" is older; it's more of a Craft than a religion. There's a focus on magic, seership, psychic experiences, ritual, and magical workings.

♦ *R/S: Tell us about EarthSpirit—*

♦ AA: Paganism is reviving within the context of a culture that *isn't* Pagan—in fact, one whose values and beliefs are positively *antagonistic* to Paganism. We've been so conditioned by our mostly-Christian culture that a lot of its specifically Christian elements have become invisible as such—they just wind up seeming "normal." **In a way, just living your life in mainstream culture is really antithetical to the core values of most pagan traditions.** So EarthSpirit is trying to develop a self-sustaining community providing means whereby people are enabled to practice Paganism not just on weekends or holidays, but every day!

Yet to propose changing the entire society to become more in line with pagan traditions is very unrealistic. Probably most people who call themselves pagans are in reality *totally* plugged into mainstream society. The middle ground is to develop a *subculture*—something that exists within the mainstream culture but is able to support a very different way of life. It's not that far-fetched. Ethnic, political and gay communities have always done this. Our emphasis is on trying to create sustainable economic models for pagan subculture survival.

Ironically, even though the word "Pagan" originally meant someone who was a rustic or farmer, the Modern Pagan movement was revived by college-educated, white middle-class urban dwellers with lots of access to information and ideas. About 20 years ago a group of us decided to form a close-knit, land-based community. **Having seen various "commune" experiments fail, we tried to develop an extended community that *didn't* require people to live together—at least until we were sure we really *could.*** Through our gatherings, classes and public rituals over the years, our community has grown to several thousand members all over the country, with a core group of about 100. Out of this, a core of about four families bought a 135-acre farm in the hills of Western Massachusetts. Seven adults and four children live here permanently or part-time, and another twenty or so consider this their other home. This was actually quite difficult; we had to make a lot of sacrifices and adjustments. Our ongoing experiment is to reclaim this land and to develop actual working models of how we can live as pagans.

The farm has several different buildings we live in. We help each other build things, everyone helps with the harvest, we share childcare—basically, we all work and play together. In paganism, besides the focus on Nature, a key focus is on the *tribal* mode of life.

Our community is not explicitly "polyamorous," but most of us don't consider ourselves as strictly monogamous, or even heterosexual. Because paganism tends to foster a sense of openness and freedom, it encourages us to be open to various possibilities that might come up. In the larger community of EarthSpirit, people are in all kinds of different relationships, from monogamous and heterosexual, to triads, group marriages, open or same-sex relationships, the whole gamut!

One reason our *intentional family* still works is that most of us have been together for 15 or 20 years. We share a long history together—more than many couples! There is a deep love, affection, commitment and understanding among us—even when we get into fights (like anybody does). Also, there is a great deal of *respect* for each other. We've all taken the same last name, which is Arthen.

♦ *R/S: How are your children being educated?*

♦ AA: Our kids attend a parent-run charter school in which we're actively involved. Conventional schools don't emphasize values we cherish, such as creativity, spontaneity, community, openness, respect, and cooperation. Developing good communication skills and qualities like sensitivity and awareness are not normally *emphasized* as children are growing up.

We start teaching our children about paganism at birth. We had a birthing room set up as a ritual space with shrines. Two children (of myself and my partner) were born there while people chanted and even danced as labor took place. Within hours of the births, a bunch of us went out in the woods and performed a Scottish "saining" ritual for the blessing and naming of the newborn child, next to a tree we connected to the child. My partner and I introduced the baby to each person; this involved ritually speaking the child's name for the first time. Everyone welcomed the child to this world. Afterwards we took the child's placenta and buried it by the tree to cement the connection between the child and the earth.

Our children have grown up with a fairly complete awareness of everything we do and are. But some pagans don't do that. Perhaps they're afraid that their child might say something embarrassing in public. Some feel they want the child to make up his or her own mind, later. I personally don't agree with these people—I feel that being pagan is *the* key thing in our lives. It binds everything together, so how are we *not* going to share that with our children? Of course, **if my children grow up and decide they don't want to call themselves pagan, that's fine with me.** But for us, paganism is our way of life. There's no way our children can grow up in our family without being exposed to it.

♦ *R/S: Your children are older now; are they still Pagan?*

♦ AA: Yes. My daughter, Isobel, is starting her training as a witch. My son Donovan, who's 14, went through one of his rites of passage last year to celebrate the fact that he is now a young man. We had a ritual that involved two days out in the woods. This happened in the context of a yearly pagan gathering we organize called Rites of Spring,

which lasts a whole week in May—this year was our 23rd year!

My son and another young man his age, Sean, went through this ritual that began on a Friday evening. They were led to the woods where they were greeted and taken into a circle of women who are central to their lives. Each woman blessed them and gave advice. Some of the women spoke frankly about their relationships with men, and what it was like to be a woman. One woman said that she had been raped, and that for a long time she had had a lot of pain, anger, and mistrust towards men. Now she was in a place where she could open more easily to men, and to these young men in particular. For our boys, this was really powerful—they had known this woman for a long time without realizing what she'd been through. The fact that she was able to trust them and share a very intimate part of her experience meant a lot to them, and it opened their eyes to some of the harsh realities that many women face in their lives, in a way that most boys that age seldom get to realize.

The next morning, on Saturday, some men who were central to their lives took them to the beach. We blindfolded them, put them in canoes, and rowed them across the water. On the other shore there were other men who greeted them, blessed them, and gave them gifts. The men talked about all the various things that being a man meant to them, and the different ways of being a man that are possible. My son and his friend were getting this prophetic *mirror* of what their lives might be like, and what they might become. Many of the men there were probably thinking, "I wish *I* had gone through something like this when I was that age!"

My son and his friend rowed the canoes back themselves, and the whole community was waiting to greet them. Those two young men felt a deep intimate kinship with all those women and men, who are all very diverse. They could see many different potential models of ways of being. And they also felt connected with the entire community that had seen them grow up, and who treasured them and valued them. ♦♦♦

EarthSpirit is a non-profit organization providing services to a nationwide network of Pagans and others following an Earth-centered spiritual path. Founded in 1980, EarthSpirit is working to develop

Pagan concepts and attitudes for living in the present age, to encourage communication and understanding among people of different traditions and ideologies, to provide opportunities for shared spiritual experience, and to help educate the general public concerning Earth-centered spirituality.

EarthSpirit offers events open to the public, including:

♦ Rites of Spring, a week-long pagan festival and gathering in Western Massachusetts near Memorial Day weekend in May.

♦ Twilight Covening, a Magical Retreat in Western Massachusetts during Columbus Day Weekend in October.

♦ Suntide, a Magical Cape Cod Weekend in July.

♦ A Feast of Lights, a Midwinter Celebration of spirit, community and the arts. See *www.earthspirit.com*. ♦♦♦

Frederic Lamond

Frederic Lamond is the author of *Religion Without Beliefs*. Interview by John Sulak.

♦ *R/S: When did you first find out about Paganism and Witchcraft?*

♦ FL: I found out about contemporary witchcraft in 1955 when I read a book by the English anthropologist Gordon Rattray Taylor, *Sex in History*. In it he described Margaret Murray's thesis about the medieval witches being the remnants of a Pagan fertility cult. The term "Paganism" didn't come into common use until the late 1960s or early 1970s.

♦ *R/S: What was your reaction when you found out about it?*

♦ FL: I was intrigued. I had had a spontaneous mystical experience of the Goddess Aphrodite in the arms of my first girlfriend, and had set out to find other worshippers of the great Goddess. G.R. Taylor's book made me start looking for books on witchcraft. It wasn't long before I found Gerald Gardner's book *Witchcraft Today* and this rang so many bells with me that I wrote to him and was in due course introduced to his coven.

♦ R/S: Describe life in Europe then. What were other Pagans like?

♦ FL: I can only speak for England. The country was still recovering from World War II and postwar austerity, and values were very conventional. But there was an active intellectual underground that was questioning and seeking to subvert the old puritanical values. England was already then, as it always has been, the most tolerant country in Europe, and in London you could do anything you wanted as long as it wasn't aggressively anti-social.

The other "Pagans" I knew were limited to the half-dozen members of my coven, but I also belonged to an organization called the Progressive League which, though firmly agnostic (if not atheistic), promoted pretty Pagan values like nudism and free love as well as socialism and world federalism.

♦ R/S: When did you meet Gerald Gardner?

♦ FL: In July 1956, after I had written to him about *Witchcraft Today*. He invited me to his flat and subsequently introduced me to the members of his coven.

♦ R/S: What was he like, and what was your relationship?

♦ FL: He was a very lovable old gentleman, unassuming, with a great sense of humour, an excellent raconteur with a fine feeling for the absurdities of human life. He was also a trickster with a very creative attitude to factual truth, especially anything to do with witchcraft and its origins.

To give you an example: Six weeks after my initiation the coven split and the older members went off with the high priestess Doreen Valiente, while the younger ones, including me, stayed with Gerald and his new high priestess, Dayonis. The breakaway coven asked if they could continue to meet in the cottage on the grounds of the nudist club owned by Gerald until they had found their own premises. Well, Gerald could have replied: "The cottage and the nudist club are my property. If you are not prepared to circle with me anymore you

can't circle on my property!" Instead he replied: "There is an ancient law dating back to the Burning Times (a favorite expression of his) that for security reasons no witch coven may meet less than 25 miles from the meeting place of another witch coven."

♦ R/S: Can you tell us about your initiation?

♦ FL: No, that is secret. But I can tell you that it made a tremendous impression on me, and I felt I was now permanently "plugged in" to the same divine power whom I had first encountered in the arms of my girlfriend.

♦ R/S: What do you know about the roots of modern Paganism?

♦ FL: Now: what I have read in Ronald Hutton's excellent book *The Triumph of the Moon*. Then: I knew intuitively it could not trace its lineage beyond the occult revival of the 1890s. Any link to the Middle Ages or even the Stone Age, which Gerald affirmed, was in my mind utterly unprovable, and didn't matter anyway.

♦ R/S: What were the Pagan rituals that you went to like? How did you celebrate the Sabbats and the Esbats?

♦ FL: The four major sabbats—Candlemas, Beltane, Lammas and Halloween are what we called them then—were bonfire picnics to which we were encouraged to invite our life-affirming friends. At the full moon esbats, we worked healing spells for those who requested it, in or out of the coven.

♦ R/S: Is what you're doing now anything like it was back then?

♦ FL: All covens are different. Some contemporary ones are much more structured and ceremonial than we were then, others much less disciplined and rather chaotic.

♦ R/S: Were you at all skeptical about what you were doing and being taught?

♦ FL: You bet! The healing spells worked well beyond pure chance, so I soon became convinced of their effectiveness. But Gerald told so many lies to newspapers, claiming that our high priestess came from a hereditary Witch coven when in fact she came from a Jewish family and had only been initiated three years before me, that I soon wondered whether Gerald had invented the whole Witchcraft setup. I had a tough three days of doubt, before an inner voice told me, "It doesn't matter! The rituals work

for you and have brought you into close contact with the Life Force and the eternal current of love. Does it matter whether they are three or three thousand years old?"

♦ R/S: Did you talk to other people about this?

♦ FL: I shared my doubts about Gerald's teachings with fellow coven members. I only told other members of the Progressive League and of Mensa about my Witch activities.

♦ R/S: How secretive were you?

♦ FL: Careful would be the right word. Not out of any fear of persecution, but because more conventional people would have regarded me as a nut case, which could have harmed my career. Besides, in England talking about your religion in ordinary conversation isn't done, and witchcraft was my religion.

♦ R/S: When did Paganism really take off, and why do you think it did?

♦ FL: In the late 1960s and 1970s. It was very much in tune with the flower child period of the late 1960s, and offered a more solid spiritual haven to disappointed flower children when that movement collapsed.

♦ R/S: Have you been a Pagan for the entire time since then?

♦ FL: Yes.

♦ R/S: Has it ever been difficult or challenging?

♦ FL: My Pagan principles: No! Life: Yes! And when lots of things started going wrong simultaneously I realized the Goddess was trying to tell me something.

♦ R/S: How has your spirituality evolved over the years?

♦ FL: I have become more tolerant of other peoples' religious beliefs and practices, and am interested in finding points of contact. Having participated in interfaith activities, I find it fascinating how some contemporary Christians are moving towards immanent pantheism, but that doesn't make me want to become a Christian.

♦ R/S: What have you learned from being a Pagan for decades?

♦ FL: That everyday life is fascinating, and much too complex to be squeezed into any religious structure, even a Pagan one. Also, that Paganism under whatever name is probably the religion of the future. ♦♦♦

Sharon Knight

Photo: Charles Gatewood

Sharon Knight is an initiated Feri priest-ess and a singer/songwriter with the tribal trance rock band, "Pandemonaeon." She has priestessed several large-scale ecstatic rituals—an example being the 1999 Ancient Ways Festival, where several hundred people invoked the goddess Kali, dancing and chanting around a bonfire on a starry night. Pandemonaeon's CD is available from their Website, *www.pande-monaeon.com.* Interview by John Sulak.

♦ **RE/SEARCH: At a Pagan ritual, you invoked the goddess Kali who is Hindu—**

♦ SHARON KNIGHT: Oh, but she's also very Pagan. Pre-Vedic Hinduism is very conducive to Pagan adaptation. In the earlier Shaka-Shaivite cults where Kali and Shiva originate, the practices resemble Pagan practices a great deal. They revere divine female power, are ecstatic in nature, and celebrate the earth rather than seek escape from her. The Hinduism most of us in the West are familiar with is Vedic, which stems from later Aryan invasions that absorbed the earlier cults and morphed them into the more orthodox approach we see today.

♦ **R/S: If you want to worship Kali, why not do it at a Hindu ceremony?**

♦ SK: I am militant about not letting myself be labeled. I don't want to be called a Buddhist or a Hindu or a Chaos Magician or a Feri initiate—although I incorporate these elements into my practice. My spirituality is very much about *movement,* where I take elements that inspire me and weave them through myself. It doesn't matter to me whether my ceremonial creations are culturally

or historically accurate—only that they move me to face the divine.

I like to say that "I am my own cult of one." Ultimately, each of us has a unique spirituality and perspective on the universe, so in a way everybody has their own religion. Ideally, on any worthwhile magical path you are peeling away layers of conditioning to find your true core, your true self. Kali is very much a part of what I resonate with.

♦ **R/S: Tell us about Kali—**

♦ SK: First of all, I have a staunch non-traditionalist attitude, so my knowledge of Kali is mostly experiential rather than scholarly. In the course of my Feri practice, Kali kept showing up as a great transformative force that I needed to work with. Both Kali and the "Tower" card in the Tarot deck fulfill the function of breaking away from what is no longer serving you. Kali can be ruthless and fierce as she cuts away illusion, but in so doing she creates the opportunity to transcend your limitations. Therefore, she's the perfect champion of the non-dogmatist.

Kali's dance is the balance between life and death. Some people look for security and material things to help shape their identity, but I think one needs to confront emptiness, too. The point is to enjoy living, without clinging to either things or rigid beliefs.

♦ **R/S: Kali is very violent and bloody—**

♦ SK: —only in one of her aspects. She is also infinitely loving and nurturing. A weakness of the Pagan community is that it can be more about frolic and celebration than doing the necessary, deeper work to refine your soul.

The function of Kali as a terrible, gory mother is to get people to confront their own fears. Of course, as humans one of our biggest fears is death. And

until you come to terms with death—although that's a lifelong struggle—you aren't free from fear; you're constantly pushing it away. A lot of what shamanic mysteries are about is exploring your demise in minute detail. Liberating yourself from the fear of death enables you to live your life more fully and passionately.

So Kali is about slaying those things that keep us from living fully, authentically and spontaneously. When I work with Kali, I sacrifice my "clingings" on the altar of the authentic self, and try to *transform* them. You never want to destroy them, because they're parts of yourself.

♦ **R/S: Where does your ritual structure come from?**

♦ SK: Some from music and belly-dancing, and some from my current coven, the Crescent Hellions. We practice *Boddhichitta,* the Buddhist practice of asking our elders, ancestors, Bodhisattvas—all enlightened beings, including parts of ourselves that may already be enlightened—for help. We end our rituals with a final completion, "Dedicating the Merit," whose purpose is to gather up all the good that has been done and concentrate it into a focus, and then share it with the entire world.

We say, "May the benefit of this act, and all acts, be dedicated unto the complete liberation and supreme enlightenment of all beings everywhere pervading space and time. May the benefit of practice—ours and others'—come to fruition ultimately and immediately, and remain in the state of presence." From there, we gather up all the energy and send it into the world with a resounding "Ah!" Raising energy can be done for everybody's good, without taking anything away from yourself. What I'm doing, I offer to everybody. Everything we do ripples out into the universe and affects people—hopefully, for the good.♦♦♦

PANDEMONAEON

Katrina Hopkins

A founding member of the Dark Flame Coven, Katrina Hopkins is a Pagan priestess, lecturer, writer, and singer-songwriter who lives in Washington, D.C. She holds a B.S. in Electrical Engineering and an M.S. in Computer Science. Her Website is *http://users.erols.com/katrina/home.htm.* Interviews by John Sulak and V. Vale.

♦ *RE/SEARCH: What's your background?*
♦ KATRINA HOPKINS: Both my parents were from North Carolina. They were part of the black migration north, between World War I and World War II. Like a lot of folks they moved north for jobs and to escape the horrors of segregation.

My grandmother was dating a Cherokee. They were sexually active and used condoms. At some point he asked her to marry him and she said *No,* so he put a hole in the condom in order to get her pregnant—it worked! In North Carolina, it was bad to be black but it was even worse to be Cherokee. My grandmother was a high yellow [light-skinned]; her family was considered upper-class, simply because they cleaned the houses of the really rich people. (They themselves lived in abject poverty, but it didn't matter.) When my great-grandparents found out who the father was, they had him "sterilized" [castrated]! My grandmother took my mother and fled to Washington, D.C. to escape the abuse from her own relatives, as well as segregation.

This was during the Harlem Renaissance, so my mother was raised in the middle of an incredible music scene sustained by thriving black businesses. When my father met my mother, he was a boxer and street hustler. He met her on the Wilson boat line—people take a little cruise and hear a little music. My father was a big player, a dangerous guy, and my mother was a little innocent. But something happened; he got sick. Of all the women he had, the only one who visited him in the hospital was a little teenage girl with a sweet face—my mother. He decided to marry her.

They got married and then he was drafted and shipped overseas—this was punishment because he refused to box the opponents the Army set up for him—he was afraid he'd kill someone. Finally he was discharged and my parents settled in Anacostia, the toughest part of Washington, D.C., and raised six children.

The schools there were horrible, so my parents sent us to Catholic school. Back then you could send a whole family for $25 a year. My neighborhood had once been huge plantations before it became a suburb for black servicemen—there weren't very many paved roads. As I grew up, these beautiful wild orchards got paved over for roads and public housing. "Urban renewal" happened, and all these poor people from another part of town got moved to my neighborhood, *apartheid*-style, to make way for "redevelopment" where they had formerly lived. Instantly, schisms developed between us and the newcomers, and my neighborhood became a gang territory. So I grew up in street gangs; every neighborhood had a gang.

I saw a lot of violence; girls were raised to know how to fight. All my role models were big, outspoken women who expressed what they wanted, and if you didn't give it, they went and got it themselves. It was expected that I could stand up to people. One woman who had a huge influence on my life worked as a historian at the Smithsonian Institute. I would go to her house and just *read;* she had all these books on the history of racism, with photographs of lynchings. I also was in a street gang. **The only white people in my life were sort of objectified—they were either nuns, priests, or policemen. They were all authority figures!**

In the 10th grade I discovered the Black Panther Party. **I started reading Mao, Franz Fanon, Angela Davis, Bobby Seale and Huey Newton. Suddenly I had a place for my anger, and an analysis.** I was immersed in Black nationalism, anti-imperialism, and Marxist-Leninism. By the time I graduated from my all-girl Catholic high school I was a stone-cold Marxist atheist. I had helped organize student demonstrations in my school where I called the Black Panthers for help—I was a follower of them but was too young to join.

I enrolled at Howard University aiming for a degree in pre-law, because I thought I could help "the movement" by being a civil rights lawyer. For the next three years I was part of several Black nationalist and anti-imperialist, communist groups—I even went to Cuba. I tried to do worker organizing in the greater D.C. area, becoming part of what was then called the "New Communist Movement" in 1976. Then I was beaten and left in the streets of New York City, purged as a "traitor" by fellow members of the communist group I had joined—that's a story in itself. By age 21, I had gone through what some people experience over 40 years! I was very disillusioned, to say the least, and decided not to become a movement lawyer.

Basically, I had to start over. I had to figure out what I believed in and what I wanted to do with my life. So I spent the next ten years rebuilding my life. I went back to school for an engineering degree, began working at the phone company and stayed away from politics for a very long time.

I still was an atheist; I had no spiritual life whatsoever. Then in 1986 I discovered that lo and behold, my father's alcoholism had had an effect on me. So I started going to A.C.O.A. (Adult Children of Alcoholics) meetings. 1986 was a very important year; it was when I discovered that I truly didn't have a concept of what people call a "Higher Power." A.C.O.A.'s precepts were: the Higher Power had to be greater than you, and it had to be capable of bringing you from insanity to sanity. So I said, "Okay, I'm assuming you guys know what you're talking about. So I'll assume you can bring me to sanity."

I had been a devout Catholic as a child, then turned to atheism for years, and now had in my life something akin to "divinity." Having found a source of spiritual nurturance, I started doing political work again. In 1991 I became associated with a Unitarian Universalist church called the "Sojourner Truth

Congregation" in D.C. Their minister became a very good friend of mine. **In 1992 I met some witches who thought just like me. We did a group reading of Starhawk's** *Spiral Dance* **and then started the Dark Flame Coven**, which still continues.

For me, being a Pagan is about recognizing the sacredness in everything. But I'm not a New Ager—I think that some things are made to die for other things, that we feed off each other, and that we're part of a much more complex organism. So I joke, "Yeah, I eat meat, but it's not because I don't appreciate it—the meat is really good!" I'm not just trying to save the clean water for the earth's benefit, but because unclean water is detrimental to my own health. The earth and my body are part and parcel of the same system: "As above, so below." [Heraclitus]

That said, most definitions of "Pagan" conveniently ignore the true diversity of earth-based spirituality. In New York, Washington, D.C. and Philadelphia, there are large urban black populations who are involved in their own African-based spirituality and don't really need European-based Pagan traditions. This spirituality makes a connection with the animal kingdom and with plants, it talks about ancestors and ancestral myths, and in general talks about doing deeper work like healing.

♦ *R/S: Why aren't more African Americans involved in Paganism?*

♦ KH: Hey—when did *I* become their spokesperson? I'll take this up at the next All Black People's Meeting and see what they come up with! People used to ask me, "Why aren't there more African Americans in the Feminism movement? I used to reply, "Just because they're not with you, doesn't mean that they're not doing their own work." A lot of Africans and people of color *are* involved in earth-based religions like Santeria, connecting to the ancestors, but within a different context. You know, it was difficult for a lot of black women to join the Feminist movement because one of the entrance criteria was turning away from men and male forms of power. I remember attending Feminist meetings where the mostly-white women present would talk about men derisively, and if you weren't able to express those same types of anger, you were *de facto* excluded from the group process.

When I was in N.O.W. (National Organization for Women) I would teach at their retreats. In one exercise, I would say to a group of Feminist women, "Imagine that you walk into a room, and it's *all men.* What would they have to do to make you feel comfortable?" The women would say things like, "There's no way I would go in! They could *never* make me feel comfortable." So now you know the answer to, "How can we make feminism more comfortable for black women?"

A lot of our future work will involve changing the language, changing the context, changing the dualistic structures, and being *responsible* for your own role in this. It's about finding the questions that illuminate. I was just talking with some people who were practically shouting, "Reclaiming is *against* hierarchy! It's *against* hegemony!" I thought, "Hmmm, they're defining themselves by what they're not." Describing yourself by what you're not is not healthy. What's needed here is *different language;* the context and dialogue need to be changed. How can we reframe this?

One of my specialties is shadow-work. It has been articulated by Jung and others. **Your shadow is the part of yourself that you discard, that you say you're not, and that you turn away from ("I couldn't possibly do** *that!").* If someone gives a strong emotional response, it's probably more shadow than anything else. And as you grow, your shadow grows. Jung also said that within your shadow there is gold. In other words, there are incredible gifts to be found in your shadow, and as long as you turn away from them, you're turning away from a source that could give you strength.

There's the idea that the first half of your life you are creating your shadow, and the second half of your life you're supposed to be re-integrating it back. One of the aspects or repercussions of not owning your shadow involves *projections,* such as "Black people are dangerous," or "Queer people are sex-crazed perverts." In our society, black people carry the society's power shadow; queer people carry the society's sex shadow. Many people in the world don't really "see" other people, they see what they project onto them. Shadow-work works to removes the projection, so you can start seeing people as they really are.

It teaches you compassion, first for yourself (because you get to see your own dark side—which can make you truly humble). Then you stop projecting on other people, and suddenly start to see the *divine* in them.

Many people believe that half of the world's trouble comes from the fact that most people *don't* do shadow work. **Most of the world's wars are about** *projections*—**demonizing other people, labeling them "evil."** As people mature, I think it's necessary to begin re-integrating things back from the shadow—look at your shadow, uncover whatever buried gifts may be there, and take the gift back consciously—which takes the power away from that shadow.

♦ *R/S: Is there any connection between what the Black Panthers were doing and your Pagan activities?*

♦ KH: Yeah! I consider myself a warrior. The Panthers set forth a context where you had to look at things far more clearly, to help shock you out of your denial. I am not a pacifist, and this distinguishes me from many other Pagans. I have not renounced violence—I'm part of a people that has been violently kidnapped from another continent. I was not a formal Panther member, but I shared their belief that we have the right to defend ourselves. But I don't believe in *unnecessary* violence.

♦ *R/S: You're affiliated with Reclaiming—*

♦ KH: I like Reclaiming because it provides a place where I can feel welcome, and where certain parts of me can be mirrored—like the fact that I'm both political and bisexual/queer—which is not so welcome, say, in Santeria.

Last year I was trying to find a way to do some healing work at a larger community level, and initiated "Connect D.C." [*www.connectdc.org*] Washington, D.C. is laid out as a diamond, with points in each of the cardinal directions. I wanted to mix in community-to-community healing with geographic focus—hence the idea of casting a magical circle around the city.

The eastern marker is in an area of D.C. that has a lot of public housing and has suffered a lot of grief. It's practically all black, and is very poor. The inhabitants have suffered from a disproportionate amount of violence, drug infestation and police over-response. A group of us Pagans cleaned up the whole area around the marker and did a ritual. A member of the Seneca Nation was present, and we asked him to come forward and sing a song of welcome for the East—the Seneca Nation still lay claim to the land up to and including the U.S. capital. This member was standing at the eastern marker next to people of African, European and Other descent—everybody performing a Wiccan ritual.

We've done this at each of the markers. To me, this was my old grass-roots organizing coming out, the priestess in me coming out, and the teacher in me coming out. This was a way to teach ritual. I called it my P.T.A. (Preacher, Teacher, Activist) activity.

♦ **R/S: Are you still involved with the Unitarian Church?**

♦ KH: Yes, with the Sojourner Truth Congregation. For a year and a half I was the acting minister. I organized all the services and performed a monthly service as part of my priestess work. I wanted to see what it was like to take responsibility for an entire community and give spiritual nurturance on a regular basis. The congregation probably found it interesting: having a witch as the acting minister!

♦ **R/S: You've been described as a computer geek—**

♦ KH: I have a Bachelor of Science in Electrical Engineering and a Master of Science in Computer Science. I'm the kind of geek that makes geeks' eyes glaze over! I've been doing research and development for a large Bell regional company for the last ten years. But with their last merger, they got rid of R&D, so now I'm an Internet Architect.

I'm also a Reclaiming teacher—I teach at witch camp—and a political activist. I think teaching is a form of priestessing—you help people move energy from one state to another, and build a container that allows transformation to happen. Often I help people transform from victim to activist.

At age 46, I'm looking back over my life and am grateful that I'm still able to be surprised and overwhelmed with grace and joy. In my coven, we joked that we didn't have a real ritual unless we had a big screw-up that would make us all laugh. **We always need a good sense of humor, even during the most sacred ritual!♦♦♦**

Selena Fox

Photo: Dr. Dennis Carpenter

Selena Fox is a prime mover behind Circle Sanctuary in Wisconsin, a non-profit Wiccan church, resource center, and nature preserve. Her enterprise encompasses publishing (*Circle* magazine is one of the largest Pagan publications, available at major chain retailers), education, and events sponsoring. She founded the Pagan Spirit Gathering, one of the first large outdoor Pagan festivals. A search for "Selena Fox" at *www.google.com* will yield a variety of documentation. Her official website is *www.circlesanctuary.org.* Interview by John Sulak.

♦ **RE/SEARCH: Tell us about your Pagan land preserve—**

♦ SELENA FOX: Circle Sanctuary, a legally-recognized Wiccan church, was founded in 1974. In 1975, we rented some rural land near Sun Prairie, Wisconsin. When our landlord found out what we were doing, he evicted us, and so it was apparent we needed our own land where we could commune with Nature and do what we wanted on a more permanent basis. In June of 1983, I had a dream about a plot of land, and shortly thereafter someone told us about a 200-acre property that had just come up for sale. It turned out to be the land I had seen in my dream.

After doing financial negotiations we felt that we needed to do a ritual before we signed the papers. So on Halloween night we did a short ritual to see if the land wanted us, and the answer was "Yes"!

From the beginning this land was to be designated and dedicated as a *sacred site,* owned by a non-profit organization rather than by an individual or group. We wanted a place where larger festivals or rituals could take place. It turned out that we had to fight a four-year legal battle.

We endured numerous zoning hearings and site visits by local officials, and it became a media circus—obviously, the issue was not zoning but our religious orientation. Finally, after a campaign which included the ACLU and others, we won—the local papers reported our victory as "Town Votes in Favor of Witchcraft Church." We had endured a rite of passage into the local area!

In 1992, when a televangelist attempted to stage a hate rally against us and get a mob to come out and disrupt our Samhain gathering, government officials including five police departments and two judges protected us. Even earlier, on Earth Day 1990, the nearby mayor invited us to give a lecture. If the township invites the local witch to talk to their youth about environmental responsibility, you know things have improved!

♦ **R/S: Describe the geography of your land—**

♦ SF: We're several miles outside of a village in a fairly conservative rural area, only a few miles from Taliesin, Frank Lloyd Wright's architectural school. Interestingly, Wright capitalized the word "Nature," and we do that as well. Taliesin means "shining brow" and it's a Welsh Pagan word. At Wright's school there's a carved inscription at the main reception hall about Celtic spirituality and the Druid roots of Taliesin. I see real parallels between Wright's work and ours—he too fought misunderstandings about what he was trying to achieve.

It's important to create ritual areas and sites within the larger sacred site for group and individual use. On our land we have a spring dedicated to Brigid, the Celtic Goddess of healing, inspiration, fire, and sacred wells and springs. Sometimes people tie a ribbon with their request for healing on one of the nearby trees—similar to the Coothie custom of Celtic Scotland, where if you had need of healing, you would petition the spirit of a local spring. So at Brigid Spring, you can see all manner of beautiful ribbons hanging.

♦ **R/S: What about Pagans who live in the city?**

♦ SF: I think you can connect with Nature no matter where you are, although it becomes a challenge when you live in a human-dominated environment. It helps to create an altar with some natural objects that come from walks outdoors. Additionally, one would do well to regularly visit an environment where one can do spiritual practice. This can be structured, in the form of a personal or group ritual, or unstructured—such as a walk through the woods, or across a prairie, or along a seashore. It's advisable to have some experience in a more natural setting at least once a year.

It's important that there be Pagan land projects throughout the country. In addition to the 200 acres run by the non-profit organization, my husband and I recently bought 33 adjoining acres so we can have some personal space. Here we are developing an international Pagan center which organizes festivals throughout the year. We have archives and a library for researchers investigating the history of Paganism. Also, we see this as a healing center. People who can't come in person can send us their ribbons along with their healing request, and we will tie them to the tree at Brigid's Spring.

We have a Stone Circle at the top of a naturally occurring mound, surrounded by a grove of oak and birch trees. On Winter Solstice 1983, eight of us weathered sub-zero temperatures and a foot of snow to do our first Solstice ritual and lay the first stones for it. Since then, thousands of stones brought by hundreds of people have been placed around this great circle atop this mound. In 1999, in connection with Circle's participation in The Parliament of World's Religions in Capetown, South Africa, we presented the Stone Circle as a gift of service to the world.

Photo: Lynnie Johnston

Over the years we've held numerous multi-cultural and inter-religious ceremonies with people from various Native American tribes; Eastern sacred traditions, such as Hinduism and Buddhism; and Christian, Jewish, and Muslim traditions. Others who may not consider themselves religious at all—humanists, agnostics, and atheists—have taken part in our multicultural celebrations. Every year we have a Mother Earth ceremony as part of Earth Day. I see Circle Sanctuary as a place where we build bridges with other people of other cultures. ♦♦♦

John Machate

This interview on the subject of Pagans in the Military raises interesting ethical issues. John Machate (veteran USAF), the founder and coordinator of the Military Pagan Network, spoke to John Sulak. See *www.milpagan.org*

The following press release was sent out from WASHINGTON, DC on May 18, 1999: U.S. Representative Bob Barr (Republican, GA) had demanded an end to the taxpayer-supported practice of witchcraft on military bases. Barr's request came in response to reports that chaplains at Fort Hood and other bases are sanctioning, if not supporting, the practice of Witchcraft as a "religion" by soldiers on military bases.

"This move sets a dangerous precedent that could easily result in the practice of all sorts of bizarre practices being supported by the military under the rubric of 'religion.' What's next? Will armored divisions be forced to travel with sacrificial animals for Satanic rituals? Will Rastafarians demand the inclusion of ritualistic marijuana cigarettes in their rations?" said Barr, in letters to military and congressional leaders.

"A print of the painting, 'The Prayer At Valley Forge,' depicting George Washington on bended knee, praying in the hard snow at Valley Forge, hangs over the desk in my office," Barr concluded. "If the practice of witchcraft, such as is allowed now at Fort Hood, is permitted to stand, one wonders what paintings will grace the walls of future generations."

Lt. Col. Benjamin Santos, Fort Hood spokesman, replied that the Army would let the Fort Hood Open Circle continue to practice on the base. "As far as we are concerned, they are a religious organization providing for the spiritual needs of our soldiers. They are proof that people with different religious beliefs are all working together successfully."

♦ **RE/SEARCH: *When was the first Pagan ritual on a U.S. military base?***
♦ JOHN MACHATE: In 1994 the first Pagan ritual occurred in the U.S. at Ft. Campbell in Kentucky. Earlier, a Wiccan service had been held in an American army base in Kaiserslautern, Germany in 1992. We estimate there are 10,000 Pagans in the military—more than the Muslims—including active duty, National Guard and their dependents. And Muslims have a full-time, active-duty military chaplain.
♦ *R/S: **How does a Pagan organization achieve military recognition?***
♦ JM: A Pagan church can become "recognized" by the Department of Defense by providing lots of paperwork, including tax-exempt paperwork, and by presenting a qualified candidate for the Chaplaincy. The only churches that have even come close are the Aquarian Tabernacle Church, Circle Sanctuary, the Sacred Well Congregation, and the Temple of Isis.
♦ *R/S: **What makes Pagan soldiers different?***
♦ JM: There's no way to differentiate a Christian soldier from a Pagan soldier— they all wear the same uniforms—except that when they go home, they worship different gods. Military personal don't give a rat's butt about what somebody else's religion is, as long as they do their job.
♦ *R/S: **Then what caused the Ft. Hood Witch hunt?***
♦ JM: Kim Sue Lia Parks, a reporter for the *Austin-American Statesman,* wrote a human interest piece on the Ft. Hood Open Circle monthly lunar ritual, which spurred Congressman Bob Barr to begin a campaign against Pagans in the military. The Pagans have a bonfire surrounded by a stone circle, with a larger stone circle around that. The stones were collected from around the base. About 150 people attend these rituals. They call the quarters, cast the circle and do participatory ritual invoking the Goddess and God. Some people wear civilian clothes and others wear robes. These services are open to everybody, even Christians—that's why they're called Open Circles.

Bob Barr is a Republican Representative from Georgia who was trying to get Clinton impeached even before the Monica Lewinsky scandal. He's opposed to gun control and there are speculations he's a racist. Barr tried to get anti-Pagan laws passed using "stealth amendments"—he would attach them to bills that *have* to pass, hoping they'd be overlooked. But he failed twice—not that he's going to give up. Senator Strom Thurmond has also supported his efforts.

A local Baptist minister named Reverend Harvey was on ABC TV screaming, "They're out there jumping around bonfires and they're probably cooking babies!" But he looked like a idiot. All this anti-Witchcraft rhetoric has simply allowed Paganism, or Wicca in particular, to come to the forefront of the media. Even Pat Robertson said, "We gotta let them do what they do, or it will fall back on us and we'll lose our rights, too."

♦ *R/S: At what point did you "come out" as a Pagan to the military?*

♦ JM: Three days into basic training, in 1989. They asked what religion I wanted listed on my dog tags. Upon responding "Wicca," they asked what it was. I told them it was a religion and they wrote it down. For six years my dog tags said "Wicca." I never had any problems with my faith in the military.

♦ *R/S: When did you start meeting other Pagans in the military?*

♦ JM: The main problem is the constant transfer of personnel from base to base. I started collecting names and putting them in a Military Pagan database. Over time I connected with people at other military bases, and eventually we became the Military Pagan Network.

A lot of Pagans in the military become Pagans after they enlisted. That poses a problem if you decide to be a pacifist, because you're still bound by the oath you took (to defend your country) when you joined the military, and oaths are very important to Pagans. You make that oath, you don't break it. Now, some Pagans are against the idea that they can't say No to what they might consider an unethical military order. Let's say you're ordered to take a hill where a village is situated. Well, you might end up killing civilians.

♦ *R/S: Also, certain Pagan activities are edgy—*

♦ JM: Right—let's say you're on active military duty while married. If the military busts you on adultery charges because you're having sex with three other women, even though your wife is watching (Pagans do not judge these types of activities), the military will still prosecute you. It falls into the category of "activities not appropriate for military personnel"—it's not considered "moral," even though everybody involved is a consenting adult.

♦ *R/S: Nevertheless, Pagans have been persecuted in the past—*

♦ JM: Covenant of the Goddess has a dissertation on their website by someone who specializes in what she calls "The Great European Witch Hunt," which covers this entire period of the so-called Burning Times. Using court records and documentation, she was able to find out how many people died, who killed them, and what the various charges were. She came up with the figure of 15,000 killed. That's a far cry from nine million, which some people have claimed. And of those 15,000, most were killed by civilian courts.

Generally, if the Catholic Church got someone who was accused of witchcraft, the person usually got off because the Church didn't recognize Witchcraft as something that even existed, not even as heresy—it wasn't "real." The book everyone cites, the *Malleus Maleficarum*—today everyone knows about it, but when it was written nobody did. The authors were two obscure monks in the middle of nowhere. More and more people are starting to recognize that the whole Burning Times myth is indeed a myth. I think Paganism might be growing up!

The Military Pagan Network is a civil rights organization; we disagree with the military on their attitude towards homosexuals. There have been soldiers dishonorably discharged because they were gay. We will allow that person to be a member of MPN, as long as their discharge was only a result of them being a homosexual.

♦ *R/S: Pagans are now becoming mainstream—*

♦ JM: The military is a litmus test for our society; they were the first to desegregate. That's why it was so important that homosexuals not be discriminated against, and unfortunately that basic freedom has not yet been attained. There may always be problems. However, Pagans have overcome one of the biggest hurdles: military approval. We're about to see more major changes, simply because we don't have to hide anymore. ♦♦♦

Chandra Krinsky, age 14

(Interview by V. Vale)

♦ *RE/SEARCH: You've been raised from Day One in a Pagan household; can you describe what makes your life "Pagan"?*

♦ Chandra Krinsky: My mom! [laughs] It's mainly *holidays*—I never celebrated Christmas. Other kids were giving me Christmas cards, and I'm like, "Am I supposed to give you something?" We celebrate Winter Solstice, which is close to Christmas, by staying up all night and giving each other presents, because the sun might not come up again! We don't celebrate the birth of Christ. It's also the way the world perceives me—I don't fit in one category, so I'm just Pagan.

There's also *jewelry;* because I wore a pentacle, everyone at school assumed I was into witchcraft. I also wear a piece of amber. I don't necessarily think it protects me, but it helps me ground; it helps me calm down if I'm nervous or stressed. I also am interested in different books, such as books about Witchcraft. And I'm definitely into Tarot—I like giving readings and I like receiving readings. Sometimes I freak my friends out!

For clothes, I have specific robes—like Celtic knotwork tie-dyes—that I wear just at Pagan events. **I'm part of a Pagan brat-pack. It's a group of kids that have all known each other since they were four and older.** We see each other three or four times a year at Pagan events, and all band together and become this roving kid-pack. It's fun, because we're really good friends and we all like each other, but it's kinda hard because we don't get to see each other very often. But at Pagan events we're inseparable: we all sleep in the same tents, we all eat together, we start food fights—it's just a bunch of kids having fun. Sometimes at Pagan events grown-ups are walking around naked and we're making fun of them: *Ha ha!*

♦ *R/S: You're accustomed to adult nudity; do you think it has traumatized you?*

♦ CK: *Noooh.* [laughs] Other than being too amusing, sometimes. I know what boys' plumbing looks like. Pagan events like Pantheacon can't be clothing-optional, but almost all other Pagan events are. I was first exposed to public nudity when I was very young, and *I* was used to running around naked—I was four, y'know. I didn't really give a care. I've just been used to it all my life. It didn't shock or surprise me, it's more, "Oh, that's nice or whatever—*now get out of my face!"*

We don't have a television at home, but I see it at other kids' homes, and I read magazines—I'm not secluded from society. I subscribe to *Teen People!* I paid for that out of my own money. But that's the only magazine I subscribe to; it's the only one I read.

♦ *R/S: What else is there to Pagan living? Do you have any hobbies?*

CK: I love to sing and act. I want to go to a college where I can have a double major in performing arts and psychology, because I want to help people with their problems—I think I'm good at that. I like hanging out with my friends, exploring new things. I read lots of books, and right now the Harry Potter books are pretty cool. There are some Teen Witch books out like the Silver Raven Wolf *Teen Witch,* but they're really bad. There's one regular TV show I like to watch: *Buffy the Vampire Slayer.* Basically it's about a girl whose destiny is to fight evil. It's interesting; sometimes it's stupid.

I also like looking at Goth comic books and sketching characters out of them. My favorites are *Johnny The Homicidal Maniac, Squee, Happy Noodle Boy* and *Lenore,* which is about a dead girl. I also collect *Archies. Squee* is about a little boy, and everything that can possibly go wrong to someone goes wrong with him. His best friend is his ripped-up teddy, his parents hate him, he gets abducted by aliens—it's kinda sad, actually. I also like *Strangers in Paradise.* One of the three main characters used to be in this all-girl mob, and she quit and it's coming back to haunt her. And she's a lesbian and in love with her best friend, who's an *overweight* straight girl—yes,

we have an overweight person in a comic book, and it's very nice, she's very pretty! And then, the lesbian has this guy who's in love with her. She's an artist; she paints. It's about how they interact and how she's trying to escape her past; it's really good and I can't wait for the next issue!

♦ *R/S: Have you had any personal relationships?*

♦ CK: I've had a boyfriend for two-and-a-half years. I have a thing for football players. We've gotten to the point where we can say we love each other—which is very good for us. He's fifteen and is a foster kid who lives in Sacramento. He's an African-American, and that presents a problem with his new foster parents because they're white and they're totally against him dating me because I'm white and he's black. So it's kinda hard. I only get to see him only once every five months or so. He used to live next door to me, so I've known him six years, although we didn't start dating until two-and-a-half years ago.

♦ *R/S: Do you have any pets?*

♦ CK: We have three cats, a dog and four snakes. We've lost three cats and a dog to cars going down our street, so our cats stay indoors now.

♦ *R/S: Can you talk about death—*

♦ CK: I've been through a lot more than most of my friends. I've seen a lot more people around me die—including close friends. My mom is a safe-sex fanatic, so I've been learning about safe sex all my life, whereas people who are my age are just learning about it now. So I think I have a better perspective and grasp. **I've had so many people die of so many different causes that I'm just kind of used to it now.** When someone close to me dies of AIDS, first there's a period of shock: "How could that be?" When I was a lot younger I'd think, "Well, they were gay . . ." Now I know that being gay and dying of AIDS are not necessarily co-related. Five months ago, a little boy who was five drowned—and this was a kid I had taught how to swim, so it made *me* feel really guilty. It made me feel I didn't do a good enough job. Personally, that was more painful, because I had actually influenced him to do something, and he had died by it.

♦ *R/S: Describe the grieving process—*

♦ CK: Usually I go into my room, cry a lot, light some incense, and think about the good things about that person, and the

experiences we shared. Sometimes I write things down. **It always helps me to write beautiful poems about people I love that have died.** When I walk down the street I feel different from everyone, because I'm a different religion. I'm sure Christ was a person, and I'm sure he died, but I didn't do anything wrong, so he didn't die for me! From the time I was nine until eleven, I went through the process of asking, "Do I really want to *be* a Pagan?"

I explored a lot of different religions, including Christianity. I went to Sunday School and Church with my friends for a couple months, and I came back to Paganism because that's who I am, and that's what I can relate to.

First of all, I don't think there's any one Supreme Being. And the gods and goddesses I relate to, I relate to on an equal level. I consider them equal to me; I don't consider them superior and I don't worship them. I talk to them and relate to them, and that's how I practice my religion.

♦ *R/S: How do you think the world came into being?*

♦ CK: My perception may change later, but for me right now, the world was always there and it just grew until it came to be the way it is today. And it's beautiful! I think Paganism focuses more on life than on a superior being. I have respect for all beings, and I don't put my peers down. If they don't have anything against me, I don't have anything against them. And I've found that for me that's a better way of life. It's a lot better way of getting along with people than going, "You suck!" [laughs]

Sometimes my mom thinks I'm rebelling because I listen to pop music. It's funny, we joke around about how other teens rebel by smoking cigarettes or listening to loud rap or metal. Me, I decided to torture her with "insipid" boy bands! The nice thing about growing up in a subculture with no TV or anything is I get to pick and choose what parts of the pop culture I'm willing to put up with.

I don't believe a lot of the crap the media sends out to the teen community and I know when I'm being fed a bunch of b/s. Other teens I know take it all too seriously and their brains are warped for life! [laughs] I've been able to pick and choose my whole life and I think it's helped me grow and establish my individuality.♦♦♦

SCI-FI BOOKS

RECOMMENDED SCIENCE-FICTION/FANTASY BOOKS

by John Sulak

Beagle, Peter S. *The Last Unicorn* (1968)
Bradley, Marion Zimmer *The Mists of Avalon* (1983), *Forest House* (1993), *Lady of Avalon* (1997), *Priestess of Avalon* (2001, w/Diana Paxson)
Clarke, Arthur C. *Childhood's End* (1953)
Clee, Mona *Overshoot* (1998) Pagans, transformation & survival after global warming devastates the environment. Cautionary, but hopeful.
Heinlein, Robert A. *Stranger in a Strange Land* (1961) A man from Mars teaches earthlings about reverence for nature, sacred sex, open relationships, ecstatic spirituality and a religion with priestesses.
The Moon is a Harsh Mistress (1966). Anarchists in a lunar colony revolt.
Kurtz, Katherine *Lammas Night* (1986) A fantasy, based on historical sources, about covens in England in WWII doing ritual magic to stop Hitler.
LeGuin, Ursula K. *Earthsea Trilogy: Wizard of Earthsea* (1968), *Tombs of Atuan* (1971), *Farthest Shore* (1972). *Left Hand of Darkness* (1969). *The Dispossessed* (1974). *Always Coming Home* (1985). *The Word for the World is Forest* (1976)
Moore, Alan (with various artists) *Promethea*, vol. 1-2. Graphic novels.
Paxson, Diana *Brisingamen* (1983), *The Wolf and The Raven* (1993). *The Dragons of the Rhine* (1995). *The Lord of the Horses* (1996), *Hallowed Isle* (2000)
Pratchett, Terry *Wyrd Sisters* (1988)
Robbins, Tom *Jitterbug Perfume* (1984)
Rowling, J.K. All *Harry Potter* books
Starhawk *The Fifth Sacred Thing* (1993), *Walking to Mercury* (1997)
Stewart, Mary *The Crystal Cave* (1970), *The Hollow Hills* (1974), *The Last Enchantment* (1979), *The Wicked Day* (1983)
Sturgeon, Theodore *More Than Human* (1953)
Tepper, Sheri S. *The Gate to Women's Country* (1988)
Tolkien, J.R.R. *The Hobbit* (1937), *The Lord of The Rings* trilogy
Varley, John *The "Gaea" Trilogy: Titan* (1979), *Wizard* (1981), *Demon* (1984)
Vinge, Joan D. *The Snow Queen* (1981)
Vonnegut, Kurt *Cats Cradle* (1963)

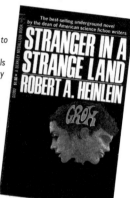

"PAGAN" FILMS

FILMS & VIDEOS OF POSSIBLE INTEREST TO PAGANS
(this list also includes animation, documentaries, sci-fi and Made-for-TV movies)

Films by Donna Read:
Burning Times
Full Circle
Goddess Remembered
Fairy Tale: A True Story
FernGully: Last Rainforest
Joseph Campbell & The Power of Myth series
Dr. Phibes (series)
Dead Birds
Mondo Magic
Mondo Cane (documentaries)
Divine Horsemen
Witchcraft Through the Ages (W.S. Burroughs narration!)
Where Green Ants Dream (Werner Herzog)
Emerald Forest,
Excalibur,
Hell in the Pacific by John Boorman
The Gods Must Be Crazy
Koyaanisqatsi
The Earthling
The Last Wave
Walkabout
Freaks

The Witches by Nicholas Roeg
White Dawn
Lair of the White Worm
The Devils
Bedknobs and Broomsticks
Bell, Book & Candle
I Married a Witch
Blue Planet
Earth [1930]
Que Viva Mexico
Black Orpheus
Orpheus
Blood of a Poet
Beauty and the Beast
Lost Horizon [1937]
Ecstasy (with Hedy Lamarr)
White Shadows of the South Seas
Trader Horn
Metropolis
Forbidden Games
Apu Trilogy
The Music Room
The Time Machine
Wild Strawberries
Seventh Seal
Mad Max

The Road Warrior
One Million Years B.C.
Woman in the Dunes
White Cargo
Most Dangerous Game
She (1965)
King Solomon's Mines
The Lost World (1925)
The Cat People (1942)
My Neighbor Totoro
Nude on the Moon
The Mask
The Naked Prey
Portrait of Jennie
Practical Magic
White Zombie
Secret Garden
Adventures of Robin Hood
Secret of the Incas
Star Trek (esp. Star Trek IV: The Voyage Home)
I, Claudius
Resurrection
Land that Time Forgot
Land of the Pharoahs
The Swimmer
Razor's Edge (1946)
Being There
Fearless
A Man Called Horse

Beetle Juice
Gandhi
Man Who Fell to Earth
My 20th Century
Blow-Up
Mists of Avalon
The Jungle Book
Sabu [any films]
Beyond The Far Reef
Blue Lagoon
Mysterious Island
I Walked with a Zombie
The Great Hunting 1984
Zoo in Budapest
Braveheart; Sirens
Knightriders
Soylent Green
Wild Women of Wonga
The Wizard of Oz
The Wicker Man
A Very Curious Girl
Faces of Death 1, 2
Twilight Zone episodes
Prehistoric Women
Green Mansions
Forbidden Planet
Critiques of Capitalism:
Land and Freedom
Modern Times

Atomic Cafe
Sweet Smell of Success
Toxic Avenger Pt. 2
The Trigger Effect
Point Blank
Man in the White Suit
Critiques of Christianity:
Passion of Joan of Arc
Dante's Inferno
Night of the Hunter
God Told Me To
Life of Brian
Day of Wrath
L'Age d'Or
La Religieuse
Simon of the Desert
Elmer Gantry
South Park [movie]
Bigger Than Life
Guyana: Cult of the Damned; The Rapture
Teorama
Last Temptation of Christ
Films by Dario Argento (warning: these are "horror" films):
Inferno
Phenomena
Suspiria

Black Sunday by Mario Bava, with the luminous Barbara Steele
Most "lost civilization," "Ancient Egypt-Greece-Rome," Medieval, South Sea Islands, "Primitive Peoples," comedy, Monte Python, wildlife/anthropology films
All Surrealist films, especially by the master of them all, LUIS BUNUEL
Films by John Waters, George/Mike Kuchar, Alejandro Jodorowsky; Maya Deren
Most Tarzan & "dinosaur" movies—especially older ones, like by Ray Harryhausen
Almost all "Exotica" music (Martin Denny, Arthur Lyman, et al) is Pagan!

PAGAN WEBSITES

RECOMMENDED PAGAN WEBSITES

by Oberon Ravenheart

Aquarian Tabernacle Church *aquatabch.org*
Betwixt & Between Community Center *betwixt.org*
Church of All Worlds *caw.org*
Circle Sanctuary *circlesanctuary.org*
Covenant of the Goddess *cog.org*
EarthSpirit *earthspirit.com*
Hexagon Hoopix *doreenvaliente.com*
Midwest Pagan Council *witchnet.org*
Pagan Educational Network *bloomington.in.us/~pen*
Pagans in Action *pactnational.org*
Paganpath *paganpath.com*
Pagan Pride Project *paganpride.org*
Sacred Earth Alliance *conjure.com/SEAhtml*
Wiccan-Pagan Educational Association *magickalcauldron.com*
Witch's Brew *witchs-brew.com*
The Witches' Web *witchesweb.com*
The Witches' Voice Inc. *witchvox.com*
(excellent for finding other Pagans in your area; news; good links)

OTHER PAGAN WEBSITES

beliefnet.com (Wiccan-heavy site)
Isaac Bonewits' site *neopagan.net*
Summerlands.com (nickname for the afterworld)
tylwytheg.com/lies.html (Lies told about Witchcraft)
webcom.com/~lstead/wicatru.html (difference between Wicca & Asatru—reconstructed Norse Paganism)
paganlibrary.com/fundies/other_people. (rebuts Jehovah's Witnesses)

RECENTLY RELEASED

MODERN PAGANS: An Investigation of Contemporary Pagan Practices

Modern Pagans is chock-full of compelling interviews and photographs that explain why Paganism is the fastest-growing "religion" today. Colorful stories of the vivid characters who sparked the current revival include Oberon, who created a genuine "Living Unicorn"; Morning Glory—wild, freedom-loving woman and creator/implementor of the controversial "polyamory" concept; Starhawk, who envisioned the advanced feminist, politically-activist, environmentalist Pagan movement of today; Isaac Bonewits, whose cutting-edge theory clarified the thinking of most Pagans alive—whether they know it or not, and many more visionaries. The ins and outs of Paganism—from rituals to child-raising to "orgies" to death rites—are explained in lucid detail. Fifty interviews, with Starhawk, Margot Adler, Diane di Prima, and members of The Pagan Federation, Druids, Asatru, EarthSpirit, Circle Sanctuary, Reclaiming, etc. 8"x9-⅞", 212 pp, 261 photos, bibliographies, filmography, Website directory, glossary, and index. PB. **$19.95.**

Real conversations #1: Henry Rollins, Jello Biafra, Lawrence Ferlinghetti, Billy Childish

A series of illuminated discussions about life, culture and politics of the 21st century—what's coming up. ♦ The Internet, dot-com backlash and SillyClone Valley ♦ sex, relationships and the population explosion ♦ celebrity, fame, and selling out to The Man ♦ mind control, Michael Jordan, branding, Levi's, consumerism ♦ Beat history, literary censorship and the fascist mentality ♦ LISTS, LISTS, LISTS of recommended books, films, websites. "Like most RE/Search books, *Real Conversations 1* flies by."—*Max.Rock&Roll.* "Very, very funny. Enthralling reading."—*A&F Quarterly* "Real Conversations 1 will stir something in the reader, be it creative juices or righteous indignation."—*Weekly Planet* "Thought-provoking ideas & good stories"—*Activist Guide.* **5"x7", 240 pages, 30 photos $12.95**

J.G. BALLARD

RE/Search #8/9: J.G. Ballard

J.G. Ballard predicted the future better than anyone else! His classic, *CRASH* (made into a movie by David Cronenberg) was the first book to investigate the psychopathological implications of the car crash, uncovering our darkest sexual crevices. He accurately predicted our media-saturated, information-overloaded environment where our most intimate fantasies and dreams involve pop stars and other public figures. Also contains a wide selection of quotations. "Highly recommended as both an introduction and a tribute to this remarkable writer."—*Washington Post* "The most detailed, probing and comprehensive study of Ballard on the market."—*Boston Phoenix.* 8½"x11", 176 pp, illus. PB. **$17.99**

Atrocity Exhibition

A dangerous imaginary work; as William Burroughs put it, "This book stirs sexual depths untouched by the hardest-core illustrated porn." Amazingly perverse medical illustrations by Phoebe Gloeckner, and haunting "Ruins of the Space Age" photos by Ana Barrado. Our most beautiful book, now used in many "Futurology" college classes. 8½"x11", 136 pp, illus. PB **$17.50 LIMITED EDITION OF SIGNED HARDBACKS**—not many left! **$50**

DANIEL P. MANNIX

FREAKS: We Who Are Not As Others

Amazing Photos! This book engages the reader in a struggle of wits: Who is the freak? What is normal? What are the limits of the human body? A fascinating, classic book, based on Mannix's personal acquaintance with sideshow stars such as the Alligator Man and the Monkey Woman. Read all about the notorious love affairs of midgets; the amazing story of the Elephant Boy; the unusual amours of Jolly Daisy, the fat woman; hermaphrodite love; the bulb-eating Human Ostrich, etc. **Put this on your coffee table and watch the fun!** 8½"x11", 124 pp, 88 photos. PB. **$15.95** Author died in 1997. **Signed, hardbound copies available for $50**

MEMOIRS OF A SWORD SWALLOWER

Not for the faint-of-heart, this book will GROSS SOME PEOPLE OUT and delight others. "I probably never would have become America's leading fire-eater if Flamo the Great hadn't happened to explode that night ..." So begins this true story of life with a traveling carnival, peopled by amazing characters—the Human Ostrich, the Human Salamander, Jolly Daisy, etc.—who commit outrageous feats of wizardry. This is one of the only *authentic* narratives revealing the "tricks" (or rather, painful skills) involved in a sideshow, and is invaluable to those aspiring to this profession. Over fifty RARE PHOTOS taken by Mannix in the 1930s and never before seen! Sideshow aficionados will delight in finally being able to see some of their favorite "stars" captured in candid moments. 8½"x11", 128 pp, 50+ photos, index, PB, **$15.99 Signed copies available for only $30**

CHARLES WILLEFORD

Wild Wives

A classic of hard-boiled fiction, Willeford's *Wild Wives* is amoral, sexy, and brutal. Written in a sleazy San Francisco hotel in the early '50s while on leave from the Army, Willeford creates a tale of deception featuring the morally-challenged detective Jacob C. Blake and his nemesis—a beautiful, insane young woman. 5x7", 108 pp. PB. **$10.99**

High Priest of California

Russell Haxby is a ruthless used car salesman obsessed with manipulating and cavorting with a married woman. A classic of hard-boiled fiction, hypocrisy, intrigue and red-hot lust. Every sentence masks innuendo, every detail hides a clue, and every used car sale is an outrageous con job. **"A tempo so relentless, words practically fly off the page."**—*Village Voice* 5x7", 148 pp. PB. **$10.99**

W.S. BURROUGHS

R/S #4/5: WS Burroughs, Brion Gysin, Throbbing Gristle

The great unknown Burroughs-Gysin treasure trove of radical ideas! Compilation of interviews, scarce fiction, essays: this is a manual of incendiary insights. Strikingly designed; bulging with radical references. **Topics discussed:** biological warfare, utopias, con men, lost inventions, the JFK killing, Hassan I Sabbah, cloning, the cut-up theory, Moroccan trance music, the Dream Machine, Manson, the media control process, prostitution, and more. Brion Gysin is an unknown genius awaiting rediscovery. 8½"x11", 100 pp, 58 photos & illus. PB, **$15.99**

William S. Burroughs T-shirt! Black & red on white, **100% cotton T-shirt.** "We intend to destroy all dogmatic verbal systems."—*WSB.* Original design hand-screened on 100% heavyweight cotton T-Shirt. **$16** Xtra Large only.

MUSIC: Read & Listen!

RE/Search #14 & #15: Incredibly Strange Music, Vol. 1 & 2—BOOKS

These are the two books that launched the mad record-collecting fad of the '90s, inspiring publications like *Cool & Strange Music*. Many records were collected for their cover—every record whose cover was reproduced has appreciated 1,000%. Focus: "Easy listening," "exotica," and "celebrity" as well as recordings by (singing) cops and (polka-playing) priests, religious ventriloquists, astronauts, opera-singing parrots, and gospel by blind teenage girls with bouffant hairdos. EACH 8½x11", 220 pp, over 200 photos, PB. Vol. 1: **$17.99**, Vol. 2: **$17.99**. Set of both Incredibly Strange Music Books, Vol. 1 & II: **$35.**

Incredibly Strange Music CDs & cassette

Incredibly Strange Music, Vol. 1

An amazing anthology of outstanding, hard-to-find musical/spoken word gems from LPs that are as scarce as hens' teeth. These tracks must be heard to be believed! (cassette only)

Incredibly Strange Music, Vol. 2 Lucia Pamela's barnyard

frenzy "Walking on the Moon"; "How to Speak Hip" by Del Close [r.i.p.] & John Brent; "Join the Gospel Express" by singing ventriloquist doll Little Marcy, and many more musical gems. Full liner notes.

Ken Nordine COLORS A kaleidoscope of riotous sound and imagery. The pioneer of "Word Jazz" delivers "good lines" which are as smooth as water, inviting the listener to embark upon a musical fantasy. Contains extra tracks not on original vinyl record.

The Essential Perrey & Kingsley Two fantastic, classic LPs (*In Sound from Way Out* and *Kaleidoscopic Vibrations*) combined on one hard-to-find CD. Contains all the tracks recorded by the Perrey-Kingsley duo. Sounds as fresh as tomorrow!

CDs: **$16** each, cassette **$12**. SPECIAL OFFER: 3-CDs, 1 cassette: **$48.**

Incredibly Strange Music Packages

1) Incredibly Strange Music Vol. One and Two (BOOKS) & their companion cassette & CD; a set which satisfies the soul. **$54.**

2) RE/Search Incredibly Strange Music Library (no books): *ISM Vol. 1* cass., and *ISM Vol. 2*, Perrey & Kingsley, and *Ken Nordine* CDs: **$54.** *Note: this is our 2nd best-seller. Many people have ordered the Incredibly Strange Music Packages and been thrilled—their lives and lusts changed forever!*

SWING

SWING! The New Retro Renaissance

Rockabilly, swing, lounge and Vegas Show Acts figure in this celebration of "born again" retro artists who feel the past is more nutritious than the crass corporate present. America used to be an amazingly lively cultural force, before monolithic mega-entertainment conglomerates turned its popular music into kitty-porn drool for the slobbering TV-worshipping masses. Fads can come and go, but the music of Lavay Smith, Big Sandy, and Sam Butera will remain with us! Learn about *the life*: vintage clothes, hairdos, shoes, cars, books, movies. Photos of bands, aerial dancers, classic cars, hairstyles, clothes, shoes, ties, accessories, and interiors of homes. Dance advice, too.

8½x11", 224 pp, with hundreds of photographs; lists of recommended books, records and films; informative essays; movie reviews; index. PB. **BOOK $17.99.**

Listen to 2 of the bands you read about in SWING!

From "Swing-from-hell" of Lee Press-On & the Nails to The New Morty Show's modern take on a '50s Vegas, Louie Prima-Keely Smith Show. These are exciting and danceable CDs—all on independent labels, impossible to find outside of San Francisco! Own a rarity! **$16 each, 2 for $25**

> *"Men never do evil so completely and cheerfully as when they do it out of religious conviction."—Pascal*
> *"Habit is probably the greatest block to seeing truth."—R.A. Schwaller de Lubicz*
> *"Dualism plus corporations will bring the death of our civilization."—E. Czerny*

Jimmy Vargas's (2) Black Dahlia CDs

Jimmy Vargas: sincerely believes he's the reincarnation of a Forties crooner. A genuine character. Was once in the punk scene, and now renews himself with these two CDs. **The Tease...the Torch & the Noir** sounds like old film noir soundtrack music. The new offering, **My Shadow Bride,** continues Vargas's journey deep into film-noirish territory: illegal nightclubs, treachery, pain & the assassin's getaway. Then remorse, regret, reincarnation, & *reunion??* For a cult audience in search of a touch of evil. Music framed in a de Chirico-like shadow landscape. **CDs $16 each.**

BLUES

ME AND BIG JOE by Michael Bloomfield

A classic coming-of-age tale, illuminating black American culture before its dilution by encroaching white American television. Bloomfield's amazing guitar artistry emblazoned Bob Dylan, Paul Butterfield Blues Band, and the Electric Flag. In this narrative, Michael befriends great blues legend Joe Lee Williams (*aka* Big Joe) and together they embark on an odyssey through the dark, smoky blues clubs of the Midwest. *Me and Big Joe* is a classic American adventure story, a must read for any blues lover or musician. "I can't recommend *Me and Big Joe* highly enough. It is a beautifully realized American miniature—nearly as scary as Melville's white whale, fully as grotesque and funny as a Fellini dreamscape and as exhilarating as Bloomfield's best solo."—*American Journal.* 5x7", 60 pp, illus., PB, **$5.99.** Impossible to find; order direct!

INDUSTRIAL

RE/Search #6/7: Industrial Culture Handbook

This book is a secret weapon—it provided an educational upbringing for many of the most radical artists practicing today! The rich ideas of the *Industrial Culture* movement's performance artists and musicians are nakedly exposed: *Survival Research Laboratories, Throbbing Gristle, Cabaret Voltaire, SPK, Non, Monte Cazazza, Johanna Went, Sordide Sentimental, R&N, & Z'ev.* **Topics include:** brain research, forbidden medical texts & films, creative crime & *interesting* criminals, modern warfare & weaponry, neglected gore films & their directors, psychotic lyrics in past pop songs, and *art brut.* This culture influenced you—without your knowledge! Many rare, powerful books are revealed. 8½x11", 140 pp, 179 photos & illust. PB, **$15.99.** Join the cult!

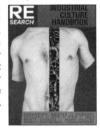

PUNK

PUNK '77: an inside look at the San Francisco rock n' roll scene, 1977 by James Stark

Covers the beginnings of the S.F. Punk Rock scene through the Sex Pistols' concert at Winterland in Jan., 1978, in interviews and photographs by James Stark. James was among the many artists involved in early punk. His photos were published in *New York Rocker, Search & Destroy* and *Slash*, among others. His posters for Crime are classics and highly prized collectors' items. Over 100 photos, including many behind-the-scenes looks at the bands who made things happen: Nuns, Avengers, Crime, Screamers, Negative Trend, Dils, Germs, UXA, etc. Interviews with the bands and people early on the scene give intimate, often darkly humorous glimpses of events in a *Please Kill Me* (Legs McNeil) style.

7½x10¼", 98 pp, 100+ photos, on archival art paper. PB, **$13.99**.

SEARCH & DESTROY: The Complete Reprint (in 2 jumbo volumes)

Facsimile editions (at 90% size) include all the interviews, articles, ads, illustrations and photos. Captures the enduring revolutionary spirit of punk rock, 1977-1978. Vol. I contains an abrasive intro-interview with Jello Biafra on the history and future of punk rock. Published by V. Vale before his RE/Search series, *Search & Destroy* is a definitive, first-hand documentation of the punk rock cultural revolution, printed as it happened! Patti Smith, Iggy Pop, Ramones, Sex Pistols, Clash, DEVO, Avengers, Mutants, Dead Kennedys, William S. Burroughs, J.G. Ballard, John Waters, Russ Meyer, and David Lynch (to name a few) discussing philosophy, creativity, their own work, & still-contemporary social issues. 10x15", 148pp, **$19.95 each, $35 for both**

PUNK VIDEO

LOUDER FASTER SHORTER
punk video by Mindaugis Bagdon

San Francisco, March 21, 1978. In the intense, original punk rock scene at the Mabuhay Gardens (the only club in town which would allow it), the AVENGERS, DILS, MUTANTS, SLEEPERS and UXA played a benefit for striking Kentucky coal miners ("Punks Against Oppression!"). One of the only surviving 16mm color documents of this short-lived era, *LOUDER FASTER SHORTER* captured the spirit and excitement of "punk rock" before revolt became style. Filmmaker Mindaugis Bagdon was a member of *Search & Destroy*, the publication which chronicled and catalyzed the punk rock "youth culture" rebellion of the late '70s. "Exceptionally fine color photography, graphic design and editing."—S.F. International Film Festival review

1980. 20 minute video in US NTSC VHS only. **$15.**

HUMOR

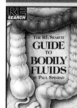

RE/Search #16 GUIDE TO BODILY FLUIDS by Paul Spinrad.

Everything you ever wanted to know about: Mucus, Menstruation, Saliva, Sweat, Vomit, Urine, Flatus, Feces, Earwax & more.

Topics include: constipation (such as its relationship to cornflakes and graham crackers!); history and evolution of toilet paper; farting; smegma and more! Ideal bathroom reading! A perfect gift for that difficult-to-shop-for person! Our funniest scientific text. Educational, yet fun.

8½x11", 148 pp., PB only. **$15.99**

D.I.Y. and POLITICAL ART

ZINES! Vol. One & Two Incendiary Interviews with Independent Publishers

In the Punk Tradition of Do-It-Yourself, these (2) books present interviews with zine creators telling why and how they publish. Some of the strangest obsessions and most gnarly personal revelations and fetishes haunt the pages of zines. Following the imperative: "Destroy the society that seeks to destroy you!", *ZINES!* #1 & 2 show how easy it is to express yourself, and thus change your world. Vol. 1: *Beer Frame, Crap Hound, Fat Girl, Thrift SCORE, Bunny Hop, Housewife Turned Assassin, Meat Hook, X-Ray* & more! Vol. 2: *Murder Can Be Fun, 8-Track Mind, McJob, Dishwasher, Temp Slave, Bruno Richard*. EACH: 8½x11", quotations, excerpts, zine directory, historical essay, index. Vol. 1: 184 pp. PB, **$18.99**; Vol. 2: 148 pp. PB, **$14.99. 2001 SPECIAL: Both for $20!**

RE/SEARCH #1, #2, #3—the shocking tabloid issues. Deep into the heart of the Control Process; Creativity & Survival, past, present & future. ◆

#1: J.G. Ballard, Cabaret Voltaire, Julio Cortazar, Octavio Paz, Sun Ra, The Slits, Conspiracy Theory Guide. **#2:** DNA, James Blood Ulmer, Z'ev, Aboriginal Music, Surveillance Technology, Monte Cazazza, Diane Di Prima, German Electronic Music Chart. **#3:** Fela, New Brain Research, The Rattlesnake Man, Sordide Sentimental, New Guinea, Kathy Acker, Pat Califia, Joe Dante, Johanna Went, SPK, Flipper, Physical Modification of Women. 11x17", Heavily illus. **$8 ea, all for $20** (Rare, fragile, and red-hot. Not at stores, direct order only)

RE/Search #11: PRANKS! (A favorite of Napster-lovers & Geeks!)

A prank is a "trick, a mischievous act, a ludicrous act." Although not regarded as poetic or artistic acts, pranks constitute an art form and genre in themselves. Here pranksters such as Timothy Leary, Abbie Hoffman, Monte Cazazza, Jello Biafra, Earth First!, Joe Coleman, Karen Finley, John Waters, Henry Rollins and more challenge the sovereign authority of words, images and behavioral convention. This iconoclastic compendium will dazzle and delight all lovers of humor, satire and irony. *Pranks!* is a classic of the *rebel literature canon*. The definitive treatment of the subject, offering extensive interviews with 36 contemporary tricksters . . . from the Underground's answer to Studs Terkel."—*Washington Post* "Pranks comes off as a statement of avant-garde philosophy–as a kind of wake-up call from an extended underground of surrealist artists."—*San Francisco Chronicle* Our heftiest book. 8½x11", 240 pp, 164 photos & illustrations, PB, **$19.99**

B-FILMS

RE/Search #10: INCREDIBLY STRANGE FILMS

First to champion Herschell Gordon Lewis, Russ Meyer, Larry Cohen, Ray Dennis Steckler, Ted V. Mikels, Doris Wishman & others who had been critically consigned to the ghettos of gore & sexploitation films, this book allowed artists to rationally explain how they made gripping dramas with zero budgets and overflowing imaginations. 13 interviews, A-Z of film personalities, "Favorite Films" list, quotations, bibliography, filmography, film synopses, & index. "Flicks like these are subversive alternatives to the mind control propagated by the mainstream media."—*Iron Horse* "The interviews are intelligent, enthusiastic and articulate."—*Small Press.* Has been used as a textbook.

8½x11", 224 pp, 157 photos & illus. PB, **$17.99**

BODY MODIFICATION and S&M

RE/Search #12: MODERN PRIMITIVES [part of our S&M Library] The *New York Times* called this "the Bible of the underground tattooing and body piercing movement." *Modern Primitives* launched an entire '90s subculture. Crammed with illustrations & information, it's now considered a classic. The best texts on ancient human decoration practices such as tattooing, piercing, scarification and more. 279 eye-opening photos and graphics; 22 in-depth interviews with some of the most colorful people on the planet. "Dispassionate ethnography that lets people put their behavior in its own context."—*Voice Literary Supplement* "The photographs and illustrations are both explicit and astounding . . . provides fascinating food for thought."—*Iron Horse* 8½x11", 212 pp, 279 photos and illus, PB. Great gift! **$19.50**

BOB FLANAGAN: SUPERMASOCHIST [part of our S&M Library] Bob Flanagan (1952-1996), born in NYC, grew up with Cystic Fibrosis (a genetically inherited, nearly-always fatal disease) and lived longer than any other person with CF. The physical pain of his childhood suffering was principally alleviated by masturbation, wherein pain and pleasure became linked, resulting in his lifelong practice of extreme masochism. Through his insider's perspective on the Sado-Masochistic community, we learn about branding, piercing, whipping, bondage and endurance trials. Includes photos by L.A. artist Sheree Rose. "…an eloquent tour through the psychic terrain of SM, discussing the most severe sexual diversions with the humorous detachment of a shy, clean living nerd. I came away from the book wanting to know this man."—*Details Magazine.* 8½x11", 128 pp, 125 photos & illustrations. PB. **$14.99.**

The Torture Garden by Octave Mirbeau This book was once described as the "most sickening work of art of the nineteenth century!" Long out of print, Octave Mirbeau's macabre classic (1899) features a corrupt Frenchman and an insatiably cruel Englishwoman who meet and then frequent a fantastic 19th century Chinese garden where torture is practiced as an art form. The fascinating, horrific narrative slithers deep into the human spirit, uncovering murderous proclivities and demented desires. "Hot with the fever of ecstatic, prohibited joys, as cruel as a thumbscrew and as luxuriant as an Oriental tapestry. Exotic, perverse . . . hailed by the critics."—*Charles Hanson Towne* 8½x11", 120 pp, 21 mesmerizing photos. **PB: $15.95. Rare Hardcover (edition of only 100; treat yourself!): $35**

Tattoo Time #3: MUSIC & SEA TATTOOS Deluxe double book issue with over 300 photos. Mermaids, pirates, fish, punk rock tattoos, etc. **$15.**

Tattoo Time #5: ART FROM THE HEART Bigger than ever before (128 pp) with hundreds of color photographs. Featuring in-depth articles on tattooers, contemporary tattooing in Samoa, a survey of the new weirdo monster tattoos, and much more! *(These are out-of-print; only a few copies are left.)* **$20**

FEMINISM

Confessions of Wanda von Sacher-Masoch Married for 10 years to Leopold von Sacher-Masoch (author: *Venus in Furs* & many other novels) whose whip-and-fur bedroom games spawned the term "masochism," Wanda's story is a feminist classic from 100 years ago. She was forced to play "sadistic" roles in Leopold's fantasies to ensure the survival of herself & their 3 children–games which called into question who was the Master and who the Slave. Besides being a compelling story of a woman's search for her own identity, strength and, ultimately, complete independence, this is a true-life adventure story–an odyssey through many lands peopled by amazing characters. Here is a woman's consistent unblinking investigation of the limits of morality and the deepest meanings of love. "Extravagantly designed in an illustrated, oversized edition that is a pleasure to hold. It is also exquisitely written, engaging and literary and turns our preconceptions upside down."—*L.A. Reader* 8½x11", 136 pp, illustrated, PB. **$13.99**

RE/Search #13: Angry Women 16 cutting-edge performance artists discuss critical questions such as: How can revolutionary feminism encompass wild sex, humor, beauty, spirituality *plus* radical politics? How can a powerful movement for social change be *inclusionary?* Wide range of topics discussed *passionately.* **Included:** Karen Finley, Annie Sprinkle, bell hooks, Diamanda Galas, Kathy Acker, Susie Bright, Sapphire. Armed with contempt for dogma, stereotype & cliché, these visionaries probe into our social foundation of taboos, beliefs & totalitarian linguistic contradictions from whence spring (as well as thwart) theories, imaginings, behavior & dreams. "The view here is largely pro-sex, pro-porn, and pro-choice."—*Village Voice* "This book is a Bible—it hails the dawn of a new era–the era of an inclusive, fun, sexy feminism. Every interview contains brilliant moments of wisdom." *American Book Review* 8½x11", 240 pp, 135 illus. PB. **$18.99**

LIBRARIES & PACKAGES

Just The RE/Search Library: All RE/Search serials #1-16 (complete set; save $25!)
Offer includes *RE/Search #1, 2 & 3* tabloids, *#4/5: Burroughs/Gysin/Throbbing Gristle, #6/7: Industrial Culture Handbook, #8/9: J.G. Ballard, #10: Incredibly Strange Films, #11: Pranks!, #12: Modern Primitives, #13: Angry Women, #14: Incredibly Strange Music, Vol. 1, #15: Incredibly Strange Music, Vol. 2,* and *#16: RE/Search Guide to Bodily Fluids.* **$175.**

The Classic RE/Search Library: All RE/Search classic reprints (Save $15!)
Offer includes *Freaks: We Who Are Not As Others, The Torture Garden, The Atrocity Exhibition, The Confessions of Wanda von Sacher-Masoch, High Priest of California* and *Wild Wives.* **$75.** Note: some of these books are in extremely short supply.

The S&M Library (Our Best-Seller!)
Includes The Torture Garden, Confessions of Wanda von Sacher-Masoch, Bob Flanagan, and Modern Primitives. **$55.** *Please call for updates and additional books available.*

ORDERING INFORMATION

**RE/SEARCH PUBLICATIONS
20 ROMOLO #B
SAN FRANCISCO, CA 94133**
tel (415) 362-1465   fax (415) 362-0742

Phone, FAX, email orders or go to our secure server!
www.researchpubs.com
info@researchpubs.com

SHIPPING USA: $4 for first item, $1 per additional item. (Add $2/item for Priority Mail USA.)
Overseas Global Air: $10 per item. For seamail (allow 2 months): **$6 for first item, $2 per additional item.**
Contact us to request a complete catalog !

INDEX

QUOTATIONS

"You cannot write a single word without a cosmology, a cosmogony."—Diane di Prima

"Religion is Culture, and Vice Versa."—Isaac Bonewits

"Monotheism is Imperialism in Religion."—James Breasted

"Belief is the enemy of knowledge."—unknown

"[S]he who is not possessed by a new theory is still in the grip of the old."—unknown

"Jazz is my religion."—Ted Joans

"Necessity is the excuse for every infringement of human freedom. It is the argument of the tyrant and the creed of the slave."—William Pitt, 1763

"The *previous* world view is Either/Or, and the Neo-Pagan world view tends to be Both/And."—Isaac Bonewits

"Christianity carries with it *totalitarianism*."—Andras Arthen

"Sex can have a great deal of healing power."—Isaac Bonewits

from "The Charge of the Goddess"*

When the moon is full, you shall assemble in some secret place
As a sign that you be free you shall be naked in your rites
Sing, feast, dance, make music and love, all in My presence
My law is love unto all beings; all acts of love and pleasure are my rituals
I Who am the beauty of the green earth and the white moon among the stars
    and the mysteries of the waters,
From Me all things proceed and unto Me they must return.

*by Doreen Valiente, 1951

FUNKUPAGAN MANIFESTO
The First National Church of the Exquisite Panic, Inc.

We must regenerate ourselves. We must create new rituals and
new mythologies to accommodate new found capabilities.

Our launching into outer space, which was considered an impossibility a mere
50 years ago, has already been accomplished. We must now have the courage to
continue this exhilarating and frightening adventure without procrastination.

It will be necessary for us to throw overboard outmoded, wasteful
ways of living. Humanity has to achieve coherence.

We must have absolute equality across the board in order for everyone to be able to
contribute to this enterprise. We will need all of the intelligence and energy we can muster.

written by Robert Delford Brown, circa 1980

www.funkup.com